THE CANADIAN YEARBOOK OF INTERNATIONAL LAW

1995

ANNUAIRE CANADIEN DE DROIT INTERNATIONAL

The Canadian Yearbook of International Law

VOLUME XXXIII   1995   TOME XXXIII

Annuaire canadien de Droit international

Published under the auspices of
THE CANADIAN BRANCH, INTERNATIONAL LAW ASSOCIATION
AND
THE CANADIAN COUNCIL ON INTERNATIONAL LAW

Publié sous les auspices de
LA SECTION CANADIENNE DE L'ASSOCIATION DE DROIT INTERNATIONAL
ET
LE CONSEIL CANADIEN DE DROIT INTERNATIONAL

UBC Press
VANCOUVER, B.C.

Printed in Canada on acid-free paper ∞

ISBN 0-7748-0566-8
ISSN 0069-0058

Canadian Cataloguing in Publication Data

The National Library of Canada has catalogued this
publication as follows:

*The Canadian yearbook of international law — Annuaire
canadien de droit international*

Annual.
Text in English and French.
"Published under the auspices of the Canadian
Branch, International Law Association and the
Canadian Council on International Law."
ISSN 0069-0058

1. International Law — Periodicals.
I. International Law Association. Canadian Branch.
II. Title: Annuaire canadien de droit international.
JX21.C3 341'.05 C75-34558-6E

Données de catalogage avant publication (Canada)

*Annuaire canadien de droit international — Canadian
yearbook of international law*

Annuel.
Textes en anglais et en français.
"Publié sous les auspices de la Branche canadienne
de l'Association de droit international et le Conseil
canadien de droit international."
ISSN 0069-0058

1. Droit international — Périodiques.
I. Association de droit international. Section canadienne.
II. Conseil canadien de droit international.
III. Titre: The Canadian yearbook of international law.
JX21.C3 341'.05 C75-34558-6F

UBC Press
University of British Columbia
6344 Memorial Road
Vancouver, BC V6T 1Z2
(604) 822-3259
Fax: 1-800-668-0821
E-mail: orders@ubcpress.ubc.ca
http://www.ubcpress.ubc.ca

Contents / Sommaire

Articles

ED MORGAN   3   Cyclops Meets the Privy Council: The Conflict in the Conflict of Laws

38   Sommaire and Summary

LUZIUS WILDHABER   41   Territorial Modifications and Breakups in Federal States

74   Sommaire and Summary

J. C. THOMAS AND SERGIO LÓPEZ AYLLÓN   75   NAFTA Dispute Settlement and Mexico: Interpreting Treaties and Reconciling Common and Civil Law Systems in a Free Trade Area

122   Sommaire and Summary

MARCIA WALDRON   123   From the Margins to the Mainstream: The Beijing Declaration and Platform for Action

148   Sommaire and Summary

TORSTEN H. STROM   149   Another Kick at the Can: Tuna/Dolphin II

183   Sommaire and Summary

Review Article

MICHAEL REISMAN   185   Metamorphoses: Judge Shigeru Oda and the International Court of Justice

221   Sommaire and Summary

Notes and Comments / Notes et commentaires

GABRIELLE MARCEAU ET 223 La première année de l'Organe de
ALAIN RICHER règlement des différends de
l'Organisation mondiale du commerce

246 Summary and Sommaire

HUGH M. KINDRED 257 The Protection of Peacekeepers

279 Sommaire and Summary

PIERRE-FRANÇOIS 281 Le rejet du concept de patrimoine
MERCURE commun de l'humanité afin d'assurer la
gestion de la diversité biologique

303 Summary and Sommaire

ALDO CHIRCOP 305 Legislating for Integrated Marine
HUGH KINDRED Management: Canada's Proposed Oceans
PHILLIP SAUNDERS Act of 1996
DAVID VANDERZWAAG 330 Sommaire and Summary

333 John Peters Humphrey — A Tribute

*Chronique de Droit international économique
en 1994 / Digest of International Economic
Law in 1994*

343 Commerce, préparé par Martin St-Amant

353 Le Canada et le système monétaire
international en 1994, préparé par
Bernard Colas

361 Investissement, préparé par Pierre Ratelle

*Canadian Practice in International Law / La
pratique canadienne en matière de droit
international public*

371 At the Department of Foreign Affairs in
1994-95 / Au ministère des Affaires
étrangères en 1994-95, compiled
by / préparé par Philippe Kirsch

395 Parliamentary Declarations in
1994-95/Déclarations parlementaires en
1994-95, compiled by/préparé par
Sapard V. M. T. N. Kalala

411 Treaty Action Taken by Canada in
1994/Mesures prises par le Canada en
matière de traités en 1994, compiled
by/préparé par André Bergeron

Cases/La jurisprudence

425 Canadian Cases in Public International
Law in 1994-95/La jurisprudence
canadienne en matière de droit
international public en 1994-95,
compiled by/préparé par
Karin Mickelson

429 Canadian Cases in Private International
Law in 1994-95/La jurisprudence
canadienne en matière de droit
international privé en 1994-95, compiled
by/préparé par Joost Blom

469 *Book Reviews/Recensions de livres*

505 *Analytical Index/Index analytique*

513 *Index of Cases/Index de la jurisprudence*

BOOK REVIEWS / RECENSIONS DE LIVRES

PAGE

Anti-dumping and Anti-trust Issues in Free-trade Areas
  By G. Z. Marceau
International Trade and Investment Law in Canada
  By Robert K. Paterson and Martine M. N. Band
The Regulation of International Trade
  By Michael J. Trebilcock and
    Robert Howse   DAVID P. STEVENS   469

International Responses to Traumatic Stress: Humanitarian,
  Human Rights, Justice, Peace, and Development
  Contributions, Collaborative Actions, and Future Initiatives
  Edited by Yael Danieli, Nigel S. Rodley,
    and Lars Weisaeth   WILLIAM A. SCHABAS   479

Le Comité international de la Croix-Rouge et la protection des
  victimes de la guerre
  Par F. Bugnion   CLAUDE EMANUELLI   481

Precautionary Legal Duties and Principles in Modern
  International Environmental Law
  By Harald Hohmann   JUTTA BRUNNÉE   484

Introduccion al derecho internacional: Relaciones Exteriores de
  los Ordenamientos Juridicos
  Par Antonio Boggiano   LOUIS PERRET   489

International Law as Law of the United States
  By Jordan J. Paust   L. C. GREEN   492

The Charter of the United Nations
  Sous la direction de Bruno Simma RENÉ PROVOST   498

Conflict of Laws in Western Europe: A Guide through
  the Jungle
  By Mathias Reimann   JOOST BLOM   501

THE CANADIAN YEARBOOK OF INTERNATIONAL LAW

INTERNATIONAL LAW

1995

ANNUAIRE CANADIEN DE DROIT INTERNATIONAL

Cyclops Meets the Privy Council:
The Conflict in the Conflict of Laws

CONFLICTS OF LAWS AND LETTERS

IN MAY 1989, a wealthy Saudi Arabian currency broker named Sheikh Abdul Ahmed Showlag died, leaving a large fortune for his heirs. Among the wealth he had accumulated in his lifetime were two deposits worth approximately £17.5m that were held in London banks. By the time of his death, these deposits had been transferred out of England into accounts held in Egypt and the island of Jersey in the name of a Panamanian company wholly owned by Abdel Moniem Mansour, an Egyptian national and former employee and assistant of Sheikh Showlag.[1] On discovering that the funds were missing, Showlag's executors and heirs first sued Mansour in England, his country of last residence and the locale of his alleged misappropriation, and subsequently brought action in Egypt, the country to which Mansour had fled and the location of at least part of the funds in issue.

Having sued abroad, Showlag's estate then came to the Channel Islands to collect the balance of the funds deposited by Mansour

* B.A. (1976, Northwestern); LL.B. (1984, Toronto); LL.M. (1986, Harvard), partner at Davies, Ward and Beck, Toronto, and special lecturer in international law at the University of Toronto, Faculty of Law. A version of this paper was initially presented at a panel on International Law Theory held at the University of Ottawa, Faculty of Law, in the fall of 1995. It was also presented at the 1996 conference on Contemporary Legal Issues at the University of Toronto, Faculty of Law. I would like to thank the organizers of and participants in both conferences for providing an opportunity to present and refine my ideas. I would also like to thank Steve Harris for his research assistance.

---

[1] *Showlag* v. *Mansour*, [1994] 2 All E.R. 129, 131 (P.C.).

into several accounts in Jersey. Under ordinary conflict of laws principles, the estate did not need to sue on the merits in the Royal Court of Jersey, since judgment had been granted in the estate's favour in England. It was simply a matter of enforcing the foreign judgment which, having been procedurally correct and defended on the merits, could not ordinarily be questioned.[2] The problem, however, was that the estate had failed to obtain judgment in Egypt, where Mansour had mounted a defence to the charge of misappropriation by successfully characterizing his receipt of the funds as a gift from the late Sheikh Showlag. Accordingly, the Jersey court was confronted with two foreign judgments that had reached opposite conclusions. Without looking behind either judgment, it was impossible for the Jersey court to know whether the funds were in Mansour's accounts as a result of a misappropriation or as a result of a gift. All the Jersey court and, ultimately, the Privy Council could do was to fashion a conflict of laws rule for enforcement of the competing judgments: either first in time or last in time would be upheld.[3]

Turning to a conflict of a different sort, the "Cyclops" chapter in James Joyce's *Ulysses*[4] presents a modernized re-enactment of the epic encounter between Odysseus and the cave dwelling one-eyed monster. Just as Odysseus was trapped and forced to deal face-to-face with his horrific nemesis, Joyce's protagonist, Leopold Bloom, is socially and psychologically trapped in a pub in a face-to-face encounter with a bellicose and belligerent adversary known as the

[2] *Owens Bank Ltd.* v. *Bracco*, [1992] 2 A.C. 443, 484 (per Lord Bridge of Harwich): "A foreign judgment given by a court of competent jurisdiction over the Defendant is treated by the common law as imposing a legal obligation on the judgment debtor which will be enforced in an action on the judgment by an English court in which the Defendant will not be permitted to reopen issues of either fact or law which have been decided against him by the foreign court."

In *Showlag, supra* note 1 at 133, the Privy Council stated with respect to the above passage in *Owens Bank*: "That statement holds good in Jersey as it does in England."

[3] *The Indian Endurance*, [1993] A.C. 410 (H.L.), citing Spencer, Bower, and Turner, *Res Judicata* 331 (2nd ed., 1969) to the effect that a foreign judgment creates a bar *per res judicata* to proceedings in England by a plaintiff relying on the same cause of action.

[4] All references are to the following edition: James Joyce, *Ulysses* (Penguin Books, 1973) (hereinafter *Ulysses*). Although the chapters in *Ulysses* are unnamed, it is Chapter 12 of the novel that is described herein and that is generally referred to as "Cyclops."

Citizen.[5] After a long and difficult ordeal, Odysseus succeeded not in killing but in blinding the Cyclops and escaped by sea to pursue his next adventure. Similarly, Bloom succeeds not in defeating but in blinding his drunken rival with rage and makes a getaway by car to the next episode in his adventurous day.

The "Cyclops" chapter is set in a way that imposes a dramatic confrontation between the Citizen's passion and Bloom's reason, or the former's narrow-mindedness and the latter's broad-mindedness. These personality traits then translate into a political discussion, with the Citizen espousing a fierce and xenophobic brand of nationalism and Bloom espousing a measured and inclusionary brand of democracy.[6] The action in the chapter is described by an unnamed narrator who displays little personality of his own and professes no insights into either the psychology or the politics of the chapter's two rival characters. Accordingly, the narrator is at a loss to evaluate the merits of either side's position in the conflict, but rather satisfies himself by describing the confrontation and determining who gets the better of whom in the mechanical sense of who stays and who leaves the pub, or who rallies the gathered crowd and who alienates it.

All of the above raises the question of what the Privy Council's judgment and James Joyce's novel have to do with each other. This article explores that relationship by suggesting certain shared traits between the legal conflict and the dramatic conflict, together with the judicial resolution and the literary resolution of the issues. In particular, the article focuses on the nature of argument, as displayed and worked through in the case law and in the novel, with a view to achieving a deeper understanding of the ways in which argumentative positions ultimately triumph or fail.

As will be seen, the parallels between the *Showlag* case and the "Cyclops" episode, and between judicial and literary efforts in general, are rather more numerous than one might at first expect. What is equally unexpected as one probes these parallels is that a reversal in the expertise of the various authors can be discerned. While the Judicial Committee of the Privy Council is highly skilled in describing a conflict and bringing it to a vivid and triumphant

---

5 For a chapter by chapter explanation of Joyce's Homeric parallels, see Blamires, *The Bloomsday Book* (Methuen & Co., 1970).

6 For an extended discussion of nationalism and political identity in the works of James Joyce, see Cheng, *Joyce, Race and Empire* (Cambridge University Press, 1995).

conclusion, James Joyce is more adept at reasoning his way through the difficulties in resolving a given conflict of arguments or laws. The further aspiration of this article, therefore, is to harness the lessons of the latter to provide insight into the former.

COMPETING FOREIGN JUDGMENTS: THE LEGAL DEBATE

One thing that is certain about the *Showlag* case is that, for the Jersey Court of Appeal, there was no certain answer. Indeed, so apparently confusing was the question of competing foreign judgments that the principal bases on which the lower courts analyzed the problem were as confused and unprincipled as could be. In effect, the Jersey courts were so taken aback by the notion that the plaintiffs would seek domestic recognition of a foreign judgment when a contrary judgment existed elsewhere that they refused to uphold either the first or the second previous judgments.[7] In fact, the third court from which the parties sought recognition placed them in an international "no exit" zone. In the words of the Jersey Court of Appeal:

The grounds for the decision appear to have been that . . . the heirs having taken proceedings against Mr. Mansour in two different jurisdictions (England and Egypt) and obtained judgment in their favour in one but not in the other could not insist upon the favourable judgment being applied in Jersey, irrespective of whether that judgment was the first or the second to be delivered.[8]

The judgment of the Privy Council was delivered by Lord Keith of Kinkle. Unlike the Jersey courts below, however, Lord Keith saw the issue not as an intractable dilemma for which there was no possible resolution, but rather as a bright choice between two clear rules.[9] While private international law was structurally incapable of providing an answer to the question of title to the disputed funds on the merits, it was perceived as at least capable of adjudicating a

[7] *Showlag, supra* note 1 at 133.

[8] *Ibid.*

[9] *Ibid.*, 133: "The appellant, representing the heirs, contends that the judgment of Hoffmann, J. being earlier in time, should prevail over the decision of the Egyptian court. The respondent on the other hand maintains that if either of the judgments is to be treated as creating an estoppel *per res judicata* it should be the later one. In their lordships' opinion the choice must indeed be between these alternatives."

resolution as between conflicting national regimes.[10] In the contest between a first-in-time doctrine and a last-in-time doctrine, Lord Keith was bound to adjudge one to be good and one to be bad.

The Privy Council perceived the issue to be one of first instance. At the same time, it saw the issue as one that called for the application of the principles and policy arguments ordinarily deployed in questions of *res judicata*. Lord Keith therefore gave weighty consideration to those aspects of English and other common law pronouncements that indicated a preference for terminating litigation upon the first adjudication. Further, he characterized this preference as being the fundamental policy underlying the *res judicata* doctrine.[11] Accordingly, the first-in-time approach was characterized from the outset as preferable, with the contrary American approach by implication being suitable only among sister states in a constitutional union where there is tight control over the compet-

10 In this, Lord Keith accentuated the "conflicts" or "private" part of this branch of international law. It is not so much that the private rights of the litigants are at stake, but rather that the "private" (as opposed to "public international") rights of the competing legal regimes are at stake. See McLeod, *The Conflict of Laws* 3, n.1 (Carswell, 1983): "private international law or conflict of laws rules are national in character. They are not rules of general application throughout the world . . . [i]t may be suggested that it is somewhat misleading to refer to the body of laws dealing with the resolution of legal disputes involving foreign elements as private international law. It is not international law in the true sense of the word."

The juxtaposition of "private" international law, which merely co-ordinates between competing national legal systems, and "public" international law, which is international law in the true sense of spanning and binding sovereign states, is truly ironic from the perspective of public international law, which has traditionally seen its own norms as representing not so much substantive limits on sovereign states but normative rules for co-ordination among the competing regimes. Thus, for example, the question is not so much whether one can attach a debtor's ship, but whether one state's legal system can intrude upon another's flag: *The Schooner Exchange* v. *McFadden*, 11 U.S. 116 (1812). Likewise, the question is not the extent of a coastal state's territorial sea, but whether the powers of sovereign states are subject to restraint: *Croft* v. *Dunphy*, [1933] A.C. 156 (P.C.) (Parliament unrestricted in its power to legislate beyond Canada's territorial sea.)

11 *Showlag, supra* note 1 at 134-36, citing (but not applying) Judgments (Reciprocal Enforcement) (Jersey) Law 1960, Art 6(1)(b): "[registration] may be set aside if the Royal Court is satisfied that the matter in dispute in the proceedings in the original court had previously to the date of the judgment in the original court been the subject of a final and conclusive judgment by a court having jurisdiction in the matter."

ing judicial processes.[12] The policy thrust of the judgment is that, for the competing systems in the international arena, a recognition and enforcement rule based on *res judicata* is necessary if endless litigation is to be avoided.[13]

To appreciate the Privy Council's point in perceiving finality to be the moving principle behind the first-in-time enforcement rule, one must make reference to the broader category of cases that relate more generally to the enforcement of foreign judgments. While the reasons provided by Lord Keith are relatively sparse, the policy concerns of the English law in the areas of recognition and enforcement have been expounded upon at some length over the past century.[14] The overriding trend has been one of expansion, with the courts moving from a territorially circumscribed notion of how legal systems operate[15] to a view bordering on full faith and credit.[16]

[12] *Showlag, ibid.*, 136: "their Lordships do not consider that the position in the United States is of assistance for present purposes."

[13] *Ibid.*: "So a judgment which is later in date than another foreign judgment which dealt with the same disputed matter is not to be recognized unless there exists some ground as discussed above which would have led to refusal to set aside the latter judgment had it been registered."

[14] In fact, English jurisprudence has recorded the recognition and enforcement of foreign judgments as far back as the seventeenth century. See *Weir's* case (1607), 1 Roll. Abr. 530K. 12; McLeod, *supra* note 10 at 581, n. 9.

[15] Dicey and Morris, *The Conflict of Laws* 985-96 (9th ed., 1973): "A foreign judgment has no direct operation in England. It cannot, thus, be immediately enforced by execution. This follows from the circumstance that the operation of legal systems is, in general, territorially circumscribed."

Accordingly, the early cases dealing with recognition and enforcement of foreign judgments were premised on a theory of comity among nations: *Cottington's* case (1678), 36 E.R. 640; *C.P.R. v. Western Union Telegraph Co.* (1889), 17 S.C.R. 151, which only later developed into a theory of legal obligation. See *Schibsby v. Westenholz* (1870), L.R. 6 Q.B. 155, 159.

[16] Unlike the equivalent English law, under the American constitutional doctrine of full faith in credit, the *lex fori*, determines the enforcement of a judgment of a sister state. See *Restatement of the Conflict of Laws* (2d), para. 99. The federal constitutional policy thereby outweighs any competing policy of the individual states in viewing the judgment of another state to be territorially circumscribed (*Milwaukee County v. M.E. Whiteco.*, 296 U.S. 268, 276-77 (1935)) although a balance is occasionally struck between the full faith in credit doctrine and the competing policy of maintaining and upholding the interest of the states where recognition and enforcement of another state's judgment would undermine a fundamental policy of the recognizing and enforcing state: *Restatement, supra*, para. 103. The starting point of any full faith in credit analysis is with recognition rather than non-recognition. See generally, *McLeod, supra* note 10, at 579-80.

The irony, of course, is that identical policy concerns in England and the United States have apparently brought about starkly divergent results.[17] While the recognition rules on which the first-in-time doctrine is ultimately premised have moved gradually from the isolated English jurisdictional stance to the interactive and cooperative American position, the actual rule with respect to competing foreign judgments adopted by the Privy Council is diametrically opposed to that embraced by the United States Supreme Court.[18] Accordingly, the following brief description of the historical development of each system may help explain the doctrinal roots and the philosophical basis for the movement of English-based law simultaneously toward and away from the American position.

The early English judgments represent a haphazard mix of principles and policies that range from unilateral extensions of comity[19] to legal obligation based on mandatory reciprocity,[20] all of which were synthesized only with the Court of Appeal's judgment in *Emanuel* v. *Symon*.[21] Considered the leading nineteenth-century authority on the enforcement of foreign judgments, *Emanuel* consolidated and exhaustively codified the circumstances in which the English courts would recognize and enforce an *in personam* foreign judgment. In doing so, the Court embraced a notion of territoriality in assessing sovereign jurisdiction that effectively sanctified the isolation of the English legal system and denigrated the unilateral assertion of jurisdiction by all other legal systems.

The facts of *Emanuel* were relatively straightforward.[22] The defendant Symon, a resident of the colony of Western Australia, entered into a partnership with several other individuals for the ownership and operation of a gold mine located within the colonial territory.

---

17 *Showlag, supra* note 1 at 136.

18 See generally, Ginsberg, "Judgments in Search of Full Faith and Credit: The Last in Line Rule for Conflicting Judgments" (1989) 82 Harv. L. Rev. 498.

19 *Weir's* case, *supra* note 14; *Roach* v. *Garvin* (1748), 1 Ves. Sen. 157, 159 (L.C.); *Wright* v. *Simpson* (1802), 6 Ves. 714, 730 (L.C.); see generally, Yntema, "The Enforcement of Foreign Judgments in Anglo-Canadian Law" (1935) 33 Mich. L. Rev. 129.

20 *Schibsby, supra* note 15 at 159; *Goddard* v. *Gray* (1870), L.R. 6 Q.B. 139, 149-50; Story, *Conflict of Laws* 24 (8th ed., 1883); Wheaton, *Elements of International Law* 112(1836). On the mix of comity, reciprocity, and obligation, see McLeod, *supra* note 10 at 581-82.

21 [1907] 1 K.B. 235 (K.B.).

22 For a more extended description of the facts, see *ibid.*, 235-36.

In 1899, Symon permanently left Western Australia and took up residence in England. In 1901, the plaintiffs, the remaining partners in the ownership and operation of the mine, commenced an action in the courts of Western Australia for the dissolution of the partnership and the taking of accounts. Symon was served in England with notice of the claim but took no steps to attend at or defend against the action. In 1903, the assets of the partnership were sold, accounts were taken, and the partnership was dissolved. On the taking of accounts, the partners were ordered by the Western Australian court to pay certain funds to rectify a deficiency in the assets of the partnership. After the dissolution, the plaintiffs brought an action against Symon in England to recover that portion of the deficiency for which Symon was liable and which, in his absence, the remaining partners had paid.

The English court of first instance gave judgment in favour of the plaintiffs.[23] In reaching this result, the Court reasoned that the defendant had effectively bargained his way into Western Australia and must therefore be deemed to have consented to the jurisdiction in which he was sued. The Court was therefore able to take on the recognition and enforcement controversy by effectively avoiding it altogether; the original jurisdiction was seen to be valid based on the acquiescence, and consequent estoppel, of the defendant.[24]

Symon appealed this finding, rephrasing the issue as one of the colonial court's essential authority for the purposes of private international law. Then, the question on appeal was cast to decide whether the courts of Western Australia had jurisdiction over Symon with respect to the partnership. The English Court of Appeal unanimously found that the courts of Western Australia did not have such jurisdiction. In overturning the lower court decision in favour of nonrecognition, Lord Alverstone, C.J. noted that the lower court decision contained essentially two different grounds for the conclusion that the defendant had submitted to the foreign jurisdiction:

first, that he was the owner of real property in the foreign country; and, secondly, that for the purpose of managing and dealing with that property he had entered into a contract of partnership in the foreign country.[25]

[23] *Ibid.*

[24] *Ibid.*, 240: "The defendant, by joining this partnership for the working of the mine in Western Australia, must, I think, be taken to have contracted that all partnership disputes, if any, should be determined by the Courts of that country, and thereby subjected himself to the jurisdiction of those Courts."

[25] [1908] 1 K.B. 302 at 306.

Lord Alverstone disposed of the first ground by citing a number of previously unsynthesized cases[26] as authority against the proposition that "mere possession of property in a foreign country is enough to give a general jurisdiction *in personam* to the Courts of the foreign country."[27] In a similar manner, Lord Alverstone disposed of the second ground, making reference to cases that until that point had stood for nothing but were now identified as decisive. Citing "authority of great weight which this Court cannot disregard,"[28] Lord Alverstone found:

in my view it is too broad a proposition to lay down that, given a contract of partnership in a foreign country, it follows that all matters arising between the partners have been submitted to the jurisdiction of the Courts of that country, although one of the partners is not a subject of, nor domiciled nor resident in, that country.[29]

The Court of Appeal was thus able to conclude that, to subject an individual to foreign legal process, there must be something connecting that individual to the foreign territory beyond that which ties him or her to the domestic court's territory:

to make a person who is not a subject of, nor domiciled nor resident in, a foreign country amenable to the jurisdiction of that country, there must be something more than a mere contract made or the mere possession of property in the foreign country.[30]

In a concurring judgment, Buckley, L.J. rejected the findings of the trial judge as unsound and set out the frequently cited rules for enforcement in England of *in personam* foreign judgments:

. . . this country will enforce [an *in personam*] foreign judgment: (1.) Where the defendant is a subject of the foreign country in which the judgment has been obtained; (2.) where he was resident in the foreign country when the action began; (3.) where the defendant in the character of plaintiff has selected the forum in which he is afterwards sued; (4.) where he has voluntarily appeared; and (5.) where he has contracted to submit himself to the forum in which the judgment was obtained.[31]

---

26 *Don* v. *Lippmoun* (1837), 5 Cl. & F. 1, 21; *Sirdar Gurdyal Singh* v. *Rajah of Faridkote*, [1894] A.C. 670, 685.

27 *Emanuel, supra* note 25 at 307.

28 *Ibid.*, 307, referencing *Schibsby* v. *Westenholz, supra* note 15 at 161, and *Sirdar Gurdyal Singh* v. *Rajah of Faridkote, supra* note 26.

29 *Ibid.*, 308.

30 *Ibid.*, 309.

31 *Ibid.*

The Court of Appeal thus determined that, in the absence of actual attornment to the foreign jurisdiction, the appropriateness of the forum was based on the residency or domicile of the defendant at the time the action was commenced. The result was a hybrid of status and contract in which a domestic national was not regarded as foreign unless he or she went to great lengths to become so.

In his concurring judgment, Kennedy, L.J. rejected the notion that appropriateness of forum could be based on a determination of which jurisdiction was most closely connected with the cause of action.[32] Citing *Sirdar Gordyal Singh* v. *Rajah of Faridkote*,[33] Kennedy, L.J. noted that an application of this latter proposed doctrine could have a burdensome result:

> [a] British subject, domiciled here, who, while temporarily in a foreign country, made a contract for a sale of goods there, must be taken to be bound by the decision of the Courts of that country in an action on the contract given merely ex parte, though he entered no appearance, and took no part in the proceedings, and had not resided in the country since the day on which he made the contract.[34]

Judicial support for the doctrine of residency and domicile therefore reflected two concerns: first, that a foreign court could otherwise be seen as having jurisdiction over a party who was territorially the subject of English jurisdiction, and second, that a defendant who was no longer resident in the foreign jurisdiction could be denied the ability to defend himself in accordance with the tenets of natural justice. The principle of territoriality therefore pushed in two directions at once, veering the English courts away from the foreign territory and causing them to circle protectively around their own. The fact that an action was intimately tied to a foreign jurisdiction or that a plaintiff might face substantial hardship in bringing an action in England was, at that moment in jurisprudential history, of no moment whatsoever.

The next stage in the development of the recognition and enforcement rules came with respect to a foreign judgment respecting personal status in the context of divorce rather than an *in personam* matter. The decision of the House of Lords in *Indyka* v. *Indyka*[35] greatly expanded the possibilities for recognition of

---

[32] *Ibid.*, 313.

[33] *Supra* note 26.

[34] *Supra* note 25 at 313.

[35] [1969] 1 A.C. 33.

foreign judgments, and, in the process, articulated a judicial policy that would be sympathetic to the finality of judgments wherever pronounced, and not only to those pronounced within the territorial confines of a given national legal authority. While the finer factual details were in dispute and remained unresolved, the essence of the controversy was the validity of a foreign divorce. Before the commencement of the Second World War, the appellant had been married under the laws of, and resided in, Czechoslovakia. With the commencement of hostilities, the appellant left his first wife to join the Czech army. When the Czech army was defeated by the Nazis, the appellant, along with many other Czech men, crossed the border into Poland and joined the Polish army. That army was, in turn, defeated by the Russians, and the appellant was captured in battle and sent to a forced labour camp in Siberia. Later in the war, the appellant was released so that he could rejoin the Polish army and once again fight against the Nazis.[36]

At the end of the war, the appellant was demobilized in England and given the choice of either staying in England or returning to Czechoslovakia. The appellant opted to stay in England. In February 1949, the first wife, who had not seen her husband for ten years, was granted a divorce by a Czechoslovakian court on the basis of deep disruption of marital relations. In 1959, the appellant, aware of the Czechoslovakian divorce, married the respondent in England. The second marriage lasted for five years, and in 1964, the respondent petitioned for divorce from the appellant. The appellant cross-petitioned for an order declaring the second marriage null and void on the basis that he was still married to his first wife. This argument assumed that the appellant's Czechoslovakian divorce was invalid in England, since the appellant had been domiciled in England at the time his divorce was granted in Czechoslovakia.

At trial, it was found that, since the appellant was domiciled in England at the time of the divorce and since, at the time of the divorce, under English law a wife could not in these circumstances validly obtain a divorce in a jurisdiction in which her husband was not domiciled, the Czech divorce was invalid in England.[37] Since the first marriage remained in full force and effect, the second marriage was declared null and void.

36 For a full rendition of the facts, see *ibid.*, 35-37.

37 *Ibid.*, 34.

When the case came before the Court of Appeal, the majority held that English courts recognized in foreign countries a like jurisdiction to that claimed for themselves.[38] Accordingly, if English rules were observed in Czechoslovakia, even though these rules did not apply and had no legal validity, the otherwise invalid Czech ruling would be recognized in England. Since the first wife had obtained a divorce after three years of residence in Czechoslovakia, and since three-year residency of a wife in England was a statutory basis upon which an English court could grant a divorce to the wife where the husband was not domiciled in England, the Czech divorce was declared valid in England. This applied even though the three-year rule was a new one for England, so that the Czech divorce would not have been valid under English law at the time it was granted.

On appeal to the House of Lords, Lord Morris of Borth-y-Gest conducted an extensive review of the law respecting the recognition of foreign decrees of divorce. He noted that the seminal case in this regard was *Le Mesurier* v. *Le Mesurier,*[39] in which it was held that foreign decrees of divorce would only be recognized in England if the parties had their domicile in that foreign jurisdiction. Reflecting the same territoriality concerns that underlay *Emanuel* v. *Symon* with respect to *in personam* judgments, the term "domicile" was narrowly construed to mean that place where the husband had elected to take up permanent residence. Concerned with the strictness of the territoriality doctrine, Lord Morris strongly approved of the significant broadening of *Le Mesurier* by a more recent Court of Appeal decision, *Travers* v. *Holley.*[40] The Court of Appeal had held in that case that where there is substantial reciprocity between jurisdictions on the basis upon which a divorce may be granted, it would be inconsistent with comity among nations for the English court to refuse to recognize a jurisdiction in a foreign court which *mutatis mutandis* it recognized for itself.[41] Since the first wife in *Indyka* did not receive her divorce on any basis that was similar to a basis for divorce available under the then applicable English law, it was sufficient to satisfy the principle of *Travers* that she could identify a basis for divorce under English law recognizable by the recognizing court.

---

[38] *Ibid.,* 36-37.

[39] [1895] A.C 517 (P.C.).

[40] [1953] 2 All E.R. 794 (C.A.).

[41] *Indyka, supra* note 35 at 75-76.

While finding that the notion of comity was a sufficient basis to uphold the decision of the Court of Appeal, Lord Morris went on to express concern with the concept of "limping marriages," where a divorce is recognized in one jurisdiction and not in another. Taking note of the speed and ease of transport that distinguished his era from the previous century, he then advanced a further and broader basis upon which he would have upheld the result arrived at in the Court of Appeal.[42] Lord Morris reasoned that where, as here, a party has a real and substantial connection to the jurisdiction within which a divorce is granted, there is no reason of privilege or policy that the decree of divorce should not be recognized in other jurisdictions.[43] This would be so regardless of the basis upon which the divorce was granted, the idea being that the connection of the subject matter to the forum should preclude all inquiry by the recognizing court.

In the words of Lord Wilberforce, concurring on this point:

the trend of legislation — mainly our own but also that of other countries with similar social systems — [is] to recognise divorces given to wives by the courts of their residence wherever a real and substantial connection is shown between the petitioner and the country, or territory, exercising jurisdiction.[44]

Taking the House of Lords' words at face value, what compelled the decision was neither the parties' consent nor an extension of pre-existing principles such as territoriality, but a driving need to update the rules of private international law and to bring them into conformity with modern litigation processes. The image is one of progress, from territorial seclusion to jurisdictional expansion, all in the name of ensuring that marital status is determined once and for all in the forum of first instance. Moreover, in Lord Wilberforce's formulation, the modern doctrine is neither artificial nor strictly procedural in terms, but rather "real and substantial" in its insistence on honouring the initial jurisdiction with which the parties are connected. The substantively identical questions of family status cannot, under the *Indyka* rationale, be litigated in subsequent jurisdictions once decided in an initial jurisdiction.

The nineteenth-century *Emanuel* rules and the twentieth-century thinking of *Indyka* came to a head in *Morguard Investments Ltd.* v.

---

[42] *Ibid.*, 76.

[43] *Ibid.*, 76-77.

[44] *Ibid.*, 105. Lord Wilberforce is cited with approval by Lord Pearson at 111.

De Savoye,[45] in which the reasoning applied by the House of Lords to judgments relating to personal status was considered by the Supreme Court of Canada in the context of a claim *in personam*. The respondents, Morguard Investments Limited and Credit Foncier Trust Company, were mortgagees of land in the Province of Alberta. The appellant, De Savoye, a resident of Alberta, was the mortgagor. In 1978, De Savoye moved to British Columbia and ceased to carry on business or reside in Alberta. The mortgages subsequently fell into default and the mortgagees brought an action in Alberta to enforce their security in the land. De Savoye was served with the claim in British Columbia in accordance with the Alberta rules for extra-provincial service, and, although properly served with process, did not appear or defend the action. There was no clause in the mortgages by which De Savoye had agreed to submit to the jurisdiction of the Alberta court, nor did he attorn to the jurisdiction. The mortgagees obtained default judgment in Alberta, sold the mortgaged property, and then commenced separate actions in British Columbia against De Savoye for recognition and enforcement of the Alberta judgment with respect to the balance outstanding on the mortgages.[46]

Judgment was granted in favour of the mortgagees in the British Columbia Supreme Court on the basis that the Alberta court had properly exercised its jurisdiction in making the orders for recovery on the mortgages.[47] De Savoye's appeal to the British Columbia Court of Appeal was dismissed on the basis that the default judgments in Alberta could be enforced in British Columbia on the basis of the reciprocal jurisdictional practice between the two provinces.[48] In reaching this conclusion, the British Columbia Court of Appeal expressly rejected *Emanuel* and applied *Travers*, acknowledging that in doing so it was extending *Travers* beyond *in rem* to *in personam* claims. The issue on appeal to the Supreme Court of Canada, therefore, was whether a personal judgment validly given in one province against an absent defendant may be enforced in another where the defendant now resides. In the absence of a constitutionalized doctrine of full faith and credit, of course, the legal relationship between Canadian provinces with

---

[45] [1990] 3 S.C.R. 1077.

[46] For a more thorough version of the facts, see *ibid.*, 1083.

[47] *Morguard Investments Ltd.* v. *De Savoye* (1987), 18 B.C.L.R. (2d) 262 (B.C.S.C.).

[48] *Morguard Investments Ltd.* v. *De Savoye* (1988), 27 B.C.L.R. (2d) 155 (B.C.C.A.).

respect to the enforcement of "foreign" provincial judgments was identical to that pertaining to fully sovereign nations.[49]

In giving judgment for the unanimous court, La Forest, J. conducted an extensive review of the historical evolution of the recognition of foreign judgments. In the first place, Buckley, L.J.'s summary in *Emanuel* of the circumstances in which an *in personam* judgment of a foreign court would be recognized in England was acknowledged as still reflecting the law of England.[50] La Forest, J. noted that attempts to expand recognition of foreign judgments beyond the limitations fixed in *Emanuel* have been firmly rejected in England,[51] and that any subsequent flexibility in the doctrine was limited to issues of family status and other claims *in rem*.[52] In Canada, the authority of *Emanuel* was consistently accepted in dealing with "foreign" judgments emanating from other provinces as well as from other sovereign nations.[53]

Not satisfied to recite tradition, the Supreme Court turned to what it considered to be an analysis of first principles. According to

[49] See the discussion, *supra* notes 15-16 and accompanying text.

[50] *Supra* note 45 at 1088.

[51] *Ibid.*, 1088-91, wherein La Forest, J. noted that *Emanuel* expressly rejected both the notion advanced in *Becquet* v. *MacCarthy* (1831), 2 B. & Ad. 951, 109 E.R. 1396 that recognition be extended to judgments respecting real estate held by defendants within the foreign jurisdiction where the cause of action arose while the defendant was within the jurisdiction, and the notion advanced in *Schibsby*, *supra* note 15 that a party may be taken to have implicitly consented to the jurisdiction of a foreign court where the party enters into a contract while residing in that jurisdiction.

[52] Subsequent to *Emanuel*, the *Travers* doctrine was expressly limited by the English Court of Appeal to judgments *in rem*. See *In re Trepca Mines Ltd.*, [1960] 1 W.L.R. 1273 (C.A.).

[53] *Morguard*, *supra* note 45 at 1091. Prior to *Morguard*, the Canadian Constitution left no room for a distinction between inter-provincial and international issues of recognition and enforcement. See, for example, *New York* v. *Fitzgerald*, [1983] 5 W.W.R. 458 (B.C.S.C.); *Walsh* v. *Herman* (1908), 13 B.C.R. 314 (B.C.S.C.); *Marshall* v. *Houghton*, [1923] 2 W.W.R. 553 (Man. C.A.); *Matter* v. *Public Trustee* (1952), 5 W.W.R. (N.S.) 29 (Alta. S.C., App. Div.); *Wedlay* v. *Quist* (1953), 10 W.W.R. (N.S.) 21 (Alta S.C., App. Div.); *Bank of Bermuda Ltd.* v. *Stutz*, [1965] 2 O.R. 121 (H.C.); *Traders Group Ltd.* v. *Hopkins* (1968), 69 D.L.R. (2d) 250 (N.W.T. Terr. Ct.); *Batavia Times Publishing Co.* v. *Davis* (1977), 82 D.L.R. (3d) 247 (Ont. H.C.), aff'd (1979), 105 D.L.R. (3d) 192 (Ont. C.A.); *Eggleton* v. *Broadway Agencies Ltd.* (1981), 32 A.R. 61 (Alta. Q.B.); *Weiner* v. *Singh* (1981), 22 C.P.C. 230 (B.C. Co. Ct.); and *Re Whalen and Neal* (1982), 31 C.P.C. 1 (N.B.Q.B.). But see, however, *Marcotte* v. *Megson* (1987), 19 B.C.L.R. (2d) 300 (B.C. Co. Ct.).

La Forest, J., the basic tenet of international law is that sovereign states have exclusive jurisdiction over their own territory, and that states are thus "hesitant to exercise jurisdiction over matters that may take place in the territory of other states."[54] Actions of foreign states were thus recognized or not on the basis of comity. Comity, however, was said to be misconstrued in the era of *Emanuel* "to be deference and respect due by other states to the actions of a state within its territory."[55] Rather, La Forest, J. offered his own more complete definition of comity:

[Comity] is neither a matter of absolute obligation, on the one hand, nor of mere courtesy and good will, upon the other. But it is the recognition which one nation allows within its territory to the legislative, executive or judicial acts of another nation, having due regard both to international duty and convenience, and to the rights of its own citizens or of other persons who are under the protection of its laws.[56]

His Lordship went on to state that the content of comity adjusts to reflect the changing nature of the world; the sociological basis for the nineteenth-century *Emanuel* rule has now apparently disappeared in a world community, even in the face of decentralized political and legal power. Accommodating the flow of wealth, skills, and people across state lines has now become the imperative. Under these circumstances, our approach to the recognition and enforcement of foreign judgments would appear ripe for reappraisal.[57]

Having established its unanimous disagreement with the rules in *Emanuel*, the Supreme Court declined further to comment on the enforcement of foreign *in personam* judgments. It is therefore difficult to discern on even the closest reading the precise principle that the Court perceived as replacing the territoriality doctrine that had been thought to govern since *Emanuel*. Addressing the case at hand, La Forest, J. found simply that a serious error had been committed when the courts transposed *Emanuel* to inter-provincial relationships,[58] and that the purpose of the Canadian Constitution was to

---

[54] *Ibid.*, 1095.

[55] *Ibid.*

[56] *Ibid.*, 1096, citing the United States Supreme Court in *Hilton* v. *Guyot*, 159 U.S. 113, 163-64 (1895), as cited in *Spencer* v. *The Queen*, [1985] 2 S.C.R. 278, 283 (per Estey, J.).

[57] *Ibid.*, 1098.

[58] *Ibid.*

create a single country with a common market where citizens are assured of economic and personal mobility across provincial lines.[59] This, combined with other constitutional and subconstitutional factors, led La Forest, J. to the conclusion that:

comity and private international law must be adapted to the situations where they are applied, and that in a federation this implies a fuller and more generous acceptance of the judgments of the courts of other constituent units of the federation.[60]

Having rejected the application of the rule from *Emanuel*, which allowed a person to avoid legal obligations in one sovereign jurisdiction by moving to another, La Forest, J. sought to establish a rule that would ensure that the plaintiff could chase the defendant across provincial lines by means of an expanded concept of the recognizing court's territorial interest. He achieved this by ensuring that the jurisdiction in which the suit is brought has relevance to the subject matter of the suit.[61] Rejecting the reciprocity approach favoured in the lower courts, La Forest, J. adopted a line of thought that the Supreme Court had previously applied to multijurisdictional tort claims in *Moran v. Pyle National (Canada) Ltd.*[62] Transposing the *Indyka* rule to a commercial litigation context, he pronounced that a court may take jurisdiction where it has a real and substantial connection to the subject matter of the dispute,[63] and that the courts of other provinces should, in turn, recognize and enforce the judgment of the court exercising jurisdiction.[64] In *Morguard*, the Alberta court had a real and substantial connection to the dispute in issue, because the property was situated in Alberta and the mortgages were executed in that province. The Alberta court therefore had jurisdiction that was recognizable and enforceable in British Columbia.[65]

The *Emanuel* doctrine was abandoned for the purpose of constitutionalizing interprovincial recognition and enforcement. Interestingly, the Supreme Court of Canada has subsequently gone on to

[59] *Ibid.*, 1099.

[60] *Ibid.*, 1101.

[61] *Ibid.*, 1103.

[62] [1975] 1 S.C.R. 393.

[63] *Morguard, supra* note 45, 1104-6.

[64] *Ibid.*, 1107.

[65] *Ibid.*, 1108.

apply the *Morguard* principle to foreign judgments by draping the federalism rationale in comity robes.[66] In this way, the "real and substantial connection" test has been treated as a near-universal statement of principle, with contemporary social and economic mobility providing the ties that bind even independent sovereigns together.[67] The notion seems to be that once a legal system has seized itself of a given dispute, the dispute must not travel with the parties but rather is wedded to the original jurisdiction by virtue of expansive recognition and enforcement rules. Claims that result in litigation, whether framed *in personam* or *in rem* and whether based on status or contract, are adjudicated once and finally in the jurisdiction of first instance. This rationale, in turn, leads to a first-in-time rule for all purposes, the territoriality of the jurisdiction being of utmost importance for the precise reason that territoriality has, in the modern era, ceased to be of any importance at all. The subsequent jurisdiction must, in a world said to be governed by comity, respect the first jurisdiction by refusing to readjudicate claims already addressed in that jurisdiction.

In the United States, both the constitutional sovereignty of the nation and the territorial and jurisdictional integrity of the states are embraced by the full faith and credit clause.[68] Since at least the

---

66 See, for example, *Amchem Products Inc. v. British Columbia (Workers Compensation Board)*, [1993] 1 S.C.R. 897. Numerous lower courts have followed suit. See *Moses v. Shore Boat Builders Ltd.* (1993), 106 D.L.R. (4th) 654 (B.C.C.A.), leave to appeal to the Supreme Court of Canada denied (1994), 23 C.P.C. (3d) 294; *Fabrelle Wallcoverings and Textiles Ltd. v. North American Decorative Products Inc.* (1992), 6 C.P.C. (3d) 170 (Ont. Gen. Div.); *McMickle v. Van Straaten* (1992), 93 D.L.R. (4th) 74 (B.C.S.C.); *Stoddard v. Accurpress Manufacturing Ltd.*, [1994] 1 W.W.R. 677 (B.C.S.C.); *Clancy v. Beach*, [1994] 7 W.W.R. 332 (B.C.S.C.); *Allen v. Lynch* (1993), 111 Nfld. & P.E.I.R. 43, 348 A.P.R. 43 (P.E.I.T.D.).

67 *Arrowmaster Inc. v. Unique Farming Ltd.* (1993), 17 O.R. (3d) 407, 411 (Ont. Gen. Div.): "I think it fair to say that the overarching theme of La Forest J.'s reasoning is the necessity and desirability, in a mobile society, for governments and courts to respect the orders made by courts in foreign jurisdictions with comparable legal systems, including substantive laws and rules of procedure.... The historical analysis in La Forest J.'s judgment, of both the United Kingdom and Canadian jurisprudence, and the doctrinal principles enunciated by the court are equally applicable, in my view, in a situation where the judgment has been rendered by a court in a foreign jurisdiction." See also *United States of America v. Ivey* (1995), 26 O.R. (3d) 533 (Ont. Gen. Div.).

68 United States Constitution, Article IV, s. 1: "Full Faith and Credit shall be given in each State to the public Acts, Records and the Judicial Proceedings of every other State. And the Congress may by general Laws prescribe the Manner in

late nineteenth century, the concept of full faith and credit has meant not only that a second jurisdiction (whether state or federal) must recognize and enforce the judgments of the first, but that a third jurisdiction must in its turn recognize and enforce the judgments of the second.[69] The irony, of course, is that the starting point for this last-in-time rule is a system governed by the principle of full faith and credit, which is the end point of the English first-in-time analysis. Again, in order to trace the development of this simultaneous move in the same and opposite directions by the two legal systems, a brief glance at the historical development of the American doctrine is called for.

Perhaps the earliest decision dealing directly with conflicting judgments is *Dimock v. Revere Copper Co.*[70] The case raised the question of enforcement in New York of two conflicting judgments, one rendered in federal court and the other in a Massachusetts state court. In January 1874, the Revere Copper Company commenced an action in Massachusetts for the enforcement of two promissory notes that had been previously executed by Dimock. Subsequently, in June 1874, Dimock filed a petition in bankruptcy with the United States federal district court for the District of Massachusetts and on March 26, 1875, Dimock was discharged by the district court of all debts and claims against his estate that had existed on June 23, 1874. On April 1, 1875, the state court, not having been advised by Dimock of the discharge from bankruptcy granted by the district court, granted judgment on the promissory notes in favour of Revere. Dimock did not pay the judgment, with the result that Revere commenced enforcement actions against Dimock in the state courts of New York where certain assets were located.[71]

In the New York action, the state court was faced with two judicial decisions, one purporting to be absolute evidence of a particular debt and the other purporting to be an absolute discharge of all debts. As a case of first instance, the dilemma admitted of no easy solution. As it happens, the New York state trial court ruled in favour of Dimock and, on appeal, the New York Court of Appeal

---

which such Acts, Records and Proceedings shall be proved and the Effect thereof.''

69 *Dimock v. Revere Copper Co.*, 117 U.S. 559 (1886).

70 *Ibid.*

71 For a more thorough elaboration of the facts and procedural history, see *ibid.*, 559-64.

ruled in favour of Revere. The issue ultimately presented to the United States Supreme Court was whether the discharge from bankruptcy acted as a bar to the New York proceeding brought to enforce the Massachusetts judgment on the promissory notes.

Justice Miller, speaking for the Supreme Court, approached the issue from the perspective of whether the Massachusetts state court judgment was valid in its own right. Upon a review of the facts, he found that the state court had valid jurisdiction that had not been challenged or ousted.[72] Citing the Supreme Court's own earlier decision in *Eyster* v. *Gaff*,[73] Justice Miller reasoned that the state court was fully competent to administer justice and, having done so, its decree could not now be treated as void. Miller, J. found that several cases pointed to Dimock's obligation to raise the defence of the discharge from bankruptcy in the state court proceedings in Massachusetts. Because Dimock had failed to do so, he was now barred from raising that defence in his action to enforce the Massachusetts state court judgment in New York.[74] Since the Massachusetts state court judgment was not barred in New York, it could be successfully sued upon in the New York state court. The Court left open the possibility that, after the discharge from bankruptcy, the Massachusetts state court could set aside its judgment on the promissory notes and thus render the judgment in favour of Revere unenforceable in other states.

The stated logic underlying the decision was that, where a defendant to an action possesses a judgment granted in a previous action that would render the pending or current action *res judicata*, and the defendant fails to produce that judgment, the defendant is to be barred from relitigating the issue decided in the second action in a different jurisdiction, on the basis of the defence created by the original judgment. In other words, as a matter of judicial policy, the last adjudication on a specific set of facts governs. The rationale was not so much one of last-in-time as one of controlling litigants' behaviour and, ultimately, judicial resources. When compared with the cognate English cases, of course, the point most worthy of note is that the identical concern for finality and the almost instinctive recoiling of the courts at the notion of relitigating a given issue led the *Dimock* court in the opposite direction.

[72] *Ibid.*, at 564.

[73] 91 U.S. 521 (1875).

[74] *Dimock, supra* note 69 at 565-66, citing *Steward* v. *Green*, 11 Paige 535; *Hollister* v. *Abbott*, 31 N.H. 442; and *Bradford* v. *Rice*, 102 Mass. 472.

What the United States Supreme Court did not address in *Dimock*, however, was the direc· effect of the second judgment on the first. Indeed, while the Supreme Court insisted that the New York court give full faith and credit to the last-in-time judgment of the Massachusetts court, the judgment rendered by the Massachusetts state court was, in turn, permitted to have no faith in and give no credit whatsoever to the first-in-time judgment of the federal Bankruptcy Court. At first blush, therefore, the rule as formulated by the Supreme Court embraced a number of substantial policies, but the practical effect was such that finality was certainly not among them. While the third court had to respect the prior two, the defendant in the second was free to use its private discretion in raising or not raising the first judgment and thereby according it equal respect. At this early stage in the development of the doctrine, therefore, the question remained as to whether last-in-time was a requirement of *res judicata* or a fundamental error in the application of the constitutional imperative to recognize the earlier judgments of sister courts.

The United States Supreme Court next visited the question of constitutional error in *Treinies* v. *Sunshine Mining Co.*[75] The *Treinies* decision was the culmination of a long and complicated set of proceedings that spanned two states, spawned a multiplicity of hearings and appeals, and generated irreconcilable decisions.[76] In *Treinies*, Mrs. Pelkes passed away leaving one-third of her estate to her daughter, Mason, and two-thirds of her estate to her second husband, John Pelkes. Mason and Pelkes elected not to observe the terms of the will and divided the estate between them, with each person choosing for him or herself the properties desired. One piece of property, mining stock in the Sunshine Mining Co., was considered valueless and not divided between the parties. By default, it remained in Pelkes's hands. Subsequently, the mining stock appreciated considerably in value and Mason brought an action in the state court of Washington to remove Pelkes as executor and dissipate the mining stock.[77] Pelkes and his assignor of the stock, Treinies, cross-petitioned for a declaration of Pelkes's ownership of the stock. At this time, Mason brought a motion for a writ of prohibition against further proceedings in the Washington state

---

[75] 308 U.S. 66 (1939).

[76] For a discussion of the procedural history, see *ibid.*, 69-70.

[77] For a thorough review of the facts, see *ibid.*, 68-69.

court on the basis of lack of jurisdiction. The Washington state court found it had proper jurisdiction over the stock and refused the writ. It then granted judgment in favour of Pelkes on the issue of ownership of the stock.

Dissatisfied with the results obtained in Washington state, Mason commenced an action in state court in Idaho, again alleging her ownership of the stock. Following the initial decision and appeal to the Supreme Court of Idaho, the state court, on directed rehearing and despite the Washington judgment of which it had been fully apprised, determined that it had jurisdiction over the issue and awarded ownership of one-half of the mining stock to Mason. Pelkes, in turn, dissatisfied with the Idaho results, commenced an action in the Washington state court alleging that the Idaho decree was invalid and reasserting his ownership of the stock. At this time, the Sunshine Mining Co. brought an interpleader action in federal court to resolve the dispute. As a result of the interpleader, Mason and Pelkes were enjoined from continuing their proceedings at the state level.[78]

In the interpleader action, Pelkes alleged that the Washington judgment should be considered effective, since it was the first decision to resolve the questions of jurisdiction and ownership of the mining stock. The argument therefore reflected a *Morguard* type of thinking, with the first adjudication being the final one on the assumption that the requisite jurisdictional link was established. Pelkes also went on to question the constitutional accuracy of *Dimock*, asserting that the failure of the Idaho court to uphold the Washington decision was contrary to rather than compelled by the full faith and credit clause. Justice Reed, speaking for the Supreme Court, refused to consider the point as worthy of serious constitutional merit:

The contention of [Pelkes] in the interpleader proceedings that the Idaho court did not have jurisdiction of the stock controversy because that controversy was in the exclusive jurisdiction of the Washington probate court must fall, because of the Idaho decision that the Washington probate court did not have exclusive jurisdiction. This is true even though the question of the Washington jurisdiction had been actually litigated and decided in favour of Pelkes in the Washington proceedings. If decided erroneously in the Idaho proceedings, the right to review that error was in those [Idaho] proceedings. While petitioner sought review from the decree of the Supreme Court of Idaho by petition for certiorari to this Court, which was denied, no review was sought from the final

78 *Ibid.*, 74.

decree of the Idaho District Court of August 18, 1936, on new findings of
fact and conclusions of law on remittur from the Supreme Court of
Idaho. . . . The holding by the Idaho court of no jurisdiction in Washington necessarily determined the question raised as to the Idaho jurisdiction. . . . The power of the Idaho court to examine into the jurisdiction
of the Washington court is beyond question. Even where the decision
against validity of the original judgment is erroneous, it is a valid exercise
of judicial power by the second court.[79]

In the result, not only must the defendant adduce the evidence
of the prior decision as a *res judicata* bar to the subsequent proceeding, but, if it fails to bar the subsequent proceeding, the defendant
must pursue all direct remedies to correct any error that occurred
in that proceeding. The failure to correct the error of the second
jurisdiction leaves the subsequent decision as *res judicata* the
relitigation of the issue in a third jurisdiction, notwithstanding any
alleged violation of the full faith and credit clause. Using logic that
can only be described as less than impeccable, the rule driven by
the requirement of recognition and equality between jurisdictions
turned out to be one that raised each subsequent jurisdiction over
and above its predecessor in such a way that no recognition could
be said to be required at all. In effect, the full faith and credit clause
required a third court to sanctify its own violation by the second
court, ignoring the sovereignty of the first court in the process.

Until the 1950s, the United States Supreme Court left open the
most perplexing aspect of the last-in-time rule — the effect of the
rule on the judgment in the initial jurisdiction. In *Sutton* v. *Leib*,[80]
Leib was liable to pay fixed monthly support to Sutton under the
terms of their 1939 divorce until such time as she remarried. On July
3, 1944, in Nevada, Sutton married Henzel, the latter having been
granted a divorce from his wife by the Nevada state court earlier in
the day. The "former" Mrs. Henzel was never served with notice of
the divorce proceedings and made no appearance at the Nevada
divorce proceedings. On August 3, 1944, Mrs. Henzel brought proceedings in the New York state court against Henzel, which were
defended by Henzel, and which resulted in the Nevada divorce being
declared null and void. Upon this finding, Sutton applied for and
was granted by the New York state court an annulment of her
marriage to Henzel. At no time was any action taken in Nevada, and
the original Nevada divorce and subsequent marriage remained

[79] *Ibid.*, 76-77.
[80] 342 U.S. 402 (1952).

unchallenged in Nevada. On the marriage of Sutton to Henzel, Leib ceased to make alimony payments to Sutton. Upon the annulment, Sutton sued Leib in the United States District Court for the Southern District of Illinois to have the alimony payments reinstituted and to require Leib to make a lump sum payment equal to the amount that would have been due up to that date but for the annulled marriage.[81]

The Illinois district and appellate courts each found that Leib was neither liable to make continuing alimony payments nor to make the lump sum payment.[82] In coming to this conclusion, the appellate court reasoned that the Nevada divorce remained valid in Nevada despite the New York ruling as to its validity and, as such, the subsequent marriage in Nevada validly terminated Leib's alimony obligations. The Court further reasoned that the subsequent annulment could not serve to reinstate the alimony obligations. The issue on appeal to the United States Supreme Court was whether the Illinois district court should give full faith and credit to the Nevada marriage or to the New York annulment.

As in *Dimock*, the Supreme Court approached the issue by addressing the validity of the second decision — in this case, the New York annulment. Justice Reed, again speaking for the Court's majority, expressed concern for the existence of "limping" judgments that lingered with validity in their initial jurisdictions but were unable to travel with the parties to sister states. With this concern in mind, he started his reasoning with various statements of principle that suggested he might embrace an English-style approach. He emphasized that the burden is on the party attacking the validity of a judgment to demonstrate its invalidity[83] and went on to assert that any such prior judgment is *res judicata* between the parties "and is unassailable collaterally."[84] In fact, Justice Reed went out of his way to point out that, in matters of family status as well as other subject areas, the decree of one state court is entitled to full faith and credit throughout the United States.[85]

Having set up the judgment for a fundamental reversal in direction, Justice Reed then slipped back onto the path that the United

---

[81] For a complete discussion of the factual background and procedural history, see *ibid.*, 405-6.

[82] *Ibid.*, 404.

[83] *Barber* v. *Barber*, 323 U.S. 77 (1944) and *Cook* v. *Cook*, 342 U.S. 126 (1951).

[84] *Sutton, supra* note 80 at 408, citing *Treinies, supra* note 75 at 76-78.

[85] *Ibid.*, citing *Milliken* v. *Mayer*, 311 U.S. 457, 462 (1940).

States courts have followed all along. Emphasizing the substantive *Morguard*-like link between the parties and, ironically, the second jurisdiction to consider the status of their marriage, the Court re-embraced the last-in-time rule in a way that bound not only the third jurisdiction but the first as well:

> As both parties were before the New York Court, its decree of annulment of their Nevada marriage ceremony is effective to determine that the marriage relationship of petitioner and Henzel did not exist at the time of filing the present complaint in Illinois for unpaid alimony. . . . [A]s to the New York decree annulling the marriage, New York had such jurisdiction of the parties and its decree is entitled to full faith throughout the Nation, in Nevada as well as in Illinois. The New York invalidation of the Nevada divorce of the Henzels stands in the same position. As Mrs. Henzel was neither personally served in Nevada nor entered her appearance, the Nevada divorce decree was subject to attack and nullification in New York for lack of jurisdiction over the parties in a contested action.[86]

The substantial connection of the parties to the last-in-time jurisdiction was deployed as the means of pulling the foundation out from under the first-in-time judgment. When combined, therefore, with the reasoning in *Treinies*, the applicable doctrine allows the defendant in the last-in-time jurisdiction to determine for his or her unilateral purposes the rule that will apply from coast to coast, even in a state whose highest court has ruled to the contrary.

Looking back over the English and American cases, it is apparent that none of the policy concerns for finality of litigation, *res judicata*, judicial resources, fundamental fairness, territoriality, sovereignty, and so on compels either a first-in-time rule or a last-in-time rule. The logical flow from first principles to both rules is internally flawed in such a way that either line could have taken a turn to the contrary at any moment in the development of the jurisprudence. Likewise, it is impossible to say that one of the rules trumps the other in a way that makes one right and one wrong. The doctrinal conflict confronted by the Privy Council in *Showlag* starts with the possibility of going either way and also ends that way. Neither rule can defeat the other on its own terms or, apparently, on any terms familiar to the legal debate.

COMPETING JUDGMENTS OF FOREIGNERS: THE LITERARY DEBATE

Unlike the *Showlag* case, whose narrative is refreshingly straight-forward, the "Cyclops" chapter in *Ulysses* stands out as a narratively

---

[86] *Sutton, supra* note 80 at 408-9.

intricate and difficult read in a book that is renowned for its narrative intricacy and difficulty.[87] In the first place, there is a narrative persona speaking in the first person who has never previously been introduced in the novel and who will never subsequently appear after the "Cyclops" episode. Thus, the opening line of the chapter, "I was just passing the time of day" is as misleading in its casual conversationalism as any opening line could be. The identity of the narrator is a mystery, and the voices that the narrator will go on to adopt throughout the chapter are anything but conversational in tone. The "Cyclops" episode, much as it is a dramatic encounter between two strong characters, is written in a series of complicated and disjointed narrative voices not easily followed by the casual reader.

The fascination with narrative and word play is, of course, both typical of Joyce and appropriate to the subject matter at hand. The protagonist, Leopold Bloom, is himself an advertising salesman, quite literally a peddlar of gimmickry through words. While Homer followed his hero, Odysseus, through various real and imagined ports of call in the ancient world, Joyce winds his hero through a single adventurous day making his appointed rounds and sales calls. In the process, where Odysseus engages the Cyclops, Bloom engages the Citizen, making for a fierce and highly visual midadventure clash. For Joyce, the high drama of the scene seems to spur an exaggerated level of narrative experimentation, with the unidentified first-person voice changing from page to page and paragraph to paragraph into an assortment of stylized parodies. At one moment the reader is immersed in the narrative of an old Celtic tale and, in the next, is confronted with legalese or romantic songs or mock parliamentary debate, etc. Just as one never knows how the confrontation with the Citizen will turn out, one never knows from page to page how the story itself will be told.

Just as *Showlag* poses a legal contest between a good rule and a bad rule, "Cyclops" poses a political contest between a good nationalist and a bad nationalist. The ironically named Citizen,

---

[87] One needs no authority whatsoever for the proposition that making one's way through *Ulysses* is both a pleasure and an ordeal. Several generations of students have verified the point through experience. *Ulysses* is, according to Virginia Woolf, a piece of work that can be described as "undergraduate," embodying both high modernist pretensions and seemingly adolescent narrative experimentation. Lecture notes for Richard Ellman's course, "The Modern Novel," Northwestern University, 1972-73, on file in the author's memory.

whose adversary, Bloom, wants nothing more than to be a citizen himself, embraces an ardent and xenophobic brand of nationalism. The Citizen is chauvinistic about Ireland and all things Irish to an extent that goes beyond stubbornness to outright ill-will. In his one-eyed world view, he sees everything through an Irish lens, dislikes the British and all other foreigners, and is open to no rational debate on the point. The Citizen spends his entire afternoon holding court in a pub rallying his troops, bullying his adversaries, and holding forth with a running beer-soaked and semi-rational commentary on Irish and world politics.

Bloom, on the other hand, is a distinctly good nationalist, seeing the world through two well-balanced eyes. At the beginning of the episode, Bloom feels socially trapped into engaging the Citizen in the pub and is compelled by his personality to answer the Citizen's boisterous passion with measured and reasoned responses. The key to his personality, of course, is that, notwithstanding that he encounters his nemesis in a pub steeped in Irish tradition, Bloom refuses to drink:

Hello, Bloom, says he, what will you have?

So they started arguing about the point, Bloom saying he wouldn't and couldn't and excuse him no offence and all to that and then he said well he'd just take a cigar.

Gob, he's a prudent member and no mistake.

Give us one of your prime stinkers, Terry, says Joe.[88]

The Citizen's prime weapon clouds his brain. Bloom's weapon, on the other hand, lets him think clearly, but makes the eyes of everyone around him tear. The image is certainly an appropriate one, given that the hero is meant to blind the one-eyed monster by the end of the encounter. Thus, while the episode proceeds with the Citizen increasingly lashing out with intoxicated fury, Bloom fights back with reason and a prime stinker as his weapon of choice.

What most characterizes the encounter between Bloom and the Citizen is that, while the Citizen's portion of the dialogue is full of bluster and lacking in all introspection or debate, Bloom's spoken lines are argumentative in the extreme. While the Citizen sees nothing but his own clouded point of view, Bloom perceives every point of debate as possessing two sides and feels obliged to articulate them. In this way, the one-eyed Citizen is contrasted startlingly

[88] *Ulysses*, 302.

with the two-eyed Bloom, much as the crude nationalist monster is contrasted with the hero as the outsider who wants nothing more than to integrate as a citizen.

By way of illustration, the conversation turns to the recent hanging of a petty criminal turned nationalist martyr. While Bloom debates the point, the Citizen pays tribute. In the brief dialogue that ensues, Joyce presents a picture of Bloom's two eyes struggling against the Citizen's one:

The memory of dead, says the Citizen taking up his pint glass and glaring at Bloom.

Ay, ay, says Joe.

You don't grasp for my point, says Bloom. What I mean is. . .

Sinn Fein! says the Citizen. *Sinn fein amhain!* The friends we love are by our side and the foes we hate before us.[89]

This type of struggle between the two characters permeates every topic of conversation. In one renowned passage that is both morbid and entertaining, the conversation turns to a local sailor, Jackie Tar, who was flogged by the captain on a British navy vessel:

That's your glorious British navy, says the Citizen, that bosses the earth. The fellows that never will be slaves, with the only hereditary chamber on the face of God's earth and their land in the face of a dozen game hogs and cotton ball barons. That's the great empire they boast about of drudges and whipped serfs.

On which the sun never rises, says Joe.

And the tragedy of it is, says the Citizen, they believe it. The unfortunate yahoos believe it.[90]

The Citizen's bluster continues to mount as he simultaneously preaches and imbibes, only to be cut off by a doubting and argumentative Bloom:

They believe in rod, the scourger almighty, creator of hell upon earth and in Jackie Tar, the son of a gun, who was conceived of unholy boast, born of the fighting navy, suffered under rump and dozen, was scarified, flayed and curried, yelled like bloody hell, the third day he arose again from the dead, steered into heaven, sitteth on his beamend 'til further orders whence he shall come to drudge for a living and be paid.

But, says Bloom, isn't discipline the same anywhere? I mean, wouldn't it be the same here if you put force against force?

89 *Ibid.*, 304.
90 *Ibid.*, 327.

Didn't I tell you? As true as I am drinking this porter, if he was at his last gasp he'd try to down face you that dying was living.

We'll put force against force, says the Citizen, we have our greater Ireland beyond the sea. They were driven out of house and home in the black 47. · · ·

Perfectly true, says Bloom. But my point was. . .[91]

At the initial stages of the encounter, it would seem that the Citizen has gotten the better of Bloom. While the former may still be a monster and the latter a potential hero, there is an attractive, almost poetic, quality to the Citizen's bluster that cannot be matched by the apparently petty logic that Bloom throws in its path.

The real stakes come out, however, when the characters finally reach the central point of their conversation. Bloom, the Jewish merchant of words, feels himself an outsider in the room full of nationalists. It is here that the political contest between good and bad, which is the centrepiece of the chapter, takes form:

Persecution, says he [i.e., Bloom], all the history of the world is full of it. Perpetuating national hatred among nations.

But do you know what a nation means? says John Wyse.

Yes, says Bloom.

What is it? says John Wyse.

A nation? says Bloom. A nation is the same people living in the same place.

By God, then, says Ned, laughing, if that's so I'm a nation for I'm living in the same place for the past five years.

So of course everyone had a laugh at Bloom and says he, trying to muck out of it:

We're also living in different places.

That covers my case, says Joe.

What is your nation if I may ask, says the Citizen.

Ireland, says Bloom. I was born here. Ireland.

The Citizen said nothing only cleared the spit out of his gullet and, gob, he spat a Red bank oyster out of him right in the corner.[92]

Bloom, of course, is a good nationalist. He wants to belong to Ireland, to be a citizen just like the Citizen. But the Citizen suffers

91 *Ibid.*, 327-28.

92 *Ibid.*, 329-30.

from the typical excesses of ultra-nationalism, espousing a doctrine that is fundamentally racist and exclusionary. To Bloom, of course, this viewpoint represents an injustice that must be exposed as such so that all with two eyes can see it for what it is. As Bloom starts to fight back against the Citizen, however, his own voice rises and subtly transforms itself from one of reason to one of passion:

Shove us over the drink, says I. Which is which?

That's mine, says Joe, as the Devil said to the dead policeman.

And I belong to a race too, says Bloom, that is hated and persecuted. Also now, this very moment, this very instant.

Gob, he near burnt his fingers with the butt of his old cigar.

Robbed, says he. Plundered. Insulted. Persecuted. Taking what belongs to us by right. At this very moment, says he, putting up his fist, sold by auction off in Morocco like slaves or cattle.

Are you talking about the New Jerusalem? says the Citizen.

I am talking about injustice, says Bloom.[93]

As Bloom's old cigar and his weapon of reason get worn down, a more intoxicating and passionate tone is adopted. Indeed, as the Citizen accelerates his own blustery intoxication, Bloom himself engages in more and more heated rhetoric until he finally storms out of the pub and into a friend's car in a barrage of drunken, shouted insults:

Mendelssohn was a Jew and Karl Marx and Mercadante and Spinoza. And the Saviour was a Jew and his father was a Jew. Your God.

He had no father, says Martin. That'll do now. Drive ahead.

Who's God? says the Citizen.

Well, his uncle was a Jew, says he. Your God was a Jew. Christ was a Jew like me.

Gob, the Citizen made a plunge back into the shop.

By Jesus, says he, I'll brain that bloody Jewman for using the holy name. By Jesus, I'll crucify him so I will. Give us that biscuitbox here.[94]

Bloom then is driven off, having successfully fired the last verbal shot back at the Citizen. As the Citizen staggered to the door to throw the biscuit tin at Bloom, his wide-open and drunken eyes

93 *Ibid.*, 331.

94 *Ibid.*, 340.

emerged from the dark pub into the bright afternoon sunshine and were momentarily blinded. Like the Cyclops in Homer's tale, the Citizen staggered back inside his lair incapacitated, and the hero escaped in time to go on to his next adventure.

On one level of the story, the hero beat the monster and the outsider beat the nationalist. On the other hand, in escalating from argumentative banality to rhetorical heights, Bloom was himself reduced to fighting the Citizen's blustering ethnic superiority with his own blustering superiority. As the story unfolds, it becomes clear that there is no good nationalism and bad nationalism, there are only competing nationalisms. While one can choose one's favourite under the circumstances, there are no principled grounds on which one can trump the other. Christ is a Jew like Bloom is an Irishman; both are true, and neither fact matters in the eyes of the adversary.

Moreover, what Joyce has made clear all along is that Bloom's real desire is to belong, to be Irish, not to be foreign. Bloom, too, is an Irish nationalist who wants to be a good nationalist, not a xenophobic and harsh one. And for that reason, Bloom has always desired to be included as a citizen in his face-off against the Citizen. Joyce's message, however, is that one cannot be a nationalist — one cannot believe in national inclusion — without simultaneously believing in exclusion. Thus, Bloom is proud to be Irish and he is proud to be a Jew, but it is in the very nature of that pride to assert some sense of difference or superior "otherness" as against the non-members. Inclusion, for Joyce, quite obviously means exclusion.

Accordingly, the nationalist debate with which the "Cyclops" episode begins turns out to be unwinnable. You cannot be both us and them, Citizen and non-Citizen, but can only choose between one or the other. In this, the contest between the good nationalist and bad nationalist is much like the contest between the last-in-time and the first-in-time rules. The good rule and the bad rule, the hero and the monster, are equally interchangeable.

THE CONFLICT OF CONFLICTS

As it turns out, both Lord Keith of Kinkle and Leopold Bloom set out to vanquish the wrong villain. For international law, whether public or private, the problem is much more profound than one of good rules and bad rules or one nationalism against another. All of the rules seem equally satisfactory when examined in isolation and equally unsatisfactory when analyzed comparatively. The Jersey

Court of Appeal in the *Showlag* case may indeed have been correct
— no rule is a good rule.[95]

The fundamental problem, played and replayed in every international law scene, is that the rhetoric of sovereignty, comity, national,
and international, cannot be overcome. International law — and in
this respect private international law or conflicts of law is the
paradigmatic case — cannot pronounce a ruling that transcends
the unilateral pronouncements of a given national jurisdiction,
because its goal is to foster and enforce respect for each nation's
laws. That is how nationhood and comity are thought to stand
together. At the same time, international law cannot protect and
enforce the sovereignty of a neighbouring nation's judgments
because it is the goal of the international legal system to submit any
given jurisdiction to its own universal norms. That is how internationalism and legal sovereignty are thought to stand together. We
simply do not know whether nations and their laws are sovereign
under international law or whether they are part and parcel of a
sovereign international system.

The conclusion of the Privy Council in *Showlag* provides a
graphic illustration of the point. In the words of Lord Keith, the
last-in-time rule is appropriate only in "an inter-state context where
the 'full faith and credit' clause of the Constitution applies."[96]
Within the United States, the states exist in union, and consequently the third jurisdiction can examine the entire package of
what came before it to assess the issue of *res judicata*. It is the fact of
collectivity — otherwise sovereign states existing under the identical meta-constitutional norms — that, for the Privy Council, distinguishes the American rule from the international rule.

Within the international system, the Privy Council reasoned, the
first-in-time rule necessarily applies. There each nation is, in effect,
on its own, and there is no question but that the proceedings of the
first jurisdiction are considered to have sprouted from a different
normative base and therefore to be qualitatively different from
those of the subsequent jurisdictions.[97] Accordingly, each successive

95 See *supra* note 7 and the accompanying text.

96 *Showlag, supra* note 1 at 136.

97 In *Showlag*, the situation was even more extreme, given the differing procedural
   routes that the various proceedings followed: "Their Lordships do not consider
   that the position in the United States is of assistance for present purposes, but
   they observe that there would clearly have been no question of Hoffmann J.'s

state must show respect to the previous one as its sovereign equal. To the extent that international law perceives states to be unified under a normative umbrella, the unification reflects a co-operative treaty regime, which is itself a product of the unilateral consent of each state rather than a legal or constitutional imperative.[98]

According to Lord Keith, the governing international convention on point is the 1968 Brussels Convention on Jurisdiction and Enforcement of Judgments in Civil and Commercial Matters, which in effect embraces the first-in-time rule.[99] This first-in-time treaty rule is posed by the Privy Council as standing in stark opposition to the last-in-time constitutional rule, the former being more appropriate to the sovereign equality and independence of states that have signed on to the treaty regime. Ironically, however, Jersey — the very state to which the rule is sought to be applied — is not a signatory to the treaty. Rather, Lord Keith reasoned, the treaty rule applies to Jersey not because it has exercised its sovereign free will, but as a matter of over-arching principle or as an international systemic rule. In Lord Keith's words:

Jersey is not one of the parties to the convention, but the circumstance that this rule finds its place in this important international convention must be of some persuasive effect in the consideration of whether a

---

judgment being capable of being founded on as [*sic*] res judicata for the purpose of the proceedings in Egypt, considering that these proceedings were primarily of a criminal character": *Ibid.*

98 Most discussions of the sources of international law identify the consent of sovereign powers as being first among sources. In effect, the consent theory has become a defence mechanism against the renowned Austinian positivist criticism of international law. See Austin, *The Province of Jurisprudence Determined* 201 (1954 ed.): "Law obtaining between nations is law improperly so called." See also *Reservations to the Genocide Convention Case*, [1951] I.C.J. 32, (Gueriero, McNair, Read, and HusMo, JJ., dissenting): "the legal basis of . . . conventions, and the essential thing that brings them into force, is the common consent of the parties"; *Asylum Case (Colombia v. Peru)*, [1950] I.C.J. 266, 277: "Custom formation based on a constant and uniform usage, accepted as law. . . ." Sovereign consent is posed as the ultimate source of a law that theoretically transcends sovereignty.

99 Article 27(5) of the Brussels Convention provides that a judgment shall not be recognized: "If the judgment is irreconcilable with an earlier judgment given in a non-contracting state involving the same cause of action and between the same parties, provided that the latter judgment fulfils the conditions necessary for its recognition in the State addressed."

similar preference for an earlier judgment in time may appropriately form part of Jersey law, in the absence of any contrary authority.[100]

Thus, while Jersey has not evidenced its accession to the first-in-time rule by exercise of sovereign consent, the rule applies to Jersey as a matter of principle; the multilateral treaty has become a quasi-constitutional rule that is appropriate for Jersey because it exists within the international legal system. This, of course, is the very thinking that justifies the last-in-time rule prevalent in the United States. American states embrace the last-in-time rule in order to respect the sovereignty and equality of each successive jurisdiction; all because, in the Privy Council's view, the several states under the constitution are somewhat less than fully sovereign. Jersey, on the other hand, embraces the first-in-time rule as a member of the international system, which overrides any need for sovereign action or consent, all in the name of respecting the full sovereignty and free legal will of the other jurisdictions with which it deals.

As the *Showlag* case demonstrates, international law is a prisoner of its own devices. Jersey and New Jersey are, effectively, equally sovereign and non-sovereign. International norms transcend sovereign jurisdictions by enforcing the rules of those very jurisdictions. At the same time, those norms protect sovereign independence — that is, uphold the various jurisdictions' independent rules — by making nations submit to systemic norms and by curtailing unilateral independent action. The real struggle of international law, as it turns out, is not the face-off between good rules and bad, last-in-time against first-in-time. Rather, the struggle in any given case is with the narrative of national independence and national submission to the law. It is this narrative that permeates and underlies the various manipulations of international law rules and forms the basis of the law's intense difficulty in overcoming intractably conflicting rules.

As for Leopold Bloom, he too may be struggling in vain against his adversary when the real enemy is far more deeply rooted in the text. The "Cyclops" episode is written in a way that intersperses the relatively sparse dialogue among more lengthy and densely descriptive passages. These passages, as indicated above, take the form of a series of exaggerated and, at times, nonsensical and parodied voices. The narrative thus ranges from the ridiculous to the sublime, from high drama to technical manual and from drunken and

---

[100] *Showlag, supra* note 1 at 136.

bawdy slang to Biblical exultations. Indeed, so prevalent are the fluctuations in narrative voice that the tone frequently changes in mid-paragraph, or even mid-sentence.

In the final scene of the chapter, Bloom escapes from the confines of the pub in which he has been trapped, while the Citizen emerges at the pub's doorway and is momentarily blinded by the sun. The scene unfolds as follows:

When, lo, there came about them all a great brightness and they beheld the chariot wherein He stood ascend to Heaven. And they beheld Him in the chariot, clothed upon in the glory of the brightness, having raiment as of the sun, fair as the moon and terrible that for awe they durst not look upon Him. And there came a voice out of Heaven, calling: *Elijah! Elijah!* And he answered with mean cry: *Abba! Adonai!* And they beheld Him even Him, ben Bloom Elijah, amid clouds of angels ascend to the glory of the brightness at an angle of forty-five degrees over Donahue's in Little Green Street like a shot off a shovel.[101]

As the final passage demonstrates, there are so many extremes, so much word play, so many changes in voice, that the text is at once highly amusing and excessively difficult. Moreover, the difficulty lies not only in following the action, but in discerning Bloom's essential personality. For Leopold Bloom, the more one reads into the chapter the more one becomes aware that the struggle for identity is not against the Citizen and his ultra-nationalism; rather the struggle for identity is against the unnamed, but ever-present, narrator. Bloom, like all the other characters in the chapter, is a captive of the very distinct narrative devices that characterize the entire episode. One simply cannot understand any given character, let alone resolve the clash between characters, without getting caught up in the extremes of descriptive technique.

Bloom's fight against the Citizen, therefore, is akin to the fight between one conflict of law rule and another. One does not know whether nationalism, or territoriality, is good or bad any more than one knows whether Leopold Bloom is Elijah the Prophet or a piece of dirt on a shovel. This struggle, so apparent in the final passage of the chapter, is foreshadowed at the outset with a subtlety that belies the extent of Joyce's insight. "Cyclops" begins with the unidentified narrator encountering a chimney sweep in what seems to be a near, and ultimately inconsequential, accident:

I was just passing the time of day with old Troy of the D.M.P. at the corner

---

[101] *Ulysses*, 343.

of Arbour Hill there and be damned but a bloody sweep came along and he nearly drove his gear into my eye.[102]

The real one-eyed monster is, in fact, the teller of the story. In a surprisingly post-modern finale to the most high-modern of novels, Joyce lets his readers know that it is the way that the story is told that is the truly interesting plot, the struggle of one character against another being a mere sideshow to the main event. Likewise, for international law, the struggle of the reasoning process and the battle between voices of sovereignty and voices of internationalism provide the interesting contest, with the arguments for and against one doctrine or another being merely a sideshow. The deep conflict, in both cases, is in the fabric of the text itself rather than in the surface colouration where the immediate contest between doctrines, characters, literary themes, and litigating parties takes place.

Joyce the dramatist pokes his narrator in the eye and opens the reader's eyes to the depth of the struggle. Lord Keith, on the other hand, the paradigm of analytic reasoning, remains both unfazed and unenlightened in his straightforward narration of the case. The lesson, of course, is that sometimes, and especially in international law, one must go far afield in order to engage a conflict and to bring its resolution home. The perspective thereby gained brings a heightened consciousness of the most conflicted aspect of the conflict of laws.

Sommaire

Le cyclope rencontre le Conseil privé: le conflit en droit international privé

Dans l'affaire Showlag, *le Conseil privé devait décider lequel de deux jugements étrangers incompatibles il allait exécuter, le plus ancien ou le plus récent. Le chapitre des "cyclopes" dans le roman* Ulysse *de James Joyce présente une version modernisée de la rencontre épique entre Odysseus et le géant cyclope qui habite dans une caverne. L'auteur examine le rapport entre le conflit juridique et le conflit évoqué dans le roman et il se penche sur le règlement judiciaire et le règlement littéraire des problèmes soulevés. L'auteur met l'accent sur la nature des arguments avancés et développés dans la décision judiciaire et dans le roman et il souligne les difficultés du droit à résoudre les problèmes posés par des règles contradictoires. Ainsi, l'auteur met*

---

[102] *Ibid.*, 290.

en lumière les tensions qui existent en droit international entre l'indépendance nationale et la soumission théorique au droit, c'est-à-dire entre les voix de la souveraineté et celles de l'internationalisme.

Summary

Cyclops Meets the Privy Council: The Conflict in the Conflict of Laws

In the Showlag *case, the Privy Council had to decide which of two conflicting foreign judgments it was to enforce, the first-in-time or the last-in-time. The "Cyclops" chapter in James Joyce's* Ulysses *presents a modernized re-enactment of the epic encounter between Odysseus and the cave dwelling one-eyed monster. The author explores the relationship between the legal conflict and the dramatic conflict, together with the judicial resolution and the literary resolution of the problems at hand. The article focuses on the nature of argument as displayed and worked through in the case law and in the novel, and points out the difficulty law has in overcoming intractably conflicting rules. In doing so, the author highlights the struggle in international law between national independence and national submission to law — the voices of sovereignty and the voices of internationalism.*

Territorial Modifications
and Breakups in Federal States

LUZIUS WILDHABER*

INTRODUCTION

THE ISSUE IN MUNICIPAL LAW

THIS ARTICLE DEALS WITH territorial modifications and breakups in federal states. It is conspicuous how incompletely and reluctantly this issue is handled by most federal constitutions. Internal territorial modifications are more readily regulated than external ones. New admittances seem conceivable, but secessions do not.

I shall discuss only the rules and practice of typical federal states.[1] It will be impossible to debate the divergencies of the various constitutional traditions, systems of government, divergent theories on sources of law, political context, and background. Of course, every federal state has its own unmistakable individuality and constitutes its own world. Nevertheless, I shall try roughly to sketch certain common features of federal systems, despite all the differences between the various countries and traditions.

---

* Professor, University of Basle, Judge of the European Court of Human Rights. This text is an updated version of an article entitled "Bestandesänderungen in Bundesstaaten," which appeared in "Recht zwischen Umbruch und Bewahrung," *Festschrift Rudolph Bernhardt* 905-33 (1995).

---

1 See generally J. Brossard, *L'accession à la souveraineté et le cas du Québec* (1976); W. Fetscherin, *Änderungen im Bestand der Gliedstaaten in Bundesstaaten der Gegenwart* (thesis) (Zürich, 1973).

THE ISSUE IN INTERNATIONAL LAW

It is striking that no federal constitution asks whether international minority or self-determination rights might have an effect on territorial modifications. Historically, this omission can easily be explained. Any minority rights that went beyond what was absolutely elementary belonged either to the reserved domain of domestic jurisdiction or else to human rights, and the self-determination of peoples was for a long time considered only a political or programmatic principle. In the practice of United Nations organs, self-determination meant no more than decolonization. Normally, minorities claiming special rights or even secession outside of a decolonization context were silenced. Instead, the sovereignty and territorial integrity of states were favoured, and non-intervention and respect for domestic jurisdiction were invoked. Secessions and newly formed states that did not originate in decolonization or voluntary agreement were accepted only reluctantly, after the success of the breakaway movement had been effectively established.

In recent years — and especially since the former Soviet Union and Yugoslavia have broken apart — the situation may well have changed. There are indications that self-determination may now go beyond decolonization, triggering claims to get rid of foreign occupations that flagrantly violate human rights and constitute an extreme repression both of the will of the majority and of popular sovereignty. These claims, to a large degree, constitute the new, post-colonial self-determination cases. It remains questionable whether current international law goes even farther. Basically, international law does not yet grant minorities a right to secede and form a new state at their own will.[2]

---

[2] See Y. Beigbeder, *International Monitoring of Plebiscites, Referenda and National Elections* (1994); C. Brölmann, R. Lefeber, and M. Zieck (eds), *Peoples and Minorities in International Law* (1993); D. Brühl-Moser, *Die Entwicklung des Selbstbestimmungsrechts der Völker unter besonderer Berücksichtigung seines innerstaatlich-demokratischen Aspekts und seiner Bedeutung für den Minderheitenschutz* (thesis) (Basel, 1994); A. Buchanan, *Secession* (1991); A. Cassese, *Self-determination of Peoples* (1995); Y. Dinstein, *The Protection of Minorities and Human Rights* (1992); F. Ermacora, H. Tretter, and A. Pelzl (eds), *Volksgruppen im Spannungsfeld von Recht und Souveränität in Mittel-und Osteuropa* (1993); T. M. Franck, R. Higgins, A. Pellet, M. N. Shaw, and C. Tomuschat, "L'intégrité territoriale du Québec dans l'hypothèse de l'accession à la souveraineté," in *Commission d'études des questions afférentes à l'accession du Québec à la souveraineté*, Exposés et études Vol. I 371-461 (1992); J. A. Frowein, R. Hofmann, and S. Oeter (eds), *Das Minderheitenrecht europäischer Staaten* (1993); H. Hannum, *Autonomy, Sovereignty, and*

The adoption of federalism can obviously reduce this dilemma, because, while respecting sovereignty, federalism can give minorities a respectable autonomy. In this way, the federal state constitutes a true model of a pluralistic society.

To be sure, federalism also has a centrifugal side, as Gregory Craven has subtly pointed out.[3] Precisely because minorities may enjoy autonomy as the member units of a federal state and because they can articulate their claims and build up their political elite and administrative infrastructure, secession is easier for them to effectuate than it would be in centralist or dictatorial regimes. Respect for minorities, which is inherent in genuine federalism, simplifies not only cohabitation but also the breaking apart. If one also claims — like the Arbitration Commission of the Conference for Peace in Yugoslavia[4] — that the borderlines between federal member units must be inviolable, one would seem to be punishing federal states for their respect for minorities and, as institutions, treating them worse than unitary states are treated.

OUTLINE OF THE ARTICLE

This article takes a comparative approach. It investigates whether federal states allow the separatist claims of their minorities for "internal modifications" on the basis of constitutional law as opposed to international law. These claims may amount primarily to (1) the formation of new member units, (2) the merger of existing member units, or (3) territorial exchanges between member units. Under international law, these issues of organization belong in principle to the domain of domestic jurisdiction. International law on the protection of minorities lacks the precision required to supersede municipal law.

Thereafter, the article proceeds to investigate whether domestic law knows any secessionist claims for "external modifications." These claims might amount primarily to (1) the formation of new

---

Self-Determination: The Accommodation of Conflicting Rights (1990); H. J. Heintze, *Selbstbestimmungsrecht und Minderheitenrechte im Völkerrecht* (1994); R. Müllerson, *International Law, Rights and Politics* (1994); A. Peters, *Das Gebietsreferendum im Völkerrecht*, (thesis) (Freiburg i. Br., 1994); K. L. Shehadi, *Ethnic Self-determination and the Break-up of States* (1993); P. Thornberry, *International Law and the Rights of Minorities* (1991); C. Tomuschat (ed.), *Modern Law of Self-Determination* (1993).

3 G. Craven, "Of Federalism, Secession, Canada and Quebec" (1991) 14 Dal. L. J. 231-65. See also *infra* notes 96-101.

4 See *infra* notes 96-99, 106.

sovereign states, (2) the merger or association with existing states or the integration into new entities, or (3) the exchange of territory with other sovereign states. These claims do not fall within domestic jurisdiction and are directly relevant under international law.

The question whether secessionist claims may be founded in international law and particularly in the self-determination of peoples will only be marginally explored. However, a comparative approach should permit a new outlook on this pervasive problem.

INTERNAL MODIFICATIONS WITHIN TYPICAL NON-COMMUNIST FEDERAL STATES

COMMON FEATURES

In typical non-communist federal states, a change in the number of the member units or territorial modifications between them are issues that are not left exclusively to the discretion of the member units directly concerned. They are of a "political" nature, insofar as the federal government — representing the whole of the federal community — must give its assent to the changes, whether they are on the level of the constitution or of legislation. Only "apolitical" rectifications of borders may normally be effected by a contract of the member units directly concerned. Since internal modifications are issues within the domestic jurisdiction of a federal state, they do not require recognition by other subjects of international law.

SIMPLIFIED PROCEDURES

Numerous federal states have set up rules for simplified modification procedures in times of expansion, change, and transition. After these phases, federal states often move on to a stage of permanent, peaceful stability and allow modifications only through more cumbersome procedures. Even then, however, modifications are not as a rule completely prohibited.

The United States and Canada

The constitutions of the United States (Article 4, section 3) and of Canada (British North America Act, 1867)[5] provided for the transformation of federal territories into member states and provinces by means of simple legislation. Thus, the United States

---

[5] 34 & 35 Victoria, c. 28. For the following developments, see Fetscherin, *supra* note 1 at 92-97, 108-12, 123-35.

expanded toward the west in five big thrusts, admitting into the federal union the territories west of the Mississippi River assigned to it in the Peace Treaty of Versailles in 1783,[6] the Louisiana Territories acquired from France in 1803,[7] Florida, which was transformed into a state in 1845, the North-West-Territories acquired in 1846,[8] and the regions taken over in the Peace Treaty with Mexico of 1848.[9] Similarly, the Canadian Parliament turned the prairie territories into provinces[10] by way of legislation.

Federal Republic of Germany

Article 29 of the Basic Law provided for a new configuration of the borders between member units (*Länder*) by means of a federal statute. The idea was to correct the fortuitous location of borders that had resulted from the military occupation of most German *Länder*. In 1976, Article 29 was amended and the obligation to reshape the borders was abolished. No *Land* has a right to ask that the federal government submit a statute concerning the new borders of member states.[11]

In Article 118 of the Basic Law, another rule concerns southern Germany. This rule came about — after a consultative vote in September 1950 — through the enactment of two federal statutes for a new formation of southern Germany in May 1951 and in a vote in December 1951. In this vote, Southern Baden voted no, but since a majority of three out of four voting regions was sufficient, the *Länder* Baden, Württemberg-Baden, and Württemberg-Hohenzollern were merged in the new *Land* Baden-Württemberg.[12]

---

6 The following states were formed: Ohio 1803, Indiana 1816, Mississippi 1817, Illinois 1818, Alabama 1819, Michigan 1837, and Wisconsin 1848.

7 The following states were formed: Louisiana 1812, Missouri 1821, Arkansas 1836, Iowa 1846, Minnesota 1858, South Dakota 1859, Kansas 1861, Nebraska 1867, North Dakota 1889, Montana 1889, Wyoming 1890, Oklahoma 1907.

8 They consisted of: Oregon 1859, Washington 1889, Idaho 1890.

9 The following states were formed: Nevada 1864, Colorado 1867, Utah 1896, Arizona 1912, New Mexico 1912.

10 Manitoba 1870, Saskatchewan and Alberta 1905.

11 Entscheidungen des Bundesverfassungsgerichts (BVerfGE) 13, 54 (73-74) (*Hessen* case, 1961).

12 Der Kampf um den Südweststaat. Verhandlungen und Beschlüsse der gesetzgebenden Körperschaften des Bundes und des Bundesverfassungsgerichtes, Vol. I (1952); BVerfGE I, 14 (1951); Fetscherin, *supra* note 1 at 81-88, 152-73.

On October 3, 1990, the German Democratic Republic (GDR) joined the Federal Republic of Germany under Article 23, sentence 2 of the Basic Law.[13] At the same time, Brandenburg, Mecklenburg-Vorpommern, Saxony, Saxony-Anhalt, and Thuringia became *Länder* of the Federal Republic of Germany, while Eastern Berlin became a part of the *Land* Berlin. These changes necessitated amendments to the constitution. The legislatures gave their assent in the form of a statute approving an international treaty (according to Article 59, section 2 of the Basic Law).[14]

India

The Constitution of India of 1949 endeavoured to transform the then nine provinces and 562 principalities into viable federal entities.[15] For a transitional period, it created four categories of states. In 1956, a federal statute reshaped the borders and split India into fourteen states[16] and six federal territories.[17] Since then, various new member states have been formed to settle ethnic, religious, or linguistic conflicts and to relieve tensions.[18] A considerable number of new member states were created in northeast

13 This was preceded by the Staatsvertrag, Wahlvertrag and Einigungsvertrag of May 18, Aug. 3 and Aug. 31, 1990, between the German Democratic Republic and the Federal Republic of Germany. See also BVerfGE 82, 316 (1990).

14 The legislators agreed with the majorities required to modify the constitution under Art. 79, para. 2 of the Basic Law.

15 As to the following, see D. Das Basu, *Constitutional Law of India*, 4th ed., 4-5, 394-985 (1985); M. P. Jain, *Indian Constitutional Law*, 4th ed., 256-58 (1987); M. V. Pylee, *Constitutional Government in India*, 4th ed. 74-89 (1984); H. M. Seervai, *Constitutional Law of India*, 3rd ed., Vol 1, 15, 173-83 (1983); K. P. Krishna Shetty, *The Law of Union-State Relations and Indian Federalism* 22-46 (1981); D. K. Singh (ed.), *V. N. Shukla's Constitution of India*, 7th ed., 3-8, 672-76 (1982).

16 Andra Pradesh, Assam, Bihar, Bombay (split up in 1960), Jammu and Kashmir, Kerala, Madya Pradesh, Madras, Mysore (called Karnataka since 1973), Orissa, Punjab, Rajasthan, Uttar Pradesh, West Bengal.

17 Delhi, Himachal Pradesh, Manipur, Tripura, Andaman and Nicobar Islands, Laccadive, Minicoy and Amindivi Islands.

18 As to the linguistic situation, see K. P. Krishna Shetty, *The Law of Union-State Relations and Indian Federalism* 398-441 (1981); as to general minority problems, see H. Harada and S. Mohaptra, *Centre-State Relations in India* 200-51 (1986); as to Punjab, see Hannum, *supra* note 2 at 151-77; as to Nagaland, L., see C. Buchheit, *Secession: The Legitimacy of Self-Determination* 189-98 (1978); as to Assam, see J. S. Wilson, "Turmoil in Assam" (1992) 15 *Studies in Conflict and Terrorism* 251-66.

India.[19] Today, there are twenty-five member states[20] and seven federal territories.[21] Various minorities still claim a right to break away from existing entities, to create a new state, or even to secede.[22] It therefore seems plausible that, in the future, the present arrangements might be subject to further modifications.

The procedure is still the same as in 1949. The constitution spells out no territorial guarantee for the member states,[23] and a mere federal statute is sufficient for internal modifications. The member state concerned has a right to be heard, but its position is not binding on the federal parliament.[24]

Brazil

Historically, all the various constitutions of Brazil included provisions on the formation of new member states and on territorial changes between member states.[25] Only the military constitutions of

---

19 Arunachal Pradesh (1987), Manipur (1971), Meghalaya (1971), Mizoram (1987), Nagaland (1962), Sikkim (1975), Tripura (1971).

20 Andra Pradesh, Arunachal Pradesh (member state since 1987), Assam, Bihar, Goa (1987), Gujarat (1960), Haryana (1966), Himachal Pradesh (1970), Jammu and Kashmir, Karnataka, Kerala, Madya Pradesh, Maharashtra (1960), Manipur (1971), Meghalaya (1971), Mizoram (1987), Nagaland (1962), Orissa, Punjab (1966), Rajasthan, Sikkim (1975), Tamil Nadu, Tripura (1971), Uttar Pradesh, West Bengal.

21 Andaman and Nicobar Islands, Chandigarh (territory since 1966), Dadra and Nagar Haveli (1961), Daman and Diu (1961), Delhi, Lakshadweep, Pondicherry (1962).

22 For instance, Telengana from Andra Pradesh, Vidarbha from Maharashtra, Uttarkhand from Uttar Pradesh, Gurkhaland from West Bengal, Bodoland from Assam, as well as Jharkhand from Bihar, Madya Pradesh, and Orissa. Movements of secession existed or still exist primarily in Nagaland, Punjab, as well as in Jammu and Kashmir.

23 *In re Berubari Union and Exchange of Enclaves*, [1960] A.I.R.(S.C.) 845, 857, (1960) 3 S.C.R. 250, 285; *State of West Bengal v. Union of India*, [1963] A.I.R. (S.C.) 1241, 1252. According to *Sri Kishan v. State*, [1957] A.I.R. (A.P.) 374, a guarantee for the continued existence of member states that existed at the time of independence is missing. Cessions of territory to other sovereign states require a constitutional basis, according to *Maganthai v. Union of India*, [1969] A.I.R. (S.C.) 783, (1969) 3 S.C.R. 254, 283 (per Hidayatullah, C.J., from whom Shah, J., differs at 299), which in turn invokes *In re Berubari Union and Exchange of Enclaves, supra.*

24 *Babulal Parate v. State of Bombay*, [1960] A.I.R. (S.C.) 51, (1960) 1 S.C.R. 605.

25 As to the following, see D. Pfirter, *Bundesstaat Brasilien* (thesis) 279-314 (Basel, 1990).

1967 and 1969 transferred the competence exclusively to the federal government. The 1946 constitution additionally demanded consultation with the legislatures of the respective member states and a plebiscite of the populace directly concerned. The new 1988 constitution did away with provincial legislature consultation, but required the consent of those directly concerned.

In the years since 1946, the territories Acre and Rondônia were transformed into member states in 1962 and 1981, the states Guanabara and Rio de Janeiro merged in 1976, Mato Grosso do Sud separated from the state Mato Grosso in 1977, Tocantins separated from the state Gioás in 1988, and finally the territories Amapá and Roraima were transformed into new member states in 1991. Today there are twenty-six member states. In 1987-88, eleven additional regions announced claims for the formation of new states.[26]

MORE COMPLEX PROCEDURES

Comparative Illustrations

As distinct from the simplified modification procedures that may be followed in times of change and transition, more complex procedures are normally required to effect modifications in federal states.

In the Federal Republic of Germany, territorial modifications must be effected by a federal statute, which then needs an approving popular vote in the *Länder* concerned (Article 29 of the Basic Law). In Austria, the constitutions of both the federal government and the *Land* concerned must be revised (*Bundesverfassungsgesetz* 1920/1945 Article 3, section 2). In Switzerland, the federal constitution is silent. The practice, as well as the views of authoritative writers, have established — mainly in discussions concerning a reunion of the two half-cantons Basel-Town and Basel-Country and the new foundation of the canton of Jura — that the constitutions of the federal government and of the cantons concerned must be revised.[27] In the United States, a federal statute is sufficient, but the member states concerned must give their approval (for instance, in the cases of the separation of Kentucky from Virginia in 1792, of Tennessee from North Carolina in 1796, of Maine from Massa-

---

[26] *Ibid.*, 314-55.

[27] See note 31 *infra.*

chusetts in 1820, and of West Virginia from Virginia in 1862).[28] In Australia, territorial modifications require the assent of the federal parliament, as well as of the parliaments and populace of the states concerned. For the formation of new states, a referendum is not obligatory (federal constitution, sections 123 and 124).[29] In Canada, the 1982 federal constitution must be revised in order to transform federal territories into provinces or to form new provinces (that is, assent of the federal parliament and two-thirds of the provinces with at least 50 per cent of the total population, Constitution Act, 1982, sections 38 and 42 (1) (e) and (f)). Territorial modifications must be approved by the provinces directly affected (section 43 (a)).[30]

Foundation of the Canton of Jura 1970-78

General Procedure

In Switzerland, during the 1970s, Northern Jura separated from the canton of Berne and formed its own canton.[31] The first step was an amendment to the Bernese cantonal constitution of 1970, which the people of the canton of Berne accepted in a vote of March 1, 1970.[32] This amendment provided for a three-step cascade of plebiscites in the Jura. In the first vote of June 23, 1974, the majority of voters in the seven jurassic districts of the canton of Berne — 36,802 yes (52 per cent) to 34,057 no (48 per cent) —

---

28 Fetscherin, *supra* note 1 at 92-97, 175; K. Loewenstein, *Verfassungsrecht und Verfassungspraxis der Vereinigten Staaten* 46-47, 90-101 (1959).

29 On that issue, see R. D. Lumb and K. W. Ryan, *The Constitution of the Commonwealth of Australia Annotated*, 3rd ed., 395-97 (1981); J. Quick and R. R. Garran, *The Annotated Constitution of the Australian Commonwealth* 974-77 (1901, reprint 1976).

30 P. W. Hogg, *Constitutional Law of Canada*, 2nd ed., 62-63 (1985).

31 Compare the messages of the Federal Council in Bundesblatt der schweizerischen Eidgenossenschaft (BBl) 1970 I 549-56, 1977 II 264-324, 1977 III 767-818; J.-F. Aubert, *Commentary of the Federal Constitution*, Art. 1 Nrs. 51-106 (1986); H. Koller, "Gebietsänderungen im Bundesstaat: Ansichten und Aussichten nach dem Laufental-Entscheid" in *Festschrift Alfred Rötheli* 173-91 (1990); D. Pfirter, "Bundesrechtliche Vorschriften für einen Kantonswechsel einzelner Gemeinden" *Zeitschrift für Schweizerisches Recht* 108 at 539-64 (1989); L. Wildhaber, "Ederswiler und Vellerat — zur Gebietsveränderung im Bundesstaat" in *Festschrift Hans Huber* 343-49 (1981).

32 With 90,358 (86.5 per cent) Yes to 14,133 (13.5 per cent) No. The seven jurassic districts voted 20,421 (90 per cent) Yes to 2,259 (10 per cent) No.

opted for the formation of the new canton.[33] In those four out of the seven districts in which a majority had voted against the formation of a new canton, additional plebiscites became possible. In the second plebiscite of March 16, 1975, the three southern districts (with the exception of the district of Laufen) decided to stay with the canton of Berne.[34] In the third round of plebiscites of September 7, September 14, and October 19, 1975, borderline communities were allowed to opt out of their district. Eight communities belonging to the bernese district of Moutier decided to join the new canton of Jura;[35] four communities of the same district decided to stay within the canton of Berne;[36] two communities of the jurassic district of Delémont opted for the canton of Berne.[37] These votes took place on the basis of cantonal law. Since their effect was to change the number of cantons and the number of members of the second legislative chamber, they needed confirmation on the federal level. On September 25, 1978, 82.3 per cent of the Swiss people and all (then twenty-five) cantons agreed to accept the formation of the new canton of Jura, as circumscribed in the three plebiscites of 1974-75.[38] Since January 1, 1979, the canton of Jura has exercised all the rights of a canton.

Much depends on the perception of minority problems, both by the majority and the minority. The leader of the separatists of the Jura, Roland Béguelin, always described the conflict as a linguistic one that opposed the Swiss-German-speaking Bernese and the French-speaking "Jurassiens." He did not mention that Berne was mainly protestant and the Jura was mainly catholic. But above all, if the issue was indeed one of language only, it is hard to see why the three northern (and French-speaking) districts wanted a new canton, whereas the three southern (also French-speaking) districts opted for Berne. The line between separatists and anti-separatists

[33] The three northern districts, Porrentruy, Delémont, and Franches-Montagnes accepted; the three southern districts, La Neuveville, Courtelary, and Moutier, as well as the Valley of Laufen, rejected.

[34] Courtelary with 10,802 (77 per cent) Yes to 3,268 (23 per cent) No; Moutier 9,947 (56.2 per cent) Yes to 7,740 (43.8 per cent) No; La Neuveville 1,927 (66 per cent) Yes to 997 (34 per cent) No.

[35] The communities Châtillon, Corban, Courchapoix, Courrendlin, Les Genevez, Lajoux, Mervelier, Rossemaison.

[36] The communities Grandval, Moutier, Perrefite, La Scheulte.

[37] The communities Rebévilier and Roggenburg.

[38] With 1,309,722 (82.3 per cent) Yes to 281,917 (17.7 per cent) No.

that was drawn in 1974-75 does not follow linguistic majorities. On the contrary, it corresponds more or less with the borders established by the Congress of Vienna in 1815, and can more logically be explained in terms of history, economy, communication, and traditional links.

The Separate Fate of the Valley of Laufen

On September 14, 1975, in the context of the third round of plebiscites, the district of Laufen voted to stay within the canton of Berne, subject to the possibility of a vote on the question of whether a procedure to join a neighbouring canton should be launched.[39] An initiative requiring such a vote came about and was accepted on June 18, 1978.[40] On January 13, 1980, a majority of those entitled to vote decided that the valley of Laufen should join either the canton of Basel-Country or the canton of Solothurn, but not the canton of Basel-Town.[41] On March 16, 1970, they then voted in favour of Basel-Country and against Solothurn.[42] In a final vote, a majority of 56.7 per cent decided on September 11, 1983, that the valley of Laufen should stay with the canton of Berne rather than join the canton of Basel-Country.[43] However, on December 20, 1988, the Federal Tribunal quashed the result of this vote, because the government of the canton of Berne had clandestinely and without any statutory basis supported the voting campaigns of the pro-Bernese side with public moneys.[44] The repetition of the vote on November 12, 1989, reversed the previous result: a majority of 51.7 per cent decided now that the valley of Laufen should join the canton of Basel-Country.[45] Because this exchange of territories between the cantons of Berne and Basel-Country was considered a modification of the federal guarantee of the territories of the cantons, it became necessary to vote on it. On September 26, 1993, a huge majority and all (twenty-six) cantons gave their consent to the

[39] With 4,216 (94 per cent) Yes to 264 (6 per cent) No.

[40] With 4,164 (65 per cent) Yes to 2,234 (35 per cent) No.

[41] 3,176 (52 per cent) voted for Basel-Country, 1,099 (32 per cent) for Solothurn, 983 (16 per cent) for Basel-Town.

[42] 4,233 (65 per cent) voted for Basel-Country, 2,315 (35 per cent) for Solothurn.

[43] With 4,675 (56.7 per cent) No to 3,575 (43.3 per cent) Yes.

[44] Entscheidungen des Bundesgerichts (BGE) 114 Ia 427. Compare also BGE 113 Ia 155.

[45] With 4,652 (51.7 per cent) Yes to 4,343 (48.3 per cent) No.

exchange of territory.[46] Since January 1, 1994, the valley of Laufen has therefore become a part of the canton of Basel-Country.

The Separate Fate of the Community of Vellerat

The original setup of the three rounds of plebiscites allowed "borderline communities" to switch allegiance and change over to the neighbouring canton.[47] When the chips were down, this arrangement left two communities that still wanted to change sides. In recent years, German-speaking Ederswiler has given up its break-away plans and decided to stay within the French-speaking canton of Jura. French-speaking Vellerat, a village of seventy inhabitants, has always been predominantly separatist and pro-Jura. After pro-tracted negotiations and federal mediation, the two cantonal governments of Berne and Jura agreed to let the community have its way, if this was properly confirmed by vote. On March 12, 1995, the voters of the canton of Berne approved a statute for the changeover of Vellerat to the canton of Jura by a large majority.[48] On June 25, 1995, the voters of the canton of Jura accepted a statute admitting Vellerat into their canton by a still clearer majority.[49] On March 10, 1996, a federal vote of the people and the cantons ratified the changeover with a huge majority.[50]

The community of Vellerat had petitioned the federal govern-ment to waive the vote on the federal level, but in vain. The Federal Council remained legalistic and stated that the exchange of a community between two cantons always constituted an exception from the federal guarantee of cantonal territory.[51] Its policy was obviously to prefer stability and even rigidity over flexibility or, worse, uncertainty.

Common Features of the More Complicated Procedures

Comparatively speaking, some internal modifications of the num-ber of member units or of territorial borders between member units

---

[46] With 1,188,941 (75.2 per cent) Yes to 392,893 (24.8 per cent) No.

[47] *Supra* at notes 33-37.

[48] 210,680 (84.3 per cent) Yes to 39,168 (15.7 per cent) No.

[49] 20,020 (92 per cent) Yes to 1,758 (8 per cent) No.

[50] 1,250,728 (91.6 per cent) Yes to 114,105 (8.4 per cent) No. All 26 Cantons said Yes.

[51] BBl 1995 III 1432 at 1437-39.

require a revision of the federal constitution, whereas, in other cases, a federal statute is sufficient. Internal modifications do not always require a constitutional revision, but, more frequently, the consents of both the federal government and the member units directly affected are required.

In some situations, solely the member units directly concerned (for example, by partitions, mergers, or transfers of territory) must agree. A federalistic contract theory, under which *all* member units would have to give their express approval to internal modifications, cannot be found anywhere.

In other situations, the consent of the member units directly affected is not sufficient *per se* to bring about modifications. Since changes in the composition or territory of member units are considered important for the whole federation, these changes require federal recognition with constitutive effect.

These findings may also be considered within the categories of the general theory of federal states. The difference between a confederation (*Staatenbund*), with its principle of unanimity, and a unitary state (*Einheitsstaat*), with its principle of majority decision, is obvious. Typical federal states apparently consider internal modifications to be a special issue that reflects the underlying character of the federal compact. While it is true that member units are not truly sovereign, the requirement of their consent to internal modifications demonstrates their lasting, state character.

Interestingly, no rule can be found for cases in which a directly affected member unit refuses its consent to an internal modification in a way that might endanger internal peace. In cases of this type, one could assert the primacy of federal law, which would allow the federal government to legislate or take direct and independent measures without the consent of the member unit concerned. This could also be considered an emergency situation in which only the federal government would be entitled to act. General solutions to this problem are difficult to find; it seems preferable to seek a specific solution to each case.

EXTERNAL MODIFICATIONS IN
NON-COMMUNIST FEDERAL STATES: ADMISSIONS

When speaking of external territorial modifications or changes in the number of member units, it is important to keep the difference between an increase or a loss of territory in mind. Most federal states are open with respect to the admission of new territories or additional member states. However, they tacitly refuse a right of secession of member units or minorities, or the possibility of a separation or breakup.

In most federal states, admission of new member states is possible by normal legislation. This has occurred in the United States (witness the admission of Texas in 1845 and of California in 1850), in Canada before 1982 (British Columbia 1871, Prince Edward Island 1873), in Australia, in the Federal Republic of Germany (Saarland 1957), and in India.[52] In Switzerland, by contrast, a revision of the federal constitution would be required (as the discussions concerning a possible admission of Northern Savoy in 1870 and of Vorarlberg in 1919 have shown);[53] the same is true in Austria.[54]

It would, in fact, seem possible to admit new territories to a federal state directly by way of an international treaty between the federal government and the territory concerned or the state from which the territory is separated or acquired.[55] The federal government would have power to enter into such treaties. Nonetheless, no federal constitutions provide for such a procedure, probably because the necessary adaptations of municipal law could hardly be anticipated in a treaty. Even where an external modification is based on an earlier treaty, it would therefore seem necessary to obtain the approval of the legislature or even a revision of the federal constitution.

EXTERNAL MODIFICATIONS IN NON-COMMUNIST FEDERAL STATES: SECESSIONS OR BREAKUPS

COMPARATIVE AND INTERNATIONAL CONSIDERATIONS

Most "classical" or "genuine" federal constitutions mention neither the possibility of disintegration nor that of secession, let alone that of exclusion. Federal unions were considered insoluble, in the same spirit in which no termination right was written into the United Nations Charter, since it was deemed improper to speak of

52 Fetscherin, *supra* note 1 at 192-214.

53 See E. Bonjour, *Geschichte der schweizerischen Neutralität*, vol. II, 2nd ed., 718-40 (1965); D. Witzig, *Die Vorarlberger Frage*, (thesis) (Basle, 1974).

54 R. Walter and H. Mayer, *Grundriss des österreichischen Bundesverfassungsrechts*, 7th ed., 77 (1992).

55 B. Kunth, *Der Abschluss völkerrechtlicher Verträge über Änderungen des Bundesgebiets*, (thesis) (Heidelberg, 1971).

divorce in the moment of marriage. The United States, Switzerland, the Federal Republic of Germany, Austria, Australia,[56] Canada, Brazil, and India[57] have included no procedures for secession or exclusion, and their practice has rejected such claims. The exclusion of a member unit, a minority, or a portion of territory without its specific consent is also considered inadmissible. As far as a secession seems conceivable, it would at any rate be subject to federal approval.

Therefore, the message of federal constitutions to their minorities and member states is that they must articulate their wishes for autonomy internally, within the federal state. A minority, a member state, or a group claiming separation without the consent of the federal government would have to overcome the argument that its claim was a breach of continuity and amounted to resistance and revolution. By remaining tacit, federal constitutions disapprove of secession. Some even declare that their territory is "inseparable."[58] This means that every secession or separation is unconstitutional and that every separatist movement runs the risk of being labelled subversive and unlawful.

By their very nature, constitutions are "introverted." Given this, no classical federal constitution shows any awareness of claims of an external right of self-determination that would not only be directly applicable as international law in domestic law, but would also claim primacy and subsequently permit a secession to member units or minorities.

Lengthy tensions and conflicts may convince a majority within a federal state that the secessionist claims of a minority may be just or at least understandable. The majority may also see no other way but secession to settle a conflict. Whichever may be the case, claims for secession or breakups will normally have to express profound and lasting divergences in order to be realistic. Secessions are not withdrawals from a club. They raise fundamental and emotional issues

---

56 See G. Craven, "The Constitutionality of the Unilateral Secession of an Australian State" (1985) 15 Fed. L. Rev. 123 and "An Indissoluble Federal Commonwealth? The Founding Fathers and the Secession of an Australian State" (1983) 14 Melb. U. L. Rev. 281-99.

57 *Cf. In re Berubari Union and Exchange of Enclaves*, Special Reference, *supra* note 23 at 845; *Ram Kishore v. Union of India*, [1966] All India Rep. 644 (S.C.); M. C. Setalvad, *Union and State Relations under the Indian Constitution* 28-29 (1974); D. K. Singh (ed.), *supra* note 15 at 5-8.

58 *Cf.* P. Häberle, "Das Staatsgebiet als Problem der Verfassungslehre," in "Kleinstaat und Menschenrechte," *Festschrift Gerard Batliner* 397 at 404-5 (1993).

of lasting effect, which can neither be initiated nor annulled at random.

The secession of a minority group remains conceivable from the point of view of international law. A unilateral declaration of independence that becomes effective in relation to the former motherland and third states may create a new state. Therefore, a successful revolution can bring about a breach of the old order and the initiation of a new one. The main issue is whether a new entity disposes of effective state power. To a large extent, this depends on the policy of the federal government. Will the federal government insist on its unity and use federal intervention (for example, financial and economic sanctions, police and army)? Or will it waive effective control of the people and territory of a rebellious new state? Will it fend off premature recognition of seceded territory by third states by qualifying such recognition as an unlawful intervention in domestic affairs?

Traditional practice is usually quite cautious in the recognition of new states. In *Madzimbamuto* v. *Lardner-Burke*, the Privy Council had to review the validity of detentions following the unilateral declaration of independence of Southern Rhodesia on November 11, 1965. On November 16, 1965, the British Parliament claimed the continued sovereignty of the United Kingdom over Southern Rhodesia. The Court held that the acts of the Southern Rhodesian government in early 1966 were invalid as long as its effective control of the new state remained uncertain: "The British Government acting for the lawful Sovereign is taking steps to regain control and it is impossible to predict with certainty whether or not it will succeed."[59]

Traditional practice considered recognition and self-determination as primarily political in character. Whereas respect for human and minority rights, democracy, and the rule of law played a minor role, states relied above all on factual effectiveness. As discussed later in this article, in the aftermath of the breakup of former Yugoslavia the international community has made a conscious endeavour to go beyond this state of affairs.

The above discussion may be illustrated by a few precedents. The breakup of the former Soviet Union, of the former Yugoslavia, and of Czechoslovakia will be dealt with later and separately, because

---

59 *Madzimbamuto* v. *Lardner-Burke*, [1969] 1 A.C. 645, 725. See also Brossard, *supra* note 1 at 105-12, 197-202, 281-87, 304-10, 398-406, 712-19; J. Crawford, *The Creation of States in International Law* 247-70 (1979).

they do not constitute cases of disintegration of "genuine" federal states. The breakups occurred because, after the disappearance of the communist dictatorships, the former regimes were incapable of giving new content to the federal constitutional structure before the long-suppressed nationalisms gained the upper hand. In the words of Karl Loewenstein, the former regimes did not succeed in time to transform a semantic into a normative federal order.[60] The former regimes had procedures for internal and external modifications that appeared simple in form, because in effect they were not intended to be used. As soon as the procedures became usable, the "semantic" federal regimes became unstable and collapsed.

American Civil War, 1861-65

The United States Constitution does not expressly speak of secession. Only a long and agonizing civil war, from 1861 to 1865, decided this issue conclusively. The union of Alabama, Florida, Georgia, Louisiana, Mississippi, and South Carolina in the "Confederate States of America," which were later joined by Arkansas, North Carolina, Tennessee, Texas, and Virginia, appeared — in the light of history and the wisdom of hindsight — as an illegal withdrawal from an indissoluble union.

In *The Federalist* (1787-88), in Alexis de Tocqueville's *De la démocratie en Amérique* (1835), and in the early cases of the Supreme Court, the thesis of a divided sovereignty between the federal government and the member states was advocated.[61] However, the great debate on nullification in 1830-33 showed that no consensus existed on the nature of the federal state and the admissibility of secession.

John C. Calhoun, the leading advocate of the nullification doctrine of the southern states, considered the member states as sovereign and independent. In his view, the people of each state, as a separate and sovereign community, had approved of the constitutional compact. The sovereignty of the member states was neither divided nor delegated. Hence, the member states could denounce at any time the compact that was at the base of the federal consti-

---

[60] K. Loewenstein, "Verfassungsrecht und Verfassungsrealität" in *Beiträge zur Staatssoziologie* 430 at 447-48 (1961).

[61] Max Beloff (ed.), *The Federalist*, nos. 39, 42 at 195-96, 216 (1948); A. de Tocqueville, *De la démocratie en Amérique* 168-69, 225, 232-33, 236-40 (1951); *Chisholm v. Georgia*, 2 Dall. (2 U.S.) 419, 435 (1793).

tution, whenever that compact became unjust, oppressive, or arbitrary.[62] They could also consider as null and void federal statutes, measures, and decisions that in their view transgressed the powers of the federal government.

The outcome of the secession war confirmed the views of Calhoun's great opponent, Senator Daniel Webster from Massachussetts. For Webster, the federal constitution was no contract, "not a league, compact or confederacy, but a fundamental law."[63] The federal constitution had founded a national, even if limited, sovereignty by enabling a representative majority to govern, thus expressing the will of the sovereign federal people.

The Supreme Court further developed these thoughts after 1865. By now it was clear that sovereignty lay with the federal government, that the union was indissoluble, that secession was illegal, and that the federal state had a contractual basis only to the extent that popular sovereignty was based on a *contrat social* and on the self-determination of a free people. In 1868, in *Texas* v. *White*, the Supreme Court rejected the nullification theory of the southern states in terms that would hardly have been so categorical before the Civil War:

> The Constitution, in all its provisions, looks to an indestructible Union, composed of indestructible States. When, therefore, Texas became one of the United States, she entered into an indissoluble relation. . . . the Act which consummated her admission into the Union was something more than a compact; it was the incorporation of a new member into the political body. And it was final. The union between Texas and the other States was as complete as perpetual, and as indissoluble as the Union between the original States. There was no place for reconsideration or revocation, except through revolution, or through consent of the States.[64]

---

[62] J. C. Calhoun, "Discourse on the Constitution and Government of the United States" in R. K. Galé (ed.), *Works 1888*, vol. I, 111-406 at 146. See also G. Ticknor Curtis, *Constitutional History of the United States*, vol. II, 1-55 (1896); A. H. Kelly and W. A. Harbison, *The American Constitution: Its Origins and Development*, 3rd ed. 300-16 (1963); F. Newton Thorpe, *The Constitutional History of the United States 1765-1895*, vol. II, 345-48, 387-440 (1901); and see generally L. Wildhaber, "Sovereignty and International Law" in R. St. J. Macdonald and D. M. Johnston (eds.), *The Structure and Process of International Law* 432-35 (1983).

[63] Thorpe, *supra* note 61 at 407.

[64] *Texas* v. *White*, 74 U.S. (7 Wall.) 227, 237 (1868); *Ex parte Siebold*, 100 U.S. 371 (1879); *Mackenzie* v. *Hare*, 239 U.S. 299, 311 (1915); *United States* v. *Curtiss-Wright Export Corp.*, 299 U.S. 304, 318 (1936); *New York* v. *United States*, 326 U.S. 572, 594-95 (1946); *Cooper* v. *Aaron*, 358 U.S. 1, 18-19 (1958).

Nova Scotia, 1867-68

A few months after the entry into force of the British North America Act, 1867, Nova Scotia elected a government inimical to the federation.[65] In February 1868, the unanimous legislature of the province and a great majority of its representatives in the federal parliament asked the Queen to dismiss the province from the federation. Nova Scotia, they argued, had never agreed to the British North America Act. In the same vein, 31,000 out of the 48,000 provincial electors signed a petition that asked for separation. The British government rejected the petition, suggested that Nova Scotia should settle its problems directly with the federal government in Ottawa, and remarked that it had "no business to inquire into the local arrangements of the North American Provinces."[66] Subsequently the provincial government negotiated with Ottawa and achieved an increase in federal grants-in-aid.

Vorarlberg, 1919; Tyrol and Salzburg, 1921

The dissolution of the Austrian-Hungarian monarchy after the First World War gave rise to the manifestation of an autonomous political will in some Austrian *Länder*. Thus, on May 11, 1919, the voters of the *Land* Vorarlberg opted, by 47,208 to 11,248 votes, to join Switzerland. The Swiss Federal Council, divided within itself, decided to accept this offer only if the conference of Paris and the federal government in Vienna expressly recognized Vorarlberg's right to self-determination. In effect, this amounted to a rejection of the offer.

Against the wishes of the federal government, votes took place in Tyrol on April 24, 1921 and in Salzburg on May 18, 1921 that resulted in overwhelming majorities of about 99 per cent in favour of adherence to Germany.[67] Following the instructions of Vienna, the vote in Salzburg was organized as a private manifestation of the political parties. A plebiscite planned on July 3, 1921 in Styria had to be cancelled. Since Article 88 of the Peace Treaty of St. Germain

---

[65] U.K., House of Commons *Parliamentary Debates*, vol. 192, col. 1658-96 (June 16, 1868); Brossard, *supra* note 1 at 275-77, 285; R. Cook, *Provincial Autonomy, Minority Rights and the Compact Theory, 1867-1921* 10-11 (Studies of the Royal Commission on Bilingualism and Biculturalism, 1969); J. A. Maxwell, "Petitions to London by Provincial Governments" (1936) 14 Can. Bar Rev. 738-49.

[66] *Ibid.*, col. 1683.

[67] In Tyrol 145,300 to 1,800 votes, in Salzburg 98,550 to 880.

of 1919 prohibited a union of Austria with the German Empire, it was impossible in any case to take into account the votes of the Austrian *Länder.* In view of the opposition of the Allies and the lack of foreign support for the policy of annexation, the secessionist tendencies were checked.[68]

Western Australia, 1933-35

In the 1930s, Western Australia felt disadvantaged by the federal government. On April 8, 1933, a two-to-one majority voted in favour of secession. Then, in 1934, the state legislature submitted a petition to the British Parliament, asking for an amendment of the Australian Constitution to allow the secession of Western Australia. A common commission of the House of Commons and the House of Lords proposed to give no heed to the petition. In the commission's view, constitutional convention demanded that the British Parliament should not intervene in the internal affairs of Australia without the consent of the federal government: "interference should only take place at the request of such Dominion . . . speaking with the voice which represents it as a whole and not merely at the request of a minority."[69]

It remained open whether secession could have been claimed if the federal government had given its consent. The upshot of the secession movement was the institutionalization of a participation of the states in the distribution of federal moneys.

Newfoundland, 1948-49

Newfoundland was a chronically indebted Dominion in 1939. At the request of the Dominion Parliament, Great Britain abrogated the constitution of Newfoundland and transferred the business of

---

[68] C. Altenstetter, *Der Föderalismus in Österreich* 12-13 (1969); F. Ermacora, *Österreichischer Föderalismus* 40-47 (1976); W. Goldinger, *Geschichte der Republik Österreich* 67-76 (1962).

[69] *Report by the Joint Committee of the House of Lords and the House of Commons Appointed to Consider the Petition of the State of Western Australia in Relation to Secession,* H. L. 75, H. C. 88, para. 7, p. viii (1935); Brossard, *supra* note 1 at 280-85; S. R. Davis (ed.), *The Government of the Australian States* 474-76 (1960); E. Russell, "Western Australian Secession Petition — Arguments Before the Joint Select Committee" (1935) 9 Aust. L. J. 141-43; R. Theoret, "Experience with the Referendum Elsewhere" in D. C. Rowat (ed.), *The Referendum and Separation Elsewhere: Implications for Quebec* 10-12 (1978). The outcome of the vote was 138,653 Yes to 70,706 No.

government to a governor who was advised by a commission. In the vote of June 3, 1948, the people of Newfoundland decided among the three alternatives, as follows: 22,300 (14.3 per cent) opted in favor of maintaining the status quo for five more years; 64,000 (41.1 per cent) were in favour of a union with Canada; and 69,400 (44.6 per cent) were in favour of re-establishing a constitutional government. In view of the lack of an absolute majority, a second plebiscite took place on July 22, 1948, with the following results: 78,300 (52.3 per cent) voted in favor of a union with Canada; 71,300 (47.7 per cent) were in favour of re-establishing the status quo as before 1933. Canada and Newfoundland then entered into a treaty of union on December 11, 1948, which the British Parliament approved by statute on March 23, 1949, without the specific assent of all Canadian provinces.[70]

Canada and Québec, 1960-95

In Canadian political history of the past thirty-five years, various problems have overlapped: the repatriation of the constitution from the United Kingdom back to Canada, the extent of centralization or regionalization, the distribution of powers between the federal government and the provinces, bilingualism, multiculturalism, the revision of the federal constitution, including constitutional amendments, a new shape of the Senate, and the protection of fundamental freedoms at the federal level. In all these respects, the relationship of Québec to Canada has played a decisive role. The issue was not so much that of an internal modification between the Canadian provinces; rather, it was the extent of autonomy of the province of Québec, the wish of some Québecers to be master in their own house, as well as the issue whether Canada constituted a union of two peoples and nations with Québec as a *société distincte* with a right of veto and withdrawal. Therefore, looming over the discussions on provincial autonomy and decentralization was the

---

70 E. R. Hopkins, *Confederation at the Crossroads: The Canadian Constitution* 262-265 (1968); H. B. Mayo, "Newfoundland's Entry into the Dominion" (1949) 15 Can. J. Ec. & Pol. Sci. 505-22; S. J. R. Noel, *Politics in Newfoundland* 255-61 (1971); R. Theoret, "The Use of the Referendum in Canada" in D. C. Rowat (ed.), *The Referendum and Separation Elsewhere: Implications for Quebec* 26-29 (1978). The referendum procedure was attacked as unconstitutional in the Newfoundland courts, but without success, in *Currie v. MacDonald* (1948) 29 Nfld. & P. E. I. R. 314 (Nfld. S.C.), (1949) 29 Nfld. & P. E. I. R. 294 (Nfld. C.A.).

threat of an external modification and of a right of self-determination understood as secession.

It would be impossible to discuss the details of these highly interesting debates.[71] The first series of debates began with the early Fulton-Favreau formula of 1964 concerning constitutional amendment, the Victoria Charter of 1971, and the Turner-Trudeau formula, and culminated in the debate on patriation and Québec's vote on sovereignty-association in 1980. Discussions continued with the non-acceptance of the Meech Lake Accord in 1987-90 and the massive rejection of the Charlottetown Agreement in a nationwide referendum on October 26, 1992, and culminated once again in the narrow rejection of a separation of Québec on October 30, 1995 (50.6 per cent versus 49.4 per cent).

On May 20, 1980, the Québec voters[72] rejected the proposal for sovereignty-association with 2,187,991 (59.56 per cent) "no" to 1,485,786 (40.44 per cent) "yes."[73] The proposal would have authorized the provincial government to negotiate a new political compact with the rest of Canada, under which Québec would have been in exclusive charge of her legislation, taxation, and external relations, but would have negotiated an economic and currency union with Canada.

Before this vote, an internal right of self-determination of Québec[74] had been accepted in Canadian public opinion to a limited extent, insofar as the federal government did not oppose the provincial plebiscite and announced that it would not use armed force.[75] It was not accepted to the extent that Québec was

---

71 See E. McWhinney, *Quebec and the Constitution 1960-1978* (1979); *Canada and the Constitution 1979-1982* (1982); J.-Y. Morin and J. Woehrling, *Les Constitutions du Canada et du Québec du régime français à nos jours* (1992); J. Woehrling, *La Constitution canadienne et l'évolution des rapports entre le Québec et le Canada anglais, de 1867 à nos jours* (University of Alberta, Centre for Constitutional Studies, 1993).

72 At that time, 82 per cent of all Franco-Canadians lived in the province of Québec and 80 per cent of the population of Québec spoke French. Québec's total population made up 28 per cent of the population of Canada.

73 See R. B. Byers, "The Referendum: Yes or No," [1980] Can. Ann. Rev. of Politics and Public Affairs 38-58.

74 In favour of such a right, Brossard *supra* note 1 at 82-89, 188-90, 304-7; D. Turp, "Le droit de sécession en droit international public" 20 Canadian Yearbook of International Law 24-78 (1982); and recently, in a very circumspect way, Woehrling *supra* note 70 at 150-67.

75 In that sense, see the Molgat-MacGuigan Committee, Special Joint Committee of the Senate and of the House of Commons on the Constitution of Canada,

not granted a free veto right in all matters of concern, and insofar as the "compact theory" was not accepted as a foundation of Canadian federalism.[76]

After the rejection of sovereignty-association in Québec, Prime Minister Pierre Trudeau decided to submit a package of proposals for the patriation of the Canadian Constitution to the British Parliament. In the famous *Patriation Reference* of September 28, 1981, the Supreme Court of Canada held that the approval of constitutional amendments by the provinces was not legally required.[77] The compact theory operated in the political realm and did not engage the law.[78] By contrast, constitutional convention required the agreement of a substantial majority of the provinces. The patriation of the constitution without such an agreement "would be unconstitutional in the conventional sense."[79] Prime Minister Trudeau and nine of the ten provincial premiers then agreed, on November 5, 1981, on a package to patriate the constitution. The Québec government vetoed this package on November 25, 1981. In the *Québec Veto Reference* of December 6, 1982,[80] the Supreme Court of Canada confirmed its earlier position. The right of veto claimed by Québec not only amounted to a denial of the unanimity rule but implicitly to the equality of the provinces. Even though the precedents invoked seemed in favour of the right of veto, the main actors had

---

Final Report, 4th Sess., 28th Parliament (1972); Prime Minister Trudeau in 1976, quoted in G. A. Beaudoin, *Essais sur la Constitution* 23, 337 (1979); the Pépin-Robarts-Commission, *A Future Together* 114-15 (Task Force on Canadian Unity, 1979).

76 As to the "compact theory," see R. Cook, *Provincial Autonomy, Minority Rights and the Compact Theory, 1867-1921* (Studies of the Royal Commission on Bilingualism and Biculturalism, 1969); G. Marchildon and E. Maxwell, "Quebec's Right of Secession under Canadian and International Law" (1992) 32 Virginia J. Int'l L. 583 at 593-98; G. Rémillard, *Le Fédéralisme Canadien* 122-40, 144-48 (1983); N. McL. Rogers, "The Compact Theory of Confederation" (1931) 9 Can. Bar Rev. 395-417; R. Romanow, J. D. Whyte, and H. Leeson, *Canada Notwithstanding: The Making of the Constitution 1976-1982* 168-76 (1984).

77 *Patriation Reference (Re Resolution to Amend the Constitution)*, [1981] 1 S.C.R. 753, 807, 125 D.L.R. (3d) 1. Martland and Ritchie, JJ. considered the approval of the provinces a legal necessity.

78 *Ibid.*, 803 (S.C.R.).

79 *Ibid.*, 909. Laskin, C.J.C. and Estey and McIntyre, JJ. rejected the existence of a "convention."

80 *Quebec Veto Reference, A.G. Que. and A.G. Can. (Re Objection by Quebec to a Resolution to Amend the Constitution)*, [1982] 2 S.C.R. 793, 140 D.L.R. (3d) 385.

lacked the conviction to operate under a legal obligation. A rule that had never been articulated or written could not be considered as a constitutional convention.[81] At that point, therefore, Canadian constitutional law rejected both the federal compact theory and Québec's right of veto.

On October 30, 1995, Québec voters narrowly rejected the proposed declaration of sovereignty for a second time with 2,361,526 (50.6 per cent) voting no to 2,308,028 (49.4 per cent) voting yes. From the vantage point of self-determination, not much had changed since 1980. It could still be stated that Québec had no right to secede unilaterally under Canadian constitutional law.[82] Nor could Québec invoke an external right of self-determination under international law without acquiescence or recognition by the federal government. The population of the province was neither colonial nor a victim of an undemocratic, discriminatory regime, nor was it exposed to flagrant violations of its human rights. However, if the federal government did not oppose such claims, international law did not impede Québec from claiming and obtaining sovereignty and independence.[83]

EXTERNAL MODIFICATIONS IN POST-COMMUNIST FEDERAL STATES

THE FAILURE OF COMMUNIST FEDERALISM

Communist federalism failed in the Soviet Union, Yugoslavia, and Czechoslovakia.[84] Although the famous Article 72 of the constitution of the Soviet Union of 1977, which went back to 1924, gave the republics a right of secession, and analogously the preambles of the constitutions of Yugoslavia (of 1974) and of Czechoslovakia (of 1968) recognized a "right of self-determination up to separation," the constitutional reality was that of authoritarian and dictatorial systems of government, in which power was centralized in the

81 *Ibid.*, 816-17 (S.C.R.).

82 *Cf.* N. Finkelstein and G. Vegh, *The Separation of Quebec and the Constitution of Canada* (1992); J. Woehrling, "Les aspects juridiques d'une éventuelle sécession du Québec" (1995) 74 Can. Bar Rev. 293-314.

83 In that sense, see T. Franck *et al.*, *supra* note 2 at 430. See also the seemingly contradictory articles of N. Finkelstein, G. Vegh and C. Joly, "Does Québec Have a Right to Secede at International Law" (1995) 74 Can. Bar. Rev. 225-60 and J. Woehrling, *supra* note 81 at 314-29.

84 A. Bebler, "Das Schicksal des kommunistischen Föderalismus. Sowjetunion, Tschechoslowakei und Jugoslawien im Vergleich" (1992) 47 Europa-Archiv 375-86.

communist party apparatus, the secret police, and the army. The right of self-determination in the form of a right of secession corresponded to the logic of Morgenstern, according to which "there cannot be, what shall not be."[85] The right existed on paper only and was considered as "consummated" by the "voluntary adherence" of the member units to the union.[86] When the authoritarian regimes collapsed and the suppressed nationalisms re-emerged, it became manifest that no culture of peaceful co-existence and respect of minorities had been built up. Hence, the right of self-determination and secession, which was believed extinct, offered itself as a possibility for minorities to take their own destiny into their hands.

SECESSION AND BREAKUP

The Breakup of the Soviet Union, 1988-91

The breakup of the Union of the Socialist Soviet Republics manifested itself in two waves.[87] First came a series of declarations of sovereignty by the union republics (and many autonomous republics and regions) between November 16, 1988, and December 15, 1990, which *inter alia* proclaimed the primacy of member unit law over union law. Then there followed a series of actual declarations of independence between March 11, 1990, and the autumn of 1991.

These declarations were preceded by those of the three Baltic states: Estonia, Latvia, and Lithuania (declarations of sovereignty of November 16, 1988, July 28, 1989, May 26, 1989; declarations of independence of March 30, 1990, May 4, 1990, March 11, 1990; referenda of independence of March 3, 1991, March 3, 1991,

---

85 C. Morgenstern, *Galgenlieder: Die unmögliche Tatsache* (1905).

86 See the references in M. Beckmann-Petey, *Der jugoslawische Föderalismus* 128-31 (1990); see also J. Bugajski, *Ethnic Politics in Eastern Europe* (1995).

87 *Cf.* M. Bothe and C. Schmidt, "Sur quelques questions de succession posées par la dissolution de l'URSS et celle de la Yougoslavie" (1992) 96 Rev. D.I.P. 811-42; G. Brunner, "Minderheiten in der Sowjetunion" 34 German Yearbook of International Law 354-412 (1991); U. W. Saxer, "The Transformation of the Soviet Union: From a Socialist Federation to a Commonwealth of Independent States" (1992) 14 Loyola of Los Angeles I.C.L.J. 581-715; T. Schweisfurth, "Vom Einheitsstaat (UdSSR) zum Staatenbund (GUS)" (1992) 52 ZaöRV 541-702; R. Yakemtchouk, "Les républiques baltes et la crise du fédéralisme soviétique" (1990) 43 Studia diplomatica, nos. 4-6 and "L'indépendance de l'Ukraine" (1993) 46 Studia diplomatica, nos. 3-5.

February 9, 1991; declaration of direct and total independence of August 20-21, 1991). Their legal position was special because they had been annexed against their will in the aftermath of the Molotov-Ribbentrop Pact of 1939. This is why, for instance, Lithuanian president Vytautas Landbergis argued that Lithuania had never belonged to the Soviet Union *de iure,* only *de facto.* Hence her declaration of independence did not constitute a secession, it merely reasserted the independence and continuity of the state of Lithuania, which had been sovereign from 1918 to 1940.[88] It is striking that the Baltic republics did not invoke the right of self-determination.[89]

In the so-called "war of the laws," the Union organs first proclaimed the primacy of union law over member unit law. Then they labelled the Baltic declarations of independence unconstitutional, null, and void. They decreed an economic boycott and endeavoured repeatedly to gain the upper hand by using force in the Baltics. On March 17, 1991, they organized a union-wide referendum, in which, however, only nine out of the fifteen republics participated. Thereafter, they provided for an extremely cumbersome separation procedure in the secession statute of April 3, 1990. The adversaries spoke of a "statute to prevent secession," but when the time came they gave no thought to observing the procedure provided in the statute.

The miscarriage of the uprising of the reactionary forces on August 19, 1991, resulted in swift and decisive change. President Yeltsin's Russia recognized Estonia and Latvia on August 24, 1991, and the Soviet Union recognized the independence of all three Baltic states on September 6, 1991. In the meantime, most West and East European states as well as the United States had also

---

[88] Quoted by R. Kherad, "La reconnaissance internationale des Etats baltes" (1995) 96 Rev D.I.P. 843 at 855. Georgia, which organized an independence referendum on Mar. 31, 1991, argued similarly that she had declared her independence on May 26, 1918; that the Government of the Soviet Union had recognized her independence in the Peace Treaty of May 7, 1920; and hence the Treaty of Alliance with the Soviet Union of May 21, 1921, inflicted on her after the annexation, was as null as the Treaty of Union of 1922. As to this, see Brunner *supra* note 86 at 369.

[89] On that issue, see A. Cassese, "Self-Determination of Peoples and the Recent Break-Up of USSR and Yugoslavia" in *Essays in Honour of Wang Tieya* 131 at 133-36 (1993). For criticism of the invocation of the right of self-determination by the non-Baltic republics, see R. Mullerson, "Self-Determination of Peoples and the Dissolution of the USSR" *ibid.,* at 567-85. See also G. Smith (ed.), *The Baltic States* (1994); A. Sprudzs (ed.), *The Baltic Path to Independence: An International Reader* (1994).

officially recognized the Baltic states. On December 21, 1991, in Alma-Ata, eleven presidents of the republics (with the exception of those of the Baltic states and Georgia) declared that the Soviet Union had terminated her existence with the formation of the Commonwealth of Independent States. They agreed that Russia should succeed to the seat of the Soviet Union in the United Nations. Shortly thereafter the international community recognized the new states.[90]

The Breakup of Yugoslavia, 1990-95

Slovenia and Croatia

Slovenia declared her sovereignty on July 2, 1990, and Croatia declared sovereignty on December 22, 1990. In the vote of December 23, 1990, the Slovenians opted for independence, and, likewise, the Croatians on May 19, 1991. On June 25, 1991, both former republics proclaimed their independence, subject to the reservation that it would prove impossible to transform Yugoslavia into a federation with far-reaching autonomy for the member republics. The remainder of Yugoslavia (Serbia and Montenegro) reacted with military force, but her army had to retreat from Slovenia on July 21, 1991. Serbian militias occupied about a third of the Croatian territory after prolonged and cruel fighting. On October 8, 1991, Slovenia and Croatia declared their independence definitively.[91]

Questions of Recognition under International Law

As late as May 24, 1991, the United States still declared that they would "not encourage or reward secession."[92] On December 16,

90 J. Charpentier, "Les déclarations des Douze sur la reconnaissance des nouveaux Etats" (1992) 96 Rev. D.I.P 343-55; Kherad, *supra* note 87 at 843-72; R. Rich, "Recognition of States: The Collapse of Yugoslavia and the Soviet Union" 4 Eur. J. Int'l L. 36-65 (1993); O. Schäfer, "Die Anerkennung von Staaten als Mittel der Kriegsverhinderung?" in *Festschrift Georg Bock* 187-208 (1993).

91 As to this and the following issue, see H. Hannum, "Self-Determination, Yugoslavia, and Europe: Old Wine in New Bottles?" (1993) 3 Trans. L. & C.P. 57-69; W. Hummer, "Probleme der Staatennachfolge am Beispiel Jugoslawien" (1993) 3 S.Z.I.E.R. 425-59; M. Weller, "The International Response to the Dissolution of the Socialist Federal Republic of Yugoslavia" (1992) 86 AJIL 569-607. According to Opinion No. 11 of the Arbitration Commission of July 16, 1993 (32 I.L.M. 1587-89), Oct. 8, 1991, is the decisive date in respect of state succession.

92 Foreign Policy Bulletin, July-Aug. 1991, 71-72.

1991, the foreign ministers of the European Communities proclaimed guidelines on the recognition of the new states in Eastern Europe and in the Soviet Union.[93] According to these guidelines, recognition would be conditional on respect for the provisions of the United Nations Charter and the Conference on Security and Cooperation in Europe (CSCE) with regard to the rule of law, democracy, human rights and minority rights, the inviolability of frontiers, the acceptance of commitments with regard to disarmament and nuclear non-proliferation, and the peaceful settlement of disputes. Entities that resulted from aggression would not be recognized.

Clearly those guidelines went considerably beyond traditional practice. Normally, solely the presence of the four formal state elements is examined. But the collapse of Yugoslavia raised issues not only of recognition, but also of self-determination. If member units express the will to separate from a federal state, it seems that they may invoke a right of secession more readily, provided that they live up to farther-reaching conditions of recognition.

Under the European Communities guidelines, some forty states recognized Slovenia and Croatia by the end of January 1992. Additional states followed suit, and on May 22, 1992, the two new states were admitted into the United Nations, along with Bosnia-Herzegovina.

Opinions of the Arbitration Commission on the Dissolution of Yugoslavia and on Self-Determination

On August 27, 1991, the European Communities appointed an Arbitration Commission, presided over by Robert Badinter. Several of the warring factions went along with this appointment, but not the remaining territory of Yugoslavia.[94] In Opinion Number 1 of November 29, 1991, the Commission stated that the federation of Yugoslavia was dissolving. In their composition and actual working, the federal organs were no longer representative. Moreover, different elements of the federation were engaged in a bloody civil war.[95]

---

[93] See 4 Eur. J. Int'l L. 72 (1993).

[94] The former federal government of Yugoslavia, in declarations of Apr. 30 and July 2, 1993 (32 I.L.M. 1581-82, 1584-85) described the "utterances" of the Arbitration Commission as invalid and not binding on it. The Arbitration Commission reacted by qualifying its opinions as "advisory" answers to questions by the chairman of the International Peace Conference on the former Yugoslavia (32 I.L.M. 1582-84).

[95] (1992) 31 I.L.M. 1494-97.

In Opinion Number 2 of January 11, 1992, the issue at stake was whether the Serbian population in Croatia and Bosnia-Herzegovina could assert a right of self-determination.[96] The Arbitration Commission found that the right of self-determination did not involve changes to those frontiers between member units that existed at the time of independence. Where various ethnic, religious, or language groups existed within a state, the identity of such groups was recognized under international law. States had to respect the minority rights of these groups. The (internal) right of self-determination served to safeguard individual human rights. Members of the Serbian population in Croatia and Bosnia-Herzegovina therefore had a right to decide which ethnic, religious, or language community they belonged to. This right did not, however, signify that they could exercise a collective right of territorial secession.[97] It would seem that the Arbitration Commission favoured a collective (external) right of self-determination of the people of a member unit with clearly defined borderlines in a collapsing federal state, provided that unit would respect human and minority rights and would not use force in violation of international law.[98]

Opinion Number 3 of January 11, 1992, dealt with the borderlines between the member republics of the former Yugoslavia. Contrary to the position taken by the Serbian government, the Arbitration Commission relied on the principle of *uti possidetis*. In its view, this was a general principle of public international law.[99] Accordingly, the frontiers between the Yugoslav member republics were protected under international law, and the alteration of such frontiers was not capable of producing any legal effect.[100]

96 In Croatia, on Dec. 19, 1991, the "Autonomous Serb Republic Krajina" was proclaimed; in Bosnia-Herzegovina, on Apr. 7, 1992, the "Serb Republic Bosnia-Herzegovina" was proclaimed; on July 3, 1992, the "Croatian Republic Herzeg-Bosnia" was proclaimed; on Sept. 10, 1993, the "Krajina of Cazin" in the enclave Bihac was proclaimed; and in Macedonia, on Apr. 5, 1992, the "Albanian Autonomous Republic Illyria" was proclaimed: *cf.* Hummer, *supra* note 90 at 441.

97 (1992) 32 I.L.M. 1497-99.

98 See above all Weller, *supra* note 90 at 589-93, 603-7; see also A. Pellet, "The Opinions of the Badinter Arbitration Committee: A Second Breath for the Self-Determination of Peoples" (1992) 3 Eur. J.I.L. 178-80.

99 *Cf. Affaire Différend frontalier (Burkina Faso c. Mali)*, [1986] I.C.J. Rep. 554 at 565-67.

100 31 I.L.M. 1499-1500 (1992). See the criticism of Hannum, *supra* note 90 at 64-69.

Bosnia-Herzegovina

The parliament of Bosnia-Herzegovina adopted a declaration of sovereignty on October 14, 1991. The Serbs of Bosnia-Herzegovina (who constituted 32 per cent of the population at that time) challenged the validity of the declaration. In an illegal plebiscite on November 10, 1991, they voted in turn for a "common state of Yugoslavia." In its Opinion Number 4 of January 11, 1992, the Arbitration Commission held "that the will of the peoples of Bosnia-Herzegovina to constitute . . . a sovereign and independent State cannot be held to have been fully established."[101] This assessment could be reviewed, however, if appropriate guarantees existed for a genuine expression of the will of the peoples of Bosnia-Herzegovina, "possibly by means of a referendum of all the citizens of the SRBH without distinction, carried out under international supervision."[102] Following this opinion, Bosnia-Herzegovina organized a referendum of independence on March 1, 1992. Apart from the Serb population, who boycotted the referendum, an overwhelming majority voted for independence. In April 1992, European Communities member states and numerous other states recognized Bosnia-Herzegovina as a new state.[103] The unfortunate former republic has ever since been ravaged by a war of rare cruelty with mass rapes, ethnic cleansing, all sorts of war crimes, and dozens of broken armistices.[104] By the autumn of 1992, Serb forces had occupied about 70 per cent of the territory of Bosnia-Herzegovina. In the autumn of 1995, the combined Bosnian and Croat forces recaptured portions of the territory, with the result that the territory was then held more or less evenly by the Serbs on one side, and the Bosnians and Croats on the other.

---

[101] (1992) 31 I.L.M. 1501-3.

[102] *Ibid.* See also Cassese, *supra* note 89 at 143.

[103] According to Opinion No. 11 of July 16, 1993, 32 I.L.M. 1587-89 (1993), Mar. 6, 1992 (i.e., the date of the proclamation of the result of the referendum) was the crucial date in respect of state succession.

[104] *Cf.* T. Meron, "Rape as a Crime under International Humanitarian Law" (1993) 87 AJIL 424-28; J. C. O'Brien, "The International Tribunal for Violations of International Humanitarian Law in the Former Yugoslavia" (1993) 87 AJIL 639-59; S. Oeter, "Kriegsverbrechen in den Konflikten um das Erbe Jugoslawiens" (1993) 53 ZaöRV 1-48; Y. Sandoz, "Réflexions sur la mise en oeuvre du droit international humanitaire et sur le rôle du Comité international de la Croix-Rouge en ex-Yougoslavie," (1993) 3 S.Z.I.E.R, 461-90; D. Thürer, "Vom Nürnberger Tribunal zum Jugoslawien-Tribunal und weiter zu einem Weltstrafgerichtshof?" (1993) 3 S.Z.I.E.R. 491-516.

Macedonia

Macedonia carried out a referendum on independence on September 8, 1991, and declared her independence on September 17, 1991. After she had completed her constitution, on November 17, 1991, by renouncing any territorial claims and by terming herself the "former Yugoslav Republic of Macedonia," she was admitted into the United Nations on April 8, 1993.[105] At the end of 1993, the European Communities states established diplomatic relations with Macedonia. The Arbitration Commission considered November 17, 1991, as the crucial date for the purpose of state succession.[106]

Kosovo

Kosovo was an autonomous province that belonged to the Republic of Serbia. The population consisted largely of Albanians. The new constitution of Serbia of September 28, 1990, forcibly incorporated Kosovo. From September 26 to 30, 1991, an illegal referendum on independence was carried out. The result was positive, but remained inconsequential. The opinions of the Arbitration Commission show that it would deny Kosovo an (external) right of self-determination in the form of a right to secession, but would grant such a right internally in form of the respect of all human and minority rights guaranteed under international law.[107]

The question remains whether the persistent, obvious, and obstinate denial of elementary human and minority rights could nevertheless lead to the foundation of a right of secession — a question that must, in my view, be answered in the affirmative.

Serbia and Montenegro

Serbia and Montenegro considered the separation of Slovenia, Croatia, Bosnia-Herzegovina, and Macedonia as illegal secessions. They therefore claimed to be identical with the former federal state of Yugoslavia as well as being her continuation. Consequently, they viewed themselves more as "trunk Yugoslavia" than as "major Serbia." On October 3, 1991, they seized power in all federal organs in a cold coup.

---

105 Opinion No. 6 of Jan. 11, 1992 (31 I.L.M. 1507-12).

106 Opinion No. 11 of July 16, 1993 (32 I.L.M. 1587-89).

107 *Supra* notes 93-97 and 100-1.

In Opinion Number 8 of July 4, 1992, the Arbitration Commission rejected the viewpoint of Serbia and Montenegro. It insisted that:

the existence of a federal state, which is made up of a number of separate entities, is seriously compromised when a majority of these entities, embracing a greater part of the territory and population, constitute themselves as sovereign states with the result that federal authority may no longer be effectively exercised.[108]

In the view of the Arbitration Commission, the former federal state had ceased to exist. Serbia and Montenegro could therefore not invoke a prior recognition of Yugoslavia *ipso facto*[109] and could not remain a United Nations member in their capacity as "Yugoslavia."[110] Under international law the former Yugoslavia had disintegrated, starting from the date when Serbia and Montenegro gave themselves a new constitution (that is, as of April 27, 1992), and when the international community began to speak of the "former Yugoslavia."[111]

The Breakup of Former Czechoslovakia (CSFR), 1992

The Czechoslovak federation (CSFR) broke up voluntarily at the end of 1992 and split into Czechia and Slovakia.[112] After the elections of June 5-6, 1992, the presidents of the two member republics agreed on the separation of the federation on June 20, 1992. On July 17, 1992, the parliament of the Slovak member republic decreed a declaration on the sovereignty of Slovakia. On November 25, 1992, the federal parliament adopted a constitutional law termi-

---

108 (1992) 31 I.L.M. 1521 at 1522.

109 Opinion No. 10 of July 4, 1992 (31 I.L.M. 1525-26).

110 See V.-D. Degan, O. E. Bring, and M. Kelly Malone, "Agora: UN Membership of the Former Yugoslavia" (1993) 87 AJIL 240-48. For a contrary view, see Y. Z. Blum, "UN Membership of the 'New' Yugoslavia: Continuity or Break?" (1992) 86 AJIL 830-33 and (1993) 87 AJIL 248-51; Hummer, *supra* note 90 at 431-37, 450-59.

111 Opinion No. 11 of July 16, 1993 (32 I.L.M. 1587-89). As to state succession, see Opinion No. 11, *supra* at 1589-98, Opinions Nos. 12-13 of July 16, 1993, and Opinions Nos. 14-15 of Aug. 13, 1993.

112 M. Bútora and Z. Bútorová, "Die unerträgliche Glattheit der Scheidung," [1993] Europäische Rundschau 93-107; M. Hosková, "Die Selbstauflösung der CSFR" (1993) 53 ZaöRV 689-735; R. Schönenfeld, "Die Auflösung der Tschechoslowakei. Glück und Ende eines Bundesstaates" (1993) 48 Europa-Archiv 228-38.

nating the Czechoslovak federation. Both governments declined to organize a referendum concerning the breakup and considered the mandate that emerged from the elections of June 1992 as sufficient.

CONCLUSION

As a rule, constitutions not only are the supreme law of a given nation-state, but they also provide for rules settling important political controversies. Federal constitutions, however, conceive only of *internal* territorial modifications between member units. They settle claims having regard to the formation of new member units, the merger of existing member units, or territorial exchanges between member units.

Numerous federal states have set up rules for simplified procedures with respect to internal territorial modifications in times of expansion and transition. After such phases, they often move on to a stage of permanent stability, allowing modifications only through more cumbersome procedures. They do not always require a revision of the constitution, but characteristically ask for a double assent by the federal government and the member units directly affected.

It would seem normal for genuine federal states to describe themselves as role models, which hold out a promise of autonomy and internal self-determination for their minorities. But *external* self-determination seems inconceivable to them. Federal constitutions do not provide for the breakaway and formation of new sovereign states, nor for the exchange of territory with other sovereign states. Such external territorial modifications are apparently revolutionary and unconstitutional.

However, here as elsewhere the facts triumph over dogma. In the first place, if a federal government agrees to a separation or secession of a member unit, that member unit may be recognized by third states and become a new sovereign state. In the second place, member units may invoke a right of external self-determination under international law if they are in a colonial situation, if their human rights are violated consistently and flagrantly, or if the federal government treats them in an undemocratic and discriminatory way and excludes them from representation. Whether and to what extent the minority groups within the secessionist member units can in turn claim internal or external self-determination, if the secession succeeds, is largely unsettled.

Sommaire

Modifications territoriales et démembrement des États fédéraux

Cet article examine comment le droit interne et le droit international traitent des questions de modifications territoriales et de démembrement des États fédéraux. L'auteur cherche à savoir si les États fédéraux autorisent les demandes séparatistes de leurs minorités qui réclament, sur la base du droit constitutionnel, des "modifications internes" telles que la formation de nouvelles entités ou la fusion d'entités existantes. Il vérifie en outre si le droit interne prévoit la présentation de demandes sécessionnistes portant sur des "modifications externes" telles que la formation de nouveaux États souverains, la fusion ou l'association d'États existants. La pratique analysée par l'auteur donne un nouvel aperçu du problème bien connu de l'autodétermination.

Summary

Territorial Modifications and Breakups in Federal States

This article considers the way in which territorial modifications and breakups in federal states are dealt with in domestic and in international law. It investigates whether federal states permit separatist claims of their minorities for "internal modifications" on the basis of constitutional law, such as the formation of new member units or the merger of existing member units, and whether domestic law knows of any secessionist claims for "external modifications," such as the formation of new sovereign states or the merger or association with existing states. The extensive practice surveyed by the author allows for a new outlook on the well-known problem of "self-determination."

NAFTA Dispute Settlement and Mexico: Interpreting Treaties and Reconciling Common and Civil Law Systems in a Free Trade Area

J. C. THOMAS* AND SERGIO LÓPEZ AYLLÓN†

INTRODUCTION

THE FIRST NAFTA CHAPTER 19 binational panel review of a Mexican anti-dumping determination[1] was decided on August 30, 1995. The review concerned "cut-to-length steel" originating in or exported from the United States, and accordingly the panel comprised Mexican and American attorneys and law professors.[2] Since it was sitting on the first case involving the review of a Mexican final determination, the panel was obliged to consider the changes effected in Mexican law as a result of NAFTA. One such issue concerned the powers of binational panels. The Secretaría de Comercio y Fomento Industrial (SECOFI), the investigating authority, argued that, when discharging its functions under Chapter 19, a

* Of Thomas & Davis, Barristers & Solicitors, Ottawa and Vancouver. Mr. Thomas is counsel to the Mexican Secretaría de Comercio y Fomento Industrial (SECOFI). The author would like to thank Alejandro Posadas for his assistance in the preparation of this paper.

† Research fellow at the Institute of Legal Research of the Universidad Nacional Autónoma de Mexico. Mr. López was an officer with SECOFI during the negotiation of the NAFTA.

[1] *Cut-to-Length Steel, Originating In or Exported From the United States of America*, MEX-94-1904-02.

[2] Although NAFTA is a trilateral agreement, the composition of Chapter 19 panels reflects the bilateral nature of that dispute settlement process. The third party does not participate in a review, nor are panelists selected from its roster. Thus, if for example a NAFTA party imposes anti-dumping duties on subject goods exported from both of the other parties, two binational panels are created rather than a single trinational panel in order to review the determination.

panel exercised only those powers granted to it by NAFTA Article 1904.8.[3] The complainants, on the other hand, argued that the panel had the powers of the Mexican court that it had replaced.

In the exercise of its judicial review function, the Mexican Fiscal Court has the unquestioned power to nullify a decision of SECOFI in appropriate circumstances. Yet, when one turns to Article 1904.8 of NAFTA to ascertain the extent of a binational panel's powers, the paragraph states only that the "panel may uphold a final determination, or remand it for action not inconsistent with the panel's decision." The question arose, therefore, whether the power to remand a decision extended to the power to nullify. SECOFI asserted that the intention of the NAFTA parties had been to preserve the discretion and autonomy of the investigating authority by expressing the panel's power solely in terms of a remand. It conceded that the practical effect of a panel finding could be to require SECOFI to revoke an anti-dumping order. However, that was a decision to be made by SECOFI in the light of one or more remands. It was not, SECOFI argued, a power that the panel could exercise in the first instance, even though the Mexican Fiscal Court could do so.

As shall be seen, the panel found against SECOFI in a three-to-two decision, for reasons that shall be discussed later in this article. The dissenting panelists expressly declined to support the majority on this issue.[4]

---

[3] Art. 1904.8 provides:

> The panel may uphold a final determination, or remand it for action not inconsistent with the panel's decision. Where the panel remands a final determination, the panel shall establish as brief a time as is reasonable for compliance with the remand, taking to account the complexity of the factual and legal issues involved and the nature of the panel's decision. In no event shall the time permitted for compliance with a remand exceed an amount of time equal to the maximum amount of time (counted from the date of the filing of a petition, complaint or application) permitted by statute for the competent investigating authority in question to make a final determination in an investigation. If review of the action taken by the competent investigating authority on remand is needed, such review shall be before the same panel, which shall normally issue a final decision within 90 days of the date on which such remand action is submitted to it.

[4] The minority stated in this regard:

> Thus, we are not deciding here whether or not the Panel has authority pursuant to Article 238 of the Federal Fiscal Code to declare the determination by SECOFI to be a nullity. Neither are we deciding on any related

In coming to its conclusion, the majority sought to discern the NAFTA parties' intentions in negotiating Chapter 19. Although NAFTA is an international agreement, the majority resorted to United States legislative history to discern the parties' intentions. The risks attendant upon taking such an approach are obvious. First, it ignores the international character of the agreement. Second, it does not follow the hierarchy of treaty interpretation established by the Vienna Convention on the Law of Treaties, which establishes that it is the language of the treaty that must be construed, first and foremost, and that the negotiating history is a supplementary means of interpretation to which reference is made only in certain limited circumstances.[5] Third, it introduces the danger that one of the parties' intentions in respect of the agreement will be taken as evidence of all the parties' intentions.

An important question, therefore, is whether in using and relying upon United States legislative history, the panel accurately captured the purpose of Chapter 19 as it was drafted by the parties to NAFTA. This article seeks to answer that question by placing the issue of the panel's powers in historical context. This requires a review of the creation of Chapter 19 in the Canada-United States Free Trade Agreement and its adaptation to NAFTA, as well as an understanding of the peculiar problems that Chapter 19 poses for Mexican law.

It will be seen that, from the beginning, Canada and the United States had different views of what they had done and how the new system would operate. Their differences, which persist to this day,[6]

---

issues, such as the assumption of the majority that Article 238 of the Fiscal Code can only be uniformly applied along with Article 239 of the Fiscal Code, or to the existence of a rule of logical sequence in the application of Article 238, much less the correct interpretation of Paragraph 1 of Article 238. Thus any assertion of the Panel regarding those issues should not be considered corroborated by us.

See the dissenting opinion of panelists John Barton and Gustavo Vega-Cánovas, MEX-94-1904-02 (North American Free Trade Agreement Binational Panel Review Minority Opinion, August 30, 1995).

[5] See Ian Sinclair, *The Vienna Convention on the Law of Treaties*, 2nd ed. 119-47 (1984).

[6] A 1995 Report by the United States General Accounting Office entitled "U.S.-Canada Free Trade Agreement: Factors Contributing to Controversy in Appeals of Trade Remedy Cases to Binational Panels" summarized the difference in views about the operation of Extraordinary Challenge Committees in NAFTA as follows:

According to U.S. and Canadian officials, ECC review of a panel's decision was meant to have a higher threshold than appellate review of a CIT

were reflected in the negotiations leading up to the Chapter's inclusion — with modifications — in NAFTA. The majority in the *Cut-to-Length Steel* review employed the American view of how Chapter 19 should operate in order to justify its claim that, like the Mexican Fiscal Court, binational panels have the power to nullify SECOFI's determinations.

It must be recognized at the outset that the panel faced a difficult task for three reasons that were peculiar to Mexican law. First, under the Mexican Constitution, as an international treaty NAFTA is self-executing and forms a part of domestic law without the enactment of implementing legislation. Thus, unlike Canada and the United States, Mexico did not go through the process of legislative amendment (at least insofar as the central provisions of Chapter 19 were concerned). The absence of consequential amendments to the domestic law deprived the panel of some valuable guidance.

Second, and partly related to the self-executing nature of NAFTA in Mexican law, Mexico did not publish an official view of what changes to the law had been effected by NAFTA. This absence of legislative history stands in sharp contrast to the practice of the United States where, when implementing an international trade agreement, the Executive Branch prepares a *Statement of Administrative Action* that sets out its view of the rights and obligations contained in the agreement and the way in which they relate to United States domestic law. This, together with the reports of congressional

---

decision by CAFC. Nevertheless, participants, including the two governments, disagreed over the interpretation of the ECC standard and where that threshold should be. As a result, the United States and Canada later took the opportunity to "clarify" the ECC role as part of their subsequent NAFTA negotiations. The final NAFTA text incorporated all the U.S. and Canadian FTA Chapter 19 provisions and extended them to Mexico, but added some clarifying language.

However, based on our review of U.S. and Canadian government documents, we believe that the new language in NAFTA regarding ECC did not resolve the fundamental difference between the parties on this issue. While U.S. and Canadian officials agreed that the new NAFTA language "made explicit what was implicit in the FTA," they unfortunately did not agree on what was implicit in the agreement. The U.S. officials characterized this as a significant change, while Canadian officials characterized it as a non-substantive change. Thus, it seems that U.S. officials expected future ECCs to be less narrow in reviewing panel decisions, and Canadian officials expected future ECCs to continue to interpret their role narrowly.

See GAO/GGD-95-175 BR at 97.

committees of jurisdiction, which normally describe Congress's legislative intent, forms part of the domestic legal context in which American courts construe the legislation that implements the international agreement.

Canada, which had no previous history of publishing such statements, began to emulate the United States when it prepared a *Statement of Implementation*, first for NAFTA and then for the World Trade Organization (WTO) Agreements.[7] Dispute settlement panels under the Canada-United States Free Trade Agreement had shown a willingness to resort to negotiating history when construing that agreement, and Canada apparently decided to prepare its version of what the international negotiations had achieved in order to counterbalance the American view of the results.

Since Mexico had not had to prepare and enact implementing legislation and did not have a practice of publishing an official account of the results of trade negotiations, there was no authoritative statement by Mexico of how Chapter 19 was intended to operate in the Mexican legal context.

Third, NAFTA's binational panel review process had been derived from a pre-existing trade agreement negotiated by two predominantly common law countries.[8] The chapter's structure was predicated upon the concept of judicial review of specialized decision-making, a concept that has been highly developed in American and Canadian administrative law jurisprudence. In Mexico, however, the law of judicial review was not so well developed (although a perusal of Article 238 of the Fiscal Code reveals civil law concepts similar to those found in the applicable United States and Canadian standards of review). The paucity of equivalent jurisprudence, together with the relative inexperience of Mexican courts in reviewing anti-dumping and countervailing duty determinations, meant that there was little relevant domestic jurisprudence beyond some in the constitutional area.[9] This will be discussed later.

The absence of implementing legislation and Mexican negotiating history, combined with the introduction into Mexican law of a

---

[7] The former was published in the *Canada Gazette* (1994). I. 68. The latter was published in the *Canada Gazette* (1994). I. 4847.

[8] In Canada, of course, Quebec adheres to the civil law, and in the United States, Louisiana continues to maintain some elements of civil law.

[9] Mexico has had a trade remedy law only since 1986, after it acceded to the General Agreement on Tariffs and Trade in 1985. Thus, there has been only a decade of trade remedy actions and little judicial review thereof.

dispute settlement process predicated on common law concepts, such as deference and decision-making by specialized agencies, therefore made the first panel proceeding truly a case of first impression in Mexican law. As such, it raised fundamental questions of treaty interpretation.

As shall be seen, NAFTA's binational panel review system is *sui generis*. On the one hand, the panels are international bodies created pursuant to the terms of an international agreement. As such, they are constituted and governed by the terms of that agreement — in particular, Article 1904, certain related annexes, and the relevant rules of procedure. On the other hand, panels are obliged to apply the standard of review and general legal principles of the country whose decision is being challenged. Panels must, therefore, sometimes confront the interaction between the international agreement and domestic law, both substantively and procedurally.

In addressing issues of this nature, the *Cut-to-Length Steel* panel had to interpret NAFTA Article 1904. In construing the article's meaning, the panel went beyond the language of NAFTA to examine the views of one party, in particular, about how Chapter 19 should operate in another context. The panel also found it helpful to refer to the practice of panels established under the Canada-United States Free Trade Agreement, a treaty to which Mexico was not a party. In doing so, the panel examined the discussions of panels reviewing Canadian determinations, and, in our view, rather imperfectly analyzed the findings of those panels.

This raises the issue of whether it is appropriate to rely on one party's account of the negotiating history (the United States), when another party (Canada) has a less well-documented account of that history, and the third (Mexico) has no equivalent account at all. The issue is especially important when the international dispute settlement body is charged with resolving a dispute concerning the latter party. There is also the related question of whether a binational panel comprising American and Mexican panelists can — at least without asking the disputing participants for detailed submissions on the point — effectively resort to the experience of panels applying the law of the third country, which has no representation on the panel.

To examine the answers to these questions, it is necessary to review the origins of FTA Chapter 19, the controversies surrounding it, its adaptation to the NAFTA, and its implementation in Mexican law. Further, it is necessary to discuss the first Mexican panel decision and order.

THE ORIGINS OF CHAPTER 19 IN THE CANADA-U.S.
FREE TRADE NEGOTIATIONS

Both Canada and the United States have had considerable experience with anti-dumping and countervailing duty laws and other trade remedy measures. Both have been among the heaviest users of anti-dumping law in the GATT, often imposing such duties on goods originating in or exported from the other. Insofar as the countervailing duty remedy is concerned, the United States by far has been the most frequent user of the remedy. Perhaps not surprisingly, given its proximity and different economy and forms of government intervention, Canada has often been on the receiving end of United States subsidy investigations.

In general form, the two countries' trade remedy laws are similar. Both employ a bifurcated investigatory process. In Canada, dumping and subsidy investigations are carried out by the Deputy Minister of National Revenue while the Canadian International Trade Tribunal is charged with the responsibility for determining "material injury" or threat thereof. In the United States, the Department of Commerce and the United States International Trade Commission respectively are responsible for the same matters.

Thus, when Canada and the United States entered into the free trade negotiations in 1986, their anti-dumping and countervailing laws and administrative regimes were somewhat similar because both were signatories to the GATT and to the 1979 Anti-Dumping and Subsidies Codes.[10] Notwithstanding the general similarities, however, United States law was far more complex, arcane, and, in many instances, more sophisticated than the Canadian. It had been applied in many cases and had been the subject of extensive interpretation by United States courts.

Like other areas of regulation in the United States, the trade remedy laws were administered under the watchful eye of Congress. The sense of Canadians familiar with the American system was that it was more susceptible to political influence than that of Canada and that Canadian exporters were sometimes victims of protectionist determinations made under political pressure. Accordingly, Canadian ministers and senior officials argued that, in addition to enhanced market access (that is, through the reduction and elim-

10 Debra P. Steger "The Dispute Settlement Mechanism of the Canada-U.S. Free Trade Agreement: Comparison with the Existing System" in McRae and Steger (eds), *Understanding the Free Trade Agreement* 49 at 56 (Ottawa: Institute for Research on Public Policy, 1988).

ination of tariffs and other barriers to trade), Canada required more "secure market access" (that is, to be insulated from United States protectionism).

Not surprisingly, the United States neither saw the basis for the latter concern nor shared the view as to the desirability of negotiating any mechanism to deal with it. Thus, despite the broad similarity of their trade remedy laws, the two countries disagreed about the laws' utility in a free trade area. Hence, their negotiating interests differed substantially.

From the outset of the free trade negotiations, therefore, Canada expressed as one of its key negotiating objectives the elimination, on trade between the two parties, of the application of their respective anti-dumping and countervailing duty laws. As far as Canada was concerned, the United States trade remedy laws had become a complainants-driven, in some cases highly-politicized and expensive, method of "harassing" Canadian exporters.[11] Thus, Canada sought an exemption from United States trade remedy law or at least a replacement regime. The United States, on the other hand, was not interested in removing or constraining its right to impose duties on dumped or subsidized goods.[12] This divergence in views nearly undermined the whole of the negotiations. It was only at the eleventh hour that a compromise was forged and an agreement became possible.[13]

THE CHAPTER 19 COMPROMISE

The compromise came in the form of a novel binational panel review mechanism for reviewing dumping and countervailing duty disputes.[14] In the negotiations, the parties had been unable to agree

[11] Shirley A. Coffield, "Dispute Settlement Provisions on Anti-dumping and Countervailing Duty Cases in the Canada-U.S. Free Trade Agreement" in McRae and Steger, *supra* note 10 at 73.

[12] Lowenfeld, "Binational Dispute Settlement Under Chapter 19 of the Canada-United States Free Trade Agreement: An Interim Appraisal" (1991) 24 N.Y.U. J. Int'l L. & P. 269 at 270.

[13] Greenberg, "Chapter 19 of the U.S.-Canada Free Trade Agreement and the North American Free Trade Agreement: Implications for the Court of International Trade" (1993) 25 L. & Pol'y Int'l Bus. 37 at 38.

[14] Steger, *supra* note 10, notes that the idea of settling trade disputes by way of a binational panel was not novel to Canada. In 1985, the Macdonald Commission, *inter alia*, recommended the establishment of a committee of ministers to adjudicate disputes over anti-dumping and countervailing duties and safeguard

to any changes to their trade remedy laws. Under the Free Trade Agreement, therefore, the parties retained their domestic anti-dumping and countervailing duty laws and investigative procedures. However, under Article 1904.1 the parties agreed to "replace judicial review of final anti-dumping and countervailing duty determinations with binational panel review." Thus, in place of national courts, binational panels would become responsible for deciding whether the importing party's "competent investigating authority" applied its anti-dumping or countervailing duty laws in a particular investigation in accordance with its domestic law.

The procedures for Article 1904 proceedings were set out in Annex 1901.2.[15] A roster of fifty individuals, half of them American, the other half Canadian, would be created. Candidates were to be of "good character, high standing and repute" and were to be chosen strictly on the basis of objectivity, reliability, sound judgment, and general familiarity with international trade law. Candidates were not to be affiliated with either party, nor were they in any event to take instructions from either party. Although not all panelists were required to be lawyers, a majority of each panel had to be lawyers in good standing.

Panels would comprise five citizens of the two countries with at least two panelists from each. While they need not all be lawyers, the chairman would be a lawyer. Their role under Chapter 19 was to replace the national courts. After a hearing at which submissions would be made by the investigating authority and other persons who, pursuant to the law of the importing party would have standing to appear and be represented, the panel would render its decision. According to Article 1904.8, a panel could uphold a final determination or remand it for action "not inconsistent with the panel's decision." The panel's decision was binding on the parties with respect to the particular matter before the panel.

To ensure the integrity of the panel process, the parties agreed to establish a code of conduct for panelists. Subject to the terms of the code of conduct and provided that it did not interfere with the performance of their duties, panelists could engage in other business during the term of the panel.[16]

---

matters. See *Report of the Royal Commission on the Economic Union and Development Prospects for Canada* (1985).

[15] Art. 1901.2.

[16] Annex 1901.2(10).

Given that anti-dumping and countervailing duty cases involve the gathering and analysis of confidential business proprietary information, the parties also provided for strict nondisclosure rules. Each agreed pursuant to Annex 1901.2(8) to establish "appropriate sanctions" for violations of protective orders (in the United States) and undertakings (in Canada) and to enforce such sanctions with respect to any person within its jurisdiction. A panelist's failure to sign an undertaking would result in the panelist's disqualification.[17]

A *SUI GENERIS* DISPUTE SETTLEMENT PROCEDURE

Chapter 19, which set out an international dispute settlement process, was created by an international agreement that required amendment to the domestic law of both countries in order to be implemented. However, unlike normal international dispute settlement (for example, Chapter 18 of the Free Trade Agreement), in which the panels were to interpret the agreement itself, Chapter 19 panels stepped into the place of a domestic court. In so doing, the panels were required to apply the domestic law to determine whether a final determination was in accordance with that law.

To enable panels to discharge this responsibility, the parties had to define the governing law. They declined to permit panels to judge the GATT-consistency of such law. For example, whether a national anti-dumping law was consistent with the GATT Anti-dumping Code was to be decided by a separate FTA Article 1903 panel or by a GATT panel. It was not for an FTA Article 1904 panel to decide; the panel "inherited" the local law and was obliged to apply it. Having restricted the panel's role to deciding whether a final determination was in accordance with the domestic law of the importing party, the parties had to specify that law. This was done in FTA Article 1904.2, which stated that "the anti-dumping law and countervailing duty law consists of the relevant statutes, legislative history, regulations, administrative practice, and judicial precedents to the extent that a court of the importing party would rely on such materials in reviewing a final determination of the competent investigating authority."

There remained the standard against which the review of the administration of the domestic law would be judged. This required the parties to introduce a standard of review into the FTA. The-

17 Annex 1901.2(8).

oretically, they could have specified a single standard of review. However, since panels were to review final decisions to determine whether they were in accordance with domestic law, it was logical to incorporate the relevant national standards of review. This was done by specifying the relevant United States and Canadian standards in Article 1911.

Finally, since much of American and Canadian administrative law is judge-made in the form of legal principles not expressed in statutes, the parties added in Article 1904.3 that panels shall apply "the general legal principles that a court of the importing Party otherwise would apply to a review of a determination of the competent investigating authority."[18]

The result was that an international dispute settlement body would be created to replace the normal reviewing court.[19] Instead of interpreting a treaty or applying an international standard of review, the panel would be inserted into what had until the FTA been a purely domestic legal proceeding. To make this system work, the parties agreed to adopt rules of procedure "based, where appropriate, upon judicial rules of appellate procedure."[20] (By the time the FTA entered into force, the parties had negotiated rules of procedure, which were published in the two countries' official journals.) The result was a single set of rules for binational panel review in both countries. Even there, however, the parties made

---

[18] Art. 1904.3.

[19] The United States House of Representatives' Committee on the Judiciary subsequently noted in this regard (at 16): "The binational panels are established to implement the FTA, an international law agreement, and the panelists will apply international law under the FTA. Panelists will be exercising authority pursuant to international law, therefore not enforcing the laws of the United States." It stated further (at 26):

> Section 401(d) of the bill makes clear that a court of the United States is not bound by a final decision of a binational panel or extraordinary challenge committee. The binational panels and extraordinary challenge committees are tribunals created by international law that will be applying international law. They are not Article III courts. Panel and committee decisions cannot be binding on U.S. courts. A court of the United States, however, may take a panel or committee decision into consideration, as it would a considered view of United States law.

Report of the Committee on the Judiciary on the United States-Canada Free-Trade Agreement Implementation Act of 1988, 100th Cong., 2d Sess. Rep't 100-816 Part 4.

[20] See Art. 1904.14.

allowance for national differences. It was necessary to provide for different definitions of "privileged information," for example, due to different national laws.[21]

It is important to note that while this *sui generis* panel process was intended to "replace" judicial review, the parties were not creating a binational court. Panels were *ad hoc* — once a panel completed its work, it was discharged. The parties clearly envisaged that panelists would act like private arbitrators rather than life-tenured judges in the sense that they would, subject to compliance with a code of conduct, continue to carry on other remunerative work before, during, and after the panel proceedings. The parties limited the scope of the issues that could be taken to binational panel review. A panel's jurisdiction was limited to the review of *final* determinations.[22] Unlike the domestic courts, a panel could not be created to review any of the investigating authority's actions before the final determination was issued.

Insofar as the review itself was concerned, a panel did not have the same panoply of powers as the domestic court that it replaced. For example, in Canada, Federal Court judges have an equitable jurisdiction[23] that permits them to make and enforce certain types of orders (such as *certiorari, mandamus,* and other prerogative writs). Federal Court judges can also award monetary damages and legal costs.[24] In contrast, the only power to fashion a remedy conferred on a binational panel was the power to uphold the determination or remand it back to the investigating authority "for action not inconsistent with the panel's decision."[25]

[21] See Rule 3 of the original version of the rules of procedure for Art. 1904 binational panel reviews.

[22] This was made clear in Art. 1904.2, which permitted the panel to review, "based upon the administrative record, a final anti-dumping or countervailing duty determination of a competent investigation authority."

[23] Section 3 of the Federal Court Act refers to it as a "court of law, equity and admiralty."

[24] Section 2 of the act defines "relief" to mean "every species of relief, whether by way of damages, payment of money, injunction, declaration, restitution of an incorporeal right, return of land or chattels or otherwise."

[25] The point is illustrated by examining the way in which Canada and the United States have implemented the NAFTA panel system in their domestic law. In Canada, an application for judicial review would be made to the Federal Court Trial Division or to the Federal Court of Appeal depending on the investigating authority being reviewed. The Trial Division has jurisdiction to hear and determine applications for judicial review made in respect of Revenue Canada

The legal situation in the United States was to similar effect. Binational panels did not possess the powers of the Court of International Trade, the court they were to "replace." As a Report of the House of Representatives Committee on the Judiciary noted in recommending the enactment of the United States-Canada Free Trade Agreement Implementation Act of 1988:

---

determinations. Subsection 18.1 of the Federal Court Act states that, on an application for judicial review, the Trial Division may:

(a) order a federal board, commission or other tribunal to do any act or thing it has unlawfully failed or refused to do or has unreasonably delayed in doing; or

(b) declare invalid or unlawful or quash, or set aside and refer back for redetermination in accordance with such directions as it considers to be appropriate, prohibit or restrain, a decision, order, act or proceeding of a federal board, commission or other tribunal.

The Federal Court of Appeal has jurisdiction to hear and determine applications for judicial review made in respect of the Canadian International Trade Tribunal. By virtue of Section 28(2) of the Federal Court Act, it has the same powers as the Trial Division.

In contrast to the wide-ranging powers held by the Canadian courts, the Canadian legislation implementing NAFTA (the North American Free Trade Agreement Implementation Act) limits the powers of a binational panel. Section 77.015(1) states:

(1) A panel shall conduct a review of a definitive decision in accordance with Chapter Nineteen of the North American Free Trade Agreement and the Rules.

(2) A panel has such powers, rights and privileges as are conferred on it by the regulations.

(3) On completion of the review of a definitive decision, a panel shall determine whether the grounds on which the review was requested have been established and *shall make an order confirming the decision or referring the matter back to the appropriate authority for reconsideration* within the period specified by the panel [emphasis added].

United States law similarly confers wide powers in respect of judicial review on the Court of International Trade. E.g., under 28 U.S.C. § 1585 "[t]he Court of International Trade shall possess all the powers in law and equity or, as conferred by statute upon, a district court of the United States," and 28 U.S.C. § 2643 gives the Court the power to enter a money judgment, order any other form of relief that is appropriate in a civil action including, but not limited to, declaratory judgments, orders of remand, injunctions and writs of mandamus and prohibition.

In contrast to these considerable powers vested in the Court of International Trade, the applicable United States statute implementing Art. 1904 of the NAFTA (19 U.S.C. § 1516a), consistent with NAFTA Art. 1904.8, refers only to a *remand* from a binational panel.

[T]here will be no injunctive relief under section 516A(c)(2) of the Tariff Act of 1930 available for determinations for which binational panel review is requested. The administering authority is given under this legislation authority to suspend liquidation in appropriate cases. The exceptions to this are cases in which a constitutional issue is raised, other than to the constitutionality of this implementing legislation as decided in new subsection (g)(4)(B) of section 516A; these cases will be before the Court of International Trade, which will continue to have the power to issue injunctions as necessary. *The binational panels will not have equity powers* [emphasis added].[26]

Thus, a panel did not possess the same powers as the United States or Canadian court that it replaced. Further, the decisions of panels were not accorded the same status in domestic law as the decisions of these courts. Article 1904.9 made it clear that binational panel decisions were binding on the parties with respect to the particular matter between them that was before the panel. However, Article 1904.10 stated that the FTA would not affect the judicial review procedures of either party or cases appealed under those procedures, with respect to determinations other than final determinations.

Paragraph 10 was an important limiting provision because it underscored the parties' intention to have the binational panel process operate as a separate form of dispute settlement. In the common law systems of both countries, a decision of a court of appeal would have precedential effects beyond the actual case under appeal; the decision would become binding on inferior courts and administrative bodies. The limiting language of paragraph 10 ensured that binational panel decisions would not enter the domestic law of the importing party and thereby affect other cases not subject to binational review.

THE EXTRAORDINARY CHALLENGE COMMITTEE

There was one exception to the rule that a binational panel's decision was final. Although it was not originally included in the "elements of agreement" document initialled by negotiators on October 3, 1987, the parties subsequently decided to include a special appeal process to protect against egregious problems that might arise from the panel process. The mechanism on which they ultimately settled was derived from the ICSID arbitration system.[27]

---

[26] Emphasis added. See *supra* note 19 at 27.

[27] ICSID stands for the International Centre for the Settlement of Investment Disputes. It is a body established by the World Bank to arbitrate disputes

Article 1904.13 thus provided that a party, within a reasonable time following a panel decision, could invoke the extraordinary challenge procedure. Paragraph 13 established a three-pronged test.[28] First, there had to be an allegation that:

(1) a member of the panel was guilty of gross misconduct, bias, or a serious conflict of interest, or otherwise had materially violated the rules of conduct

(2) the panel had seriously departed from a fundamental rule of procedure

(3) the panel had manifestly exceeded its powers, authority, or jurisdiction set out in this Article [1904].[29]

Second, any of the above actions had to have "materially affected the panel's decision." Third, such action had to "threaten the integrity of the binational panel review process."[30]

To staff the extraordinary challenge procedure, Annex 1904.13 required the parties to establish a ten-person roster (five from each party) of judges or former judges of a federal court of the United States or a superior court of Canada. There was no requirement that they have any particular knowledge or experience in international trade law. When a party requested that an extraordinary challenge committee be established, each party would select one member, and the third would be selected from the roster by the two members chosen by the parties or, if necessary, by lot from the

---

between investors and host states. Art. 50 of the ICSID Rules of Procedure for Arbitration Proceedings, which deals with "Interpretation, Revision and Annulment of the Award," sets out the grounds for seeking an *ad hoc* review committee. The grounds are very similar to those ultimately included in Article 1904.13.

[28] Art. 1904.13 requires a party to "allege" rather than establish these three prongs.

[29] Art. 1904.13(a). The language in NAFTA Art. 1904.13(a)(iii): "for example, by failing to apply the appropriate standard of review" was not included in the FTA. Canada, in its *Statement on Implementation for NAFTA* (at 204), stated that the inclusion of this clause "does not expand the scope of an extraordinary challenge proceeding from what had been negotiated under the FTA." Instead, Canada asserted that it merely made explicit what was implicit in the FTA. The United States, in its *Statement of Administrative Action*, H. Doc. 103-59, Vol. 1, 103d Cong., 1st Sess. at 644, saw the change as more significant.

[30] Art. 1904.13(b).

roster.[31] Once selected, the committee was to render a decision "typically within 30 days of its establishment."[32]

If a committee was satisfied that the grounds set out in Article 1904.13 were met, then it would either vacate the original decision or remand it to the original panel for action not inconsistent with the committee's decision. If vacated, then a new panel had to be established; if the grounds for review were not met, then the decision of the binational panel would stand. Finally, the committee's decision was binding on the parties with respect to the matter decided.[33]

The Peculiarities of the New System

Even at the time of the FTA's entry into force on January 1, 1989, there were questions about how the Chapter 19 system would work in practice. First, from the Canadian perspective, it seemed obvious that it would act differently than the courts it replaced. Otherwise, why bother to change the existing systems of judicial review? The replacement of one or three judges who were more expert in the process of judicial review than in the intricacies of trade remedy law with panels of five non-judges who were more expert in trade remedy law than in judicial review could be expected to have some effect — even if the panels thought they were acting as the domestic court would act.

Second, there was the question of how well lawyers schooled in the law of one country could grasp not only the mainstream principles of administrative law in the other country but also the more subtle points that become the almost intuitive knowledge of the experienced practitioner. This was perforce the case for those panelists who were not lawyers. In fact, there was a question whether economists, political scientists, and others of recognized standing in their respective communities could grasp the complexities of performing judicial review in either their own or a foreign legal system.

Third, and related to the second issue, was the whole question of differences in legal reasoning. The method of analyzing a legal problem varies not only between lawyers and judges, but also

---

[31] Unlike a panel established pursuant to Annex 1901.2, no peremptory challenges are available.

[32] Annex 1904.12(2).

[33] Annex 1904.13(3).

between lawyers and judges schooled in different legal systems. One obvious difference between Canada and the United States concerned the use of legislative history. In the United States, legislative history is commonly used when construing the meaning of statutes. In Canada, although the tradition has been relaxed in recent years, courts have followed the reticence of English courts in resorting to extrinsic interpretative aids outside the statute's language.

Fourth, as foreshadowed by the imprecision of the language of Article 1904 in describing the governing law (the law consists of the "relevant statutes . . . and judicial precedents to the extent that a court . . . would rely on such materials," and the panel shall apply the standard of review and "the general legal principles that a court . . . otherwise would apply"), there was a question about a panel's ability to discern what the relevant law was and then properly apply it. This problem was not eased by the fact that administrative law — although highly developed and voluminous in both countries — is sometimes imprecise. It is an area of law in which, having recited the general principles, the domestic courts themselves frequently encounter problems in applying the law. The inconsistency of much of the jurisprudence in both countries, combined with the case-specific factual features of court decisions and the discretionary nature of judging may cause reasonable and conscientious lawyers and judges to disagree about the application of the law in any given case. This is not an area of law in which clear, objective, and easily applied principles of law govern.[34]

---

[34] The GAO Report, *supra* note 6 adverted to this fact when it discussed United States concerns that binational panels were creating a separate jurisprudence. It commented:

> Determining what constitutes substantial evidence involves subjective judgment and is the subject of ongoing debate in U.S. administrative law. Questions regarding the application of the standard, such as how much evidence is required to support an agency decision, involve the discretion of the reviewing court or panel. The criteria that have been articulated by appellate courts for the application of the standard have not necessarily provided clear guidance for individual cases.

Consequently, comparing the panels' treatment of the substantial evidence standard with that of CIT is difficult because different judges themselves have applied the standard differently. Some participants told us that they see CIT judges apply the standard of review in a range of ways — that is, not uniformly. In the judicial process, the boundaries for CIT judges applying the standard of review are established through review of these decisions by higher courts,

Taken together, these factors exposed the Chapter 19 panel process to potential criticism.[35] It was entirely predictable and perhaps inevitable that disappointed litigants would complain about the panels' behaviour, analysis, and decisions. Given the inherent imprecision and difficulty in measuring how a court conducts judicial review over time, it would not be particularly difficult to level accusations about the panels' performance.

In fact, as events transpired, many FTA Chapter 19 panel decisions would be unanimous. This suggested that panelists had made their decisions in a collegial fashion and were able to overcome any difficulties in discharging their responsibilities. However, the possibility remained that one day an important case could go before a panel and the worst outcome could result — that is, a split among panelists along national lines. This is precisely what happened at the later stages of the biggest dispute to go before an FTA binational panel — the *Softwood Lumber* dispute.[36]

---

namely CAFC. However, under FTA, while an ECC can review a panel decision, the standard for this subsequent review is different (GAO Report at 35).

[35] The GAO Report, *ibid.*, commented in this regard:

> While panels perform the same function and are charged with applying the same legal standard of review as CIT, they are different in their composition and in their practices. Participants in the panel process had opposite views about whether some panel decisions were in keeping with or contrary to what CIT would have decided. Furthermore, participants noted procedural differences between the panel process and the judicial process. (See App. III.)

These differences could add to the controversy over the process because they are not what some U.S. participants are used to encountering in the U.S. system. For example, several participants noted that panels and panelists were easier targets for criticism than courts and judges were. This is because panelists served *ad hoc*, were otherwise colleagues of the other participants, may have represented clients on similar issues before the administering agencies, and did not have the same stature as judges. Some suggested that permanent panelists may be needed in the future, while others thought that the private parties should have a role in selecting panelists. In updating FTA binational panel provisions during NAFTA negotiations, U.S. officials sought to encourage a more judicial character in panels by adding a "requirement that the United States include judges and former judges on the panelist rosters to the fullest extent practicable (*ibid.*, 99).

[36] This is addressed in a forthcoming paper co-authored by J. C. Thomas and T. M. Apsey, entitled, "Lessons of the Softwood Lumber Dispute: Politics, Protectionism, and the Panel Process."

DIFFERENT VIEWS OF WHAT HAD BEEN ACCOMPLISHED

It is clear from this quick sketch of the binational panel review process that it was a far cry from Canada's original negotiating objective. Indeed, both parties retained their existing laws. What was achieved was a change in the review of the administration of the laws. It warrants noting that although the two parties were able to agree on the treaty language that set out the Chapter 19 regime, they held strikingly different views of what they had actually achieved.

To Canada, the replacement of a court (with one or three judges sitting, depending on which national court was being replaced) with an *ad hoc* binational panel comprising five trade law and policy experts would lead to much greater scrutiny of the decisions by investigating authorities, even if the panels applied the same standard of review that a domestic court would apply. Given the fact that courts themselves vary as to the degree of judicial activism in review of agency decisions, the Canadian view was that a change in the composition of the reviewing body would make a difference to the result. Put simply, five experts would be more likely than one or three generalist judges to subject the final determination to rigorous review.

To the United States, Chapter 19 was designed to reduce the often lengthy backlog of judicial review applications (and had the salutary effect of making previously unreviewable Canadian deputy ministerial determinations of dumping and subsidization now reviewable).[37] Although some officials may privately have thought differently, the administration was officially of the view that the

---

37 The House Committee on the Judiciary noted in this regard:

> The creation of binational panel, in combination with other features of the FTA, offer concrete benefits for United States persons and businesses. First, the panels will apply the same standard of review as a court but it must make its decisions in a much shorter time period, and, thereby enhance the "ability to calculate the economic costs and benefits . . . [involved in appealing a case]." Second, the use of dispute resolution panels over the next five to seven years is designed as a prelude to the development of permanent substantive changes in the trade laws of the two countries. It has been argued that familiarity with the laws of the other nation will facilitate this development. Third, to American exporters the FTA presents a specific improvement by authorizing review of certain decisions concerning anti-dumping and countervailing duty cases in Canada that are not currently subject to judicial review in Canadian courts. Finally, the use of binational panels permits the interested private parties to utilize, in appropriate cases, the legal assistance of government attorneys in the panel process. This indirect type of assistance to United States exporters could help reduce the legal costs to the parties, especially to small businesses (*supra* note 19 at 3).

panels would not or should not act in a different way from the domestic courts they replaced. It pointed in this regard to Article 1904.3, which stated that the panel shall apply the standard of review applied by the domestic court.

This difference in views has persisted ever since Chapter 19 entered into force. The 1995 United States General Accounting Office study of Chapter 19's operation prepared for then-Senator Bob Packwood[38] identified the difference in negotiating perspectives as follows:

In compromising, U.S. and Canadian negotiators had common goals for the panel process. These goals were to protect sovereignty, create trade benefits, reduce political tension, and provide a fair and expeditious review process. However, their expectations of how the panel process would accomplish each of these goals differed. For example, on one hand Canadian negotiators expected that the panel process would address the complaints of Canadian producers that United States political pressures disposed United States agency officials to side with United States industry complainants. They also expected that the new forum would make panel review speedier, less costly, and more rigorous than CIT [Court of International Trade] review of United States agency actions. On the other hand, United States negotiators expected that quicker resolution of [trade] issues would minimize unnecessary bilateral trade friction, while reliance on United States trade law meant that the panel review would be comparable to CIT review. Thus, the panel process was a compromise that left the underlying concerns about the use of trade remedy laws unresolved.[39]

The GAO returned to this difference in view later in its Report when it commented:

Although U.S. and Canadian officials reached agreement on the details of the panel process — panels would (1) give the appearance of greater objectivity, (2) be less politicized, and (3) be quicker (and therefore less costly) than the judicial review process — they emphasized different aspects when describing their agreement publicly during their legislative approval processes. However, U.S. officials believed that panel decisions would be no different from U.S. court decisions. The United States emphasized that panels would employ the same standard of review and same general legal principals as national courts and could not substitute their judgment for that of the agencies'. However, Canadian officials

---

[38] Senator Packwood was a leading ally of the "Coalition for Fair Lumber Imports," a trade group that had successfully petitioned for a countervailing duty against imported Canadian lumber only to see the duty eliminated after a series of sometimes rancorous binational panel decisions and an Extraordinary Challenge Committee proceeding.

[39] *Supra* note 8 at 3.

emphasized their belief that panelists' expert opinions would improve oversight of U.S. agency actions, and that panels would not be as deferential as the U.S. courts were. Panels were seen as an improvement because Canadians believed that CIT was "passive" in its review of United States agency actions, and that politics, not the law, guided agency determinations.[40]

This fundamental difference in view about the way in which binational panels would conduct reviews persisted and has endured to this day. Being the smaller partner, Canada has seen the panels as bodies that can ensure that the trade remedy laws are applied in a depoliticized and impartial fashion. Canada has expected the binational panels to hold the investigating authority to a higher standard of accountability. The United States continually has asserted that the decision of a binational panel in a particular case should be the same as that which would emerge from the domestic court it replaced.[41] The United States therefore has asserted that the decisions of the investigating authority should be accorded the same deference as that which would be accorded by a judge or panel of judges unschooled in the arcane complexities of trade remedy law.

THE POSSIBILITY OF A SUBSTITUTE REGIME

In addition to agreeing upon a novel review mechanism, the FTA parties agreed to further "negotiations" or "discussions" — depending on which party was speaking — on trade remedy law reform. Under the FTA, the binational panel review process was originally intended to be a temporary mechanism. In Article 1907, the parties agreed to establish a working group that would seek to develop more effective rules and disciplines concerning the use of government subsidies and a substitute system of rules for dealing with unfair pricing and government subsidization, and consider any problems that may arise in implementing Chapter 19. Where appropriate, the working group was to recommend solutions.

Interestingly, at the time the FTA was concluded, the Canadian government's hopes were placed more on the prospects of negotiating a substitute regime than on the temporary binational panel

---

[40] *Ibid.*, 38-39.

[41] This difference of view manifested itself in the NAFTA negotiations when Chapter 19 arose as an issue. The United States was disinclined to continue Chapter 19. To Canada, this was unacceptable; Chapter 19 was a *sine qua non* of a successful outcome to the negotiations. Ultimately, Chapter 19 was included, but not without important modifications.

process. This can be seen in the annotation of Chapter 19 that was prepared by Canada to accompany the first public release of the FTA.[42]

After the FTA entered into force, working parties were duly established to develop the substitute regime, but in reality there was little interest on the American side to do anything. Article 1907 had been regarded by American negotiators as a sop to Canada designed to allow ministers to "declare victory and go away." In addition, two years after the FTA entered into force, Mexico expressed its interest in negotiating either accession to the FTA or a separate bilateral agreement with the United States. Thus, the process contemplated in Article 1907 was overtaken by events.

CHAPTER 19 OF NAFTA

During the NAFTA negotiations, the three parties did not address the institutional and dispute settlement provisions until close to the end of the negotiations. By the spring of 1992, the parties began to turn their minds to Chapter 19. By that time, with over three years of experience with the FTA, far from converging, Canadian and American attitudes about Chapter 19's utility and efficacy remained unreconciled and arguably were even further apart. Insofar as the original commitment to seek to develop a new regime was concerned, nothing had been done other than to hold a few desultory meetings of officials. Moreover, throughout the NAFTA negotiations, United States officials had consistently reiterated the United States' position that no substantive changes to the trade remedy laws would be contemplated.

[42] The annotation stated:

> Article 1907 provides that the two governments will work towards establishing a new regime to address problems of dumping and subsidization to come into effect no later than at the end of the seventh year. During the course of the current negotiations, the two sides recognized that developing a new regime was a complex task and would require more time. The goal of any new regime, however, will be to obviate the need for border remedies, as are now sanctioned by the GATT Anti-dumping and Subsidies Codes, for example, by developing new rules on subsidy practices and relying on domestic competition law. Thus the goal of the two governments remains the establishment of a new regime to replace current trade remedy law well before the end of the transition period.
>
> In the meantime, Chapter 19 includes provisions to prevent abuse of the current system, thus allowing Canadian exporters to compete in the U.S. market on a more secure, predictable, and equitable footing.

As for the binational panel process, the challenge for Canada was how to make permanent in NAFTA what was originally conceived in the FTA as a temporary dispute settlement mechanism pending the development of a substitute regime. For its part, the United States queried whether the mechanism should be continued at all. In the three years that had elapsed since the FTA entered into force, the United States had lost some important cases and had launched two Extraordinary Challenge Committee proceedings, both of which it had lost.[43] There was growing discontent among United States industries who used the trade remedy laws and their congressional allies. With Mexico, a civil law country, a party to the negotiations, the American opponents of Chapter 19 saw an opportunity to argue that the introduction of panelists schooled in the civil law would further complicate what they saw was already an unacceptable situation.

To Canada, however, the very things that made Chapter 19 suspect in American eyes were its strengths: for example, the fact that five-person panels had in some, if not all cases, subjected final determinations to greater scrutiny than the domestic courts, and the fact that the United States had lost some major cases because panels had found that the investigating authority had not properly applied the law. Thus, Canada informed the United States that it could not agree to a NAFTA that did not include Chapter 19.

Mexico saw the force of the Canadian position and lent its weight to Chapter 19's inclusion. A key point for Mexico was that the central protection of "secure" market access for Canada could not be continued on a purely bilateral basis. If Canada made Chapter 19 the *sine qua non* of its becoming a party to NAFTA, Mexico would have to have the benefits (and disciplines) of Chapter 19 as well.

Judging that the negotiation could not conclude without the inclusion of Chapter 19 in the Agreement, the United States negotiators sought to strip out as many objectionable features of Chapter

---

43 The first ECC resulted from a panel review of the International Trade Commission's injury determination in *Fresh, Chilled, and Frozen Pork from Canada*. In the first review, the panel found that the injury determination was not supportable and remanded it to the ITC. The ITC's determination on remand was then reviewed and the panel again sent it back, this time with instructions to find no injury. The ITC protested the panel's decision as "counterintuitive, counterfactual, and illogical, but legally binding." The United States then commenced an ECC proceeding alleging that the panel had manifestly exceeded its powers, authority, or jurisdiction. The ECC rejected all of the United States arguments and dismissed the complaint ((1991) 4 T.C.T. 7037). The second ECC adopted the same approach in *Live Swine from Canada* ([1993] F.T.A.D. No. 4).

19 as possible. The Canadians were equally determined to retain as much of the original text as possible. The end result was a chapter that retained a substantial resemblance to its FTA counterpart but also contained some significant changes.

The original commitment in FTA Article 1907 to seek to develop a substitute regime was watered down to an agreement "to consult" on "the potential to develop" a substitute system of rules and disciplines.[44] Annex 1901.2, which sets out the terms for establishing panels, contained new language on panelists' qualifications. In addition to the old requirements of "objectivity, reliability, sound judgment and general familiarity with international trade law," the Annex now contained language that was manifestly the product of compromise: "The roster shall include judges or former judges to the fullest extent practicable."[45] Thus, while the United States preference for judicial generalists was recognized, Canada and Mexico retained the right not to appoint judges because it was not "practicable." The United States administration later declared that this was a "significant procedural change." Its *Statement of Administrative Action* for the NAFTA implementing legislation commented:

There are several advantages to having judges and former judges serve as panelists. *For example, the participation of panelists with judicial experience would help to ensure that,* in accordance with the requirement of Article 1904, panels review determinations of the administering authorities *precisely as would a court of the importing country* by applying exclusively that country's AD [anti-dumping] and CVD [countervailing duty] law and its standard of review. *In addition, the involvement of judges in the process would diminish the possibility that panels and courts will develop distinct bodies of U.S. law"* [emphasis added].[46]

The extraordinary challenge procedure was also changed in important respects. The third ground for extraordinary challenge review, namely, that "the panel manifestly exceeded its powers, authority or jurisdiction" was amended to include the illustrative example of "for example, by failing to apply the appropriate standard of review." This too was heralded by the United States as necessary to protect the panel system. The *Statement of Administrative Action* commented:

[44] Art. 1907.2.

[45] Annex 1901.2, para. 1.

[46] *Statement of Administrative Action* at 644.

Strict adherence by binational panels to the requirement in Article 1904(3) that panels apply the judicial standard of review of the importing country is the cornerstone of the binational panel process. Scholars have noted the potential within the system for disuniformity of panel decisions with each other and established U.S. law. See A.F. Lowenfeld, *Binational Panel Dispute Settlement Under Chapters 18 and 19 of the Canada-United States Free Trade Agreements: An Interim Appraisal* 81 (December 1990). In order to ensure that such disuniformity does not develop through panel decisions under the NAFTA, binational panels must take care to apply properly the importing country's law and standard of judicial review.

In light of the central importance of this requirement, any *failure* by a binational panel to apply the appropriate standard of review, if such failure materially affected the outcome of the panel process and threatened the integrity of the binational panel review process, would be grounds for an ECC to vacate or remand a panel decision.

The decisions of a few binational panels convened under the CFTA have underscored the importance of the NAFTA's emphasis on the proper application of the judicial standard of review. *In specific, these decisions have raised the question of whether these panels have correctly applied the standard of review.* Where, in the Administration's view, panel decisions have failed to apply the appropriate standard of review or they have otherwise manifestly exceeded their powers, authority or jurisdiction, there could be recourse to the extraordinary challenge procedure under Article 1904(13) [emphasis added].[47]

The length of time for an Extraordinary Challenge Committee review was lengthened from thirty days to ninety days from the committee's establishment, and the committee's mandate was more explicitly defined than previously to permit "examination of the legal and factual analysis underlying the findings and conclusions of the panel's decision in order to determine whether one of the grounds set out in Article 1904.13 has been established."[48] Once again, the *Statement of Administrative Action* commented:

By expanding the period of review and requiring ECCs to look at the panel's underlying legal and factual analysis, the changes to Annex 1904 clarify that an ECC's responsibilities do not end with simply ensuring that the panel articulated the correct standard of review. Rather, ECCs are to examine whether the panel analyzed the substantive law and underlying facts.[49]

---

[47] Emphasis added. *Ibid.*, 195-96.

[48] The FTA's equivalent language had been less explicit, simply referring to the possibility that there would be a "finding that one of the grounds set out in paragraph 13 . . . has been established."

[49] *Statement of Administrative Action* at 196.

NAFTA also introduced an entirely new mechanism in Article 1905, entitled "Safeguarding the Panel Review System." This was designed primarily to meet a concern that had not arisen in the implementation of the FTA in the two common law countries, namely, the question of finality and bindingness of panel decisions. Under Mexican law, the potential for an *amparo* challenge of SECOFI's implementation of a binational panel remand led the other two NAFTA parties to seek a treaty mechanism that would ensure the effective implementation of panel decisions.[50]

Finally, NAFTA Chapter 19 included an illustrative list of features that were considered to be "desirable in the administration of anti-dumping and countervailing duty laws."[51] These ranged from the presentation of facts and arguments to the provision of a statement of reasons. Having listed such features, however, in keeping with the design of the original Chapter 19, the parties sought to ensure that the features did not become an independent standard against which the administration of a party's law could be judged in a particular case: "Inclusion of an item . . . is not intended to serve as guidance to a binational panel reviewing a . . . determination pursuant to Article 1904 in determining whether such determination was in accordance with the law of the importing Party."[52]

CHAPTER 19 IN MEXICAN LAW

NAFTA represented a turning point in Mexican law because, due to the extent of its legal consequences,[53] it re-opened an old debate not yet resolved in Mexico, regarding the place of international agreements in Mexican law.[54] The incorporation of international

[50] This is discussed further below.

[51] Art. 1907.3.

[52] *Ibid.*

[53] Héctor Fix Fierro and Sergio López-Ayllón, "E'l Tratado de Libre Comercio de América del Norte y la globalización del derecho. Una visión desde la sociología y la política del derecho" in Jorge Witker (ed.), *El Tratado de Libre Comercio de América del Norte. Análisis, diagnóstico y propuestas jurídicas*, vol. 1, 19 at 54 (Mexico: UNAM, 1993).

[54] The bibliography on these issues is extensive. E.g., note Jorge Witker, *ibid.*, vol. 1 at 79-108; Guillermo Aguilar Alvarez, "Marco jurídico del Tratado de Libre Comercio de América del Norte" in Rubén Valdez Abascal and J.E. Romero (eds), *La modernización del derecho mexicano* 601-34 (Mexico: Porrúa, 1994); Carpizo, Jorge, "La interpretación del artículo 133 constitucional" in *Boletín Mexicano de Derecho Comparado*, año II, no. 4, Jan.-Apr. 1969 at 3-33; Antonio

agreements is governed by Article 133 of the Mexican Constitution,[55] which states that international agreements concluded by the president of the Republic, approved by the Senate, and that conform to the constitution, are the supreme law of all of the unions.[56] In other words, subject to the conditions established by Article 133, international agreements are "law," and are of direct application. Thus, as a general rule, there is no need in Mexico for further legislative acts to implement treaties in domestic law, due to their self-executing nature.

Notwithstanding this, Mexican legal doctrine acknowledges that certain provisions of international agreements, called "hetero-executives," require, to be operative, additional legislative action. In the case of Chapter 19 of NAFTA, a limited amount of legislative action was necessary to allow the Article 1904 review system to function. In the first instance, certain procedural features of trade remedy investigations that had not been implemented in Mexican law (those listed in Article 1904.15), were implemented through the enactment of a new Law of Foreign Commerce and its regulation.[57] Second, it was necessary to amend Articles 94, 97, and

Martínez Báez, "La Constitución y los tratados internacionales" in *Revista de la Escuela Nacional de Jurisprudencia,* t. VIII, no. 30, Apr.-June 1946 at 167-81; Jorge Palacios Treviño, *Tratados: legislación y práctica en México* (Mexico: Secretaría de Relaciones Exteriores, 1986); M. Seara Vázquez, *Derecho internacional público* (Mexico: Porrúa, 1976); F. Vázquez Pando, "Jerarquía del Tratado de Libre Comercio en el sistema constitucional mexicano" in *Panorama jurídico del Tratado de Libre Comercio* 35 ff. (Mexico: Universidad Iberoamericana, 1992).

55 Art. 133 reads: "This Constitution, the laws of the Congress of the Union that emanate from it and all the treaties that conform to it, concluded or to be concluded by the President of the Republic, with the approval of the Senate, will be the Supreme Law of the Union. The State judges will conduct themselves under such Constitution, laws, and treaties, notwithstanding the provisions to the contrary, that may be found in the States' Constitutions or laws." Other constitutional articles that apply to the international sphere are Art. 15; Art. 76, para. 1; Art. 89, para. 10; Art. 104; Art. 107; and Art. 117, para. 1.

56 This article, introduced for the first time in the Mexican Constitution of 1857, is inspired by the second paragraph of Art. 6 of the constitution of the United States of America. See F. Tena Ramírez, *Derecho constitucional mexicano,* 18th ed., 413 ff. (Mexico: Porrúa, 1981).

57 The Law on Foreign Trade was published in the *Official Gazette of the Federation* (*Diario Oficial de la Federación*) on July 27, 1993, and its regulations on December 30, 1993. Some scholars in Mexico have pointed out that these amendments were "a hasty and naive homologation on the field" that left the national productive sectors in a state of "legal impairment provoked by the mechanical

98 of the Foreign Commerce Law, Article 202 of the Fiscal Code of the Federation, and Articles 15 and 24 of the Organic Law of the Fiscal Tribunal of the Federation,[58] to modify the existing regime for judicial review of SECOFI's final determinations on anti-dumping and countervailing duties, and to make available any alternative dispute mechanism negotiated in an international agreement.

This legislative activity was not the same as the process of enacting implementing legislation necessary in Canada and the United States because its objective was limited to ensuring that underlying anti-dumping and countervailing duty laws were common enough in the three parties that the Chapter 19 review mechanism would function in a relatively balanced fashion. The amendments did not address the specific procedures, powers, and authority of Article 1904 panels because those had already been specifically addressed by the provisions of the NAFTA.

In other words, the operation of binational panels in Mexico is governed directly by the provisions of the NAFTA, and there is no domestic statute adapting Chapter 19 to the Mexican legal system or to guide panels on the interpretation and extent of Chapter 19. This raises a number of issues.

As explained earlier, Chapter 19 was negotiated under difficult circumstances. It is no exaggeration that, for the Mexican negotiators, merely obtaining the chapter's inclusion in NAFTA was a major negotiating objective in itself. In an address to the Senate of the Republic on the conclusion of the negotiations, the Mexican secretary of commerce, Dr. Jaime Serra Puchi, later affirmed that "a fundamental aspect of the negotiation was to ensure to the Mexican exporters that they would not be subject to the arbitrary and

---

homologation to anglo-saxon laws": see Jorge Witker and Hernández Susana, "Resolución de controversias en materia de antidumping y cuotas compensatorias en el TLCAN" in *El Tratado de Libre Comercio de América del Norte, supra* note 53, vol. 1 at 268. We consider this opinion unjustified, because the legislative and regulatory amendments in Annex 1904.15 had the basic purpose of allowing Chapter 19 of NAFTA to work. In fact, the same annex includes the commitments of the United States and Canada to legislative and regulatory amendments.

58 See *Decreto que reforma, adiciona y deroga disposiciones de diversas leyes relacionadas con el Tratado de Libre Comercio de América del Norte,* published in the *Official Gazette of the Federation* on December 22, 1993 (*Diario Oficial*).

unjustified application of the defense measures against unfair trade practices of the United States and Canada."[59]

Since the panel system's essential attributes had already been defined, when, after delicate negotiations, the United States and Canada agreed to extend Chapter 19 to Mexico, the potential for adapting the chapter or even changing the wording of some of its main provisions was very limited and, in some instances, non-existent. The changes to which the parties agreed were only those strictly necessary for the chapter to be applied to Mexico and to accommodate the negotiations between Canada and the United States as to how much NAFTA Chapter 19 should be changed from FTA Chapter 19.

This had at least two important consequences. First, NAFTA Chapter 19 preserves a great deal of the language of its parent chapter of the Canada-United States FTA. Thus, many of its concepts and its underlying logic came from the common law and, due to the way in which treaties operate in Mexico, became incorporated directly into Mexican domestic law. The interpretation of these concepts in the context of the Mexican civil law system is not easy, particularly where there are no equivalent or similar concepts in the Mexican law.[60] Second, the interpretation of many of the articles requires a detailed knowledge of the history of the negotiations and of the way in which the Canadian and American unfair trade practices systems, for which Chapter 19 was originally conceived, work. Without this knowledge, it is easy to imply results that inadvertently modify the intended operation of the provisions of Chapter 19.

One example concerns the limits of Article 1904.1, which establishes that the parties "shall replace judicial review of final anti-dumping and countervailing determinations with binational panel review." The wording of this paragraph could be taken to suggest that the panels replace the Fiscal Tribunal of the Federation, thus acquiring the same functions and powers. This interpretation is clearly wrong. As indicated earlier, a panel is an alternative to judicial review, but its legal nature, powers, and rules of procedure are governed exclusively by the provisions of NAFTA or by rules

[59] Dr. Jaime Serra Puche, Secretary of Commerce and Industrial Development, address on the achievements of the negotiation of the Free Trade Agreement between Mexico, Canada, and the United States, to the Commerce Commission of the H. Senate Chamber, on August 14, 1994.

[60] E.g., the concept of "standard of review" was not usually used in the Mexican legal system.

trilaterally agreed pursuant to NAFTA. The first paragraph of Article 1904 establishes only that the parties agreed to an alternative to the usual domestic tribunal.

Another example concerns the panels' purpose, which is to review whether the final determinations of the investigating authorities were made in conformity with the "anti-dumping or countervailing law" of the importing country. Article 1904.2 defines that law as the "relevant statutes, legislative history, regulations, administrative practice and judicial precedents to the extent that a court of the importing party would rely on such materials in reviewing a final determination of the competent investigating authority." This definition poses important questions in Mexico, including: Does the definition include international agreements, specifically the WTO Agreements on Anti-dumping and Subsidies and Countervailing Measures (and their predecessors)? Does it allow the panels to analyze the constitutionality of the determinations of SECOFI? And, based on the relative absence of precedents in Mexican law on the subject-matter, are panels authorized to rely on the decisions of other panels (which apply foreign law under a different treaty) to support their decisions? These are questions that can be answered only after detailed analysis.

NAFTA Article 1904.2 was incorporated without modification from Article 1904.2 of the FTA. The reason FTA Article 1904.2 did not refer to international treaties and to the parties' respective constitutions in the definition of "anti-dumping and countervailing laws" is relatively simple. Since the relevant treaties were not self-executing in either Canada or the United States, they are not applied directly by the local courts, unless they are implemented through legislation. Insofar as constitutional issues are concerned, the United States and Canada evidently concluded that the panels should not decide them. The major issues had already been settled and procedural fairness issues were already well addressed in the administrative law of both parties. The omission of references to constitutions and international treaties, therefore, was not a "technical mistake"[61] as the *Cut-to-Length Steel* panel suggested.

---

[61] In its decision in *Cut-to-Length Steel*, the majority found that the English version of NAFTA, due to a "technical mistake does not explicitly acknowledge international agreements as a direct source of application of antidumping law." It affirmed also that due to a "technical mistake," Art. 1904 "does not make any reference to the constitutions of the parties as a potential source of antidumping law."

The case of Mexico is different. The self-executing character of the treaties means that, under Article 133 of the Mexican Constitution, they are to be considered as "law." The Supreme Court of Justice has concluded that Article 133 "adopts the rule that international law is part of the national legal system."[62] Thus, for the case of Mexico, it must be held that the expression "laws" includes international agreements. Another interpretation would prevent the use by the panels of an important source of anti-dumping legislation that is binding on both the Mexican administrative authorities and the domestic tribunals.

However, this interpretation raises the problem of reciprocity; in other words, whether the United States and Canada are also obliged to apply international agreements of that kind, since the governing law's definition of the "relevant statutes" does not include such agreements. At the level of international law, it is clear that the obligation to apply the international agreements on unfair trade practices is the same for the three countries; the difference lies in the way each country adopts and implements its international obligations in its domestic legal system; in the United States and Canada, treaties are binding only through implementing statutes (which allow the drafters to make choices on how they will implement the international obligation domestically). In Mexico, the treaties apply directly, and there is no "legislative intermediation."

The interpretation of constitutions is more delicate. We believe that, *prima facie*, because of their powers and arbitral nature, there is a serious question under Mexican law of whether panels can interpret the constitution. Arguably, their mission must be limited to applying the anti-dumping or countervailing duty law in light of the applicable standard of review and the relevant general principles of law.

---

62 Semanario Judicial de la Federación, 6a. época, vol. 151-56, Part 6, at 186. In another thesis in relation to the binding force of the *Paris Convention for the Protection of Industrial Property*, the Supreme Court of Justice concluded that "it must be held that in conformity with Article 133 of the General Constitution of the Republic, it has the category of supreme law of the Union, thus, the competent authorities are obliged to follow it": Semanario Judicial de la Federación, 7a. época, vol. 115-20 at 101. In a recent decision concerning contradictory decisions of two Circuit Collegiate Tribunals, and thus establishing a mandatory precedent (*jurisprudencia*), the Court in full, examining the application of the Protocol on Uniformity of the Legal Regime for Powers, concluded that "its rules must be understood incorporated into the national law, according to articles 133 of the Fundamental Law, and thus, must be of obligatory observance, and of direct application on the subject-matter": Contradiction of proposition 3/92, Supreme Court of Justice, March 2, 1994.

The *Cut-to-Length Steel* panel concluded that by "mistake," the constitutions of the parties were not included in the relevant NAFTA article. We consider this to be questionable. Reference to the rest of the text of NAFTA shows that every time the parties wanted to refer to their constitutions, they did so expressly (see for example, Article 601, Annex 1-7, especially Annex 3). Specifically, the definition of "domestic law" of Article 1905.1 (Safeguarding the Panel Review System), which expressly includes the constitution, suggests that omitting a reference to the constitution was intentional and not an oversight. Article 1904.2 did not intend panels to construe a party's constitution. The panel's mandate is limited to reviewing the legality of administrative acts in light of Article 238 of the Fiscal Code and the relevant general principles of law.

Finally, it must be emphasized that, unlike the case in the United States and Canada, judicial precedents on unfair trade practices are very rare in Mexico.[63] This is due in part to the relatively young Mexican trade remedy system. Thus, panels reviewing final determinations of Mexican authorities face the problem of a very limited number of precedents to guide them in their work.

This does not justify panels compensating for the gap by using precedents from other international agreements or the judicial precedents of the other countries. In that respect, the final phrase of NAFTA Article 1904.2 is clear. The "judicial precedents" are part of the anti-dumping legal provisions only "to the extent that a court of the importing party would rely on such materials in reviewing a final determination. . . ." Neither the Fiscal Tribunal nor the federal tribunals would ever use the decisions of other courts as a source of domestic law. Thus, faced with little precedent, panels reviewing Mexican determinations must render decisions that are faithful to the Mexican standard of review and general principles of law, even though there is little specific guidance open to them in that regard!

---

[63] By 1995, only four SECOFI determinations had been challenged before the Fiscal Court. Also, by March 1995, 60 of SECOFI's final determinations had been challenged under the *amparo* procedure (see text following note 79, *infra*). Of those, in nine cases the *amparo* was granted, 40 cases were dismissed, and 11 were under consideration by the federal courts. See Leycegui, Beatriz, "A Legal Analysis of Mexico's Anti-dumping and Countervailing Regulatory Frameword" in B. Leycegui, W. Robson, and Dahilia Stein (eds), *Trading Punches: Trade Remedy Law and Disputes Under NAFTA* 56-57 (Washington DC: ITAM-C.D. Howe-NPA, 1995).

Article 1904.3 establishes that panels must apply "the standard of review set out in Annex 1911 and the general legal principles that a court of the importing party otherwise would apply to a review of a determination of the competent investigating authority." In the case of Mexico, this paragraph raises two problems: the first on the adequacy of the stipulated standard of review, Article 238 of the Fiscal Code, when applied to the area of unfair trade practices, and the second on the definition of "general legal principles" insofar as Mexico is concerned.

The concept of "standard of review" as such has not been part of the Mexican legal lexicon.[64] In the Mexican context, it will be comparable to other phrases elaborated by Mexican mandatory precedents (*jurisprudencia*), in particular, to the "rules on preferential review of concepts of violation or wrong" (*"reglas de estudio preferente de conceptos de violación o agravios"*) or simply to that of "hypothesis of illegality" (*"causales de ilegalidad"*). In the case of NAFTA, the standard of review was identified in Annex 1911 as Article 238 of the Fiscal Code of the Federation.[65] The problem is not its identification, but whether it fits a subject such as that of unfair trade practices. This article establishes the standard that the Fiscal Tribunal of the Federation uses to judge the illegality of administrative determinations, especially those of fiscal nature (i.e., investigations conducted by tax authorities). This standard has

---

[64] This concept does not appear in any edition of *Diccionario Jurídico Mexicano* (Mexico: Instituto de Investigaciones Jurídicas-Porrúa, 1988).

[65] This article, as amended on December 15, 1995, reads:

An administrative determination shall be declared illegal, when one of the following hypotheses is proven: I. Lack of jurisdiction of the officer issuing, ordering or conducting the procedure, out of which the determination stems. II. Omission of the formal requirements demanded by law affecting any defense of the person, and transcending the outcome of the challenged determination, including absence of basis or motivation, as the case may be; III. Defects on the procedure affecting the party's defense and transcending the outcome of the challenged determination. IV. If the facts that motivated it were not realized, or they were different, or they were erroneously appreciated, or the determination was issued breaching the provisions that should be applied, or the correct provisions were not applied. V. When the administrative determination, in exercising discretionary powers, does not correspond to the ends for which the law grants those powers. The Fiscal Tribunal of the Federation could bring into the record, on its own motion, for being a public matter, the lack of jurisdiction of the authority to issue the challenged determination, and the total absence of basis and motivation of such determination.

been applied by the Fiscal Tribunal in a very rigorous and formalistic way.[66]

The trade remedy law area has specific attributes that make it different from the fiscal area.[67] It is enough to consider, for example, the objective and circumstances under which the verification visits are conducted or the different results that may arise from the application of different methodologies when calculating dumping margins. If we were to strictly apply the formal standard, many decisions could conceivably be declared a nullity,[68] and thus the investigating authority would be constrained in addressing unfair trade practices. In other words, it seems necessary to adapt Article 238 to the particular characteristics of the unfair trade practices area.

The second issue relates to "general principles of law." These principles are different in each country. Thus, the definition embodied in Article 1911 of NAFTA,[69] taken from the FTA, is only an illustrative list. In the case of Mexico, there is no authority establishing the identity of the principles.[70] For example, the *Diccionario Jurídico Mexicano* says: "It is not possible to make an exhaustive list of the general principles of law . . . nevertheless, some can

---

[66] James F. Smith, "Confronting Differences in the United States and Mexican Legal Systems in the Era of NAFTA" (1993) 1 U.S.-Mexico L. J. 1, 85.

[67] E.g., the purpose of the fiscal area is to collect taxes. It is governed by strict principles of legality regarding taxation, determination, and collection, and its regulation belongs to the domestic field. A compensatory duty seeks to neutralize the negative effects of an unfair trade practice. To establish the amount of this duty, complex calculations must be made to determine both the existence of dumping and the level of injury (which is frequently the object of review). In dumping regulation, international agreement is of paramount importance.

[68] Consider, e.g., the effects that the strict application of Art. 238, para. 4: "the facts that motivated it were not realized, or they were different, *or they were erroneously appreciated*" and its procedural consequences, as established in Art. 239 of the same statute (absolute nullity), would have on the area of anti-dumping.

[69] Art. 1911 states that "general legal principles includes principles such as standing, due process, rules of statutory construction, mootness and exhaustion of administrative remedies."

[70] E.g., Art. 14 of the Civil Code establishes that civil trials must be resolved in accordance with the literal wording or interpretation of the law, and, if this is not possible, "upon the general legal principles and equity," but does not explain the specific content of the latter. Art. 17 of the Federal Labour Law also refers to the "general principles of law and equity" without stating their specific content.

be mentioned, i.e: equity, in other words, the fair application of the law to the concrete case; good faith or faithfulness to your word; the duty to fulfil the covenants; the right to self-defense."[71]

In addition, some scholars in Mexico have raised the question whether the panels should refer to general principles of domestic law or to the general principles of international law.[72] The answer is that the panels reviewing final determinations of SECOFI can only apply the general principles of law that a Mexican tribunal would use, in other words, those considered part of the domestic legal system.

In relation to the standard of review, it is important to underline that Chapter 19 is constructed upon the working logic of the Canadian and American systems, particularly the principle of deference applied by the reviewing courts with regard to the decisions of the specialized administrative agencies. The principle of deference, extensively elaborated through case law, means that the reviewing court will normally respect the decisions of the administrative agency, especially on findings of fact and interpretations of the agency's constituting statute, due to the specialized technical knowledge that it possesses. Thus, generally speaking, even if the court differs on how the facts were assessed or the law was applied, it will confirm the decision of the agency, if reasonable.

In Mexican law, neither the doctrine, nor the tribunals, have developed the principle of deference as such. Nevertheless, we find that there are two principles that if brought together, because they lead to similar results, could be considered equivalent. The first refers to the presumption of legality that administrative acts and determinations enjoy. This principle is embodied in Article 8 of the Federal Law of Administrative Procedure[73] and Article 68 of the Fiscal Code of the Federation.[74]

The second principle is the exercise of so-called "discretionary authority." This prerogative implies "the power of free assessment over the content of their acts or actions," that the law recognizes

---

71 *Diccionario Jurídico Mexicano, supra* note 64, vol. 4, 2543.

72 Luis Malpica de la Madrid, *El sistema mexicano contra prácticas desleales de comercio internacional y el TLCAN* 166-67 (Mexico: UNAM, 1996).

73 "Article 8: The administrative act will be valid until, and only when, the administrative or jurisdictional authority, where appropriate, declares it a nullity."

74 "Article 68: The acts and determinations of the fiscal authorities are to be presumed legal."

and confers on administrative agencies. This freedom, authorized by law, can be to a greater or lesser degree and is evident when the authority must choose between two possible decisions."[75] The doctrine admits that this power, to be exercised by the authority, must be provided by a statute establishing its limits. Regarding its jurisdictional control, the tribunals admit the principle that the judge must respect its exercise, provided that the agency stays within the limits of the statute:

The use of the discretionary power, implies a subjective judgment by the authority exercising it. This subjective judgment escapes the control of the federal judicial authorities, because they do not possess full jurisdiction on the *amparo* trial, and thus, they cannot substitute their judgment for that of the responsible authorities.[76]

Nevertheless, this principle is not absolute, and the Supreme Court has established its limits basically to be when the subjective judgment is not reasonable, but arbitrary and capricious, and when it is patently unjust and unfair.[77] Thus, even when there is an acknowledgment of the administrative body's discretionary power the jurisdictional control depends in great measure on the court.

Insofar as Mexican anti-dumping and countervailing duty law is concerned, it would be helpful to legislate the precise extent of the authority's discretionary powers. This seems appropriate because of the specialized nature of the administrative agency's decisions and due to the need for an appropriate, properly defined scope of action. This would add certainty to the system and would provide guidance in the assessment of the investigating authority's decisions by tribunals and panels.

A hotly debated issue in Mexico is the extent of the powers of the panels, in particular, the meaning of the expression "the panel may uphold a final determination or *remand it* for action. . ." [emphasis

---

[75] *Diccionario Jurídico Mexicano*, vol. 4, 178 (Mexico: UNAM, 1983).

[76] Semanario Judicial de la Federación, 4th period, vol. 73, Sept. 3, 1942, "Amparo administrativo en revisión," 4, 753-42. Unanimity de 4 votos.

[77] "Facultades discrecionales. Apreciacion del uso indebido de ellas en juicio de amparo." I.e., The use of judgment or of the discretionary power granted to the administrative authority can be censored on the *amparo* suit, when it is exercised in an arbitrary or capricious way, when the decision does not refer to the circumstances that concretely deal with the case at issue, when these (the circumstances) have been modified or the facts upon which the decision is based are erroneous, or when the reasoning upon which it is based is against the rules of logic. Apéndice al Semanario Judicial de la Federación 1917-75, proposition 396, part 3, Segunda Sala, at 653.

added], included in Article 1904.8 of NAFTA. The concept of a "remand" is found in the common law tradition and has no exact equivalent in Mexican law. In general, a remand is the act of a reviewing court, sending a case back to the original tribunal, ordering it to have a limited re-hearing, to conduct a whole new hearing, or to take another kind of action.[78] NAFTA defines remand in Article 1911 as "a referral back for determination not inconsistent with the panel or committee decision." The reason for having a remand procedure relates to the *ad hoc* nature of panels, and to the principle of deference implicit in Chapter 19. Panels must leave the authorities a certain freedom of action regarding the conduct to follow in response to the panel's decision. The obligation imposed on authorities is "to take action not inconsistent with the panel decision."

In Mexican law, the effects of the decisions of the Fiscal Tribunal of the Federation are found in Article 239 of the Fiscal Code of the Federation. This article establishes that the tribunal may:

(1) recognize the validity of a challenged determination

(2) declare the nullity of the challenged determination

(3) declare the nullity of the challenged determination for certain effects, defining clearly the way and manner in which the authority must comply with it, except when discretionary powers are involved.

As can be seen, the remand power that is conferred on panels does not have the same effect and is particularly different from that provided in paragraphs (ii) and (iii) of Article 239.

The important point is that the powers of the panels are governed by NAFTA and not by the Fiscal Code of the Federation. The former prescribes different powers than those prescribed by the latter. Thus, the panels could not declare a nullity "for certain effects," since this is a power only of the Fiscal Tribunal. The panel must limit itself to remanding the determination to the authority. It is for the authority to then act "in a way not inconsistent with the the panel's decision."

Finally, the last part of Article 1904.11 establishing that "no party may provide in its domestic legislation for an appeal from a panel decision to domestic courts," is the object of debate in Mexican law, and, as we will see, a question not yet resolved. This raises the

[78] *Black's Law Dictionary* 896 (6th ed., abridged, St. Paul, West Publishing Co., 1991).

difficult problem of the *amparo* in Mexican law.[79] The *amparo* covers various procedural instruments and has become, for historical reasons, the judicial review mechanism of all Mexican legal proceedings. El juicio de Amparo (the suit of protection) is established in Articles 103 and 107 of the federal constitution and is regulated in the Amparo Law, which has been amended frequently over the years, with numerous amendments, the most recent dating from 1995. These are the five sectors it presently comprises:

(1) as the equivalent of *habeas corpus*, to protect the freedom of the individual

(2) as an instrument to challenge laws (*amparo against laws*), including laws enacted by Congress, regulations of the executive branch and international treaties

(3) as a remedy to challenge the final decisions of all judges and courts of the country, as the equivalent of a *federal cassation*[80]

(4) as an administrative lawsuit with respect to acts or determinations of administrative authorities that cannot be challenged before administrative or judicial courts

(5) as an instrument that establishes procedural advantages for peasants subject to agrarian reform (agrarian amparo).

In all cases, the amparo determinations have individual effects only (the so-called "Otero clause").

In relation to Chapter 19, one dimension of the issue is that treaties are "law" in Mexico. As such, the authorities are obliged to

79 On *amparo*, see Fix-Zamudio, Héctor and Fix-Fierro, "Mexico — Constitutional Law" in R. Blanpain (ed.), *International Encyclopedia of Laws* (Deventer: Kluwer Law and Taxation Publishers, 1994); Fix-Zamudio, Héctor, "A Brief Introduction to the Mexican Writ of Amparo" (1979) 9 Calif. West. Int'l L. J. 306; Baker, *Judicial Review in Mexico, A Study of the Amparo Suit* (Austin: University of Texas Press, 1971).

80 This is probably the most difficult part of *amparo*. In fact, the original principles of the *amparo* (judicial review of the constitutionality of laws practised by judges and courts of the United States, as described by de Tocqueville in *Democracy in America*) underwent a significant transformation in the second half of the nineteenth century. Contrary to the text of Art. 8 of the Amparo Law of 1869, the Supreme Court of Justice accepted the *amparo* against judicial decisions; that is, not only when such decisions dealt with a question of constitutionality, but also when the incorrect application of a secondary law was alleged. In other words, the exact application of the law became an "individual guarantee" as a result of a liberal interpretation of the ambiguous wording of Art. 14 of the constitution. See Fix-Zamudio and Fix-Fierro, *ibid.*, 108-12.

abide by their provisions, and their actions are subject to jurisdictional control. Therefore, if the act of an authority is contrary to the provisions of the treaty (for example, if Mexico denies the creation of a panel when a person has standing to request one, or if SECOFI refuses to comply, or inadequately complies with the order of the panel) an aggrieved person could request through an *amparo*, that SECOFI be ordered to comply with Mexico's treaty obligations.

A second dimension of the issue concerns the meaning of the final phrase of Article 1904.11. This provision admits two interpretations. The first one, held by some scholars,[81] is that it precludes the launching of an *amparo* action. The second interpretation is that it must be interpreted to mean that no ordinary jurisdictional defence is available (judicial review *strictu sensu*), not that it denies the constitutional defence (the *amparo*). If the first interpretation is accepted, the issue of the constitutionality of the NAFTA's exclusion of the *amparo* suit would immediately arise. According to Articles 103 and 107 of the constitution, the *amparo* can always be brought against any act of any authority that violates the individual rights of a person (including those of legality), except when the same constitution states otherwise.

The second interpretation does not raise the issue of the constitutionality of the treaty, because the *amparo* is formally not a means of controlling legality, but a means of controlling constitutionality. What would happen if a federal tribunal granted an *amparo* against a determination of SECOFI implementing an order of a panel? This could be considered to be contrary to Mexico's obligations under the NAFTA, and Canada and the United States could activate the safeguard mechanism contemplated in Article 1905 of NAFTA. This reaction would not be different from that Mexico would take if those countries declared the unconstitutionality of the review system of Chapter 19 of the treaty.

A more careful look, and taking into consideration certain procedural principles of the *amparo* (*principio de definitividad, acto consentido, acto de autoridad, interés legítimo*, etc.), leads to the conclusion that an *amparo* would hardly succeed. Nevertheless, it is an open question that will be resolved only if the issue is put before a federal court.[82]

[81] E.g., Malpica de la Madrid, *supra* note 72 at 221.

[82] Ruperto Patiño Manfer, "Recursos ordinario y jurisdiccionales en materia de prácticas desleales de comercio internacional" in Jorge Witker (ed.), *Resolución de controversias comerciales en América del Norte* 379-80 (Mexico: UNAM, 1994).

THE BINATIONAL PANEL DETERMINATION IN *CUT-TO-LENGTH STEEL*

The following comments should not be taken to be unduly critical of the panel's decision in *Cut-to-Length Steel*, because the magnitude of the challenge that confronted the panel can hardly be overstated. It was presented with a major case, with many complaints about the final determination — an unusual set of facts in that the unit of SECOFI that had conducted the investigation had been constituted in different forms during the investigation (thus raising thorny issues of constitutional law concerning the authority of officials to act), and the fact that the investigation had been conducted under an old anti-dumping law that was no longer in effect.

Compounding this was the fact that, as noted earlier, Mexican administrative law regarding anti-dumping and countervailing duties is comparatively less well developed than its American and Canadian equivalents, while Mexican constitutional law is impressively rigorous and formalistic when viewed from a foreign perspective. The absence of implementing legislation and legislative history made the Mexican situation stand in stark contrast to the situation in Canada and the United States, where the governments had drafted and enacted implementing legislation that gave Chapter 19 effect in their domestic legal systems (and statutory guidance to panels). In short, the panel faced a daunting challenge and the following comments should be read in light of the authors' recognition of the magnitude of the undertaking.

It will be recalled that one of the issues that the panel had to address was the nature of its powers. Just as the other NAFTA parties had expressly incorporated their relevant standards of review into Annex 1911, Mexico had stipulated Article 238 of the Fiscal Code. Article 239 establishes that where certain breaches of Article 238 occur, the appropriate remedy is to nullify the authority's determination. In the *Cut-to-Length Steel* case, the complainants argued, therefore, that for certain violations of Article 238, Article 239 of the Fiscal Code allowed the Fiscal Court to nullify rather than remand and the panel must do likewise. However, only Article 238 and not the neighbouring articles that dealt with the Fiscal Court's remedial powers had been included in Annex 1911 of the NAFTA. The question, therefore, was whether the panel's power to remand conferred by Article 1904.8 extended to the power to nullify. This was one of the threshold issues that the panel had to confront.

In beginning its analysis, the majority also had to confront an important drafting question. The NAFTA's description of the governing law (which had been derived without change from the equivalent FTA provision) was silent on two sources of law that, in the Mexican domestic legal context, were particularly relevant. As mentioned earlier, the two sources were the Mexican Constitution and international treaties. The reason for the omission of references to constitutions and international treaties in the Canada-United States FTA seems to be that the two parties did not contemplate constitutional issues being raised in panel reviews (largely because constitutional issues have largely been settled insofar as the trade remedy law is concerned, and questions of procedural fairness are addressed in mainstream administrative law) and, due to the dualist tradition of both FTA parties, international trade agreements did not have direct legal effect. Therefore, although such treaties might on occasion be relevant to questions of interpretation of the domestic statute, they would not form a central role as a primary source of the substantive law governing a review.

In Mexico, the situation was quite different and in analyzing its function and responsibility under NAFTA Chapter 19, the majority of the panel found it necessary to read the constitution and treaty law into the Article 1904.2 description of the governing law (i.e., "statutes, legislative history, regulations, administrative practice and judicial precedents"). It did so on the basis that while panels were to replace the courts, they were "not intended to apply a different *substantive law* than would be applied by the local court, nor are they intended to apply a different *standard of review* than would be applied by the local court."[83]

In supporting this statement, the majority asserted that "there has been *broad recognition* of the fact that binational panels are *not* to develop a separate jurisprudence in anti-dumping cases from the jurisprudence developed by local tribunals."[84] The evidence for this statement was contained in footnote 65 which stated:

This conclusion, of course, flows from the language of the Treaty itself. Articles 1901 and 1902 make it clear that each country *retains* its existing domestic anti-dumping law without change, but is free to amend that law. Under Article 1903, a procedure is established whereby any such amendment can be challenged for its consistency with the treaty. Various statements made by the United States Congress also make this point indisputably clear. In the Statement of Administrative Action to the North American Free Trade Agreement Implementation Act, *reprinted in*

---

[83] Decision (English courtesy translation) at 16. (Emphasis in the original.)

[84] *Ibid.*, 16.

H. Doc. 103-159, Vol. 1, 103d Cong., 1st Sess. at 195, for example, the United States Congress made the following statement: "There are several advantages to having judges and former judges serve as panelists. For example, the participation of panelists with judicial experience would help to ensure that, *in accordance with the requirement of Article 1904, panels review determinations of the administering authorities precisely as would a court of the importing country* by applying exclusively that country's AD and CVD law and its standard of review. In addition, the involvement of judges in the process would *diminish the possibility that panels and courts will develop distinct bodies of U.S. law* [emphasis added]."

The argument expressed by the Statement of Administrative Action quoted by the majority was unquestionably made by the United States. However, it reflected a United States concern that has never been shared by Canada (nor had Mexico expressed a view on the matter since it had not arisen previously in the Mexican context). Indeed, as we have seen, the "separate jurisprudence" argument had become a major issue in Washington because United States industries that had lost Chapter 19 panel proceedings had argued that the panels were too rigorous and less deferential to the investigating authorities than the United States courts. From the Canadian perspective, the greater scrutiny to which panels had subjected the authorities' decisions was seen as evidence of the system's value. Canadian officials saw the argument about preventing the emergence of a separate jurisprudence as the United States' desire to return to less rigorous review of the type practised by generalist judges who were less expert in the matters under review than five expert *ad hoc* panelists.

The irony of the situation is that, whether intentionally or not, the majority in *Cut-to-Length Steel* used a position articulated by one NAFTA party to justify *restraint* in panel activism to support a position that *expanded* the panel's powers in another NAFTA party. Then, in deciding that the express inclusion of only one article of the Fiscal Code (Article 238 — the standard of review) in the NAFTA did not preclude it from also including the neighbouring Articles 237 and 239, the majority reasoned that since the panel "replaced" the Fiscal Court, it must be able to apply Articles 237 and 239 to the extent possible. The first reason it cited in support of the conclusion was "*the basic policy consideration,* expressed on numerous occasions by one or more NAFTA governments, that binational panels ought not to create a separate anti-dumping jurisprudence from that created by the local courts."[85]

[85] *Ibid.*, 22.

This reliance on the views of one party — the majority was simply incorrect in implying that the view had been expressed by more than one government — was inappropriate. The United States view had emerged over the years and had manifested itself in congressional criticism of the FTA's Chapter 19. It was factually incorrect to suggest that this criticism had become a "basic policy consideration" relating to Chapter 19's operation expressed by more than one of the NAFTA parties. What was particularly hard to accept from the Mexican perspective, was the fact that this was used to justify a claim of *additional* powers. By claiming the power effectively to order a nullity, the majority was expanding its powers beyond that expressly conferred upon a panel by Article 1904.8. In the Canadian or American context this would be analogous to a panel claiming that the exercise of equitable jurisdiction was necessary in order for it to effectively apply the standard of review included in Annex 1911.

The majority's subsequent grounds were also faulty. It argued that without the power to nullify under Article 239 the panel could find itself "in the unacceptable position, once having determined that fundamental constitutional provisions had been violated by the investigating authority, that it had no effective remedy for such violation."[86] In fact, the investigating authority had freely acknowledged at the hearing that after one or more remands, it could be obliged to revoke a final determination. SECOFI's point was that the structure and context of Article 1904.8 made it clear that, unlike the Fiscal Court, the panel could not issue a nullity order. It could only remand the determination for action "not inconsistent with the panel's decision." SECOFI accepted that a panel's decision might find a final determination defective enough that upon reviewing the decision, SECOFI might conclude that it could not remedy the situation by taking action "not inconsistent with the panel's decision" and would therefore have to revoke the determination. Thus, the majority had raised an objection that SECOFI itself had not advanced.

The third reason offered by the majority was that the practice of panels reviewing Canadian decisions under the FTA showed that although only one statute, which sets out the standard of review (the Federal Court Act), had been included in Article 1911, panels had felt free to refer to another statute (the Special Import

---

[86] *Ibid.*, 23.

Measures Act) when applying that standard of review. This was unpersuasive for two reasons. First, the other statute merely gave guidance to how the Federal Court Act's standard of review was to be applied in a particular type of review and said nothing about the panel's powers.[87] Second, it seemed to be overreaching to use Canadian cases where panels had referred to another statute to employ a more restrictive and deferential standard of review in certain types of cases, to justify the claim to a judicial power that was not expressly conferred by Article 1904.

The panel then considered the Canadian panel experience in the context of remedies. It noted that panels had adverted to the fact that Canadian courts had found that a breach of natural justice would render a decision invalid (i.e., a nullity). In fact, however, of all of the binational panel reviews of Canadian determinations under the FTA and NAFTA, no panel has ever done so (which the majority was forced to admit when it stated "[a]lthough no panel has found cause to rule affirmatively when reviewing under this standard").[88] The fact was that no binational panel review of a Canadian determination has yet to confront the extent of the panel's powers so there was, strictly speaking, no "Canadian experience," only *obiter dicta.*[89]

Should the issue ever arise in the Canadian context, a panel would have to confront the fact that Parliament has expressly spelt out the extent of the panel's remedial powers in s. 77.015 of the Special Import Measures Act that implements Chapter 19 in Canadian law. The relevant provisions are as follows:

[87] This was the so-called "privative clause" of the Special Import Measures Act, which stated that decisions of the Canadian International Trade Tribunal were "final and conclusive." This has generally meant in Canadian administrative law that, rather than the "reasonableness" test being applied as the standard of review, the more deferential "patently unreasonable" test is to be applied. This had nothing to do with a panel's powers to fashion a remedy as a result of a review of a Canadian final determination.

[88] Decision, *supra* note 83 at 27. In fact, however, of all of the binational panel reviews of Canadian determinations under the FTA and NAFTA, no panel has rendered a decision invalid. The majority was forced to admit this fact when it stated "[a]lthough no panel has found cause to rule affirmatively when reviewing under this standard."

[89] Any Canadian binational panel proceeding that considered the issue of nullifying a final determination would have to confront the fact that, by its implementing legislation and regulations, Canada has expressly limited the binational panels' powers to those powers described in Art. 1904.8: *supra* note 25.

Conduct of review. A panel shall conduct a review of a definitive decision in accordance with Chapter Nineteen of the North American Free Trade Agreement and the rules. [1993, c.44, s. 219].

Disposition after review. On completion of the review of a definitive decision, *a panel shall determine whether the grounds on which the review was requested have been established and shall make an order confirming the decision or referring the matter back to the appropriate authority for reconsideration within the period specified by the panel* [emphasis added].[90]

Thus, the language of the Canadian implementing statute tracks Article 1904.8 (in marked contrast to the powers granted to the Federal Court and Federal Court of Appeal).

Finally, the panel noted the fact that in the United States, in *Certain Softwood Lumber Products from Canada,* a binational panel ordered the authority to "make certain determinations that were specifically designed to bring the case to an end."[91] However, the example cited (the *Pork* and *Live Swine* cases that were not cited by the panel but which were to similar effect as *Softwood Lumber*) actually proved SECOFI's point, namely, that the panels reviewing United States decisions had never purported to issue orders of nullity in the first instance. In each case, the investigating authority had been given an opportunity to take action "not inconsistent with the panel's decision." No FTA or NAFTA panel has yet claimed the power to nullify an authority's determination in the first instance.

While it is correct to say that the panel in *Softwood Lumber,* on a second remand, sent back a number of issues for specific findings, which, if adopted, would logically lead to the termination of the proceedings, it is of significance that this direction was given only after the investigating authority failed to respond sufficiently to the panel's first remand and that, even on the second remand, the panel did not order the investigating authority to terminate the proceedings.

The majority in *Cut-to-Length Steel* apparently did not consider the findings of the panel in *Fresh, Chilled, or Frozen Pork from Canada,* which specifically addressed the extent to which a panel may do more than merely remand a determination for further action. In *Pork,* the panel was faced with a situation where, upon a second review, it was not satisfied with action taken by the investigating authority pursuant to the panel's initial decision. The panel's dis-

---

[90] 1993, c.44, s. 219 (emphasis added).

[91] Decision, *supra* note 83 at 29.

cussion of the issue is both instructive and persuasive. The panel was of the view that a

> Chapter 19 Panel does not have the authority to do other than affirm or remand, in appropriate circumstances with instructions. On the other hand, Article 1904(8) speaks of a "final decision." The use of these words in the FTA, in the very Article describing the duty of the Panel, indicates that the Panel states its view with as much finality as the case permits.
>
> The Panel is supported in this view by the action of an earlier panel, *Red Raspberries from Canada*, U.S.A-89-1904-01 (Opinion of the Panel upon Remand, April 2, 1990). There the Department of Commerce, having twice failed "to provide an adequate explanation" of its failure to use home market sales as the basis for determining foreign market value, had the matter remanded "with instructions" that it recalculate foreign market value using home market sales.
>
> A similar result is justified in a case such as this, in which the ITC's Record has been combed not once but twice in the search for substantial evidence of a threat of material injury. Clear direction from the Panel is essential if the Panel is to answer the FTA's insistence on a "final decision" at this stage (Article 1904.8) and its repeated calls for expedition in the settling of matters such as these (Articles 1904.4, 1904.6, 1904.8, 1904.13, 1904.14 and 1904.15(g)(ii)) and in light of the need for respect of Panel review as an institution brought by the FTA into the domestic laws of Canada and of the United States, not as an indicative suggestion but as "binding" (Article 1904.9).[92]

Ironically, the *Cut-to-Length Steel* majority's discussion of United States and Canadian panel decisions under the FTA was in response to SECOFI's argument that Article 1904.8 limits the remedial authority of binational panels. The majority had this to say:

> SECOFI in effect suggests that while the Fiscal Tribunal demonstrably has authority to order the "nullification" of an agency proceeding, a binational panel, considering identical facts, may not do so. The end result of identical cases brought before the Fiscal Tribunal and before a Chapter 19 panel would therefore, on this reasoning, be very different. The Panel believes that such a result was not intended by the NAFTA Parties.[93]

It is curious that the majority apparently considered SECOFI to be incapable of acting in a manner "not inconsistent with the panel's decision" such that the end result would be "very difficult" from that which would have occurred in judicial review before the

---

[92] Memorandum Opinion and Order Regarding ITC's Determination on Remand In the Matter of *Fresh, Chilled and Frozen Pork from Canada*, USA-98-1904-11 (Art. 1904 Binational Panel Review Under the United States-Canada Free Trade Agreement, January 22, 1991) at 5.

[93] *Cut-to-Length Steel* panel decision, *supra* notes 1, 4 at 26-8.

Fiscal Tribunal. In each of the FTA panel decisions cited by the majority (and many others not cited), the investigating authority responded appropriately, albeit with great reluctance in *Softwood Lumber*. Why should SECOFI not have been given the same opportunity to take corrective action?

CONCLUSION

This article has described the history of a central feature of NAFTA and sought to draw a lesson about international treaty interpretation. The lesson is that panels must approach their tasks with caution and should be careful to pay particular attention to the express terms and structure of the treaty that they have been charged with applying. The *Cut-to-Length Steel* case is an excellent illustration of the wisdom of the Vienna Convention on the Law of Treaties' insistence that the first priority of treaty interpretation is to examine the plain language of the treaty and, only in certain circumstances, should resort to extrinsic materials be had. Where extrinsic materials are employed, it is critically important to differentiate between the persuasiveness of different types of such materials.

For example, the panel had the actual legislation enacted by Canada and the United States to implement Chapter 19 put before it. That legislation showed that panels have much more narrowly defined powers than the domestic courts they "replace." The majority did not address this actual practice of the other parties (in terms of how they implemented Article 1904 in their domestic law). Instead, it relied on the legislative history of one party and, in so doing it is respectfully submitted, misunderstood the significance of that legislative history. It also failed accurately to employ the Canadian panel materials available to it. The panel's reliance on these materials was, in our view, erroneous.

As noted earlier, it is ironic — but also illustrative of the risks attendant in taking this approach — that the majority of the panel relied on United States arguments for restraint by binational panels to justify an activist interpretation of the powers conferred upon it by the treaty. The result was that it interpreted its powers more broadly than a plain reading of Article 1904.8 would support. Of course, this was a three-to-two decision. The question is whether future panels reviewing Mexican determinations will take the same approach.

Sommaire

Le mécanisme de règlement des différends de l'ALÉNA et le cas du
Mexique: l'interprétation des traités et la réconciliation des systèmes de common law et de droit civil dans une zone de libre-
échange

*Le premier groupe spécial binational qui a été formé en vertu du chapitre 19
de l'ALÉNA pour examiner une décision mexicaine concernant une affaire
d'antidumping a soulevé des questions importantes à propos de l'interprétation des traités. Comme le Mexique, qui est un pays de droit civil, avait
appliqué l'ALÉNA d'une manière différente, le groupe spécial devait donc
examiner un processus de mise en application qui différait de celui des
juridictions de common law du Canada et des États-Unis. Les auteurs
soutiennent qu'en interprétant l'ALÉNA, le groupe spécial s'est fondé sur
l'historique des négocations d'une seule partie, soit les États-Unis, pour en
arriver à une décision qui ne représentait pas l'intention des trois parties.
Par conséquent, le groupe spécial formé en vertu du chapitre 19 a exercé,
dans cette affaire concernant le Mexique, une compétence différente de celle
qui est normalement exercée par les groupes spéciaux à l'égard des décisions
des deux autres parties à l'ALÉNA.*

Summary

NAFTA Dispute Settlement and Mexico: Interpreting Treaties and
Reconciling Common and Civil Law Systems in a Free Trade Area

*The first NAFTA Chapter 19 binational panel review of a Mexican anti-
dumping determination raises important questions about the interpretation
of treaties. In confronting the different way in which Mexico, a civil law
country, had implemented NAFTA, the panel had to deal with a process of
implementation different from that in the common law jurisdictions of
Canada and the United States. The authors argue that in interpreting
NAFTA, the panel relied on the negotiating history of one party, the United
States, to reach a conclusion that did not represent the intentions of the three
parties, and led to the exercise of a jurisdiction by a Chapter 19 panel in
respect of Mexico that is different from that exercised by Chapter 19 panels
reviewing determinations from the other two NAFTA parties.*

From the Margins to the Mainstream: The Beijing Declaration and Platform for Action

MARCIA WALDRON*

INTRODUCTION

THE UNITED NATIONS FOURTH World Conference on Women was held in September 1995 in Beijing, China. It was the fourth United Nations conference to deal specifically with the human rights of women[1] and the latest in a series of high profile United Nations conferences held since the United Nations Conference on the Environment and Development in 1992.[2] The conference was notable both for the unprecedented number of delegates at a United Nations conference and for the intense level of media scrutiny accorded to it.[3] Though not without controversy and disagreement, it presented an important occasion for the international community to assess and develop its political commitment to the protection of the human rights of women and toward equality for women by the year 2000.

---

* B.A. (McGill), M.A. (Toronto) LL.B. (Ottawa); of the Bar of Ontario. I wish to acknowledge the helpful comments of Daniela Napoli.

---

[1] The three previous conferences were held in Mexico City in 1975, in Copenhagen in 1980, and in Nairobi in 1985.

[2] These conferences were the 1993 World Conference on Human Rights, the 1994 International Conference on Population and Development, and the 1995 World Summit for Social Development.

[3] S. Faison, "Women's Meeting Agrees On Right to Say No To Sex," *New York Times* (Sept. 1, 1995) A1; S. Faison, "Women Carry Hopes As Conference Ends," *New York Times* (Sept. 16, 1994) A5.

THE BEIJING DECLARATION AND PLATFORM FOR ACTION

The product of the conference, the Beijing Declaration and Platform for Action, sets out an agenda for women's empowerment through the implementation of the Nairobi Forward Looking Strategies For the Advancement of Women, which stemmed from the previous United Nations world conference on women.[4] It aims to remove obstacles to women's active participation in all spheres of public and private life in order for them to have a full and equal share in economic, social, cultural, and political decision-making. The entire document is divided into two main sections, the Declaration and the Platform for Action. The key part of the document, the Platform for Action, sets out twelve interrelated and interdependent critical areas of concern: poverty, education, health care, violence, effects of armed or other kinds of conflict, the economy, power and decision-making, institutional mechanisms, human rights, media, environment, and the girl child. Based on these critical areas of concern, it outlines strategic objectives as well as interlinked and mutually reinforcing concrete actions to be taken by various actors to achieve these objectives.

Although it is a non-binding agreement under international law, the Beijing Declaration and Platform for Action puts the human rights of women on the international agenda by taking a rights-based approach to the empowerment of women. Previous approaches concentrated on humanitarian and social policy-making.[5] The Declaration reaffirms the commitment of governments to the full implementation of the human rights of women and of the girl child as an "inalienable, integral and indivisible part of all human rights and fundamental freedoms."[6] It further affirms that "women's rights are human rights."[7] The Platform for Action states that "the advancement of women and the achievement of equality between women and men are a matter of human rights and a condition for

---

[4] World Conference On Women, *Report of the Fourth World Conference On Women*, UN GAOR, Doc.A/Conf. 177/20, 1985 [hereinafter Declaration or Platform for Action]. See also *Report of the World Conference to Review and Appraise the Achievements of the United Nations Decade For Women: Equality, Development and Peace*, UN GAOR, Doc. A/Conf. 116/28, 1985.

[5] D. Sullivan, "Women's Human Rights and the 1993 World Conference on Human Rights" (1994) 88 AJIL 152 at 164.

[6] Declaration, *supra* note 4, Annex 1, para. 9.

[7] *Ibid.*, para. 14.

social justice and should not be seen in isolation as a women's issue."[8] It deems the lack of respect for and inadequate promotion and protection of the human rights of women as a critical area for concern[9] and calls for the full realization of all human rights and fundamental freedoms of all women as essential for the empowerment of women.[10]

By having a separate section on human rights, the Platform for Action, at least symbolically, affirms that the international system can no longer regard women's rights as separate from human rights. The term "women's rights" is somewhat of a misnomer. Women's rights are supposed to be human rights, enshrined in all United Nations documents beginning with the United Nations Charter. Yet, far from being redundant, women's rights cannot be taken for granted as constituting an integral part of the human rights agenda. Instead, "women's rights are human rights" is a rallying cry, an aspirational concept rather than a statement of the existing situation under the international human rights system. Women's issues and concerns have usually been marginalized within this system and dealt with in specialized instruments and machineries.

The development of separate enforcement mechanisms to deal with the human rights of women is not necessarily detrimental. Those who work within this specialized system often have greater awareness, knowledge, experience, and commitment to women's issues than those who operate solely within the mainstream. Certainly, the specialized system has an essential role to play in the codification and enforcement of women's rights. However, critiques of the specialized machineries and instruments for women's human rights point to their weaker enforcement mechanisms as compared to those of the mainstream.[11] Specialized mechanisms tend to have weaker implementation procedures, fewer financial resources, less United Nations Secretariat support, and are accorded less attention

---

8 Platform for Action, *ibid.*, ch. 3, para. 41.

9 *Ibid.*, para. 44.

10 *Ibid.*, ch. 2, para. 9.

11 S. Coliver, "United Nations Machineries on Women's Rights: How They Better Help Women Whose Rights are Being Violated" in Lutz et al., *New Directions in Human Rights* 25 (Philadelphia: University of Pennsylvania Press, 1989); T. Meron, "Enhancing the Effectiveness of the Prohibition of Discrimination Against Women" (1994) 84 AJIL 213; L. Reanda, "Human Rights and Women's Rights: The United Nations Approach" (1981) 3 Hum. Rts Q. 11.

and prestige by governments and non-governmental organizations (hereinafter NGOs) than the more mainstream instruments and machineries. The limits of this system must be recognized. Its existence must not be used as a justification for limiting the implementation of women's rights within the more mainstream human rights system.[12] The conceptual, political, and pragmatic dilemma that arises with any focus on the mainstream machineries is that one may risk perpetuating their centrality and thereby marginalize the specialized system.[13] Nevertheless, the endeavour is necessary and useful. Primary focus on the specialized system can only limit the effectiveness of any comprehensive strategy for eradicating some of the most pernicious forms of human rights violations.

LAW AND RIGHTS

The need for integration of gender perspectives has been one that the United Nations human rights system has highlighted over the past several years in various policy declarations and resolutions, such as the Vienna Declaration and Program of Action, the product of the United Nations World Conference on Human Rights, and a recent resolution from the United Nations Commission on Human Rights.[14] In essence, the Platform for Action continues much of this work. Most of its twelve sections deal specifically with the issue of

[12] In an institutional sense, the "mainstream" means those generally Geneva-based institutions that are responsible for general human rights matters — e.g., the UN Commission on Human Rights. More substantively, however, the "mainstream" encompasses those human rights guarantees within the "general" human rights instruments, particularly the International Covenant on Civil and Political Rights and the Covenant on Economic, Social and Cultural Rights. For an excellent analysis of the analytical and institutional treatment of women's human rights under the international human rights system, see A. Byrnes, "Women, Feminism and International Human Rights Law: Methodological Myopia, Fundamental Flaws or Meaningful Marginalisation? Some Current Issues" (1992) 12 Aust. Y.B. Int'l L. 205, 208; A. Byrnes, "Towards a More Effective Enforcement of Women's Human Rights through the Use of International Human Rights Law and Procedures" in R. J. Cook (ed.), *Human Rights of Women: National and International Perspectives* 190 (Philadelphia: University of Pennsylvania Press, 1994).

[13] Byrnes, "Women, Feminism and International Human Rights Law" *supra* note 12, 205 at 208.

[14] See World Conference on Human Rights, *Vienna Declaration and Programme of Action*, UN GAOR, Doc. A/Conf. 157/23, 18 at para. 37 and 20 at para. 42, 1993; Commission on Human Rights, *Report of the 51st Session*, UN ESCOR, Supp. No. 4, Doc. E/CN.4/176, 1995.

integrating or mainstreaming gender into the human rights framework to varying degrees. For example, the section on poverty states that the failure to adequately mainstream a gender perspective in all economic analysis and planning, as well as the failure to address the structural causes of poverty, are contributing factors to the disproportionate number of women living in poverty.[15] It calls for the development of concepts and practical methodologies for incorporating gender perspectives into all aspects of economic policy-making, including structural adjustment planning and programs.[16] The section on the economy calls for an active and visible policy of mainstreaming a gender perspective in all policies and programs.[17]

The human rights section is the key section on the treatment of gender within the international human rights system. It states, "the equal rights of men and women are explicitly mentioned in the Preamble to the Charter of the United Nations. All the major international human rights instruments include sex as one of the grounds upon which States may not discriminate."[18] The clearest statement on gender mainstreaming is paragraph 221, which states:

The human rights of all women and of the girl child must form an integral part of United Nations human rights activities. Intensified efforts are needed to integrate the equal status and the human rights of all women and girls into the mainstream of United Nations system-wide activities and to address these issues regularly and systematically throughout relevant bodies and mechanism.[19]

Any policy of mainstreaming will require both a substantive and institutional reorientation of focus on the part of governments, NGOs, and regional and intergovernmental organizations. The international human rights system will have to struggle with the issue of whether current conceptual and procedural frameworks are adequate to deal with women's human rights. International human rights law operates within a narrow conceptual framework that has often excluded women's concerns from the agenda. Despite the fact that all major international human rights instruments include sex as one of the grounds upon which states cannot

15 Platform for Action, *supra* note 4, ch. 4, para. 48.

16 *Ibid.*, para. 67.

17 *Ibid.*, para. 164

18 *Ibid.*, para. 214.

19 *Ibid.*, para. 221.

discriminate, women's human rights have been largely neglected within the United Nations human rights system.

An important reason for this is the conceptual and institutional primacy of civil and political rights (the so-called first generation rights) over economic, social, and cultural rights (the second generation rights). Feminist legal analysts have argued that women's human rights violations are often the result of an unequal share of economic and social power, and therefore a narrow focus on civil and political rights fails to address many of the underlying causes of the violations of their human rights.[20] This dichotomy has also been challenged by scholars from the south who view the prioritization of civil and political over social, economic, and cultural rights as fitting into a western model of human rights.[21]

The Platform for Action addresses this dichotomy. It reaffirms that "all human rights — civil, cultural, economic, political and social, including the right to development — are universal, indivisible, interdependent and interrelated."[22] This section is notable for several reasons. First, there is the absence of any mention of third generation rights — for example, the right to self-determination. Second, the inclusion of both first and second generation rights entails a more integrated and expanded approach to dealing with women's human rights than traditionally has been the case. An approach to the eradication of human rights violations that is not based on an understanding of the interrelationship between the full spectrum of human rights cannot effectively improve the status of women in many societies.[23]

Even within the traditional framework of civil and political rights, a conceptual framework that divides society into a public and private sphere has worked to exclude the fundamental issues relating to women's experience from the international human rights

[20] H. Charlesworth, "What are Women's International Human Rights" in R. J. Cook (ed.), *supra* note 12, 58 at 74-75 (Philadelphia: University of Pennsylvania Press, 1994). See also C. Bunch, "Women's Rights as Human Rights: Toward a Re-vision of Human Rights" (1990) 12 Hum. Rts Q. 486 at 494-95.

[21] See generally A. O. Ilumoka, "African Women's Economic, Social, and Cultural Rights — Toward a Relevant Theory and Practice" in R. J. Cook, (ed.), *supra* note 12 at 306 (Philadelphia: University of Pennsylvania Press, 1994).

[22] Platform for Action, *supra* note 4, ch. 4, para. 213.

[23] R. J. Cook, "Women's International Human Rights Law: The Way Forward" in R. J. Cook (ed.), *supra* note 12, 3 at 13-14.

agenda.[24] Under traditional human rights law, society is divided into two separate spheres, the public and the private. The public sphere — that is, the workplace, economics, politics, and intellectual and cultural life are viewed as the proper sphere for state intervention. Since the law traditionally operates in this sphere, human rights violations committed at the hands of the state or of its agents may engage state responsibility for these violations. On the other hand, the private sphere, such as the family, does not necessarily engage state responsibility for human rights violations.

Greater importance and value are attached to the public than to the private sphere. Although what is considered public in one society may be considered private in another, there is a consistent pattern across societies of devaluating the sphere that women inhabit.[25] Yet, this dichotomy between public and private is politically, rather than inherently, constructed.[26] What is considered a human rights violation is public and fits more closely to the male experience of human rights violations. According to Professors Charlesworth and Chinkin, in the major human rights treaties, "rights are defined according to what men fear will happen to them."[27] Since men are more likely to suffer from human rights violations at the hands of the state than from the private sphere, legal responsibility attaches to the state for the eradication of these violations. Excluding the private sphere, particularly the family, from state regulation essentially relieves the state from any obligation to intervene and thus from any responsibility for those violations that most affect women. The prioritization of the public over the private sphere and the limits of state responsibility for human rights violations operate to exclude women's concerns from the ambit of both first and second generation rights. Unfortunately, this dichotomy has operated at the international level. Those working in the international system have often failed to adequately

24 See generally, H. Charlesworth, C. Chinkin, and S. Wright, "Feminist Approaches to International Law" (1991) 85 AJIL 613; C. Romany, "Women as Aliens: A Feminist Critique of the Public/Private Distinction in International Human Rights Law" (1993) 6 Harv. Hum. Rts J. 87.

25 Charlesworth, *supra* note 20, 58 at 69-70.

26 See Bunch, *supra* note 20. See also N. Burrows, "International Law and Human Rights — the Case of Women's Rights" in Campbell et al. (eds), *Human Rights From Rhetoric to Reality* 80 at 82 (London: Blackwells, 1986).

27 H. Charlesworth and C. Chinkin, "The Gender of Jus Cogens" (1993) 15 Hum. Rts Q. 63 at 69.

consider the gender implications of their mandate, even when the procedure or law exists to enable this to be done.[28]

The ambit of state responsibility under international law has expanded in such a way that the state may be held accountable for acts not directly attributed to it, such as failure to investigate or prosecute a violation, failure to meet an obligation, failure to exercise due diligence to prevent, eliminate, reduce, or mitigate a violation, failure to provide effective access to non-discriminatory law enforcement or judicial remedies, and failure to ensure equal application of the law.[29] The state may also have a positive duty to repeal legislation that perpetuates human rights violations.[30] The challenge for feminists is to deconstruct accepted concepts of what constitutes a human rights violation in order to further expand the doctrine of state responsibility for acts occurring at the hands of non-state actors.

The Platform for Action does address the issue of state responsibility in a limited sense. It calls for governments to take "urgent action to combat and eliminate all forms of violence against women in private and public life, whether perpetrated or tolerated by the state or private persons."[31]

The discourse on the public/private dichotomy raises the broader issue of the limits of rights discourse under the current international human rights system. Can the neglect of gender issues be remedied within the current framework? Two important issues are raised. First, the debate over the public/private dichotomy must consider the issue of systemic inequalities and historical deprivations. Failure to challenge underlying structural inequalities in society will not lead to any significant improvement in the human rights situation of women. The Platform for Action states:

If the goal of full realization of human rights for all is to be achieved, international human rights instruments must be applied in such a way as to

[28] For an analysis of the importance of the victim's sex for the work of the UN Special Rapporteur on Torture, see International Human Rights Law Group (Women in the Law Project), *Token Gestures: Women's Human Rights and UN Reporting, The UN Special Rapporteur on Torture* 1 (International Human Rights Law Group, 1993). See also Byrnes, "Towards a More Effective Enforcement of Women's Human Rights through the Use of International Human Rights Law and Procedure" *supra* note 12, 190 at 194.

[29] See R. J. Cook, "State Responsibility for Violations of Women's Human Rights" (1994) 7 Harv. Hum. Rts J. 125 at 143; Romany, *supra* note 24, 87 at 110-11.

[30] Cook, *ibid.*, 149; Romany, *supra* note 29, 105.

[31] Platform for Action, *supra* note 4, ch. 4, para. 225.

take more clearly into consideration the systematic and systemic nature of discrimination against women that gender analysis has clearly indicated.[32]

There may have to be some reconsideration by the United Nations human rights system of the underlying approach of international human rights bodies in dealing with the elimination of systemic discrimination against women. Gender inequality may be perpetuated with any legal norm or model based on the treatment of men as the applicable standard for which discrimination against women is measured.[33] Since men and women have not achieved equality in society, the use of male or even so-called gender neutral standards for defining equality for women may perpetuate discrimination. Gender neutral language ignores discriminatory treatment based on legal, cultural, and religious traditions as well as the fact that the law is based on male-defined concepts and harms. Those who are unlike cannot be treated alike.[34]

Unfortunately, this model is the one that has been used by international and regional human rights tribunals.[35] Human rights scholars have argued that a better approach would consider how women actually function in society, with particular recognition of any disadvantage they may suffer as a group based on law, tradition, or culture.[36] To establish the fact of discrimination, a member of a disadvantaged group would have to show that a distinction based on the characteristics of that group is not imposed on others, and either continues or worsens the disadvantage.[37] Achieving equality may necessitate differential treatment of men and women, including the use of systemic remedies such as special measures or employment equity.[38] Such an approach will also address the systemic nature of civil, political, economic, traditional, social, and

---

[32] *Ibid.*, para. 222.

[33] Feminists have argued that this model, "the similarity and difference" model will force women to look at their situation on the basis of how similar or different their treatment under the law is from that of men. For discussions of the principles of equality and non-discrimination, see A. F. Bayefsky, "The Principle of Equality or Non-Discrimination in International Law" (1990) 11 Hum. Rts L. J. 1; K. E. Mahoney, "Canadian Approaches to Equality Rights and Gender Equity in the Courts" in R. J. Cook (ed.), *supra* note 12 at 439.

[34] Bayefsky, *ibid.*, 11. Mahoney, *supra* note 33 at 442.

[35] Cook, *supra* note 23 at 156.

[36] This is the "disadvantage" model: see Cook, *ibid.*, 155-56; Mahoney, *supra* note 33 at 441-49.

[37] Mahoney, *supra* note 33 at 445.

[38] Mahoney, *ibid.*, 443; Bayefsky, *supra* note 33 at 28-33.

cultural impediments to the empowerment of women, which may operate to devalue or ignore issues traditionally associated with women, such as reproductive health and work in the home. In such cases, there are no comparable male standards with which to assess the content and reach of the law.

The second factor to be considered regarding the efficacy of the current institutional system for the international protection of women's human rights is recognition of the limit of legal solutions to pervasive societal factors that marginalize women or accord them subordinate status in society. The Platform for Action states that eradication of human rights violations can be realized only if effective *de facto* equality is achieved through the enforcement of "family, civil, penal, labour and commercial laws or codes, or administrative rules and regulations intended to ensure women's full enjoyment of human rights and fundamental freedoms."[39] International bodies entrusted to deal with human rights must consider both the *de jure* and the *de facto* situation of women in any given society. Because there are often differences between the content and application of the law and what society condones, any emphasis on the legal rather than on the *de facto* situation may lead to the neglect of the disempowerment of women as a result of custom and tradition.[40] Human rights specialists will have to look beyond the law to effect change for women by integrating theories and policies derived from such disciplines as sociology, education, anthropology, and economics.

Competing Conceptions of Gender and Rights

To mainstream gender is to assume that gender is the determinative factor for women across borders. Is it ever possible to speak meaningfully of women's voice in an international framework? Is it inaccurate to speak of a single "women's voice"? There are two major limits to conceptualizing and institutionalizing gender within the current United Nations human rights system: multiple barriers or forms of discrimination and differing cultural conceptions of human rights and women's role in society.

Both the Declaration and the Platform for Action recognize the multiple barriers to full equality and advancement faced by some women because of their race, age, language, ethnicity, culture,

---

[39] Platform for Action, *supra* note 4, ch. 4, para. 219.

[40] L. Reanda, *supra* note 11 at 15.

religion, socio-economic class, disability, or because they are indigenous people, migrant workers, displaced women, or refugees.[41] The document consistently recognizes these barriers throughout the various sections. The issue, however, is not mere recognition of these multiple barriers, but a full integration of the experiences lived through these barriers into a comprehensive gender perspective.

Despite societal and cultural differences between women, women in all cultures face oppression because of their gender. Is gender the factor that connects women across class, race, and culture? Angela Harris has critiqued the tendency of feminists to essentialize the concept of gender so that it becomes the determinative category for analysis and factors such as race and religion operate merely as variables on this concept.[42] The problem with gender essentialism is that it conceptualizes gender as the paradigmatic experience of women, independent of race, ethnicity, class, and sexual orientation or other social or legal factors that greatly affect women's lives. It is often difficult to conceptualize a "woman's voice" because of the variety of experiences faced by women.

If there can be no essential "women's voice," the United Nations human rights system is faced with many conceptual as well as procedural nightmares. To what extent can gender determine the analytical framework of the specific issue under discussion? How can gender be integrated into other issues under discussion such as torture, race, or contemporary forms of slavery? How does it interplay with these factors in determining the form that the human rights violations may take? As Professor Byrnes argues:

the institutional allocation of responsibility for "human rights issues" and "women's issues" within a system such as the United Nations human rights system may make it important to ask whether every human rights violation suffered by a women is violation of women's rights or whether the fact that race, class or political opinion are the determinative factors in many human rights violations against women, perhaps to the exclusion of sex and gender, means that women "just happen to be the victims of them and gender plays no significant role and if so, which ones they are.[43]

The violations that women suffer may be indistinguishable from those suffered by men of the same social group. The form of the

41 Platform for Action, *supra* note 4, ch. 2, para. 32 and ch. 4, paras. 46, 225.

42 See A. P. Harris, "Race and Essentialism in Feminist Legal Theory" (1990) 42 Stanf. L. Rev. 581.

43 Byrnes, "Women, Feminism and International Human Rights Law," *supra* note 12, 205 at 216.

violation may differ because of gender.[44] However, certain violations are gender-specific, even though experienced differently across class, race, and culture.[45] The United Nations human rights bodies are faced with the daunting task of determining which social factor (race, class, gender, etc.) is determinative for any given human rights question under discussion, because the system is institutionalized to consider violations under separate treaties and enforcement mechanisms. Pragmatically, this means that the prioritization of one factor over another may be inevitable. The inherent problem with such an approach is that it would presuppose a neat categorization of human rights violations. In reality, many violations are linked in such a way that, in essence, what one is left with are categories requiring unique analytical frameworks.

The difficulty with the use of single categories is most acute when gender is considered with other forms of discrimination, such as race or ethnicity. The interplay of these two factors is not an infrequent event in this age of ethnic conflict. The United Nations currently has two treaties that deal with discrimination — the Convention on the Elimination of Racial Discrimination and the Convention on the Elimination of All Forms of Discrimination Against Women. Both race and sex are also set out as grounds on which one cannot discriminate under more general human rights instruments, such as the Universal Declaration on Human Rights. The issue for international human rights experts is to determine the quantitative and qualitative effect that one factor has on the other. The two factors are often inextricably linked. For example, how does one examine the situation of a female migrant worker from an ethnically marginalized group who receives lower wages than both her male counterpart and women from the host country? How does one examine the systematic rape of women as part of a policy of "ethnic cleansing?" In short, is race a variable on gender, or is gender a variable on race? Or, are the two factors synthesized to create the necessity for new concepts, procedures, and direction in the human rights system? The institutional, if not the conceptual, dilemma has not been fully appreciated by those working in the mainstream human rights system.

[44] *Ibid.*, 215.

[45] Byrnes, "Towards a More Effective Enforcement of Women's Human Rights Through the Use of International Human Rights Law and Procedure" *supra* note 12, 190 at 194.

Notably, the Beijing Platform for Action does recognize multiple barriers in many of its sections and thus avoids the tendency to isolate them into one section.[46] The human rights section expands the recognition of multiple barriers toward a recognition that these barriers may lead to marginalization of some women in society and thus to further barriers to access to information and to recourse to mechanisms for resolving cases of human rights violations.[47] The international human rights system must move beyond mere recognition of these barriers to systematic analysis of the quantitative and qualitative interplay of these factors. The Platform for Action does attempt to do this by calling for the need to fully integrate multiple barriers into a comprehensive gender analysis for research and studies. It calls for the dissemination of gender-disaggregated data and information by age, sex, socio-economic status, and "other relevant indicators" for program and policy planning.[48]

The second major limitation of gender categorization at the international level is the differing cultural concepts of human rights and the role of women in societies. This issue of cultural relativism is not a new one under international human rights law.[49] Although, arguably, the international human rights community has achieved some consensus as to the duty of states to resolve and uphold certain rights as universal, in the specific context of

46 Sullivan criticizes the Vienna Declaration and Programme of Action for isolating women's rights in one section, rather than integrating them into the entire document. See Sullivan, *supra* note 5, 152 at 159.

47 Platform for Action, *supra* note 4, ch. 4, para. 225.

48 *Ibid.*, para. 206. There is no specific mention of race and ethnicity although, presumably, they are subsumed under "other relevant indicators." Notably, there is also no mention of sexual orientation, despite support by some states, such as Canada, for its inclusion.

49 Cultural relativism challenges the view that there is a universal normative order. Human values, including human rights, vary depending on the particular culture. Human rights are little more than culturally specific norms. This view is opposed by the concept of universalism, which argues that values, including human rights, are constant across cultures. The obligations to human liberty and dignity are universal. See generally A. A. An'Naim, "Towards a Cross-Cultural Approach to Defining International Standards of Human Rights: The Meaning of Cruel, Inhuman, or Degrading Treatment or Punishment" in A. A. An'Naim (ed.), *Human Rights in Cross-Cultural Perspectives: A Quest for Consensus* (Philadelphia: University of Pennsylvania Press, 1992); J. Donnelly, "Cultural Relativism and Universal Human Rights" (1984) 6 Hum. Rts Q. 400; A. Dundes Renteln, "The Unanswered Challenge of Relativism and the Consequences For Human Rights" (1985) 7 Hum. Rts Q. 514.

women's human rights it has failed to fully resolve the debate between cultural relativism and universalism. The tension between the two is evident in the Declaration and Platform for Action, resulting in an outcome that is contradictory and difficult to implement. On the one hand, there is reaffirmation and commitment to the universal nature of human rights and to the full implementation of the human rights of women and of the girl child as an "inalienable, integral and indivisible part of all human rights."[50] In even stronger language, the Platform for Action states that the universal nature of these rights is "beyond question."[51] On the other hand, the Platform for Action calls for the empowerment of women while "recognizing national, regional, historical, cultural and religious particularities."[52] Many states also made reservations to the various sections of the document where it was viewed as going against religious law or values.[53] In trying to resolve the two conceptual positions, the document ends up with little more than an untenable marriage of universalism, cultural relativism, and state sovereignty. It states:

> The full realization of all human rights and fundamental freedoms of all women is essential for the empowerment of women. While the significance of national and regional particularities and various historical, cultural and religious backgrounds must be borne in mind, it is the duty of States, regardless of their political, economic and cultural systems, to promote and protect all human rights and fundamental freedoms. The implementation of this Platform, including through national laws and the formulation of strategies, policies, programs and development priorities, is the sovereign responsibility of each State, in conformity with all human rights and fundamental freedoms, and the significance of and full respect for various religious and ethical values, cultural backgrounds and philosophical convictions of individuals and their communities should contribute to the full enjoyment by women of their human rights in order to achieve equality, development and peace.[54]

This section affirms the sovereign responsibility of each state to determine its own religious values. Religion is further affirmed as a universal cultural right in public or private, while there is recognition of the negative impact, such as violence and discrimination, that

---

[50] Declaration, *supra* note 4, Annex 1, para. 9; Platform for Action, *supra* note 4, ch. 4, 216.

[51] Platform for Action, *supra* note 4, ch. 4, para. 211.

[52] *Ibid.*, ch. 1, para. 9.

[53] *Ibid.*, ch. 5.

[54] *Ibid.*, ch. 2, para. 9.

extremism has on women.[55] Yet, who determines what is extreme? Can the violation of women's human rights be said to result solely from extremism? On one hand, women must challenge universalistic concepts of human rights as well as any tendency toward gender essentialism. On the other hand, they must challenge the cultural traditions within their society — traditions that are not necessarily extreme but may nevertheless exclude them from economic, social, and political participation.[56] References to extremism do not deal with what one commentator terms as the issue of cultural practices that encompass cultural sanctions of gender discrimination and gender-based violence. For example, deference to the family often shields domestic violence from scrutiny.[57]

The difficulty for those engaged in mainstreaming gender is one of trying to tie local and regional "particularities" into a single unifying concept of what it is that constitutes a women's voice under international human rights law. This issue has been translated into strategic choices for those working in the field. One such strategy has been the choice of violence as a focus of inquiry at the international level, because it is viewed as a cross-cultural human rights violation. At the Vienna World Conference on Human Rights, violence was a strategic choice in rallying women around the world to attention to women's human rights.[58] For the first time, violence was treated as a mainstream human rights violation, resulting in the post-conference appointment by the United Nations Commission on Human Rights of a Special Rapporteur Against Violence.[59] The issue of violence merits its own section in the Platform for Action. It is recognized as essentially deriving from cultural patterns, particularly as a result of the "harmful effects of certain traditional or customary practices and all acts of extremism linked to race, sex, language or religion that perpetuate the lower status accorded to women in the family, the workplace, the community and society."[60]

---

55 *Ibid.*, para. 24.

56 Sullivan, *supra* note 5, 152 at 157-58.

57 *Ibid.*, 158.

58 Julie A. Mertus and Pamela Goldberg, "A Perspective on Women and International Human Rights after the Vienna Declaration: The Inside/Outside Construct" (1994) 26 N.Y.U. J. Int'l L. & P. 201 at 206-7.

59 Commission on Human Rights, *Report on the Fifth Session*, UN ESCOR Supp. No. 4, Doc. E/1994/24-E/CN.4/1994/132.

60 Platform for Action, *supra* note 4, ch. 4, para. 118.

It calls for the prohibition and elimination of violence resulting from any harmful aspect of certain traditional customary or modern practices that violate the rights of women.[61]

The mainstream regional and international human rights systems must at least recognize cultural traditions within any given society that do not accord with international standards for the treatment of women. This does not necessarily entail acceptance of those standards but, rather, a willingness to facilitate dialogue between those who advocate differing conceptions of cultural norms. Abdullah A. An'Naim argues for a method whereby societies would engage in intracultural dialogue as a starting point for any consideration of implementing international human rights law.[62] Those who do not belong to a particular society must avoid the tendency to dictate the terms of such dialogue, while encouraging the enforcement of international human rights law.[63]

The challenge therefore is to empower women within particular societies to expand or change the provisions of particular laws and practices that may exclude them from meaningful participation in society, while identifying and striving to eliminate the harmful effects of such traditions and entrenched practices. This may require mobilization at the grassroots level as well as use of the language of rights within the cultural context of a society in order to advance specific claims.[64] This will further entail a full appreciation of the complex interplay of economic, social, and political factors that abound to maintain these traditions.[65] Without such an understanding, international human rights norms will fail to find legitimacy within a society.[66]

There must, however, be strict scrutiny of proclamations of cultural norms when these are used as justification to reject international human rights standards. Many cultural norms are contestable, subject to a variety of interpretations and practices, and are often ambiguous.[67] There must also be scrutiny of those who claim

---

[61] *Ibid.*, para. 224.

[62] See A. A. An'Naim, "State Responsibility under International Human Rights Law to Change Religious and Customary Laws" in R. J. Cook (ed.), *supra* note 12 at 177.

[63] *Ibid.*, 179.

[64] See Ilumoka, *supra* note 21.

[65] An'Naim, *supra* note 62 at 178.

[66] *Ibid.*, 176-77.

[67] *Ibid.*, 173.

to have the right to determine cultural norms to decide whether they, in fact, have the power to do so. As the embodiment of an agreement between a large number of states, the Platform for Action should, as a minimum, serve as a barometer against which the *de facto* and *de jure* situations of women across borders are measured by the international community. Despite recognition of cultural "particularities," the document makes strong statements about the universal nature of women's human rights. The right to enjoy one's culture is a human right. What must be avoided is the tendency to dichotomize women's rights on the one hand and the right to enjoy one's culture or religion on the other.

Those active on the international scene may have to consider the need to focus more on regional than on international dialogue and procedures. Regional systems, in areas where there is similarity of culture, language, religion, and economies, provide opportunities to establish consensus over human rights norms that may not yet exist at the international level.[68] Presumably, a regional focus would generate different sets of priorities and concerns across regions instead of arguments against the universality of women's human rights. During the preparatory process that led up to the Beijing conference and during the conference, the themes advanced by the European Union and western countries were in many respects similar to those advanced by delegations from the south — for example, the recognition of women's contribution to the economy and the participation of women in the decision-making processes.[69] However, delegations from the south lay equal emphasis on issues relating to access to education, health, land and property rights, and development resources from industrialized countries.[70] Nevertheless, a regional focus on women's rights may appear antithetical to international human rights law, because it does not resolve the stalemate between universalism and cultural relativism.

In the final analysis, the document fails to resolve the tensions between the universality of the rights that it exhorts, state

[68] R. J. Cook, "Women's International Human Rights Law: The Way Forward" in R.J. Cook (ed.), *supra* note 12 at 167.

[69] World Conference on Women, *Regional Platform for Action: Women in a Changing World — Call for Action from an ECE Perspective*, UN ESCOR, Doc. E/CN.6/1995/5. See also European Commission (1995) 9 Bulletin of the European Union 1.

[70] E.g., see regional platforms of actions for Africa, E/ECA/ACW/RC.V/EXP/WP.6/Rev.4, and for the Arab region, E/ESCW/SD/1994/IG.1-WOM/L.4.

sovereignty, and cultural conceptions of human rights. There remains the danger that interpretations of the Platform for Action may result in a multi-tiered system of human rights, with its implementation based on a country's level of development, its human rights record, and its inherent or proclaimed cultural traditions. For some governments, the document will serve only as a minimum set of standards for the development of legal mechanisms and policy programs. For others, it may serve as a document encompassing objectives that cannot be fully implemented given current conditions. For still others, it may include policies that have to be adapted to society or that will be rejected outright as going against cultural norms.

MAINSTREAM, MARGINALIZATION, AND PROCEDURE: INSTITUTIONAL RESPONSES

Any attempt to integrate gender within the United Nations human rights system must grapple with several institutional aspects of mainstreaming issues related to gender, because women's issues and concerns have yet to be established as constituting an integral part of all international human rights machineries. First, there will have to be strong political commitment at the highest level by both governments and by the United Nations. Second, there will have to be effective co-ordination of mandates at the international level. Finally, the international human rights system will have to deal with equitable representation by sex at the national and international level.

The Beijing Declaration and Platform for Action is a large document that emphasizes the need for concrete action by the international community for improving the human rights situation of women globally. The Platform for Action calls for the United Nations system to give full, equal, and sustained attention to the human rights of women in the exercise of their respective mandates, including those in the areas of civil, cultural, economic, political, and social rights.[71] To implement this platform, it will be necessary to develop a comprehensive policy program for mainstreaming advisory services, technical assistance, reporting methodology, gender impact assessments, co-ordination, public information, and human rights education.[72] This policy program must be both "active and visible."[73]

[71] Platform for Action, *supra* note 4, ch. 4, para. 231.

[72] *Ibid.*

[73] *Ibid.*

To meet the policies of such an action-oriented document, concerted efforts must be made to incorporate a gender perspective into all human rights policies and procedures at the national, regional, and international levels. Attention to women's rights affects the entire content of rights and influences the need to adopt particular responses.[74] The various actors in the system will need to make concerted efforts to integrate gender-specific policies. There is scope to do so under current instruments and machineries.

The treaty-based bodies, such as the Human Rights Committee (hereinafter HRC) and the Committee on the Elimination of Racial Discrimination (hereinafter CERD) must regard distinctions based on sex as a basis for human rights violations.[75] This is particularly important in light of the fact that, unlike the Committee for the Elimination of Discrimination Against Women (CEDAW), some of these bodies have established a quasi-judicial individual complaints procedure.[76] These bodies may present the only forum for women to lodge individual complaints against states parties to a treaty when their rights have been violated.

The United Nations Secretariat also has an important role to play in mainstreaming gender-related issues into the human rights system. The Platform for Action calls for all United Nations officials to receive training in the human rights of women in order to recognize the necessity of applying gender analysis when appropriate to do so.[77] There must also be improved co-operation and co-ordination between the various human rights divisions, particularly

---

[74] Byrnes, "Women, Feminism and International Human Rights Law," *supra* note 12 at 211.

[75] A. F. Bayefsky argues that distinctions based on sex, like those based on race, are suspect because they are most likely to be unjustified and thus are deserving of the highest scrutiny: "The Principle of Equality Or Non-Discrimination in International Law" (1990) 11 Hum. Rts L.J. 1 at 18-24. See also H. Charlesworth and C. Chinkin, "The Gender of Jus Cogens" (1993) 15 Hum. Rts Q. 63, who argue for the inclusion of sex into the accepted category of *jus cogens* or peremptory norms of human rights from which no derogation is permitted. This category usually includes race but excludes sex as a ground against which one cannot discriminate.

[76] International Convention on the Elimination of All Forms of Racial Discrimination, March 7, 1966, Can. T.S. 1970, no. 28, art. 14; First Optional Protocol to the International Covenant on Civil and Political Rights, December 19, 1966, Can. T.S. 1976, No. 47; Convention Against Torture and Other Forms of Cruel, Inhuman or Degrading Treatment or Punishment, December 17, 1984, Can. T.S. 1987, no. 36, art. 22.

[77] Platform for Action, *supra* note 4, ch. 4, para. 231.

between the Division for the Advancement of Women, the United Nations Centre for Human Rights, and specialized agencies such as the International Labour Organization.[78] Non-governmental organizations also have an important role to play within the system, since their information often provides the only reliable source of the actual human rights situation in a country, particularly where governments have failed to take reasonable steps to prevent violations or to investigate and punish human rights violations. However, their role can be effective only if their access to the United Nations system is developed to the extent that they can effectively participate in important United Nations human rights meetings. Governments must also institutionalize procedures for consultation with non-governmental organizations at the national and regional levels.

No policy of mainstreaming women's rights at the international level can be effective without commitment and active co-operation at the national level. The Platform for Action calls for governments to include gender aspects, including gender disaggregated data, in all of their reports submitted under the various human rights conventions.[79] Improvement in the situation of women can only be realized if there is a thorough reporting of the factual situation of human rights within states. Data can expose the *de facto* situation of women in a specific country and can thus help in holding states accountable for violations of women's rights.[80] What is needed is both events-based data (data on individual violations) and standards-based data (state compliance with violation of economic, social, and cultural rights).[81] However, any gender disaggregated data must incorporate the systematic interplay of gender with all other forms of human rights barriers such as age, disability, sexual orientation, race, and ethnicity.

Ultimately, the United Nations system is only as good as the sum of its parts and often only that of its weakest link. For any human rights policy to be successfully implemented, there will have to be strong and consistent commitment at the political level. United Nations human rights bodies, such as the Commission on Human Rights and the Commission on the Status of Women must continue

---

[78] *Ibid.*

[79] *Ibid.*, para. 230.

[80] R. J. Cook, "State Responsibility for Violations of Women's Human Rights" (1994) 7 Harv. Hum. Rts J. 125 at 175.

[81] *Ibid.*

to call for the United Nations human rights system to integrate a gender perspective into their work. All thematic and country specific rapporteurs who are appointed by the Commission on Human Rights must specifically relate their mandate to a consideration of the impact of gender on rights. Special rapporteurs have an important role to play in documenting the *de facto* situation of women's human rights, and their work can complement the effects of the United Nations treaty-based procedures. The treaty bodies are limited in their ability to eradicate human rights violations, since they can only consider the human rights situation of state parties to a particular treaty. However, the special rapporteurs have a wider scope to highlight the human rights situation within states that have not ratified international human rights treaties.[82]

Political commitment must be evident at the highest levels.[83] The United Nations General Assembly, the Security Council, and the Economic and Social Council must consider political and economic sanctions for human rights violations on the basis of a state's treatment of the human rights of women. Governments must incorporate the human rights situation of women into their foreign policy. The High Commissioner for Human Rights, who is responsible for system-wide co-ordination of human rights, must effectively combine quiet diplomacy and good offices, where necessary, with publicizing violations of women's human rights in specific countries. Political commitment must be backed up by the allocation of financial resources.

The integration of women's rights perspectives will entail the adoption of policies for effective co-ordination at the international level. These policies should translate into the streamlining of institutional functions and the avoidance of duplicate mandates. The Platform for Action states, "cooperation is also needed to strengthen, rationalize and streamline the United Nations human rights system and to promote its effectiveness and efficiency, taking into account the need to avoid unnecessary duplication and overlapping of mandates and functions."[84] However, a pragmatic tension may develop between the avoidance of duplication on one hand and a policy of integrating gender on the other. Unless

---

82 See Committee On the Elimination of Racial Discrimination, *Report of the Committee on the Elimination of Racial Discrimination*, UN GAOR, 49th Sess., Supp. No. 18, Doc. A/49/18, 1995.

83 Platform for Action, *supra* note 4, ch. 5, para. 308.

84 *Ibid.*, ch. 4, paras 221, 231.

gender is regarded as an integral analytical factor under all human right mandates, a tendency may develop to avoid duplication by prioritizing the particular human rights issue that is under consideration. As a result, the impact of other issues, such as gender, may be neglected or minimized. For example, CERD may regard women's issues as within the scope of CEDAW and minimize or ignore their impact. CEDAW in turn may view race as the domain of CERD and ignore or minimize its impact.

A scenario of this type, while seemingly efficient, will likely produce distorted realities of the situation of human rights within any given state by minimizing the complex interplay of multiple forms of barriers and their effect on any given right. A sophisticated analytical and procedural framework must identify all possible grounds on which a person can be discriminated against in a particular society as systemic factors that quantitatively and qualitatively affect whatever is the specific human right issue under consideration. All relevant grounds for discrimination, such as gender, socio-economic status, religion, ethnicity, or race are variables that must consistently and systematically be applied to human rights mandates, whether that mandate is race, sex, contemporary forms of slavery, torture, election monitoring, war crimes, poverty, or development. Again, this process will combine data disaggregated by gender with other demographic or societal grounds that are relevant to a particular state or region.

A policy of integrating gender issues must also recognize the important issue of representation at the national and international levels. The issue is not just what gets into the agenda but also who has the power to decide it. Professors Mertus and Goldberg term the situation "insider-outsider," whereby those who suffer from discrimination are deemed "insiders" in the sense of being those who suffer from or are most likely to suffer from human rights violations on the basis of belonging to one group or another.[85] Women as a group are thus "insiders." On the other hand, those on the "outside" are those who do not experience or are less likely to experience human rights violations. Those on the "outside" of oppression are, unfortunately, the most visible at the national and international level, on national delegations, on international bodies, and within mainstream human rights NGOs and research institutes. On the other hand, those on the "inside" of oppression,

---

[85] See generally, Mertus and Goldberg, *supra* note 58.

who have first-hand experience of particular violations and thus can contribute much to the human rights debate, are often invisible from groups that are theorizing about human rights or from key decision-making bodies.

One factor that leads to the absence of gender perspectives in the international human rights system is the dominance of men on most human rights bodies.[86] This invisibility of women from key decision-making roles must be recognized as operating on several levels. At the international level, it operates to exclude women from appointment to mainstream human rights treaty and political bodies. The Platform for Action mission statement recognizes that women are under-represented at decision-making United Nations levels.[87] The section on power and decision-making calls for an equitable balance of gender in the appointment of candidates to United Nations bodies and specialized agencies, particularly at senior professional levels.[88] Yet, although the United Nations has had a policy of gender parity, women are absent from senior level positions within the United Nations Secretariat.[89] At the national level, governments must appoint women to national delegations to the United Nations and to other international forums.[90] Even those countries with otherwise "good" human rights records must strive to achieve gender parity on their delegations. Those countries that have had relative success in appointing women to their delegations must be diversified with respect to other barriers — notably, race, ethnicity, and religion. In order for United Nations bodies to establish equitable representation, states must actively recruit and nominate female candidates and candidates from cultural and racial minorities for national delegations and for appointments to the United Nations. Equitable gender representation at the United Nations is positively related to gender representation at the national level, since many United Nations officials are recruited from national delegations or governments.

Women's rights advocates and mainstream NGOs must deal with the problem of the relative absence at the international level of

---

[86] E.g., CERD currently only has one woman member, Mrs. Shanti Sadiq Ali.

[87] Platform for Action, supra note 4, ch. 2, para. 28.

[88] *Ibid.*, ch. 4, para. 192.

[89] Secretary-General, *Advancement of the Status of Women in the Secretariat: Report of the Secretary-General*, UN GAOR, 48th Sess., Doc. A/48/513, 1993.

[90] Platform for Action, *supra* note 4, ch. 4, para. 192.

women from marginalized groups within particular societies, some of whom may not have the power or means to speak for their group. The Platform for Action notes that, as a group, women who suffer multiple forms of discrimination are marginalized within society by a general lack of knowledge and recognition of their human rights as well as by obstacles to access to information and to recourse to mechanisms in cases of violations of their human rights.[91] Still, NGOs must deal with the issue of those women who face multiple forms of discrimination, who have knowledge of and access to international human rights procedures, but who may still choose to shun action at the international level. These women may feel marginalized within the women's human rights community and perceive that they are excluded from "the inside" — that is, from the influential groups that have informal and formal access to government officials and funding. Moreover, some women may believe that the fight for human rights should remain at the national level, perhaps involving men of the same group, and that the limited resources are best used for improving national procedures, rather than being spent on seemingly inefficient international procedures. The situation of women's rights on another continent, while unfortunate, may not take on the necessary immediacy for a move into the international arena.

The argument for equitable representation of women on human rights bodies presupposes that the inclusion of those most likely to experience the particular human rights violation under discussion will make a qualitative difference to the work being done. Presumably, the appointment of women on these bodies may lead to substantive changes in current analytical and procedural frameworks for international human rights norms. The presence of women also may increase the chances that new claims based on women's experience will be successful.[92] The United Nations cannot ignore the necessity for actively seeking and recruiting women from all geographic, cultural, religious, and ethnic groups. This activity may involve looking beyond recruitment from governments and academics toward non-traditional sources, such as NGOs that focus on women's human rights.

---

[91] *Ibid.*, ch. 2, para. 31 and ch. 4, para. 225.

[92] Byrnes, "Towards a More Effective Enforcement of Women's Human Rights through the Use of International Human Rights Law and Procedure," *supra* note 12 at 200.

However, representation must ultimately be based on the presentation of ideas and perspectives as much as on membership within a particular group. Representation based on "insider" status may be futile in practice. Most people are at once insiders and outsiders depending on the particular criteria under consideration. Any policy based largely on representation will be untenable in practice, measured on belonging to a particular group without reference to the representation of ideas. The United Nations must establish a policy of integrating women's rights perspectives with a policy of equitable representation by sex.

CONCLUSION

Operating within the mainstream may mean working within it while challenging some of its accepted practices. As two commentators have noted, the problem facing women who are working to enhance human rights protection of women is "how to work effectively within a hierarchical, complex, and constraining system without being corrupted by that system; or how to play the game and break the rules at the same time."[93] By calling for the international system to implement strategies for a comprehensive rights framework, to tackle systemic discrimination, and to deal with violence against women in the non-state sector, the Platform for Action should lead to some improvement in current conceptual and institutional frameworks. In the short term, the eradication of these frameworks is neither necessary nor desirable. There is scope within the present system for adapting or even expanding these frameworks more fully to reflect the needs of women. The implications of such adaptation and the level of improvement effected can be measured only in the long term. Those active on the international scene may have to recognize the limits of tinkering with, rather than dismantling, the system.

It is somewhat ironic to address the issue of the mainstream within the context of a women's human rights document that stemmed from a women's conference and was drafted by the United Nations Division on the Advancement of Women. Focus on the mainstream must not lead to the marginalization of those instruments and machineries that were set up to deal specifically with women's rights. Instead, the effective implementation of women's human rights under the international system as it now

93 Mertus and Goldberg, *supra* note 58 at 215.

exists must regard the specialized machineries and those of the mainstream as complementary systems. Each has weaknesses that must be recognized by those working in the field. Working within the mainstream is just one component of a general strategy for the advocacy of women's human rights at the international level.

Sommaire

De la marginalité au courant dominant: la déclaration de Beijing et la plate-forme pour l'action

La quatrième Conférence mondiale des Nations Unies sur les femmes a donné à la communauté internationale une excellente occasion d'évaluer et d'élargir son engagement politique envers la protection des droits de la personne des femmes. L'auteur examine la déclaration de Beijing et la plate-forme pour l'action qui ont été produites par la Conférence et se demande si les mécanismes internationaux conviennent à la mise en oeuvre de droits qui ont été traditionnellement marginalisés. Tout en reconnaissant les limites passées et actuelles des mécanismes internationaux, l'auteur souligne l'importance de travailler au sein des institutions dominantes et d'élaborer des procédures spéciales indépendantes, si l'on veut s'assurer que le système international reflète les besoins des femmes.

Summary

From the Margins to the Mainstream: The Beijing Declaration and Platform for Action

The United Nations Fourth World Conference on Women provided an important occasion for the international community to assess and to develop its political commitment to the protection of the human rights of women. The author discusses the Beijing Declaration and Platform for Action that resulted from the conference and considers whether international machineries for the enforcement of rights will be adequate to deal with rights that traditionally have been marginalized. Recognizing the past and current limitations of international mechanisms, the author argues that working within mainstream institutions as well as developing independent special procedures are necessary measures to ensure that the international system reflects the needs of women.

Another Kick at the Can: Tuna/Dolphin II

TORSTEN H. STROM*

INTRODUCTION

O N AUGUST 16, 1991, a GATT[1] dispute settlement panel submitted its report to the parties in a matter concerning United States import restrictions on canned yellowfin tuna originating in the Eastern Tropical Pacific Ocean.[2] That report, although it has never been tabled in the GATT Council[3] for consideration by the

---

* LL.B., LL.M., of the Bar of Ontario. This article is based on a section of an LL.M. thesis that more generally examines the trade/environment "conflict." The views expressed in this article are personal and should not be interpreted as representing the views of the government of Canada or of its Department of Natural Resources where the author is employed as a policy analyst.

---

1 See *General Agreement on Tariffs and Trade*, Oct. 30, 1947, 55 UNTS 194 [hereinafter "GATT"]. GATT has now been replaced by GATT 1994 as part of the Uruguay Round Final Act, MTN/FA, 15 December 1993, which is the package of agreements, decisions, and understandings that constitute the new GATT/ WTO framework.

2 See GATT Dispute Settlement Panel Report *United States Restrictions on Imports of Tuna*, submitted to the Parties Aug. 16, 1991, reprinted in (1991) 30 I.L.M. 1594. [hereinafter Tuna/Dolphin I] Although it was the practice of GATT not to release panel reports until they had been adopted by the Council, this report was leaked to the public and, following pressure from both Mexico and the United States, the GATT decided to release it officially.

3 In the new World Trade Organization (WTO), the old GATT Council has been replaced by a two-tiered system, involving a General Council, which sits as the Dispute Settlement Body (DSB) when it considers panel reports, and three new councils dealing with trade in goods, trade in services, and trade-related intellectual property matters. In a significant reversal, panel reports are now automat-

Contracting Parties,[4] became the focal point of a heated debate that continues today. The debate focuses on the perceived conflict between the goals of trade liberalization — primarily sought to be achieved through the political/legal framework provided by the GATT and its sister agreements — and national and international efforts to protect the earth's natural environment.

Although Tuna/Dolphin I has yet to be adopted by the GATT Council, it has been assailed by environmentalists as the "smoking gun," which proves not only that the GATT is heedless of environmental concerns, but that it is downright hostile to them.[5] The findings and reasoning of that panel, it has been said, put into jeopardy the use of environmental trade measures (ETMs) to achieve legitimate environmental protection and natural resource conservation objectives.[6] Recent commentaries have expressed a more moderate view[7] of the potential impact of the panel's findings on international environmental protection, but the reality remains that the reasoning of the panel may have a profound impact on the GATT's treatment of ETMs in the future, to the extent that they fall within its scope of regulation.[8]

---

ically adopted by the DSB unless there is unanimous agreement not to do so. This differs from the old system, which required unanimity to adopt a panel report, and will raise the stakes considerably for disputes brought before a GATT panel. For a more complete discussion of the new dispute resolution system, see A. F. Lowenfeld, "Remedies Along with Rights: Institutional Reform in the New GATT" (1994) 88 AJIL 477.

4 Mexico has apparently pushed for its consideration by the GATT Council: see S. Charnovitz, "Dolphins and Tuna: An Analysis of the Second Panel Report" (1994) 24 ELR: News and Analysis 10567 at 10568, note 8.

5 See, e.g., P. Goldman, "Resolving the Trade and Environment Debate: In Search of a Neutral Forum and Neutral Principles" (1992) 49 Wash. and Lee L. Rev. 1279.

6 See, e.g., D. Mayer & D. Hoch, "International Environmental Protection and the GATT: The Tuna/Dolphin Controversy" (1993) 31 Am. Bus. L.J. 187 at 191.

7 Interestingly, Steve Charnovitz believes that environmentalists pose a greater threat to GATT than GATT does to the environment. He has written, "[t]he latent threat to the world economy is not what GATT may do to the environment, but rather what environmentalists may do to the GATT." See S. Charnovitz, "The Environment vs. Trade Rules: Defogging the Debate" (1993) 23 Env'l L. 475 at 488.

8 Some commentators have asserted that the impact of GATT on environmental protection will continue to be minimal, and point to the paucity of disputes that have arisen in the GATT context relating to environmental measures. They also point to the comment by the Tuna/Dolphin I panel that GATT, "imposes few constraints on a contracting party's implementation of domestic environmental

It should also be said, however, that Tuna/Dolphin I served an important and useful purpose because it galvanized both the environmental and the trade communities into action. It has led to a running debate among academics, activists, trade officials, and government leaders on the proper role of the WTO/GATT in the field of environmental protection, and on the appropriate balance to strike between the objectives of liberalizing trade and those of ensuring the protection of the natural environment.[9] Unfortunately, perhaps, this debate has not yet resulted in many concrete results.[10]

The completion of the Uruguay Round of multilateral trade negotiations without a concerted effort[11] by the Contracting Parties to alter the *status quo* toward a clear resolution of the perceived

---

policies." See, e.g., P. Sorsa, "The General Agreement on Tariffs and Trade (GATT)," in J. Kirton and S. Richardson (eds), *Trade, Environment and Competitiveness: Sustaining Canada's Prosperity* 181 at 182 (Ottawa: NRTEE, 1992); E.-U. Petersmann, "International Trade Law and International Environmental Law: Prevention and Settlement of International Environmental Disputes in GATT" (1993) 27 J. World T. 43 at 77-78. Others disagree, pointing to the global scale of many environmental problems and the threat that GATT poses to any environmental initiatives outside national boundaries, or that require international cooperation. See, e.g., E. Brown Weiss, "Environment and Trade as Partners in Sustainable Development: A Commentary" (1992) 86 AJIL 728 at 733.

9 The trade/environment debate has generated an overwhelming volume of scholarly comment. See, *inter alia*, J. Jackson, "World Trade Rules and Environmental Policies: Congruence or Conflict?" (1992) 49 Wash. & Lee L. Rev. 1227; T. J. Schoenbaum, "Free International Trade and Protection of the Environment: Irreconcilable Conflict?" (1992) 86 AJIL 700; T. E. Skilton, "GATT and the Environment in Conflict: The Tuna-Dolphin Dispute and the Quest for an International Conservation Strategy" (1993) 26 Cornell Int'l L.J. 455; and D. J. Black, "International Trade v. Environmental Protection: The Case of the Embargo on Mexican Tuna" (1992) 24 Law & Pol'y Int'l Bus. 123.

10 Steve Charnovitz has pointed out that "[a]lthough there are some important disagreements about values that separate the different sides of the debate, much of the conflict may result from misunderstandings." He has also asserted that "[t]here is no easy way to characterize the sides of the debate" because environmentalists may also consider themselves as trade proponents and trade experts usually also see themselves as being sensitive to environmental concerns. See Charnovitz, *supra* note 7 at 490.

11 The conclusion of the Uruguay Round did bring certain changes to the WTO/GATT organizational framework that could be interpreted as progress in the quest for a reconciliation of the apparent conflict, as well as the insertion of a statement on sustainable development in the preamble to the Marrakesh Agreement establishing the WTO. However, none of this has brought about any real change so far, although it must be conceded that at the time of writing the new framework has been in force for less than one year.

GATT-environment conflict promises to keep the debate going for some time. Moreover, the publication of the second GATT panel report[12] dealing with the tuna/dolphin conflict provides further indication of the uncertain state of the GATT law concerning environmental trade measures.

This paper will examine the reasoning of the GATT panel in Tuna/Dolphin II and compare it with that of Tuna/Dolphin I. While it could be said that Tuna/Dolphin I has been superseded by Tuna/Dolphin II, the status of both reports is not yet settled. Thus, it is still possible that either one or the other, or both, may eventually be adopted by the WTO Dispute Settlement Body and become an authoritative statement of GATT law.[13]

First, the background to the two disputes, as well as the applicable national legislation and GATT rules, will be outlined. Second, the findings of the two panel reports will be reviewed and analyzed. Finally, the perceived shortcomings of the panel reports will be examined, and some conclusions offered as to the quality of the reasoning found in the two reports, the potential (and need) for future panels to "refine" the principles set out in them, and the likely impact of Tuna/Dolphin I and II on the trade and environment debate.

TUNA/DOLPHIN I

THE FACTS

The disputes in the two tuna/dolphin cases arose because the United States placed an import embargo on Mexican-produced tuna taken in the Eastern Tropical Pacific (ETP),[14] as well as an intermediary ban on all tuna imported from countries that imported tuna taken by Mexican[15] fishing vessels in the ETP.[16] The

---

12 See GATT Dispute Settlement Panel Report, *United States Restrictions on Imports of Tuna*, as reprinted in (1994) 33 I.L.M. 839 [hereinafter Tuna/Dolphin II].

13 For a discussion of the role of GATT panels in the creation of international trade law, see Par Hallstrom, *The GATT Panels and the Formation of International Trade Law* (Stockholm: Juristforlaget, 1994).

14 For a more complete review of the facts, see Tuna/Dolphin I, *supra* note 2 at 1598-1601, paras 1.1-2.12.

15 The countries subject to the primary embargo were, at various times, Mexico, Vanuatu, Ecuador, Panama, and Venezuela. The embargo extended to all yellowfin tuna taken with purse seine nets in the ETP. The intermediary nations affected by the embargo included, at various times, Costa Rica, France, Italy,

primary and intermediary embargoes were imposed on the basis of various provisions in the Marine Mammal Protection Act (MMPA),[17] a United States federal statute first enacted in 1972 to prohibit the "taking" of marine mammals without specific authorization.[18] That act required, *inter alia*, countries exporting tuna to the United States to demonstrate that they had dolphin conservation requirements similar to those of the United States — especially with regard to the yellowfin tuna-fishing industry active in the ETP.[19]

Because Mexico failed to meet the requirements set out in the MMPA, the United States imposed the embargo on all tuna originating in Mexico that had been caught in the ETP. Mexico complained that the legislation violated the GATT and, when conciliation failed to resolve the dispute, a panel was established to examine the matter.

ARTICLE III.4 — "LIKE PRODUCTS" VERSUS PRODUCTION
AND PROCESSING METHODS

Mexico based its complaint principally on the assertion that the United States' primary and intermediary embargoes did not conform to Article XI.1 of the GATT, which stipulates, *inter alia*, that Contracting Parties shall not impose quantitative restrictions on imports. Mexico also argued that the regulatory provisions of the

---

Japan, Panama, Canada, Colombia, Ecuador, Indonesia, Korea, Malaysia, the Marshall Islands, Netherlands Antilles, Singapore, Spain, Taiwan, Thailand, Trinidad and Tobago, and the United Kingdom.

16 For a vivid, first-hand description of the methods used to catch yellowfin tuna in the Eastern Tropical Pacific, and the impact that these methods had on dolphins, see K. Brower, "The Destruction of Dolphins" (1989) 263 The Atlantic Monthly 35.

17 P.L. 92-522, 86 Stat. 1027, as amended by P.L. 100-711, 102 Stat. 4755 (1988) and P.L. 101-627, 104 Stat. 4467 (1990), codified as 16 U.S.C, paras 1361-1421(h).

18 The MMPA underwent a number of amendments following its enactment, but the key changes occurred in 1988, when the United States imposed requirements on foreign fishing vessels not to exceed by more than 1.25 times the number of dolphin actually taken by the United States fishing fleet in the ETP. See Section 101(a)(2)(B).

19 The United States only enforced its own legislation following a court order issued by a federal court in *Earth Island Institute* v. *Mosbacher*, 746 F. Supp. 964 (Cal. 1990), 929 F.2d 1452 (9th Cir. 1991), a case brought by an environmental group.

MMPA violated Article III[20] because they discriminated between domestic and imported "like products." Mexico argued that domestic yellowfin tuna and imported yellowfin tuna were "like products" within the meaning of Article III.4, notwithstanding the difference in their production and processing methods. In any event, Mexico argued, "a measure regulating a product could not legally discriminate between domestic and imported products based solely on the production process."[21] Mexico further requested the panel to find that the measures taken by the United States could not be justified under the GATT and asked the panel to recommend that the United States "bring its measures into conformity with its obligations under the General Agreement."[22]

The United States, on the other hand, suggested that the regulatory measures of the MMPA conformed with Article III.4, seeking to qualify them as internal regulations that were applied consistently to imported and domestic products. The United States did not seek to avoid the characterization of the regulations in question as being aimed at a production and processing method. Instead, the United States argued that:

> Where the United States had requirements in place regarding the production method for a particular product, such as in the current proceeding on tuna, the United States could then exclude imports of that product that did not meet the United States [*sic*] requirements, provided that such regulations were not applied so as to afford protection to domestic production, and as long as the treatment accorded the imported product was no less favourable than the treatment accorded the like domestic product.[23]

---

[20] Art. III provides, in part, that "regulations and requirements affecting the internal sale, offering for sale, purchase, transportation, distribution or use of products . . . should not be applied to imported or domestic products so as to afford protection to domestic production"(Art. III:1).

. . .

"The products of the territory of any contracting party imported into the territory of another contracting party shall be accorded treatment no less favourable than that accorded to like products of national origin in respect of all laws, regulations and requirements" (Art. III:4).

[21] Tuna/Dolphin I, *supra* note 2 at 1603, para. 3.16. For good measure, Mexico went on to argue, rather weakly, that the MMPA requirement was not even a PPM because its purpose was to protect dolphins, not to regulate the production of tuna as such: para. 3.17.

[22] *Ibid.*, 1601, paras 3.1-3.5

[23] *Ibid.*, 3.19.

In other words, the United States claimed that it was treating Mexican tuna no less favourably than it was treating tuna caught by its own tuna fleet, and that, in fact, it was giving Mexican tuna better treatment because the allowable incidental "taking" of dolphin for Mexican tuna fishing vessels was 1.25 times the allowable incidental taking for the United States tuna fleet. As such, the regulations in the MMPA were not providing domestic tuna production with protection against imports. Therefore, Article III had not been violated.

The panel quickly disposed of the American contention that Article III.4 applied by finding that Article III only deals with "products as such," not with production and processing methods that had no bearing on product characteristics. In its findings, the panel found that Article III.4 actually requires internal regulations to meet three obligations: they must provide MFN treatment in accordance with Article I.1;[24] they cannot be applied so as to afford protection to domestic production pursuant to Article III.1; and they must accord to the imported product treatment no less favourable than that accorded to like products of national origin pursuant to Article III.4.[25]

The panel noted the frequent use of the word "product" in Article III and in the note to Article III,[26] and suggested that Article III was meant only to cover "products as such." It then sought to buttress this view by referring to the report of a GATT Working Party on border tax adjustments, which had been adopted in

[24] Art. I:1 states in part that:

> With respect to customs duties and charges of any kind . . . and with respect to all matters referred to in paragraphs 2 and 4 of Art. III, any advantage, favour, privilege or immunity granted by the contracting party to any product originating in or destined for any other country shall be accorded immediately and unconditionally to the like product originating in or destined for the territories of all other contracting parties.

[25] Tuna/Dolphin I, *supra* note 2 at 1617, para. 5.9.

[26] Annex 1, (1969) 4 BISD 62 at 63. The Ad Art. III states:

> Any internal tax or other internal charge, or any law, regulation or requirements of the kind referred to in paragraph 1 which applies to an imported *product* and to the like domestic *product* and is collected or enforced in the case of the imported *product* at the time or point of importation, is nevertheless to be regarded as an internal tax or other internal charge, or a law, regulation or requirement of the kind referred to in paragraph 1 [of Art. III], and is accordingly subject to the provisions of Art. III [emphasis added].

1970.[27] The panel relied on the Working Party's conclusion that "there was a convergence of views to the effect that *taxes directly levied on products were eligible for tax adjustments,*"[28] and that "certain taxes that were not directly levied on products were not eligible for adjustment,"[29] as an analogy for arguing that if border tax adjustments were available only for taxes levied directly on products, then Article III.4 could only be used to justify regulations that related directly to a product. In examining the measures in question, the panel concluded that:

These regulations could not be regarded as being applied to tuna products as such because they would not directly regulate the sale of tuna and could not possibly affect tuna as a product. . . . Article III.4 calls for a comparison of the treatment of imported tuna *as a product* with that of domestic tuna *as a product.* Regulations governing the taking of dolphins incidental to the taking of tuna could not possibly affect tuna as a product. Article III.4 therefore obliges the United States to accord treatment to Mexican tuna no less favourable than that accorded to United States tuna, whether or not the incidental taking of dolphins by Mexican vessels corresponds to that of United States vessels.[30]

Some commentators have asserted that the distinction drawn by the panel between "products" and "process and production methods," or PPMs, is novel and not entirely supported by the material used by the panel to justify its finding.[31] As will be discussed below, there may be reasons for finding fault with the panel's reasoning but, it will be submitted, the interpretation given by the panel cannot be said to be wrong. Furthermore, while some fault may be sought in the reasons, it cannot be found in the outcome.

By relying on the distinction between PPMs and "products as such" to dismiss the arguments of the United States government regarding Article III.4, the panel also avoided the much thornier issues that had been raised, namely, the relationship between

---

[27] See Doc. L/3464, BISD (18th Supp.), adopted on Dec. 2, 1970, 97.

[28] *Ibid.*, 100, para. 14 [emphasis inserted in quote provided in Tuna/Dolphin I, *supra* note 2, at 1618, para. 5.13].

[29] *Ibid.*

[30] Tuna/Dolphin I, *ibid.*, 1618, paras 5.14-5.15. Emphasis in the original.

[31] See, e.g., S. M. Spracker and D. C. Lundsgaard, "Dolphins and Tuna: Renewed Attention on the Future of Free Trade and Protection of the Environment" (1993) 18 Col. J. of Env'l L. 385 at 395-96; Charnovitz, *supra* note 4 at 493. But see Jackson, *supra* note 9, at 1242-43.

Article III and Article XI,[32] and whether a measure that meets the Article III requirements can nevertheless be invalidated under Article XI.[33] These issues, however, will not be addressed here.

After finding that Article III.4 could not apply to the measures taken by the United States, the panel had no trouble concluding that the import embargo violated the Article XI prohibition on quantitative restrictions.[34]

ARTICLE XX — THE EXCEPTIONS

The United States sought to justify the primary and intermediary bans on the grounds that they were measures that were "necessary to protect human, animal, or plant life or health," and/or "relating to the conservation of exhaustible natural resources," as allowed under Article XX(b) and (g).[35]

Article XX(b)

The United States argued that its measures were justified under Article XX(b) because they "served solely the purpose of protecting dolphin life and health and were 'necessary' within the meaning of that provision."[36] The measures were necessary, it was said, because there were no alternative means reasonably available to protect dolphins outside United States jurisdiction.[37] The panel found, however, that, based on an assessment of a number of factors, including the drafting history of the provision, its purpose, and the consequences that the United States interpretation would

---

32 See S. Charnovitz, "Green Roots, Bad Pruning: GATT Rules and Their Application to Environmental Trade Measures" (1994) 7 Tulane Env'l L.J. 299 at 307; GATT, *Canada: Administration of the Foreign Investment Review Act*, BISD (30th Supp.), adopted Feb. 7, 1984, 140 at 162, para. 5.14; and GATT, *Canada: Import, Distribution and Sale of Certain Alcoholic Drinks by Provincial Marketing Agencies*, BISD (39th Supp.), adopted Feb. 18, 1992, 27 at 84, para. 5.28.

33 See the arguments put forward by the United States and Mexico in Tuna/Dolphin I, *supra* note 2 at 1602, paras 3.11-3.12.

34 *Ibid.*, 1618, paras 5.17-5.18. The panel duly noted in para. 5.18 that the United States, "did not present to the Panel any arguments to support a different legal conclusion regarding Art. XI."

35 *Ibid.*, 1601-2, paras 3.6-3.9. The United States also sought to rely on Art. XX(d), but those arguments were rejected for reasons not germane to this paper. See *infra* note 55.

36 *Ibid.*, 1619, para. 5.24.

37 *Ibid.*

and the consequences that the United States interpretation would have, "for the operation of the General Agreement as a whole,"[38] the extrajurisdictional application of trade measures, was not within the scope of Article XX(b). After examining the negotiating history of Article XX, the panel concluded that "the record indicates that the concerns of the drafters of Article XX(b) focused on the use of sanitary measures to safeguard life or health of humans, animals or plants within the jurisdiction of the importing country."[39] The panel went on to note that:

[I]f the broad interpretation of Article XX(b) suggested by the United States were accepted, each contracting party could unilaterally determine the life or health protection policies from which other Contracting Parties could not deviate without jeopardizing their rights under the General Agreement.[40]

Further, the panel found that, even if extrajurisdictional application was possible, the United States had not met the "necessity" standard of Article XX(b) because it had not exhausted "all options reasonably available to it" to address the problem through GATT-consistent means, such as "international cooperative agreements."[41] This finding has been widely criticized[42] because it ignores determined efforts by the United States to establish a multilateral framework for dolphin conservation, efforts that eventually led to an agreement in which Mexico participated.[43]

Finally, the panel noted that even if the measure in question — that is, the import embargo — was the only means "reasonably available" to the United States, it could not be considered "necessary" within the meaning of Article XX(b) because, given the criteria to be met, "the Mexican authorities could not know whether, at a given point in time, their policies conformed to the United States' dolphin protection standards."[44]

---

38 *Ibid.*, 1620, para. 5.25.

39 *Ibid.*, para. 5.26.

40 *Ibid.*, para. 5.27.

41 *Ibid.*, paras 5.26-5.28.

42 See, e.g., J. McDonald, "Greening the GATT: Harmonizing Free Trade and Environmental Protection in the New World Order" (1993) 23 Env'l L. 397 at 434-35. This point will be addressed in more detail below.

43 See *infra*, note 52.

44 Tuna/Dolphin I, *supra* note 2, at 1620, para. 5.28.

Article XX(g)

Under Article XX(g), the United States suggested that its measures were "primarily aimed at the conservation of dolphin [*sic*], and that the import restrictions . . . [were] 'primarily aimed at rendering effective restrictions on domestic production or consumption' of dolphin [*sic*]."[45] As in its disposition of the Article XX(b) arguments, the panel rejected the submissions of the United States government under Article XX(g), on the grounds that the article did not allow for measures with extrajurisdictional application, and that, in any event, the measures could not be "regarded as being primarily aimed at the conservation of dolphins."[46] The panel based its conclusions on the reasoning that "a country can effectively control the production or consumption of an exhaustible natural resource only to the extent that the production or consumption is under its jurisdiction."[47] To the panel, this suggested that Article XX was not meant to include measures aimed at the conservation of extrajurisdictional exhaustible resources.

As with Article XX(b), the panel also found that the measures in question — even assuming that trade measures with an extrajurisdictional reach were within the scope of Article XX(g) — were too "unpredictable," from the standpoint of the conservation of exhaustible natural resources, to be considered as being "primarily aimed at the conservation of dolphins."[48] That unpredictability stemmed from the retroactive nature of the calculation of the annual allowable incidental taking of dolphin by the Mexican tuna fleet, as described above.

It should be noted that the panel relied in part on a policy argument to reject the United States submissions concerning the extrajurisdictional reach of measures taken pursuant to Article XX. The panel expressed concern that, if an extrajurisdictional scope was read into the Article XX exceptions, it would allow individual Contracting Parties unilaterally to impose their life and health protection policies or conservation policies on other Contracting

---

[45] *Ibid.*, 1620, para. 5.30. The term "primarily aimed at" stems from an earlier GATT report that had elaborated on the meaning of the terms "relating to" and "in conjunction with." See GATT, *Canada — Measures Affecting Exports of Unprocessed Herring and Salmon*, BISD (35th Supp.), adopted Mar. 22, 1988, 98.

[46] *Ibid.*, 1621, paras 5.31-5.33.

[47] *Ibid.*, para. 5.31.

[48] *Ibid.*, para. 5.33.

Parties through trade measures. Such an interpretation, the panel suggested, would mean that:

The General Agreement would then no longer constitute a multilateral framework for trade among all Contracting Parties but would provide legal security only in respect of trade between a limited number of Contracting Parties with identical internal regulations.[49]

This double fear of extrajurisdictionality and unilateralism is the underlying problem, and, it is submitted, the principal reason why the Tuna/Dolphin I panel ruled as it did, notwithstanding its efforts to clothe its conclusions in a strictly technical legal interpretation of Article XX. The fear of "unilateralism" has been one of the focal points of the debate about trade and the environment. While that fear has been severely criticized on varied grounds by many commentators,[50] it should be noted that the panel's rejection of unilateralism is also supported by several eminent trade experts and academics, and is in accord with one of the underlying policy objectives of the WTO/GATT framework of promoting multilateral solutions to international trade conflicts.[51] Unilateralism is dealt with further by the panel in Tuna/Dolphin II, although it also fails to respond fully to the need to resolve the issues in a manner that is both balanced and principled.

Finally, after having established the GATT-inconsistency of the primary embargo, the panel turned to the intermediary embargo and, using essentially the same reasons as for the primary embargo, concluded that the intermediary embargo was also inconsistent with United States' GATT obligations.

TUNA/DOLPHIN II

BACKGROUND

The second tuna/dolphin panel report was based essentially on the same facts as Tuna/Dolphin I. The report was released to the public in May 1994 by the Office of the United States Trade Representative, despite the fact that it had not yet been considered

---

49 *Ibid.*, 1620, para. 5.27.

50 See, e.g., S. Charnovitz, "Environmental Trade Measures: Multilateral or Unilateral?" (1993) 23 Env'l Pol'y & L. 154 at 154, col. 1, who has written that "the choice between multilateralism and unilateralism is, in many respects, a false one." See also B. Anderson, "Unilateral Trade Measures and Environmental Protection Policy" (1993) 66 Temple L. Rev. 751 at 784.

51 See, e.g., Jackson, *supra* note 9, at 1241.

by the GATT Council. The Tuna/Dolphin II report was the result of a complaint filed jointly by the European Community (EC) and the Netherlands (on behalf of the Dutch Antilles) in GATT concerning the intermediary embargo imposed by the United States on tuna products from Contracting Parties that imported tuna originating in Mexico. At one point, twenty countries, including Canada, were targetted by the embargo. The EC brought its complaint when it became clear that for political reasons Mexico would not push for the adoption of the first tuna/dolphin panel report in the GATT Council.[52]

ARTICLE III.4 AND ARTICLE XI

Unlike the situation in Tuna/Dolphin I, Article III.4 did not figure prominently in the arguments before the Tuna/Dolphin II panel, although the panel addressed the provision at length in its findings. The United States, having lost its argument on Article III in Tuna/Dolphin I, chose not to pursue that issue and once again did not put forward any submissions on Article XI. Instead, it focused its efforts on the Article XX exceptions. The EC essentially repeated the Tuna/Dolphin I panel's interpretation of Article III — a submission the second panel had no trouble accepting without apparent critical analysis. Consequently, the panel found that, "Article III calls for a comparison between the treatment accorded to domestic and imported like *products*, not for a comparison of the policies or practices of the country of origin with those of the country of importation."[53] Examining the measures in question, the panel concluded that:

[T]he [U.S.] import embargoes distinguished between tuna products according to harvesting practices and tuna import policies of the exporting countries; that the measures imposed by the United States in respect of domestic tuna similarly distinguished between tuna and tuna products according to tuna harvesting methods; and that none of these practices,

---

52 Mexico decided not to press for the adoption of the report because at the time it was engaged in NAFTA negotiations, and it feared that United States environmental groups would pressure Congress to reject any deal if the Tuna/Dolphin I panel report was officially adopted by the GATT Council. In fact, following the release of the panel report in Tuna/Dolphin I, Mexico was one of the parties to a multilateral agreement to take steps to protect dolphins in the ETP. See *Agreement of June 1992 for the Reduction of Dolphin Mortality in the Eastern Pacific Ocean*, reprinted in (1994) 33 I.L.M. 936. See also Charnovitz, *supra* note 50, at 154, col. 2.

53 Tuna/Dolphin II, *supra* note 12 at 889, para. 5.8 [emphasis in original].

policies and methods could have any impact on the inherent character of tuna as a product.[54]

As was mentioned earlier, this view of the scope of Article III, which will be examined in detail below, has been criticized.

Like its predecessor in Tuna/Dolphin I, the panel found without any difficulty that the United States import embargo violated the Article XI.1 proscription of quantitative restrictions.

ARTICLE XX — NEW ARGUMENTS, NEW REASONS, OLD RESULTS

The arguments in the Tuna/Dolphin II proceedings focused almost exclusively on Article XX,[55] foreshadowing the probability that it is within Article XX that changes to the GATT are most likely to occur in terms of accommodating environmental concerns.[56] The European Community argued that the measures did not fit within the scope of the general exceptions in Article XX for two main reasons. First, the EC relied on the findings of the Tuna/Dolphin I panel report that Articles XX(b) and XX(g) did not cover measures with an extrajurisdictional scope.[57] Second, the EC argued that, regardless of the extrajurisdictional element, the United States measures could not be said to be "necessary" within the meaning of Article XX(b)[58] or "primarily aimed at" the conservation of an exhaustible natural resource within the meaning of Article XX(g).[59]

---

[54] *Ibid.*, 889-90, para. 5.9.

[55] The United States also sought to rely on Art. XX(d) in its arguments for upholding the intermediary embargo, but the panel found that Art. XX(d) was only available if the laws or regulations (in this case the regulation mandating the primary embargo) that formed the basis for the impugned measures were otherwise consistent with GATT. Because the panel had found that the primary embargo violated Art. XI, it found that Art. XX(d) arguments were not available to the United States. See *Ibid.*, 898, paras 5.40-5.41.

[56] See, e.g., D. Esty, *Greening the GATT: Trade, Environment, and the Future* (Washington, DC: Institute for International Economics, 1994).

[57] Tuna/Dolphin II, *supra* note 12 at 853, para. 3.15 *et passim.*

[58] *Ibid.*, 871, para. 3.75. According to the Community, the United States had failed to exhaust other options reasonably available to it to achieve its policy goal through means consistent with GATT, such as an international agreement. Furthermore, it was not "necessary" to protect dolphins because the number of incidental dolphin deaths represented "much less than 1 percent of the total dolphin population in the eastern tropical Pacific."

[59] *Ibid.*, 867, para. 3.53. The Community cited the "unpredictable conditions" caused by the uncertainty of the actual United States rates of incidental dolphin

In its submissions on the Article XX exceptions, the United States focused on both technical legal arguments and statutory interpretation, as well as on policy considerations relating to the growing importance of environmental protection and resource conservation efforts on both a national and global scale.[60] The difficult hurdle the United States faced, and which ultimately it could not overcome with the possible exception of the extrajurisdictionality question, was the reasoning and conclusions of the panel in Tuna/Dolphin I. The United States placed much emphasis on the extrajurisdictionality argument in its submissions to the Tuna/Dolphin II panel[61] and succeeded in convincing the panel that the Tuna/Dolphin I panel had indeed made a mistake.[62] Unfortunately for the United States, that success proved to be insufficient. In the end, the Tuna/Dolphin II panel reached the same conclusion as the Tuna/Dolphin I panel — that the United States measures did not fit within the scope of the Article XX general exceptions — although it did so via a somewhat different route.

In evaluating the arguments of the parties with respect to Article XX, the Tuna/Dolphin II panel introduced a three-step analysis.[63] It first examined whether the stated policy goal of the measure fell within the scope of Article XX exception. Then, the panel considered whether the measure itself fit within the scope of either Article XX(b) or XX(g). If it passed the first two steps, the measure was to be tested to determine whether it conformed with the preamble of Article XX.

Contrary to the findings in Tuna/Dolphin I, the second panel found that Article XX could, in principle, accommodate measures that extended beyond the jurisdiction of the country taking the measures, so that the natural resource sought to be conserved, or the animal life or health sought to be protected, could be located outside the territory of the regulating state.[64] The panel first noted

---

deaths in determining the allowable Mexican rates, as precluding the possibility that the measures could be "primarily aimed" at the conservation of exhaustible natural resources. The Community also questioned whether dolphins could even be considered as a natural resource "in any economic sense of the word" (*ibid.* at 867, para. 3.52).

[60] *Ibid.*, 852-73, paras 3.7-3.83.

[61] *Ibid.*, 853-61, paras 3.15-3.34.

[62] *Ibid.*, 893, para. 5.20, and at 896, para. 5.33.

[63] *Ibid.*, 890-91, para. 5.12.

[64] *Ibid.*, 892-93, para. 5.20.

that there was nothing in Article XX itself that indicated a limitation
on the location of either the "exhaustible natural resource" or the
"human, animal or plant life and health" sought to be protected.[65]
The panel then pointed to other provisions within Article XX to
demonstrate that there was no absolute proscription on measures
related to "things or actions outside the territorial jurisdiction of the
party taking the measure."[66] The panel concluded that there was no
reason to limit the application of either Article XX(b) or Article
XX(g) to the territory of the party imposing the measure.[67] The
panel's findings also seem to imply that the measures could extend
to "exhaustible natural resources" or "human, animal or plant life
and health" located not only extrajurisdictionally, but also within the
territory of another country, because the panel did not draw any
distinction between extrajurisdictionality and extraterritoriality in its
conclusions that Article XX did not place limitations on the geographical scope of the impugned trade measures.

The panel also found, however, in the second step of its analysis,
that the United States measures could not be considered as "relating to" the conservation of exhaustible natural resources because
they were not "primarily aimed" at such an objective.[68] This conclusion was based on the panel's assessment that the measures in
question could only achieve their intended effect[69] if they were
followed by changes in the policies and practices of third countries

---

[65] *Ibid.*, 891, para. 5.15.

[66] *Ibid.*, para. 5.16.

[67] *Ibid.*, 892-93, para. 5.20.

[68] A previous GATT panel had interpreted the "relating to" and "in conjunction
with" requirements in Art. XX(g) as meaning "primarily aimed" at the conservation of the resource, and "primarily aimed" at rendering effective the restrictions
on domestic production or consumption. See the GATT panel report, *Canada —
Measures Affecting the Exports of Unprocessed Herring and Salmon*, BISD (35th Supp.),
adopted Mar. 22, 1988, 98 at 114, para. 4.6. [hereinafter the *Herring/Salmon*
case] The panel in Tuna/Dolphin II, following the lead of the panel in Tuna/
Dolphin I, adopted this interpretation. See *ibid.*, 893, para. 5.22.

[69] The Tuna/Dolphin II panel found that "primarily aimed" meant not only the
objective of the measure in question, but also its effect. In other words, a
measure could only be considered "primarily aimed" at the conservation of a
resource if it was effective. It may be inferred, however, from the panel's
remarks about the effectiveness of the measure having to rely on other countries changing their policies and practices, that the panel did not believe that
the dramatic decline in the incidence of dolphin mortality in the ETP since the
inception of the United States measures could be a true indicator of the
effectiveness of the measure by itself: *Ibid.*, 893, para. 5.22.

from which the tuna was originally exported.[70] The panel then resorted to the same policy argument used by the panel in Tuna/ Dolphin I to make the dispositive finding that:

> [M]easures taken so as to force other countries to change their policies, and that were effective only if such changes occurred, could not be primarily aimed at either the conservation of an exhaustible natural resource, or at rendering effective restrictions on domestic production or consumption, in the meaning of Article XX(g).[71]

Finally, it should also be observed that the Tuna/Dolphin II panel did not, in the light of its conclusion on the second step of its three-pronged test, go on to consider in detail whether the measures in question would have met the requirements found in the preamble to Article XX.

TUNA/DOLPHIN I AND TUNA/DOLPHIN II: A MISSED OPPORTUNITY?

ARTICLE III

The central concern expressed by environmentalists concerning Article III relates to the Tuna/Dolphin I panel's rejection of the relevance of processing and production methods (PPMs) in determining the "likeness" of a product for regulatory purposes.[72] It has been argued that there is nothing in the GATT to support a finding that Article III refers only to the regulation of the product itself, and that it was open to the two panels to find that PPMs are a valid criterion on which to determine the likeness of products in cases of products involving environmentally damaging processing and production methods.[73]

It should be noted that PPMs have not been ruled to be inappropriate means to establish "likeness" in all cases. In fact, PPMs have been used as the basis for determining likeness in cases involving food and sanitary standards, for the reason that it is not always

---

[70] *Ibid.*, 893-94, paras 5.23-5.24.

[71] *Ibid.*, 894, para. 5.27.

[72] See, e.g., H.L. Thaggart, "A Closer Look at the Tuna-Dolphin Case: 'Like Products' and 'Extrajurisdictionality' in the Trade and Environment Context" in P. Demaret et al. (eds), *Trade and the Environment: The Search for Balance*, Vol. 1, 69 (London: Cameron May, 1994).

[73] See, however, Jackson, *supra* note 9 at 1242-44, who says that the rejection of PPMs can be inferred from GATT as a whole, and on the basis of policy considerations.

possible to determine whether a product meets a standard by examining the product itself. In those situations, the production or processing method has been examined as an indicator of whether the resulting product characteristics will meet sanitary or health standards. These types of PPMs must be distinguished from those that cannot affect the characteristics of the product itself. One commentator[74] has argued that the Tuna/Dolphin I panel declared the use of all PPMs irrelevant in the determination of "likeness" under Article III, and expressed the fear that, "if Article III cannot justify regulations regarding a method of production, then a nation may be forced to accept products that it believes are chemically or morally tainted."[75] This view of the panel's reasoning is mistaken. The panel emphasized that "likeness" is not affected by a PPM that cannot possibly affect the characteristics of the product, as such.[76] It did not say that PPMs are never relevant in establishing "likeness" for the purposes of Article III.

In the eyes of the panel, the PPM could not be considered a product standard because it did not relate to the final characteristics of the product itself.[77] Because the United States measure was not considered a product standard, Article III was not relevant to determining the GATT legality of that measure. Critics of the ruling assert that there is no intrinsic reason why PPMs[78] cannot be used to determine likeness. They point to the flexible, case-by-case approach taken by GATT panels in the past when faced with "likeness" issues and argue that products manufactured or harvested using different PPMs may not be "like products," at least in the eyes of consumers.[79] Furthermore, it is argued, there are other examples of the use of non-product-related factors to differentiate between products.[80]

---

[74] See Charnovitz, *supra* note 4 at 10573.

[75] *Ibid.*

[76] The panel stated that "Article III covers only those measures that are applied to the product as such." A PPM-based standard that relates directly to product characteristics meets this requirement. See Tuna/Dolphin I, *supra* note 2, at 1618, para. 5.14.

[77] Tuna/Dolphin I, *ibid.*

[78] For the remainder of this article, the term PPMs will refer to non-product-characteristic-based production and processing methods; that is, PPMs that do not affect the final characteristics of a product.

[79] See Charnovitz, *supra* note 4 at 10577.

[80] *Ibid.*

It is true that there is no clear precedent for rejecting PPMs as a valid criterion for determining "likeness."[81] Moreover, despite the efforts by the tuna/dolphin panels to "read" such an exclusion into the language of Article III, it could be argued that the force of the panels' logic was questionable.[82] In future cases, it is not inconceivable that methods of production should be given consideration in deciding on the likeness of two products. It is submitted that it would not have contravened previous GATT decisions for the panel to have accepted the United States' argument that the trade measure was an internal regulation imposing a product standard, but also to have found that, in this case, the difference in the harvesting methods did not make the imported and domestic tuna different products for the purposes of national treatment under Article III.4. Such a ruling would have preserved the outcome of the dispute but maintained flexibility for future GATT panels to examine other production and processing methods in the context of an Article III dispute. Of course, GATT panel reports are not binding on future panels, and, in this case at least, the panel report has not even been adopted by the GATT Council, so perhaps there is no formal need to preserve such flexibility. Yet, GATT panels tend to rely on past panel decisions for principles of interpretation, as demonstrated by the Tuna/Dolphin II panel's adoption of the findings in Tuna/Dolphin I concerning Article III and PPMs.

There is, however, a compelling policy reason for rejecting the use of PPMs as a valid criterion in establishing the "likeness" of two products for the purposes of Article III in the two tuna/dolphin cases. It stems from the role of the GATT in international trade and the objectives of the Contracting Parties in establishing the GATT. By allowing the consideration of PPMs as potential determinants of the "likeness" of products for the purposes of Article III, the GATT would improve the ability of Contracting Parties to devise trade measures that can serve as protectionist non-tariff barriers to trade, while making it more difficult for GATT panels to find such trade

[81] Much effort has gone into an examination of GATT negotiating history to establish whether the contracting parties intended Art. III to encompass the use of PPMs, but that examination has yielded little direct evidence that PPMs were intended to be included. Conversely, there is little direct evidence that they were meant to be excluded. See Charnovitz, *ibid.*, 10577; but see also Jackson, *supra* note 9.

[82] See Charnovitz, *supra* note 32; Thaggart, *supra* note 72; but see also Sorsa, *supra* note 8, for a contrary view.

measures GATT-illegal.[83] As has been observed elsewhere,[84] environmental trade measures are notoriously difficult to expose as being protectionist in their intent. Allowing PPMs — particularly on the basis that they have different environmental impacts — to become acceptable criteria for differentiating between two otherwise "like products" will make it far easier for countries to select any stage or aspect of a manufacturing or processing method of a given product, assert that it has a detrimental environmental impact, and then claim that its trade measure does not discriminate because the domestic "like" product is produced in a slightly different manner. A GATT panel faced with such an argument would have no criteria at its disposal for evaluating such an argument, provided that it could be demonstrated that there was some environmental impact associated with the PPM. This would be a step backwards for the trading system because it would ask panels to evaluate factual findings and arguments relating to environmental protection that go far beyond the GATT itself.[85] Such an inquiry would, at the very least, fit better into the general exceptions found in Article XX.

"Green traders"[86] have proposed two ways in which the use of a PPM could potentially be put forward as a valid criterion in determining "likeness." The first accepts consumer preference as a valid means to establish the likeness of two products.[87] For example, if consumers demonstrate a marked preference for "dolphin-safe" tuna over other tuna, it is argued that the two are not "like" products and therefore not subject to Article III national treatment.

---

83 This argument has not been adequately addressed by proponents of the inclusion of PPMs as relevant criteria in the "likeness" determination under Art. III. See, e.g., Jackson, *supra* note 9 at 1242-43. Charnovitz acknowledges this difficulty but does not address it in detail; see Charnovitz, *ibid.*, 322.

84 See Esty, *supra* note 56 at 24.

85 Rejecting PPMs as determinants of "likeness" may make it more difficult in some cases for GATT/WTO members to protect the environment. This is the fundamental tension between GATT and environmental protection. Also, with the new dispute settlement mechanism, which includes the possibility of using expert advisory bodies to assist panels in making factual determinations, such an exercise may be made simpler. This fact, however, does not alter the problem of the vacuum that exists in the rules for adjudicating these conflicts.

86 In using this term, I am referring to those academics and commentators who favour interpreting GATT to make it more amenable to the perceived needs of those who are making efforts to protect the natural environment.

87 Charnovitz, *supra* note 4 at 10577 asserts that consumer attitudes affect the "likeness" determination.

Yet, consumer preference is not immutable,[88] and surely the two products could still be considered as substitutable and therefore competing. In that sense, consumer preference cannot be said to alter "the inherent character of tuna as a product."[89]

The second potential use of PPMs in determining likeness focuses more directly on the environmental impact of the production/processing/harvesting of the product in question. Although the nature and quality of the imported product itself may not be affected, environmentalists argue that, as a matter of policy, the differential environmental impact of the production processes of the imported product and the competing domestic product should be used to determine "likeness" for the purposes of Article III. This approach, however, creates a couple of problems that would be very difficult to resolve.

The first problem relates to the economic theory of comparative advantage on which the merits of international trade are based. That theory holds that, because nations are different in their characteristics, including natural resource endowment, social structure and policies, skills, labour force, and the like, they differ in their abilities to produce certain goods.[90] The comparative advantage that one nation has in the production of a particular good encourages that nation to specialize and to trade for other goods that it needs. Specialization in production among nations leads to greater efficiency and greater overall wealth. Economists argue that environmental and natural resource policies are also factors that contribute to comparative advantage. Thus, to allow trade measures that seek to neutralize the comparative advantage caused by environmental and natural resource policies would negate the natural efficiency of the trading system and, in the long

---

88 If "likeness" is to be determined by consumer preference, this creates the prospect of a single imported product changing from being "like" to "unlike" and *vice versa*, as consumer preferences shift over time and for reasons that may be completely unrelated to environmental factors.

89 See Tuna/Dolphin II, *supra* note 12 at 889-90, para. 5.9.

90 For a general discussion, see P. R. Krugman and M. Obstfeld, *International Economics: Theory and Policy* (Boston: Scott, Foresman and Co., 1988). For a critique of the role of the doctrine of comparative advantage as a justification for the treatment given to ETMs by the GATT, see W. J. Snape III & N. B. Lefkovitz, "Searching for GATT's Environmental *Miranda*: Are 'Process Standards' Getting 'Due Process?'" (1994) 27 Cornell Int'l L.J. 777 at 799-803.

run argue economists,[91] actually lead to greater damage to the natural environment.

The second problem relates to the determination of whether a particular PPM should be considered valid as a criterion for differentiating between two otherwise competing products. Surely not all PPMs, regardless of the context, can be accepted as a valid basis for differentiating between products. Such a view could lead to the massive introduction of PPM-based trade measures as justification for avoiding the national treatment obligation of Article III. Perhaps we can say that only environmentally-related PPMs should be considered as potentially valid criteria for determining "likeness." But even then, there must be some form of a test to establish whether the environmentally-related PPM has an environmental impact of sufficient significance to merit being viewed as a relevant criterion for demonstrating product differentiation.

Assume, for example, that the environmental impact of the Mexican PPM (setting on dolphins to catch tuna), which was the basis for the United States' import embargo, could be viewed, in principle, as a valid criterion for determining "likeness" in the context of Article III, because the incidental taking of dolphins is generally accepted as a PPM-based environmental impact. What factors could or should a GATT panel rely on to accept it as a relevant criterion for allowing different treatment for Mexican tuna (or European tuna, for that matter) by the United States? The factors that come readily to mind, given that the principal policy reason for accepting PPMs as relevant criteria is the protection of the environment, are the need for dolphins to be protected and the efficacy of the trade measure in achieving that goal. But what about the protectionist or discriminatory effects of the measure? Should these factors be weighed against the environmental objective and/or efficacy? In the case of the tuna/dolphin dispute, it was not at all clear whether dolphins needed protection, either because they were not endangered or because the dolphin mortality rate had already fallen significantly in response to the measures imposed by the United

---

91 See, e.g., GATT, *Trade and the Environment*, GATT Doc. 1529, Feb. 13, 1992, reprinted in GATT, *International Trade*, Vol. 1, 90-91 (Geneva, 1992). An important distinction must be made, however, between environmental impacts with purely local effects and environmental impacts with cross-border or "spill-over" effects, or global effects. See, e.g., J. Bhagwati, "Trade and the Environment: The False Conflict" in D. Zaelke et al. (eds), *Trade and the Environment: Law, Economics and Policy* 159 (Washington, DC: Island Press, 1993).

States on its domestic tuna fleet.[92] It could be argued that the environmental objective in that case was less than compelling, which is precisely what the European Community asserted.[93]

But what about other environmental "crises," such as global warming, where the case for urgent measures may be stronger? How would a panel establish the validity and/or urgency of the environmental objective? And how would it establish the efficacy of the trade measure in achieving the objective?[94] Should the determination of "likeness" also be subject to some form of a proportionality test weighing the environmental impact against the benefits of the products involved? These extremely difficult methodological questions are not answered by environmentalists, who at the same time criticize GATT tuna/dolphin panels for failing to introduce completely new criteria and requirements into an Article III evaluation of a non-tariff barrier to trade. Surely, it cannot be left to a GATT panel to introduce a whole new approach to interpreting the meaning and scope of Article III.[95]

For these reasons, while it may be conceivable for PPMs, in theory, to have some relevance in determining the "likeness" of products for the purposes of determining whether the "national treatment" obligation in Article III is being violated, the inherent difficulties in devising an appropriate "test" for when and how PPMs should be relevant and compelling factors in an Article III

---

[92] See the arguments of the European Community in Tuna/Dolphin II, cited *infra* note 93. If the issue does not turn on conservation, it could be characterized as a competitiveness problem, with United States tuna fishermen not wanting to compete with the Mexican "free riders." Yet, how detrimental is the competitiveness factor if studies show that environmental compliance is, on average, 1-2 per cent of production costs? Can it be demonstrated that the United States tuna fleet incurs significantly higher costs as a result of having to employ different tuna fishing methods?

[93] Tuna/Dolphin II, *supra* note 12 at 871, para. 3.75.

[94] See, e.g., B. F. Chase, "Tropical Forests and Trade Policy: The Legality of Unilateral Attempts to Promote Sustainable Development Under the GATT" (1994) 17 Hastings Int'l & Comp. L. Rev. 349, who, in discussing the Austrian effort to persuade Malaysia to develop a sustainable development approach to its forestry industry, brings out effectively the complexities inherent in countries trying to achieve global environmental objectives through unilateral trade measures.

[95] Contrast this with Steve Charnovitz's argument, *supra* note 4 at 10576, that GATT panelists should not be able to rewrite the rules to match their individual policy preferences. The question arises, whose policy preferences should they rely on when "rewriting" the rules?

argument — whether that test is formulated by a GATT panel or by
the WTO General Council — make it highly inadvisable, if not
practically impossible, for Article III to play a significant role in any
"shift" in the interpretation of the GATT to accommodate the use
of trade measures for environmental purposes. In that sense, both
of the GATT panels in the tuna/dolphin disputes reached the right
conclusion in disposing of the Article III arguments put forward by
the United States. At the same time, it is perhaps regrettable that
little flexibility was preserved for future panels to re-examine a PPM
argument under different circumstances.

ARTICLE XX

Most commentators who favour an adjustment in the GATT to
take account of environmental concerns have focused on the potential for Article XX to be used as a means to accommodate the GATT
and trade measures with environmental objectives,[96] and often it is
the two exceptions in Article XX(b) and (g) that have been given
attention.[97] Unfortunately, because Article XX has not been dealt
with in many GATT panel reports, there is very little material to
draw on in trying to establish definitively the meaning and scope of
the Article XX exceptions.

The GATT panel in Tuna/Dolphin II used a three-step approach
in examining the conformity of United States trade measures with
the Article XX exceptions. It first considered whether the policy
behind the measure "fell within the range of policies"[98] aimed at
conserving natural resources or protecting human, animal, or plant
life and health. Second, it determined whether the measure itself
met the criteria set out in either of the two exceptions. Third, it was
supposed to establish whether the requirements of the Article XX
preamble were met. Because the panel found that the United States
measure did not meet the requirements in the second step,
however, it never examined whether the requirements of the preamble had been met. This omission is regrettable because the
preamble to Article XX may potentially play a more significant role

---

[96] See, e.g., Charnovitz, *supra* note 7; Esty, *supra* note 56.

[97] It has also been proposed by some commentators that an explicit exception
should be added that refers to measures relating to the environment, as well as
an exception for trade measures relating to an international environmental
agreement.

[98] Tuna/Dolphin II, *supra* note 12 at 890, para. 5.12.

in ensuring that protectionist trade measures disguised as ETMs are rejected. This potential will be discussed further below.

Article XX(b)

Article XX(b) provides for an exception to the normal GATT obligations for measures "necessary to protect human, animal or plant life or health." For the GATT panels that have examined this exception,[99] the key issue has been the definition of "necessary."

The first GATT panel to consider the meaning and scope of the word "necessary" had been asked to examine the use of a trade measure enacted by the United States to enforce its patent laws.[100] The United States sought to rely on Article XX(d), which also uses the word "necessary."[101] In its report, the panel found that:

[A] contracting party cannot justify a measure inconsistent with another GATT provision as "necessary" in terms of Article XX(d) *if an alternative measure which it could reasonably be expected to employ and which is not inconsistent with other GATT provisions is available to it.* By the same token, *in cases where a measure consistent with other GATT provisions is not reasonably available, a contracting party is bound to use, among the measures reasonably available to it, that which entails the least degree of inconsistency with other GATT provisions* [emphasis added].[102]

That definition of "necessary" was adopted by another GATT panel, but in the context of Article XX(b).[103] That panel saw no reason why the meaning of "necessary" in the two provisions

---

[99] Charnovitz has examined the historical background of the clause in his article, "Exploring the Environmental Exceptions in GATT Art. XX" (1991) 25:5 J. of World Trade 37. He argues that not only does the historical record support the view that Art. XX was meant to include ETMs — as opposed to sanitary measures only — but also that GATT panels have put an unduly restrictive meaning on Art. XX(b), thus making it far too difficult to justify even legitimate ETMs as allowable exceptions to the GATT. Professor Jackson takes issue with Charnovitz's reliance on drafting and negotiating history, describing these tools as merely, "ancillary means of interpreting treaties": see Jackson, *supra* note 9 at 1241.

[100] GATT, *United States — Section 337 of the Tariff Act of 1930*, BISD (36th Supp.), adopted Nov. 7, 1989, 345 [hereinafter the *Section 337* case].

[101] Art. XX(d) relates to measures that are "necessary to secure compliance laws or regulations which are not inconsistent with provisions of this Agreement, including those relating to . . . the protection of patents."

[102] The *Section 337* case, *supra* note 100 at 392, para. 5.26 (emphasis added).

[103] GATT, *Thailand — Restrictions on Importation of and Internal taxes on Cigarettes*, BISD (37th Supp.), adopted Nov. 7, 1990, 200 at 223, para. 74 [hereinafter the *Thai Cigarette* case].

should be different, given that the objectives of the two provisions were identical, even if the specific subject matter of the trade measures in question was different.[104]

This "narrow" approach to Article XX(b) has been severely criticized on a number of grounds, including the absence of clear intention among GATT Contracting Parties to define "necessary" in those terms and the difficulty in going from a theoretical formulation to practical application.[105] While it may be true that the theoretical formulation is complex, however, it is surely not an argument for the interpretation being wrong.

On the contrary, the theoretical formulation of the meaning of the word "necessary" makes sense if one considers that these are exceptions, and as such are to be construed narrowly,[106] without at the same time making them completely inaccessible. Additionally, as Anne McCaskill has put it, "[I]t is not clear why this [definition of 'necessary'] should be considered an unreasonable condition,"[107] because it surely requires a state seeking to justify the ETM to choose, from among the methods available to it, the one that is the least GATT-inconsistent. As expressed in the *Section 337* case, the definition does not require the state to compromise its chosen level of protection, and there is no proportionality test required to weigh the objective of the ETM against its impact.[108]

---

104 *Ibid.*

105 See, e.g., Charnovitz, *supra* note 99 at 49.

106 See Tuna/Dolphin I, *supra* note 2 at 1619, para. 5.22, citing two previous GATT panel reports that had been adopted: *Canada — Administration of the Foreign Investment Review Act*, BISD (30th Supp.), adopted Feb. 7, 1984, 140 at 164, para. 5.20, and *United States — Section 337 of the Tariff Act*, BISD (36th Supp.), adopted Nov. 7, 1989, 345 at 393, para. 5.27.

107 A. McCaskill, "Dangerous Liaisons: The World Trade Organization and the Environmental Agenda" in K. H. Christie (ed.), *New Directions: Environment, Labour and the International Trade Agenda* 93 at 97 (Ottawa: Carleton University Press, 1995). After all, she continued, "it is difficult to understand why it should be permissible to apply measures that are *more* trade restrictive than necessary" (emphasis in the original).

108 In the *Section 337* case, *supra* note 100 at 393, para. 5.26, the panel made it clear that Art. XX(d) (and by extension XX(b)) did not require the GATT member to change, "its desired level of protection of [the] law [in question]." The test, as enunciated in that panel report, does not require a proportionality test to weight the costs against the benefits; it merely requires that the measure chosen be carefully tailored so as to achieve the objective without unnecessarily restricting trade.

The key to the "necessary" test, however, lies in its application by the GATT panel, and that is where both tuna/dolphin panels appear to have run into problems. In fact, both panels introduced new elements to the test without actually explaining those elements in a broader sense, and neither based its conclusions regarding the GATT consistency of the United States trade measure on a true application of the test as set out in the *Section 337* and *Thai Cigarette* cases cited above.

In Tuna/Dolphin I, the panel based its reasoning primarily on the "extrajurisdictional" nature of the import ban caused by the focus on the production and processing methods of the Mexican fishing fleet. For that panel, the issue turned on whether the scope of Article XX(b) included measures with an extrajurisdictional element. As noted above, the panel found that it did not include these measures because to allow extrajurisdictional measures would lead to countries taking unilateral measures to impose their own policies on other GATT members.

Almost as an afterthought, the panel also remarked that, regardless of the extrajurisdictionality issue, the United States did not meet the "necessity" requirement because it had not "exhausted all options reasonably available to it to pursue its dolphin conservation objectives through measures consistent with the General Agreement, in particular through the negotiation of international cooperative arrangements."[109] Aside from the questionable accuracy of that statement, given the efforts made by the United States to develop an international framework to protect dolphins since the early 1970s,[110] it appears to open the door to the possibility that ETMs based on international agreements will receive more sympathetic treatment before GATT panels, an assertion with which other GATT commentators have not agreed.[111] The GATT

---

[109] Tuna/Dolphin I, *supra* note 2 at 1620, para. 5.28.

[110] See Charnovitz, *supra* note 4 at 10571.

[111] In fact, the GATT itself, in its much maligned report on trade and the environment, *supra* note 94 at 24-25, appears to reject the possibility of even ETMs in multilateral international agreements meeting GATT requirements, but later in its report it seems to take a more positive view of ETMs as instruments for achieving international environmental objectives: *supra* note 94 at 35-36. Also, the now defunct GATT Group on Environmental Measures and International Trade, in its second report to the GATT Council, also seems to express reservations about the GATT-consistency of ETMs in international environmental agreements, although its tone is more cautious and ambivalent. See

panel should have explored more vigorously the factual issue of whether the prospects for an international environmental agreement were realistic, and if not, whether the United States measure truly represented the least GATT-inconsistent measure available. This exercise became superfluous, however, in the light of the policy imperative identified by the panel of not allowing unilateral trade measures with extrajurisdictional dimensions because of their potential impact on the multilateral trading system as a whole. The point is that the introduction of such a policy imperative was inserted into the factually-based "necessary" test devised by previous panels.

The "extrajurisdictionality" limitation imposed by the Tuna/ Dolphin I panel has rightly been challenged by a number of commentators[112] as having no basis in either the GATT text itself or in its negotiating history. Furthermore, it is contradicted by the existence of an extrajurisdictional element in other provisions within Article XX.[113]

What was more disturbing about the reasoning of the Tuna/ Dolphin I panel was its failure to examine more closely the elements of the "necessary" test. Clearly, the panel feared that opening up the Article XX exceptions to unilateral trade measures that extended beyond national borders would have a negative impact on GATT as a multilateral forum for negotiations. If individual countries could enact trade measures — ostensibly for environmental or conservation purposes — that were aimed at the policies and practices of other countries, stronger GATT members, such as the United States or the European Union, would use their economic leverage to bypass negotiations at a multilateral level.[114] These considerations are, however, more policy-oriented and should not form part of a "necessary" test that, as it was enunciated in previous panel reports, is factual in nature.

GATT, *Report by Ambassador H. Ukawa (Japan), Chairman of the Group on Environmental Measures and International Trade, to the 49th Session of the Contracting Parties,* Doc. L/7402, Feb. 2, 1994 at 3-8.

[112] See, e.g., McDonald, *supra* note 4, at 432-33; P. L. Lallas et al., "Environmental Protection and International Trade: Toward Mutually Supportive Rules and Policies" (1992) 16 Harv. Env'l L. Rev. 271 at 284-85.

[113] See, e.g., Art. XX(e), which allows measures, "relating to the products of prison labour."

[114] Arguably, that is what the United States achieved, because Mexico decided not to pursue the adoption of the panel report in the GATT Council.

In Tuna/Dolphin II, the extrajurisdictionality issue was quickly laid to rest, with the panel flatly contradicting the findings of the previous panel that the Article XX exceptions did not allow for measures with an extrajurisdictional scope. The panel considered the negotiating history of the provision, the wording of the article as a whole, and the findings of two previous GATT panels,[115] and concluded that trade measures with an extrajurisdictional component fell within the range of policies covered by Article XX.[116]

Next, the panel referred to the "necessary" test established in the two GATT reports cited above,[117] but it did not go on to consider whether the United States trade measure was in fact the least GATT-inconsistent measure reasonably available. Instead, it focused on the "effectiveness" of the measure in terms of its objective — dolphin conservation — and concluded that the measure could not, by itself, achieve that objective. It could only achieve that objective if the countries affected by the import ban changed their tuna-fishing practices and policies.[118] It then noted that Article XX(b) was not explicit about allowing measures to be effective that required other countries to change their policies and practices, and remarked that Article XX, as an exception to GATT obligations, must be construed narrowly "and in a way that preserves the basic objectives and principles of the General Agreement."[119] This finding led the panel to the conclusion that measures that rely on the targeted countries changing their practices and policies in order to achieve their objectives could not be said to be "necessary," because they would seriously impair the objectives of the General Agreement.[120]

---

115 See *Canada — Measures Affecting the Exports of Unprocessed Herring and Salmon,* BISD (35th Supp.), adopted Mar. 22, 1988, 98; and *United States — Prohibitions of Imports of Tuna and Tuna Products from Canada,* BISD (29th Supp.), adopted Feb. 22, 1982, 91.

116 Tuna/Dolphin II, *supra* note 12 at 893, paras 5.20, 5.33. Curiously, the panel, agreeing that Art. XX(b) was wide enough to cover extrajurisdictional measures, made reference to the United States pursuing its policy within its jurisdiction and over its nationals and vessels. This would clearly be irrelevant in this context, given that the focus of the measure was the conservation of dolphins located outside United States jurisdiction.

117 *Supra* notes 100 and 103.

118 Tuna/Dolphin II, *supra* note 12 at 897, paras 5.36, 5.37.

119 *Ibid.,* para. 5.38.

120 *Ibid.* at 897-98, paras 5.38, 5.39.

While the Tuna/Dolphin II panel appeared to dismiss the extra-jurisdictionality argument, the wording of the panel is confusing in that it refers to countries regulating their own nationals outside the national territory. Does this mean that the extrajurisdictional quality of a trade measure is only consistent with the Article XX exceptions to the extent that it is limited to the activities of its own nationals? Such an interpretation would seem to render the extra-jurisdictional aspects of the exceptions moot.

The panel's approach also fails to address the criteria set out in the "necessary" test in the *Section 337* panel report. The panel did not actually examine whether the measure was the least GATT-inconsistent measure available that would also accomplish the underlying objective — namely, dolphin conservation.

While fears over the negative impact of the use of unilateral trade measures are valid and important from the point of view of preserving the multilateral regulatory framework, the panel in Tuna/Dolphin II, like its predecessor in Tuna/Dolphin I, has muddied the waters by misapplying the "necessary" test to achieve the "right" result. By changing their focus from the issue of whether the measure in question is the least GATT-inconsistent measure available to the realm of the underlying policies of GATT in determining whether a measure is "necessary," the two tuna/dolphin panels have raised more questions than they have answered.

Article XX(g)

The problems found in the two panels' approach to Article XX(b) are also present in their respective approaches to Article XX(g). In both reports, the two panels relied substantially on the same reasons for eliminating Article XX(g) as they did for rejecting Article XX(b) as a source of legitimacy for the United States tuna import ban.

The Tuna/Dolphin I panel considered the "primarily aimed" test, but its basis for eliminating Article XX(g) as an exception for the United States trade measure was that Article XX(g), as written, did not extend to natural resources located outside the jurisdiction of the GATT member imposing the trade measure. The panel considered that a country could not readily control either production or consumption of natural resources located outside its jurisdiction. Therefore, measures that focused on resources outside national boundaries could not be "primarily aimed" at the conservation of those resources. Following this interpretation of the "primarily aimed" test, it seems that the trade measures must be considered as "primarily aimed" at domestic conservation in order to be effective. At the same time, no serious consideration was given as to whether the measures were in fact effective. In fact, of course, an extrajurisdictional measure would never be treated by a panel as "primarily aimed" at conservation, regardless of its efficacy, because the finding is based on policy grounds.

In its findings, the panel in Tuna/Dolphin II, like its predecessor, appears to have blended two concepts. The first was the policy consideration that extrajurisdictional unilateral trade measures by GATT members would lead to a form of "eco-imperialism" that could endanger the multilateral trading system. This idea was first expressed by the Tuna/Dolphin I panel. The second concept was the requirement that the measure be "primarily aimed at" conservation, first expressed by the GATT *Herring/Salmon*[121] panel and adopted by Tuna/Dolphin I.

After finding that the United States measure could only achieve its conservation objective by "forcing" other countries to change their policies and practices, the Tuna/Dolphin II panel observed that Article XX should be construed narrowly,[122] and that interpreting Article XX to allow unilateral measures would seriously impair the balance of rights and obligations among the Contracting Parties.[123] It then inserted this policy argument into the "primarily aimed" requirement and found that measures taken with the objective of forcing countries to change their policies and practices could not "be primarily aimed either at the conservation of an exhaustible natural resource or at rendering effective restrictions on domestic production or consumption, within the meaning of Article XX(g)."[124] As such, the measure did not meet an essential requirement of Article XX(g).[125] It should be noted that nowhere is

---

[121] *Supra* note 68.

[122] This interpretation is adopted from two previous GATT panel reports. See GATT panel report in *Canada — Administration of the Foreign Investment Review Act, supra* note 32 at 164, para. 5.20; GATT panel report in *United States — Section 337 of the Tariff Act of 1930*, BISD (36th Supp.), adopted Nov. 7, 1989, 345 at 393, para. 5.27.

[123] Tuna/Dolphin II, *supra* note 12 at 894, para. 5.26.

[124] *Ibid.*, para. 5.27.

[125] Although reference is made only to the panel's findings with regard to Art. XX(g), substantially the same reasoning was followed to invalidate the arguments of the United States government under the Art. XX(b) exception. See Tuna/Dolphin II, *ibid.*, 895-98, paras 5.28-5.39.

the actual impact of the trade measure in terms of dolphin conservation considered by the panel.

The panel's interpretation also must mean that the "primarily aimed at" test cannot relate solely to the objective of the trade measure, because clearly a trade measure can, from a factual viewpoint, be "primarily aimed" at the conservation of a resource while using the means of an import ban to induce exporting countries to change their environmental policies. The issue is not only the objective of the measure but its perceived efficacy, including not only whether it is contingent upon the exporting country responding appropriately, but also on whether the measure is in fact effective by itself. Yet, the Tuna/Dolphin II panel also makes it clear that, if the trade measure has an extrajurisdictional unilateral component, it will not matter how effective the measure is, because policy considerations will not allow such a measure to be considered as being "primarily aimed" at conservation.

This reasoning has confused rather than clarified the scope of the Article XX exceptions. The Tuna/Dolphin II panel appears to be allowing for measures that have an extrajurisdictional application, but not where, to be effective, they must induce other Contracting Parties to alter their environmental policies. While this interpretation is perhaps somewhat broader than that of Tuna/Dolphin I, it raises the important question of what types of measures could be considered as falling within the scope of the panel's interpretation of Articles XX(b) and XX(g). Unfortunately, the panel does not provide any illustrative assistance.

The Preamble

The preamble to Article XX reads as follows:

Subject to the requirement that such measures are not applied in a manner that would constitute a means of arbitrary or unjustifiable discrimination in countries where the same conditions prevail, or a disguised restriction on international trade, nothing in this agreement shall be construed to prevent the adoption or enforcement by any contracting party of measures.

Neither panel considered whether the United States trade measure met the requirements of the preamble or determined whether the measure constituted "a means of arbitrary or unjustifiable discrimination in countries where the same conditions prevail" or "a disguised restriction on international trade." This is unfortunate because the preamble may be the more appropriate tool to ensure that ETMs are not used as disguised protectionist trade measures. The preamble has been considered in previous GATT panel reports, and a definition of the key phrases has been established. That definition has been criticized, however, for failing to provide the type of narrow scope that has been given to the definitions of the qualifying measures themselves.[126] If Article XX represents exceptions, then the whole article, including the preamble, should be construed narrowly and strictly against the party seeking to rely on it.

In one case, a GATT panel found that, if a measure is "publicly announced" as a trade measure, it cannot be considered as a "disguised restriction" on international trade.[127] This soft approach to what constitutes a "disguised restriction" arguably makes the requirement worthless, since it is too easily met.[128] A better approach would be to treat the "disguised restriction" requirement in a similar manner as under Article III. This way, a panel will be able to use the test to distinguish between ETMs enacted for protectionist purposes or with protectionist effects and those ETMs with valid objectives and without protectionist effects.[129]

Furthermore, the requirement that the measure should not constitute an "arbitrary or unjustifiable discrimination between countries where the same conditions prevail" also has potential to be used as a check against trade measures with extrajurisdictional reach that represent a unilateral attempt by one country to impose its own environmental policies on another. The phrase could be interpreted so that such a measure would be considered "unjustifiable discrimination." This would allow GATT panels to avoid having to inject policy issues into the factual determinations associated with the "necessary" and "primarily aimed" tests under Article XX(b) and (g).

---

[126] See Charnovitz, *supra* note 98 at 47-48.

[127] See GATT, *United States — Prohibition of Imports of Tuna and Tuna Products from Canada*, BISD (29th Supp.), adopted Feb. 22, 1982, 91 at 108, para. 4.8 [hereinafter the *U.S.-Canada Tuna* case].

[128] Professor Jackson calls the preamble requirements a "softened measure of 'national treatment' and MFN obligations": see Jackson, *supra* note 9 at 1240.

[129] Charnovitz suggests that this was the original intent behind the preamble requirements when the GATT was negotiated: *supra* note 98 at 47. It also assumes that the ETMs failed the test under Article III. A PPM-based measure would probably fall into this category.

CONCLUSIONS

Although it may be said that Tuna/Dolphin II has amended the "extrajurisdictionality" element read into Articles XX(b) and (g) by the Tuna/Dolphin I panel, it cannot be said that the Tuna/Dolphin II panel report, when read as a whole, has taken us very much further down the road to a set of clear or uncontroversial principles for resolving GATT/environment conflicts when those conflicts stem from unilateral ETMs. Clearly this is a problem, given that the vast majority of ETMs are still driven by domestic considerations rather than by international negotiations. That having been said, the reasoning of the panels in the two tuna/dolphin reports does provide — though inferentially — a more coherent approach for judging the GATT-legality of ETMs that stem from international multilateral agreements.

The "failure" of the Tuna/Dolphin II panel to resolve the concerns of "green traders" does not necessarily mean that the panel's interpretation of Articles III and XX is completely wrong-headed. GATT exists to provide a regulatory framework for preventing or minimizing trade distortions brought about by discriminatory and protectionist behaviour by its member states. It was not created, nor is it equipped in terms of clear principles and rules, for adjudicating international disputes involving conflicts between environmental concerns and individual countries' trade and economic policies. While some analysts are critical of the panel's stated concern that unilateral trade measures will jeopardize the multilateral trading system — that is, the GATT framework — it must be noted that giving powerful trading states the right to use unilateral measures to achieve environmental policy goals, however worthy in the eyes of some environmentalists, may lead to, at best, environmental "vigilantism," and at worst, increased trade protectionism in the guise of ETMs, aimed at nullifying the comparative advantage enjoyed by the exporters of a given product usually coming from a developing country.

At the same time, there is clearly scope for altering GATT's approach to the two Article XX exceptions and to the requirements of the preamble, so that the nature of an inquiry into the application of GATT exceptions in the context of an ETM does not become too confused by a mix of factual elements and the policy imperatives that underlie the GATT.

Sommaire

Variations sur le même thon: la deuxième affaire Thons/Dauphins

La décision rendue par le deuxième groupe spécial du GATT dans l'affaire Thons/Dauphins fait ressortir à nouveau le soi-disant conflit entre les buts poursuivis par la libéralisation du commerce et les mesures nationales et internationales destinées à protéger l'environnement. L'auteur examine le raisonnement élaboré par le groupe spécial dans la deuxième affaire Thons/Dauphins et le compare à celui de la première affaire. Il se demande ensuite si les règles juridiques du GATT sont compatibles avec les préoccupations environnementales. Bien qu'il critique une partie du raisonnement des groupes spéciaux dans les deux affaires Thons/Dauphins, l'auteur soutient que les rapports fournissent implicitement une méthode cohérente pour évaluer, à la lumière du GATT, la légalité des mesures commerciales de nature environnementale que l'on retrouve dans plusieurs conventions multilatérales internationales.

Summary

Another Kick at the Can: Tuna/Dolphin II

The decision of the second GATT panel in the Tuna/Dolphin *dispute again focuses attention on the perceived conflict between the goals of trade liberalization and national and international efforts to protect the earth's natural environment. The author reviews the reasoning of the panel in* Tuna/Dolphin II, *compares it with that of* Tuna/Dolphin I, *and considers the adequacy of GATT law to deal with environmental concerns. Although he criticizes some of the reasoning of the panels in the two tuna/dolphin cases, the author argues that the reports do provide — though inferentially — a coherent approach for judging the GATT-legality of environmental trade measures that stem from international multilateral agreements.*

Review Article

Metamorphoses: Judge Shigeru Oda and the International Court of Justice

MICHAEL REISMAN*

L ET TWO THINGS BE SAID at the outset of the review of this
interesting and important book.[1] First, the idea for this series is
excellent and timely — truly one of those rueful "Why-didn't-
I-think-of-that?" ideas. Second, this reviewer nevertheless has many
reservations about key jurisprudential assumptions and strategic
choices that were made in developing the idea and about the ways
those assumptions and strategies have been implemented.

Two assumptions must undergird this enterprise: first, that the
unique character and "value-structure" of each judge is an important variable in the application, if not incremental formation, of
international law; and second, that the International Court is an
important institution and has played a significant role, as the title
puts it, in "the progressive development of international law." One
of the most curious features of this book is that the first assumption,
although virtually a prerequisite to judicial biography, is shared by
Professor McWhinney in a most confined and restrictive way. The
second assumption, which is legally problematic, factually doubtful,
and, in the opinion of the reviewer, corrosive of the future role of

* Hohfeld Professor of Jurisprudence, Yale Law School. The editorial assistance of
Juan Millán, Yale J.D. 1996 is gratefully acknowledged. Mahnoush H. Arsanjani,
Myres S. McDougal, Yasuaki Onuma, and Andrew Willard read early drafts and
made useful comments and criticisms. Cheryl DeFilippo supervised the prepara-
tion of the manuscript. This review was completed in November 1995. ©
Michael Reisman, 1995. All rights reserved.

1 E. McWhinney, *Judge Shigeru Oda and the Progressive Development of International
Law: Opinions (Declarations, Separate Opinions, Dissents) on the International Court of
Justice, 1976-1992*, Vol. I of *The Judges* (1993).

the Court, is embraced by Professor McWhinney here, as in his previous books,[2] as an article of faith.

Volume I of *The Judges* consists of three parts. The first part is a biography of Judge Shigeru Oda, the distinguished scholar, international practitioner, and three-term judge of the International Court of Justice, which includes an assessment of his judicial *oeuvre* and a bibliography, in English, of his principal work. The second part is a wide-ranging international constitutional law essay by Professor McWhinney that describes and analyzes in broad terms the constitutional contribution of the Court and Judge Oda's role in it. The third part provides photocopies of the texts of Judge Oda's dissenting and concurring opinions. *The Judges* initiates a series of volumes "collecting and synthesizing the opinions of leading international judges of the contemporary era who have contributed significantly to the progressive development of International Law."[3]

Given the ambitiousness of this new series, Professor McWhinney, one of the leading commentators on the work of the Court and leading champions of its expanded role, is the obvious candidate for an enterprise undertaking to create a new genre in international law. His is a challenging project, and it has its perils. The book under review, although it has many achievements, has not avoided all of them. That may be less the fault of Professor McWhinney than of certain problems that this genre will encounter in international law itself.

THE IMPORTANCE OF THE JUDGE'S PERSONALITY

Why write a biography of an international judge and why collect the judge's separate opinions? In contrast to the situation in the United States, judicial decision has always been a marginal part of the international political system. Thus, although serious and searching biographies have been written of critical international

---

[2] See e.g., E. McWhinney, *Judicial Settlement of International Disputes: Jurisdiction, Justiciability and Judicial Law-Making on the Contemporary International Court* (1991) (hereinafter McWhinney, *Judicial Settlement*); E. McWhinney, *The International Court of Justice and the Western Tradition of International Law* (1987) (hereinafter McWhinney, *Western Tradition*); E. McWhinney, *The World Court and the Contemporary International Law-Making Process* (1979) (hereinafter McWhinney, *Law-Making Process*).

[3] E. McWhinney, *Judge Shigeru Oda and the Progressive Development of International Law* vii (1993).

personalities[4] from Woodrow Wilson on,[5] there has not been such biographical interest in international judges. (Max Huber is a possible exception, but, in Huber's case, the interest was stimulated by his management of the International Committee of the Red Cross during the Second World War and not by his sometime judicial role.) For most of the past century, moreover, the adjudications that have occurred have been by consent of the states concerned. The issues submitted were carefully circumscribed, as often were the principles of law to be applied. There was neither invitation nor much room for judicial creativity. In addition, the persons selected to decide the issues operated *ad hoc* so that, outside claims commissions, few international lawyers could expect to decide more than one or two cases in their careers. The result was that there was neither a "who" nor a "what" worth studying.

There is another, more troubling, obstacle to the development of this type of literature in public international law. The assumption necessary for examining the personalities of judges — that is, that the judges were independent and were actually making their own choices — was at best awkward during the Cold War. Throughout this period, totalitarian dictatorships contributed a significant number of judges to the International Court of Justice. Unpleasant as it may be to state, there is no reason to believe that the judges appointed to external arenas by those dictatorships were allowed to be any more independent than those appointed to internal arenas. Where judges, myth system notwithstanding, are subject to an operational code of direct political control, their personalities are not critical to understanding how the power process operates.[6]

Many of these factors have changed dramatically. There is now a permanent judicial institution that is getting many more cases than in the past. Though the statute of the Court does not envisage lifetime appointments, a significant number of judges have been

---

4 See, e.g., A. Bullock, *Hitler: A Study in Tyranny* (1962); E. H. Erikson, *Gandhi's Truth on the Origins of Militant Nonviolence* (1969): See Jean Claude Fauez, *Une Maison Impossible: Le CICR les déportations et les camps de concentration nazis* (1988), especially at 38-39 et seq.

5 See, e.g., S. Freud and W. C. Bullitt, *Thomas Woodrow Wilson, Twenty-Eighth President of the United States: A Psychological Study* (1967); A. L. George and J. L. George, *Woodrow Wilson and Colonel House* (1956).

6 Professor McWhinney would presumably disagree, since he thinks that suspicions of "Cold War-induced concealed ideological bases within the Court's ranks" were "irrational and ill-founded . . . at the time and [seem] even more so in retrospect." See McWhinney, *supra* note 3 at 98.

elected to two or more consecutive terms. In a simple quantitative sense, there is now ample "who" and "what," and Professor McWhinney believes and argues, in the very thoughtful, though controversial, essay that comprises one of the chapters (and which will be considered below), that judicial judgment is an important dimension of international politics. In short, with the end of the Cold War and the apparent triumph of the liberal democratic constitutional model, characterized by an independent judiciary, there may be good reason to expect renewed and widespread focus on the personality of international judges.

Any inquiry into judicial biography presupposes certain jurisprudential assumptions. In classic positivism, law is a body of rules and judges are technicians. Judges, according to Article 2 of the Statute of the International Court, require only legal expertise and high moral character. Lapses in high moral character may be investigated but, beyond that, searching biographical inquiry exceeds professional need. The personality of the judge may be the subject of vulgar curiosity or, in highly sanitized form, may provide grist for an introduction to those dreaded postprandial celebratory speeches at bar associations. Since, in this theory, the judge is not considered central in shaping the law, information about the judge's personality is not supposed to be useful for the predictive or explanatory tasks of the practitioner or legal scholar.

American legal realism effected a paradigm shift in jurisprudence that was no less radical than Copernicus's in astronomy and theology.[7] The Realists appreciated that one could not explain past decisions or predict future decisions (the essential practice of law in Holmes's famous apothegm) by reference to the extrapolation of rules in rigorous logical exercises. Explaining why past decisions had been made the way they were and predicting future decisions required observer or practitioner, as the case might be, to take account of history, culture, current politics, economics, and, in some contexts, the personality of the judge. The judges of United States domestic law were moved centerstage; the rules were moved to the wings. Methodologies for studying judges proliferated, ranging from Jerome Frank's grotesque distortion of Freudian thought to jurimetrical techniques that incorporated modern statistics. The biography of the judge became a legitimate focus of legal scholarship.

---

[7] Other intellectual traditions developed comparable insights. Marx, for example, insisted on more contextuality and the Frankfurt School, incorporating Freud's insights, also looked to the personality variable.

The working assumptions of biography as a tool of political scientific research have advanced dramatically. The earliest efforts were what Lasswell derisively called "political taxidermy." The invention of psychoanalysis and the rediscovery of the unconscious coincided with this interest and generated a variety of techniques and interpretive systems for conducting searching examinations of the personality. The classical Freudian view was that "rationality" was a micrometrically thin veneer, stretched to the limit over deep personality forces agitated by undigested memories and trauma. From a Freudian perspective, one's psychological makeup could be read in everything one did in much the way that one's distinctive DNA can be read in every cell in the body.

Lasswell adapted Freud's insights for the purposes of political biography and considerably refined them, asking questions about personality, culture, class, gender, and crisis exposure. But whether one accepts the approach of Sigmund Freud, Anna Freud, Lasswell, Erikson, or other masters of this method, the essential assumptions that underlie it are the same and are now common to virtually all serious biography: among the forces that shape how each of us perceives, values, and acts are the culture or cultures in which we have been shaped, the great historical events we have experienced, the class in which we have been socialized, our gender, and, not the least and in many ways the cumulation of all of the preceding, our individual personality dynamics and the crises we have undergone. Of course, modern biographical research addresses these factors in varying ways and with varying emphases.

Since individual responses to crises vary so widely, crisis has become a particularly important focus for the contemporary political biographer. For some, crises are indelible trauma, paralyzing or sterilizing experiences; for others, such as Leonardo, Luther, and Gandhi (all subjects of acutely perceptive and imaginative psycho-biographies),[8] crises stimulate creative responses that liberate so effectively the individuals experiencing them that these persons then become models, emulated by others who find themselves similarly situated. In this respect, these personal responses to, and triumphs over, crisis can change the world.

In a way, modern biographical methods have proved profoundly democratic. The unique drama of each of our lives is indispensable

---

[8] See, e.g., Erikson, *supra* note 4; E. Erikson, *Young Man Luther: A Study in Psychoanalysis and History* (1958); S. Freud, *Leonardo da Vinci: A Psychosexual Study of an Infantile Reminiscence* (A.A. Brill, trans., 1916).

to understanding us and what we do. No drama is richer or more important than any other, but some of us are more influential than others. This is especially true if, following a struggle, we discharge roles that project and amplify our inner lives to embrace many others in our community and, eventually, in other communities. This particular distinction is not limited to the great charismatic spiritual or political leaders. Judges, too, are in a special situation. They are empowered to issue binding judgments that confirm, adapt, or rework whatever basic values of society are at stake in current controversies, and certainly in the great "trouble cases"[9] of each era. If personality is one factor accounting for what each of us does, the personality of the judge in his or her judicial role may be of substantial and immediate importance, regardless of whether the court in question thinks it is practising "active" or "passive" virtues.

Because of the way judges work, an inquiry into their personalities is, in some ways, easier than a similar inquiry into other decision-makers. Every decision-maker leaves material that can be studied, but judges, particularly dissenting or concurring judges, leave a distinctive spoor, a written corpus in which the evidence of how they reacted to events and how they rationalized their reactions can be examined in terms of the forces that worked on and in their personalities. Studying that material can help the biographer explain how decisions are made, how law evolves, how the writer "ticked," and how all of these factors interacted. In any case, the biographer needs a method, whatever it may be, and needs to dig.

Professor McWhinney's approach to the function and utility of judicial biography for international judges is, in many ways, close to the classic positivist conception (of which he is critical on other grounds): the plenary and, in particular, the inner life of the judge is simply *not* relevant to legal inquiry. Another biographer might have asked why Judge Oda *always* writes a dissenting opinion or separate opinion. Professor McWhinney, in the fashion of William of Occam, would answer "because he disagrees." If the other biographer then asked "why," Professor McWhinney answers:

[T]he *rôle* of a judge on any tribunal is determined by the combination and interaction of special institutional and processual elements historically developed on that court and also of the judge's own personal

9 See K. N. Llewellyn and E. A. Hoebel, *The Cheyenne Way: Conflict and Case Law in Primitive Jurisprudence* 28-29 (1941).

culture as refined and concretized in legal terms by his academic education and professional experience.[10]

You will note that the personality variable is missing in this formula. Instead of an inquiry into Oda, the man, Professor McWhinney has opted for an entirely different theory of the relevant components of judicial biography: the jurisprudential theories imbibed from teachers, professional experience, the historic moment, the texts produced, and the dynamics of the court on which the judge under examination serves or served. McWhinney paraphrases Bentham: "The Law, as Jeremy Bentham remarked, is not made by Judge alone but by Judge and Company."[11] More attention is vouchsafed Company than Judge. We are presented with a biographical method that looks beyond, around, and away from its subject.

Thus, the legal formation of Judge Oda is presented as a microcosm of the evolution of an authentic "Japanese School of International Law," which was then overlaid by his exposure to the policy-sciences approach at Yale, all of which was further affected by what Professor McWhinney believes is the transformation of the Court itself. As Professor McWhinney synthesizes it, the method shaped by Yokota and Taoka in Japan is essentially a model of interpretation. The method

[i]nsisted on clarifying the socio-historical circumstances in which a claimed existing norm of International Law had been first formed. Such [a] clarification process was based on the premise that it was necessary to analyze the original social function of the legal norm in question so as to ascertain limitations implied thereby on its practical operation or utility in subsequent time periods.[12]

On to this, according to Professor McWhinney, was added the approach of McDougal and Lasswell, which the author describes as:

A blend or synthesis, in measure, of ideas already in circulation, from the 1920s onwards, by the two rather different, but complementary, American

---

[10] McWhinney, *supra* note 1 at 22.

[11] *Ibid.*, 96.

[12] *Ibid.*, 10. This reviewer is not familiar with Japanese jurisprudence, but is informed that there were major differences in approaches between Yokota and Taoka. Taoka was a socio-historicist whereas Yokota was a disciple of Kelsen and sought to minimize the influence of these factors. For an authoritative discussion of the different international legal schools in Japan in this period, see Y. Onuma, "Japanese International Law in the Postwar Period: Perspectives on the Teaching and Research of International Law in Postwar Japan" (1990) 33 *Japanese Annual of International Law*.

Legal Realist and American Sociological Schools of Law. Both of these had challenged the *status quo* of legal theory of traditional, "black letter law," analytical positivism. McDougal and Lasswell added to them, however, by a much more rigorous systemization and classification, and also by injecting a neo-Hegelian, normative-style, or purposive element in which the emphasis was to be on a conscious shaping and sharing of community values, in concrete decision-making, in the quest for an ultimate "International Law of Human Dignity."[13]

In addition, McWhinney finds Oda's diplomatic exposure, concurrent with his academic appointment and *oeuvre*, to be a critical factor, and he recites, without detail or analysis, the many conferences and trips that Oda made on behalf of the Japanese government.

With this sort of approach, the biographical section reads at times like something in an alumni bulletin: a chatty curriculum vitae in the context of the activities of the school and the alumni association as told by the witty, polyglot, and delightfully erudite class historian. It tells us nothing about Oda's parents, his class origins, his childhood, his adolescence, his faith and religious struggles, the formation of his sexuality, his relation to those closest to him in his family, his culture, and, in particular (and one would have thought indispensably), how he dealt with the collective trauma of Japan that ripped the country during his formative years — for Judge Oda is a member of what the Japanese call the "mid-war" generation, those who were shaped by the pre-war political culture but came of age in the immediate post-war, with virtually all of their cultural preparation shattered, indeed atomized, into irrelevance. Professor McWhinney tells us nothing of Judge Oda's inner life.

Indeed, Professor McWhinney's narrative seems to go out of its way to avoid even getting close to basic curriculum vitae material that would have forced further inquiry. For example, the narrative mentions rather blandly that Judge Oda was already a university student and "on military service" at the time the war ended and that he then returned to the university. In fact, as Judge Oda himself has mentioned to students he has addressed in the United States, he was trained as a *kamikaze* pilot, the quintessential expression of the war catechism, "[t]o match our training against their numbers and our flesh against their steel."[14] Oda was destined to

---

[13] *Ibid.*, 17.

[14] R. Benedict, *The Chyrsanthemum and the Sword: Patterns of Japanese Culture* 24 (1946).

die in a suicide attack if atomic bombs had not brought the war to an abrupt end.

Another biographer might have been moved to inquire into the inner dynamics of a man whose life was saved by the weapon that destroyed so many of his countrymen, indeed, so much of Japan, and the memory of which continues to traumatize so many members of subsequent generations. Another biographer might inquire about the implications for Judge Oda of then directly entering the law faculty of a private university in the United States that was well-known for its influential contacts with the American government, and to study there with a man who had held a high post in that government during the war, supported the decision to drop the bombs, and, indeed, had led the international legal defence of post-war atmospheric testing of atomic and hydrogen bombs in the Pacific.[15]

As Kenzaburo Oë, the brilliant Japanese novelist who became a sort of spokesman for the post-war generation (and who is mentioned by McWhinney in a footnote with regard to a different matter), has related:

[T]hroughout the war, a part of each day in every Japanese school was devoted to a terrible litany. The Ethics teacher would call the boys to the front of the class and demand of them one by one what they would do if the Emperor commanded them to die. Shaking with fright, the child would answer: "I would die, Sir, I would rip open my belly and die." Students passed the Imperial portrait with their eyes to the ground, afraid their eyeballs would explode if they looked His Imperial Majesty in the face.[16]

The empire collapsed. The emperor, a god-king and the linchpin of the world of the Japanese, was revealed as an ordinary human being. Moreover, in a Confucian society in which the authority of superiors was unquestioned, the superiors were exposed as wicked, criminal, and unworthy of trust. John Nathan, translator of Oë's novel, *A Personal Matter*, writes of the continuing, perhaps lifelong consequences for a Japanese of that period of having been denied his "ethical inheritance":

15 See Benedict's interesting comments on the behaviour of Japanese prisoners of war: *ibid.*, 40-41. For McDougal's essay, see McDougal and Schlei, "The Hydrogen Bomb Tests in Perspective: Lawful Measures for Security" (1955) 64 Yale L.J. 64.

16 J. Nathan, "Translator's Note" in Kenzaburo Oë, *A Personal Matter* viii (1968). For a moving depiction of a child's life at the time of Japan's surrender, see K. Oë, "The Day the Emperor Spoke in a Human Voice," *New York Times* (May 7, 1995) (Magazine) 103.

The values that regulated life in the world he knew as a child, however fatally, were blown to smithereens at the end of the war. The crater that remained is a gaping crater still, despite imported filler like Democracy.[17]

To be sure, in this century much of this is not a uniquely Japanese phenomenon. It has recurred, *mutatis mutandis*, in other settings, for Germans after the war,[18] for lapsed Catholics for whom God has died, for lapsed communists at various times in this century (particularly after Khruschev's exposure of Stalin's crimes and then the collapse of the Soviet Union), and so on. But in few places could it have been more individually wrenching than in Japan, a fact that makes Japanese intellectuals of this period so fascinating, and their literature, which has tried to describe and plumb the experience, such haunting human documents of remarkable intensity and brilliance.

Judge Oda survived the experience, but we are told nothing of the trauma he may have suffered in the process of the disintegration and reconstruction of his inner world and the ways in which that process might relate to the remarkably consistent jurisprudence to be found in his opinions.

There are other aspects of Judge Oda's judicial *oeuvre* and his distinctive professional style that Professor McWhinney recounts but that simply cry out for deeper inquiry. Consider, for example:

· Judge Oda, the "loner": the sheer number of dissents and separate opinions he has produced, some differing only slightly from the majority, and the fact that in none of them was he joined by another member of the Court.[19] Yet the dissents do not reveal a "wrecker," a person who is at all "anti-institutional." Indeed, in reading through the corpus of Judge Oda's work, one is struck by the number of cases, especially in the latter part of his career, in which Judge Oda expresses serious doubts about the core issue of

---

[17] Ibid., viii.

[18] Indeed, still occurs: see R. Atkinson, "Germans Still Grapple with Apocalypse of '45," *International Herald Tribune* (May 8, 1995), at 6:4-8.

[19] Indeed, Judge Oda himself has expressed curiosity on this. In a protocol visit to the International Law Commission in its 1995 session, Judge Oda observed that it was curious that he was virtually always in lone dissent. "Bien que l'esprit de contradiction ne soit pas un trait de sa personnalité, c'est un fait que dans l'exercice de ses fonctions de juge, il lui arrive souvent de se trouver minoritaire, ce qui l'a conduit à rédiger de nombreuses opinions dissidentes ou individuelles." UN Doc. A/CN.4/SR.2412 (July 11, 1995).

the majority opinion or acknowledges a personal difference[20] and then supports the majority. One wonders what the function of the separate opinion is for him.

· Judge Oda's distinctive *ex cathedra* style: the extraordinarily detailed and systematic exposition of every step in the logical process, as if the writer were unwilling to allow himself to make a leap or to take anything for granted. At one place, Professor McWhinney refers to this as a sort of *Begriffsjurisprudenz*,[21] though to this reviewer it does not manifest the "[e]xcessive preoccupation with concepts considered in abstraction from the conditions under which they have to be applied in real life," as Professor Hart has put it.[22] Far less than a tyranny of concepts (for it is not conceptual), it is a demand for the most explicit rationality and an extraordinary concern and respect for the political and legal commitments actually made and discoverable by digging into texts and legislative histories. Nor are Oda's positions, for example, his commitment to equidistance in maritime boundary delimitation, impractical or impracticable. Policy differences aside, equidistance is far more practical than equitable principles! Elsewhere, Professor McWhinney attributes Judge Oda's penchant for long opinions to his limited "mastery of an acquired, foreign language."[23] This sort of explanation is the sort of self-deprecating statement one would expect from Judge Oda himself. It is simply not persuasive, because his English is refined and nuanced when he speaks impromptu. Moreover, he has written short opinions — one of his most recent is, as mentioned, two sentences — and the longer opinions owe their length to the complexity of the problem, which Judge Oda acknowledges and addresses explicitly. Not all of the opinions are equally persuasive, but none is wordy or windy.

· Judge Oda's extraordinary self-control in personal comportment: who has ever seen him angry, indeed less than perfectly courteous?

· Judge Oda's remarkable independence and strength of will — one example will suffice. Although he studied with Myres McDougal for

---

20 *Request for an Examination of the Situation in Accordance with Paragraph 63 of the Court's Judgment of 20 December 1974 in the Nuclear Tests Case (New Zealand v. France)* (1995) I.C.J., 288 (Order of Sept. 22) (declaration of Judge Oda).

21 McWhinney, *supra* note 1 at 23.

22 H. L. A. Hart, *Jhering's Heaven of Concepts and Modern Analytical Jurisprudence*, in Franz Wieacker and Christian Wollschlager (eds), *Jherings Erbe* 68 (1970).

23 McWhinney, *supra* note 1 at 89; see *ibid.*, 23.

three years and won his close and lifelong friendship, Judge Oda was one of the few students who largely resisted the influence of McDougal, who was a magnetic and overpowering personality.[24] Instead, he selected and incorporated only those concepts, techniques, and linguistic components from the master's *oeuvre* that served his own purposes.[25]

It is particularly regrettable that these sorts of questions were not pursued, for Judge Oda, though always dignified, is not aloof or compulsively private. He is open and reflective about his background, and with friends, among whom Professor McWhinney is especially close, has always addressed and tried to be responsive to questions not dealing with immediate cases. Moreover, Japanese intellectuals of his generation who have been involved in exploring their national history through personal experience have, in my own experience, responded to sympathetic questions, precisely because these questions assisted them in their own quest.

We turn to biography to learn how the life of the subject has influenced his work and, through it, us all. Although Judge Oda may well have had the most dramatic inner life of any judge now on the Court, in this book we learn nothing of it.

Professor McWhinney tells us that he has elected this restrictive form of biography — and it is plainly a considered decision — but there is no methodological survey of the alternatives or explanation of why this form has been chosen. He simply does not tell us why he approaches the problem as he does. It can hardly be because he is unfamiliar with the literature on the relevance of the personality variable in politics and law. McWhinney is a leading international lawyer and publicist, trained initially in the sociological school of international law of the late Julius Stone, of whom he was a most prized student, and then, as a contemporary of Judge Oda, in the legal realist-policy science approach of Myres S. McDougal and Harold D. Lasswell at Yale, which puts special emphasis on depth psychology. All of McWhinney's work has been marked by an interdisciplinary conception of problems and a consultation of a

---

24 See R. A. Falk, "Casting the Spell: The New Haven School of International Law," (1995) 104 Yale L.J. 1991, 1997.

25 Consider, in this regard, his doctoral dissertation, which conceives of the oceans as a resource in classic McDougal fashion, but then proceeds in a manner that is distinctively not McDougal. See S. Oda, *The Riches of the Sea and International Law* (1953) (unpublished J.S.D. dissertation, Yale Law School).

dazzlingly wide spectrum of scientific literatures in many languages. To be sure, Professor McWhinney executes the "company" method he has selected very well, as one would expect. Skilfully, he exposes affection and enlightenment networks on the Court and is always poised, as readers of his books know, to identify larger institutional trends. But when all is said and done, this particular effort results in a rather wooden, impersonal approach to judicial biography. We are perforce left to speculate on why this method was selected.

As a practical matter, Professor McWhinney may feel that there is no other way of writing about a living and sitting judge. The Roman maxim *de mortuis nil nisi bonum* certainly does not apply to biographers. But do sitting judges, after the searing examination before appointment, thereafter benefit from a principle of *de judicibus vivis nil nisi nugas*? Perhaps national culture acts as a restraint, and this reviewer is guilty of parochialism and cross-cultural insensitivity. In some countries, perhaps including Canada, a probing inquiry into the life of a judge might be considered unduly intrusive and violative of privacy. In the United States, however, the relevance of psychological factors on the current behaviour of politicians is taken for granted, and searching biographies of living political figures, including psychobiographies that range from the refined and academically respectable to the vulgar and sensationalistic, are deemed permissible and in the public interest. This is not to suggest that the biographical treatment of judges is or must be *per se* gross impertinence. Professor Gunther, in his recent treatment of Learned Hand,[26] manages, in a very refined way, to present a great deal of data about the insecurity and identity crisis of the young Learned Hand and the effect it exercised on his professional substance and persona.

Professor McWhinney is not a positivist, but his reticence about engaging in deeper biographical inquiry may derive from deference to the myth system of positivism as applied to the International Court. The notion that a critical factor in the Court's decisions may be those individuals who are able to dominate what has been until this past July a college of fifteen middle-aged and elderly males, along with their undigested memories and possibly neurotic compulsions, could well reduce the future acceptability of the Court. Perhaps the editor believes that puncturing the myth of an autonomous body of law at the international level could undermine the International Court.

Most readers of biography implicitly acknowledge two things: first, that our cumulative inner lives profoundly shape what we

26 G. Gunther, *Learned Hand: The Man and the Judge* (1994).

currently do, and that self-understanding empowers the individual and makes him or her more responsible; and second, that a general understanding of the role of personality enables all of us to be better citizens and people. That is why biography is relevant to the theory and practice of law and politics. The question is whether the biographical method that the editor of the book under review has chosen — or, arguably, the method that is required by the sensitivity of the subject — can teach us something valuable. If it cannot, and if, as a practical matter, another more searching method simply cannot be undertaken, a biographical series on the judges of the International Court may make little sense.

THE COURT AS INTERNATIONAL LAWMAKER

The second critical assumption of this book, and the series of which it will be the flagship, is, as the title makes clear, that the International Court is properly engaged in the "progressive development of international law." Often juxtaposed with the word "codification," the term "progressive development" means lawmaking. Is the International Court of Justice accepted as an international lawmaker, authorized to make and apply new law in the individual cases before it? As a matter of international policy, should it be? For Professor McWhinney, the answer to both questions is so strongly affirmative that an examination of criticisms and alternatives is unnecessary. He writes:

> The cause of the progressive development of International Law, in accord with the UN Charter mandate to that effect, can be joined by judge, legal scholar, and professional negotiator, without any necessary and inevitable opposition between them.[27]

Now, obviously, a decision institution that reasons its awards and then publishes them will ineluctably affect expectations. When the Permanent Court of International Justice was under design, Balfour, surely thinking of a court far more restrained than one afire with a mission of progressive development, still observed that "the decision of the Permanent Court cannot but have the effect of gradually molding and modifying international law." And he added cryptically, "This may be good or bad."[28]

[27] McWhinney, *supra* note 1 at 96.

[28] PCIJ Documents concerning the Action taken by the Council of the League of Nations under Article 14 of the Covenant, p. 38, cited in *Continental Shelf*

This is not what Professor McWhinney has in mind. His proposition is redolent of positions espoused by the leading international judicial romantic of this century, the great Sir Hersch Lauterpacht, and his worthy successor at Cambridge and the Court, Judge Sir Robert Jennings. Sir Robert has said recently:

> *Ad hoc* tribunals can settle particular disputes; but the function of the established "principal judicial organ of the United Nations" must include not only the settlement of disputes but also the scientific development of general international law . . . there is therefore nothing strange in the ICJ fulfilling a similar function for the international community.[29]

Is there a United Nations Charter or, for that matter, customary mandate for the International Court or, indeed, for anyone to engage in "progressive development" or legislation?

It may be useful to pause for a moment and consider the genesis of the concept of "progressive development." Traditionally, doctrinal international law has allowed for formal and informal lawmaking. The formal method of making international law is by agreement, either bilaterally or after multilateral conference. The informal method is by practice, which is both generative and indicative of custom. The United Nations Charter itself is a manifestation of this first method. For the scholar, of course, the contemporary international law-making process is seen as far richer, a coaxial process of communication in which messages of content, authority, and control-intention are modulated among all politically relevant actors, with continuing assessments of prescriptions of law.[30] But the scholarly apparatus appropriate for the role of the scholar is not necessarily appropriate for the role of the judge. For a court or tribunal of specific powers — especially one that has been endowed with a choice-of-law clause, such as Article 38 of the International Court of Justice Statute — assignment or self-assignment of a new power of "progressive development" seems to contradict the very idea of specific powers. Where does progressive development fit into the scheme of the Charter and Statute?

(Tunisia v. *Libyan Arab Jamahiriya)*, (1981) I.C.J. 23, 29 (Apr. 14) (separate opinion of Judge Oda).

29 Sir Robert Jennings, *The Role of the International Court of Justice in the Development of International Environmental Protection Law,* cited in *East Timor (Port.* v. *Austl.)* (1995) I.C.J., 90 (June 30) (separate opinion of Judge Ranjeva).

30 For elaboration, see W. M. Reisman, "International Lawmaking: A Process of Communication" (1981)75 Proc. Am. Soc'y Int'l L. 101.

The term "progressive development of international law" is a *hapax legomenon* in the Charter. The Charter mentions it in connection with one of the assignments of the General Assembly of the United Nations, but by no stretch of the imagination or feat of deconstruction can it be construed as authorizing the Assembly to engage in a legislative function. Article 13 states, in relevant part: "The General Assembly shall initiate studies and make recommendations for the purpose of . . . promoting international co-operation in the political field and encouraging the progressive development of international law and its codification."[31]

Progressive development is a curious creation. Development is development. The redundant word "progressive" in the formulation is the product of a compromise at San Francisco between those who wanted the General Assembly to have a broad revisory capacity over the inherited corpus of international law and those who wanted, at the most, a considerably more modest competence. The term "progressive" seems first to have appeared in the comments and amendments to the Dumbarton Oaks proposal made by Ecuador, to give the General Assembly the "power to establish or progressively amend the principles and rules" of international law.[32] In later discussions, the activity came to be referred to as "progressive development."[33] The apparently innocuous change of

---

[31] UN Charter, Art. 13(1).

[32] See Doc. 2, G/7(p), 3 UNCIO Docs 404 (1945); see also Doc. 42, P/10, 1 UNCIO Docs. 369 (1945) (statement by chairman of Ecuadorian Delegation, Apr. 30, 1945).

[33] The Chinese proposals of May 1, 1945, called for "[t]he Assembly [to] be responsible for initiating studies and making recommendations with respect to the development and revisions of the rules and principles of international law." Doc. 1, G/1(a), 3 UNCIO Docs. 24 (1945). When Committee II/2 met on May 9 to consider what would become Article 13, it approved the Vandenberg (U.S.) proposal, drawn from amendments offered by the four sponsoring powers, that "[t]he General Assembly should initiate studies and make recommendations . . . for the encouragement of the development of international law." Doc. 203, II/2/8, 9 UNCIO Docs 21-22 (1945). Despite this vote, the committee reopened the issue on May 21 to consider four questions posed by Subcommittee II/2/A, see Doc. 416, II/2/A/3, 9 UNCIO Docs 345-47 (1945). The committee now approved the Assembly's powers to initiate studies and make recommendations for both the "codification" and "revision" of international law. Doc. 507, II/2/22, 9 UNCIO Docs 69-70 (1945).

Thus, on June 5, Subcommittee II/2/B met to consider the language approved on May 9, taking into account the vote of May 21. The subcommittee apparently agreed that "codification" merited a separate reference but

an adverb to an adjective, often done to facilitate the drafting or rationalization of translations when negotiations are conducted simultaneously in different but equally authentic languages, appears, in this instance, to have introduced a qualitative difference. The adverb imports simply moving through space or advancing point-by-point on an agenda; the adjective carries, more clearly, implications of the advocacy of progress or reform. And reform, like beauty, is in the eye of the beholder. For the purposes of Article 13, the beholder is the General Assembly.

Not that the grammatical changes should have made any difference. In many ways, the final arguments in Committee II/2 on June 7, 1945, over the use of the word "revision" rather than "progressive development" had become classic tweedle-dee and tweedle-dum; by then, in both formulas, it was agreed that, however the activity was designated, it would be contained within the Assembly's competence to initiate studies and make recommendations encouraging development or revision.[34] A rose is a rose, and studies and recommendations for the purpose of developing international law are studies and recommendations.

It is thus clear both from text and from legislative history that the Charter does not authorize the General Assembly to take binding decisions. Its "progressive development" is essentially an authoriza-

---

debated whether the "development" language of the Vandenberg proposal adequately covered "revision." Two formulations were considered. Version A, which received five votes, gave the Assembly the power to initiate studies and make recommendations "for the codification of international law, the encouragement of its development, and the promotion of its revision." Version B, which gathered three votes, gave such power "for the encouragement of the progressive development of international law and for its codification." Both versions were advanced to Committee II/2. Doc. 795, II/2/B/11, 9 UNCIO Docs 423-24 (1945).

On June 7, the full Committee II/2 met yet again to consider the language to be inserted. Proponents of Version A argued that "development," even coupled with the term "progressive," did not necessarily imply the power to revise, which the committee had clearly approved on May 21, while supporters of Version B maintained that "'[p]rogressive development' would establish a nice balance between stability and change, whereas 'revision' would lay too much emphasis on change." By a vote of 28-8, the second alternative was approved. Doc. 848, II/2/46, 9 UNCIO Docs. 177-78 (1945).

Subsequently, the Coordinating Committee laconically noted the tortured history of the passage: "This particular phrase had represented a considerable compromise in the Committee." WD 292, CO/119, 17 UNCIO Doc. 100 (1945).

34 See Doc. 848, II/2/46, 9 UNCIO Docs 177-78 (1945).

tion to clarify *lex ferenda* and then to recommend its findings to the member states. In their thorough commentary on the Charter of the United Nations, Professor Simma and his colleagues concluded that "all attempts to give the [General Assembly] any power to establish the content of international law with binding force were rejected."[35]

By a curious irony of history, the term "progressive" took on other meanings and came, in some quarters, to have important positive identifications and properties. During the heyday of the Non-Aligned Movement (NAM), the leadership was composed of *soi-disant* "progressive" states — Castro's Cuba, Nasser's Egypt, Tito's Yugoslavia, Sukarno's Indonesia, and so on. The natural arena of NAM operation was the General Assembly. By virtue of the fact that the NAM leadership had appropriated the adjective, the changes they pressed for in international law were "progressive"; hence, "progressive development" of international law meant, for them, lawmaking or legislation of a certain decided cast. This occurred after the phrase had been championed in Committee II/2 as the more conservative option under consideration![36] Given that this orientation was strongly resisted in many quarters, "progressive development" acquired a conflictive rather than scholarly overtone.[37]

In 1947, the Assembly created the International Law Commission to engage in "codification and progressive development." In fact, the ILC Statute was slightly less generous in its grant of competence with regard to progressive development: progressive development generally requires a reference from the General Assembly while codification does not.[38] However the ILC Statute is interpreted,

---

[35] Carl-August Fleischhauer, "Article 13," in Bruno Simma (ed.), *The Charter of the United Nations: A Commentary* (1994).

[36] See *supra* note 33.

[37] Professor McWhinney once preferred to characterize the process of international lawmaking, as "dialectical" because "to talk, for scientific-legal purposes, of a 'progressive development' of international law is either to lend oneself to a conscious semantic confusion or else to engage, in the end, in professions of rival political faiths": McWhinney, *Law-Making Process, supra* note 2 at 1.

[38] See Statute of the International Law Commission and Other Resolutions of the General Assembly Relating to the International Law Commission, UN Doc. A/CN.4/4, at 4-6 (1949) (Arts 16-18); Fleischhauer, *supra* note 35 at 269. But see Report of Committee on the Progressive Development of International Law,

nemo dat quod non habet: the International Law Commission was given no competence to bind states by its *ipse dixit* because the Assembly simply does not have that power to delegate. The Commission's function is to prepare drafts for the General Assembly that may, if it deems appropriate, convene an international conference. The conference can then rework the draft into the form of a draft treaty that will then become binding on individual states only upon their ratification. ILC drafts may propose developmental changes, but it is ultimately not the Assembly but the individual states that dispose. In short, the Charter does not authorize or empower the General Assembly, or any subordinate entity the General Assembly may create, to engage in legislation.

How, then, does Professor McWhinney transfer the limited notion of "progressive development" that the Charter assigned to the Assembly and the Assembly, in turn, delegated to the International Law Commission, to the International Court of Justice? Professor McWhinney sees a broader, undefined "Charter mandate" for which three groups are the cadres of progressive development: negotiators, legal scholars, and the judges of the International Court of Justice. To be sure, there are certain features that are common to the Charter mandate we have just reviewed and the function of the "professional negotiator." The latter may certainly invent new bilateral or multilateral normative regimes. Indeed, the negotiator's explicit function may include the fashioning of new arrangements, and, even if the authority granted the negotiator's principal does not give such power, whatever arrangements are designed are still, in parallel to the recommendations of the Assembly, *ad referendum.*

As for the "legal scholar," only a sterile representative of the breed would believe that our task is limited to inventorying and summarizing decisions that have been taken and scholarly views about them. The legal scholar should certainly consider the clarification of *lex ferenda* as part of the professional turf. If the term "progressive development" is simply a new way of describing this, then it is not disquieting. It is also unlikely to be particularly effective. But surely it would be professionally improper and

GAOR (II) 6th Comm., Annex I, at 178 (1946) which, perhaps more realistically, acknowledged that the distinction between the two activities could not be "rigidly maintained in practice." Nor, one may add, is the distinction of practical importance, for the ILC's *oeuvre* must always be approved by the Assembly and then referred to States for their approval for it to become law.

personally dishonorable for the scholar to assume that the role now included an inherent progressive development component that would be effected by engaging in explicit misstatements — that is, by presenting his or her personal policy preferences as if they *were* law or, at least, reflected in the expectations of the community. I do not believe Professor McWhinney is proposing this.

As a practical matter, neither the negotiator nor the scholar is an explicit lawmaker. Each can play a role in the development of international law by study and recommendation, but the actual force of the role will derive only from the cogency and quality of the recommendations, not from an implied authority in the role-player who puts them forward.

Does the international judge who, with the collegium, renders a final judgment, have a lawmaking competence *ad referendum* of the sort the Charter allows the Assembly, or practice allows the negotiator, and scholarship allows and demands of the scholar? It is difficult for me to see how the judge might found such a power. For the Court, there is no principal *ad referendum.* Its decisions are final and unappealable. Nor is there explicit or implied authority. The Charter does not authorize the Court to engage in this function. Article 38 of the Statute of the Court — which is the choice-of-law clause of that tribunal — states that its "function is to decide in accordance with international law." If Article 38 stopped there, one might argue that "international law" has come, by operation of customary law, to include some sort of general "progressive development" competence. But Article 38 proceeds to designate the material to which the Court is to have reference. It makes no mention of progressive development.

The Court, like any other international arbitral body, is assigned limited powers; excursions beyond those powers may lead to the annulment of their putative awards. The litigants may explicitly authorize the Court and similar entities to look beyond *lex lata,* as in the *Libya-Tunisia Continental Shelf* case,[39] and the parties may also authorize the Court to ignore the law and to decide *ex aequo et bono.* And, implicitly, parties may authorize a court or other implementing agency to elaborate and supplement when the assignment is the application of an instrument of general provisions (for example, certain human rights instruments) to a wide and not always anticipated range of factual situations.

---

[39] *Continental Shelf (Tunis. v. Libyan Arab Jamahiriya)* (1982) I.C.J. 18, 23 (Feb. 24) (Article I of Compromise).

Arguably, parties referring certain cases, such as contested boundary decisions, can be presumed to want an answer. In these cases, if existing prescriptions or the compromissory formulations do not provide the answer, some judicial creativity is appropriate.[40] The alternative is a judgment of *non liquet*. But, properly understood, *non liquet* is an extremely rare occurrence, because no legal system and no code prescribes for *every* eventuality. The law is full of holes. Decision-makers are constantly and routinely plugging them by analogy, teleology, the application of more general community policies, and other types of generative logic that are central to the juridical method. Only when it becomes clear that no accepted community policy exists and that the community has decided to leave certain matters or sectors unregulated or in a "civic order,"[41] and the legal system does not instruct the court to act as a legislator in these circumstances,[42] does the question of rendering a judgment of *non liquet* arise.

There may be circumstances in which the appropriate judicial response would be to conclude that, while the Court can supplement law in some circumstances, in the instant case: (1) the community has not arrived at a decision regarding regulation of a certain problem or sector; (2) the community is prepared *faute de mieux* to live with the costs and consequences of this specific anomie; and (3) politically significant groups are unwilling to suffer the imposition of a legal regime on the issue. Thus, *non liquet* shares a place with discretionary judicial self-limitations such as the political question doctrine, non-justiciability, and the doctrine of inherent limitations of the judicial function, as developed by the International Court in the *Northern Cameroons* case.[43] Needless to say, decisions to make law, no less than decisions to duck a case, are very serious and may be undertaken only when warranted.

---

[40] See *Egypt-Israel Arbitration Tribunal: Award in Boundary Dispute Concerning the Taba Area* (1988) 27 I.L.M. 1421 (Award of Sept. 29, 1988).

[41] M. S. McDougal et al., "Nationality and Human Rights: The Protection of the Individual in External Arenas" (1974) 83 Yale L.J. 900.

[42] As does Switzerland: "A défaut d'une disposition légale applicable, le juge prononce selon le droit coutumier et à défaut d'une coutume, selon les règles qu'il établirait s'il avait à faire acte de législateur." Cc. Art. 1 (Switz.). But, significantly, the last paragraph of Art. 1 obliges the judge performing this role to be guided by appointed legal doctrine and case law, suggesting that a more limited supplementation rather than an extensive revision is contemplated.

[43] *Northern Cameroons (Cameroon v. U.K.)* (1963) I.C.J. 15 (Dec. 2).

Does an international court, notwithstanding, have a general licence to legislate or "progressively develop" international law in the cases that come before it? Since the International Court of Justice requires an explicit authorization to engage in decision *ex aequo et bono*, it seems clear that the Statute was not intended to bestow a general power of equitable decision. I take it that, in Professor McWhinney's view, the fifteen members of the contemporary International Court, as members of an "emerging constitutional court," have acquired the competence to engage in lawmaking under the rubric of progressive development.

Professor McWhinney has long espoused an active lawmaking role for the Court, "a new, community policy-making rôle."[44] Part of what lends legitimacy to the Court's forays into such policymaking, in Professor McWhinney's view, is his belief that the "International Court is now, in a very real sense, a representative tribunal, whose membership, in its ethno-cultural, legal-systemic, political-ideological, and even geographical make-up, fully reflects the new, plural, inclusive World Community of today."[45] For Professor McWhinney, representativeness is fundamental to legitimacy when the conception of the judicial role has shifted from impartial forum to quasi-legislature.[46] But law is authority *and* control. Professor McWhinney never seriously questions whether representativeness of the sort seen on the Court is sufficient, of itself, to confer legitimacy in the eyes of important international actors. The United States' continuing resistance to the Court's new politics is portrayed as illegitimate without considering whether China or Russia, to name only two other permanent members of the Security Council, are any less resistant. Such a query could point to some important systemic dynamics with which the law must contend.

If there is a problem with the legitimacy of the fifteen members of the Security Council making law through Chapter 7 and Article

---

44 McWhinney, *Judicial Settlement, supra* note 2 at xv.

45 *Ibid.*, 106 (noting that the success of candidates is tied to geographic and legal-systemic origins and the degree of commitment to "progressive development of international law"): *ibid.*, 31, 99.

46 *Ibid.*, 114-15. Professor McWhinney makes it plain that the representation of different groups is central to the election of judges to the International Court, and he thinks that the success of those efforts for adequate representation makes "the International Court judges' claims to constitutional-legal legitimacy in the exercise of such a new, community policy-making role . . . at least as great as those of any of the great national, Special Constitutional Courts . . . of our times": *ibid.*, xv.

25, as prescribed by the Charter, why is it repaired by a fifteen-member court-making law without even the sanction of the Charter? And is the Court, with its appropriately restrictive evidentiary rules and judicial procedures designed for bilateral cases, an efficient or even adequate forum for the inherently political process of testing resistance and support and hammering out legislation for the entire world? The area into which the Court has rushed most explicitly to make law is the law of the sea, and its efforts in that area have hardly been satisfactory. Its straight baseline creation in 1951[47] was so ill-conceived that, in addition to setting off a sea-rush, the Court itself, by 1982, was ignoring straight baselines in maritime boundary delimitations.[48] And its invention, in 1969, of the *grundnorm* of maritime boundary limitation, the rule of equitable principles,[49] must surely stand as one of the most bizarre creations in the history of international law.

For Professor McWhinney, legitimacy is representativeness. The element that he ignores, however, is the need for authority's minimal congruence with patterns of effective power. "Representative" votes of formal legitimacy that purport to make international law may lack real legitimacy because they do not reflect the desires of effective decision-makers. The strength of the oft-criticized Charter regime is that it is based on reality.

The "representative" International, Court embarked on "progressive development," is transforming a fifteen-member court into an international legislator. How many actors will accept this transformation and its legislative output? Professor McWhinney is one of the leading comparatists of the judiciaries in the advanced industrial legal systems.[50] In many of the courts on which he has written authoritatively, contingent lawmaking competences are accepted as legitimate, if not mandatory, functions of the courts concerned; the quality of the work of the courts engaged in this function is, in large part, judged by the quality of its creativity. The point to be emphasized is that these various courts operate in political contexts in which this contingent judicial lawmaking function is accepted. Professor McWhinney's view, which has also been expressed by certain

---

47 *Fisheries (United Kingdom v. Norway)* (1951) I.C.J. 116 (Dec. 18).

48 *Continental Shelf (Tunisia v. Libyan Arab Jamahiriya)* (1982) I.C.J. 4 (Feb. 20).

49 *North Sea Continental Shelf (Federal Republic of Germany v. Denmark; Federal Republic of Germany v. Netherlands)* (1969) I.C.J. 3 (Feb. 20).

50 See, e.g., E. McWhinney, *Supreme Courts and Judicial Law-Making* (1986); E. McWhinney, *Comparative Federalism* (1965).

judges (notably former president Nagendra Singh and former president Sir Robert Jennings), is not shared by Judge Oda.

With respect, Professor McWhinney may be mistaken in seeing only one alternative available to the Court if it does not seize the "progressive development" role he recommends. For him, the remaining alternative is "the claimed mechanical, 'neutral' task of logical interpretation of already existing legal rules, divorced from the particular societal facts in which those rules had their historical origins."[51] But these polarities are no more satisfactory than the more familiar ones of "activism" as opposed to "strict construction" or "original meaning." The proper judicial role, I would submit, is neither general "progressive development" nor the caricature of blind application of "rules," legislation, or agreements. It is, rather, a conception of a judicial role, restricted like any other, with limitations that are accepted and honoured by the role player. Within this role, rules are properly seen as communications carrying relevant and authoritative policy information that must be shaped in the idiosyncratic texture of each controversy, to provide a decision that best approximates the minimum order and larger policy objectives of the community. Make no mistake: this is no easy task, not the least because of the constant possibility of infiltration, whether in factual characterization or legal specification, of personal preferences and prejudices, some operating at levels of consciousness so deep that the judge may be unaware of them. Hence the need for techniques of self-scrutiny.[52] For jurists and the systems they serve, biographical and autobiographical methods are not, in this perspective, mere entertainment or luxuries. They are indispensable judicial skills, directly related to the protection of public order.

To be sure, the judicial function involves "supplementing and policing"[53] or, in Professor McWhinney's formulation, "affirmative re-writing or re-casting of old rules in accord with contemporary

---

51 McWhinney, *Judicial Settlement of International Disputes, supra* note 2 at 91.

52 H. Lasswell & M. S. McDougal, *Jurisprudence for a Free Society: Studies in Law, Science, and Policy* 591 ff. (1992). See also W. M. Reisman, "The Tormented Conscience: Applying and Appraising Unauthorized Coercion" (1983) 32 Emory Law J. 499; W. M. Reisman, *A Jurisprudence from the Perspective of the Political Superior*, Siebenthaler Lecture, Chase College of Law, Northern Kentucky University (March 2, 1995) 23 Northern Kentucky Law Review 603 (1996).

53 M. S. McDougal et al., *The Interpretation of International Agreements and World Public Order* (1994).

[one might interpose here the word "authoritative"] policy imperatives that the Lasswell-McDougal Policy Science school would imply [or identify]."⁵⁴ Supplementing and policing are particularly urgent in periods of rapid transition. This is not judicial activism, but an appropriate discharge of the judicial function, and it is quite distinct from an active lawmaking role that deems itself entitled to ignore expressions of authoritative policy and assumes a competence to determine itself, case-by-case and "progressively," what the law *should* be. That seems to me to be the conception adopted over two decades by a shifting majority of the International Court and endorsed *ex cathedra* by Professor McWhinney.⁵⁵ Until now, Judge Oda and a minority of other judges have steadfastly dissented.

While some of the majority's initiatives have won praise in some quarters, they have, in the view of others, led the Court to major and sometimes disastrous initiatives in international constitutive change. For one thing, the Court elaborated a theory of jurisdiction no longer based on consent. Judge Oda rather consistently resisted this initiative. The majority's initiatives have also led to the Court's assumption, especially in the area of maritime boundary delimitation, that it is entitled to change the law on a case-by-case basis. Here again, Judge Oda's work is marked by a consistent and detailed examination of existing prescriptions, on the basis of which he tries to fashion the appropriate legal response. Indeed, in the major cases that Professor McWhinney believes are the building blocks of the emerging constitutional role for the International Court, Judge Oda has raised a voice of reservation and opposition.

In my view, Judge Oda is right. The Court has engaged in lunges for jurisdiction in cases in which there was no consent and legislative exercises that, in addition to being unauthorized, do not reflect the common interests of the world community. These practices, for all the technical skill of those who engage in them, inescapably take on a shabby character, involving legal tricks, gimmicks, and gambits, and forced interpretations that ill-befit any great court and certainly not the "principal judicial organ of the United Nations." But a far-reaching judicial lawmaking role requires subterfuge and

---

⁵⁴ McWhinney, *supra* note 1 at 92.

⁵⁵ Of course, when Professor McWhinney describes the process of discovering international law, he does so in a subtle and nuanced way; but despite his own language, he seems to disregard whether the "principal actors affected" truly have accepted and acted on legal propositions later declared law by the Court. See McWhinney, Western Tradition, *supra* note 2 at 144-46.

misstatement. Article 38 of the Statute is clear, so when the Court is engaging in "progressive development," it cannot say, "Formula A is the law, but we are now putting on our judicial-legislative hats and are going to decide on the basis of formula B, in the exercise of our competence to engage in discretionary 'progressive development.'" In the pretense that formula B is the law, the Court confuses the community as to the methods by which law is to be inferred, undermines confidence in legal expectations, and undermines the confidence of others in itself. All of these have proliferating consequences for the international legal system.

Beyond the erosion of stability of expectation, these lawmaking initiatives often have high institutional costs. States are not obliged to turn to the Court for the resolution of their disputes. When they do, their legal advisers have presumably studied the relevant parts of international law and enter Court with some confidence that it will be applied. To have the Court *ad hoc* "progressively develop" new norms with retroactive effect will hardly encourage responsible legal advisers to refer cases to the Court. The Court's efforts at progressive development, well-intentioned I am sure, have harmed the Court's reputation and eroded confidence in international law.

JUDGE ODA'S DECISIONS: THE ANALYSIS

The opportunity to study what emerges as one judge's coherent and intellectually rigorous jurisprudence is one of the dividends of this first volume of Professor McWhinney's series. Yet there are some structural problems in the genre that Professor McWhinney has shaped here, and they are particularly apparent with respect to Judge Oda's *oeuvre*. Common law lawyers, for whom the judgment is the critical epistemic unit, study separate and dissenting opinions of collegial tribunals because they provide a window on internal cameral deliberations — that is, the points that members of the tribunal agreed and disagreed upon. The publication only of the separate opinions as "stand alone" documents does not facilitate this. (Many of Judge Oda's opinions are an exception, for they are close to free-standing essays.) The utility of these documents alone may show continuities in the thinking of the judge under study, but will not convey the influence the dissenting or concurring judge had on the outcome of the majority decision or the fundamental points of difference.

Curiously, the approach taken in this series may actually ascribe more importance to judges who wrote more but exercised less influence. A prerequisite of a judge on a large collegiate tribunal is diplomatic ability — that is, the capacity to persuade (and be persuaded), to lead or participate in the shaping of as large a majority view as possible. This last ability may be as important as intellectual power. The judges who have the greatest influence on the Court will be those who write the majority opinion (which of course appears anonymously in the Court's practice) or those who, in cameral deliberations, had the greatest influence on shaping the judgment. The author of the separate opinion, whether concurring or dissenting, in effect acknowledges that the position he or she espoused was not accepted by the majority. On the other hand, if one accepts Holmes's notion that dissents are communications to subsequent tribunals and invitations to revisit and reconsider previous decisions, then the dissent may prove to be an important resource for scholarship and for the formation of policy.

This property of the genre that Professor McWhinney has created is particularly problematic with regard to Judge Oda. Judge Oda's personal judicial *oeuvre* may be the largest in the history of the Permanent and the International Court. It is theoretically consistent and provides a picture window on the jurisprudence and intellectual *modus operandi* of its creator. But it is comprised of dissents and of separate opinions that sometimes read like dissents. It has been a minority view — always a minority of one — and does not reflect, other than in a negative sense, the views and trends of the Court as a whole. If one were to translate these various documents into a sociogram, in which the *dramatis personae* of the Court were distributed spatially in accordance with their degree of influence, one feels, in rereading these opinions that Judge Oda is not in a vertical cluster, but over to the side.

These problems notwithstanding, Professor McWhinney analyzes in considerable detail the corpus of Judge Oda's judicial work. The appraisal is precise and fair, but often critical, for in contrast to the highly activist judicialist theory that Professor McWhinney so vividly propounds here and in his other books, Judge Oda's jurisprudence, as it appears in his work, is marked by a more restrictive, consistent, and non-opportunistic approach. Professor McWhinney, for example, speaks of the Court's majority "opting for an ample, beneficial approach to exercising jurisdiction in a great political-legal *cause célèbre*."[56] This means, I presume, that if the majority really wants to

---

56 McWhinney, *supra* note 1 at 94.

decide the case, it will "hokey up" jurisdiction, even if there is no consent under the ordinary usages of construction.

Judge Oda has not been party to this vision. His *oeuvre* shows, first, his concern for strict procedural integrity, even where fulfilling its requirements would defeat jurisdiction in a particular case; second, his meticulous examination and high degree of respect for the expressed expectations of the parties with regard to jurisdiction; and, third, a comparably meticulous examination of the sources of international law, as prescribed by the choice of law clause of the statute, and respect for these laws in deciding the merits of disputes. As Judge Oda said in the *Gulf of Fonseca* case, in a sentiment that runs through many of his dissents: "[M]y dissent is a result of my understanding of the contemporary as well as the traditional law of the sea, an understanding which seems to be greatly at variance with the views underlying the present judgment."[57] These are not empty words. Judge Oda's opinions are thoroughly researched and argued, and whether one is persuaded or not, the conclusions are reasoned.

Judge Oda's treatment of specific international constitutional issues is marked by respect for the political autonomy of the institution under review. In the *WHO Headquarters* case, his first separate opinion, he concluded:

It is not desirable, of course, that the Organization, the functions of which are situated in the field of world health, emphatically not a political but a humanitarian problem, should decide to shift the Office for political motives. Yet once the Organization, in its considered judgment, which the Court is not concerned with, finds it unnecessary or impossible to carry out its functions through the Office at Alexandria, the transfer or removal of the latter certainly falls within the competence of the World Health Assembly.[58]

Fifteen years later, in the *Lockerbie* case, he reproved the Security Council for making a decision three days after the close of oral argument, which it knew would influence proceedings. Yet he acknowledged the autonomy of the Council and the limitations of the Court:

I do not deny that under the positive law of the United Nations Charter a resolution of the Security Council may have binding force, irrespective of

[57] *Land, Island and Maritime Frontier Dispute (El Salvador v. Honduras: Nicaragua Intervening)* (1992) I.C.J. 351, 733 (Sept. 11).

[58] *Interpretation of the Agreement of Mar. 25, 1951 Between the WHO and Egypt* (1980) I.C.J. 73, 153 (Dec. 20).

the question whether it is consonant with international law derived from other sources. There is certainly nothing to oblige the Security Council, acting within its terms of reference, to carry out a full evaluation of the possibly relevant rules and circumstances before proceeding to the decisions it deems necessary. The Council appears, in fact, to have been acting within its competence when it discerned a threat against international peace and security in Libya's refusal to deliver up the two Libyans accused. Since, as I understand the matter, a decision of the Security Council, properly taken in the exercise of its competence, cannot be summarily reopened, and since it is apparent that resolution 748 (1992) embodies such a decision, the Court has at present no choice but to acknowledge the pre-eminence of that resolution.[59]

But in the important case of the *Arbitral Award of 31 July 1989*,[60] in which the Court was petitioned to review an arbitral award, Judge Oda, although joining the majority, did indulge in observations about the merits. These observations strike one as inconsistent with his scrupulous concern for the autonomy of other institutions.

In the administrative review function of the Court, Judge Oda has tended to be rather bureaucratic (as, for example, in the *Yakimetz* case[61] and in the *Mortished* case[62]) in contrast to Judge Lachs, who often used these cases as an opportunity to reflect more broadly on administrative and review functions. On a constitutional issue, Judge Oda inclined to agree with a number of the dissenters on the essentially appeal function that the Court should exercise with regard to the judgments of the administrative tribunal.

On procedural issues, Judge Oda has argued against the majority view for a broad right of intervention in *Tunisia/Libya*[63] and in *Libya/Malta*.[64] Yet, in the *Nicaragua* case, he joined the majority in rejecting El Salvador's right of intervention, despite the fact that it effectively decided the merits. He expressed his "unease at . . .

---

59 *Questions of Interpretation and Application of the 1971 Montreal Convention Arising from the Aerial Incident at Lockerbie (Libyan Arab Jamahiriya v. U.K.)* (1992) I.C.J. 3, 17 (Order of Apr. 14) (declaration of Judge Oda).

60 *Arbitral Award of 31 July 1989 (Guinea-Bissau v. Senegal)*, (1991) I.C.J. 53, 81 (Nov. 12) (separate opinion of Judge Oda).

61 *Application for Review of Judgment No. 333 of the United Nations Administrative Tribunal* (1987) I.C.J. 18, 83 (May 27) (separate opinion of Judge Oda).

62 *Application for Review of Judgment No. 273 of the United Nations Administrative Tribunal* (1982) I.C.J. 325, 389 (July 20) (separate opinion of Judge Oda).

63 *Continental Shelf (Tunisia v. Libyan Arab Jamahiriya)* (1981) I.C.J. 3, 23 (Feb. 24) (separate opinion of Judge Oda).

64 *Continental Shelf (Libyan Arab Jamahiriya v. Malta)* (1984) I.C.J. 3, 90 (Mar. 21) (dissenting opinion of Judge Oda).

unfortunate aspects of the procedure" in that case,[65] but that unease was not disturbing enough to push him into dissent. In the *Gulf of Fonseca* case, he insisted, in dissent, that a non-party intervener was bound by the ensuing judgment.[66] In *Gulf of Maine*, he supported the Court's refashioning of the institution of chambers, but insisted on making clear that this was essentially the parties' decision.[67] Professor McWhinney has interesting and useful observations on the background of this constitutional change.[68]

Professor McWhinney sees the law of the sea as a major contribution of the Court. This student finds little coherence in the Court's case law here and sometimes wonders if the law in this area might have fared better if the Court, going back as far as the *Anglo-Norwegian Fisheries* case,[69] had never had the opportunity to tamper with it. In contrast, Judge Oda's dissents are refreshingly consistent. He dissented against the majority in *Tunisia/Libya*, in which the majority produced an essentially unreasoned judgment. Judge Oda developed a "qualified equidistant" method that would have given a larger portion of the shelf to Tunisia.[70]

In the *Border and Transborder Armed Actions* case, Judge Oda stated his jurisdictional article of faith:

> When considering the jurisdiction of the International Court of Justice in contentious cases, I take as my point of departure the conviction that the Court's jurisdiction must rest upon the free will of sovereign States, clearly and categorically expressed, to grant to the Court the competence to settle the dispute in question.[71]

A review of the corpus, however, indicates that he has not always been strictly true to this credo. For example, in *Border and Trans-*

---

[65] *Military and Paramilitary Activities (Nicaragua* v. *U.S.)* (1984) I.C.J. 215, 220 (Order of Oct. 4) (separate opinion by Judge Oda).

[66] *Land, Island and Maritime Frontier Dispute (El Salvador* v. *Honduras: Nicaragua Intervening), supra* note 57 at 619

[67] *Delimitation of the Maritime Boundary in the Gulf of Maine Area (Canada* v. *U.S.)* (1982) I.C.J. 3, 10 (Order of Jan. 20) (declaration of Judge Oda).

[68] See McWhinney, *supra* note 1 at 33-37.

[69] *Fisheries (U.K.* v. *Norway)* (1951) I.C.J. 116 (Dec. 18); see W. M. Reisman and G. S. Westerman, *Straight Baselines in International Maritime Boundary Delimitation* (1992).

[70] *Continental Shelf (Tunisia* v. *Libyan Arab Jamahiriya)* (1982) I.C.J. 18, 270 (Feb. 24) (dissenting opinion of Judge Oda).

[71] *Border and Transborder Armed Actions (Nicaragua* v. *Honduras)* (1988) I.C.J. 69, 109 (Dec. 20) (separate opinion of Judge Oda).

border, he supported jurisdiction after expressing doubts about it. In the jurisdictional phase of *Nicaragua,* he voted with the majority, but effectively reversed his conception of jurisdiction in the Merits phase. In the *Nauru* case, Judge Oda did not allow his concern for the preservation of the environment to generate a jurisdiction when there was none. In his view, Nauru's claim had not been raised at the time of independence or for fifteen years thereafter, during which period it, itself, was responsible for the phosphate mining. Since it had "not taken any steps towards the rehabilitation of the lands it has itself worked . . . equity requires the conclusion that Nauru, by this conduct, combined with lack of due diligence, has disqualified itself from pursuing any allegation of Australian responsibility."[72] In the recent *New Zealand* v. *France Nuclear Test* case, Judge Oda joined the majority in refusing the New Zealand request on the grounds of the law, but concluded: "[A]s the Member of the Court from the only country which has suffered the devastating effects of nuclear weapons, I feel bound to express my personal hope that no further tests of any kind will be carried out under any circumstances in the future."[73]

But if Judge Oda has felt that jurisdiction was properly founded, he has been inclined to exercise it to the fullest, even if there was a possibility of negotiation. Thus, in the *Passage through the Great Belt* case, in which the Court sent strong signals to the parties of its interest in seeing a negotiated settlement, Judge Oda seemed very anxious to have the Court decide the case "as speedily as possible."[74]

In other judgments rendered since the appearance of Professor McWhinney's book, the approach apparent in the major lines of Judge Oda's jurisprudence has continued. In the confusing *Qatar* v. *Bahrain Boundary* case, Judge Oda was the lone dissenter in the first phase. Even Bahrain's *ad hoc* judge joined the majority. Judge Oda argued logically and persuasively that the Court simply lacked competence to compel the parties to take any action before its own jurisdiction had been established, and that the Court was carving a

---

[72] *Certain Phosphate Lands in Nauru (Nauru v. Australia)* (1992) I.C.J. 240, 324 (June 26) (dissenting opinion of Judge Oda).

[73] *Request for an Examination of the Situation in Accordance with Paragraph 63 of the Court's Judgment of 20 December 1974 in the Nuclear Tests Case (New Zealand v. France)* (1995) I.C.J. (Order of Sept. 22) (declaration of Judge Oda).

[74] *Passage through the Great Belt (Finland v. Denmark)* (1991) I.C.J. 12, 27 (Order of July 29) (separate opinion by Judge Oda).

new role for itself (or perhaps, one might add, adopting the role that Judge Bedjaoui, then president of the Chamber, had experimented with in one phase of the *Burkina Faso* v. *Mali* case). Judge Oda concluded:

> Neither the "1987 Agreement" nor the "1990 Agreement" can be deemed to constitute a basis for the jurisdiction of the Court in the event of a unilateral application under Article 38(1) of the Rules of Court and . . . the Court is not empowered to exercise jurisdiction in respect of the relevant disputes unless they are jointly referred to the Court by a special agreement under Article 39(1) of the Rules, which, in my view, has not occurred in this case. The Court has nonetheless opted for the role of conciliator instead of finding, as I believe it ought to have done, that it lacks jurisdiction to entertain the Application filed by Qatar.[75]

In fact, one might add, elements on the Court were engaged in more than conciliation, for in "fix[ing] . . . the time-limit within which the Parties are, jointly or separately, to take action to this end,"[76] the Court was already exercising a compulsory jurisdiction, which, necessarily, implied a finding of consent. And, indeed, in the second phase, the Court confirmed consent.[77] Now four other judges dissented, although none joined Judge Oda. In his dissent in this phase, Judge Oda carefully pointed out that the records of the meetings of the parties could not be plausibly construed as conferring contingent jurisdiction by a subsequent unilateral application, that the unilateral application was actually selective of issues in contention, and that, procedurally, Bahrain had not been given a meaningful opportunity to present its views.[78]

In *East Timor*, Judge Oda joined the majority's conclusion that Portugal's application was inadmissible because of lack of jurisdiction. But while the majority rested its judgment on the fact that the rights and obligations of a third party, which had not given its consent, were at the center of the dispute, Judge Oda felt that Portugal lacked *locus standi*.[79] In this respect, his view seems to be truer to *Namibia* and is a clear indictment of the nonfeasance of the

---

75 *Maritime Delimitation and Territorial Questions between Qatar and Bahrain* (1994) I.C.J. 112, 149 (July 1) (dissenting opinion of Judge Oda).

76 *Ibid.*, 126.

77 *Maritime Delimitation and Territorial Questions between Qatar and Bahrain* (1995) I.C.J. 6 (Feb. 15).

78 *Ibid.*, 40 (dissenting opinion of Judge Oda).

79 *East Timor (Portugal v. Australia)* (1995) I.C.J., 90 (June 30) (separate opinion of Judge Oda).

political branch — that is, the United Nations. The majority opinion delicately sidesteps this point in formulae that are unpersuasive and, in places, hypocritical.

AN EMERGING CONSTITUTIONAL ROLE FOR THE COURT?

After analyzing Judge Oda's "judicial mind and faith" through his written decisions, Professor McWhinney turns at last to his central thesis, the International Court of Justice as "emerging Constitutional Court along the lines of the great continental European, specialized national constitutional tribunals of the post-World War II era."[80] He cites three decisions of the 1992 term that indicate, to his satisfaction, that the Court has definitively moved beyond a limited, black-letter-law conception of its role. The first, the *Lockerbie* case, drew the Court into a debate over its relation to other United Nations institutions. The second, the *Nauru* case, presented the "opportunity" for the Court to venture into new areas of law, such as environmental protection and good neighbourliness. The third, the final judgment of the Special Chamber in the *Land, Maritime and Island Frontier Dispute*, allowed the Court, this time with Judge Oda as part of the deciding body, to assay the status of certain aspects of the law of the sea.

By this point, it should come as no surprise to the reader that Judge Oda is curiously tangential to this narrative, sometimes in opposition to the position that Professor McWhinney espouses and sometimes hardly registering at all. For example, in *Lockerbie*, Judge Oda joins in the majority opinion, which holds that Security Council resolutions, properly taken, are preeminent under United Nations law; but he files a declaration in which he advocates greater judicial self-restraint by deciding the case on narrower grounds (namely, that the Libyan application was not timely because the question under consideration was an interpretation of the Montreal Convention and not the protection of sovereign rights under international law). Professor McWhinney's opinion of this interpretation becomes clear when he writes that Judge Oda's emphasis on deciding cases on technical grounds where available "is an aspect of that positivist, technical approach to the judicial process and judicial reasoning":[81]

---

80 McWhinney, *supra* note 1 at 97.

81 *Ibid.*, 106.

[T]hat form of historical positivism, based on rigorous scientific research and analysis of legal source materials (treaty, judicial, and doctrinal), and their logical projection and extension to present problem-situations, that Judge Oda had acquired from his great Japanese law teachers and that is reflected in all his Separate Opinions throughout his term on the Court.[82]

In contrast, Professor McWhinney describes the separate opinion of Judge Lachs in *Lockerbie* in these terms:

This is judicial self-restraint exercised in the larger intellectual dimension of a postulated consciously policy-making rôle for the Court. It has echoes of the doctrine of self-restraint applied by the Court, much earlier, in *Nuclear Tests*, when it managed to produce a judicial majority in support of a then legally *avant-garde* international environmental protection norm, but by the legal indirection of an essentially adjectival law-based ruling. . . . While the Court, in the present case, will defer to the Security Council in the exercise of a styled "concurrent jurisdiction," it is indicated that this is to be limited to the particular, Chapter VII of the United Nations Charter, decisions involved, and that the Court reserves its own full legal competencies in other respects.[83]

Professor McWhinney finds Judge Lachs's approach laudable in that it preserves the potentiality for Court *activism*. It respects, in the specific case, the proper competence of the Security Council within its sphere, but does not let slip the opportunity to reaffirm a "full complementarity of powers which should sensibly be exercised with inter-institutional comity and cooperation,"[84] and certainly does not refuse to address the issue on "technical" grounds (especially, it would seem, if a "progressive" norm can be slipped in by using such a device). Judge Oda, in contrast, does not see the Court playing a major lawmaking role and does not strain for verbal formulations that preserve that potentiality. To characterize this approach as "technical" is to mistake style for substance. It is a position that respects the Charter's constitutional allocations.

In *Certain Phosphate Lands in Nauru*, while three other judges dissented on certain points at the stage of Australia's objections to jurisdiction, Judge Oda was the lone dissenter on four additional points. Judge Oda's votes, Professor McWhinney argues, went counter to:

[a] perceptible trend in the Court's *jurisprudence* . . . not to allow the opportunity to rule on major substantive law issues to be frustrated or

[82] *Ibid.*, 116.
[83] *Ibid.*, 107 (internal citations omitted).
[84] *Ibid.*, 106.

diverted by an overly precise or rigid insistence on the prior exhaustion of procedural forms or rules as a pre-condition to the Court's exercise of jurisdiction in a case coming before it.[85]

Professor McWhinney believes that this "trend in the Court's *jurisprudence . . .* seems confirmed and extended with the Court judgment . . . and with the margins of the Court majorities on the separate points raised in the case" and that, on balance, this is a good thing "where the opportunity for a useful Court contribution to World Community law-making would otherwise be lost."[86] Judge Oda, just as clearly, believes the Court best serves as a predictable and accepted forum for dispute resolution.

CONCLUSION

Because Volume 1 of *The Judges* is as much a condensed restatement of major themes developed in Professor McWhinney's *oeuvre* as it is an examination of Judge Oda's career, it is perhaps fitting that the volume closes by examining one final case from the 1992 term: the *Land, Maritime and Island Frontier Dispute*. We find Judge Oda playing the role of lone dissenter again and, ironically enough, in a case centrally involving the law of the sea. As in his discussion of *Lockerbie*, Professor McWhinney again links Judge Oda with the losing side in his vision of the "New Court" and its progressive development of international law. Judge Oda is, in the McWhinney view, part of that "positivist approach on the Court [that] was reduced, with the successive elections to the Court, to a lonely, last-ditch intellectual-legal position."[87]

In fact, that assessment is proving wrong. The "New International Constitutional Court" may prove as enduring as the abortive experiment of a "New International Economic Order" and the

---

[85] *Ibid.*, 108. This is a significant change because only two years earlier Professor McWhinney had written:

> The actual record of the International Court's jurisprudence in the post-South West Africa Second Phase era, shows a tribunal that is increasingly confident in its new community policy-making role; but a tribunal, nevertheless, that as an important element in that new judicial and legal sophistication, will still be cautious about venturing into policy pronouncements in law unless the essential procedural, adjectival law pre-conditions for a Court ruling are properly met[.]

McWhinney, *Judicial Settlement, supra* note 2 at 136.

[86] McWhinney, *supra* note 1 at 109.

[87] *Ibid.*, 25.

unlamented "New International Information Order." In recent cases, the majority, reinforced by new judges, has moved the Court back to the role assigned it in the Charter and the Statute. In the Court's Order of September 22, 1995, in which Judge Oda was part of a twelve to three majority, he appended, as mentioned,[88] a two-sentence declaration, supporting the Court on the law, but expressing a "personal hope" that there would be no further tests. Judge Shahabuddeen concluded his separate, but concurring, opinion as follows:

[I]t is right to recall that the title of the Court is the "International Court of Justice." However, it is also useful to bear in mind that the "Justice" spoken of is not justice at large; as in the case of courts of justice generally, it is "the primary function of the Court to administer justice based on law."

. . . .

It does not follow from the fact that the Court may also be described as a court of law that it administers the law mechanically. Lacking the full measure of the judicial power available to some national courts, it has nevertheless found opportunity for enterprise and even occasional boldness. Especially where there is doubt, its forward course is helpfully illuminated by broad notions of justice. However, where the law is clear, the law prevails.[89]

The words could have been penned by Judge Shigeru Oda. As to why Judge Oda has so consistently taken this view, rather than the proactively legislatistic approach of some of his colleagues, the reader puts down Volume I of *The Judges* entertained and provoked, but no more informed than when he took it up.

---

[88] See *supra* note 73 and accompanying text.

[89] *Request for an Examination of the Situation in Accordance with Paragraph 63 of the Court's Judgment of 20 December 1974 in the Nuclear Tests Case (New Zealand v. France)* (1995) I.C.J. (Order of Sept. 22) (separate opinion of Judge Shahabuddeen).

Sommaire

Métamorphoses: Juge Shigeru Oda et la Cour internationale de justice

Une série consacrée aux juges de la Cour internationale de justice devrait se fonder sur deux postulats. Le premier, que la personnalité et le système de valeurs de chaque juge constituent un facteur important dans l'application et même l'évolution du droit international; le second, que la Cour internationale est un organisme important qui a joué un rôle considérable dans le développement progressif du droit international. Le critique salue l'idée de cette série. Il estime toutefois que l'auteur n'a pas donné l'importance qu'il fallait à ces deux postulats. Il émet aussi des réserves à l'égard de certains choix stratégiques et déductions jurisprudentielles de l'auteur. Il considère de plus que ce dernier a fait une application discutable de ces choix et déductions.

Summary

Metamorphoses: Judge Shigeru Oda and the International Court of Justice

A series about the judges of the International Court must be based on two postulates: first, that the unique character and, of course, "value-structure" of each judge is a variable of some importance in the application, if not incremental formation, of international law; and second, that the International Court is an important institution and has played a significant role in "the progressive development of international law." While welcoming the idea of this series, the reviewer has reservations about the way these postulates have been embraced and adopted by the author and outlines his reservations about key jurisprudential assumptions and strategic choices that were made in designing the idea and about the ways those assumptions and strategies have been implemented.

Notes and Comments /
Notes et commentaires

La première année de l'Organe de règlement des différends de l'Organisation mondiale du commerce*

I INTRODUCTION

L'ORGANISATION MONDIALE DU COMMERCE (l'OMC) a été créée le 1er janvier 1995. Les gouvernements avaient achevé les négociations du Cycle d'Uruguay le 15 décembre 1993 et les ministres ont donné leur sanction politique aux résultats de ces négociations lors d'une réunion tenue à Marrakech en avril 1994. Le Mémorandum d'accord sur les règles et procédures régissant le règlement des différends (le Mémorandum d'accord) fait partie intégrante de l'Accord instituant l'OMC. L'Organe de règlement des différends (l'ORD) a été institué pour administrer le Mémorandum d'accord. Le système de règlement des différends de l'OMC est un élément essentiel pour assurer la sécurité et la prévisibilité du système commercial multilatéral.

Dans cette note, nous exposerons brièvement la structure juridique de l'OMC, dont fait partie l'ORD, ainsi que sa structure institutionnelle. Dans un deuxième temps, nous soulignerons les principaux changements résultant du Mémorandum d'accord, dont l'administration relève de l'ORD, ainsi que les principales fonctions et obligations de l'ORD et des Membres. Enfin, nous ferons un survol des activités de l'ORD en 1995 tant sur le plan administratif qu'en ce qui concerne le règlement des différends.

---

* Les auteurs aimeraient remercier Bill Davey et Mireille Cossy pour leurs commentaires. Les opinions exprimées dans cette note sont strictement personnelles et ne lient pas le Secrétariat de l'OMC. Toute erreur ne peut être imputée qu'aux auteurs.

II   La structure juridique et institutionnelle de l'OMC

A   La structure juridique

Comme il ressort du tableau 1 figurant à la fin de cette note, l'Accord de Marrakech instituant l'Organisation mondiale du commerce forme un tout ("single undertaking"). L'adhésion "à la carte" qui prévalait pour le GATT et les Codes du Tokyo Round et la fragmentation[1] des disciplines qui en a résulté, d'une part, et la crainte de voir certains pays bénéficier des résultats des négociations sans contrepartie ("free-riding"), d'autre part, avaient incité les parties contractantes du GATT à favoriser la conclusion d'un traité unique qui contiendrait toutes les règles relatives au commerce international et dont l'adhésion serait globale et générale. C'est pour mieux éviter cette fragmentation et pour veiller à ce que les questions relatives au commerce international soient examinées dans un même cadre institutionnel que les partenaires commerciaux ont institué l'OMC[2] et l'ont dotée des pouvoirs nécessaires pour la conduite des relations commerciales entre les Membres de l'OMC en ce qui concerne toutes les questions liées aux accords multilatéraux négociés durant le Cycle de l'Uruguay.

Les fonctions de l'OMC sont beaucoup plus étendues que celles du GATT qui, rappelons-le, n'était qu'un simple traité multilatéral autour duquel s'était développé des arrangements pratiques institutionnels. L'article III de l'Accord de Marrakech instituant l'Organisation mondiale du commerce définit les fonctions de l'OMC comme suit:

(a) Faciliter la mise en oeuvre, l'administration et le fonctionnement de l'Accord instituant l'OMC et des Accords commerciaux multilatéraux et favoriser la réalisation de leurs objectifs, et servir aussi de cadre pour la mise en oeuvre, l'administration et le fonctionnement des Accords commerciaux plurilatéraux.

[1] Durant les négociations du Tokyo Round il avait été décidé que l'adhésion aux nouveaux codes (subventions, dumping, obstacles techniques au commerce, etc. . . .) serait facultative. Ainsi, plusieurs parties contractantes du GATT n'ont jamais adhéré à certains des codes. En matière de dumping par exemple, des règles différentes s'appliquaient selon que les parties au différend étaient ou non membres du Code antidumping.

[2] Contrairement au GATT qui n'avait pas de personnalité juridique distincte de ses Membres, l'Accord de Marrakech instituant l'Organisation mondiale du commerce prévoit à l'article VIII:1 que l'OMC aura la personnalité juridique et se verra accorder, par chacun de ses Membres, la capacité juridique qui pourra être nécessaire à l'exercice de ses fonctions.

(b) Être l'enceinte pour les négociations entre ses Membres au sujet de leurs relations commerciales multilatérales concernant des questions visées par les accords figurant dans les Annexes du présent accord. L'OMC pourra aussi servir d'enceinte pour d'autres négociations entre ses Membres au sujet de leurs relations commerciales multilatérales, et de cadre pour la mise en oeuvre des résultats de ces négociations, selon ce que la Conférence ministérielle pourra décider.

(c) Administrer le Mémorandum d'accord sur les règles et procédures régissant le règlement des différends.

(d) Administrer le Mécanisme d'examen des politiques commerciales.

Par ailleurs, en vue de rendre plus cohérente l'élaboration des politiques économiques au niveau mondial, l'OMC doit coopérer, selon qu'il sera approprié, avec le Fonds monétaire international et avec la Banque internationale pour la reconstruction et le développement et ses institutions affiliées.[3]

La création d'un cadre institutionnel commun ne remédiait cependant pas à elle seule au fait que les négociations dans tous les secteurs s'étaient déroulées en vase clos, un peu à la façon du Tokyo Round. Il fallait ramener le résultat de toutes ces négociations sous un même toit. Le mécanisme juridique choisi afin de confirmer le caractère unique et global de l'Accord de Marrakech fut d'incorporer, à titre d'annexes, les Accords multilatéraux à l'Accord instituant l'Organisation mondiale du commerce. L'Accord sur l'OMC est donc composé d'un accord fondamental — l'Accord instituant l'OMC — et de trois annexes. Ces annexes "font partie intégrante" de l'Accord instituant l'OMC et "sont contraignantes pour tous les Membres."[4] Comme il ressort du tableau 1, l'Annexe 1 regroupe l'Annexe 1A qui comprend les accords multilatéraux sur le commerce des *marchandises*,[5] l'Annexe 1B relative à l'Accord sur le

---

[3] Article III:5 de l'Accord de Marrakech instituant l'Organisation mondiale du commerce.

[4] Article II:2 de l'Accord instituant l'OMC.

[5] La première composante de cette Annexe 1A est le GATT de 1994. Le GATT de 1994 est constitué:

    (a) des dispositions de l'Accord général sur les tarifs douaniers et le commerce, en date du 30 octobre 1947, annexé à l'Acte final adopté à la clôture de la deuxième session de la Commission préparatoire de la Conférence des Nations Unies sur le commerce et l'emploi tel qu'il a été rectifié, amendé ou modifié par la suite (ci-après dénommé le "GATT de 1947") et,

    (b) des dispositions des instruments juridiques mentionnés ci-après qui sont entrés en vigueur en vertu du GATT de 1947 avant la date d'entrée en

commerce des *services* et l'Annexe 1C qui contient l'Accord sur les aspects des droits de *propriété intellectuelle* qui touchent au commerce. L'Annexe 2 comprend le Mémorandum d'accord sur les règles et procédures régissant le règlement des différends (ainsi que les règles particulières ou supplémentaires prévues dans les accords spécifiques) et l'Annexe 3 les règles régissant le Mécanisme d'examen des politiques commerciales. Les Annexes 2 et 3 sont d'application horizontale en ce sens qu'elles s'appliquent à tous les Accords multilatéraux.

Les accords prévus aux Annexes 1, 2 et 3 ne sont pas des accords autonomes indépendants les uns des autres puisqu'ils font tous partie intégrante du même traité. Ils auraient pu être intitulés "chapitres" ou "sections" comme dans l'ALÉNA ou le Traité établissant la CEE, afin d'indiquer qu'ils sont interreliés quant à la forme et au fond. Toutefois, comme les négociations se sont

---

vigueur de l'Accord sur l'OMC:
(i)   protocoles et certifications concernant les concessions tarifaires;
(ii) protocoles d'accession (à l'exclusion des dispositions *(a)* concernant l'application provisoire et la dénonciation de l'application provisoire et *(b)* prévoyant que la Partie II du GATT de 1947 sera appliquée à titre provisoire dans toute la mesure compatible avec la législation en vigueur à la date du Protocole);
(iii) décisions sur les dérogations accordées au titre de l'art. XXV du GATT de 1947 et encore en vigueur à la date d'entrée en vigueur de l'Accord sur l'OMC;
(iv) autres décisions des PARTIES CONTRACTANTES du GATT de 1947;
(c) des Mémorandums d'accord mentionnés ci-après:
(i)   Mémorandum d'accord sur l'interprétation de l'art. II:1 (b) de l'Accord général sur les tarifs douaniers et le commerce de 1994;
(ii) Mémorandum d'accord sur l'interprétation de l'art. XVII de l'Accord général sur les tarifs douaniers et le commerce de 1994;
(iii) Mémorandum d'accord sur les dispositions de l'Accord général sur les tarifs douaniers et le commerce de 1994 relatives à la balance des paiements;
(iv) Mémorandum d'accord sur l'interprétation de l'art. XXIV de l'Accord général sur les tarifs douaniers et le commerce de 1994;
(v)   Mémorandum d'accord concernant les dérogations aux obligations découlant de l'Accord général sur les tarifs douaniers et le commerce de 1994;
(vi) Mémorandum d'accord sur l'interprétation de l'art. XXVIII de l'Accord général sur les tarifs douaniers et le commerce de 1994; et
(d) du Protocole de Marrakech annexé au GATT de 1994.

Le GATT de 1994 est donc juridiquement distinct du GATT de 1947. Concernant la transition du GATT à l'OMC, voir G. Marceau "Transition from the GATT to the WTO: a Most Pragmatic Operation," J.W.T., vol. 29, n° 4, p. 147.

déroulées de façon autonome dans tous les secteurs et que ce n'est qu'à la fin qu'il fut décidé de fondre l'ensemble des résultats des négociations en un seul traité, l'expression "accord" ("agreement") a été maintenue.

Une quatrième annexe reprend les quatre Accords commerciaux *plurilatéraux*, soit l'Accord sur les marchés publics, l'Accord sur le commerce des aéronefs civils, l'Accord international sur le secteur laitier et celui sur la viande bovine. Les accords et instruments juridiques connexes repris dans l'Annexe 4 font également partie de l'Accord instituant l'OMC pour les Membres qui les ont acceptés et sont contraignants pour ces Membres seulement. Les Accords commerciaux plurilatéraux ne créent ni obligations ni droits pour les Membres qui ne les ont pas acceptés.[6]

Sur le plan institutionnel, des corps administratifs et politiques appelés "Conseils," "Comités," "groupes de travail" et "groupes de négociations" sont établis en vertu des accords figurant dans les Annexes de l'Accord instituant l'OMC.

B LA STRUCTURE INSTITUTIONNELLE DE L'OMC

Comme il ressort du tableau 2, la *Conférence ministérielle*, composée de représentants de tous les Membres, est au sommet de l'organigramme institutionnel de l'OMC. La Conférence ministérielle, qui se réunit au moins une fois tous les deux ans, exerce les fonctions de l'OMC et prend les mesures nécessaires à cet effet. Elle prend les décisions sur toutes les questions relevant de tout Accord commercial multilatéral, si un Membre en fait la demande, conformément aux prescriptions spécifiques applicables concernant la prise de décisions.[7]

Dans l'intervalle entre les réunions de la Conférence ministérielle, ses fonctions sont exercées par le *Conseil général* qui est également composé de représentants de tous les Membres et qui se réunit selon qu'il est approprié.[8] Alors que, sous le règne du GATT ("General Agreement on Tariffs and Trade"), le Conseil des représentants veillait à l'administration générale des activités et des opérations des Parties Contractantes, y compris le règlement des différends, l'Accord instituant l'OMC a attribué l'administration du mécanisme de règlement des différends exclusivement à l'ORD.

---

6 Art. II:3 de l'Accord instituant l'OMC.

7 Art. IV:1 de l'Accord instituant l'OMC.

8 Art. IV:2 de l'Accord instituant l'OMC.

Selon l'article IV:3 de l'Accord instituant l'OMC, c'est au Conseil général de s'acquitter des fonctions de l'ORD. L'ORD n'est donc autre que le Conseil général exerçant un rôle particulier en vertu de procédures particulières.[9] Il faut bien noter que l'ORD est juridiquement distinct du Conseil général et a son propre président, ainsi que le prévoit l'article IV:3 de l'Accord instituant l'OMC:

> Le Conseil général se réunira, selon qu'il sera approprié, *pour s'acquitter* des fonctions de l'Organe de règlement des différends prévu dans le Mémorandum d'accord sur le règlement des différends. L'Organe de règlement des différends pourra avoir son propre président et établira le règlement intérieur qu'il jugera nécessaire pour s'acquitter de ces fonctions.

L'article IV:4 prévoit une disposition similaire en ce qui concerne l'Organe d'examen des politiques commerciales.

Pour veiller à la bonne administration des Accords commerciaux multilatéraux figurant aux Annexes 1A, 1B et 1C respectivement, un Conseil du commerce des marchandises, un Conseil du commerce des services et un Conseil des aspects des droits de propriété intellectuelle qui touchent au commerce ont été établis.[10] Ces Conseils exercent les fonctions qui leur sont assignées par les accords respectifs et par le Conseil général et ont établi avec l'approbation du Conseil général leur règlement intérieur respectif. Les représentants de tous les Membres peuvent participer à ces Conseils qui se réunissent selon qu'il est nécessaire pour s'acquitter de leurs fonctions. Ces Conseils ont également le pouvoir d'établir des organes subsidiaires. Le tableau 2 énumère les comités — plusieurs d'entre eux existaient déjà dans le cadre du GATT — groupes de travail et groupes de négociation qui ont ainsi été établis.

Les comités suivants relèvent directement de la Conférence ministérielle: le Comité du commerce et du développement,[11] le

---

9 Une distinction fondamentale existe relativement au droit de vote. En ce qui concerne le Conseil général, l'Accord instituant l'OMC prévoit des règles précises qui varient selon le genre de question faisant l'objet du vote. L'ORD n'agit que par consensus.

10 En vertu de l'art. IV:5, le Conseil du commerce des marchandises supervise le fonctionnement des Accords commerciaux multilatéraux figurant à l'Annexe 1A. Le Conseil du commerce des services supervise le fonctionnement de l'Accord général sur le commerce des services (l'AGCS). Le Conseil des ADPIC supervise le fonctionnement de l'Accord sur les aspects des droits de propriété intellectuelle qui touchent au commerce (l'Accord sur les ADPIC).

11 Selon l'art. IV:7, dans le cadre de ses fonctions, le Comité du commerce et du développement examinera périodiquement les dispositions spéciales des

Comité des restrictions appliquées à des fins de balance des paiements, le Comité du commerce et de l'environnement et le Comité du budget, des finances et de l'administration. Ils exercent les fonctions qui leur sont assignées par l'Accord instituant l'OMC ainsi que par les Accords commerciaux multilatéraux, et toutes fonctions additionnelles qui leur sont assignées par le Conseil général. La Conférence ministérielle pourra établir des comités additionnels auxquels elle confiera les fonctions qu'elle pourra juger appropriées.[12]

III LES PRINCIPAUX CHANGEMENTS RÉSULTANT DU MÉMORANDUM D'ACCORD SUR LE RÈGLEMENT DES DIFFÉRENDS

Plusieurs auteurs ont déjà examiné les nouvelles règles prévues par le Mémorandum d'accord.[13] Le système de règlement des différends de l'OMC est généralement considéré comme l'un des piliers du nouvel ordre commercial multilatéral. Déjà, en vertu de la décision adoptée lors de la réunion de mi-parcours de Montréal, des modifications avaient été apportées en vue d'accroître l'automaticité des décisions relatives à l'établissement, au mandat et à la composition des groupes spéciaux de façon à ce que ces décisions ne dépendent plus de l'assentiment des parties à un différend.[14] Le tableau 3 décrit, de façon schématique, les étapes du mécanisme de règlement des différends.

Le Mémorandum d'accord a renforcé le système existant en étendant le principe d'automaticité à l'adoption des rapports des groupes spéciaux et du nouvel Organe d'appel. Les nouvelles règles ont ainsi modifié le principe du consensus, un principe fondamental du GATT. Auparavant, la plupart des décisions relatives au règlement des différends nécessitaient le consensus des PARTIES CONTRACTANTES. Or, depuis le 1er janvier 1995, le Mémorandum d'accord prévoit une série d'événements juridiques qui se

---

Accords commerciaux multilatéraux en faveur des pays Membres les moins avancés et fera rapport au Conseil général pour que celui-ci prenne les mesures appropriées.

12 Art. IV:7 de l'Accord instituant l'OMC.

13 Voir notamment les n°s 3 et 4 du vol. 29 du *JWT* qui sont consacrés en grande partie au mécanisme de règlement des différends dans le cadre de l'OMC.

14 Décision prise par les PARTIES CONTRACTANTES le 12 avril 1989 sur les améliorations des règles et procédures de règlement des différends du GATT, IBDD 36S/64.

produisent automatiquement à moins que les Membres n'en arrêtent le déroulement par consensus.[15] Il s'agit du principe du "consensus renversé" ("reverse consensus") en ce sens qu'il faut un consensus pour "renverser" la suite des événements.

Le Mémorandum d'accord a également établi un système "intégré" de règlement des différends permettant aux Membres de l'OMC de fonder leurs revendications sur tout Accord commercial multilatéral (les accords visés) figurant dans les Annexes de l'Accord instituant l'OMC. La plupart des Codes du Tokyo Round prévoyaient leur propre mécanisme de règlement des différends. Cela avait donné lieu à d'importants problèmes de "forum shopping"[16] étant donné qu'un différend pouvait être porté à la fois devant le GATT (en vertu des articles XXII et XXIII) et devant les comités institués par les Codes pour entendre les litiges résultant de la mise en application de leurs dispositions. C'est pour éviter cette "fragmentation" que les négociateurs ont établi un système intégré en réunissant en un seul accord l'ensemble[17] des règles relatives au règlement des différends et en instituant un organe de règlement des différends unique.[18] Pour ce qui est de l'ensemble des règles et procédures qui avaient été établies au cours des ans et qui avaient été partiellement codifiées lors de la réunion de mi-parcours de Montréal, le premier paragraphe de l'article 3 du Mémorandum d'accord prévoit ce qui suit:

Les Membres affirment leur adhésion aux principes du règlement des différends appliqués jusqu'ici conformément aux articles XXII et XXIII du GATT de 1947, et aux règles et procédures telles qu'elles sont précisées et modifiées dans le présent mémorandum d'accord.

[15] Une décision sera réputée avoir été prise par consensus si aucun Membre, présent lorsque la décision est prise, ne s'oppose formellement à la décision proposée.

[16] Surtout dans le domaine des règles commerciales (antidumping et subventions).

[17] Certains accords commerciaux prévoient des dispositions particulières en ce qui concerne le règlement des différends. Ces règles "spéciales ou additionnelles" l'emportent sur les règles plus générales du Mémorandum d'accord (art. 1:2) et sont récapitulées à l'Appendice 2 du Mémorandum. Elles sont tout ce qui reste des mécanismes spécifiques de règlement des différents qui figuraient dans plusieurs accords commerciaux. Ce n'est qu'à la toute fin des négociations, lorsqu'il fut décidé d'établir un système intégré, que ces mécanismes disparurent à l'exception de certaines dispositions particulières.

[18] Les nouvelles règles du Mémorandum d'accord et celles contenues dans les Accords multilatéraux sont reproduites dans la publication de l'OMC, *Les Procédures de règlement des différends de l'OMC*, 1995.

Certains prétendent que cette disposition fait en sorte que les anciennes règles ne s'appliquent pas en tant que telles aux différends de l'OMC et ont été "absorbées" dans le Mémorandum d'accord aux termes de l'article 3.[19] Elles n'évolueraient donc plus en tant que "corps de règles autonome" indépendamment des règles prévues au Mémorandum d'accord.

Comme nous l'avons indiqué dans la section précédente, l'ORD a été établi afin de veiller à l'administration générale du Mémorandum d'accord sur le règlement des différends, y compris les dispositions particulières contenues dans les accords visés. L'ORD a donc le pouvoir d'établir des groupes spéciaux, d'adopter les rapports de groupes spéciaux et de l'Organe d'appel, d'assurer la surveillance de la mise en oeuvre des décisions et recommandations, et d'autoriser la suspension de concessions et d'autres obligations qui résultent des accords visés. L'ORD doit également informer les Conseils et Comités compétents de l'OMC de l'évolution des différends en rapport avec des dispositions des accords visés respectifs; il doit, maintenant que des délais stricts ont été mis en place et que de nombreuses procédures écrites sont nécessaires, faire fonction de "greffe" et ainsi recevoir et enregistrer toutes les demandes et autres communications des Membres prévues par les dispositions du Mémorandum d'accord. Du fait de son pouvoir général d'administration, l'ORD a aussi le pouvoir d'adopter les règles de procédure nécessaires au bon fonctionnement du Mémorandum.

Le tableau 4 énumère les fonctions de l'ORD et les communications que les Membres se sont engagés à transmettre à l'ORD aux fins du règlement de leurs différends. Comme il ressort du tableau 3, lorsqu'un différend n'est pas réglé par voie de consultations,[20] le Mémorandum d'accord prescrit qu'un groupe spécial sera établi[21] au plus tard à la réunion de l'ORD suivant celle à laquelle la demande aura été présentée à moins que l'ORD se prononce par consensus contre cet établissement. Le Mémorandum d'accord prévoit également des règles et des délais spécifiques pour les

---

[19] Il faut toutefois noter que l'Accord sur les marchés publics du Tokyo Round toujours en vigueur et l'Accord sur les aéronefs prévoient que le Mémorandum d'accord concernant les notifications, les consultations, le règlement des différends et la surveillance — Décision de 1979 du Tokyo Round — leur est toujours applicable.

[20] Art. 4:7 du Mémorandum d'accord.

[21] Art. 6:1, *idem.*

décisions à prendre concernant le mandat[22] et la composition des groupes spéciaux.[23] Les groupes spéciaux devront normalement être composés de trois personnes[24] ayant des compétences et une expérience appropriées et venant de pays dont le gouvernement n'est pas partie au différend.[25] Le Secrétariat tiendra une liste indicative d'experts satisfaisant à ces critères.[26]

La procédure des groupes spéciaux est exposée en détail dans le Mémorandum d'accord.[27] Un groupe spécial devra normalement achever ses travaux dans un délai de six mois ou, en cas d'urgence, dans les trois mois.[28] Son rapport devra être adopté dans un délai maximal de soixante jours à compter de sa distribution, à moins que l'ORD ne décide par consensus de ne pas l'adopter, ou que l'une des parties ne notifie à l'ORD son intention de faire appel.[29] La possibilité de porter le différend en appel est un nouvel élément important du Mémorandum d'accord. Un Organe d'appel a été institué à la première réunion de l'ORD. Il est composé de sept membres, dont trois siégeront pour une affaire donnée.[30] Les appels seront limités aux questions de droit couvertes par le rapport du groupe spécial et aux interprétations du droit données par celui-ci.[31] La durée de la procédure d'appel ne devra généralement pas dépasser soixante jours à compter de celui où une partie a formellement notifié sa décision de faire appel.[32] Un rapport établi en appel sera adopté par l'ORD et accepté sans condition par les parties au différend dans les trente jours suivant sa distribution aux Membres, à moins que l'ORD ne se prononce par consensus contre son adoption.[33]

---

[22] Art. 7, *idem.*

[23] Art. 8, *idem.*

[24] Art. 8:5, *idem.*

[25] Art. 8:3, *idem.*

[26] Art. 8:4, *idem.*

[27] Art. 12 et Annexe 3 du Mémorandum d'accord.

[28] Art. 12:8, *idem.*

[29] Art. 16:4, *idem.*

[30] Art. 17, *idem.*

[31] Art. 17:6, *idem.*

[32] Art. 17:5, *idem.*

[33] Art. 17:4, *idem*; les rapports qui portent sur les subventions prohibées ou les subventions qui peuvent donner lieu à une action doivent être adoptés dans un délai de 20 jours (art. 4.9 et 7.9 de l'Accord sur les subventions et les mesures compensatoires).

Les règles relatives à la surveillance et aux sanctions ont également été renforcées. Après l'adoption du rapport d'un groupe spécial ou de l'Organe d'appel, l'ORD veillera à la mise en oeuvre des recommandations jusqu'à ce que la question soit résolue. Trente jours après l'adoption du rapport, la partie concernée devra faire connaître ses intentions concernant la mise en oeuvre des recommandations adoptées.[34] S'il est irréalisable pour la partie concernée de s'y conformer immédiatement, celle-ci se verra accorder un "délai raisonnable," qui sera fixé soit par accord des parties dans un délai de quarante-cinq jours à compter de l'adoption du rapport,[35] soit sur proposition du Membre concerné avec l'approbation de l'ORD,[36] soit par arbitrage dans un délai de quatre-vingt-dix jours à compter de l'adoption.[37] En cas de désaccord au sujet de l'existence ou de la compatibilité avec un accord visé de mesures prises pour se conformer aux recommandations et décisions, les parties peuvent avoir recours au groupe spécial initial ou à un autre groupe spécial qui devra alors rendre son rapport dans les quatre-vingt-dix jours.[38]

De nouvelles dispositions énoncent les règles relatives à la compensation ou à la suspension de concessions au cas où les recommandations ne seraient pas mises en oeuvre volontairement par la partie concernée. Si le Membre concerné ne met pas la mesure jugée incompatible avec un accord visé en conformité avec ledit accord ou ne respecte pas autrement les recommandations et décisions dans le "délai raisonnable," les parties pourront, dans un délai spécifié, entreprendre des négociations en vue de se mettre d'accord sur une compensation mutuellement acceptable. Si ces négociations ne peuvent aboutir dans les vingt jours, une partie au différend pourra demander à l'ORD l'autorisation de suspendre l'application de concessions ou d'autres obligations à l'égard de l'autre partie concernée.[39] L'ORD devra maintenant accorder cette autorisation dans un délai de trente jours à compter de l'expiration du délai raisonnable pour la mise en oeuvre. Malgré l'automaticité de cette décision de l'ORD, en cas de désaccord au sujet des

---

[34] Art. 21:3 du Mémorandum d'accord.

[35] Art. 21:3(b), *idem.*

[36] Art. 21:3(a), *idem.*

[37] Art. 21:3(c), *idem.*

[38] Art. 21:5, *idem.*

[39] Art. 22:2, *idem.*

principes ou du niveau des suspensions proposées,[40] la question pourra être soumise à l'arbitrage.[41] En principe, les concessions devraient être suspendues dans le même secteur que celui qui est en cause dans l'affaire examinée par le groupe spécial.[42] Si cela n'est pas possible ou efficace, la suspension pourra intervenir dans un secteur différent au titre du même accord.[43] Si, là encore, cela n'est pas possible ou efficace et si les circonstances sont suffisamment graves, la suspension de concessions pourra intervenir au titre d'un autre accord[44] ("cross-retaliation").

Le Mémorandum d'accord contient un certain nombre de dispositions qui tiennent compte des intérêts spécifiques des pays en développement et des pays les moins avancés.[45] Il prévoit également certaines règles spéciales pour le règlement des différends lorsque, malgré le fait qu'il n'y a pas eu violation d'obligations découlant d'un accord visé, un Membre estime que des avantages découlant pour lui d'un accord se trouvent annulés ou compromis[46] ("non-violation").

Le Mémorandum d'accord condamne toute action unilatérale et réaffirme, c'est l'une de ses dispositions essentielles, que les Membres ne doivent pas eux-mêmes déterminer qu'il y a eu violation, ni suspendre des concessions, mais plutôt appliquer les règles et procédures de règlement des différends du Mémorandum d'accord.[47]

IV RAPPORT DES ACTIVITÉS DE LA PREMIÈRE ANNÉE D'OPÉRATION DE L'ORD

À la réunion du 31 janvier 1995 du Conseil général de l'OMC, l'Ambassadeur Kenyon (Australie) a été nommé Président de l'ORD. L'ORD s'est réuni onze fois et a également tenu plusieurs rencontres informelles. Ses principales activités sont décrites ci-après.

[40] Art. 22:4 du Mémorandum d'accord: "Le niveau de la suspension de concessions ou d'autres obligations autorisées par l'ORD sera équivalent au niveau de l'annulation ou de la réduction des avantages."

[41] Art. 22:7, *idem.*

[42] Art. 22:3(a), *idem.*

[43] Art. 22:3(b), *idem.*

[44] Art. 22:3(c), *idem.*

[45] Art. 3:12, 4:10, 8:10, 12:10, 12:11, 22:7, 22:8, 24, 27:2, 27:3 du Mémorandum d'accord.

[46] Art. 26, *idem.*

[47] Art. 23, *idem.*

A ORGANE D'APPEL PERMANENT

a Institution de l'Organe d'appel

L'Organe d'appel a été institué à la première réunion de l'ORD, le 10 février 1995, conformément à l'article 17:1 du Mémorandum d'accord sur le règlement des différends.

b Désignation des membres de l'Organe d'appel

La sélection des membres de cet Organe d'appel fut l'une des opérations politiques les plus délicates de l'année. Un comité de sélection fut établi à cette fin sous la présidence de l'Ambassadeur Kenyon. Outre le président de l'ORD, ce comité de sélection était composé du président du Conseil général, des présidents du Conseil des marchandises, du Conseil des services et des ADPIC et du Directeur général. Le Comité préparatoire, établi afin de faciliter la transition vers l'OMC, avait déjà élaboré des lignes directrices afin d'aider le comité de sélection. La sélection des membres allait inévitablement poser de très sérieux problèmes eu égard, notamment, à la diversité des partenaires commerciaux de l'OMC, au nombre restreint de membres à sélectionner (sept) et aux critères généraux qui sont énoncés dans le Mémorandum d'accord sur le règlement des différends. Les dispositions pertinentes de l'article 17 prévoient ce qui suit:

(2) L'ORD désignera les personnes qui feront partie de l'Organe d'appel. Leur mandat sera de quatre ans et, pour chacune, sera renouvelable une fois. Toutefois, les mandats de trois personnes tirées au sort parmi les sept personnes désignées immédiatement après l'entrée en vigueur de l'Accord sur l'OMC arriveront à expiration après deux ans. Dès qu'ils deviendront vacants, les postes seront repourvus. Une personne désignée pour remplacer une personne dont le mandat ne sera pas arrivé à expiration occupera le poste pendant la durée restante du mandat de son prédécesseur.

(3) L'Organe d'appel comprendra des personnes dont l'autorité est reconnue, qui auront fait la preuve de leur connaissance du droit, du commerce international et des questions relevant des accords visés en général. Elles n'auront aucune attache avec une administration nationale. La composition de l'Organe d'appel sera, dans l'ensemble, représentative de celle de l'OMC. Toutes les personnes qui feront partie de l'Organe d'appel seront disponibles à tout moment et à bref délai et se maintiendront au courant des activités de l'OMC en matière de règlement des différends et de ses autres activités pertinentes. Elles ne participeront pas à l'examen d'un différend qui créerait un conflit d'intérêt direct ou indirect.

Les Membres furent d'abord invités à soumettre des candidatures pour ces postes. Vingt-deux pays soumirent trente-trois noms. À la réunion de l'ORD du 25 avril 1995, le Président présenta la liste de tous les candidats mis en nomination et invita les délégations à faire valoir leurs points de vue à cet égard à un "Comité des Six" qui examinerait les candidatures. Une série de consultations bilatérales et multilatérales eu lieu avec cinquante-quatre délégations.

Le Comité des Six dut retarder la présentation de son rapport à plusieurs reprises faute de consensus sur la sélection des membres. Les Américains et Européens souhaitaient initialement avoir deux sièges chacun, ce qui aurait évidemment laissé très peu de place aux autres pays dont notamment les pays en voie de développement.

À la réunion d'octobre de l'ORD, le Président informa les Membres que les conclusions auxquelles était parvenu le "Comité des Six" au sujet de la composition de l'Organe d'appel avaient été communiquées aux trente-trois candidats et que quelques délégations avaient demandé un délai de réflexion. En novembre, le président, au nom du Comité des Six, soumit à l'ORD pour approbation la liste des membres proposés ci-après:

M. James Bacchus (États-Unis)
M. Christopher Beeby (Nouvelle-Zélande)
Professeur Claus-Dieter Ehlermann (Allemagne)
Dr Said El-Naggar (Égypte)
M. le Juge Florentino Feliciano (Philippines)
M. Julio Lacarte Muro (Uruguay)
Professeur Mitsuo Matsushita (Japon)

Après de nombreux débats, l'ORD approuvait, le 1er décembre, la proposition du Comité des Six. Ces sept premiers membres furent assermentés le 14 décembre 1995. L'Organe d'appel, en consultation avec le Président de l'ORD et le Directeur général, est en train d'élaborer des procédures de travail qui seront communiquées aux Membres pour leur information. Ces procédures devront être achevées incessamment, compte tenu du fait que l'Organe d'appel pourrait être saisi de sa première affaire avant la fin de l'hiver 1996.[48]

---

[48] Art. 17:9 du Mémorandum d'accord.

B RÈGLEMENT INTÉRIEUR DES RÉUNIONS DE L'ORGANE DE RÈGLEMENT DES DIFFÉRENDS

Lors de la première réunion de l'ORD, le Président, conformément à l'article IV:3 de l'Accord instituant l'OMC, proposa que l'ORD adopte le règlement intérieur proposé par le Comité préparatoire[49] à l'exception de deux questions en suspens, à savoir la question de l'élection du Président (et, éventuellement, d'un vice-président) et celle de la participation d'organisations internationales en qualité d'observateurs à l'OMC, questions sur lesquelles l'ORD reviendrait lorsqu'elles auraient fait l'objet d'un accord. À la réunion de l'ORD du 25 avril 1995, il fut décidé que l'ORD n'aurait pas de vice-président; la question de la participation d'organisations internationales n'a toujours pas été réglée.

C CALENDRIER DES RÉUNIONS DE L'ORGANE DE RÈGLEMENT DES DIFFÉRENDS

À la réunion de mars 1995, le Président proposa un calendrier pour les réunions ordinaires de l'ORD prévues en 1995, calendrier qui pouvait être modifié au besoin. Il convient de noter que ce calendrier ne diminue en rien le droit des Membres de convoquer l'ORD en tout temps,[50] notamment pour l'établissement d'un groupe spécial,[51] l'adoption des rapports des groupes spéciaux[52] et l'inscription en appel,[53] comme prévu dans le Mémorandum d'accord sur le règlement des différends.

D CODE DE CONDUITE CONCERNANT LES DIFFÉRENDS VISÉS PAR LE MÉMORANDUM D'ACCORD

Des négociations ont eu lieu entre les Membres de l'OMC, sous la présidence de l'Ambassadeur Armstrong (Nouvelle-Zélande), en vue de parvenir à une entente sur un ensemble de règles que les

---

49 PC/IPL/9

50 L'art. 2:3 du Mémorandum d'accord est clair à cet égard: ''L'ORD se réunira aussi souvent qu'il sera nécessaire pour s'acquitter de ses fonctions dans les délais prévus par le présent memorandum.''

51 Voir *supra* note 5 relative à l'art. 6 du Mémorandum d'accord.

52 Voir l'art. 16 du Mémorandum d'accord sur le règlement des différends et les art. 4.8 et 7.6 de l'Accord sur les subventions et les mesures compensatoires.

53 Voir l'art. 16 du Mémorandum d'accord sur le règlement des différends et les art. 4.8 et 7.6 de l'Accord sur les subventions et les mesures compensatoires.

personnes participant au processus de règlement des différends devraient observer. En novembre 1994, les États-Unis avaient soumis un premier projet à cet effet qui a servi de base aux négociations. Ces règles de conduite portent sur la confidentialité, les conflits d'intérêt, l'indépendance et l'impartialité. Elles s'appliqueraient aux membres des groupes spéciaux et de l'Organe d'appel ainsi qu'au personnel du Secrétariat et de l'Organe d'appel qui est chargé de les aider. Au moment de la rédaction de cette note, on était parvenu à s'entendre sur le texte de ce Code de conduite mais la possibilité d'appliquer certaines de ces règles aux activités de l'Organe de supervision des textiles faisait toujours l'objet de négociations.

E   LISTE INDICATIVE DE PERSONNES AYANT OU NON DES ATTACHES
    AVEC DES ADMINISTRATIONS NATIONALES APPELÉES À FAIRE
    PARTIE DE GROUPES SPÉCIAUX

Conformément à l'article 8:4 du Mémorandum d'accord sur le règlement des différends, le Secrétariat doit tenir une liste indicative de personnes ayant ou non des attaches avec des administrations nationales appelées à faire partie de groupes spéciaux ("panelists"). En 1995, le Président de l'ORD a donc invité les délégations à soumettre les noms de candidats (avec leur curriculum vitae) qui pourraient être portés sur la liste indicative. À la suite de consultations informelles, il fut décidé de ne pas effectuer d'évaluation préalable des candidats. Les délégations auront donc la possibilité de faire ajouter en tout temps des noms à la liste indicative en les soumettant à tout moment à l'ORD pour approbation. Comme il revient toujours aux parties à un différend de choisir les personnes qui feront partie du groupe spécial, l'évaluation des candidats se fera dans le cadre de différends particuliers.

À la réunion qu'il a tenu en septembre, l'ORD a décidé de mettre la première liste indicative en distribution non restreinte.[54]

F   PRATIQUES CONCERNANT DES QUESTIONS PROCÉDURALES

L'ORD a également mis en place, à titre expérimental, quelques "pratiques" concernant des questions procédurales. Il convient de noter qu'il ne s'agit pas de véritables décisions qui lient les Membres mais plutôt de pratiques proposées par le Président de l'ORD

[54] Voir document WT/DSB/W/8.

qui pourront être révisées et qui pourraient, à terme, être adoptées formellement. On peut envisager que même si elles n'étaient jamais adoptées formellement, ces pratiques pourraient acquérir un caractère obligatoire à titre de coutume internationale. Par ailleurs, l'article 31.3(c) de la Convention de Vienne sur le droit des traités prévoit qu'une pratique ultérieure peut servir de base pour confirmer l'interprétation à donner à une disposition d'un traité.

31.2 Aux fins de l'interprétation d'un traité, le contexte comprend, outre le texte, préambule et annexes inclus:
. . .
31.3 Il sera tenu compte, en même temps que du contexte:
. . .
(b) de *toute pratique ultérieure* suivie dans l'application du traité par laquelle est établi l'accord des parties à l'égard de l'interprétation du traité.

Ainsi, si les Membres de l'OMC prennent l'habitude d'adhérer à de telles pratiques, on pourra possiblement déduire de cette "pratique ultérieure" que les Membres ont l'intention que ces pratiques aient un caractère obligatoire.

a   *"Date de transmission," "date de distribution"*[55]

Certains délais énoncés dans le Mémorandum d'accord étant de rigueur, il devenait impératif que les règles relatives à la computation de ces délais, notamment les points de départ et d'échéance, soient clarifiés. À titre d'exemple, les articles 4:11 et 16:4 du Mémorandum d'accord prévoient ce qui suit:

4.11 Chaque fois qu'un Membre autre que les Membres qui prennent part aux consultations considérera qu'il a un intérêt commercial substantiel dans les consultations tenues en vertu du paragraphe 1 de l'article XXII du GATT de 1994, du paragraphe 1 de l'article XXII de l'AGCS ou des dispositions correspondantes des autres accords visés,[56] il pourra

[55] Cette pratique s'applique également aux rapports des groupes spéciaux adoptés en vertu des art. 4.8, 4.9, 7.6 et 7.7 de l'Accord sur les subventions.

[56] Les dispositions correspondantes des accords visés relatives aux consultations sont les suivantes: Accord sur l'agriculture, art. 19; Accord sur l'application des mesures sanitaires et phytosanitaires, par. 1 de l'art. 11; Accord sur les textiles et les vêtements, par. 4 de l'art. 8; Accord sur les obstacles techniques au commerce, par. 1 de l'art. 14; Accord sur les mesures concernant les investissements et liées au commerce, art. 8; Accord sur la mise en oeuvre de l'art. VI du GATT de 1994, par. 2 de l'art. 17; Accord sur la mise en oeuvre de l'art. VII du GATT

informer lesdits Membres ainsi que l'ORD, *dans les 10 jours suivant la date de transmission de la demande de consultations au titre dudit article*, de son désir d'être admis à participer aux consultations.
. . .
16.4 Dans les 60 jours suivant la *date de distribution* du rapport d'un groupe spécial aux Membres, ce rapport sera adopté à une réunion de l'ORD,[57] à moins qu'une partie au différend ne notifie formellement à l'ORD sa décision de faire appel ou que l'ORD ne décide par consensus de ne pas adopter le rapport. Si une partie a notifié sa décision de faire appel, le rapport du groupe spécial ne sera pas examiné par l'ORD, en vue de son adoption, avant l'achèvement de la procédure d'appel. Cette procédure d'adoption est sans préjudice du droit des Membres d'exprimer leurs vues sur le rapport d'un groupe spécial.

À la réunion de mars 1995, le Président de l'ORD a informé les Membres qu'il avait tenu des consultations informelles au sujet du sens à donner aux expressions "date de transmission" ou "date de distribution" figurant dans le Mémorandum d'accord sur le règlement des différends (et dans ses règles additionnelles et spéciales) et constituant le point de départ de computation de délais. Afin d'éviter toute ambiguïté à cet égard, l'ORD a décidé, à titre d'essai, que lorsqu'il était fait référence à la "date de transmission" ou à la "date de distribution" dans le Mémorandum d'accord, la date à utiliser sera la date imprimée sur le document de l'OMC à distribuer, le Secrétariat donnant l'assurance que cette date sera la date à laquelle ce document est effectivement mis dans les casiers des délégations dans les trois langues de l'OMC. Cette solution a été appliquée avec succès.

b   Communications effectuées en vertu du Mémorandum d'accord sur le règlement des différends

Selon l'article 4:4 du Mémorandum d'accord, "[t]outes les demandes de consultations . . . seront notifiées à l'ORD et aux

---

de 1994, par. 2 de l'art. 19; Accord sur l'inspection avant expédition, art. 7; Accord sur les règles d'origine, art. 7; Accord sur les procédures de licences d'importation, art. 6; Accord sur les subventions et les mesures compensatoires, art. 30; Accord sur les sauvegardes, art. 14; Accord sur les aspects des droits de propriété intellectuelle qui touchent au commerce, art. 64.1; et les dispositions correspondantes des Accords commerciaux plurilatéraux relatives aux consultations, telles qu'elles sont déterminées par les organes compétents de chaque Accord et notifiées à l'ORD.

57 S'il n'est pas prévu de réunion de l'ORD pendant cette période, à un moment qui permette de satisfaire aux prescriptions des par. 1 et 4 de l'art. 16, l'ORD tiendra une réunion à cette fin.

Conseils et Comités compétents par le Membre qui demande l'ouverture de consultations." Pour simplifier le travail des délégations, les Membres ont été invités à envoyer leurs notifications en un seul exemplaire au Secrétariat (Division du Conseil) et à indiquer dans le texte quels sont les autres Conseils ou Comités compétents auxquels elles souhaitaient les adresser. Le Secrétariat s'est engagé à les communiquer à ces organes.

c *Délais prévus par le Mémorandum d'accord sur le règlement des différends et les autres accords visés qui expirent un jour non ouvré*

À la réunion de juillet 1995, le Président indiquait qu'un certain nombre de délégations avaient demandé comment traiter les délais prévus dans les dispositions du Mémorandum d'accord qui venaient à expiration un jour non ouvré à l'OMC. Des consultations informelles ont permis d'élaborer un projet d'entente en vertu duquel lorsqu'un délai expire un jour non ouvré à l'OMC, toute communication à faire ou démarche à entreprendre avant l'expiration de ce délai est acceptée le premier jour ouvré à l'OMC qui suit la date d'expiration. Il est toutefois entendu que les délais eux-mêmes ne seront pas modifiés. Ce projet a été adopté à la réunion qu'a tenue l'ORD en septembre. Jusqu'à maintenant, cette règle n'a pas été utilisée.

G LES ACTIVITÉS DE L'ORD DANS LE CADRE DES PROCÉDURES DE RÈGLEMENT DES DIFFÉRENDS

En 1995, vingt-cinq demandes de consultation ont été notifiées à l'ORD. Il convient de noter que douze de ces demandes ont été soumises par des pays en voie de développement. Cela constitue certainement un fait nouveau par rapport aux années précédentes où tout donnait à croire que le mécanisme de règlement des différends du GATT n'était utilisé que par les pays "riches." Cette nouvelle participation peut s'expliquer de plusieurs façons.

Premièrement, les nouvelles règles applicables au processus de règlement des différends sont plus "juridiques" et moins "politiques" qu'auparavant, l'adoption automatique des rapports des groupes spéciaux en étant peut-être le meilleur exemple.

Ensuite, l'existence de dispositions substantielles plus favorables aux pays en voie de développement a pu inciter ces derniers à avoir recours au système de règlement des différends. À titre d'exemples, les pays en voie de développement peuvent maintenant exiger que la durée des procédures d'un groupe spécial soit abrégée;[58] ils

---

[58] Art. 3:12 du Mémorandum d'accord.

peuvent également demander l'intervention du Directeur général lors des consultations et en demander l'extension;[59] une attention spéciale est accordée aux problèmes et intérêts particuliers des pays en voie de développement lors des consultations,[60] dans le rapport du groupe spécial[61] et lors de la mise en oeuvre des recommandations et décisions;[62] de plus, si un pays en voie de développement est partie à un différend contre un pays développé, le groupe spécial comprendra un ressortissant d'un pays en voie de développement si le pays en voie de développement le demande.[63] L'article 24 du Mémorandum d'accord, concernant les pays Membres les moins avancés, dispose qu'à tous les stades de la détermination des causes d'un différend et d'une procédure de règlement des différends concernant un pays Membre moins avancé, une attention particulière sera accordée à la situation spéciale des pays Membres les moins avancés. À cet égard, les Membres devront faire preuve de modération lorsqu'ils soulèveront des questions concernant un pays Membre moins avancé. Aucune de ces disposition n'ayant encore été analysée par un groupe spécial, il est encore trop tôt pour conclure qu'elles auront une incidence réelle sur les droits des pays en voie de développement.

La dernière raison pouvant expliquer la nouvelle participation des pays en voie de développement est qu'en vertu de l'article 27 du Mémorandum d'accord, il est maintenant expressément prévu qu'une assistance technique est offerte aux pays en développement qui en font la demande. Le deuxième paragraphe de l'article 27 dispose comme suit:

À la demande d'un Membre, le Secrétariat lui apportera son concours dans le règlement d'un différend, mais il sera peut-être aussi nécessaire de donner des avis et une aide juridique additionnels aux pays en développement Membres en ce qui concerne le règlement des différends. À cette fin, le Secrétariat mettra à la disposition de tout pays en développement Membre qui le demandera un expert juridique qualifié des services de coopération technique de l'OMC. Cet expert aidera le pays en développement Membre d'une manière qui permette de maintenir l'impartialité du Secrétariat.

59 Art. 12:10, *idem.*

60 Art. 4:10, *idem.*

61 Art. 12:11, *idem.*

62 Art. 21:2, 21:7 et 21:8, *idem.*

63 Art. 8:10, *idem.*

Les pays en voie de développement ont eu recours aux services d'un expert juridique dans tous les différends dans lesquels ils étaient parties.

L'ORD a procédé à l'établissement de groupes spéciaux pour les trois différends suivants.[64]

a Différend sur l'essence (Vénézuéla/Brésil c. États-Unis)

À sa réunion du 10 avril 1995, l'ORD a établi un groupe spécial pour examiner la décision finale adoptée le 15 décembre 1993 (en vigueur depuis le 1er janvier 1995) par l'Agence pour la protection de l'environnement des États-Unis, *Réglementation concernant les combustibles et les additifs pour combustibles* — normes pour l'essence nouvelle et anciennes formules (Réglementation sur l'essence). Le Vénézuéla estimait que la Réglementation sur l'essence contrevenait aux obligations qui incombaient aux États-Unis au titre du GATT de 1994 et de l'Accord sur les obstacles techniques au commerce. Selon le Vénézuéla, la Réglementation favorisait l'essence produite aux États-Unis et dans un pays tiers au détriment de l'essence vénézuélienne et était donc incompatible avec les obligations d'accorder le traitement national et le traitement de la nation la plus favorisée prévues aux articles I et III du GATT de 1994. La Réglementation enfreindrait également les articles 2.1 et 2.2 de l'Accord sur les obstacles techniques au commerce car elle créerait des obstacles non nécessaires au commerce et serait, de ce fait, plus restrictive pour le commerce que nécessaire. Le Brésil, qui avait engagé des consultations avec les États-Unis sur le même sujet, s'est joint au différend le 22 mai. Le groupe spécial devrait présenter son rapport au début de l'année 1996.

b Différend au sujet des coquilles St-Jacques (Canada, Pérou et Chili c. CE)

À la réunion de juillet de l'ORD, le Canada a déclaré qu'il considérait que la mesure prise par la France en matière d'étiquetage applicable aux pectinidés était incompatible avec les obligations des Communautés européennes dans le cadre de l'OMC, notamment leurs obligations au titre de l'article 2 de l'Accord sur

---

[64] L'ORD a également établi un groupe spécial dans le conflit entre la CE et le Canada concernant les droits de douanes imposés sur certaines céréales mais il semble que ce différend sera résolu sans qu'il soit nécessaire de poursuivre les procédures.

les obstacles techniques au commerce et des articles I et III du GATT de 1994. Le Canada et les Communautés européennes ont tenu, sans succès, des consultations et le Canada a demandé et obtenu l'établissement d'un groupe spécial.

Le Pérou et le Chili ont également tenu des consultations au sujet de cette réglementation française et, le 11 octobre 1995, l'ORD établissait un groupe spécial conjoint pour ces deux pays en application de l'article 9.1 du Mémorandum d'accord sur le règlement des différends concernant les demandes multiples qui prévoit ce qui suit:

Procédures applicables en cas de pluralité des plaignants

Dans les cas où plusieurs Membres demanderont l'établissement d'un groupe spécial en relation avec la même question, un seul groupe pourra être établi pour examiner leurs plaintes, en tenant compte des droits de tous les Membres concernés. Chaque fois que possible, il conviendra d'établir un seul groupe spécial pour examiner ces plaintes.

Deux groupes spéciaux (Canada et Pérou/Chili) avaient donc été établis pour examiner des plaintes relatives à la même question. Dans un tel cas, l'article 9.3 du Mémorandum d'Accord prévoit ce qui suit:

Si plusieurs groupes spéciaux sont établis pour examiner des plaintes relatives à la même question, les mêmes personnes, dans toute la mesure du possible, feront partie de chacun de ces groupes et le calendrier des travaux des groupes spéciaux saisis de ces différends sera harmonisé.

Les mêmes individus ont effectivement accepté de faire partie des deux groupes spéciaux et le calendrier des deux groupes spéciaux a été harmonisé. Les rapports finaux sont prévus pour le printemps 1996.

c *Différend concernant des taxes imposées sur certaines boissons alcooliques (CE, Canada et États-Unis c. Japon)*

À la réunion de juillet 1995, les Communautés européennes, le Canada et les États-Unis ont demandé l'établissement d'un groupe spécial chargé d'examiner les taxes perçues au Japon sur certaines boissons alcooliques. Les Communautés ont indiqué qu'elles se préoccupaient de cette question depuis un certain temps. Déjà, en 1986, par suite d'une procédure de règlement des différends, un groupe spécial avait présenté un rapport dont les conclusions corroboraient, selon elles, son interprétation de la situation.[65] Depuis,

65 L/6216.

malgré des contacts constants avec le Japon, il n'y avait eu aucune amélioration satisfaisante de la situation. Les Communautés ont donc engagé une nouvelle procédure dans le cadre de l'OMC. Les consultations en vue d'arriver à une solution satisfaisante n'ayant pas permis de surmonter les difficultés, les Communautés ont demandé l'établissement d'un groupe spécial.

Le Canada et les États-Unis se sont joint à la demande de la CE alléguant l'illégalité du régime de taxation des alcools en vigueur au Japon qui prévoit différents taux de taxation selon les catégories de boissons alcooliques distillées. Le Japon a consenti à l'établissement du groupe spécial conjoint conformément à l'article 9.1 du Mémorandum d'accord, dès la première demande des parties. Le rapport du groupe spécial devrait être remis aux parties d'ici l'été 1996.

V Conclusion

Un plus grand nombre de différends sont soumis au nouveau mécanisme de règlement des différends de l'OMC. En 1995, il y a eu vingt-cinq demandes de consultations contre sept en 1994.[66] Un pays en développement avait initié le différend pour près de la moitié (douze) de ces affaires. Cela constitue un changement important considérant qu'entre 1948 et 1994 un pays en développement n'avait initie un litige que dans onze des 126 différends.

La plupart de ces différends ont fait l'objet d'un règlement avant que les membres d'un groupe spécial aient été choisis. Le caractère plus automatique et plus prévisible du mécanisme explique peut-être sa plus grande "efficacité," les parties à un différend réalisant qu'à terme une décision véritablement contraignante (compte tenu du principe du consensus "renversé") sera rendue par un groupe spécial.

[66] Comme il était encore trop tôt pour qu'une affaire de droit anti-dumping ou de droit compensateur ne soit présentée au titre de l'OMC, les sept demandes de consultations de 1994 ne comprennent que les différends relatifs à l'Accord général et ne comprennent pas ceux qui sont intervenus dans le cadre des codes du Tokyo Round concernant les droits antidumping et les droits compensateurs. Les mesures transitoires prévues dans l'Accord antidumping (art. 18.3) et l'Accord sur les subventions (art. 32.3) de l'OMC prescrivent que les nouveaux accords ne s'appliquent qu'aux mesures imposées par suite d'une enquête ouverte après le 1er janvier 1995. Comme il s'écoule habituellement plus d'un an entre la date d'ouverture de l'enquête et celle de l'imposition de la mesure commerciale contestée, aucune demande de consultation n'a été présentée au titre de ces accords.

L'augmentation du nombre de différends portés devant l'OMC, la plus grande participation des pays en voie de développement et la rapidité avec laquelle ces différends sont résolus témoignent de la confiance accrue de tous les Membres envers le mécanisme de règlement des différends de l'OMC.

GABRIELLE MARCEAU ET ALAIN RICHER
Organisation mondiale du commerce

Summary

The First Year of the Dispute Settlement Body of the World Trade Organization

The first year of the World Trade Organization (WTO) has been a great success. Various institutional matters, including those related to the transition from the old GATT 1947 to the new organization, the implementation of extended national legislation notification and review procedures, the setting up of new committees on trade and environment, regional arrangements and least developed countries, as well as the nomination of many chairpersons and the seven new "judges" for the Appellate Body, are but a few of the numerous accomplishments of the WTO members in 1995. Interestingly, developing countries' participation in the WTO system has increased drastically, namely through their repeated use of the new dispute settlement rules; in fact, 50 per cent of the dispute requests have been initiated by developing countries. The WTO has clearly triggered a process from which there is no turning back.

Sommaire

La première année de l'Organe de règlement des différends de l'Organisation mondiale du commerce

La première année de l'Organisation mondiale du commerce (OMC) fut un grand succès. Les Membres de l'OMC ont notamment mis en place tout le nouveau système de notification préalable et de révision des législations nationales, et mis sur pied les nouveaux comités sur l'environnement, sur les arrangements régionaux et sur les pays les moins avancés. En plus d'assurer l'achèvement des activités GATT 1947 et la transition formelle en faveur de l'OMC, les Membres ont également procédé à la nomination des présidents de plusieurs comités et des "juges" du nouvel organe d'appel. L'élément peut-être le plus impressionnant du départ de cette nouvelle organisation est la participation particulièrement active des pays en développement au nouveau système obligatoire de règlement des différends; la moitié des vingt-cinq requêtes pour consultation ont été initiées par ceux-ci. Quel changement alors qu'entre 1948 et 1994, les pays en développement n'avaient initié que onze des 126 différends. En fait l'OMC a déclenché un nouveau processus pour lequel il n'y a pas de marche arrière possible.

TABLEAU 1 Structure juridique de l'accord instituant l'organisation mondiale du commerce

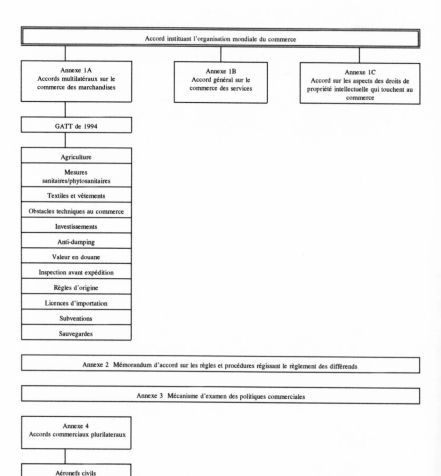

Accord instituant l'organisation mondiale du commerce

Annexe 1A
Accords multilatéraux sur le commerce des marchandises

Annexe 1B
Accord général sur le commerce des services

Annexe 1C
Accord sur les aspects des droits de propriété intellectuelle qui touchent au commerce

GATT de 1994

Agriculture

Mesures sanitaires/phytosanitaires

Textiles et vêtements

Obstacles techniques au commerce

Investissements

Anti-dumping

Valeur en douane

Inspection avant expédition

Règles d'origine

Licences d'importation

Subventions

Sauvegardes

Annexe 2 Mémorandum d'accord sur les règles et procédures régissant le règlement des différends

Annexe 3 Mécanisme d'examen des politiques commerciales

Annexe 4
Accords commerciaux plurilateraux

Aéronefs civils

Marchés publics

Secteur laitier

Viande bovine

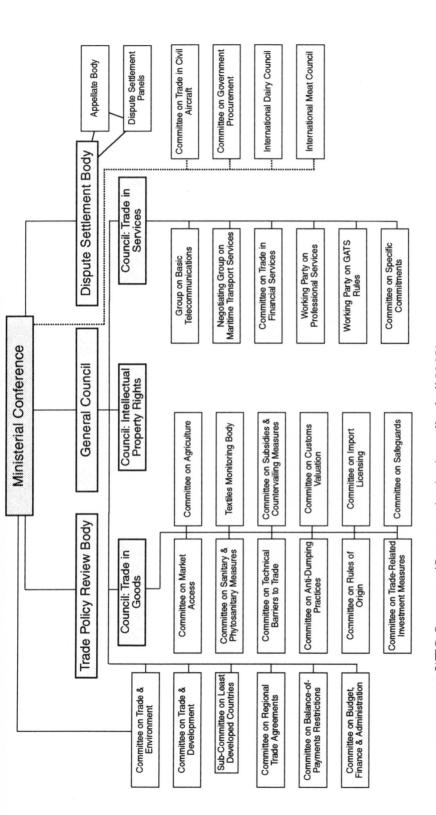

Ministerial Conference

- **Trade Policy Review Body**
- **General Council**
- **Dispute Settlement Body**
  - Appellate Body
  - Dispute Settlement Panels

- Committee on Trade & Environment
- Committee on Trade & Development
- Sub-Committee on Least Developed Countries
- Committee on Regional Trade Agreements
- Committee on Balance-of-Payments Restrictions
- Committee on Budget, Finance & Administration

Council: Trade in Goods
- Committee on Market Access
- Committee on Sanitary & Phytosanitary Measures
- Committee on Technical Barriers to Trade
- Committee on Anti-Dumping Practices
- Committee on Rules of Origin
- Committee on Trade-Related Investment Measures
- Committee on Agriculture
- Textiles Monitoring Body
- Committee on Subsidies & Countervailing Measures
- Committee on Customs Valuation
- Committee on Import Licensing
- Committee on Safeguards

Council: Intellectual Property Rights

Council: Trade in Services
- Group on Basic Telecommunications
- Negotiating Group on Maritime Transport Services
- Committee on Trade in Financial Services
- Working Party on Professional Services
- Working Party on GATS Rules
- Committee on Specific Commitments

- Committee on Trade in Civil Aircraft
- Committee on Government Procurement
- International Dairy Council
- International Meat Council

TABLEAU 2 WTO Structure (Structure institutionnelle de l'OMC)

TABLEAU 3 Mécanisme de règlement des différends de l'OMC

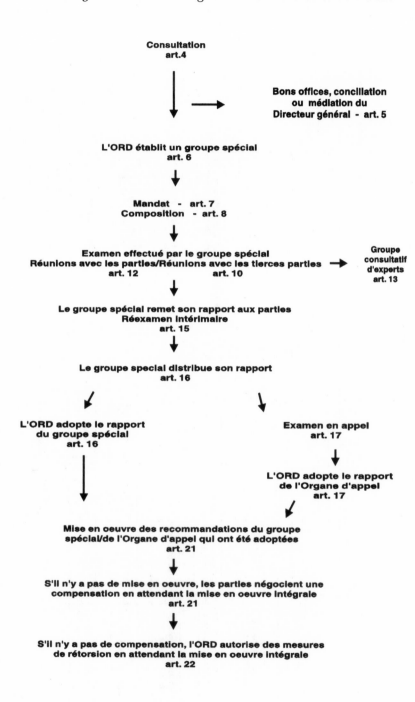

TABLEAU 4 Fonctions/devoirs de l'ORD et des Membres aux termes du Mémorandum d'accord

(A) Généralement

(1) L'ORD administre le Mémorandum et, sauf disposition contraire d'un accord visé, les dispositions des accords visés relatives aux consultations et au règlement des différends. En conséquence, l'ORD a le pouvoir d'établir des groupes spéciaux, d'adopter les rapports de groupes spéciaux et de l'organe d'appel, d'assurer la surveillance de la mise en oeuvre des décisions et recommandations, et d'autoriser la suspension de concessions et d'autres obligations qui résultent des accords visés (article 2:1). Du fait de son pouvoir général d'administration, l'ORD a aussi le pouvoir d'adopter les règles de procédure nécessaires au bon fonctionnement du Mémorandum.

(2) L'ORD informe les Conseils et Comités compétents de l'OMC de l'évolution des différends en rapport avec des dispositions des accords visés respectifs (article 2:2).

(3) L'ORD fait fonction de "greffe" et, à ce titre, reçoit notification de toute demande et autres communications des Membres prescrites par diverses dispositions du Mémorandum d'Accord et ci-après détaillées.

(4) Les accords sur le recours à l'arbitrage doivent être notifiés à tous les Membres — assez longtemps avant l'ouverture effective de la procédure d'arbitrage — (article 25:2); les décisions arbitrales doivent également être notifiées à l'ORD — et au Conseil ou Comité de tout accord pertinent — (article 25:3).

(5) Les parties aux Accords plurilatéraux notifie à l'ORD toute décision établissant les modalités d'application du Mémorandum, y compris toute règle ou procédure spéciale ou additionnelle.

(6) S'agissant de la liste indicative de personnes appelées à faire partie de groupes spéciaux, l'ORD approuve ou non les noms des personnes qui pourraient être suggérés par les Membres pour être inclus dans la liste indicative (article 8:4).

(7) Concernant l'Organe d'appel, l'ORD
  (a) doit instituer l'Organe d'appel permanent pour connaître des appels concernant des affaires soumises à des groupes spéciaux (article 17:1).
  (b) désigne les personnes qui feront partie de l'Organe d'appel (article 17:2).
  (c) administre les dispositions du Mémorandum relatives à l'Organe d'appel, y compris la notification des inscriptions en appel, les demandes de prorogation des délais, la surveillance de la mise en oeuvre des rapports de l'Organe d'appel et l'autorisation d'imposer des sanctions.

(B) Dans le cadre des opérations des groupes spéciaux

(8) Au stade des procédures de consultation,
  (a) toutes les demandes de consultations doivent être notifiées à

l'ORD par le Membre qui demande l'ouverture de consultations (article 4:4).

(b) chaque Membre autre que les Membres qui prennent part aux consultations informe lesdits Membres et l'ORD de son désir d'être admis à participer aux consultations (article 4:11).

(c) si les Membres auxquels la demande de consultations est adressée y consentent, ils en informent l'ORD (article 4:11).

(9) L'ORD établit les groupe spéciaux (une réunion de l'ORD peut être convoquée sur demande à ce sujet),

(a) établissement d'un groupe spécial — disposition générale — articles 2:1 et 6 du Mémorandum.

(b) établissement d'un groupe spécial en vertu de l'article 17.5 de l'Accord antidumping.

(c) établissement d'un groupe spécial en vertu de l'article 4.4 (subventions prohibées) de l'Accord sur les subventions et les mesures compensatoires.

(d) établissement d'un groupe spécial en vertu de l'article 7.4 (subventions pouvant donner lieu à une action) de l'Accord sur les subventions et les mesures compensatoires.

(10) Lorsqu'il établit un groupe spécial, l'ORD peut autoriser son président à en définir le mandat en consultation avec les parties au différend. Le mandat ainsi défini est communiqué à tous les Membres (article 7:3).

(11) L'ORD reçoit les demandes des Membres parties à un/des différend(s) "en relation avec la même question" afin qu'un seul groupe spécial soit établi pour examiner leurs plaintes — procédures applicables en cas de plurilatéralité des plaignants — (article 9:1).

(12) Les tierce parties qui ont un intérêt substantiel dans une affaire portée devant un groupe spécial et qui désirent se faire entendre par ce groupe spécial et lui présenter des communications écrites doit en informer l'ORD (article 10).

(13) En cas de retard dans la procédure de règlement des différends,

(a) le groupe spécial doit informer l'ORD des raisons pour lesquelles il ne peut pas remettre son rapport dans le délai prescrit de six mois — ou de trois mois en cas d'urgence — (article 12:9).

(b) l'Organe d'appel doit informer l'ORD des raisons pour lesquelles il ne peut présenter son rapport dans les 60 jours prescrits — 30 jours dans le cas d'une subvention prohibée selon l'article 4.9 de l'Accord sur les subventions — (article 17:5).

(14) S'agissant des rapports des groupes spéciaux, l'ORD doit

(a) adopter ces rapports dans les 60 jours suivant la date de distribution aux Membres — sauf appel ou consensus (article 16:4).

(b) adopter les rapports concernant les subventions prohibées ou les subventions qui peuvent donner lieu à une action dans les 30 jours à compter de la communication du rapport à tous les Membres (articles 4.8 et 7.6 de l'Accord sur les subventions).

(15) L'ORD reçoit les demandes d'appel,
    (a) disposition générale (article 16:4).
    (b) appel d'un rapport concernant des subventions prohibées (article 4:8).
    (c) appel d'un rapport concernant des subventions pouvant donner lieu à une action (article 7:6).

(16) l'ORD doit adopter les rapports de l'Organe d'appel (sauf consensus),
    (a) disposition générale — dans les 30 jours suivant sa distribution aux Membres (article 17:14).
    (b) en ce qui concerne les subventions prohibées et les subventions pouvant donner lieu à une action, dans les 20 jours suivants la communication du rapport aux Membres (articles 4.9 et 7.7 de l'Accord sur les subventions).

(C) Dans le cadre de la surveillance de la mise en oeuvre des recommandations et décisions

(17) Après l'adoption du rapport du groupe spécial ou de l'Organe d'appel, l'ORD doit tenir sous surveillance la mise en oeuvre des recommandations ou décisions adoptées (articles 2:1, 21:6 et 22:8).

(18) L'ORD doit tenir une réunion dans les 30 jours* suivant la date d'adoption du rapport du groupe spécial ou de l'Organe d'appel, afin que le Membre concerné informe l'ORD de ses intentions au sujet de la mise en oeuvre des recommandations et décisions de celui-ci (article 21:3).

(19) S'il est irréalisable pour un Membre de se conformer immédiatement aux recommandations et décisions, ce Membre disposera d'un délai raisonnable pour le faire; ce délai raisonnable devra être approuvé par l'ORD (article 21:3).

(20) Il va de soi que dans les cas où il y aura désaccord au sujet de l'existence ou de la compatibilité avec un accord visé de mesures prises pour se conformer aux recommandations et décisions, et que ce différend est réglé suivant les procédures de règlement des différends du Mémorandum d'accord, y compris, dans tous les cas où cela sera possible, avec recours au groupe spécial initial, il sera donné avis à l'ORD de ces nouvelles procédures (article 21:5).

(21) Le groupe spécial initial, un autre groupe spécial ou un arbitre transmettra son rapport à l'ORD dans les 90 jours suivant la date à laquelle il aura été saisi de la question. Lorsque le groupe spécial estimera qu'il ne peut pas présenter son rapport dans ce délai, il devra informer l'ORD par écrit des raisons de ce retard et lui indiquera dans quel délai il estime pouvoir présenter son rapport (article 21:5).

(22) A moins que l'ORD n'en décide autrement, la question de la mise en oeuvre des recommandations ou décisions sera inscrite à l'ordre

---

* S'il n'est pas prévu de réunion de l'ORD pendant cette période, celui-ci tiendra une réunion à cette fin.

du jour de la réunion de l'ORD après une période de six mois suivant la date à laquelle le délai raisonnable pour se conformer aux recommanda-tions et décisions aura été fixée et restera inscrite à l'ordre du jour des réunions de l'ORD jusqu'à ce qu'elle soit résolue. Dix jours au moins avant chacune de ces réunions, le Membre concerné présentera à l'ORD un rapport de situation écrit indiquant où en est la mise en oeuvre des recommandations ou décisions (article 21:6).

(23) Pays en développement

    (a) S'il s'agit d'une affaire soulevée par un pays en développe-ment Membre, l'ORD étudiera quelle suite il pourrait en outre y donner, qui soit appropriée aux circonstances (article 21:7).

    (b) S'il s'agit d'un recours déposé par un pays en développement Membre, en examinant quelles mesures il pourrait être approprié de prendre, l'ORD devra tenir compte non seule-ment des échanges visés par les mesures en cause mais aussi de leur incidence sur l'économie des pays en développement Membres concernés (article 21:8).

(D) Dans le cadre des mesures de compensation et suspension des concessions

(24) Si aucune compensation satisfaisante n'a été convenue dans les 20 jours suivant la date à laquelle le délai raisonnable est venu à expiration, toute partie ayant invoqué les procédures de règlement des différends peut demander à l'ORD l'autorisation de sus-pendre, à l'égard du Membre concerné, l'application de conces-sions ou d'autres obligations au titre des accords visés (article 22:2).

(25) Dans ces circonstances, l'ORD doit accorder, sur demande, l'auto-risation de suspendre des concessions ou d'autres obligations dans un délai de 30 jours à compter de l'expiration du délai raison-nable, à moins qu'il ne décide par consensus de rejeter la demande (article 22:6).

(26) L'ORD n'autorisera pas la suspension de concessions ou d'autres obligations si un accord visé interdit une telle suspension — par exemple, selon l'article XXII:7 de l'Accord sur les marchés publics, tout différend survenant dans le cadre de cet accord n'entrainera pas la suspension de concessions qui résultent de tout autre accord (article 22:5).

(27) Lorsque le Membre concerné conteste le niveau de la suspension proposée, ou affirme que les principes et procédures applicables n'ont pas été suivis dans les cas où une partie plaignante a demandé l'autorisation de suspendre des concessions ou d'autres obligations, la question sera soumise à l'arbitrage et il faut s'attendre à ce qu'elle soit notifiée à l'ORD (article 22:6).

(28) L'ORD sera informé dans les moindres délais de la décision d'arbitrage et accordera, sur demande, l'autorisation de suspendre des concessions ou d'autres obligations dans les cas où la demande sera compatible avec la décision de l'arbitre, à moins que l'ORD ne décide par consensus de rejeter la demande (article 22:7).

(29) Conformément au paragraphe 6 de l'article 21, l'ORD continuera de tenir sous surveillance la mise en oeuvre des recommandations ou décisions adoptées, y compris dans les cas où une compensation aura été octroyée ou dans les cas où des concessions ou d'autres obligations auront été suspendues, mais où des recommandations de mettre une mesure en conformité avec les accords visés n'auront pas été mises en oeuvre (article 22:8).

(E) Aux termes de l'Accord sur les subventions

(30) L'ORD, si la demande lui est faite, devra engager la procédure pour obtenir des pouvoirs publics du Membre qui accorde la subvention les renseignements nécessaires pour établir l'existence et le montant du subventionnement, et la valeur des ventes totales des entreprises subventionnées ainsi que les renseignements nécessaires pour analyser les effets défavorables causés par le produit subventionné (article 2 de l'Annexe V de l'Accord sur les subventions).

(31) En ce qui concerne les subventions prohibées, l'ORD devra accorder au Membre plaignant l'autorisation de prendre des contre-mesures appropriées, à moins que l'ORD ne décide par consensus de rejeter la demande (article 4.10 de l'Accord sur les subventions).

(32) Dans le cas où le Membre n'aura pas pris des mesures appropriées pour éliminer les effets défavorables de la subvention ou retirer la subvention dans un délai de six mois à compter de la date à laquelle l'ORD aura adopté le rapport du groupe spécial ou le rapport de l'Organe d'appel, et en l'absence d'accord sur une compensation, l'ORD accordera au Membre plaignant l'autorisation de prendre des contre-mesures proportionnelles au degré et à la nature des effets défavorables dont l'existence aura été déterminée, à moins que l'ORD ne décide par consensus de rejeter la demande (article 7:9).

(F) Aux termes de l'Accord sur les services

(33) Le Conseil du commerce des services ou l'ORD pourra, à la demande d'un Membre, entrer en consultation avec un ou plusieurs Membres, sur une question pour laquelle une solution satisfaisante n'aura pas pu être trouvée au moyen des consultations prévues au paragraphe 1 (article XXII:2 de l'Accord sur les services).

(34) Si l'ORD considère que les circonstances sont suffisamment graves pour justifier une telle mesure, il pourra autoriser un ou plusieurs Membres à suspendre, à l'égard de tel autre ou tels autres Membres, l'application d'obligations et engagements spécifiques conformément à l'article 22 du Mémorandum d'accord sur le règlement des différends (article XXIII:2 de l'Accord sur les services).

The Protection of Peacekeepers*

INTRODUCTION

THE EXPANSION OF PEACEKEEPING operations by the United Nations in this decade has been a bold, but problem-filled, initiative. One unwelcome but perhaps inevitable problem is the protection of the peacekeepers themselves. The sheer increase in the numbers of peacekeepers is enough to ensure that the risk of casualties, hitherto small, would be realized on regrettably frequent occasions. Twenty-four Pakistani soldiers on peacekeeping duty in Somalia were ambushed and murdered in one tragic incident alone.[1]

In addition, the character of United Nations operations has changed radically, exposing the peacekeepers to much greater risk of harm than before. Traditionally, peacekeeping involved a thin line of troops in blue berets patrolling a cease-fire zone by agreement with the parties in conflict. Now the United Nations takes a much more active and interventionist role in the search for peace, security, and stability in an area of crisis. In addition to its traditional observer and monitoring functions (both military and civilian), the United Nations undertakes preventive diplomacy, political confidence building, and other peacemaking strategies even involving

---

* This comment is based on lectures delivered at the Lester B. Pearson Canadian International Peacekeeping Training Centre, Cornwallis, Nova Scotia, in September 1995.

---

[1] In total, 115 peacekeepers lost their lives in the service of United Nations Operations in Somalia II.

military enforcement.[2] In short, the United Nations now mounts complex multidimensional operations that may change and develop as the circumstances of the crisis in question demand. These kinds of proactive roles place United Nations personnel in the midst of ongoing conflicts, exposing them to much greater risks of accidental injury and also to deliberate attack.

The great variety of activities now undertaken by the United Nations has also drawn personnel with much more diverse expertise and experience into peacekeeping operations. Military forces must now operate in co-ordination with numbers of police and civilian personnel, who may be United Nations officials, contracted experts, non-governmental organization staff, or local employees.[3] While each individual requires the same protection of his or her physical well-being and human dignity, the different functions and legal status of peacekeeping personnel require different means of securing their safety.

The right to protection of peacekeeping personnel has many facets. Legal protection has both civil and criminal dimensions. Laws of both international and national origin proscribe the mistreatment of peacekeepers and prescribe the prosecution of wrongdoers. Certain classes of personnel may also claim inviolability of their person and immunity from legal process in particular circumstances. All peacekeeping personnel who become the victims of criminal or other wrongful behaviour may expect to be compensated for their injuries. In the last resort, failing respect for their right to protection, peacekeepers may act in self-defence in proportion to the danger being faced.

Since the problems of protecting peacekeepers has only recently come to the fore, such relevant legal provisions that exist lie scattered among many sources. In addition, until the new United Nations Safety of Personnel Convention[4] was concluded in 1994,

---

[2] See United Nations secretary general, "An Agenda for Peace. Preventive Diplomacy, Peacemaking and Peace-Keeping. Report of the Secretary-General Pursuant to the Statement Adopted by the Summit Meeting of the Security Council on 31 January 1992," UN SCOR, 1992, UN Doc. A/47/277, S/24111, (1992) 31 I.L.M. 953.

[3] Cf. S. Ogata, "The Interface between Peacekeeping and Humanitarian Action" in D. Warner (ed.), *New Dimensions of Peacekeeping* 119 (Dordrecht: Martinus Nijhoff, 1995).

[4] Convention on the Safety of United Nations and Associated Personnel, GA Res. 49/59, UN GAOR, 49th Sess., UN Doc. A/RES/49/59 (1995).

there was no international convention that dealt directly with peacekeeping. The protection currently available arises from general references and interpretative inclusions of peacekeepers in treaties principally directed to other persons and problems.

In these circumstances, the object of this comment is to gather together and to correlate the different legal sources of protection with the different types of peacekeeping personnel. It will proceed first by describing all the personnel who may be involved in peacekeeping activities and then by exploring the various legal rights that attach to each class of persons. It will conclude with a discussion of the new United Nations Safety of Personnel Convention, and an analysis of the scope of its protection.

CLASSES OF PEACEKEEPING PERSONNEL

Modern United Nations peacekeeping mandates frequently demand a mixture of military, police, and civilian components. There were always some civilian United Nations personnel who provided administrative support to an operation, but the bulk of the force was constituted by the Blue Berets, who provided the traditional cease-fire monitoring service. Now, however, military personnel are engaged in new ways, and a great variety of civilians, from non-governmental as well as intergovernmental organizations (hereinafter IGOs), now work with the United Nations alongside the troops. To understand the protection afforded to all the people likely to be involved in peacekeeping operations, it is necessary to distinguish the status of each class of personnel subsumed under these three broad headings.

MILITARY PERSONNEL

A soldier is a soldier everywhere, but his or her legal status under a United Nations operation will vary depending on the scope of the mandate and the rules of engagement. A United Nations force consists of contingents of trained military personnel seconded from member states, united under a commander who is responsible to the secretary general, and identified by the United Nations emblem in white on distinctive light blue berets. As peacekeepers in the traditional sense, they participate in consent operations under Chapter 6 of the United Nations Charter and do not use force, even if they have the means, except as a last resort of self-defence. In essence, peacekeeping is done by non-combatant forces. In addition, the United Nations is now likely to undertake peace-enforcing actions authorized by the Security Council under Chapter 7. In other words, the troops may become combatants. The clearest example of a mission of this character was Operation Desert Storm to drive the Iraqi aggressors out of Kuwait.[5]

Not every action under Chapter 7 of the Charter is an enforcement operation. In Bosnia, for example, although operations were authorized under Chapter 7, the United Nations Protection Forces (hereinafter UNPROFOR) were present with the consent of the recognized government and were principally engaged in the defensive activities of ensuring local security, monitoring no-fly zones, and protecting the delivery of humanitarian assistance.[6] There appears to be developing, therefore, a functional distinction within the peace-enforcing mandate of the United Nations in the use of military personnel as combatants or non-combatants. While the United Nations has not defined the term "combatant," its meaning may reflect the practice under the Geneva or Red Cross Conventions concerning humanitarian law.[7]

It is also possible that military forces other than United Nations Blue Berets may be engaged in peacekeeping operations. Rarely, multinational forces not of United Nations origin or authorization may undertake peacekeeping missions. One successful instance was the multinational force and observers emplaced in the Sinai in 1982.[8] But a severe limitation on their use is that, being outside the United Nations Charter, they can only be mounted and continued with the full consent of all concerned. More commonly, the collective forces of regional intergovernmental organizations, like the North Atlantic Treaty Organization (hereinafter NATO) and the Organization of American States (hereinafter OAS), may execute peacekeeping functions. Chapter 8 of the Charter recognizes their independent involvement in the maintenance of international

---

[5] See SC Res. 678 (1990), UN SCOR, 45th Sess., UN Doc. S/RES/678 (1990).

[6] For a review of the United Nations Protection Forces, see V.-Y. Ghebali, "UNPROFOR in the Former Yugoslavia: The Misuse of Peacekeeping and Associated Conflict Management Techniques" in D. Warner (ed.), *supra* note 3 at 13.

[7] See *infra* note 45 and accompanying text.

[8] For a brief review of this operation, see J. P. Baratta, *International Peacekeeping: History and Strengthening* 42 (Washington: Center for U.N. Reform Education, 1989). See also N. A. Pelcovits, *Peacekeeping on Arab-Israeli Fronts: Lessons from the Sinai and Lebanon* (Boulder: Westview Press, 1984).

peace and security,[9] but not to the extent of enforcement action without Security Council approval.[10] Thus the OAS took the first initiative in trying to resolve the crisis over the democratically elected government in Haiti. So far, however, the deployment of forces by regional organizations has been in co-operation with, and upon the authorization of, the United Nations as a kind of franchise for the execution of the operation in question. Thus NATO has conducted air strikes in the Bosnian theatre of action when called upon by the United Nations secretary general pursuant to Security Council authority.[11] Similarly, the Economic Community of West African States was delegated to intervene in the civil war in Liberia.[12] Since these operations have been undertaken on behalf of the United Nations, the military personnel may be classified for the purpose of establishing their status in the same functional way as genuine United Nations forces.

POLICE PERSONNEL

Though regularly spoken of along with military and civilian personnel, police are ordinarily treated separately by reason of their particular law enforcement authority and functions. But, as regards their personal protection, the more important consideration seems to be whether they are military or civilian police. If they are military police, their legal status will be determined by their association with a particular force and its functions. If they are civilian police, their rights are more likely to be fixed according to the status of the civilian authority by which they were engaged and to which they answer. It is possible to imagine a complicating crossover of status if civilian police happened to be attached to a military force in an auxiliary capacity. For the purposes of this comment, however, it is sufficient to note that the protection afforded to police personnel follows their military or civilian lines of authority within the particular United Nations operation.

---

9 Article 52.

10 Article 53. Except possibly in collective self-defence under Article 51.

11 For a short review of NATO's role, see E. Marcuse, "The Former Yugoslavia: NATO's Role," in D. Warner (ed.), *supra* note 3 at 173.

12 Retroactively franchised might be a more apt description of the United Nation's action. See United Nations-Cyprus Status of Forces Agreement, SC Res. 788 (1992), UN SCOR, 47th Sess., UN Doc. S/RES/788 (1992).

CIVILIAN PERSONNEL

The civilian complement of a peacekeeping operation may be made up of officials or of private individuals. Most of these kinds of personnel have long been regularly engaged in humanitarian activities in the field, but the expanded scope of United Nations peacekeeping operations has now brought them into close contact, if not co-ordinated action, with the military forces.

Amongst the officials of IGOs, one may distinguish, first, the officers and experts from the United Nations itself; second, those from United Nations subsidiary organs; and third, those from United Nations specialized agencies. United Nations officials deployed in peacekeeping operations might include the secretary general or his or her special representative in the particular conflict, regular United Nations staff who provide administrative support for the military forces, and experts contracted by the United Nations for specific onsite activities. A similar mix of officials and experts might be put in the field by such United Nations subsidiary organs as the United Nations Development Programme (UNDP), United Nations High Commissioner for Refugees (UNHCR), United Nations High Commissioner for Human Rights (UNHCHR), and United Nations Children's Fund (UNICEF), which runs an emergency relief fund. Some United Nations specialized agencies, such as the Food and Agriculture Organization (FAO), through its joint administration of the World Food Program with the United Nations, also find they have staff and other employees in the field of an United Nations peacekeeping operation.

Amongst the hundreds of private associations or non-governmental organizations (hereinafter NGOs) concerned about human welfare, perhaps about a dozen large ones deliver the bulk of humanitarian assistance around the world in centres of conflict and need. The most longstanding internationally is the International Committee of the Red Cross (hereinafter ICRC). Some other equally well-known names are Oxfam, CARE, Médecins sans Frontières, and Feed the Children. These NGOs put expatriate staff members and locally hired employees in the places of stress according to the humanitarian needs of the population. Since most of the IGO and NGO personnel are in the field not because a peacekeeping mission has been organized, but primarily to supply emergency relief and long-term development assistance to the local community, they are frequently on sight before the United Nations operation is mounted and even before the conflict that gives rise to it has broken out.

Existing Protection of Peacekeeping Personnel

Every peacekeeping operation is given a specific mandate and predetermined rules of engagement. Preferably these are agreed with the parties in conflict. In consent operations, by definition, this is so. In enforcement actions, only some or none of the hostile parties may have concurred in the operation. When there is consent, the United Nations will usually try to make a status of forces or status of operation agreement with the host government(s). Only if such a status of forces agreement has been concluded is there likely to be any particular provision for the protection of individual peace-keepers. These agreements usually cover questions about the status of personnel, criminal and civil jurisdiction, taxation, customs, premises, freedom of movement, use of transport facilities and public utilities, liaison with local authorities, and dispute settlement.[13] As this list indicates, these agreements are chiefly concerned with the execution of the United Nations' mandate. They emphasize the peacekeepers' rights to act rather than their protection and security concerns, so that additional rights of personal protection must be sought in the general sources of international law. As it happens, a wide variety of relevant treaties affect the specific classes of personnel that may be engaged in peacekeeping activities.

MILITARY PERSONNEL

On the military side, the distinction between combatant and non-combatant forces is critical to their expectation of treatment. It is clear that combatants must be accorded the rights under the humanitarian laws of armed conflict, in particular the 1907 Hague Conventions, the 1925 Gas Protocol, and the 1949 Geneva or Red Cross Conventions with their Additional Protocols.[14] Thus combatant troops are entitled to expect, and must themselves respect, the limits on the methods of warfare and the rights of the sick and

---

[13] See, e.g., UN-Cyprus Agreement 1964, 492 UNTS 57.

[14] Convenient collections of these international humanitarian laws may be found in A. Roberts and R. Guelff (eds), *Documents on the Laws of War*, 2d ed. (Oxford: Clarendon Press, 1989) and D. Schindler and J. Toman (eds), *The Laws of Armed Conflict*, 3rd rev. ed. (Dordrecht: Martinus Nijhoff, 1988).

wounded, prisoners of war, and others *hors de combat.* As combatants, however, they are legitimate targets of deliberate attack and capture.

Non-combatant forces, that is, peacekeepers *par excellence,* may hope to be extended the same consideration as civilians under these humanitarian laws — that is to say, they may not be attacked but should be respected and treated humanely. For example, seizing UNPROFOR troops and officers as hostages and compelling them to act as shields to protect military targets from attack, as the Bosnian Serbs did in May 1995, is not acceptable conduct. Non-combatant peacekeepers should not, however, depend on the right to receive humane treatment, because they are not a class of personnel envisaged by the Geneva Conventions.[15] The best assurance that peacekeepers may currently obtain against mistreatment is, at the time they consent to the peacekeeping operation, to secure the explicit agreement of each party to the conflict to apply, at a minimum, the laws of the Geneva Conventions to the United Nations troops and other peacekeeping personnel. Recognizing this gap in the structure of the laws of armed conflict, the United Nations has recently moved to close it with a new convention. Since the convention also deals with non-military personnel, discussion of it will be reserved until later. In addition, since a United Nations force acts as a subsidiary organ of the United Nations, its personnel may claim the protections and immunities of United Nations officials.[16] Since these rights are most apposite to civilian personnel, they are discussed in the next subsection concerning United Nations officials and experts. As a last resort, military personnel may use proportionate force in their own self-defence. Finally, in the event that they are wounded or disabled, they may expect to be assisted and compensated by their national authorities. In Canada, for example, a variety of veterans' programs are available.

UNITED NATIONS OFFICIALS AND EXPERTS

Among civilians, more provision has been made for IGO officials than for NGO staff. A general statement of immunity for inter-

---

15 For the simple reason that peacekeeping had not been invented by the United Nations when the conventions were concluded in 1949. See also L. C. Green, *The Contemporary Law of Armed Conflict* 325 (Manchester: Manchester University Press, 1993).

16 United Nations, *The Blue Helmets,* 2d ed. 408 (1990). See also UN-Cyprus Status of Forces Agreement, *supra* note 13, Art. 23.

national civil servants is included in the United Nations Charter itself. Article 105 provides in part that "officials of the Organization shall . . . enjoy such privileges and immunities as are necessary for the independent exercise of their functions in connexion with the Organization." Abbreviated and general though it may be, Article 105 provides a firm foundation for the protection of peacekeeping officials.

More specific protection has since been arranged by a series of conventions respecting different classes of IGO officials. The prototype is the 1946 Convention on the Privileges and Immunities of the United Nations.[17] By Article 5, section 18, officials of the United Nations shall:

(a) be immune from legal process in respect of words spoken or written and all acts performed by them in their official capacity;
. . . .
(d) be immune . . . from immigration restrictions and alien registration;
. . . .
(f) be given . . . the same repatriation facilities in time of international crises as diplomatic envoys[.]

These limited immunities are meant to protect officials in the performance of their functions. This functional character is reinforced by Article 5, section 20:

Privileges and immunities are granted to officials in the interests of the United Nations and not for the personal benefit of the individuals themselves. The Secretary-General shall have the right and the duty to waive immunity of any official in any case where, in his opinion, the immunity would impede the course of justice and can be waived without prejudice to the interests of the United Nations[.]

Implicit in this section is the obligation of United Nations officials to respect local law in their activities. Indeed, Article 5, section 21 places a duty on the United Nations to co-operate in the local administration of justice and to prevent officials from abusing their immunities.

The Convention draws a distinction between permanent officials and experts with whom the United Nations contracts for specific activities. Article 6 grants experts who are performing missions for the United Nations "such privileges and immunities as are necessary for the independent exercise of their functions." In particular, section 22 accords them:

17 (1949) 43 A.J.I.L. Supp. 1.

(a) immunity from personal arrest or detention and from seizure of their personal baggage;
(b) in respect of words spoken and acts done by them in the course of the performance of their mission, immunity from legal process of every kind[.]

As with officials, by section 23 the secretary general has the power to waive an expert's immunity when appropriate. Thus experts are given immunities that are comparable to those of United Nations officials but adapted to their particular functions and circumstances.

In addition, the United Nations may issue its officials with *laissez-passer* as travel documents, in place of passports, for entry to and transit through member countries. Experts are not provided with *laissez-passer* but are given certificates to indicate that they are travelling on United Nations business.[18]

Although passing reference is made to "comparable officials of specialized agencies,"[19] a subsequent convention was specially prepared about them. The Convention on the Privileges and Immunities of the Specialized Agencies[20] grants designated officials of the specialized agencies practically the same immunities as United Nations officials. The functional character of these rights is enhanced by the additional statement that the Convention's provisions "must be interpreted in the light of the functions with which that agency is entrusted."[21]

Unlike the Convention on the Privileges and Immunities of the United Nations, however, this Convention is not applicable in the territory of states immediately upon their adherence to it. It operates as a standard set of provisions to which each specialized agency must also individually adhere. Thus, Article 1, section 1 lists the specialized agencies to which the Convention is addressed. This list includes, for instance, the FAO, which is jointly responsible with the United Nations for the World Food Program and its operation in peacekeeping situations. Article 10, section 37 requires each specialized agency to inform the United Nations secretary general that it accepts the standard clauses and any annex relevant to its particular field of responsibilities. In addition, each country that accedes to the Convention must also notify the secretary general toward which specialized agencies it considers itself bound. This two-step process

18 Art. 7, sections 24 and 26 respectively.
19 Art. 4, section 28.
20 33 UNTS 261, 290 (1947).
21 Art. 10, section 24.

of application is a necessary mechanism to create legal obligations between a particular agency and a particular state. It also demonstrates that the Convention is not generally applicable and serves as a warning to officials of a particular agency to check whether they can rely on its provisions in the specific territory in which they will be operating.

A further noticeable difference between this Convention and that related to the United Nations is the absence of any provisions for experts, as opposed to officials. This class of personnel is dealt with in a series of annexes to the Convention that cover each individual adhering agency. Thus Annex 2 describes the position of experts, other than officials, of the FAO. The different annexes are, however, strikingly similar on this topic and provide immunities that closely parallel those afforded to experts on mission for the United Nations.

OTHER IGO OFFICIALS

The two previous conventions deal with the immunities of officials and experts within the family of United Nations organizations. They extend approximately equivalent rights to peacekeeping personnel who are posted by the United Nations itself, by one of its subsidiary organs, such as the United Nations High Commissioner for Refugees, or by a specialized agency of the United Nations. Therefore, they are likely to cover most of the United Nations personnel sent on peacekeeping operations. However, officials of other IGOs not affiliated with the United Nations may also be engaged in peacekeeping activities. This is increasingly likely to occur if the United Nations continues to franchise its operational power to regional and other international organizations. Although the OAS, for instance, had a leading role in the measures taken in Haiti, its officials are outside the scope of the two conventions on the immunities of the United Nations and the specialized agencies, and so are afforded no protection by them. It is not possible to regard OAS officials or experts as being on mission for the United Nations merely because the Security Council authorized their IGO's involvement in its peacekeeping operation; they would probably need to be directly contracted by a United Nations body to fall under its umbrella of protection.

It is customary, however, for an IGO to be given legal identity and status by its constitution or charter within the territory of its member states. It is possible, therefore, that an official of a regional IGO engaged in a peacekeeping operation in the region would have comparable immunities to United Nations officials, provided the host state is a member of that IGO. The exact scope of these rights will, of course, depend upon the membership and the constitution of the IGO.

The immunity of the person set forth in this group of treaties is a distinct advantage to United Nations and other IGO personnel, such as field administrators, monitors, and refugee officers, in peacekeeping situations. Their inviolability protects them from arrest and detention. It is a defensive right, however, that places no duty on the local government or hostile parties to take active measures for their safety in the midst of the conflict. In truth, these conventions were drafted with peacetime missions in mind, and not the kinds of crises with which peacekeeping operations have to contend. The right of repatriation in time of international crisis, mentioned previously as part of the available immunities of officials, underlines the limited scope of application of these conventions on the ground.

There is a convention, however, that was concluded to protect international representatives and officials from terrorist attacks and is broad enough in scope to include peacekeeping personnel in its coverage. The Convention on the Prevention and Punishment of Crimes Against Internationally Protected Persons, Including Diplomatic Agents[22] defines the class of protected personnel very broadly. Article 1(b) includes, in addition to heads of state, heads of government and ministers of foreign affairs:

any representative or official of a state or any official or other agent of an international organization of an intergovernmental character who, at the time when and in the place where a crime against him, his official premises, his private accommodation or his means of transport is committed, is entitled pursuant to international law to special protection from any attack on his person, freedom or dignity, as well as members of his family forming part of his household.

States parties to the Convention are required to proscribe in their criminal law any intentional commission, threat, or attempt to murder, kidnap, or attack a protected person or his or her official premises, private accommodation, and means of transport in a way that endangers him or her. When they apprehend an alleged offender, they are bound to arrest and prosecute or extradite. States

22 1035 UNTS 167 (1973), 1977 Can. T.S. No. 43.

are also expected to co-operate in the prevention of these crimes by taking active measures to stop preparations for their commission. Thus an IGO official who is entitled to immunity may additionally expect criminal law protection from personal attacks while engaged in peacekeeping activities in those countries that are party to this Convention. Finally, IGO officials who pursue missions in the face of conflict may also rely for their security on such other legal rights that exist for civilian peacekeepers who do not share their official standing.

ICRC STAFF

In turning attention to other civilian peacekeepers, such as NGO staff members, it is noticeable that no general treaty for their protection is currently in place. The sole exception is the ICRC by reason of its special status in connection with the Hague and the Geneva Conventions. As the leading exponent of the humanitarian law found in this family of treaties, it is not surprising that the ICRC is granted a protected status in certain circumstances. The protection is afforded by use of the red cross emblem. Article 44 of Convention I[23] states:

With the exceptions of the cases mentioned in the following paragraphs of the present Article, the emblem of the red cross on a white ground and the words "Red Cross," or "Geneva Cross" may not be employed, either in time of peace or in time of war, except to indicate or to protect the medical units and establishments, the personnel and material protected by the present Convention and other Conventions dealing with similar matters. . . .

The international Red Cross organizations and their duly authorized personnel shall be permitted to make use, at all times, of the emblem of the red cross on a white ground[.]

This provision is remarkable for both its complexity and its comprehensiveness. Several aspects should be noted. First, the red cross emblem may only be used in restricted circumstances — so restricted, in fact, that the article prohibits its use except in the situations specifically announced. This restraint is necessary to maintain the historically significant symbolism of the emblem. Second, the emblem may have an indicative or a protective function. The immediate circumstances of its use will determine the purpose to which it is being put. Third, the ICRC has general authority to

---

[23] *Supra* note 14. See also J. S. Pictet (ed.), *Commentary*, vol. 1 (Geneva: ICRC, 1952).

make use of the emblem at all times. This authorization is without reservation, and hence the emblem may be used by ICRC personnel for its protective value wherever and whenever the nature of their work requires. Fourth, the extent of protection encompasses the full range of immunity and security provided in all the related conventions. The precise protection that ICRC personnel may expect depends upon the character of the peacekeeping work they are engaged in and the conditions of conflict in which they are operating. In general, use of the emblem commands full protection. Thus, for example, medical personnel of the belligerent forces, who are entitled to display the red cross emblem, "shall be respected and protected in all circumstances."[24] In practice, the ICRC studiously guards its protected position by carefully trying to maintain a disinterested neutrality. Without such protection, ICRC personnel would not only be personally exposed, but also, in many instances, they would not be able to do their humanitarian work.

CIVILIAN PERSONNEL GENERALLY

While civilian peacekeepers other than ICRC personnel are not specific objects of protection in any operable treaty, they are entitled to the same respect as civilians generally under international humanitarian and human rights laws. Thus those parts of the Geneva Conventions, particularly Convention IV as enlarged by the two Additional Protocols, should be applied to NGO, as well as IGO, staff within the conflict zone, at the very least when in occupied territory during an international armed conflict. These protections, however, do not extend to the full range of the Conventions, because these personnel are not entitled to bear the red cross emblem and all that it entails.[25]

The keystone of the protections of civilians under Convention IV[26] is expressed in Article 27 as follows:

Protected persons are entitled, in all circumstances, to respect for their persons, their honour, their family rights, their religious convictions and practices, and their manners and customs. They shall at all times be humanely treated, and shall be protected especially against all acts of violence or threats thereof and against insults and public curiosity.

[24] Geneva Convention I, *supra* note 14, Art. 24.
[25] See Pictet, *supra* note 23.
[26] *Supra* note 14.

These rights are elaborated in subsequent articles of the Convention in considerable detail. However, the essential thrust of Geneva Convention IV is to protect civilians from the abusive use of the power that local authorities hold over the population. It is noticeably concerned with the plight of unengaged civilians who happen to be located in enemy or occupied territories. It does not particularly address the general dangers from opposing forces resulting from the recourse to hostilities and conflict, and yet it is these risks that peacekeeping civilians, by reason of their active involvement, regularly and with foresight have to face.

General human rights laws may also afford protection to civilians in specific situations. National human rights prescribed in the country of operations may offer remedies for peacekeepers if they are still operable. International human rights standards, found in such documents as the Universal Declaration of Human Rights,[27] the International Covenant on Civil and Political Rights,[28] and the Convention against Torture,[29] are not so readily suspended in times of conflict and so may be resorted to in the event of mistreatment — in particular, "Everyone has the right to liberty and security of the person;"[30] "No one shall be subjected to arbitrary arrest and detention;"[31] "No one shall be subjected to torture or to cruel, inhuman or degrading treatment."[32] These protections apply to peacekeepers without discrimination.

In addition, international criminal laws may prevent mistreatment of peacekeepers through their deterrent effect. The operation of this complex body of proscriptions against war and offences against peace and humanity may depend upon the character of the conflict in which the United Nations operation takes place. Thus "grave breaches" of the Geneva Conventions are limited to circumstances of international armed conflict in which the conventions apply. Other international crimes are more generally subject to the criminal laws. Such crimes against humanity as murder, imprisonment, and torture

---

27 UNGA Res. 217 (III), UN GAOR, 3rd Sess., Supp. No. 13, p. 71, UN Doc. A/810 (1948) (hereinafter UDHR).

28 999 UNTS 171 (1966); 1976 Can. T.S. No. 47 (hereinafter ICCPR).

29 Convention Against Torture and Other Cruel, Inhuman or Degrading Treatment or Punishment, 1987 Can. T.S. No. 36; reprinted in 23 I.L.M. 1027 and 24 I.L.M. 535. (hereinafter Torture Convention)

30 UDHR Art. 3, ICCPR Art. 9.

31 UDHR Art. 9, ICCPR Art. 9.

32 UDHR Art. 5; ICCPR Art. 7; Torture Convention *passim.*

as proscribed by customary international law probably do not depend on the presence of armed conflict. Similarly, the group of conventions concluded to combat international terrorism[33] are effective under all conditions, provided they have been ratified or adopted by the particular state or states where the United Nations is engaged in peacekeeping. For example, the International Convention Against Taking Hostages[34] makes hostage-taking an international crime and binds states either to prosecute or to extradite offenders. Importantly, this convention applies to everyone, civilian or military, involved in a peacekeeping operation.

The common feature that can be observed in surveying these bodies of law about humanity is that none of them is directly intended to resolve the problems of peacekeepers. Whether international humanitarian laws, human rights standards, or criminal prohibitions affect the condition of peacekeepers depends upon their scope for adaptation to new circumstances and for application by analogy. If there is a central common limitation to the protection that these laws can provide, it is that they do not envisage peacekeeping personnel who must function in the midst of hostilities. They do not expect non-combatants to be actively involved in the armed conflict, so they do not directly oblige the hostile parties to take affirmative measures to protect peacekeepers.

THE NEW UNITED NATIONS SAFETY OF PERSONNEL CONVENTION

The absence of explicit obligations on hostile regimes to provide for the safety of peacekeepers, whether non-combatant forces, police, IGO officials, or NGO staff, in the midst of their conflict has not gone unnoticed. In December 1992, the United Nations General Assembly included the protection of peacekeeping personnel on its agenda. "Acknowledging the vital importance of the involvement of United Nations personnel in preventive diplomacy, peacemaking,

[33] See the Tokyo Convention on Offences and Certain other Acts on Aircraft 704 UNTS 219 (1963), 1970 Can. T.S. No. 5; Hague Convention for the Suppression of Unlawful Seizure of Aircraft 860 UNTS 105 (1970), 1972 Can. T.S. No. 23; Montreal Convention for the Suppression of Unlawful Acts Against the Safety of Civil Aviation 974 UNTS 177 (1971), 1973 Can. T.S. No. 6; Montreal Protocol for the Suppression of Unlawful Acts of Violence at Airports Serving International Civil Aviation (1988) 27 I.L.M. 627; Convention for the Suppression of Unlawful Acts Against the Safety of Maritime Navigation (1988) 27 I.L.M. 672; and Protocol for the Suppression of Unlawful Acts Against the Safety of Fixed Platforms Located on the Continental Shelf (1988) 27 I.L.M. 685.

[34] 1316 UNTS 205 (1979).

peace-keeping, peace-building and humanitarian operations," and "noting with grave concern the growing number of fatalities and injuries among United Nations peace-keeping and other personnel resulting from deliberate hostile actions in areas of deployment,"[35] the General Assembly began to consider how to ensure their safety. Within two years, the General Assembly adopted a Convention on the Safety of United Nations and Associated Personnel.[36] It was open for signature throughout 1995 and will come into force thirty days after twenty-two states have formally adhered to it.[37]

The key provision of the new Convention is Article 7. It reads:

Duty to ensure the safety and security of United Nations and associated personnel
(1) United Nations and associated personnel, their equipment and premises shall not be made the object of attack or of any action that prevents them from discharging their mandate.
(2) States Parties shall take all appropriate measures to ensure the safety and security of United Nations and associated personnel. In particular, States Parties shall take all appropriate steps to protect United Nations and associated personnel who are deployed in their territory from the crimes set out in article 9.
(3) States Parties shall cooperate with the United Nations and other States Parties, as appropriate, in the implementation of this Convention, particularly in any case where the host State is unable itself to take the required measures.

In essence, paragraph 1 forbids the host authorities from attacking peacekeeping personnel or from inhibiting their activities,[38] while paragraph 2 requires them to take positive steps to prevent attacks or interference by others. When the local regime is non-existent or

---

[35] Protection of Peace-Keeping Personnel, UNGA Res. 47/72, Annex UNGAOR, 47th Sess., Doc. A/RES/47/72 (1993).

[36] UNGA Res. 49/59 Annex, UNGAOR, 49th Sess, UN Doc. A/RES/49/59 (1995). See P. Kirsch, "Convention on the Safety of United Nations and Associated Personnel" (1994) 23 Can. Council Int'l L. Proc. 182.

[37] Arts 24 and 27.

[38] Art. 8 reinforces the general obligation in Art. 7(1) not to interfere with UN peacekeepers by specific directions in the event of their capture or detention. It reads:

> Except as otherwise provided in an applicable status-of-forces agreement, if United Nations or associated personnel are captured or detained in the course of the performance of their duties and their identification has been established, they shall not be subjected to interrogation and they shall be promptly released and returned to the United Nations or other appropriate authorities. Pending their release such personnel shall be treated in accordance with universally recognized standards of human rights and the principles and spirit of the Geneva Conventions of 1949.

incapable of fulfilling these obligations, paragraph 3 obliges other governments involved in the crisis to ensure the safety of the peacekeepers.

The specific crimes alluded to in Article 7(2) and enumerated in Article 9 include murder, kidnapping, and attacks upon peacekeepers or threats or attempts to attack them, as well as violent attacks upon their premises, accommodation, or means of transport. Thus seizing members of United Nations forces as hostages, firing mortars and missiles at their headquarters, ambushing their motorized patrols, and threatening them at gun point, all of which have occurred in Somalia or Bosnia, for example, are prohibited. On becoming parties to the Convention, states undertake to prescribe these as crimes in their national laws and to assign penalties "which shall take into account their grave nature."[39] They are also bound to assert jurisdiction on the principles made familiar and well established by the anti-terrorism conventions, namely, *aut dedere, aut judicare*. Thus states parties must exercise their jurisdiction to apprehend offenders and to submit them for prosecution or to extradite them to another state that is willing and able to prosecute them.[40]

Several other articles of the Convention provide preventive and co-operative support for these penal measures. Thus states parties are bound to take practicable action to prevent attacks and other offences against peacekeepers. They are also obliged to co-operate in the prevention and prosecution of offences by sharing information about preparations for criminal acts and providing assistance in identifying offenders and obtaining evidence of crimes.[41] The Convention also extends protection both to alleged offenders, by requiring fair treatment in their investigation, prosecution, and trial,[42] and to host countries, by demanding that peacekeepers respect local laws and regulations.[43]

The application of the Convention's protections, however, does not extend to all classes of peacekeepers. The Convention precisely specifies the persons it will protect. Article 2 states:

(1) This Convention applies in respect of United Nations and associated personnel and United Nations operations, as defined in Article 1.

[39] Art. 9(2).
[40] Arts. 10, 13-15.
[41] Arts. 11, 12, 16.
[42] Art. 17.
[43] Art. 6.

(2) This Convention shall not apply to a United Nations operation authorized by the Security Council as an enforcement action under Chapter VII of the Charter of the United Nations in which any of the personnel are engaged as combatants against organized armed forces and to which the law of international armed conflict applies.

The exclusion in paragraph 2 of certain United Nations enforcement actions is made in very exacting yet still uncertain terms. Enforcement action may only be taken by the United Nations under Chapter 7, but not every enforcement action is necessarily military. For instance, economic sanctions are typically applied as a means of enforcement before any military action is taken. Even if an operation involves military personnel authorized under Chapter 7, they may not be engaged in enforcement activities. Thus, military protection of humanitarian convoys of foodstuffs and medical supplies should not attract the operation of paragraph 2. Only on those occasions when military personnel can be said to be "combatants" are they excluded from the Convention. The meaning of this term has yet to be determined in practice. Would it include, for instance, the pilots of the NATO airplanes who, at the request of the United Nations, attacked Bosnian Serb ammunition depots, air defence radar and communications sites, and command posts?[44] The reference at the end of the paragraph to the application of the law of international armed conflict suggests that the meaning of "combatant" in that law (that is, *inter alia*, the Hague and Geneva Conventions) will influence the interpretation of the same term in the new United Nations Convention.

The exclusion of combatant military personnel in Article 2 paragraph 2 is an exception to the classes of peacekeepers protected by paragraph 1. They are defined in Article 1 as follows:

For the purposes of this Convention:

(a) "United Nations personnel" means:
   (i) Persons engaged or deployed by the Secretary-General of the United Nations as members of the military, police or civilian components of a United Nations operation;
   (ii) Other officials and experts on mission of the United Nations or its specialized agencies or the International Atomic Energy Agency who are present in an official capacity in the area where a United Nations operation is being conducted;

---

44 The official view seems to be that the use of force in these circumstances was only a backup measure for the fulfilment of UNPROFOR's humanitarian objectives. See the comments in V.-Y. Ghebali, *supra* note 6 at 20.

(b) "Associated personnel" means:
  (i) Persons assigned by a Government or an intergovernmental organization with the agreement of the competent organ of the United Nations;
  (ii) Persons engaged by the Secretary-General of the United Nations or by a specialized agency or by the International Atomic Energy Agency;
  (iii) Persons deployed by a humanitarian non-governmental organization or agency under an agreement with the Secretary-General of the United Nations or with a specialized agency or with the International Atomic Energy Agency,
  to carry out activities in support of the fulfillment of the mandate of a United Nations operation; and
(c) "United Nations operation" means an operation established by the competent organ of the United Nations in accordance with the Charter of the United Nations and conducted under United Nations authority and control:
  (i) Where the operation is for the purpose of maintaining or restoring international peace and security; or
  (ii) Where the Security Council or the General Assembly has declared, for the purposes of this Convention, that there exists an exceptional risk to the safety of the personnel participating in the operation[.]

These clauses appear complex, even bewildering, but they are designed to describe the different classes of personnel who are likely to be present in the field of a peacekeeping operation. An example under each clause may clarify the definitions. Paragraph (a) comprises the various United Nations officers. Subparagraph (i), for example, covers the Blue Berets of the military component as well as United Nations civilian officials. Subparagraph (ii) includes officials of United Nations subsidiary organs like UNHCR and UNICEF relief officers who happen to be present in the theatre of peacekeeping operations even though they are engaged on their own complementary, yet technically separate, missions.

Paragraph (b) gathers in officials and staff who are not United Nations officers but are employed on United Nations business. Subparagraph (i) would have covered the coalition forces assigned by national governments to the Iraq/Kuwait crisis and the NATO pilots deployed in air strikes against the Bosnian Serbs. Subparagraph (ii) would include truck drivers engaged by the World Food Program as part of its relief mandate in an United Nations operation. Subparagraph (iii) would protect NGO staff, provided they are under contract to the United Nations or a specialized agency in connection with a peacekeeping operation. Thus CARE or Oxfam workers deployed by arrangement with UNHCR as part of a United Nations operation would come within the scope of the Convention. The personnel and NGOs engaged of their own initiative in humanitarian and development work will not be protected by the Convention, even though they are operating within the area of a peacekeeping operation.

Thus the Convention carefully draws a line of inclusion around United Nations humanitarian activities. It excludes combatant forces as not humanitarian in objective and it leaves out private humanitarian efforts by NGOs.[45] The combination of requirements of a United Nations mandate and a humanitarian character are further emphasized by Article 1, paragraph (c), which confirms that the operation must be a peacekeeping or other extremely risky mission established and conducted under the United Nations Charter (viz. Chapters 6 or 7). Thus, a peacekeeping operation mounted by a group of countries as a measure of collective self-defence or by a regional IGO would not be covered by the Convention unless and until it received the delegated authority of the United Nations.

From a practical point of view, the right to protection under the Convention will not be respected if it is not obvious who is so entitled. Article 3 of the Convention therefore calls for distinctive identification of all components of a United Nations operation together with their property, equipment, and personnel. It is also easier to conduct a peacekeeping mission and more likely that the safety of the peacekeepers will be assured if it is a consensual operation. Hence, Article 4 calls on the host state to conclude as soon as possible an agreement on the status of the United Nations operation and all its personnel, including the privileges and immunities for its military and police components.[46] In the last resort, as Article 21 points out, peacekeepers have a right to act in self-defence.

---

45 During the negotiations, some states wanted to exclude NGO personnel altogether, even when working under contract to a UN agency. See Ad-Hoc Committee on the Elaboration of an International Convention Dealing with the Safety and Security of United Nations and Associated Personnel, *Report of the Ad-Hoc Committee on the Work Carried Out during the Period from 28 March to 8 April 1994 Annex*, UNGAOR, 49th Sess., Supp. 22, at p. 21 para. 44, UN Doc. A/AC.242/2 and *Report of the Ad-Hoc Committee on the Elaboration of An International Convention Dealing with the Safety and Security of United Nations and Associated Personnel*, UNGAOR, 49th Sess., Supp. 22, p. 17, UN Doc. A/AC.242/2 (1994). The difficulties encountered in negotiation are described by P. Kirsch, *supra* note 36, 182 at 185.

46 Why immunities for military and policy personnel are singled out is not obvious. Civilian peacekeepers are equally in need of immunities and presumably will be included since the operative clause of Art. 4 refers to "all personnel engaged in the operation."

REMEDIES FOR INJURED PERSONNEL

In the event that civilian peacekeeping personnel are injured or their property or equipment is damaged, the ordinary remedies of the civil law are available to them. Injured military peacekeepers may also have these remedies, but their needs are usually taken care of by the national force in which they serve. Rights to compensation and restoration of property exist under both national and international law. The injured individual may personally sue the wrong-doer under the local law of civil wrongs (tort or delict) and under human rights law, where practicable. Frequently a more likely course of redress is a claim on the international plane. The national state of the victim is entitled to reparations for the injured national from the host government for the mistreatment or denial of human rights that its state officials committed or failed to take reasonable precautions to prevent private individuals from committing.[47]

When the victim is also an IGO official, the International Court of Justice has determined in the *Reparations* case[48] that the organization may make a complementary claim on account of its loss of services of the injured individual. In the case of the United Nations, a universal organization, this right of reparation is enforceable against all countries in the world. Other IGOs may be limited to claiming against member states of the particular organization.[49] However, the scope of the right will still be substantially the same for those IGOs whose membership is widely spread throughout the world. Finally, injured peacekeepers may look to their employer for compensation. Both IGOs and NGOs involved in emergency and humanitarian relief take out insurance against injury to their property and personnel. Entitlement to appropriate compensation for "death, disability, injury or illness attributable to peace-keeping service" in United Nations operations is expressly preserved in the new Safety of Personnel Convention.[50]

---

[47] See H. M. Kindred et al., *International Law Chiefly as Interpreted and Applied in Canada*, 5th ed. (Toronto: Emond Montgomery Publications, 1993) at Chap. 9 — State Responsibility.

[48] [1949] I.C.J. Rep. 174 (Adv. Op.).

[49] In the *Reparations* case, *ibid.*, the International Court of Justice determined that the United Nations has "objective international personality and not merely personality recognized by [member states] alone." Other IGOs of lesser universality in membership and purposes cannot assert objective personality.

[50] *Supra* note 36, Art. 20(e).

CONCLUSION

This catalogue of partial powers and protections of peacekeeping personnel is not neat and tidy, but its cumulative legal effect is a substantial body of rights. The sooner the new Safety of Personnel Convention is brought into force, the better will be the operational context of peacekeeping for nearly everybody. Two significant *lacunae* in the widespread net of protection will, however, continue to exist. The first concerns the uncertainty surrounding the characterization of peacekeepers as combatants so as to separate them and to subject them potentially to attack or capture as prisoners of war. The second is the exclusion of IGO and NGO personnel who are engaged in military supervision, governmental reconstruction, humanitarian assistance, and emergency relief in places of conflict over which the United Nations has not chosen to exercise its peacekeeping powers. These situations are in fact more numerous around the world than even the increasing numbers of crises in which the United Nations has intervened.

Finally, it has to be recognized that the expression of legal powers and protections for peacekeepers is no guarantee that their safety will be assured at the conflict-filled site of their operations. In practice, their best course of protection may be to try to establish good relations with all the parties to the conflict on the ground and to maintain that goodwill by visible impartiality in their actions.

HUGH M. KINDRED
Faculty of Law, Dalhousie University

Sommaire

La protection des gardiennes et gardiens de la paix

À la lumière des risques croissants auxquels sont exposés aujourd'hui un plus grand nombre de gardiennes et gardiens de la paix qui oeuvrent dans des milieux hostiles, l'auteur passe en revue les sources juridiques relatives à leur sécurité et à leur protection. En premier lieu, l'auteur énonce les catégories de personnel qui peuvent prendre part à des opérations de maintien de la paix et examine ensuite la protection que le droit leur offre. Il démontre que de nombreuses conventions, notamment celles concernant l'immunité du personnel des Nations Unies ainsi que les traités portant sur le droit humanitaire et les droits de la personne, renferment des dispositions générales pouvant être interprétées de manière à viser les gardiennes et gardiens de la paix. Mais aucune convention ne traitait directement de leurs problèmes et de leur protection jusqu'à ce que les Nations Unies adoptent, à l'automne 1994, la Convention sur la sécurité du personnel des Nations Unies et du personnel associé. Quand cette convention sera en vigueur, elle imposera des devoirs positifs aux États afin d'assurer la sécurité et la protection des gardiennes et gardiens de la paix et elle appliquera des sanctions pénales contre les individus qui attaquent leur personne ou leurs biens. L'auteur conclut que la nouvelle convention assure une large protection aux gardiennes et gardiens de la paix, mais il est d'avis qu'elle comporte deux lacunes importantes. Elle ne s'appliquera pas aux gardiennes et gardiens de la paix qui sont des combattants (et les critères servant à déterminer ce statut ne sont pas clairs), ni au personnel qui prend part à des opérations de maintien de la paix ne relevant pas des Nations Unies.

Summary

The Protection of Peacekeepers

In light of the increased risks nowadays faced by much greater numbers of peacekeepers in hostile environments, the author surveys the legal sources for their safety and protection. The article first describes the kinds of personnel that may be engaged in peacekeeping operations before exploring the legal rights of protection that attach to each of them. It shows that many conventions, especially those relating to immunities of United Nations personnel as well as humanitarian and human rights treaties, contain general provisions that may be interpreted to include peacekeepers, but that none are aimed directly at their problems and protection. None, that is, until the United Nations adopted the Convention on the Safety of United Nations and Associated Personnel in the fall of 1994. When that Convention comes into force, it will impose affirmative duties on states to ensure the safety and security of peacekeepers and will apply criminal sanctions against individuals who attack them or their property. The article concludes that the new convention casts a wide net of protection over peacekeepers but suffers from two significant lacunae. *It will not cover peacekeepers who are combatants (and the criteria for that characterization are unclear) or personnel engaged in non-United Nations peacekeeping operations.*

Le rejet du concept de patrimoine commun de l'humanité afin d'assurer la gestion de la diversité biologique*

INTRODUCTION

L A CONVENTION SUR LA DIVERSITÉ biologique[1] fut signée le 5 juin 1992, après quatre ans de négociations, lors du Sommet de la Terre qui se tint à Rio de Janeiro. Cette convention ne satisfait pas les environnementalistes[2] et pour cause: elle n'est pas obligatoire; aucune liste de zones à protéger n'a été arrêtée; le principe de zones d'intérêt mondial, sortes de réserves internationales de protection de ressources génétiques les plus représentatives du milieu, n'a pas été retenu puisqu'il était considéré comme une atteinte à la souveraineté nationale des États; et finalement, la question du financement n'a pas été résolue.[3] En revanche la Convention donne satisfaction aux pays en développement[4] en leur reconnaissant une souveraineté permanente sur des ressources déclarées

---

* L'auteur est avocat et détient une matrise en environnement de l'Université de Sherbrooke. Ce texte a été préparé à partir d'un chapitre de mémoire présenté en 1995, en vue de l'obtention d'un D.E.A. en droit et économie du développement à l'Institut du droit de la paix et du développement de l'Université de Nice — Sophia Antipolis. Le mémoire qui a obtenu la meilleure note avait pour titre: "L'évolution du concept de patrimoine commun de l'humanité appliqué aux ressources naturelles."

---

[1] *Convention sur la diversité biologique*, 5 juin 1992. Texte reproduit dans (1992) R.G.D.I.P. aux pp. 952-74.

[2] M.-A. Hermitte, "La Convention sur la diversité biologique" (1992) A.F.D.I. 844.

[3] *Ibid.* à la p. 859.

[4] Ci-après P.E.D.

patrimoine national au même titre que le sont les ressources minérales de leur sous-sol, mettant fin à la pratique du libre accès des
prospecteurs. Les pays développés[5] bien qu'insatisfaits des dispositions de l'entente, ont néanmoins pour la plupart décidé de la
signer et les États-Unis ont finalement choisi d'y adhérer malgré
leur hostilité initiale. La Convention est d'ailleurs entrée en vigueur
le 29 décembre 1993.

Jusqu'au moment de l'entrée en vigueur de la Convention sur la
diversité biologique, l'accès aux ressources génétiques ainsi que
leur prélèvement se faisaient sans qu'aucune compensation financière ne soit exigée par les P.E.D., si bien que l'on pouvait considé-
rer que cette procédure constituait un "code de conduite" découlant d'une perception générale à l'effet que les ressources
génétiques étaient une sorte de patrimoine commun de l'humanité.[6] Cette conception du "libre accès gratuit" fut cependant
remise en question par les P.E.D. lors de la tenue au sein du
Programme des Nations unies pour l'environnement,[7] à partir de
1988, des travaux de préparation de la Convention sur la diversité
biologique.[8] Les P.E.D. considéraient injuste d'accorder le libre
accès à un patrimoine génétique qui pourrait par la suite faire
l'objet de brevets obtenus par des entreprises de P.D., qu'ils
n'auraient par la suite pas la possibilité d'acquérir faute de ressources financières.[9] Les P.D. avaient en effet donné une valeur
économique aux ressources génétiques prélevées dans les P.E.D. en

[5] Ci-après P.D.

[6] Ci-après P.C.H. M.-A. Hermitte, *supra* note 2 à la p. 845.

[7] Ci-après P.N.U.E.

[8] Le P.N.U.E. constitua en 1988 le Groupe spécial d'experts juridiques et techniques, devenu en mai 1911 le Comité de négociation intergouvernemental,
qu'il chargea de l'élaboration d'une convention sur la diversité biologique.
Après sept sessions de négociations, le Conseil d'administration du P.N.U.E.
adopta le 22 mai 1992 la version définitive d'un texte qui deviendra la *Convention sur la diversité biologique.* J. Untermaier, "La Convention de Rio sur la
conservation durable de la diversité biologique" dans M. Prieur et S. Dombe-
Bille, dir., *Droit de l'environnement et développement durable*, Limoges, Presses universitaires de Limoges, 1994, 351 à la p. 104.

[9] Selon la Commission mondiale sur l'environnement et le développement, ci-
après la C.M.E.D., la part des P.E.D. dans le nombre total de brevets délivrés
dans le monde en 1980 n'était que de 6 %. Commission mondiale sur l'environnement et la développement, *Notre avenir à tous*, Montréal, Éditions du fleuve,
1989 à la p. 105. Les droits de propriété industrielle pouvaient couvrir des
ressources aussi vitales pour les P.E.D. que de nouvelles variétés de semences à
haut rendement alimentaire.

permettant la brevetabilité de micro-organismes obtenus à la suite de manipulations effectuées sur ces ressources. Le débat qui ne portait à l'origine que sur la préservation de zones de diversité biologique prit rapidement les allures d'un règlement de comptes des P.E.D. à l'égard des P.D. en matière de développement,[10] amenant le rejet par les P.E.D. de l'application du concept de P.C.H. aux ressources génétiques. Ces derniers considéraient en effet que les ressources génétiques ne constituaient pas des ressources naturelles communes de l'humanité. C'est donc paradoxalement la recherche par les P.E.D. d'une plus grande équité dans leurs rapports avec les P.D. quant à la gestion des ressources génétiques qui amena le rejet de leur part du concept de P.C.H. appliqué à ces ressources.

Le Comité du P.N.U.E. chargé de l'élaboration d'une convention disposait d'un projet de convention préparé par des associations de protection de la nature,[11] dans lequel une approche "conservationniste" était prédominante par rapport aux questions économiques et faisait des ressources génétiques un bien possédant plusieurs des caractéristiques propres à un bien qualifié P.C.H.[12] Les États qui devenaient en quelque sorte de simples gardiens de la diversité biologique, devaient établir des zones de protection représentatives du plus grand nombre d'espèces possibles retrouvées sur leur territoire, l'objectif du projet étant de créer un réseau international de réserves de conservation. Le document, fort louable d'un point de vue environnemental, ne fut pas retenu à cause de l'opposition des P.E.D. d'appuyer un système qui ne laissait aucune place à leurs préoccupations avant toutes relatives à leur développement économique.

L'arrêt de mort du projet "conservationniste" fut signé par le Directeur exécutif du P.N.U.E., Mostapha Tolba, qui déclara lors de la seconde session du Comité de négociation intergouvernemental tenue à Genève, en juin 1990, que "le concept de patrimoine

---

[10] M.-A. Hermitte, *supra* note 2 à la p. 846.

[11] Regroupés au sein de l'Union internationale pour la conservation de la nature (U.I.C.N.). P. W. Birnie et A. E. Boyle, *International Law and the Environment*, New York, Oxford University Press, 1993 aux pp. 484-86.

[12] Ce projet, assez curieusement, ne qualifiait pas la diversité biologique de P.C.H. et il fut avancé que cela était une "conséquence du statut philosophique choisi pour la diversité biologique. Si elle avait une valeur pour elle-même, protégée au-delà des aspects simplement utilitaristes elle était plus qu'un simple patrimoine" M. -A. Hermitte, *supra* note 2 à la p. 850.

commun de l'humanité est inadéquat, que les ressources génétiques relèvent de la souveraineté permanente sur les ressources
naturelles, et qu'il est néanmoins indispensable qu'il y ait libre
accès de tous à ces ressources."[13]

Cette déclaration était contradictoire en ce que seule l'adoption
du concept de P.C.H. permettait à tous les États d'avoir un libre
accès aux ressources génétiques et qu'au contraire le concept de
souveraineté permanente sur les ressources naturelles était une
limitation potentielle à cette possibilité. Le représentant du
P.N.U.E. souhaitait que les P.D. échangent leurs technologies contre des droits d'accès aux ressources,[14] principe qui ne sera pas
maintenu dans la version finale de la Convention en raison du
désaccord des P.D. Quant aux autres aspects de la déclaration de M.
Tolba, notamment la question cruciale de la souveraineté permanente des États sur les ressources génétiques, ils emporteront
l'adhésion des P.E.D. et seront repris dans la version finale de la
Convention. La déclaration de M. Tolba donna une certaine légiti-
mité à la position des P.E.D. qui consistait à rejeter l'application du
concept de P.C.H. à ces dernières et à soumettre les ressources
génétiques à la souveraineté des États sur les ressources naturelles.
D'autres facteurs, cette fois-ci extérieurs au débat qui portait sur la
diversité biologique, exercèrent une influence non négligeable sur
ce dernier et amenèrent l'application du concept de souveraineté
permanente sur les ressources naturelles aux ressources génétiques.
Il n'en demeure pas moins qu'il s'agit d'une application inusitée de
ce principe consacré dans de multiples résolutions de l'Assemblée
générale des Nations unies,[15] notamment dans la Déclaration concernant l'instauration d'un nouvel ordre économique international
et dans la Charte des droits et devoirs économiques des États, toutes
deux adoptées en 1974.[16]

---

[13] *Ibid.* aux pp. 852-53.

[14] Les P.E.D. croyaient pouvoir, dans les années 60, échanger leurs matières
premières contre des brevets et techniques des P.D., ce qui ne fonctionna
guère. *Ibid.* à la p. 853.

[15] Ci-après A.G.N.U. Pour une étude de ces Résolutions voir G. Abi-Saab, "La
souveraineté permanente sur les ressources naturelles" dans *Mélanges René-Jean
Dupuy*, Paris, Pédone, 1991 aux pp. 643-44.

[16] Respectivement Résolutions (A/RES/3201/S-6VI, 1974) et (A/RES/3201/
XXIX, 1974); *Ibid.* Ces Résolutions et celles qui furent adoptées antérieure-
ment ne faisaient aucune distinction entre les ressources vivantes et non
vivantes. De plus, elles ne faisaient pas mention d'un devoir de conservation à la

Le débat sur la diversité biologique et le statut juridique conféré aux ressources génétiques ne peuvent se comprendre qu'en faisant l'analyse du concept de P.C.H. (première partie). Nous ferons par la suite l'étude des facteurs extérieurs au débat sur la diversité biologique, qui outre la position tenue par M. Tolba, conditionnèrent le statut juridique qui fut attribué aux ressources génétiques (deuxième partie).

I L'ANALYSE DU CONCEPT DE P.C.H.

Le concept de P.C.H. évolua sous l'impulsion constante que lui donnèrent les P.E.D. depuis la grande période de décolonisation des années 60, jusqu'à la conclusion des travaux de la Commission mondiale sur l'environnement et le développement[17] desquels naquit le concept de "développement durable." L'analyse du concept de P.C.H. sera faite à travers la genèse de ce concept (A), en définissant son contenu juridique (B) et en expliquant sa maturation à travers le concept de développement durable (C).

A LA GENÈSE DU CONCEPT DE P.C.H.

L'accession à la souveraineté politique de nombreux États au cours des années 60 contribua à l'évolution du droit international qui, jusqu'à cette période, était en grande partie un droit qui avait pour finalité de servir les intérêts des puissances européennes et de certaines autres dont la culture et les traditions en faisaient des États qui avaient le privilège d'accéder au "concert des grands."[18] Les nouveaux États indépendants, qui pour la plupart accusaient un retard important dans le niveau de leur développement lors de leur accession à la souveraineté politique par rapport aux États membres des Nations unies, utilisèrent le concept du droit des peuples à disposer d'eux-mêmes afin d'affirmer leur souveraineté sur les ressources naturelles localisées sur leur territoire.[19] Après

---

charge des États. P. W. Birnie *et al.*, *supra* note 11 à la p. 113. Ce principe qui fit son apparition aux Nations unies au début des années 50, dans le sillage des premières indépendances d'après-guerre, servit de fondement au contrôle des investissements étrangers et à la nationalisation et l'expropriation de biens étrangers. G. Abi-Saab, *supra* note 15 aux pp. 648-61.

[17] Ci-après C.M.E.D.

[18] C. Zorgbibe, "Communauté internationale ou concert des grands?" dans *Mélanges René-Jean Dupuy*, *supra* note 15 aux pp. 372-82.

[19] G. Abi-Saab, *supra* note 15 à la p. 643.

s'être assurés la maîtrise de celles-ci, les nouveaux États en vinrent à revendiquer leur juste part des ressources naturelles appartenant à la communauté internationale qui devaient selon eux être partagées selon la maxime "à chacun selon ses besoins."[20]

L'initiative de l'élaboration du concept de P.C.H. en tant qu'instrument de développement des P.E.D. revient à M. Arvid Pardo qui, pour la première fois en 1967, exposa à l'A.G.N.U. que les ressources des grands fonds marins devaient être exploitées en priorité dans l'intérêt de l'humanité toute entière, en tenant compte tout particulièrement des besoins des pays pauvres.[21] L'Accord sur la Lune et les corps célestes, adopté en 1979,[22] fera des ressources contenues dans ces astres un P.C.H. dont la finalité sera la même que celle du P.C.H. constitué par les grands fonds marins, soit le relèvement du niveau de vie des pays pauvres. L'introduction du concept de P.C.H. s'est donc faite sous l'influence des P.E.D. et répondait à "l'incapacité des P.E.D. de bénéficier effectivement des libertés dont jouissent les États les plus puissants" à cause des limites technologiques et financières qui s'imposaient à eux.[23]

Les années 80 seront celles de la prise de conscience par la communauté internationale des graves problèmes environnementaux affectant certaines ressources naturelles communes de l'humanité et de la nécessité d'apporter des correctifs à court terme à des situations menaçant la survie de l'espèce humaine à plus ou moins brève échéance. Lorsque les ressources étaient peu utilisées, la vision traditionnelle de ressources abondantes, voire inépuisables, semblait garantir des opportunités égales quant à leur utilisation. Mais la constatation que beaucoup d'entre elles étaient épuisables et certaines autres menacées par la pollution obligea à rechercher de nouveaux mécanismes visant leur répartition équitable tant pour les générations présentes que pour les générations futures.[24] Des références constantes seront faites à l'humanité dans les différents

---

[20] M. Bedjaoui, *Droit international, bilan et perspectives*, t. 2, Paris, Pédone, 1991 aux pp. 1263-64.

[21] A.-C. Kiss, "La notion de patrimoine commun de l'humanité" (1982) 175: 2 R.C.A.D.I. 99 aux pp. 114-15.

[22] Accord ré gissant les activités des états sur la lune et les autres corps célestes, 5 décembre 1979, 18 I.L.M. 1434, 20 Ind. J.I.L. 399 (en vigueur le 11 juillet 1984).

[23] A. D. Roth, *La prohibition de l'appropriation et les régimes d'accès aux espaces extra-atmosphériques*, Paris, Presses universitaires de France, 1992 à la p. 111.

[24] *Ibid.* à la p. 110.

traités qui seront signés dans le domaine environnemental, mais le concept de P.C.H. y sera absent, du moins dans le verbe, puisque son essence y sera à travers un concept d'une grande efficacité pour les P.E.D. quant à leurs revendications: le développement durable.[25] Les Traités qui seront signés afin de protéger les ressources naturelles communes de l'humanité auront donc tout autant comme finalité la protection de la ressource que la promotion du développement économique des P.E.D.[26]

Le P.C.H., compris dans le sens d'une répartition équitable des bénéfices provenant de l'exploitation de ressources naturelles communes, ne serait pas un concept juridique reconnu pour certains, en raison du fait que les deux seules conventions internationales où il y est fait référence, soit la Convention des Nations unies sur le droit de la mer et l'Accord sur la Lune et les corps célestes, n'auraient pas à ce jour été ratifiées par suffisamment d'États représentatifs des intérêts de la communauté internationale dans les domaines d'application de ces Traités. D'autres soutiennent que les références fréquentes faites à cette notion à l'A.G.N.U. ainsi que l'application volontaire de certaines dispositions de ces Traités par les États, surtout en droit de la mer, auraient créé une coutume internationale qui servirait de fondement à une acceptation par les États des principes fondamentaux du concept de P.C.H.[27]

B   LE CONTENU JURIDIQUE DU CONCEPT DE P.C.H.

La proposition Pardo est à la base du régime juridique que les États signataires de la Convention des Nations unies sur le droit de

---

25 Le concept de développement durable a été élaboré par la C.M.E.D. et présenté dans un rapport diffusé en avril 1987 sous le titre français de "Notre avenir à tous" ("Our Common Future"). La C.M.E.D., qui reçut son mandat de l'A.G.N.U., définit le développement durable comme: "un développement qui répond aux besoins du présent sans compromettre la capacité des générations futures de répondre aux leurs." C.M.E.D., *Notre avenir à tous, supra* note 9 à la p. 51.

26 Certains considèrent que les traités relatifs à la protection de ressources communes dans le domaine de l'environnement n'auraient comme finalité que la défense d'intérêts communs, comme c'est le cas en ce qui concerne le patrimoine culturel et naturel. K. Kouassi, "Le concept de patrimoine commun de l'humanité et l'évolution du droit international public" (1985) Revue juridique et politique, 949 à la p. 952; P.-M. Dupuy, *Droit international public*, Paris, Dalloz, 1992 à la p. 505.

27 Sur cette question et sur les opinions à ce sujet, voir P.-M. Dupuy, *supra* note 26 aux pp. 232-235.

la mer conféreront aux grands fonds marins en 1982, en faisant de ceux-ci un P.C.H. ayant les caractéristiques fondamentales données à ce concept par M. Pardo dans les différentes interventions qu'il fit à ce sujet à l'A.G.N.U.[28] L'expression même de P.C.H. impliquera à partir de la première intervention de M. Pardo un contenu juridique spécifique, que la doctrine précisera[29] et que les États refuseront de conférer à certains biens lorsqu'ils choisiront des expressions telles que "apanage de l'humanité"[30] ou "préoccupation de l'humanité toute entière,"[31] ces biens pouvant toutefois revêtir une ou plusieurs des caractéristiques propres à un bien qualifié de P.C.H.

Un bien peut être considéré P.C.H. si la gestion qu'on en fait répond aux six principes suivants:[32] (1) le bien ne doit être susceptible d'aucune appropriation nationale; (2) le bien doit être utilisé exclusivement à des fins pacifiques; (3) le bien doit être accessible à tous afin d'y effectuer de la recherche scientifique et les résultats doivent être publics; (4) l'utilisation du bien ou de ses ressources doit tenir compte du renouvellement de la ressource lorsqu'il s'agit d'une ressource non renouvelable[33] et de l'intérêt des générations futures tout autant que de celui des générations présentes;[34] (5) l'exploitation du bien et celle des ressources qu'il comporte

---

[28] *Ibid.* aux pp. 114-19.

[29] A.-C. Kiss, *supra* note 21 à la p. 135 et les références qu'il cite à la note 86.

[30] Expression retenue pour qualifier l'espace extra-atmosphérique à l'art. premier du *Traité sur les principes devant régir les activités des États dans le domaine de l'exploration et de l'utilisation de l'espace extra-atmosphérique, y compris la Lune et les autres corps célestes*, entré en vigueur le 27 janvier 1967. R.T. Lan. 1967, no. 19, 610 R.T.N.U. 205.

[31] Expression retenue pour qualifier l'atmosphère dans le préambule de la *Convention cadre sur les changements climatiques* (C.C.C.C.), adoptée à Rio de Janeiro le 15 mai 1992. Texte dans le rapport de la C.M.E.D., *Notre avenir à tous*, *supra* note 9 aux pp. 237-58.

[32] C. C. Joyner, "Legal implications of the concept of the common heritage of mankind" (1986) vol. 35, part. 1, I.C.L.Q. 191 aux pp. 191-92.

[33] A.-C. Kiss, *supra* note 21 à la p. 241.

[34] Ce principe serait inhérent au concept de P.C.H. "L'humanité d'aujourd'hui serait considérée comme le *trustee*, le dépositaire des ressources naturelles de la planète avec l'obligation de les transmettre aussi complètement que possible aux générations à venir." *Ibid.* à la p. 129. En ce qui concerne les droits des générations futures, voir A. D'amato, E. Brown Weiss et L. Gündling, "Agora: What obligation does our generation owe to the next? An approach to global environmental responsibility" (1990) 84 A.J.I.L. 190; P. W. Birnie et A. E. Boyle, *supra* note 11 aux pp. 211-12.

doivent être faites dans l'intérêt de l'humanité toute entière en portant une attention toute particulière aux pays les plus pauvres; (6) la gestion du bien doit être faite par un organisme représentant les intérêts de tous les États.

Le bien considéré P.C.H. peut être tout autant un bien dont l'exploitation permet de réaliser des revenus qu'un bien qui nécessite des investissements afin d'en assurer la protection. L'espace extra-atmosphérique, la Lune et les grands fonds marins, entreraient dans la première catégorie, tandis que les biens visés par la Convention sur le patrimoine mondial, culturel et naturel entreraient dans la deuxième. Les ressources de l'environnement communes de l'humanité, telles l'atmosphère et le patrimoine génétique, entreraient dans les deux catégories puisque leur exploitation dans un premier temps permet la réalisation de revenus et leur surexploitation dans un second requiert des investissements afin d'assurer leur réhabilitation. L'application du concept de P.C.H. se ferait toujours dans un esprit d'inégalité compensatoire au profit des P.E.D., ces derniers devant jouir d'une proportion plus élevée des revenus provenant de l'exploitation des biens compris dans la première catégorie et les P.D. assumant une part plus importante des sommes requises pour assurer la protection des biens compris dans la deuxième catégorie. Un bien considéré P.C.H. peut être sous la souveraineté d'un État comme le sont les biens visés par la Convention sur le patrimoine mondial, culturel et naturel ou n'être soumis à aucune juridiction étatique particulière comme l'est l'atmosphère.

C LA MATURATION DU CONCEPT DE P.C.H. À TRAVERS CELUI DE DÉVELOPPEMENT DURABLE

L'évolution du concept de P.C.H. suit celle de la recherche d'un nouvel ordre économique international[35] par les P.E.D. en constituant un élément indispensable à sa réalisation et en devenant même le symbole de son accomplissement.[36] La raison de la juxtaposition de ces deux notions opérée par les P.E.D. dans leurs

35 Ci-après N.O.E.I.

36 En parlant du début des travaux de la Conférence sur le droit de la mer, R.-J. Dupuy note: "Le départ de la Conférence, en 1974, coïncidait d'ailleurs avec celui des négociations sur le nouvel ordre économique international dont le régime des fonds marins devait, pour le Tiers-Monde, marquer un modèle et un test." R.-J. Dupuy, *La clôture du système international: La Cité Terrestre*, Paris, Presses universitaires de France, 1989 à la p. 42.

rapports avec les P.D. visant l'établissement de nouvelles règles dans le domaine économique, s'explique par les similitudes qui existent entre les idéologies à la base même de ces concepts.

Les P.E.D. formulèrent leur première demande à l'effet que les questions de développement soient abordées par une approche globale destinée à l'instauration d'un N.O.E.I. lors du IVᵉ Sommet des pays non alignés, tenu à Alger en septembre 1973, par 77 P.E.D.[37] L'A.G.N.U. adopta par la suite, en mai 1974, la Déclaration et le programme d'action concernant l'instauration d'un N.O.E.I.[38] et en décembre de la même année la Charte des droits et devoirs économiques des États. Ces documents qui détaillent les demandes des P.E.D. constituent "le point d'orgue des revendications du Tiers-Monde . . . en insistant particulièrement d'une part sur la protection de la souveraineté des États et d'autre part sur le droit au commerce sur une base équitable."[39]

Le nouvel ordre demandé comportait deux axes de revendications: l'égalité souveraine des États qui ne pouvait se concrétiser que par une indépendance économique accrue des P.E.D. par rapport aux P.D. et l'appel à une plus grande solidarité de la communauté internationale, par un traitement préférentiel accordé aux P.E.D. afin de corriger les inégalités de fait entre les États.

Les P.E.D. considéraient que les règles du libre marché devaient être adaptées par des mesures compensatrices afin d'en réduire les rigueurs à leur égard et que devaient être instaurés à plus long terme des mécanismes institutionnels, assurant leur participation dans un esprit d'équité à la mise en place de normes économiques.[40] Cette démarche, qui concernait dans un premier temps les relations commerciales entre États, s'étendit par la suite à d'autres domaines qui concernaient la gestion des ressources naturelles communes de l'humanité comme les grands fonds marins,

---

37 Cet événement fut précédé de deux autres importants dans la genèse du N.O.E.I.: la première Commission des Nations unies pour le commerce et le développement (C.N.U.C.E.D.), tenue à Genève en 1964, et la proclamation en 1970 de la *Stratégie des Nations unies pour la deuxième décennie pour le développement*. N. Quoc Dinh, P. Daillier et A. Pellet, *Droit international Public*, Paris, L.G.D.J., 1994 à la p. 978.

38 Résolutions 3201 (S-VI) et 3202 (S-V); M. Bennouna, "Droit international et développement" dans M. Bedjaoui, dir., *Droit international, bilan et perspectives*, t. 1, Paris, Pédone, 1991 à la p. 666.

39 N. Q. Dinh *et al.*, *supra* à la p. 978.

40 *Ibid.* aux pp. 979-80.

l'espace extra-atmosphérique, la Lune et les corps célestes, pour finalement atteindre des secteurs relatifs à la préservation de l'environnement global comme les questions de la stabilisation du climat, de la protection de la couche d'ozone et de la diversité biologique. Les P.E.D. cherchent maintenant à assurer une gestion équitable des ressources environnementales dans un esprit marqué par une idéologique proche de celle qui animait le N.O.E.I., le concept de P.C.H. devenant en quelque sorte un instrument de la réalisation du N.O.E.I. quant à la gestion de certaines de ces ressources, comme l'atmosphère et la couche d'ozone. Les ressources génétiques feraient exception à cette règle puisque le concept de P.C.H. leur serait inapplicable. Les P.E.D. considèrent, en effet, qu'il est équitable de ne permettre l'accès des P.D. aux ressources situées sur le territoire des P.E.D. qu'en contrepartie d'un accès préférentiel consenti par les P.D. aux P.E.D. sur les brevets accordés pour des créations génétiques issues de prélèvements effectués sur le territoire de P.E.D.

Les P.E.D. modifieront leur stratégie dans leur façon de revendiquer l'équité à la base du N.O.E.I. à partir des années 80. Trois facteurs seront à l'origine de ce changement: (1) les graves problèmes financiers, monétaires et énergétiques qu'ils doivent résoudre;[41] (2) le constat du refus des P.D. d'accéder à leur demande d'un N.O.E.I.; (3) la survenance de problèmes environnementaux globaux qui préoccupent les P.D. et qui requièrent la collaboration des P.E.D. pour leur résolution.

Bien que les P.E.D. continueront, par le biais de résolutions adoptées à l'A.G.N.U., d'affirmer leur volonté de voir s'instaurer un N.O.E.I. et de définir des stratégies afin d'atteindre cet objectif,[42] leurs efforts porteront plus à partir des années 80 sur des solutions immédiates à leurs problèmes; ainsi les stratégies de développement des P.E.D. pour les années 80 et 90 seront moins empreintes que ne l'étaient les précédentes d'une vision du développement axée sur la mise en place de programmes globaux à long terme caractéristiques du N.O.E.I.[43] Les P.E.D. qui chercheront plutôt des solutions "à la pièce" à leurs problèmes de développement utiliseront moins fréquemment le terme même de N.O.E.I. dans leur discours officiel.

---

[41] *Ibid.* à la p. 979.

[42] Voir les *Stratégies des Nations-unies pour les troisième et quatrième décennies pour le développement* adoptées par les Résolutions 35/56 du 5 décembre 1980 et 45/199 du 21 décembre 1990.

[43] N. Q. Dinh *et al*, *supra* note 37 à la p. 979.

La survenance de certains événements menaçant la survie de l'espèce humaine donna cependant l'opportunité aux P.E.D. de revendiquer non pas la réalisation du N.O.E.I. en tant que tel mais celle de ses éléments constitutifs. En réponse à la demande de collaboration faite par les P.D. aux P.E.D. en vue de l'adoption de mesures propres à assurer la préservation de l'environnement à l'échelle planétaire, les P.E.D. demandèrent en échange la prise en compte de leurs revendications exprimées dans le N.O.E.I., en se fondant sur le concept de développement durable.[44] Dans ces nouveaux rapports de force Nord-Sud qui caractérisèrent les années 80, les P.E.D. prirent conscience qu'ils ne pouvaient faire valoir leurs doléances en faveur de leur développement, que dans un contexte de conditionnalité et qu'en ne leur trouvant la monnaie d'échange qui leur avait fait défaut dans les négociations portant sur l'espace extra-atmosphérique, la Lune et les grands fonds marins. Cette monnaie d'échange leur était désormais fournie par les problèmes environnementaux globaux.[45] Les P.E.D., qui semblaient avoir

---

[44] Pour certains, le développement durable serait une notion issue du N.O.E.I. et constituerait le véhicule permettant la réalisation des nouveaux objectifs de la communauté internationale. N. Q. Dinh *et al.*, *supra* à la p. 979. Nous sommes d'avis que le développement durable est avant tout le compromis auxquels les P.D. et les P.E.D. arrivèrent afin que puisse se faire la promotion de leurs intérêts propres. En vertu du compromis obtenu, les P.D. s'engagent à collaborer avec les P.E.D. à la réalisation des éléments constitutifs du N.O.E.I. et les P.E.D. s'engagent en contrepartie à collaborer avec les P.D. à la mise en place de mesures visant la protection de l'environnement global. Le développement durable serait porteur des éléments constitutifs du N.O.E.I. Il suffit, pour se convaincre de cette affirmation, de se reporter au chapitre 3 du rapport de la C.M.E.D. intitulé "Le rôle de l'économie mondiale" dans lequel la C.M.E.D. traite des revendications traditionnelles des P.E.D. en faveur d'un N.O.E.I.: (1) allégement de la dette externe (pp. 87-89); (2) accroissement de l'aide internationale (pp. 90-93); (3) stabilisation du cours des matières premières (pp. 94-98); (4) réduction du protectionnisme (p. 98); (5) facilitation des transferts de technologie (pp. 104-06); (6) établissement d'un code de bonne conduite pour les firmes transnationales (pp. 101-04); (7) établissement de garanties contre les fluctuations des recettes d'exportation (pp. 94-95) et on retrouve finalement, à la p. 255 du rapport, la promotion de l'industrialisation des P.E.D. Seule la réforme du système monétaire international ne semble pas être envisagée. Voir au sujet du N.O.E.I., M. Bettati, *Le nouvel ordre économique international*, Paris, Presses universitaires de France, 1983.

[45] La disparition des régimes communistes de l'Europe de l'est, au début des années 90, aurait peut-être compromis les revendications des P.E.D. en faveur d'un N.O.E.I. si des problèmes environnementaux globaux permettant l'application du concept de développement durable n'étaient pas survenus

abandonné au cours des années 80 la recherche d'un N.O.E.I.
imprégné de l'idéologie socialiste qui caractérisait leurs revendications au cours des années 70, poursuivirent néanmoins dans le
domaine environnemental, à partir du milieu des années 80, la
recherche de la réalisation des éléments constitutifs du N.O.E.I.
Les succès remportés par les P.E.D. ne furent guère meilleurs en
ce qui concerne l'application du concept de P.C.H. aux ressources
qu'ils considéraient communes à l'humanité qu'ils ne le furent en
ce qui concerne l'établissement d'un N.O.E.I. Lorsqu'ils parve-
naient à ce qu'une ressource obtienne le statut de P.C.H., comme
ce fut le cas pour les grands fonds marins et la Lune, les P.D. usaient
de tous les moyens dilatoires possibles afin de retarder l'application
du concept ou utilisaient tous les pouvoirs dont ils disposaient afin
d'enlever au concept toute sa portée originelle. La vague de néoli-
béralisme suscitée par la chute de l'ex-U.R.S.S. constitua un handi-
cap supplémentaire à l'établissement de structures propres à
assurer la gestion de P.C.H. La survenance des problèmes environnementaux globaux permit encore aux P.E.D. d'intégrer dans les
mécanismes de gestion des ressources menacées par la pollution,
des dispositions assurant des résultats similaires à ceux qui auraient
été obtenus si le concept de P.C.H. leur avait été appliqué. Ainsi,
s'appuyant sur des vocables tels que "préoccupation pour l'humanité toute entière,"[46] ou à partir de conventions ne faisant tout
simplement pas référence au concept d'humanité,[47] les P.E.D. ten-
tèrent de faire en soi que ces ressources soient utilisées au profit de
l'humanité toute entière à la manière de véritables P.C.H.

II Les facteurs extérieurs au débat qui eurent une
   influence sur le choix du statut juridique conféré aux
   ressources génétiques

Les débats sur la diversité biologique et la portée de la Convention qui en résulta doivent être analysés à la lumière des négociations parallèles qui se déroulaient entre P.D. et P.E.D. dans d'autres

---

dans les années 80. En effet, l'échec des pays d'Europe de l'est dans l'instauration d'un régime dont l'idéologie était fondée sur une répartition équitable des
richesses au niveau national, donnait des arguments aux détracteurs de l'idéologie du N.O.E.I.

[46] Voir la note 31.

[47] Par exemple, la *Convention de Vienne sur la protection de la couche d'ozone*, Texte
dans R. Elliot Benedick, *Ozone Diplomacy: New Directions in Safeguarding the Planet*,
Cambridge, Harvard University Press, 1991 aux pp. 218-29.

secteurs qui concernaient l'exploitation de ressources naturelles communes (A). Ils doivent aussi être analysés à la lumière des travaux de la C.M.E.D., qui donna son aval à l'exercice par les P.E.D. d'une souveraineté sur les ressources génétiques (B).

A   LES NÉGOCIATIONS PARALLÈLES QUI SE DÉROULAIENT DANS
     D'AUTRES SECTEURS QUI CONCERNAIENT L'EXPLOITATION DE
     RESSOURCES NATURELLES COMMUNES

L'insatisfaction des P.E.D. quant au statut juridique de l'espace extra-atmosphérique est bien connue. Les P.E.D. avaient toujours soutenu, depuis l'adoption du Traité sur l'espace extra-atmosphérique,[48] que les principes de liberté d'exploration et de liberté d'accès ne servaient que les intérêts des P.D. et que la notion d'"apanage de l'humanité" devait être remplacée par celle de P.C.H. qui était susceptible d'assurer un partage plus équitable de cette ressource. L'Accord sur la Lune et les corps célestes qui faisait des ressources naturelles de ces astres un P.C.H., bien qu'en vigueur depuis 1979, n'avait pas été ratifié par les puissances spatiales. L'exploitation des ressources naturelles qui se trouvaient sur ces astres, comme le prévoyaient les dispositions du Traité, semblait devenir un objectif de plus en plus hypothétique.[49]

La Convention des Nations unies sur le droit de la mer qui, à sa Partie XI faisait de la Zone internationale constituée par les grands fonds marins un P.C.H. dont on avait prévu les modalités de partage, n'était pas en vigueur dû au nombre insuffisant de ratifications. Le régime d'exploitation de la Zone était de plus compromis par le refus d'importants pays industrialisés d'adhérer à la Convention, en appuyant leur décision sur le fait qu'ils jugeaient insatisfaisantes les dispositions qui concernaient précisément le régime retenu pour l'exploitation de la Zone.

Les discussions entourant la gestion de l'atmosphère étaient très âpres et bien que des progrès aient été faits en ce qui concernait la préservation de la couche d'ozone, la problématique demeurait entière en ce qui avait trait aux modifications climatiques. Les P.D. opposaient une fin de non-recevoir aux P.E.D. qui souhaitaient que soient incluses des dispositions prévoyant l'application du concept de P.C.H. à l'atmosphère, ce qui aurait ainsi permis une utilisation

---

[48] Voir la référence au Traité à la note 30.
[49] Voir la référence au Traité à la note 22.

équitable de cette ressource entre les États et la création d'une autorité internationale afin d'en assurer la gestion.

La position de négociation des P.E.D. était toutefois meilleure dans le domaine de l'atmosphère qu'elle ne l'était dans les domaines qui concernaient l'espace extra-atmosphérique, la Lune et les grands fonds marins. En effet, les P.D. n'avaient d'autres choix pour résoudre la problématique atmosphérique que de s'assurer la collaboration des P.E.D.; aucune action efficace à l'échelle de la planète n'étant envisageable si les P.E.D. n'adoptaient pas dans le futur des comportements différents de ceux que les P.D. avaient eus jusqu'à présent.

En ce qui concernait la diversité génétique, les P.E.D. disposaient d'un atout de négociation supplémentaire: la plus grande partie de la ressource naturelle à préserver se trouvait sur leur territoire.[50] Cet élément, qui revêtait une importance capitale dans les pourparlers entre les deux groupes, servait d'autant plus les intérêts des P.E.D. que les causes directes qui menaçaient l'intégrité de la diversité biologique, originaient d'activités qui se déroulaient sur leur territoire: culture extensive, déforestation et croissance démographique.[51] De plus, l'appui du Directeur exécutif du P.N.U.E. aux P.E.D. était de taille et permit à ces derniers de soutenir une position difficilement défendable d'un point de vue environnemental si l'on considère que la communauté internationale possède un intérêt légitime dans la préservation de cette ressource.[52]

L'attitude des P.E.D. fut cependant avant tout leur réponse à l'évolution du droit des brevets qui en vint à reconnaître la brevetabilité généralisée des organismes vivants. Un Comité d'experts, mis sur pied par le Comité du P.N.U.E. lors de la deuxième session de ses travaux et chargé de réaliser une étude sur les rapports entre droits de propriété intellectuelle et accès aux ressources génétiques,[53] donna la justification aux P.E.D. pour qu'ils agissent dans ce sens, en affirmant que "dans l'hypothèse où le lobbying des biotechnologies aboutissait à obtenir des Offices de brevets la brevetabilité des gènes, des cellules, des tissus et, *in fine*, de tous les

---

[50] C.M.E.D., *Notre avenir à tous, supra* note 9 à la p. 181.

[51] *Ibid.* aux pp. 181-85.

[52] Dans le même sens, voir *infra* note 76.

[53] L'étude que le Comité devait réaliser devait porter en plus sur ces deux autres aspects: Les coûts de la conservation et les mécanismes de financement. Pour un résumé de l'étude sur ces deux aspects voir: M.-A. Hermitte, *supra* note 2 aux pp. 854-55.

organismes vivants, il devenait cohérent de supprimer le libre accès aux ressources génétiques sauvages des pays du Tiers-Monde."[54] Le Comité admettait tout de même que la solution la plus respectueuse de "l'intérêt général" était de maintenir le libre accès aux ressources sans possibilité de brevetabilité des créations génétiques, mais qu'une protection relative de l'invention pouvait être accordée afin de récompenser l'innovation.[55] La solution avancée par le Comité était bien loin de celle d'un accès préférentiel aux techniques brevetées suggéré par le Directeur exécutif du P.N.U.E. Ainsi, au nom d'un nouvel "ordre environnemental mondial"[56] le patrimoine génétique de l'humanité était échangé contre certaines promesses des P.D. en matière de développement.

B   L'AVAL DE LA C.M.E.D. QUANT À L'EXERCICE D'UNE
    SOUVERAINETÉ PAR LES P.E.D. SUR LES RESSOURCES
    GÉNÉTIQUES

Le rapport de la C.M.E.D. et les travaux de préparation de la Conférence des Nations unies sur l'environnement et le développement eurent un impact important sur l'attitude des P.E.D. d'appliquer le concept de souveraineté permanente sur les ressources naturelles à la diversité génétique. Ces deux événements, qui portaient les germes du N.O.E.I. ou, à tout le moins, les éléments constitutifs de ce N.O.E.I. que les P.E.D. réclamaient sous la forme renouvelée du débat environnemental, imprégnèrent le statut juridi-

---

54 *Ibid.* à la p. 856.

55 En fait, le Comité souhaitait une généralisation du système du "droit d'obtention végétale" qui existait déjà et qui donnait "un monopole d'exploitation aux obtenteurs d'une nouvelle variété végétale, sans empêcher les concurrents d'utiliser les ressources génétiques contenues dans cette variété pour obtenir une nouvelle variété qui comprendra une partie des qualités de la première." *Ibid.* à la p. 855. Ce système avait l'avantage de permettre un libre accès pour les concurrents à la ressource contenue dans l'invention et d'accorder au propriétaire du terrain sur lequel les gènes étaient prélevés, souvent un agriculteur, le privilège d'utiliser les semences faites à partir de ces gènes sans devoir payer de redevances à l'inventeur. *Ibid.* aux pp. 855-56.

56 Le Directeur exécutif du P.N.U.E. déclara en effet, lors de la seconde session du Comité de négociation intergouvernemental tenue à Genève en juin 1990, qu'un nouvel ordre politique et économique international devait être institué et que la fin de l'affrontement Est-Ouest était l'occasion de mettre sur pied un "nouvel ordre environnemental" qui serait fondé sur une coexistence harmonieuse entre économie et développement. M.-A. Hermitte, *supra* note 2 aux pp. 852-53.

que conféré à la biodiversité dans la Convention qui fut signée. Le statut juridique retenu et les mécanismes de protection de cette ressource soulèvent néanmoins de sérieuses interrogations quant à leur efficacité et leur pertinence d'un point de vue environnemental. La C.M.E.D. aborda la question de la diversité biologique à la deuxième partie de son rapport intitulée "Problèmes communs" et plus précisément au chapitre 6 dont le titre est: "Espèces et écosystèmes: les ressources au service du développement." Aucune référence ne fut faite par la C.M.E.D. à la diversité biologique au chapitre 10 de son rapport qui traitait de "La gestion du patrimoine commun." La C.M.E.D. n'aborda en effet à ce chapitre que les problèmes relatifs aux océans, à l'espace extra-atmosphérique et à l'Antarctique, d'un point de vue environnemental il va sans dire, mais aussi en faisant ressortir les éléments de la problématique Nord-Sud quant à la gestion de ces ressources.

En ce qui concerne les océans, la C.M.E.D. invitait les "grandes puissances technologiques"[57] à ratifier la Convention des Nations unies sur le droit de la mer afin que puisse entrer en vigueur le plus tôt possible les dispositions qui concernaient la protection de l'environnement. La C.M.E.D. faisait toutefois référence aux grands fonds marins et à ses ressources déclarés P.C.H., "notion qui représente une étape dans le domaine de la coopération internationale"[58] dont l'exploitation dépendait, bien que la C.M.E.D. ne le dit pas expressément, de la ratification de l'entente par les mêmes "grandes puissances technologiques."

Dans le domaine de l'espace extra-atmosphérique, la C.M.E.D. parla de mesures à mettre en oeuvre de façon à prévenir la pollution de l'espace orbital par les débris de fusées ou de satellites hors d'usage et de celles à adopter de façon à minimiser les risques de contamination sur Terre dans l'éventualité où des engins spatiaux défectueux fonctionnant à l'énergie nucléaire tomberaient sur Terre.[59] La C.M.E.D. aborda cependant la question de la répartition équitable de l'utilisation de l'orbite géosynchrone entre P.D. et P.E.D.[60]

Le troisième et dernier élément abordé par la C.M.E.D. dans ce chapitre était l'Antarctique. Il y était souligné la nécessité de

---

[57] C.M.E.D., *Notre avenir à tous, supra* note 9 à la p. 329.

[58] *Ibid.* à la p. 328.

[59] *Ibid.* aux pp. 332-33.

[60] *Ibid.* à la p. 331.

préserver l'environnement de ce continent et de ne réserver son usage qu'à des fins pacifiques et de recherche scientifique dans un esprit de coopération internationale.[61] Il était aussi abondamment fait état de la nécessité d'assurer une participation équitable entre P.D. et P.E.D. dans la gestion du continent et, bien que la C.M.E.D. ne recommandait pas de lui donner le statut de P.C.H.,[62] elle mentionnait que "bon nombre estiment que le système mis en place dans le cadre des Traités sur l'Antarctique est l'apanage exclusif des pays riches et technologiquement avancés"[63] et, abordant la question des richesses minérales du continent, elle suggérait que des efforts soient faits par la communauté internationale afin de modifier les Traités sur l'Antarctique pour les rendre plus universels, plus ouverts, pour qu'ils répondent "aux expressions des préoccupations et des intérêts matériels et légitimes dans l'Antarctique."[64]

Il est assez clair que la stratégie de la C.M.E.D. consistait à traiter de l'exploitation plus équitable au profit des P.E.D., de ce qu'elle considérait être des ressources naturelles communes de l'humanité, ayant toutes potentiellement le statut de P.C.H. ou un statut qui en était proche. La C.M.E.D. utilisa le couvert de la protection de l'environnement de ces milieux pour aborder la question de leur gestion équitable, ce dernier élément semblant poser dans l'optique de la C.M.E.D. des difficultés tout aussi importantes pour la communauté internationale que le premier. Le fait que la C.M.E.D. n'ait pas abordé la question des ressources génétiques dans ce chapitre indique qu'elle ne considérait pas que celles-ci constituaient des ressources les assimilant à un P.C.H., mais aussi et surtout que la répartition des avantages résultant de leur exploitation ne poserait pas de problèmes aux P.E.D. dans l'avenir. En effet, en vertu du principe de l'exercice de leur souveraineté permanente sur ces ressources, que la C.M.E.D. reconnaissait implicitement, ils devenaient maîtres en quelque sorte de l'imposition de conditions qui les satisferaient quant à leur exploitation.

---

[61] *Ibid.* à la p. 335.

[62] La C.M.E.D. mentionne qu'il "n'existe pas d'accord général sur la question de savoir si l'Antarctique fait partie du patrimoine international" dans une section où elle fait état de l'insatisfaction des P.E.D. quant au statut existant. *Ibid.* à la p. 336. Parlant d'un régime régissant l'exploitation des minéraux elle dit: "Des questions nouvelles concernant le caractère équitable de ce régime contiennent des défis qui pourraient remodeler le contexte politique du continent au cours de la prochaine décennie." *Ibid.* à la p. 335.

[63] *Ibid.* à la p. 336.

[64] *Ibid.* à la p. 342.

Il est difficile de mesurer l'influence que le traitement accordé aux ressources génétiques par la C.M.E.D. dans son rapport eut sur le choix que firent les rédacteurs de la Convention de retenir le statut de ressources naturelles soumises à la souveraineté des États comme applicable aux ressources génétiques. On peut cependant affirmer que la position tenue par les représentants de certains P.E.D., lors des travaux de préparation de la Conférence des Nations unies sur l'environnement et le développement, démontre sans équivoque qu'un certain lien s'établit entre le rapport de la C.M.E.D. et les discussions qui se déroulaient au sein du P.N.U.E. en vue de l'élaboration de la Convention sur la diversité biologique. Cette constatation semble conforme au fait que le rapport de la C.M.E.D. devait servir de base de discussion en vue du sommet de Rio au cours duquel la Convention devait être adoptée. Ainsi, au début de l'année 1991, le représentant du Mexique fit une déclaration à l'A.G.N.U. dans laquelle il y affirma le principe de la souveraineté absolue des États sur les ressources génétiques.[65] Cette question fut débattue au sein du Comité préparatoire de la Conférence des Nations unies sur l'environnement et le développement[66] et le responsable du Comité soutint que "la diversité biologique au sens matériel du terme est patrimoine national des pays qui la possèdent."[67]

Une certaine osmose s'établit donc entre les travaux de préparation de la Conférence de Rio et ceux du P.N.U.E. relatifs à l'élaboration d'un projet de Convention sur la diversité biologique,[68] donnant ainsi la saveur d'instrument de réalisation des éléments constitutifs du N.O.E.I. à une Convention dont on continue de dire à tort qu'elle a pour objectif premier d'assurer la pérennité des ressources génétiques de la biosphère. Il apparaît ainsi dans le domaine de la protection de la diversité biologique, comme cela fut le cas dans celui de la protection de l'atmosphère, qu'en se servant du concept de développement durable, les États ont tenté de faire en soi que la protection de l'environnement se fasse harmonieusement avec la progression du développement. La juxtaposition de ces deux concepts dont la concrétisation s'est faite autour du principe de la souveraineté permanente des États sur les ressources naturelles, semble cependant

---

[65] M-A. Hermitte, *supra* note 2 à la p. 856.

[66] A/Conf. 151/PC/L.30.

[67] M-A. Hermitte, *supra* à la p. 857.

[68] A.-C. Kiss et S. Dombe-Bille, *La Conférence des Nations unies sur l'environnement et le développement* (1992) t. XXXVIII, A.F.D.I. à la p. 836.

n'offrir aucune chance véritable quant à la mise sur pied d'un système adéquat de protection de la biodiversité.

La Convention dans son préambule dispose que la diversité biologique est une "préoccupation commune de l'humanité" et que les États ont des droits souverains sur leurs ressources biologiques. L'article 15 détermine les modalités d'accès aux ressources génétiques et il est indiqué que "le pouvoir de déterminer l'accès aux ressources génétiques appartient aux gouvernements et est régi par la législation nationale," tandis que l'article 16 détermine les modalités d'accès aux technologies d'exploitation des ressources génétiques ainsi que leur transfert, lesquels "sont assurés et/ou facilités pour ce qui concerne les P.E.D. à des conditions justes et plus favorables, y compris à des conditions de faveur et préférentielles s'il en est ainsi mutuellement convenu."

L'efficacité de la Convention repose donc sur la réalisation de l'hypothétique équilibre entre l'accès par les P.D. aux ressources génétiques et celui par les P.E.D. aux technologies du génie génétique, ce qui en constitue d'ailleurs le coeur.[69] Cette façon de concevoir la protection de ressources qui, bien qu'étant localisées sur le territoire de certains États, intéressent tout de même l'humanité et qui consiste à donner à chaque groupe d'États, P.D. d'un coté et P.E.D. de l'autre, une monnaie d'échange[70] qui leur permettra de réaliser leurs objectifs, a cependant comme limite l'intérêt économique de l'entreprise. Autrement dit, si l'exploitation de certaines espèces végétales ou animales s'avérait n'avoir aucun intérêt commercial, le pays n'aurait plus qu'un intérêt moral à protéger l'espèce menacée.

CONCLUSION

Le principe de la souveraineté permanente sur les ressources naturelles appliqué aux ressources génétiques est le résultat de l'échec des P.D. de faire participer les P.E.D. sur une base équitable

---

[69] Voir l'art. 1 de la Convention, mais surtout l'art. 4 où il est mentionné que: "Les P.E.D. ne pourront s'acquitter effectivement des obligations qui leur incombent en vertu de la Convention que dans la mesure où les P.D. s'acquitteront effectivement des obligations qui leur incombent en vertu de la Convention." M.-A. Hermitte, *supra* note 2 aux pp. 865-67.

[70] Parlant de l'attitude des P.E.D. lorsqu'ils prirent conscience de la valeur potentielle de la diversité génétique, un auteur indique: "l'idée s'impose que la diversité génétique représente un trésor qu'il faut s'approprier au plus vite pour le monnayer, puisqu'il est à la base de la mise en oeuvre des biotechnologies." M. Chauvet et L. Olivier, *La biodiversité, enjeu planétaire. Préserver notre patrimoine génétique*, Paris, Éditions Sang de la terre, 1993 à la p. 299.

au développement des biotechnologies. La présence très marquée
de dispositions concernant le développement économique des
P.E.D. dans la Convention constitue la réaction des P.E.D. à un
système qu'ils considèrent ne servir que les intérêts des P.D.
Les P.E.D. considèrent ainsi que "le développement économique
et social et l'éradication de la pauvreté sont les premières priorités
des P.E.D. qui prennent le pas sur toutes les autres"[71] et que la
responsabilité première de la protection de la diversité biologique
incombe aux P.D., qui devront prendre à leur charge le financement des mesures de conservation mises de l'avant puisque "le fait
d'assurer des ressources financières nouvelles et additionnelles
ainsi qu'un accès satisfaisant aux techniques pertinentes devrait
influer sensiblement sur la mesure dans laquelle le monde sera à
même de s'attaquer à l'appauvrissement de la diversité biologique.[72] La protection de la biodiversité dépend donc de l'acceptation par les P.D. de leurs obligations en matière de développement,[73] mais aussi de la reconnaissance par les P.E.D. de la
pertinence et de la suffisance des mesures mises de l'avant.

L'un des principaux problèmes de l'application du principe de
souveraineté permanente sur les ressources naturelles à des
ressources naturelles communes de l'humanité, tient au fait que la
protection de ces ressources ne peut se faire que par la conclusion
d'accords imposant des restrictions aux États quant à l'exercice de
leur souveraineté sur ces ressources.[74] De plus, le principe de la
souveraineté permanente sur les ressources naturelles donne des
pouvoirs tels aux États qu'il est difficile d'imaginer un contrôle
efficace de la communauté internationale sur les décisions prises
par un État et qui seraient contraires à la protection des ressources
génétiques.[75]

[71] Préambule de la Convention dont la référence est citée à la note 1, *supra*.

[72] *Ibid.*

[73] M.-A. Hermitte, *supra* aux pp. 867-68.

[74] P. W. Birnie et al., *supra* note 11 à la p. 113.

[75] L'art. 2, al. 1, de la Charte des droits et devoirs économiques des États, dispose
que: "Chaque État détient et exerce librement une souveraineté entière et
permanente sur toutes ses richesses, ressources naturelles et activités économiques, y compris la possession et le droit de les utiliser et d'en disposer." Le droit
de disposer serait restreint par le pouvoir d'*imperium* à travers lequel une
nouvelle tendance "préservatrice" émergerait en droit de l'environnement et
qui aurait pour but de protéger des intérêts futurs ou plus larges. G. Abi-Saab,
supra note 15 aux pp. 646-47.

Quel P.D. pourrait alors reprocher à un P.E.D. de ne pas défendre avec conviction une ressource que lui-même il n'a pas défendue avec une dose suffisante de courage afin qu'elle soit consacrée P.C.H., la mesure du courage devant dans ce cas comme dans bien d'autres se mesurer par l'importance des fonds qu'il était prêt à consacrer pour la protection de la ressource.

Il est à souhaiter que les P.D. n'aient pas concédé ce que beaucoup d'observateurs éclairés considéraient comme étant indéniablement un patrimoine de l'humanité,[76] en se disant qu'en cas de refus de collaborer des P.E.D., ils avaient à la limite les moyens de s'approprier par l'usage de la force les ressources dont l'accès leur serait refusé.[77] Le développement est un préalable à la protection de l'environnement, qui elle-même est un préalable à la paix internationale. Il est difficile de réaliser concurremment ces trois objectifs, c'est en tout cas ce que la C.M.E.D. a fait croire à notre génération avec le concept de développement durable. Il est à espérer que nos enfants seront plus critiques que nous.

PIERRE-FRANÇOIS MERCURE
Université de Nice — Sophia Antipolis

[76] A.-C. Kiss affirme qu'en ce qui concerne l'appauvrissement du patrimoine génétique "seules des solutions globales sont envisageables — Il convient donc de s'interroger comme certains auteurs le font sur l'opportunité d'évoquer le concept de patrimoine commun de l'humanité dans la recherche de solutions juridiques à ces problèmes." A.-C. Kiss, *Droit international de l'environnement,* Paris, Pédone, 1989 à la p. 189. Dans le même sens, C. De Klemm, *Conservation of Species, the Need for a New Approach* (1982) vol. 9, Environmental Policy and Law, à la p. 117; M. Bedjaoui affirme quant à lui: "Ce concept novateur de patrimoine commun de l'humanité" pourrait "recevoir des applications pour" le patrimoine génétique animal et végétal dont il importe de préserver la richesse et la variété pour les générations futures." M. Bedjaoui, *Droit international, bilan et perspectives,* t. 2, Paris, Pédone, 1991 à la p. 1264.

[77] Une telle éventualité serait possible si l'on considère l'intervention des P.D. au Koweït, lors de la guerre du Golfe, alors que l'Iran menaçait l'accès des P.D. aux ressources pétrolières sur lesquelles ils n'avaient aucune emprise juridique. A. Lipietz, *Les négociations écologiques globales; enjeux Nord-Sud* (1994) t. XXXV, n°. 137, Revue Tiers-Monde à la p. 342.

Summary

Rejecting the Concept of the Common Heritage of Mankind in Order to Ensure Biological Diversity

With the enactment of the Convention on Biological Diversity, genetic resources of the biosphere are subject to state jurisdiction within the territory in which they are located, in accordance with the concept of permanent sovereignty over natural resources. The idea that these resources could be managed by the international community to benefit mankind, in line with the concept of the common heritage of mankind, was rejected because of the attitude of the developed countries, who refused to grant preferential treatment to developing countries with regards to the transfer of knowledge and biotechnological patents, in exchange for free access to genetic resources.

Rejection of the concept of the common heritage of mankind by developing countries can further be explained by their loss of faith in its application to other common natural resources, and the treatment reserved for biological diversity by the World Commission on Environment and Development in its report. Developing countries, relying on the concept of sustainable development, intend to pursue the realization of the new international economic order constituents through genetic resource management.

Sommaire

Le rejet du concept de patrimoine commun de l'humanité afin d'assurer la gestion de la diversité biologique

Avec l'entrée en vigueur de la Convention sur la diversité biologique, les ressources génétiques de la biosphère sont soumises à la juridiction de l'État à l'intérieur du territoire où elles se trouvent, conformément au principe de la souveraineté permanente des États sur les ressources naturelles. L'idée d'une gestion de ces ressources par la communauté internationale au profit de l'humanité, selon les caractéristiques propres du concept de patrimoine commun de l'humanité, n'a pu être retenue à cause de l'attitude des pays développés. Ces derniers refusaient d'établir des mécanismes de préférence à l'égard des pays en développement, quant à la transmission des connaissances et des brevets en matière de biotechnologie, en échange de leur libre accès aux ressources génétiques.

Le rejet du concept de patrimoine commun de l'humanité par les pays en développement a été encouragé par leur désillusionnement quant à son application à d'autres ressources naturelles communes, ainsi que par le traitement fait à la diversité biologique par la Commission mondiale sur l'environnement et le développement dans le rapport qu'elle a produit. Les pays en développement, s'appuyant sur le concept de développement durable, entendent poursuivre la réalisation des éléments constitutifs du nouvel ordre économique international à travers la gestion des ressources génétiques.

Legislating for Integrated Marine Management: Canada's Proposed Oceans Act of 1996

INTRODUCTION

IN 1995, EIGHT YEARS after the idea was first mooted in a ministerial policy paper,[1] an Oceans Act was placed before Parliament for consideration. It began life as Bill C-98 (1995) and subsequently became Bill C-26 (1996).[2]

If Canada is to assert its jurisdictional rights and fulfil its management responsibilities for its vast marine areas, it requires a coherent statutory framework for the administration of ocean spaces and resources,[3] as well as the capacity to develop management plans and policies. Bill C-26 is intended to address this general requirement for the "integrated management of oceans and marine resources."[4]

---

[1] Department of Fisheries and Oceans, *Oceans Policy for Canada: A Strategy to Meet the Challenges and Opportunities on the Oceans Frontier* (Ottawa: Government of Canada, 1987).

[2] Bill C-98, An Act Respecting the Oceans of Canada, 1st Sess., 35th Parl., 1994-95 (1st reading June 14, 1995, reprinted as amended by the Standing Committee on Fisheries and Oceans as reported to the House on Dec. 8, 1995). The bill died on the order paper when the House was prorogued on Feb. 2, 1996, but, upon the unanimous approval of a government motion in the new session, the bill was reinstated as Bill C-26, 2d Sess., 35th Parl., 1996 (1st reading April 17, 1996) and was moved forward immediately to the committee report stage that it had reached in the last session. Debate and concurrence in the bill at the report stage was concluded on June 12, 1996.

[3] At the same time, it may be noted that Canada already has over thirty federal statutes with extensive supporting subsidiary legislation dealing with various specific aspects of Canada's oceans.

[4] Bill C-26, Preamble.

The managerial challenge is not, however, a new one. Canada first extended jurisdiction over a 200-nautical-mile fishing zone in 1977[5] and has functioned without a comprehensive Oceans Act since that time. There are at least three factors that may have acted as stimuli to the introduction of Bill C-26 at this time. First, Canada is preparing to ratify[6] the 1982 United Nations Convention on the Law of the Sea (hereinafter Law of the Sea Convention),[7] a move that would be a precursor to the extension and rationalization of its jurisdictional claims in the offshore. Second, it has been the policy of this government to reduce the size of the public service, whether through privatization of services, amalgamation of agencies, or the introduction of user fees. This process has touched on oceans interests in a number of areas, including fisheries (increased licence fees to help finance fisheries management), marine transportation (user fees for navigational services), and environmental protection (privatization of oil spill response and introduction of a user-pay system). Third, a number of significant changes have been made and further changes proposed in legislation for sectors such as fisheries and transport.[8]

The introduction of an Oceans Act did not take place in isolation from these developments, as is reflected in the explicit and implicit functions of Bill C-26, which may be described in the following three ways:

---

[5] C.R.C. 1978, cc. 1547 and 1548, pursuant to the Territorial Sea and Fishing Zones Act, R.S.C. 1985, c. T-8, s. 4.

[6] House of Commons, Minutes of Proceedings and Evidence of the Standing Committee on Fisheries and Oceans, No. 19 (Oct. 20, 1994) at 35-37.

[7] UN Doc. A/Conf.62/122, (1982), 21 I.L.M. 1261 (in force Nov. 16, 1994).

[8] In the fisheries sector, Bill C-115, An Act Respecting Fisheries, 1st Sess., 35th Parl., 1994-95, proposed the merger of the Fisheries Act, R.S.C. 1985, c. F-14 and the Coastal Fisheries Protection Act, R.S.C. 1985, c. C-33, into one statute to provide a comprehensive instrument to address fisheries management and enforcement both domestically and extraterritorially, although this bill died on the order paper and has not been reintroduced. The Canada Shipping Act, R.S.C. 1985, c. S-9, has also seen extensive amendment over the past few years in the area of vessel-source pollution, partly as a result of Canada's accession to various international conventions, including the International Convention on Oil Pollution Preparedness, Response and Cooperation, 1990,(1991) 30 I.L.M. 735, and the International Salvage Convention, 1989, reprinted in G. Brice, "The New Salvage Convention: Green Seas and Grey Areas," [1990] L.M.C.L.Q. 32 at 54.

(1) It serves as *preparatory* legislation prior to ratification of the Law of the Sea Convention, so that Canada will be able to maximize its benefits under the Convention.

(2) It is *integrative* legislation, in that it provides a common policy framework for the numerous federal statutes dealing with oceans issues.

(3) It functions as *organizational* legislation, concentrating and strengthening the authority of the Minister of Fisheries and Oceans to play a lead role, or at least a co-ordinating role, on most oceans issues. A related benefit of improved organization is that it would ostensibly render ocean management more efficient and cost-effective.

Canada is not, of course, alone in facing the challenges of implementing the Law of the Sea Convention, nor in seeking the benefits of improved integration and organization of ocean management functions. It is, however, unusual in the extent to which it has sought to deal with these various requirements through a single umbrella piece of legislation. Numerous coastal states have enacted legislation formalizing their maritime zone claims,[9] but few of those states have actually adopted legislation that combines assertion of maritime jurisdiction with a framework for ocean management in a comprehensive Oceans Act.[10] Bill C-26 does this through three

---

[9] Activity on this front was particularly pronounced during the Third United Nations Conference on the Law of the Sea (1973-82) and after the adoption of the Law of the Sea Convention. For examples of such legislation from around the world, see *The Law of the Sea: National Legislation on the Exclusive Economic Zone and the Exclusive Fishery Zone* (New York: Office of the Special Representative of the Secretary-General for the Law of the Sea, United Nations, 1986).

[10] Two countries that provide interesting comparisons with Canada are Mexico and Poland. In 1985, Mexico enacted the Federal Act Relating to the Sea as principal legislation to enable it to maximize its benefits under the Law of the Sea Convention (published Jan. 8, 1986 in the *Diario Oficial de la Federacion*, 1986, and available in (1986) 7 Law of the Sea Bulletin 53-66). This instrument reproduces, *in grosso modo*, the text of the Law of the Sea Convention, concentrating on national ocean policy formulation, the establishment of a legal regime for the exploration and exploitation of ocean resources, maritime security, and marine environmental protection. The instrument aims at implementing the National Development Plan, but stops short of developing an institutional framework. Poland's Act Concerning the Maritime Areas of the Polish Republic and the Marine Administration, Mar. 21, 1991, reproduced in (1992) 21 Law of the Sea Bulletin 66-86, goes further. In addition to defining Poland's maritime zones and jurisdictions, the act identifies the minister of transport and marine economy as the country's marine administration with

broad sets of provisions: it sets out and consolidates jurisdictional claims; it attempts to define a framework for a national oceans management strategy and integrated management plans; and it redefines organizational responsibilities for oceans issues, based largely on lead and co-ordinating roles for the Department of Fisheries and Oceans.

Bill C-26, then, represents an ambitious effort to integrate ocean management activities in a manner, and to a degree, that may be appropriate to the regime set out in the Law of the Sea Convention, but which has not been enthusiastically endorsed in the practice of other states. This comment, while not attempting a detailed analysis of all aspects of Bill C-26 and related legislation, provides a general assessment of its provisions with respect to the key integrative functions set out above. First, a review of the jurisdictional claims contained in the bill is provided, because the assertion of jurisdiction sets the stage for the other measures. Second, those provisions that define the bill's approach to an oceans management strategy are examined and critiqued, including reference to how well they reflect the emerging principles of sustainable development. Third, the bill's division of governmental (and non-governmental) roles in ocean management is briefly described, and some concerns noted with respect to the extent and nature of consolidation of functions. Finally, some general conclusions are suggested as to the efficacy of this proposed legislation, and what it says of the future of oceans management in Canada.

ASSERTING JURISDICTION

The sovereign authority exercised in Part 1 of Bill C-26[11] takes up for Canada, for the first time, the full extent of coastal jurisdiction permitted under the Law of the Sea Convention and associated customary international law. The Convention came into force in November 1994, and although Canada, a signatory,[12] is not yet a party, it is known to be preparing for ratification.[13] The Department of Justice has been requested to draft implementing legislation, and

---

wide powers including not only maritime transport and safety of life at sea, but also living resource utilization, marine environment protection, and coastal zone management.

[11] Ss. 4-27.

[12] Dec. 10, 1982, the date of the conclusion of the Conference.

[13] *Supra* note 6.

the Geological Survey of Canada is mapping the full extent of the Canadian continental shelf and its resources,[14] in preparation for making a claim to sovereign rights on the shelf beyond 200 nautical miles before the Commission on the Limits of the Continental Shelf.[15]

Previously Canada drew its maritime boundaries in accordance with the Territorial Sea and Fishing Zones Act (hereinafter the Territorial Sea Act),[16] which principally asserted a 12-nautical-miles territorial sea configured from a combination of low-water marks and straight baselines between prescribed coastal points. Canada also exercised fishing jurisdiction in historically claimed waters and beyond the territorial sea to a distance of 200 nautical miles from the coastal baselines.[17] In addition, Canada asserted environmental jurisdiction and control in northern waters under the Arctic Waters Pollution Prevention Act (hereinafter the Arctic Act)[18] out to a distance of 100 nautical miles from the coastline.[19] Although several statutes specifically extend to these areas, it was not until the Canadian Laws Offshore Application Act (hereinafter the Offshore Laws Act)[20] was passed in 1990 that federal and provincial laws were made generally applicable to adjacent offshore areas.

Bill C-26 substantially overtakes this patchwork of enactments. It consolidates the provisions of the Territorial Sea Act and the Offshore Laws Act (but not the Arctic Act) and declares three new maritime zones — contiguous zone, exclusive economic zone, and

14 Geological Survey of Canada, *Canada and Article 76 of the Law of the Sea, Defining the Limits of Canadian Resource Jurisdiction Beyond 200 Nautical Miles in the Atlantic and Arctic Oceans* (Open File 3209, Ron McNab (ed.), May 15, 1994).

15 In accordance with Art. 76(8) and Annex 2 of the Law of the Sea Convention, a broad margin state, such as Canada, that intends to establish the outer limits of the continental shelf beyond 200 nm of its baselines has ten years from the date the Convention comes into force to submit the particulars of the claimed limits to the Commission, together with supporting scientific and technical data. The Commission would consider the submission and may make recommendations in accordance with Art. 76, and then the limits of the shelf "established by the coastal state on the basis of these recommendations" would become final.

16 R.S.C. 1985, c. T-8.

17 C.R.C. 1978, cc. 1547-1549, pursuant to s. 4 of the Territorial Sea Act.

18 R.S.C. 1985, c. A-12.

19 Between the 60th parallel of north latitude and the 141st meridian of west longitude. See the definition of "arctic waters" in s. 2 of the Arctic Act.

20 S.C. 1990, c. 44. Section 7, applying provincial laws in offshore areas, has not been proclaimed in force.

continental shelf. As a prerequisite to these legitimate claims, it is necessary to fix the baselines for their measurement around the whole of Canada's coasts. Bill C-26 does so in the same way as the Territorial Sea Act did, and additionally closes the gaps that existed by declaring connecting baselines across the outer limits of bodies of water, like the Gulf of St. Lawrence, over which Canada has traditionally asserted historic title, as part of its sovereign territory.[21]

The territorial sea of Canada[22] will continue to be a marine zone of 12 nautical miles width measured from the established baselines.[23] The new contiguous zone[24] consists of a belt of sea 12 nautical miles wide immediately beyond the territorial sea. Its function is to prevent infringement of Canada's customs, fiscal, immigration, and sanitary laws in the territorial sea. Federal officials may prevent offences from being committed against Canadian territory and may arrest suspects for offences committed in Canada.

The exclusive economic zone[25] (EEZ) overlaps the contiguous zone and extends beyond the territorial sea a further 188 nautical miles. Consistent with the Law of the Sea Convention,[26] Canada will acquire both resource rights and environmental responsibilities. Canada has sovereign rights to explore, exploit, conserve, and manage the living and non-living resources of the waters, the seabed, and its subsoil. Bill C-26 also declares Canada's jurisdiction to regulate the establishment and use of artificial islands and structures, such as oil platforms, to conduct scientific research, and to protect the marine environment.[27] These rights are all expressly available to the coastal state under the Law of the Sea Convention, but they must be affirmatively claimed, as Bill C-26 now does. The bill also distinctively elaborates these powers by proclaiming Canadian authority to harness economically the energy potential of the water, currents, and winds in and over the EEZ.[28] The fishing zones originally declared under the Territorial Sea Act are now to be

---

21 Bill C-26, s. 5.
22 Territorial Sea Act, s. 3.
23 Bill C-26, s. 4.
24 *Ibid.*, s. 10-12.
25 *Ibid.*, s. 13-16.
26 Part 5, Arts. 56-75.
27 Bill C-26, s. 14.
28 *Ibid.*

rolled into the new jurisdiction, partly within internal waters claimed by historic title and partly under the EEZ.[29] The formal declaration of an EEZ in Bill C-26 has removed any uncertainty as to the full extent of Canadian environmental jurisdiction in the offshore. The assertion of EEZ jurisdiction for the protection and preservation of the marine environment is made pursuant to the entitlement in Part 5 of the Law of the Sea Convention. The exercise of this jurisdiction is "as provided for in the relevant provisions of this Convention,"[30] which include those in Part 12, headed Protection and Preservation of the Marine Environment. It is worth noting that Article 234, within Part 12 of the Convention, enables Arctic states to provide for special and more stringent protection of ice-covered areas than would normally be the case in other areas.[31] This special protection for the unique and fragile polar environments was included mainly as a result of Canada's vigorous promotion of it at the Third United Nations Conference on the Law of the Sea.[32] Canada's success at the Conference was due in no small measure to its initially controversial Arctic Act.

Curiously, the special needs for environmental protection in the Arctic do not seem to have been factored into Bill C-26. Although the Canadian EEZ will obviously extend for 200 nautical miles over the oceans all around the country, the unamended definition of "arctic waters" will ensure that Canada's special environmental protection in the Arctic will continue to apply only 100 nautical miles seaward. Perhaps it can be argued that Canada's principal area of concern is not so much the offshore as the inshore and interconnecting waters in the northern archipelago. If this is indeed the case, Canada's environmental jurisdiction in the Arctic will operate with two regimes in two separate belts of sea, in effect

---

[29] *Ibid.*, s. 16.

[30] Art. 56(1)(b).

[31] "Coastal States have the right to adopt and enforce non-discriminatory laws and regulations for the prevention, reduction and control of marine pollution from vessels in ice-covered areas within the limits of the EEZ, where particularly severe climatic conditions and the presence of ice covering such areas for most of the year create obstructions or exceptional hazards to navigation, and pollution of the marine environment could cause major harm or irreversible disturbance of the ecological balance. Such laws and regulations shall have due regard to navigation and the protection and preservation of the marine environment based on the best available scientific evidence."

[32] See D. M. McRae and D. J. Goundrey, "Environmental Jurisdiction in Arctic Waters: The Extent of Article 234" (1982) 16 U.B.C.L. Rev. 197 at 209-15.

creating the type of fragmentation that Bill C-26 is supposed to remedy by promoting integrated management of oceans and marine resources.[33] In the seaward belt (that is, outside 100 nautical miles to the limit of the EEZ), the applicable regime will be the general regulation of marine environmental protection consisting of a mixture of the Canadian Environmental Protection Act,[34] Fisheries Act,[35] Canada Shipping Act, [36] and supporting regulations. In the "arctic waters" proper, the Arctic Act will continue to be the principal piece of legislation. This division between the two marine belts is unnecessary, because Article 234 of the Law of the Sea Convention applies to all EEZ areas. The easier solution would have been for Bill C-26 to extend the definition of "arctic waters" from 100 to 200 nautical miles by amending the Arctic Act.

The continental shelf is a geomorphological feature over which Canada has previously exercised jurisdiction consistent with the 1958 Geneva Convention on the Continental Shelf.[37] Bill C-26[38] now takes up the full extent of jurisdiction as the continental shelf is legally conceived in the Law of the Sea Convention.[39] This means that Canada may control the seabed on the Pacific coast for certain purposes to a distance of 200 nautical miles (that is, co-extensive with the EEZ) even though there is only a minor continental shelf in the geographic sense. On the Atlantic coast, Canadian jurisdictional rights will extend over substantially the whole of the juridical continental margin (that is, shelf, slope, and rise) to its outermost limits, even though they exceed 200 nautical miles from the coastal baselines. In fact, it is estimated that over one million square kilometres of the seabed in the Atlantic will be added to the area of Canada's jurisdictional rights beyond 200 nautical miles offshore.[40] The authority exercisable by the coastal state in the continental shelf continues to be the right to explore and exploit the mineral and non-living resources, together with the sedentary species of

[33] The preamble makes this clear.

[34] R.S.C. 1985 (4th Supp.), c. 16.

[35] R.S.C. 1985, c. F-14.

[36] R.S.C. 1985, c. S-9.

[37] 499 UNTS 311, Can. T.S. 1970 No. 4.

[38] Ss. 17-21.

[39] Part 6, Arts. 76-85.

[40] *Supra* note 14 at 22. The Report's preliminary assessment is that the combined additions of jurisdiction beyond 200 nm in the Atlantic and the Arctic will represent an area nearly equal to the three Prairie provinces.

living organisms, on the seabed or in the subsoil. In this context, the significance and urgency of the Geological Survey of Canada's current efforts to map this submarine area[41] are obvious. The substance of the Canadian Laws Offshore Application Act is extended into the new marine zones. Curiously, while provincial laws may be declared applicable by federal regulations in the territorial sea, nothing is expressly said about the status of federal laws in that zone.[42] Further, while provision is made for both federal and provincial laws in connection with the continental shelf,[43] nothing is directly said about the regulation of the waters of the EEZ. A close reading of Bill C-26, however, reveals that the application of provincial laws in the EEZ is indirectly provided for. By section 20, federal laws apply to installations and artificial islands on Canada's continental shelf and the safety zones established around them. By section 21, provincial laws may be made to apply by regulations "to the same extent as federal laws apply pursuant to section 20 in any area of the sea . . . that forms part of the exclusive economic zone . . . or is above the continental shelf of Canada." Thus, provincial laws may operate in the EEZ under section 21 but only through the restraining filter of section 20. The scope of provincial laws capable of extension to the EEZ is thereby limited to activities associated with the continental shelf that obtrude into the superjacent waters. There will be no general application of provincial laws in the EEZ as there is in the territorial sea. As to federal laws, Parliament, in the exercise of its constitutional jurisdiction over shipping, fisheries, and navigable waters, has already passed numerous pieces of legislation that apply specifically to the oceans. Therefore, the drafters of Bill C-26, it seems, did not think it necessary to make any further general reference to the application of federal laws in the territorial sea and EEZ. In any event, the bill grants the minister of justice regulatory power to extend federal and provincial laws into any parts of Canada's oceans as circumstances demand.[44]

ENABLING OCEANS MANAGEMENT

While the preamble to Bill C-26 boasts of Canada's wish to reaffirm its role as a world leader in oceans and marine resource man-

[41] *Ibid.*
[42] Bill C-26, s. 9.
[43] *Ibid.*, ss. 20 and 21.
[44] *Ibid.*, s. 26(1)(k).

agement, Part 2 of the act, the key section devoted to planning and strategizing, is far from inspiring and only makes general commitments. The minister of fisheries and oceans, in collaboration with various federal agencies, provincial and territorial governments, aboriginal organizations, and coastal communities, is required to lead the development and implementation of a national oceans management strategy.[45] The strategy is to be based on the principles of sustainable development, integrated management, and the precautionary approach. The minister of fisheries and oceans is also required to facilitate the development and implementation of integrated management plans,[46] and such planning must include the development of a national system of marine protected areas.[47]

At least three areas of disappointment stand out in the proposed Part 2, which calls for development of a national oceans management strategy. These areas, discussed in the following subsections of this comment, are limited commitment to the principles of sustainable development, lack of details and clarity for the oceans management strategy, and limited embrace of integrated management planning.

LIMITED COMMITMENT TO SUSTAINABLE DEVELOPMENT PRINCIPLES

Bill C-26 fails to impose a firm obligation on all government departments and agencies to follow the principles of sustainable development in oceans related decision-making. Instead, the Bill merely requires the national strategy to be based on sustainable development principles.[48]

Although the Bill specifically articulates two key principles of sustainable development, namely integration[49] and precaution,[50] the proposed legislation omits reference to other guiding princi-

---

[45] *Ibid.*, s. 29.

[46] *Ibid.*, s. 31.

[47] *Ibid.*, s. 35(2).

[48] *Ibid.*, s. 30.

[49] For a discussion of the multiple meanings of the integration principle, see R. Kenchington and D. Crawford, "On the Meaning of Integration in Coastal Zone Management" (1993) 21 Ocean and Coastal Management 109-27.

[50] For recent reviews of the precautionary principle, see T. O'Riordan and J. Cameron (eds), *Interpreting the Precautionary Principle* (London: Cameron May, 1994), and H. Hohmann, *Precautionary Legal Duties and Principles of Modern International Environmental Law* (London: Graham and Trotman/Martinus Nijhoff, 1994).

ples, including pollution prevention, polluter pays, public participation, community-based management, intergenerational equity,
and indigenous rights.[51] The impression is left of a bill that was
hurriedly drafted in a conservative style, with only a token reference
to sustainable development and the principles of the Rio Declaration,[52] and without any attempt to articulate the relevant elements
of Agenda 21,[53] in particular Chapter 17 on oceans. These documents provide important and complementary policy and management frameworks for the Law of the Sea Convention, within which
Canadian oceans policy is inevitably situated.

LACK OF DETAILS AND CLARITY FOR THE OCEANS
MANAGEMENT STRATEGY

Besides calling for the development of a principled national
oceans management strategy, Bill C-26 leaves the contents, time-
frame, and procedures to ministerial discretion. No checklist of
priority issues that the ocean strategy must address is provided. No
deadline for completion of an oceans management strategy is established. No independent review process, such as a multi-stakeholder
sustainable seas commission or council, is guaranteed to ensure
critical and detailed review.

A list of crucial issues to be considered in an oceans management
strategy might include some or all of the following:

· actions to implement the concept and principles of sustainable
  development
· options for further reducing fragmentation in governmental
  approvals and decision-making related to estuarine, coastal, and
  marine areas
· priorities and processes to be followed for designating marine
  protected areas

51 For a recent review on the importance of principles in guiding law reform, see
   D. VanderZwaag, *Canada and Marine Environmental Protection: Charting a Legal
   Course towards Sustainable Development* (London: Kluwer Law International,
   1995), chap. 1.
52 *Rio Declaration on Environment and Development,* UN Doc. A/CONF. 151/5/Rev.1,
   (1992) 31 I.L.M. 874.
53 *United Nations Conference on Environment and Development (UNCED), Agenda 21:
   Programme of Action for Sustainable Development,* UN Doc. A/CONF.
   151/26/Rev.1, Vol. 1, 1992, reprinted in S. P. Johnson, *The Earth Summit: The
   United Nations Conference on Environment and Development* 125 (London: Graham
   and Trotman/Martinus Nijhoff, 1993).

- integration and co-ordination of maritime enforcement
- environmental standard-setting within the principles of precaution and pollution prevention
- research priorities for marine science
- content of and process for developing integrated management plans
- need for regional ocean management strategies
- appropriate dispute resolution mechanisms for conflicts of use in estuarine, coastal, and marine areas
- methods for strengthening regional and bilateral ocean management agreements and arrangements
- methods for implementing Canada's international obligations affecting estuarine, coastal and marine ecosystems

The lack of a clear mandate to develop regional ocean management strategies is of particular concern. In the context of a country like Canada, which borders on three oceans with fundamentally different marine environments, there is a risk that a purely national oceans management strategy will be simplistic and not sensitive to regional differences and challenges. The physical configuration, the resources, and the environment of the eastern, western, and northern coastal zones are different. The Atlantic cod and Pacific salmon fisheries, for example, cannot be regulated the same way. It will be necessary for the minister, in co-operation with other federal bureaucracies, relevant provinces, and other actors, to initiate a process to develop regional management strategies that are more attuned to the particular coastal and ocean management needs and aspirations of the communities in the various regions concerned. In any case, some provinces have already taken steps to develop their own coastal zone management plans.[54]

Although not an oceans act *per se*, New Zealand's Resource Management Act 1991[55] provides a legislative precedent[56] for including

---

54 E.g., Nova Scotia has recently launched *Coastal 2000* as an initiative for public discussion. See Nova Scotia Department of the Environment and Nova Scotia Department of Fisheries, *Coastal 2000: A Consultation Paper* (July 1994).

55 Statutes of New Zealand 1991, No. 69.

56 For recent reviews of the Resource Management Act 1991, see M. Phillipson, "Implementing Sustainable Development in New Zealand: The Resource Management Act 1991" (1994) 4 J.E.L.P. 222, and O. Furuseth and C. Cocklin, "An Institutional Framework for Sustainable Resource Management: The New Zealand Model" (1995) 35 Nat. Res. J. 243.

content requirements, a time limitation, and an independent inquiry provision. Section 57 requires preparation of a New Zealand coastal policy statement,[57] while Section 58 spells out specific policy areas to be addressed, such as national priorities for preserving the natural character of the coastal environment. An appointed board of inquiry is required to review and report on the policy statement.[58] The Resource Management Act 1991 also requires the minister of conservation to prepare a draft New Zealand coastal policy statement within one year.[59]

Bill C-26 also fails to distinguish clearly the development of a national oceans management strategy from the broader challenge of forging a national oceans policy. A national oceans policy is something more than a management strategy. A national oceans policy is an authoritative statement issued at the highest level of government indicating values, interests, and directions for the pursuit of national oceans interests, domestically and internationally.[60] A management strategy should be a plan of action to implement aspects of the national policy and to ensure coherence, co-ordination, efficiency, equity, and effectiveness. The drafters of Bill C-26 seem to have blended the two, not without some confusion.

LIMITED EMBRACE OF INTEGRATED MANAGEMENT PLANNING

Although Bill C-26 requires the minister of fisheries and oceans to lead and facilitate the development and implementation of integrated management plans for estuarine, coastal, and marine waters,[61] great discretion is left with the minister. The minister *may* establish advisory or management bodies and *may* establish marine environmental quality guidelines, objectives, and criteria.[62] No geo-

---

[57] The policy statement was issued in 1994. For an overview and the text see "New Zealand: New Zealand Coastal Policy Statement 1994" (1995) 10 Int'l J. Mar. & Coastal L. 431.

[58] *Supra* note 55, ss. 27 and 46.

[59] *Ibid.*, s. 431 (one year after the date of commencement of the act).

[60] For a discussion of the various meanings of national oceans policy, see R. W. Knecht, "National Ocean Policy in the United States: Less Than the Sum of Its Parts," in P. Fabbri (ed.), *Ocean Management in Global Change* (London: Elsevier Applied Science, 1992) 184-85.

[61] Bill C-26, s. 31.

[62] *Ibid.*, s. 32(c), (d).

graphical priorities or zones are set out for planning purposes. No time obligation is imposed.[63]

Bill C-26 also, in some areas, fails to take integrated coastal and ocean management seriously. It appears to stop short of clearly authorizing joint coastal-ocean management committees or boards with the provinces and territories. Section 32(c) provides only that the minister *may* take into consideration the views of provincial and territorial governments in the process of establishing advisory or management bodies. The bill also provides no guaranteed budget to foster integrated management planning. The critical need for financial support and technical assistance to local authorities and communities has been noted by various authors.[64] Indeed, the main thrust of the United States Coastal Zone Management Act of 1972[65] was to provide financial incentives for states to undertake coastal zone management planning exercises.[66]

An important improvement on the first draft of Bill C-26, however, was made in the revised bill, which removed a significant amount of discretion from the minister in implementing integrated management plans. Instead, the revised bill placed a series of legal obligations on the minister to "develop and implement policies and programs" and to "coordinate" with other agencies their implementation in coastal and marine waters.[67] By a simple legislative stroke, what were originally purely discretionary planning activities of federal bureaucrats have become matters of legal obligation that must be undertaken in collaboration with a range of involved actors, including ministers other than the minister of fisheries and oceans, other federal boards and agencies, the governments of the provinces and territories, bodies established under land claims settlements, and coastal communities. The stipulation of an all-inclusive process in planning satisfies an essential element in the principle of integration — namely, that all actors with coastal and marine management responsibilities or interests should be part

[63] Compare, e.g., New Zealand's Resource Management Act 1991, s. 432, which requires regional councils to prepare coastal plans within two years.

[64] See, e.g., E. J. Norrena, "Stewardship of Coastal Waters and Protected Spaces: Canada's Approach" (1994) 18 Mar. Pol'y 153 at 160.

[65] 16 U.S.C. § 1451.

[66] See, e.g., R. W. Knecht, "The U.S. National Coastal Management Program — Problems and Opportunities in the Next Phase" (1987) 15 Coastal Management 103.

[67] Bill C-26, s. 32(a) and (b).

and parcel of both macro and micro strategies and plans.[68] Curiously, however, the minister's powers again become discretionary when it comes to entering into agreements with other ministers or agencies and to consultation. These two areas are central to the pursuit of co-operation with other actors.[69]

Bill C-26 is also very general and enabling regarding the designation and management of marine protected areas. While the minister of fisheries and oceans is to lead and co-ordinate the development and implementation of a national system of marine protected areas, the governor in council retains the power to make regulations in such areas as zoning requirements and prohibitions on classes of activities.[70] In addition, Bill C-26 does not appear to have resolved the fragmentation and potential "turf battles" that surround the designation and management of marine protected areas in Canada. Parks Canada, within the Department of Canadian Heritage, issued a revised National Marine Conservation Areas Policy[71] in 1994 with the intention of establishing national marine conservation areas pursuant to the National Parks Act[72] or under new legislation to be developed.[73] A National Marine Conservation Areas System Plan,[74] published in 1995, develops further the goal of establishing a national marine conservation area within each of twenty-nine distinct marine regions of Canada. Meanwhile, 1994 amendments to the Canada Wildlife Act[75] authorize the governor in council to establish marine protected areas within any fishing

---

68 Similarly, the revised bill removed the minister's discretion in favour of a legal obligation to co-operate with other ministers, federal and provincial agencies, aboriginal organizations, and coastal communities in the exercise of the powers, duties, and functions in the bill: *ibid.*, s. 33(1)(a).

69 *Ibid.*, s. 33(1)(b) and (2).

70 *Ibid.*, s. 35(2) and (3).

71 See Canadian Heritage, Parks Canada, *Guiding Principles and Operational Policies* 43-61 (Ottawa: Minister of Supply and Services Canada, 1994).

72 R.S.C. 1985, c. N-7 (as am. R.S.C. 1985 (4th Supp.), c. 39).

73 Parks Canada is in the process of seeking Cabinet authorization for a new National Marine Conservation Areas Act. Personal communication, Mr. Dave McBurney, Marine Areas Coordinator, National Parks Directorate, Ottawa (Apr. 17, 1996).

74 Canadian Heritage, Parks Canada, *Sea to Sea to Sea: Canada's National Marine Conservation Areas System Plan* (Ottawa: Ministry of Supply and Services, 1995).

75 R.S.C. 1985, c. W-9 (as am. S.C. 1994, c. 23).

zone.[76] The Department of Canadian Heritage Act[77] allocates jurisdiction over national parks and national marine conservation
areas[78] to the minister of Canadian heritage.[79]

Although one of the key law reform implications of the integration principle is to streamline legislation and regulations in the
environmental protection field,[80] Bill C-26 avoids tackling the frag-
mented array of marine environmental protection legislation. For
example, the Canadian Environmental Protection Act[81] will still
govern toxic chemicals management[82] and ocean dumping.[83] The
Canada Shipping Act[84] and the Arctic Act focus on control of vessel-
source pollution. The Fisheries Act[85] governs pollution control at
the federal level, through, among other things, a prohibition on the
deposit of deleterious substances into water frequented by fish[86]
and a prohibition on causing harmful alteration, disruption, or
destruction of fish habitats.[87]

In addition to the shortcomings described above, Bill C-26 has
not overcome the tension between the need for an integrated
approach to planning and management for coastal and marine
areas and the constraints of constitutional federal-provincial pre-
rogatives. Modern coastal and ocean management, largely as a
result of better understanding of the importance of activities in

[76] *Ibid.*, The minister of the environment is authorized to provide advice and to
carry out conservation measures in marine wildlife areas: *ibid.*, s. 4.1(1).

[77] S.C. 1995, c. 11. Act has now been proclaimed.

[78] *Ibid.*, s. 4(2)(e).

[79] The jurisdiction is limited, however, to matters over which Parliament has
jurisdiction "not by law assigned to any other department, board or agency of
the Government of Canada": *ibid.*, s. 4(1). Some efforts at collaboration are
ocurring through an interdepartmental Marine Protected Area Steering Committee initiated in 1995 and consisting of representatives from Environment
Canada, Parks Canada, Fisheries and Oceans and Natural Resources Canada.
See E. J. Zurbrigg, *Towards an Environment Canada Strategy for Coastal and Marine
Protected Areas* (Hull, PQ: Canadian Wildlife Service, 1996).

[80] See D. VanderZwaag, *supra* note 51 at 9.

[81] *Supra* note 34.

[82] *Ibid.*, Part 2.

[83] *Ibid.*, Part 6.

[84] *Supra* note 36.

[85] *Supra* note 35.

[86] *Ibid.*, s. 36(3).

[87] *Ibid.*, s. 35.

watersheds and their impact on the marine environment, increasingly looks at the continuum between land and sea as a unity. Marine pollution remains predominantly of land-based origin, whether through terrestrial or atmospheric pathways. And yet, a fundamental premise for the development of an oceans management strategy in the bill is the exclusion of rivers and lakes in deference to provincial authority.[88] Although such a stipulation may be inevitable in a federal initiative, perhaps a fundamental weakness of the process of developing Bill C-26 was that at no time was any effort made to build a "partnership bill" that would involve all relevant levels of government and other important actors. As a result, the bill inevitably became narrow. The principle of integration enunciated in Bill C-26 necessarily includes spatial integration (that is, integrated planning for coastal and marine areas, not just *waters*) in order to facilitate integrated coastal zone management and the management of land-based activities and sources of pollution.

ORGANIZING GOVERNMENT RESPONSIBILITIES

Part 3 of Bill C-26 consists largely of provisions that address the problem of departmental responsibilities and the organization of government to pursue ocean management tasks. Some of these aims are met through numerous consequential amendments to existing laws and the repeal of others,[89] but it is the division of authority over oceans activities that is of interest here. While any assessment of the reorganization provisions is bound to be premature so long as their implementation is incomplete, it is useful to consider three broad issues that are raised in Part 3. These issues, explored in the following subsections of this comment, are the organizational structure imposed by the bill, the treatment of marine science, and the role of ocean policy research and education.

ORGANIZATIONAL STRUCTURE

The most significant substantive provisions in Part 3 are those that address the question of ministerial authority. In general, the minister of fisheries and oceans is granted authority over all oceans

---

88 Bill C-26, s. 28.

89 *Ibid.*, ss. 53 and 56-108 make consequential amendments. Ss. 54 and 55 repeal the Territorial Sea Act, *supra* note 16, and the Offshore Laws Act, *supra* note 20, respectively.

matters not assigned to anyone else.[90] This inclusive power is more particularly designated with respect to the Canadian Coast Guard and its services, fisheries and other marine sciences, and hydrographic services.[91] However, the department cannot possibly fulfil all its functions independently.

The pursuit of integrated ocean management necessarily involves a wide range of governmental and non-governmental actors. Other countries have addressed the question of inter-agency concerns through the establishment of inter-agency co-ordinating committees. The Netherlands has had a particularly successful experience in this regard.[92] Canada's past experience with an inter-agency committee for oceans has been less successful, and the committee has fallen into disuse. Bill C-26 could have strengthened inter-agency coordination by institutionalizing an inter-agency committee rather than leaving the responsibility for co-ordination purely in the hands of one minister. The minister will have discretionary power to establish advisory or management bodies in relation to the implementation of integrated management plans,[93] but this is much less than an inter-agency committee for oceans generally. In any case, despite past experience, it will become necessary for the minister to establish an inter-agency co-ordinating committee to ensure multi-departmental support and minimize potential bureaucratic conflicts.

Bill C-26 reinforces the Department of Fisheries and Oceans' lead role in the oceans and further clarifies its mandate. However, despite its wide range of responsibilities concerning the national oceans management strategy and integrated management plans,

90 *Ibid.*, s. 40. Including, of course, the continuing and contentious problems of the fisheries.

91 *Ibid.*, ss. 41-45.

92 The Netherlands' institutional framework for ocean management includes three co-ordinating mechanisms: (1) the North Sea Committee of the Public Works Council; (2) the Interdepartmental Coordinating Committee for North Sea Affairs (ICONA), which has an independent chairperson; and (3) the Ministerial Co-ordinating Committee for North Sea Affairs (MICONA). See *Harmonization of Netherlands North Sea Policy 1989-1992*, Second Chamber of the States General, 1989-90 Session, Items 44-45. There is also a Parliamentary Commission for the Seas, with representatives from all political parties, and an overall co-ordinating minister for North Sea Affairs, who is the minister of transport and public works. For a commentary on this system, see Ton IJlstra, "The Organisation of the North Sea Policy in the Netherlands" (1990) 2 Water Law 127-32.

93 Bill C-26, s. 32(c)(i), discussed in text at and following note 62 *supra*.

fisheries science, hydrography, oceanography, and other marine sciences, it will not be possible for the department to exercise its responsibilities with reference to all ocean uses, and even less for coastal uses. There are other major ocean uses — for example, marine transportation and offshore oil and gas — in which the department's role will be peripheral at best. Further, there are other functions in Bill C-26 that are the responsibility of other ministries. Thus provisions formerly in the Offshore Laws Act will continue to be administered by the minister of justice.[94] Similarly, provisions taken from the Territorial Sea Act will continue to attach to the minister of foreign affairs and international trade.[95] The latter will also have a role to play in connection with permits for marine scientific research by foreign nationals.[96]

The strengthening of the Department of Fisheries and Oceans has occurred at the expense of other federal agencies, notably the Department of Transport. In this regard, it is worth reviewing the experience of the ministre de la mer of France, which was originally conceived as an oceans ministry but has now suffered diminished status as a result of inter-bureaucratic warfare. The process of defining and consolidating Canada's new Department of Fisheries and Oceans has not been smooth. The transfer of the Coast Guard from the Department of Transport to Fisheries resulted in a split of management and regulatory responsibilities for marine transportation that again contradicts the message of integration that Bill C-26 is supposed to convey. The rationale behind the change was to concentrate oceans responsibilities in one agency to the extent possible and, at the same time, merge the Fisheries and Oceans and Coast Guard fleets that were managed in parallel. As a result, the Coast Guard has been split from the Ship Safety and Ports and Harbours Directorates, which will remain with the Department of Transport. Ship Safety would remain responsible for safety, vessel-source pollution prevention, and onboard regulation of commercial and fishing vessels (construction, equipment, crewing, operational standards). The Coast Guard would remain responsible for enroute safety systems and services, including search and rescue.[97]

94 *Ibid.*, s. 26.

95 *Ibid.*, s. 25.

96 *Ibid.*, s. 44.

97 *Ibid.*, s. 41. See also "Ship Safety Responsibilities," a communication to clients by Michael Turner, assistant deputy minister of transport dated Sept. 19, 1995,

MARINE SCIENCE

The availability of timely, accurate, and appropriate scientific information is essential to the conduct of ocean management in the modern era. This is clearly reflected in the overall scheme of the Law of the Sea Convention, whether in the structure of the fisheries management approach and its demand for policies based on the "best available scientific information,"[98] or in the data-intensive (optional) approach to determination of seaward shelf limits.[99] Part 3 of Bill C-26 states the Canadian government's approach to the organization of marine science. The question is whether this structure is adequate to meet the demands that will be placed on it in coming years.

The approach to marine science is in essence quite similar to that of other parts of the proposed legislation. As many functions as possible are consolidated within the Department of Fisheries and Oceans, and the minister is given the power (but not the obligation) to carry out those functions. The bill provides that the minister *may* carry out a number of activities in "performing the duties and functions assigned by . . . the *Department of Fisheries and Oceans Act*,"[100] including *inter alia* the following:[101]

· collect data for the purpose of understanding oceans and their living resources and ecosystems
· conduct hydrographic and oceanographic surveys of Canadian and other waters

---

and Minutes of the Canadian Marine Advisory Council, Ottawa, Oct. 3-5, 1995 meeting, issued on Jan. 31, 1996, by the Canadian Coast Guard.

98 See, e.g., Law of the Sea Convention, Art. 61(2): "The coastal State, taking into account the best scientific evidence available to it, shall ensure through proper conservation and management measures that the maintenance of the living resources of the zone is not endangered by over-exploitation."

99 *Ibid.*, Art. 76(4).

100 R.S.C. 1985, c. F-15, s. 4(1)(c). This section simply provides that the powers and duties of the minister of fisheries and oceans over "hydrography and marine sciences" extends to all matters within Parliament's jurisdiction and "not by law assigned to any other department, board or agency of the Government of Canada."

101 Bill C-26, s. 42. The only amendment to this section by the Standing Committee was the addition of subs.(j) respecting the use of traditional ecological knowledge.

· conduct marine scientific surveys relating to fisheries resources and their supporting habitat and ecosystems
· conduct basic and applied research related to hydrography, oceanography, and other marine sciences
· carry out investigations for the purpose of understanding oceans and their living resources and ecosystems
· conduct studies to obtain traditional ecological knowledge for the purpose of understanding oceans and their living resources and ecosystems.

In carrying out this impressive array of functions, the minister is to exercise three distinct types of powers or responsibilities. First, the minister is to be "responsible for coordinating, promoting and recommending national policies and programs with respect to fisheries, science, hydrography, oceanography and other marine sciences"[102] — a clearly non-operational, hortatory role. Second, the minister is empowered to engage more directly in the field and "conduct or cooperate with persons conducting basic and applied research" and "for that purpose maintain and operate ships, research institutes, laboratories and other facilities."[103] Finally, the minister has an advisory role, and "may provide marine scientific advice, services and support to the Government of Canada and . . . to the governments of the provinces, to other states, international organizations and to other persons."[104]

The basic structure of this model for organizing research is clear. Within the limitations imposed by the constitution and by other statutory allocations of research responsibilities, control of this function is to continue under the centralized direction of the Department of Fisheries and Oceans[105] and is to be exercised

---

102 *Ibid.*, s. 43(a).

103 *Ibid.*, s. 43(b)(i) and (ii). A minor interpretation problem arises from the phrasing of subs.(b), which states that these operational powers apply "in carrying out his or her responsibilities *under this section*" [emphasis added]. Given that the powers to "conduct . . . research" and "maintain and operate ships, research institutes, laboratories and other facilities" seem to be directly related to the functions addressed in s. 42, it is likely that it was intended to cover responsibilities under this Part. Note also that under s. 45 the minister has similar operational powers relating to hydrographic activities.

104 *Ibid.*, s. 43(c).

105 There is provision for outside input into the research process through the Fisheries and Oceans Research Advisory Council, constituted of scientists, departmental representatives, universities, the fishing industry, and the public:

largely at the discretion of the minister. These two characteristics, centralization and discretion, raise questions as to the appropriateness of this approach to the organization of Canada's marine science research effort. The extent of ministerial discretion under Bill C-26 has been dealt with above, and the problems identified there are repeated in the context of marine science. Although it may be dangerous to attempt an overly restrictive definition of ministerial responsibilities for a scientific program that is necessarily flexible and adaptive, it might at least have been possible to identify a mandatory process by which research functions could be prioritized and reviewed.

The more fundamental difficulty, however, lies in the consolidation of most research functions in one department. To subject marine scientific research to the direct operational control of the minister and the bureaucracy, particularly under such a discretionary regime, raises the real danger that research priorities will be dictated, not by scientific requirements, but in accordance with the policy considerations of the day. While it is acknowledged that science can readily generate its own ossified bureaucracies and internal politics, the present model of hands-on governmental control of research is excessively vulnerable to political interference with research priorities.

Nor is it necessary to assume bad faith, for there are systemic problems with this approach that justify serious concern, particularly in the highly charged case of fisheries research.[106] Integration of science functions within the department charged with fisheries management will tend to subordinate basic research to the exigencies of the management process, since the minister and

---

Fisheries and Oceans Research Advisory Council Act, R.S.C. 1985, c. F-16, s. 4. By s. 10, the Council advises the minister, *inter alia*, on "fisheries research and the marine sciences" and "the scope and adequacy of the science policies and programs of the Department of Fisheries and Oceans." This is, however, a purely advisory function, and there is no obligation on the minister to listen, and no power for the Council to conduct research.

106 The role of science has been front and centre in the post-collapse debates over the northern cod fishery. See, e.g., J. Hutchings and R. Myers, "The Biological Collapse Of Atlantic Cod Off Newfoundland and Labrador: An Exploration of Historical Changes in Exploitation, Harvesting Technology, and Management" in R. Arnason and L. Felt (eds), *The North Atlantic Fisheries: Successes, Failures and Challenges* (Charlottetown: Institute of Island Studies, 1995) and A. Finlayson, *Fishing for Truth: A Sociological Analysis of Northern Cod Stock Assessments from 1977-1990* (St. John's: Institute of Social and Economic Research, Memorial Univ., 1994).

managers will naturally tend to concentrate on those functions that most immediately demand both their attention and a decision.[107] As a result, the fundamental understanding of resources and eco-systems, which is ultimately necessary to the management effort, is less likely to be advanced, and new approaches that might challenge the orthodoxy of assessment techniques will not emerge.[108]

Despite the benefits to be gained by integrative approaches to management and planning, it is possible that marine science, on which an oceans strategy should be based, may not be an appropriate candidate for full integration, given the difficulties suggested here. Consideration should have been given, first, to the categorization of research functions and the assignment of these to the departments (or other agencies) identified as the most appropriate location.[109] Such an exercise might still have resulted in extensive consolidation, but on the basis of rational choice rather than reflexive amalgamation.

The second option that deserves greater attention is the creation of an "arm's length" body for the conduct of some marine scientific research, particularly that which is not directly tied to the day-to-day management effort. Such a body could be given its status and mandate in the statute but operate under the direction of a highly qualified board. An independent voice of this type, guided by the available scientific knowledge and not by the policy of the day, could enhance the quality of understanding of the oceans and the ability to ensure their sustainable use.

---

[107] See, e.g., P. Underwood, "To Manage Quotas or Manage Fisheries?" (1995) 18 Dal. L.J. 36 at 39: "Feeding the assessment models with data and calculating all of the various TACs became the bread and butter for Department of Fisheries and Oceans ... science. Integrated research into ecosystem dynamics fell by the wayside." Nor was this argument only made in hindsight. See, e.g., the concerns raised in 1972 over a proposed merger of the Fisheries Research Board and the Department of Fisheries in K. Johnstone, *The Aquatic Explorers: A History of the Fisheries Research Board of Canada* 254 (Toronto: University of Toronto Press, 1977).

[108] Underwood, *ibid., passim.*

[109] Such an approach is not without precedent. See, e.g., the division of research functions in Australia, with activities such as managerial statistics, basic research, and industrial research split among different institutions and under different statutes. See Australian Institute of Marine Science Act 1972-1973, Vol. 1, Acts of the Parliament 1901-1973 (basic research), Science and Industry Research Act 1949-1973, Vol. 10, Acts of the Parliament 1901-1973, Fisheries Management Act 1991, No. 162, Acts of the Parliament 1991.

This is not a new model for Canadian marine (and particularly fisheries) research. The Fisheries Research Board of Canada (FRB) operated for decades under the supervision of an independent board and with a general mandate handed down by statute.[110] Unlike the current Fisheries and Oceans Research Advisory Council, the FRB had an operational mandate to plan and conduct research activities. It was under a duty to report back to the minister, but for most of its life this was done as a relatively independent entity, and not as an operational part of the departmental bureaucracy.[111]

The FRB model was not perfect, and leaving scientific functions beyond the direct reach of government is problematic in times of shrinking resources.[112] Nonetheless, the experience of recent years indicates that a marine science program run solely under the control of a managerial department and directed at an operational level by the minister and bureaucrats presents its own flaws. A return to a fully independent approach may not be possible or desirable, but it should not automatically be assumed that the other extreme, consolidation within one department, is the only other option. The role of marine science in ensuring that Canada can fulfil its obligations under the Law of the Sea Convention, and in allowing sustainable use of our marine resources, is far too important for it to be corralled in this way.

OCEAN POLICY RESEARCH AND EDUCATION

Despite the difficulties suggested above, Bill C-26 clearly seeks to promote the conduct of marine scientific research through the provisions of Part 3. In a broader context, however, it takes a somewhat narrow and conservative approach to research. While strong in calling for applied marine scientific research and increased study of marine ecosystems, the bill fails to recognize the

110 Fisheries Research Board Act, R.S.C. 1970, c. 121 (substantially amended and retitled Fisheries and Oceans Research Advisory Council Act by the Government Organization Act 1979, S.C. 1978-79, c. 13, ss. 8-12).

111 R.S.C. 1970, c. 121, s. 6 provided: "The Board has charge of all federal fishery research stations in Canada, and has the conduct and control of investigations of practical and economic problems connected with marine and fresh water fisheries . . . and such other work as may be assigned to it by the Minister."

112 For a review of the accomplishments of the FRB, and of the factors that led to its absorption as a unit of government by the 1970s, see Johnstone, *supra* note 107, *passim.*

need to lend support to social science research in marine affairs. Given the recent crises in fisheries management, which appear to have serious social, economic, political, and ethical roots,[113] it is rather surprising not to see some legislative reference to the need for policy-oriented studies. Canada's legislators might have "borrowed" from the experiences of the United States, where the federal government has for over twenty-five years supported a National Sea Grant Program to facilitate research and education in marine-related problems facing the country.[114]

On a related point, Bill C-26 also fails to emphasize the importance of public education in fostering sustainable development and management in ocean and coastal areas. The bill requires the minister of fisheries and oceans to "gather, compile, analyze, coordinate and disseminate information."[115] While this responsibility should permit public access to oceans information and data, it does not require programs of public education that are so necessary for the institution and fulfilment of an integrated and sustainable oceans management strategy.

CONCLUSION

The core of Bill C-26 is a new and global approach to the management of the oceans and their resources within Canadian jurisdiction. That jurisdiction is extended by Part 1 of the bill through the territorial sea, the contiguous zone, the exclusive economic zone, and the continental shelf to the fullest extent permitted to Canada under international law. Part 2 of the bill constitutes a modest first step in the development of a comprehensive policy and legal framework to guide integrated coastal and ocean development in Canada. It is a pioneering statute that, compared to other oceans laws around the world, is significantly more advanced in legislating for integrated marine management. Its underlying direc-

[113] For an excellent overview of the numerous dimensions of fisheries management, see the recent special issue of the Dalhousie Law Journal: "After the Collapse" (1995), 18 Dal. L. J.

[114] For a description of the program and previous advocacy of a similar program for Canada, see R. Coté, C. Lamson, and D. VanderZwaag, "Getting the Oceans Act Together" (1990) Policy Options 23 at 26. Congress established the National Sea Grant College Program in 1966 and the secretary of commerce has designated 29 Sea Grant College Programs in coastal and Great Lake states and in Puerto Rico.

[115] Bill C-26, s. 33(1)(c).

tive is clear: in the development of oceans strategy, the best modern environmental principles should be applied and incorporated.

However, there are significant weaknesses in Part 2. A bold task, such as the laying of a framework for a national oceans management strategy, required a more concrete and innovative approach and a better response to important principles of sustainable development. Bill C-26 does not go far enough to integrate these principles in the legislative structure, and thus neglects an opportunity to reflect the conclusions of the United Nations Conference on Environment and Development in a meaningful manner in the oceans context.

According to Part 3 of the bill, the minister of fisheries and oceans will act as the co-ordinator and facilitator of the new oceans management strategy and has been given an enhanced scope of authority to do so. The minister is granted plenty of statutory and regulatory powers with which to exercise that authority but fewer complementary obligations, especially regarding the involvement of other actors, than the new integrative approach would seem to require. It remains to be seen what sort of integrated management strategy for Canada's oceans and marine resources will ultimately be constructed.

ALDO CHIRCOP
HUGH KINDRED
PHILLIP SAUNDERS
DAVID VANDERZWAAG
Marine and Environmental Law Programme, Faculty of Law, Dalhousie University

Sommaire

Instauration d'une gestion intégrée des océans: le projet de loi de 1996 concernant les océans du Canada

Le projet de loi C-26 vise à instaurer une gestion intégrée des océans et des ressources marines qui relèvent de la compétence du Canada. Le projet de loi énonce les droits souverains que la Convention des Nations Unies sur le droit de la mer reconnaît au Canada sur ses zones maritimes, soit la mer territoriale, la zone contiguë, la zone économique exclusive et le plateau continental. Il établit le cadre d'une stratégie nationale de gestion des océans qui repose sur le développement durable, la prévention et la gestion intégrée des ressources et des activités côtières et marines. Ces dispositions, bien que prometteuses, témoignent cependant d'un engagement limité envers les prin-

cipes du développement durable. Elles manquent de précision et de clarté quant à la stratégie de gestion des océans proposée et elles ne favorisent pas une planification intégrée de la gestion. En outre, le projet de loi redéfinit les responsabilités relatives à la gestion des océans du Canada. Il accroît notamment le rôle du ministre des Pêches et des Océans de façon considérable. Toutefois, pour atteindre une véritable gestion intégrée du projet de loi C-26, le ministre devra partager avec d'autres intervenants un plus grand nombre de responsabilités que ne le prévoit le projet.

Summary

Legislating for Integrated Marine Management: Canada's Proposed Oceans Act of 1996

Bill C-26 is intended to provide for the integrated management of the oceans and marine resources within Canada's jurisdiction. The bill sets out Canadian jurisdiction in the territorial sea, the contiguous zone, the exclusive economic zone, and the continental shelf in accordance with the United Nations Law of the Sea Convention. It defines a framework for a national oceans management strategy based on sustainable development, a precautionary approach, and integrated management plans for oceans and coastal resources and activities. These promising provisions suffer from limited commitment to sustainable development principles, lack of details and clarity about the intended oceans management strategy, and limited embrace of integration in management planning. The bill also redefines the organizational responsibilities for Canada's oceans in a way that significantly enhances the role of the minister of fisheries and oceans. In fulfilling these functions, the minister is likely to have to share responsibilities with other stakeholders rather more than Bill C-26 actually requires, if its integrative management objectives are to be attained.

John Peters Humphrey — A Tribute

THE EDITORS WISH TO RECORD the passing of the distinguished Canadian international lawyer John Humphrey, a man who made a singular contribution to the field of human rights and who continued as a scholar and teacher up until shortly before his death. Author of several books and numerous articles, recipient of countless honorary degrees and awards, including the John Read Medal awarded by the Canadian Council on International Law, John Humphrey had for many years been a familiar figure on the landscape of international law in Canada.

John Humphrey began his career between the First and Second World Wars. After studying at Mount Allison University, McGill University, and the University of Paris, Humphrey began the practice of law in Montreal in 1930. In 1936, he was appointed to McGill Faculty of Law and became Gale Professor of Law, teaching Roman law and international law. What would have been an illustrious career as law professor and Dean of Law was interrupted when John Humphrey joined the United Nations Secretariat in 1946 as director of the Division of Human Rights.

In that position, John Humphrey was intimately involved in one of the most auspicious legal events of the post-war era — the drafting of the Universal Declaration on Human Rights. As director of the Division of Human Rights, Humphrey was responsible for the preparation of the secretariat draft of what ultimately became the Universal Declaration.

As a tribute to that work and to the man John Humphrey and in memory of his outstanding contribution to the field of international law, we are reproducing below the text of that first manuscript draft prepared in John Humphrey's handwriting.

The manuscript is in the law library at McGill University. The text is taken from that prepared by A. J. Hobbins, senior librarian of McGill University, to whom the editors record their thanks.

SHEET 1

The preamble shall enunciate the following principles:

(1) that there must be respect for human if [*sic*] rights and freedoms if the world is to know peace;

(2) that man does not have rights only: he owes duties to the society (both national and international) of which he forms part.

(1) The provisions of this International Bill of Rights shall be deemed fundamental principles of international law and of the national law of each of the member States of the United Nations. Its observance is therefore a matter of international concern and it shall be within the jurisdiction of the United Nations to discuss any violation thereof.

(1a) It is the duty of the State to respect and maintain the rights enunciated in the Bill of Rights.

(1b) Every one owes a duty of loyalty to his State and to the international community of which he forms part. He must accept his fair share of responsibility for the performance of social duties and also his share of any sacrifices made necessary by the exigencies of life in common.

(2) In the exercise of his rights every one is limited by the rights of others and by the just requirements of the democratic State.

(3) Every one has the right to life.
torture. [very faint aide-mémoire to insert text appears on sheet 4]

(4) Every one has the right to personal liberty.

SHEET 2

PREAMBLE

Man does not have rights only, he owes duties to the society (national and international) of which he forms part

(1) It is solemnly declared that the principles here enunciated are matters of international concern. No plea of sovereignty shall

ever again be allowed to permit any nation to deprive [inserted from lower on the page]

RIGHTS AND DUTIES WITHIN THE STATE

Right to liberty and freedom
Right to social security
Right to equality and protection against discrimination
  limitations

RIGHTS AND DUTIES AS MEMBER OF INTERNATIONAL COMMUNITY

Right to live out his days secure from war and the fear thereof. Incorporation of declaration into national law (see Inter-American).

SHEET 3

DECLARATION OF INTERNATIONAL CONCERN

It is solemnly declared that the principles enunciated by this International Bill of Rights are matters of international concern and within the jurisdiction of the United Nations. No plea of sovereignty shall (ever again) be allowed to permit any state to deprive men and women within its borders of the rights established by it.

The provisions of this International Bill of Rights shall be deemed fundamental principles of International law and of the national law of each of the member states of the United Nations to be realized by appropriate action of international and national agencies. Respect for these principles is therefore a matter of international concern and it shall be within the jurisdiction of the U.N. to discuss any violation thereof.

It is the duty of the state to respect and maintain the rights enunciated in this Bill of Rights. [Appears upside down at the bottom of the page]

SHEET 4 (VERSO OF SHEET 3)

This right can be denied only when the person concerned has been convicted under general law of some crime against society to which the death penalty is attached. [This is an addition to (3) on Sheet 1.]

No one shall be subjected to torture or to any unusual punishment, *torture* or indignity. [Text for aide-mémoire on torture on Sheet 1]

[The remaining two paragraphs appear upside-down at the bottom of the sheet.]

THE ENJOYMENT OF RIGHTS

Every one, moreover, owes a duty of loyalty to the society *whether* both national *or* and international of which he forms part. He must accept his just share of responsibility for the performance of social duties and *accept* also his share of any *common* sacrifice made necessary by the exigencies of life in common. [Variant text for (1b) on Sheet 1]

SHEET 5

There shall be full equality before the law in the enjoyment of the rights enunciated in this Bill of Rights and no one shall suffer any discrimination whatsoever because of race, sex, language or religion.

Having regard to UNESCO
UNESCO is, of course, interested in the freedom of information and has expressed a desire to *cooperate with the U.N.* be represented at the proposed int. conference on that subject.
Under

The Council may therefore wish to request the G.A. to change the date of the

[These notes refer to the possible rescheduling of the International Conference on Freedom of Information (eventually held at Geneva in March-April 1948), given UNESCO's expressed interest. Having nothing to do with the draft they probably represent some work interruption and the utilization of a handy piece of paper.]

SHEET 6 (VERSO OF SHEET 5)

Every one has a right to own personal property. His right to share in the ownership of industrial, commercial and other profit-making enterprises is governed by the laws of the State of which he is a citizen.

Every one shall
[The remaining two paragraphs are written upside-down at the bottom.]
and to live in healthy pleasant surroundings.
[This hanging phrase is written in ink and represents concluding phraseology, eventually not used, for Article 31.]
Every one has the right to good food and to housing, and to live in surroundings that are pleasant and healthy.

SHEET 7

Subject to the laws governing slander and libel there shall be full freedom of speech and of expression by any means whatsoever, and there shall be reasonable access to all channels of *information* communications. Censorship shall not be permitted, [one illegible word erased]

There shall be free access to all sources of information both within and beyond the borders of the State. [This erasure became Article 17, Sheet 10.]

The press is bound by a sacred duty towards society to present the news in a fair and impartial manner. [Cf. Article 19, Sheet 11]

SHEET 8

[At this point draft articles are given Roman numerals beginning with X.]

(X)   No one shall be convicted of crime except for violation of a law in effect at the time of the commission of the act charged as an offense [text corrected from "offence" to reflect this spelling], nor be subjected to a penalty greater than that applicable at the time of the commission of the offense.

SHEET 9 (FIGURE 3)

(XI)   No one shall be subjected to arbitrary searches or seizures or to unreasonable interferences with his person, *home, correspondence* family relations, [this phrase was substituted for the erasure], reputation, privacy, activities, *and* or personal property.

(XII)   The sanctity of the home and the secrecy of correspondence shall be respected. [This clause appears to have been added afterwards, presumably when the concept was removed from Article 11, causing renumbering up to at least Article 22.]

(XIII)   Slavery and compulsory labour are inconsistent with the dignity of man and therefore prohibited by this Bill of Rights. But a man may be required to perform his just share of any public service that is equally incumbent upon all, and his right to a livelihood is conditioned by his duty to work. Involuntary servitude may also be imposed as part of a punishment pronounced by a court of law.

SHEET 10

(XIV)   Subject to any general law adopted in the interest of national welfare or security, there shall be liberty of movement and free choice of residence within the borders of each State.

(XV)   The right of emigration and expatriation shall not be denied.

(XVI)   There shall be full freedom of conscience and belief and of religious worship. Every one has the right to form, to hold, and to receive opinions.

(XVII)   There shall be free access to all services of information both within and beyond the borders of the State.

SHEET 11

(XVIII)   Subject only to the laws governing slander and libel, there shall be full freedom of speech and of expression by any means whatsoever, and there shall be reasonable access to all channels of communication. Censorship shall not be permitted.

(XIX)   The press is bound by a sacred duty towards society to present the news in a fair and impartial manner.

SHEET 12

(XX)   There shall be full freedom of peaceful assembly.

(XXI)   There shall be full freedom to form association for purposes not inconsistent with this Bill of Rights.

(XXII)   Every one has a right to own personal property. His right to share in the ownership of industrial, commercial and other profit-making enterprises is governed by the law of the State of which he is a citizen.

SHEET 13

(XXIII)   Every one is entitled to the nationality of the State where he is born unless and until on attaining majority he declares for the nationality open to him by virtue of descent.

No one shall be deprived of his nationality by way of punishment or be deemed to have lost his nationality in any other way unless he concurrently acquires a new nationality.

Every one has the right to renounce the nationality of his birth, or previously acquired nationality, upon acquiring the nationality of another State.

SHEET 14

(XXIV)   No alien who has been legally admitted to the territory of a State may be expelled except in pursuance of a judicial decision or recommendation as a punishment for offences [British variant used here but transcribed "offenses" in first typed draft] laid down by law as warranting expulsion.

(XXV)   Every one has the right to take an effective [adjective added later] part in the government of the State of which he is a citizen. The State has a duty to conform to the wishes of the people as manifested by democratic elections.

(XXVI)   Every one has the right, either individually or in association with others, to petition the government of his State or the United Nations for redress of grievances.

SHEET 15

(XXVII)   Every one has the right to education. Each State has the duty to require that every child within its territory receive a primary [adjective added later] education. *Within the limits of its economic capacity and development, the State must maintain*
The State shall maintain, within the limits of its economic capacity and development, adequate and free

facilities for such education. It shall also promote facilities for higher education.

(XXVIII) Every one has the right and the duty to perform socially useful work.

(XXIX) Every one has the right to good working conditions.

SHEET 16

(XXX) Every one is entitled to adequate food and housing.

(XXXI) *Every one has the* [change from "a"] *right to social security. To this end the State must promote measures* [measures was erased earlier than the remainder of the paragraph] *public health and safety. This right includes the right to health in so far as*

(XXXI) Every one has the right to leisure. [Cf. Article 31, Sheet 18]

(XXXII) Every one has the right to culture and to the enjoyment of the arts. [Cf. Article 32, Sheet 18]

(XXXIII) Every one has the right to share in the benefits of science. [Cf. Article 33, Sheet 18]

(XXXIV) *Every one has the right*
The State shall promote public health and safety.

(XXXIV) *Every one has the right to social security. To this end each State shall within the limits of its economic capacity and development promote public health and safety, and establish*

SHEET 17 (VERSO OF SHEET 16)

(XXXIV) Every one has the right to live and work in healthy surroundings and a right to medical care.

(XXXV) Every one has the right to social security. To this end, each State shall, within the limits of its economic capacity and development, promote public health and safety. *and establish systems of social insurance and social agencies.* It shall also *make effective provisions for public* maintain *or ensure that there are maintained* effective arrangements for the prevention of unemployment, for the provision of adequate insurance *compensation in the event of* against the risks of unemployment, accident, disability, ill health, sickness, old age or other involuntary loss of livelihood. *including*

SHEET 18

(XXX)   Every one has the right to a *fair share reasonable* just wage
         and standard of living. [This is the last entry in pencil,
         the remainder of the manuscript being in ink.]
(XXX)   Every one is entitled to adequate food and housing.
(XXXI)   Every one has the right to a fair share of rest and leisure.
(XXXII) Every one has the right to participate in the cultural life
         of the community and to enjoy the arts.
(XXXIII) Every one has the right to share in the benefits of
         science.
(XXXIV) Every one has the right to social security. To this end
         each State shall, within the limits of its economic capac-
         ity and when necessary in cooperation with other States,

Chronique de Droit international économique en 1994 / Digest of International Economic Law in 1994

I Commerce

préparé par
MARTIN ST-AMANT*

L'ANNÉE 1994 fut marquée par un événement des plus importants pour le Canada, soit l'entrée en vigueur, le 1ᵉʳ janvier, de l'Accord de libre-échange nord-américain.[1] Rien d'étonnant donc à ce que nous décidions d'y consacrer la totalité de la présente chronique.

C'est dès juin 1990 que le Mexique signifia son intention d'amorcer des discussions avec les États-Unis en vue de la conclusion d'un accord de libre-échange. Le gouvernement mexicain d'alors considérait un tel accord comme un puissant outil de modernisation économique en facilitant notamment l'intégration du Mexique dans l'économie nord-américaine, tout en encourageant l'investissement et le rapatriement des capitaux mexicains. Dans un monde s'orientant vers la création de grands marchés régionaux, le Mexique prit ainsi le pari qu'il ne pourrait faire bande à part. Par ailleurs, désireux d'obtenir un accès accru au marché américain et de contourner toute velléité protectionniste de la part des États-

---

* Avocat, Joli-Coeur, Lacasse, Lemieux, Simard, St-Pierre, s.e.n.c.; Doctorat en Droit commercial international, Université de Paris I (Panthéon-Sorbonne).

---

[1] Voir *Accord de libre-échange entre le gouvernement du Canada, le gouvernement des États-Unis d'Amérique et le gouvernement des États-Unis du Mexique*, signé le 17 décembre 1992, en vigueur le 1ᵉʳ janvier 1994 (ci-après dénommé l'ALÉNA). La loi canadienne de mise en œuvre de l'Accord de libre-échange a été adoptée par la Chambre des communes le 27 mai 1993. Voir *Loi portant mise en œuvre de l'Accord de libre-échange nord-américain*, L.C. 1993, c. 44.

Unis, le Mexique cherchait à atteindre les mêmes objectifs que ceux qui avaient amené le Canada à conclure un accord semblable avec les États-Unis.[2]

Le Canada, quant à lui, après quelques hésitations, décida néanmoins de participer aux négociations, jugeant somme toute qu'il ne pouvait se permettre de rester en marge des négociations bilatérales, lesquelles pouvaient donner lieu à des modifications substantielles des courants d'échanges et d'investissements en Amérique du Nord. Le Canada se devait toutefois de rester vigilant puisqu'une participation directe au processus de négociations comportait un risque élevé, soit celui que les États-Unis tentent de renégocier certains points de l'Accord de libre-échange Canada-États-Unis, points sur lesquels ils n'ont pas rencontré leurs objectifs lors des premières négociations.[3] Dans ce contexte, la conservation de l'accès au marché des États-Unis à des conditions au moins aussi favorables que celles qui seraient consenties au Mexique, l'assurance de l'existence d'une protection continue pour certains secteurs névralgiques de son économie et subsidiairement l'obtention d'un accès au marché mexicain, furent dans l'ordre les trois principaux objectifs que s'était fixé le Canada dans le cadre de ces négociations.[4]

Les prochaines pages présentent un bref aperçu des principaux éléments de l'ALÉNA portant sur le commerce des biens et des services. Une prochaine chronique fera quant à elle le point sur la libéralisation dans les domaines des marchés publics et de la propriété intellectuelle et sur les divers mécanismes de règlement des différends prévus par l'ALÉNA.

[2] Voir *Accord de libre-échange entre le gouvernement du Canada et le gouvernement des États-Unis d'Amérique*, signé le 2 janvier 1988, en vigueur le 1er janvier 1989. Réimprimé (1988) 27 I.L.M. 281 (ci-après dénommé l'Accord de libre-échange Canada-États-Unis).

[3] On pense notamment ici aux industries culturelles, aux subventions déloyales et aux mécanismes de règlement des différends.

[4] Notons que les flux commerciaux entre le Canada et le Mexique sont relativement faibles. Le Mexique se classe en effet au dix-septième rang comme marché pour les exportations canadiennes et moins de 1,5 pour cent des exportations mexicaines sont destinées au Canada. Bilatéralement, ces échanges s'établissaient à 2,3 milliards de dollars en 1989, ce qui est peu comparé aux échanges canado-américains qui représentaient la même année, 185,8 milliards de dollars. Voir *Statistiques Canada*, 1989. Quant aux circuits d'investissement, ils sont demeurés très faibles. Toutefois, le potentiel de croissance des échanges bilatéraux est intéressant. L'accroissement du niveau de vie, dans un pays de plus de quatre-vingt millions d'habitants, laisse entrevoir, pour le Canada, la perspective de marchés considérables et croissants.

I COMMERCE DES BIENS

Outre l'incorporation des dispositions relatives au traitement national prévues à l'Accord général sur les tarifs douaniers et le commerce,[5] les trois pays ont convenu d'éliminer progressivement les droits de douane dans leur commerce trilatéral selon un calendrier à quatre étapes. Un premier groupe de produits entrera en franchise de droits dès l'entrée en vigueur de l'ALÉNA, tandis que les autres verront l'élimination des droits s'établir sur une période égale à cinq, dix ou même à quinze années.[6]

Il importe de noter qu'entre le Canada et les États-Unis, le calendrier d'élimination des droits continuera d'être régi par l'Accord de libre-échange Canada-États-Unis.[7] Par ailleurs, des dispositions fort complexes sur les règles d'origine indiquent si un produit exporté par l'une des parties peut bénéficier des avantages conférés par l'ALÉNA.[8] Le programme des "Drawback" visant le remboursement des droits de douane sur les intrants importés de produits subséquemment exportés sera d'autre part supprimé entre le Canada et les États-Unis, non plus le 1er janvier 1994 tel que le

5 Voir *Accord général sur les tarifs douaniers et le commerce*, (1950) 55 R.T.N.U. 188, R.T. Can. n° 27 (ci-après dénommé Accord général). Voir aussi ALÉNA, *supra* note 1, art. 301(1). En ce qui concerne les états et les provinces canadiennes, ils devront accorder aux biens d'une autre partie un traitement aussi favorable que celui qu'ils accordent à leurs propres biens et aux produits de tout autre état ou province. *Ibid.* art. 301(2).

6 ALÉNA, *supra* note 1, art. 301(2) et annexe 301.2(1). Soulignons que ce sera seulement certaines exportations mexicaines à destination des États-Unis qui seront touchées par une réduction des droits s'échelonnant sur quinze ans. Les parties pourront par ailleurs, si elles le souhaitent, accélérer le calendrier d'élimination des droits de douane. *Ibid.* art. 302(3).

7 Voir *supra* note 2 et note chronique antérieure sur cet accord; M. St-Amant, "Chronique de droit économique international en 1988," (1989) 27 A.C.D.I. 344.

8 En règle générale, les produits fabriqués avec des composantes provenant de l'extérieur de la zone de libre-échange seront assimilés à des produits nord-américains si les transformations apportées ont pour effet de changer la classification du produit dans le système harmonisé de désignation et de codification des marchandises. ALÉNA, *supra* note 1, art. 401(b). Dans quelques cas, les produits, en plus d'un changement de classification, devront, pour satisfaire aux règles d'origine, inclure un pourcentage précis de valeur ajoutée nord-américaine. Dans d'autres cas, seule l'exigence d'une teneur nord-américaine est requise. *Ibid.* art. 401(d). Si, d'autre part, la valeur des compostantes non originaires de la zone ne dépasse pas 7 pour cent de son prix ou de son coût total, un produit pourra néanmoins être considéré comme un produit nord-américain en vertu de la clause *de minimis*. *Ibid.* art. 405.

prévoyait initialement l'Accord de libre-échange Canada-États-Unis, mais à partir du 1er janvier 1996.[9] Dans le commerce avec le Mexique, la suppression du programme est prévue pour le 1er janvier 2001.[10] Les trois pays renoncent également à toute forme de restrictions à l'importation et à l'exportation, outre celles autorisées par les articles XI et XX de l'Accord général.[11]

La réduction des barrières tarifaires et non tarifaires dans les domaines de l'industrie automobile, du textile et des vêtements et de l'agriculture fait l'objet de dispositions particulières dans l'ALÉNA. En ce qui concerne l'automobile, l'ALÉNA élimine les obstacles au commerce des véhicules (automobiles et camions) et des pièces.[12] Le Traité de 1965 entre le Canada et les États-Unis sur le commerce des produits de l'automobile est quant à lui maintenu tout comme dans l'Accord de libre-échange Canada-États-Unis.[13] En outre, de nouvelles règles d'origine moins ambiguës sont adoptées.[14] Dans le secteur du textile et des vêtements, l'ALÉNA prévoit généralement des règles d'origine plus strictes que ce qui était prescrit dans l'Accord de

9 ALÉNA, *supra* note 1, art. 303(1), 303(7) et annexe 303.7. Par la suite, un mécanisme de remboursement partiel des droits sera instauré. *Ibid.* art. 303(1). Ce mécanisme permettra aux producteurs canadiens d'obtenir un remboursement équivalent au moindre montant entre les droits de douane payés sur les intrants importés et les droits de douane applicables aux exportations de produits finis aux États-Unis ou au Mexique.

10 *Ibid.*

11 ALÉNA, *supra* note 1, art. 309(1).

12 ALÉNA, *supra* note 1, annexe 300-A. L'Accord prévoit ainsi entre le Canada et le Mexique une réduction de 50 pour cent des droits de douane sur les automobiles dès l'entrée en vigueur de l'Accord et le reste en neuf étapes annuelles finissant le 1er janvier 2003. Une même réduction de 50 pour cent sur les camions légers le 1er janvier 1994 et le reste en quatre étapes annuelles finissant le 1er janvier 1998. Enfin, l'Accord prévoit une élimination progressive des droits sur une période de dix ans sur la plupart des autres véhicules.

13 ALÉNA, *supra* note 1, annexe 300-A-1. Voir aussi *Accord entre le gouvernement canadien et le gouvernement des États-Unis d'Amérique concernant les produits de l'automobile*, (1967) R.T. Can. n° 14, réimprimé (1965) 4 I.L.M. 302. Le pacte de l'automobile a pour objectif de libéraliser le commerce de l'automobile en permettant l'entrée en franchise de la plupart des véhicules et pièces reliés à cette industrie.

14 ALÉNA, *supra* note 1, art. 403. La teneur du contenu nord-américain est en effet plus détaillée, ce qui laissera place à des calculs plus exacts. Pour les automobiles, les camions légers, les minibus ainsi que leur moteur et leur transmission, la règle d'origine est fixée à 62,5 pour cent du contenu nord-américain et à 60 pour cent pour les autres véhicules ainsi que leur moteur, transmission et autres pièces.

libre-échange Canada-États-Unis. Ainsi, en ce qui concerne les vêtements, les pays signataires ont incorporé la règle de la triple transformation[15] et pour le textile, la règle de la double transformation[16]. Outre l'élimination progressive des droits de douane, l'ALÉNA augmente sensiblement par rapport à l'Accord de libre-échange Canada-États-Unis les contingents tarifaires autorisés à l'exportation de produits du Canada vers les États-Unis.[17]

Dans le secteur de l'agriculture, l'ALÉNA comporte d'abord deux volets trilatéraux, l'un en matière de soutien interne afin que les politiques des trois pays ne faussent pas les échanges[18] et l'autre en matière de subventions à l'exportation[19]. Deux ententes bilatérales, l'une entre le Mexique et les États-Unis et l'autre entre le Mexique et le Canada, ont par ailleurs été conclues relativement à l'accès au marché.[20] Le commerce entre le Canada et les États-Unis est pour sa part toujours régi par le chapitre 7 de l'Accord de libre-échange Canada-États-Unis.[21] Des engagements en matière de

---

[15] ALÉNA, *supra* note 1, annexe 401. Un vêtement sera de ce fait originaire de la zone de libre-échange s'il est coupé et cousu en Amérique du Nord et que le tissu et le fil proviennent également de la région.

[16] *Ibid.* Pour respecter la règle d'origine, le textile doit être fabriqué dans la zone de libre-échange tout comme le fil principal. Pour les tissus incluant plusieurs matériaux différents, c'est l'ensemble des fils qui doit provenir de la zone.

[17] ALÉNA, *supra* note 1, liste 6.B.1.

[18] ALÉNA, *supra* note 1, art. 704. Les parties reconnaissent cependant la possibilité sous réserve des obligations aux termes de l'Accord général, de modifier leurs mesures de soutien interne. *Ibid.*

[19] ALÉNA, *supra* note 1, art. 705. Bien que les trois pays ne se sont pas engagés formellement à éliminer les subventions à l'exportation, ils prennent acte que ces dernières peuvent perturber leurs marchés. *Ibid.* art. 705(2). Des obligations de préavis et de consultations sont prévues afin que les intérêts des parties soient dûment pris en compte préliminairement à l'octroi des subventions. *Ibid.* art. 705(3) et (4). Par ailleurs, un groupe de travail examinera les possibilités d'éliminer les subventions à l'exportation. *Ibid.* art. 705.6.

[20] ALÉNA, *supra* note 1, annexe 703.2 et annexe 702.1. En ce qui concerne le Canada et le Mexique, il fut entendu que la suppression des droits de douane et autres mesures non tarifaires se fera graduellement, soit pour certains produits dès l'entrée en vigueur de l'Accord, soit pour d'autres sur une période de cinq ou dix ans. Notons toutefois que le système canadien de gestion de l'offre est préservé pour ce qui est du secteur laitier, avicole et des œufs. Des clauses de sauvegarde spéciales ont par ailleurs été insérées dans l'Accord, clauses qui n'auront cependant d'effet qu'au cours des dix premières années. *Ibid.* art. 703 (3) et (4).

[21] Sur les dispositions de cet Accord en matière d'agriculture, voir M. St-Amant, *loc. cit.*, *supra* note 7 aux pp. 346-47.

mesures sanitaires et phytosanitaires (MSP) furent également pris par les trois pays et ce avec pour objectif avoué que de telles mesures n'aient pas pour effet de créer des obstacles déguisés au commerce ou un traitement discriminatoire envers une autre partie.[22]

II Commerce des services

L'ALÉNA s'appuie ici en grande partie sur l'expérience de la négociation menée dans le cadre de l'Uruguay Round et sur le chapitre 14 de l'Accord de libre-échange Canada-États-Unis.[23] La libéralisation du commerce des services dans le cadre de l'ALÉNA vise à réduire le nombre d'obstacles inutiles auxquels font actuellement face les fournisseurs de services des trois pays. Dans cette perspective, tous les services, à l'exception des services financiers, des télécommunications de base, des services aériens et des transports maritimes, sont soumis aux clauses de la nation la plus favorisée, du traitement national et du droit de non-établissement.[24] Toutefois, les parties pourront inscrire des réserves dans le but de maintenir toute mesure non conforme existante ou de préserver leur capacité d'adopter de nouvelles mesures non conformes dans certains secteurs particuliers ou activités particulières.[25] Par ailleurs, les pays signataires ont indiqué à l'annexe V de l'ALÉNA les restrictions quantitatives qu'ils entendaient maintenir.[26] Au moins tous les

[22] ALÉNA, *supra* note 1, art. 712(3) et (6). Ces engagements s'apparentent à ceux sur les normes techniques: recherches d'équivalences, référence aux normes internationales, justification basée sur des principes scientifiques, obligation de notification, diffusion de l'information et coopération technique. Le droit de fixer le niveau de protection jugé approprié est par ailleurs sauvegardé. *Ibid.* art. 712(2) et 715.

[23] Voir sur cet Accord, M. St-Amant, *loc. cit.*, note 7 aux pp. 351-54.

[24] ALÉNA, *supra* note 1, art. 1201(2), 1202, 1203 et 1205. Le droit de non-établissement vise à interdire à une partie d'imposer à un fournisseur de services d'une autre partie une présence commerciale sur le territoire aux fins de la fourniture transfrontière d'un service.

[25] ALÉNA, *supra* note 1, art. 1206. Quant aux mesures non conformes existantes des états ou provinces, les pays signataires auront jusqu'au 1er janvier 1996 pour dresser leurs listes d'exception. *Ibid.* Les mesures non conformes actuellement en vigueur au niveau municipal ou local peuvent par ailleurs être maintenues et n'ont pas à faire l'objet de réserve.

[26] ALÉNA, *supra* note 1, art. 1207(1). C'est ainsi que le Canada a inscrit dans sa liste le privilège exclusif de la Société canadienne des postes quant à la cueillette, la transmission et la distribution des lettres sur le territoire canadien.

deux ans, les parties devront chercher à négocier la libéralisation ou la levée de ces restrictions quantitatives.[27] En ce qui concerne plus particulièrement les services transfrontières de transport terrestre, l'ALÉNA établit un calendrier pour la libéralisation du transport par autocar et par camion ainsi que pour l'adoption de normes techniques et de sécurité compatibles.[28] Soulignons qu'aucun pays ne supprimera ses restrictions sur les services intérieurs de transport de marchandises par camion. Quant au secteur du transport maritime, il est de nouveau exclu de l'ALÉNA, comme ce fut d'ailleurs le cas avec l'Accord de libre-échange Canada-États-Unis. Il en est de même en ce qui a trait au transport aérien.[29] Dans le domaine des télécommunications, l'ALÉNA a pour objet principal de garantir un accès raisonnable et non discriminatoire aux services de télécommunications. Les dispositions de l'ALÉNA ne s'appliquent cependant pas aux mesures adoptées ou maintenues par l'une ou l'autre des parties et qui concernent la diffusion ou la distribution par câble d'émissions radiophoniques et télévisuelles.[30] D'autre part, l'accès et le recours aux réseaux et

---

Soulignons d'autre part que les parties ont un an pour y inscrire les restrictions quantitatives existantes maintenues par un état ou une province. *Ibid.* art. 1207(2).

[27] ALÉNA, *supra* note 1, art. 1207(4). Soulignons qu'une partie pourra refuser d'accorder à un fournisseur de services d'une autre partie les avantages de l'Accord, si les services en question sont fournis par une entreprise possédée ou contrôlée par des ressortissants d'un pays de l'extérieur de la zone de libre-échange et que cette entreprise n'exerce aucune activité commerciale importante sur le territoire de l'une ou l'autre des parties. *Ibid.* art. 1211(2).

[28] ALÉNA, *supra* note 1, annexe 1. Ainsi, à titre d'illustration, trois ans après l'entrée en vigueur de l'Accord, le Mexique autorisera les entreprises canadiennes et américaines de transport par autocar à exploiter des circuits internationaux à destination et en provenance de n'importe quel point de son territoire. Six ans après l'entrée en vigueur de l'Accord, le Mexique accordera en outre aux entreprises de camionnage canadiennes et américaines l'accès à la totalité de leur territoire si l'origine ou la destination est hors du Mexique. D'autre part, le Mexique, sept ans après l'entrée en vigueur de l'Accord, permettra aux canadiens et américains de détenir 51 pour cent des intérêts dans les secteurs du transport par autocar et du camionnage. Une participation de 100 pour cent sera autorisée mais seulement le 1er janvier 2004.

[29] Les services aériens spécialisés tels que notamment les services de cartographie et de photographie font toutefois l'objet d'une certaine libéralisation. Voir ALÉNA, *supra* note 1, annexe 1.

[30] ALÉNA, *supra* note 1, art. 1301(2). Une exception est prévue lorsqu'il s'agit de protéger l'accès aux réseaux publics de transport des communications. *Ibid.*

services publics de transport des télécommunications est dorénavant assuré pour les personnes de l'une ou l'autre des parties.[31] Les conditions régissant la fourniture de services améliorés ou à valeur ajoutée doivent au demeurant ne pas être discriminatoires tout en étant transparentes.[32] Par ailleurs, si un monopole d'état fournit un service ou un réseau public de transport de télécommunications, il lui sera interdit de profiter de sa position de monopole pour agir de manière anticoncurrentielle dans les marchés non monopolistiques des services améliorés ou à valeur ajoutée.[33] Finalement, en ce qui concerne les services professionnels, l'ALÉNA prévoit des dispositions relatives à l'autorisation d'exercer et à la reconnaissance professionnelle et ce afin d'éviter des obstacles non nécessaires au commerce. Chacune des parties devra ainsi s'efforcer de veiller à ce qu'une mesure relative à l'autorisation d'exercer et à la reconnaissance professionnelle soit basée sur des critères objectifs et transparents, tels la capacité d'offrir le service en question et la compétence professionnelle. De plus, une telle mesure devra ne pas imposer plus de difficultés qu'il n'est nécessaire pour assurer la qualité du service et ne pas constituer une restriction déguisée à la prestation du service.[34] Dans un autre ordre d'idées, une partie, bien que pouvant reconnaître les qualifications et les autorisations professionnelles obtenues sur le territoire d'une autre partie, ne sera pas obligée d'accorder cette reconnaissance à l'éducation, à l'expérience ou au titre professionnel obtenu dans une autre partie.[35] Dans les deux années suivant l'entrée en vigueur du présent Accord, chacune des parties devra, en outre, avoir éliminé toute exigence de citoyenneté ou de résidence permanente à un professionnel étranger qui voudrait exercer sur le territoire de l'une ou

---

[31] ALÉNA, *supra* note 1, art. 1302.

[32] ALÉNA, *supra* note 1, art. 1303. Notons que par services améliorés ou services à valeur ajoutée on entend des services de télécommunications faisant appel à certaines applications de traitement informatique modifiant les données. Il s'agit, à titre d'exemple, des services à valeur ajoutée de transmission, de stockage et de traitement des données à distance. *Ibid.* art. 1310. Par ailleurs, aucune partie ne pourra obliger une personne à fournir au public en général des services de télécommunications à valeur ajoutée ou à justifier ses tarifs pour ses services. *Ibid.* art. 1303(2).

[33] ALÉNA, *supra* note 1, art. 1305.

[34] ALÉNA, *supra* note 1, art. 1210(1).

[35] ALÉNA, *supra* note 1, art. 1210(2).

l'autre des parties.[36] Soulignons en terminant que les parties devront s'efforcer d'élaborer des normes et des critères mutuellement acceptables relativement à l'autorisation d'exercer et à la reconnaissance professionnelle.[37]

[36] ALÉNA, *supra* note 1, art. 1210(3). Si cette obligation n'est pas respectée, les autres parties pourront appliquer ou rétablir des conditions équivalentes dans le même secteur de services. *Ibid.*

[37] ALÉNA, *supra* note 1, annexe 1210.5(2).

II Le Canada et le système monétaire international en 1994

préparé par

BERNARD COLAS*

L'IMPORTANCE DES ORGANISATIONS FINANCIÈRES internationales n'est plus à démontrer. Cinquante ans après la création des institutions de Bretton Woods, elles jouissent d'une place centrale dans le système financier et monétaire international (I). Leur intervention s'inscrit de plus en plus dans une économie mondialisée, façonnée par les mesures de libéralisation prises en application notamment des accords de l'Organisation mondiale du commerce (OMC) et de l'Accord de libre-échange nord-américain (ALÉNA) (II). Les actions qu'elles mènent sont complétées des normes prudentielles adoptées principalement dans le cadre du Comité de Bâle sur le contrôle bancaire (III).

I Coopération monétaire et financière internationale

L'année 1994 marque le cinquantenaire de la Conférence de Bretton Woods (juillet 1944) et de la naissance de la Banque mondiale ainsi que du Fonds monétaire international (FMI). La commémoration de cet événement a donné lieu à de nombreuses manifestations et à une réflexion sur le rôle futur de ces institutions. Au Canada, elles furent la cible d'un vaste plan de réformes énoncé à l'issue de l'examen de la politique étrangère mené en 1994/95.[1] Ce plan propose que ces institutions financières inter-

---

* Avocat au Barreau du Québec, Docteur en droit, vice-président de la Société de droit international économique (SDIE).

---

[1] Rapport du *Comité mixte spécial chargé de l'examen de la politique étrangère du Canada: La politique étrangère du Canada: Principes et priorités pour l'avenir (1994)* et Chambre des communes du Canada, *De Bretton Woods à Halifax et au-delà: Vers un 21ᵉ sommet pour relever le défi du XXIᵉ siècle (1995)*.

nationales poursuivent une politique destinée à alléger la pauvreté, à favoriser le développement humain durable et à accroître la stabilité des marchés financiers et monétaires. Ces suggestions sont conformes à la position traditionnelle que prend le Canada particulièrement au sein des institutions financières internationales.[2]

Dans le cadre de la Banque mondiale, le Canada en 1994 a contribué à réapprovisionner le Fonds pour l'environnement mondial (FEM) et a continué à favoriser l'intégration des critères environnementaux dans les programmes de prêts. Ce Fonds, qui est le principal mécanisme de règlement des questions environnementales mondiales, vient de recevoir 2 milliards $US en prévision des débours pour les dix prochaines années, dont 111 millions $CAN du Canada. Par ailleurs, un Fonds de participation de 300 millions $US a été créé en 1994 (lequel a été réapprovisionné plus tard dans l'année d'un montant de 200 millions $US). Il sert à appuyer la participation des bénéficiaires dans la conception, la mise en oeuvre et le suivi des opérations de la Banque mondiale ainsi que les régions rurales participantes aux activités de prêts de la Banque.[3]

Au sein du FMI, des mesures ont été prises afin d'accroître son aide financière et de renforcer ses pouvoirs de surveillance. C'est à regret toutefois que les pays industrialisés et en développement n'ont pas réussi à s'entendre sur la Dixième révision générale des quotes-parts, qui s'est achevée en décembre 1994, ni sur une nouvelle allocation de droits de tirage spéciaux (DTS), laquelle aurait permis d'allouer des DTS à un grand nombre de membres, y compris la Russie, qui se sont joints au FMI depuis la dernière allocation en 1979.

En 1994, le FMI est parvenu à prolonger jusqu'au 30 avril 1995 la Facilité de transformation systémique (FTS), facilité créée en 1993 pour aider la Russie et d'autres pays à planification centrale à relever les défis que présente le passage à une économie de marché.[4] Le Canada a également appuyé le renouvellement de la Facilité d'ajustement structurel renforcé (FASR) convenue le 23 février

---

[2] Dans le cadre de la huitième augmentation générale des ressources de la Banque interaméricaine de développement (BID) complétée en 1994 (40 milliards $US), le Canada s'est déclaré satisfait que le soutien de la Banque aux programmes social et de lutte contre la pauvreté soit porté à 40 pour cent du total des prêts et à 50 pour cent du nombre des opérations. *Rapport annuel de la BID 1994* (1995) à la p. 9.

[3] *Rapport annuel de la Banque mondiale* (1995) à la p. 23.

[4] Cette facilité permet d'accorder une aide financière aux pays qui ont des problèmes de balance des paiements attribuables à une chute marquée des exportations ou à une hausse importante du coût de l'énergie importée.

1994. Il a en outre veillé à ce que cette facilité renouvelée consacre une plus grande attention aux filets de sécurité sociale et mette davantage l'accent sur la qualité des dépenses publiques. La contribution du Canada au FASR a consisté en un prêt de 200 millions DTS et en une aide sous forme de subvention de 60 millions DTS.[5]
Le Conseil des gouverneurs du FMI a en outre décidé de relever la limite annuelle d'accès des États membres au Compte des ressources générales du FMI de 68 pour cent à 100 pour cent de la quote-part, et ce pour une période de trois ans.[6] La limite cumulée reste inchangée, à 300 pour cent de la quote-part. Elle peut être toutefois exceptionnellement dépassée, comme l'atteste le montage financier approuvé en 1994/95 en faveur du Mexique. Le montage mexicain représente la plus importante aide jamais approuvée par le FMI en faveur d'un État membre, tant pour le montant que pour le pourcentage global de la quote-part.[7] Cette mesure a été prise afin de soutenir les autorités mexicaines dans l'application d'un programme d'ajustement vigoureux destiné à lutter contre une grave crise des marchés des capitaux et des changes.[8] Pour prévenir à l'avenir ce type de crise, il a été proposé de renforcer le pouvoir de surveillance du FMI sur les politiques de change.[9] Cela lui donnerait ainsi les moyens d'intervenir plus efficacement auprès de ses membres, qui voient la solidité de leur système financier menacée dans un contexte de libéralisation et de déréglementation.

II Libéralisation des services financiers

L'*Acte final reprenant les résultats des négociations commerciales multilatérales du Cycle d'Uruguay*, signé le 15 avril 1994 à Marrakech (Maroc), intègre pour la première fois dans un accord commercial au niveau mondial les échanges de services.[10] L'entente qui libéra-

---

5 Ministère des finances du Canada, *Rapport sur les opérations effectuées en vertu de la Loi sur les accords de Bretton Woods et des accords connexes 1994* (1995) à la p. 12.

6 *Rapport annuel du FMI* (1995) aux pp. 40-41.

7 Le 1er février 1995, le Mexique s'est vu accorder, à l'appui d'un programme économique et financier pour 1995-1996, un accord de confirmation de 12 milliards DTS, dont 5,3 milliards DTS ont été décaissés d'emblée, *op. cit.* aux pp. 132-33.

8 Pour une brève explication de la crise mexicaine, lire: *Rapport annuel de la BRI* (1995) à la p. 8.

9 *Rapport annuel du FMI* (1995) aux pp. 45-53.

10 GATT, *Résultats des négociations commerciales multilatérales du Cycle d'Uruguay: Textes juridiques* (1994).

lise ces échanges s'intitule "Accord général sur le commerce des services (GATS)" et comprend une annexe consacrée aux *services financiers*. Conformément à cet accord, le Canada a notamment accepté de supprimer les restrictions imposées aux étrangers relatives à la propriété d'institutions financières canadiennes. Ainsi la limite individuelle de 10 pour cent et la limite collective de 25 pour cent imposées jusqu'à maintenant à la propriété par des étrangers des institutions financières canadiennes régies en vertu des lois fédérales (les règles dites des 10/25) et la règle qui limitait à 12 pour cent la part de marché national aux banques étrangères ont été éliminées.

Des mesures semblables avaient été prises par le Canada en application de l'Accord de libre-échange Canada-États-Unis (ALÉ) et de l'Accord de libre-échange nord-américain (ALÉNA) (entré en vigueur le 1er janvier 1994)[11] sans que cela entraîne une augmentation importante de la propriété étrangère.[12] Encore aujourd'hui, les banques étrangères contrôlent environ 10 pour cent de l'actif des banques canadiennes.[13]

Cependant la limite de 10 pour cent imposée à toute personne en matière de propriété individuelle d'une banque de l'Annexe I est maintenue.[14] La loi sur les banques exige également des banques étrangères qui veulent s'établir au Canada qu'elles le fassent par le biais de l'incorporation d'une filiale canadienne — plutôt que d'une succursale — et qu'elles s'enregistrent en vertu de l'Annexe II.[15] L'approbation ministérielle est exigée lorsqu'une filiale d'une banque étrangère souhaite ouvrir plus d'une succursale. Ces mesures sont justifiées principalement pour des raisons prudentielles. Certaines poursuivent les mêmes objectifs que ceux fixés au niveau international par le Comité de Bâle sur le contrôle bancaire.[16]

---

[11] *Loi de mise en oeuvre de l'Accord de libre-échange nord-américain*, c. 115, sanctionnée le 23 juin 1993.

[12] E. Leroux, *Le libre-échange nord-américain et les services financiers* (Montréal: Éditions Yvon Blais, 1995) aux pp. 25-28, 101-04.

[13] D. Clarke, "Du GATT au GATS," *Le Banquier*, 1er octobre 1994 aux pp. 26-30.

[14] *Loi de mise en oeuvre de l'Accord sur l'Organisation mondiale du commerce*, c. 47, sanctionnée le 15 décembre 1994.

[15] M. H. Ogilvie, "The Legal Regulation of Foreign Banks Doing Business in Canada," (1991) 4 C.U.B.L.R. 39-62.

[16] Le Comité de Bâle sur le contrôle bancaire, auquel appartient le Canada, est un comité d'autorités de contrôle bancaire institué en 1975 par les gouverneurs des banques centrales des pays du Groupe des Dix [ci-après Comité de Bâle].

III Renforcement des règles prudentielles

L'Accord de 1988 sur les fonds propres,[17] élaboré par le Comité de Bâle, a fait l'objet en 1994/95 de nombreux amendements et propositions de modifications. Cet accord détermine un pourcentage de fonds propres (également connu sous le nom de *ratio Cook*) que les banques actives sur la scène internationale doivent respecter pour contenir les risques de crédit.

Cet accord a récemment été amendé. Les modifications adoptées en 1994 ont porté sur la reconnaissance de la *compensation bilatérale* dans l'évaluation du risque de crédit aux fins de l'adéquation des fonds propres.[18] À la satisfaction du secteur bancaire canadien, cet amendement laisse chaque autorité de tutelle nationale libre d'élaborer les procédures que les banques doivent suivre pour reconnaître la pleine validité juridique des accords de compensation. Le Comité de Bâle ne publiera aucune liste de conventions acceptables. Dans la mise en oeuvre de cet amendement, il veillera à promouvoir un processus de consultation entre autorités afin de faciliter le contrôle du respect des conditions prescrites.

Par ailleurs, il a été proposé de modifier la définition des *pays de l'OCDE* aux fins de calcul des exigences de fonds propres relatives aux créances transfrontières sur les administrations centrales et les banques. Sous réserve de consultations nationales, le groupe OCDE serait défini, à partir de 1995, comme "l'ensemble des membres actuels de l'OCDE ou des pays signataires des Accords généraux d'emprunt, à condition que ces pays n'aient pas rééchelonné leur dette extérieure souveraine dans les cinq années précédentes." Cette proposition d'amender l'Accord de 1988 fait suite à l'adhésion du Mexique à l'OCDE ainsi qu'à l'ouverture de négociations d'adhésion avec des pays en transition dont la stabilité financière

---

17 *Convergence de la mesure et des normes de fonds propres* (1988), Bâle [ci-après *Accord de 1988*].

18 Comité de Bâle sur le contrôle bancaire, *Accord de Bâle sur les fonds propres: Traitement du risque de crédit lié à certains instruments de hors-bilan* (1994). Ce document soumettait à consultation deux autres propositions visant à reconnaître les effets de la compensation dans le calcul des majorations de fonds propres relatives au risque de crédit potentiel futur lié à certains instruments hors-bilan; et à élargir le tableau des facteurs de majoration relatifs à ces risques figurant dans l'*Accord de 1988*, afin de mieux rendre compte du risque de crédit potentiel explicitement couvertes dans l'Accord. Ces propositions ont été intégrées à l'Accord de 1988 en 1995; voir: Comité de Bâle sur le contrôle bancaire, *Accord de Bâle sur les fonds propres: traitement du risque potentiel lié aux instruments de hors-bilan* (1995).

n'est pas suffisamment fiable[19] pour pouvoir bénéficier de coeffi-
cients de pondération différenciés. En vertu des dispositions de
l'Accord de 1988, les prêts accordés à des pays de l'OCDE sont
considérés suffisamment sûrs qu'ils n'ont pas à entrer dans le calcul
des 8 pour cent de fonds propres requis.[20]

Le Comité de Bâle a également proposé d'étendre l'Accord de
1988 aux *risques de marché*.[21] Ces risques sont définis comme "les
risques de pertes sur des positions du bilan et du hors-bilan résultant de variations des prix du marché."[22] Ils couvrent les risques
relatifs aux titres de créance et de propriété du portefeuille de
négociation ainsi que le risque de change et le risque sur produits
de base pour l'ensemble de la banque. Conformément à cette
proposition, les banques seraient tenues de mesurer ces risques de
marché et de leur appliquer des exigences de fonds propres,
comme cela est le cas pour les risques de crédit. Le compromis
élaboré pour l'évaluation de ces risques de marché se rapproche de
la position exprimée par les banques canadiennes. L'amendement
proposé permettrait aux banques d'utiliser leur propre modèle
interne, sous réserve du respect de certaines conditions et de
l'approbation des autorités de contrôle nationales, plutôt que de
recourir uniquement à un dispositif standardisé comme cela avait
précédemment été suggéré.[23] Le Comité a reconnu, après analyse,
la fiabilité des modèles internes des banques pour mesurer les
risques de marché.[24]

---

[19] B. Colas, *L'Organisation de coopération et de développement économiques et l'évolution du droit international de l'économie et de l'environnement* (1995), Thèse de doctorat, Université de Paris I aux pp. 127-37.

[20] Les créances relatives aux administrations centrales et aux banques centrales des pays de l'OCDE reçoivent une pondération de 0 pour cent et les créances, autres que les instruments de fonds propres à l'égard des banques de pays de l'OCDE, reçoivent une pondération de 20 pour cent.

[21] Comité de Bâle sur le contrôle bancaire, *Projet d'extension de l'accord sur les fonds propres aux risques de marché*, Proposition soumise à consultation (1995). Voir: Canada, *Rapport annuel du Bureau du surintendant des institutions financières 1994-1995* (1995) à la, p. 11.

[22] *Projet d'extension*, *supra* note 21 à la p. 1.

[23] Cet amendement fait suite aux propositions diffusées en avril 1993. À ce sujet, voir B. Colas, "Chronique de droit international économique" (1994) 32 A.C.D.I. 293-95.

[24] Comité de Bâle sur le contrôle bancaire, *Exigences de fonds propres pour les risques de marché: Approche fondée sur les modèles internes*, Proposition soumise à consultation (1995).

Enfin, après de nombreuses années de discussions, le Comité de Bâle et le Comité technique de l'Organisation internationale des commissions de valeurs (OICV) sont finalement parvenus à adopter des principes de base équivalents sur la saine gestion des risques dans les activités sur *instruments dérivés*.[25] Remarquant que les activités des banques et maisons de titres sur instruments dérivés donnent lieu à des risques comparables, ces organismes ont chacun diffusé le 27 juillet 1994 des lignes directrices pour la gestion des risques liés aux instruments dérivés.[26] Soulignons également la publication d'un rapport sur la surveillance prudentielle des conglomérats financiers, préparé conjointement par le Comité de Bâle, l'OICV et l'Association internationale des responsables de la surveillance de l'activité d'assurance (IAIS).[27]

Ainsi, la mondialisation des marchés financiers génère de nouveaux risques auxquels les organismes internationaux, tant publics que privés, s'efforcent de répondre. Les initiatives prises en 1994/95 sont nombreuses. Elles marquent un renforcement et un élargissement de la coopération internationale destinée à assurer la stabilité du système bancaire et financier et à étendre les bénéfices de la libéralisation des échanges.

[25] Comité de Bâle sur le contrôle bancaire, *Lignes directrices pour la gestion des risques liés aux instruments dérivés* (1994). Ces principes prévoient notamment le suivi approprié par le conseil d'administration et la direction générale de l'établissement, un processus adéquat de gestion des risques comportant en permanence la mesure, la surveillance et le contrôle des risques, des systèmes d'information de la direction précis et fiables, une notification en temps opportun à la direction et des procédures détaillées d'audit et de contrôle.

[26] *International Organization of Securities Commissions: Annual Report 1994* (1995) à la p. 7.

[27] *The Supervision of Financial Conglomerates: A Report by the Tripartite Group of Bank, Securities and Insurance Regulators*, Bâle (1995).

III Investissement

préparé par

PIERRE RATELLE*

E n 1994, le paysage juridique canadien a été le théâtre d'un
événement majeur qui a éclipsé tous les autres.[1] Il s'agit de
l'entrée en vigueur, le 1er janvier, des dispositions en matière
d'investissement de l'Accord de libre-échange nord-américain
(ALÉNA).[2]

I Entrée en vigueur de l'ALÉNA

A dispositions en matière d'investissement

Les dispositions de l'ALÉNA en matière d'investissement sont
regroupées principalement dans le chapitre 11. Ce chapitre est

---

* Avocat au Barreau de Montréal spécialisé en droit des affaires internationales,
Docteur en droit international économique de l'Université de Paris I (Panthéon-Sorbonne), Chargé de cours en droit international public et en droit
commercial international aux départements des Sciences juridiques, de la Gestion et des Sciences politiques de l'Université du Québec à Montréal (UQAM).

---

1 On peut citer notamment: (1) la *Loi portant mise en oeuvre de l'Accord instituant
l'Organisation mondiale du commerce*, S.C. 1994, c. 47, entrée en vigueur le 1er
janvier 1995, et qui inclut, en particulier, l'Accord sur les mesures d'investissement liées au commerce de l'Acte final de l'Uruguay Round du GATT; (2)
l'*Accord entre le gouvernement du Canada et le gouvernement de l'Ukraine pour l'encouragement et la protection des investissements*, signé à Ottawa, le 24 octobre 1994.

2 Voir *Loi portant mise en oeuvre de l'Accord de libre-échange nord-américain*, S.C. 1993,
c. 44. Ci-après "Loi de mise en oeuvre de l'ALÉNA." Pour un compte-rendu
plus exhaustif, d'un point de vue canadien, concernant les dispositions
d'ALÉNA en matière d'investissement, et reprend en paine cette chronique,
voir Ministère des Affaires Extérieures, *Ènoncé canadien demise en oeuvre de
l'ALÉNA* dans Gaz. c. 1er janv. 1994. I. 147-60.

divisé en deux parties: A (Dispositions générales) et B (Règlement des différends entre une Partie et un investisseur de l'autre Partie).

a Dispositions générales

Aux termes de l'article 1101, la partie A vise toute mesure prise par une Partie (c'est-à-dire pour le Canada, tout palier gouvernemental) et agissant sur: (1) les investisseurs d'une autre Partie (soit les sociétés-mères ou particuliers mexicains ou américains); (2) les investissements effectués par les investisseurs d'une autre Partie (filiales ou éléments d'actifs situés au Canada); et (3) pour les fins des dispositions concernant les prescriptions de résultats et les mesures environnementales, tous les investissements effectués au Canada. Les mesures visées par le chapitre 14 (Services financiers) échappent à la portée de la partie A.

L'article 1101 confirme le droit de chaque Partie d'exercer des fonctions (par exemple, l'exécution des lois) et d'assurer des services comme la sécurité sociale et les services de santé. Il confère également au Mexique l'exercice exclusif des activités économiques énumérées à l'annexe III, soit celles qui relèvent du domaine public en vertu de la constitution mexicaine. Par contre, les investissements qu'autorisent les autorités mexicaines dans ces secteurs (par marché de services, entente de partage de production ou autrement) sont assujettis aux dispositions de l'ALÉNA. Certains articles instaurent des dérogations supplémentaires; l'article 1108, entre autres, prévoit que l'obligation du traitement national ne s'applique pas aux subventions.

L'article 1102 précise l'obligation fondamentale des gouvernements, qui est d'accorder le traitement national aux investisseurs et aux investissements dans l'établissement, l'acquisition, l'expansion, la direction, l'exploitation, la vente ou autre aliénation de ceux-ci. Dans cet article, il est expliqué que le traitement national interdit aux Parties d'exiger d'un investisseur d'une autre Partie qu'il accorde à ses ressortissants une participation minimale dans l'entreprise en cause et d'obliger, en raison de sa nationalité, à vendre son investissement. Les investisseurs étrangers sont donc assurés de bénéficier des mêmes avantages que les intervenants intérieurs, lors de l'établissement comme par la suite.

L'article 1103 stipule que chaque Partie accordera aux investisseurs d'une autre Partie un traitement non moins favorable que celui qu'elle accorde aux investissements provenant d'un pays tiers.

L'article 1104 précise en outre l'obligation d'accorder le traitement national ou, s'il est plus avantageux, celui de la nation la plus favorisée.

L'article 1105 ajoute que le traitement accordé doit être conforme au droit international. Cette précision a pour but de garantir une norme minimale de traitement aux investisseurs originaires des pays signataires. Chaque Partie est également tenue de s'abstenir de toute discrimination dans la compensation de pertes résultant d'un conflit armé ou d'une guerre civile. Le dernier paragraphe de l'article institue cependant une exception précisément circonscrite qui exempte les programmes de subvention existants de l'obligation relative au traitement national.

L'article 1106 interdit l'imposition ou l'application de diverses prescriptions de résultat (pourcentage d'exportations, contenu national, etc.) en ce qui concerne l'établissement, l'acquisition, l'expansion, la gestion, la direction ou l'exploitation d'un investissement. Il interdit également aux Parties de subordonner à ces prescriptions l'octroi d'avantages (subventions, incitatifs fiscaux, etc.), de privilégier la production intérieure et de relier l'accès à leur marché à la valeur des exportations. Ces contraintes ne valent pas dans le cas de subventions accordées en retour d'installation d'usine de production à un endroit désigné, de la prestation d'un service, de la formation ou de l'embauche de travailleurs, de l'érection ou de l'agrandissement d'installation ou de l'exécution de travaux de recherche et de développement. L'article ne limite pas le recours à diverses mesures (notamment de protection de l'environnement) exigeant un contenu national donné ou favorisant les biens ou services d'origine intérieure, à la condition qu'elles ne soient pas appliquées de façon arbitraire, ni ne constituent une restriction déguisée au commerce ou à l'investissement international. Les mesures indispensables à la protection de la vie et de la santé des personnes et des animaux et à la préservation des végétaux sont expressément permises.

L'article 1107 interdit aux Parties d'imposer quelque exigence de nationalité que ce soit à l'égard des dirigeants en ce qui concerne les investissements effectués par des investisseurs d'une autre Partie. Cette disposition permet donc à ces investisseurs d'embaucher les personnes de leur choix (dans le respect des lois intérieures régissant l'immigration). Par contre, une Partie peut exiger que la majorité des membres du conseil d'administration soit recrutée parmi ses propres citoyens ou résidents, à la condition que cette exigence ne compromette pas de façon importante la capacité de l'investisseur à contrôler son investissement.[3]

Les articles 1102, 1103 et 1107 ne s'appliquent pas aux marchés publics et aux subventions.

L'article 1108 énumère les exceptions admises à l'égard des obligations prescrites dans les articles 1102 (TN), 1103 (TNP), 1106 (Prescriptions de résultat) et 1107 (dirigeants et conseils d'administration). Il établit également la relation entre la présente partie et les annexes I, II, III et IV.

L'annexe I dresse la liste des mesures qui, actuellement, ne répondent pas aux exigences des articles 1102, 1103, 1106 et 1007. Aucune de ces mesures ne peut désormais devenir plus contraignante; toute mesure de libéralisation devient en outre définitive. On peut voir, dans la même annexe, la liste de mesures fédérales que chaque État désire voir maintenues. Les mesures non conformes des États ou des provinces seront exemptées les deux années qui suivront l'entrée en vigueur de l'ALÉNA, soit jusqu'au 1er janvier 1996. Après cette période, seules seront reconduites celles qui figurent à l'annexe I. Les mesures prises par des administrations locales peuvent aussi être maintenues sans être inscrites à l'annexe I.

Toutes les mesures existantes non conformes du gouvernement fédéral du Canada bénéficient d'une clause d'antériorité et sont inscrites à l'annexe I. Toutes les mesures américaines non conformes du gouvernement fédéral américain bénéficient également d'une clause d'antériorité et sont inscrites à l'annexe I. Le Mexique, pour sa part, a fait inscrire à la même annexe les mesures considérables qu'il entend prendre pour libéraliser sa réglementation relative aux investissements. Il s'engage notamment à hausser sensiblement les seuils d'examen des prises de contrôle étrangères, à réduire ou à supprimer de nombreuses contraintes sectorielles à l'investissement étranger et à éliminer graduellement ses prescriptions de résultat qui nuisent au libre exercice du commerce.

---

[3] À titre d'exemple, au Canada, la *Loi sur les sociétés par actions*, L.R.C. 1985, c. C-44, prescrit que le conseil d'administration des sociétés constituées en vertu des lois fédérales soit en majorité simple composé de résidents canadiens; dans certains secteurs réglementés (par exemple les services aériens), la proportion peut être encore plus élevée. L'annexe I de l'ALÉNA garantit le maintien de ces exigences. Dans la liste canadienne ajoutée à cette dernière, on précise que le Canada conserve le droit d'imposer des contraintes à la propriété étrangère et d'exiger la présence d'une proportion donnée de citoyens et de résidents canadiens parmi les dirigeants et le conseil d'administration de société et d'actifs publics et privatisés.

À l'annexe II, on retrouve les secteurs et activités à l'égard desquels les mesures non conformes actuelles et futures échappent à la
portées des articles 1102, 1103, 1106 et 1107.[4] À cet égard, l'interdiction d'exiger la vente d'investissements existants pour des raisons de nationalité reste totale.

L'annexe III dresse la liste des secteurs relevant exclusivement du
domaine public en vertu de la constitution mexicaine et précise les
dispositions applicables au Mexique dans la privatisation des
sociétés d'États.[5]

L'annexe IV précise les exceptions admises à l'article 1103
(TNP); y figurent notamment toutes les ententes bilatérales et
multilatérales déjà conclues, ainsi que les projets d'ententes concernant l'aviation, la pêche, les questions maritimes et les télécommunications.

L'article 1109 oblige chacune des Parties à permettre que soient
effectués librement et sans retard tous les transferts se rapportant à
un investissement (bénéfices, remboursements de prêts, liquida-
tions, etc.). Il interdit par ailleurs à un gouvernement de forcer le
rapatriement de capitaux, mais prévoit des exceptions relatives à
l'application des lois de nature générale, par exemple celles qui ont
trait à la faillite ou au négoce des valeurs mobilières.[6]

En vertu de l'article 1110, aucune des Parties ne peut exproprier
un investissement effectué par un investisseur d'une autre Partie,
sauf pour une raison d'intérêt public, sur une base non discriminatoire, en conformité avec l'application régulière de la loi et moyen-

---

4 Les secteurs choisis par le Canada sont les suivants: affaires autochtones, propriété foncière exclusivement réservée aux résidents le long des littoraux
océaniques, télécommunications, obligations gouvernementales, affaires des
minorités ethniques, services sociaux (y compris la sécurité ou la garantie des
revenus, la sécurité et l'assurance sociale, le bien-être social, l'éducation publique, la formation publique, la santé et la garde des enfants), services aériens
spécialisés, cabotage et, dans le domaine maritime, droit d'imposer des mesures
équivalentes aux mesures américaines.

5 Le Mexique conserve le droit d'imposer à la propriété étrangère les contraintes
établies lors de l'autorisation de l'investissement intérieur. Dans les secteurs
ouverts aux intérêts privés entre le 1er janvier 1992 et l'entrée en vigueur de
l'ALÉNA, il peut également limiter la participation étrangère dans la première
acquisition, mais pour un maximum de trois ans. Les dispositions de l'art. 1108
interviendront au rythme de la libéralisation des politiques mexicaines; ainsi,
dès qu'un secteur s'ouvre à la propriété étrangère, aucune contrainte ne pourra
être remise en place; de même, toute exception devrait être inscrite à l'annexe I.

6 Il est à noter que l'article 2104 de l'ALÉNA institue une autre exception, bien
circonscrite, à l'égard de problèmes relatifs à la balance des paiements.

nant le versement d'une indemnité. Celle-ci doit équivaloir à la juste valeur marchande de l'investissement, additionnée d'intérêts calculés selon un taux commercial raisonnable. Si elle n'est pas versée dans une devise du Groupe des Sept, elle doit être établie de manière à tenir compte de toute fluctuation du taux de change entre la date de l'expropriation et celle du paiement. L'article ne s'applique pas à la délivrance de licences obligatoires, ni à l'annulation, à la limitation ou à la création de droits de propriété intellectuelle, pour autant que soient respectées les dispositions du chapitre 17 (Propriété intellectuelle).

L'article 1111 permet aux Parties de prescrire des formalités spéciales, notamment en ce qui concerne la constitution légale des investisseurs, à la condition que ces formalités ne réduisent pas sensiblement les protections accordées par le chapitre. Il autorise également les Parties à demander à un investisseur d'une autre Partie de fournir à l'égard de son investissement des renseignements d'usage qui ne serviront qu'à des fins de statistique.

En cas d'incompatibilité entre le chapitre traitant de l'investissement et les autres chapitres de l'ALÉNA, l'article 1112 fait en sorte que ces derniers prévalent dans la mesure de l'incompatibilité et, en conséquence, que leurs dispositions particulières aient priorité sur les clauses plus générales du chapitre 11.[7]

L'article 1113 permet à une Partie de refuser d'accorder les avantages conférés par le chapitre à un investissement provenant d'une entreprise d'une autre Partie, quand cette entreprise est contrôlée par des investisseurs originaires d'un pays non signataire de l'ALÉNA, avec lesquels la Partie qui refuse d'accorder les avantages n'entretient pas de relations diplomatiques ou à l'égard duquel elle adopte ou maintient des mesures qui interdisent les transactions commerciales ou qui seraient contournées si les avantages étaient accordés. Une Partie peut également refuser d'accorder ces avantages à des investissements "fantômes," c'est-à-dire en l'absence d'une activité commerciale importante dans un pays signataire.

Le premier paragraphe de l'article 1114 stipule que chaque Partie est en droit d'adopter des mesures de protection de l'environnement et de les faire appliquer, sous réserve qu'elles soient

---

[7] Si, par exemple, une Partie oblige un fournisseur de services d'une autre Partie à verser un cautionnement avant de pouvoir fournir un service sur son territoire, le c. 11 s'appliquera au cautionnement, mais non à la fourniture de ce service transfrontière.

conformes aux dispositions du chapitre, c'est-à-dire mises en oeuvre sur la base du TN. Le second paragraphe s'intéresse à la laxité des politiques de lutte à la pollution. Les Parties s'y engagent à reconnaître qu'il n'est pas approprié d'encourager l'investissement en assouplissant les mesures nationales qui se rapportent à la santé, à la sécurité ou à l'environnement, en y renonçant ou en y dérogeant. La Partie qui estime qu'une autre Partie a offert un tel encouragement pourra demander la tenue de consultations.

Aux termes de l'article 1139, le terme "investissement" porte les participations minoritaires, les placements de portefeuille et les biens immobiliers au même rang que les mises de fonds procurant un intérêt majoritaire, que leur auteur soit canadien, américain ou mexicain. Alors que l'Accord de libre-échange Canada-États-Unis[8] ne visait que leurs investissements réciproques, l'ALÉNA s'appliquera à tous ceux que réalisent des sociétés constituées dans les pays signataires, de quelque origine qu'elles soient.

b Règlement des différends entre une Partie et un investisseur de l'autre Partie

La partie B du chapitre 11 de l'ALÉNA, soit les articles 1115 et 1138, propose aux investisseurs privés, qui se trouvent en conflit avec une Partie autre que celle dont ils sont originaires, des mécanismes d'arbitrage en vue du règlement du litige.

Toutefois, ni ces mécanismes, ni la procédure "gouvernement-à-gouvernement" décrite au chapitre 20 de l'ALÉNA ne peuvent être utilisés à l'égard des décisions prises en vertu de la *Loi sur Investissement Canada*[9] ou par la Commission nationale mexicaine d'examen de l'investissement étranger (*Comisión Nacional de Inversiones Extranjeras*).

B MODIFICATIONS À LA LÉGISLATION CANADIENNE

Comme nous venons de le voir, le chapitre 11 permet au Canada de conserver les mesures existantes non conformes inscrites à la liste qu'il a fait insérer dans l'annexe I. Le Canada convient par ailleurs: (1) d'étendre à tous les pays signataires de l'ALÉNA (c'est-à-dire le Mexique) les avantages consentis aux États-Unis en vertu de l'Accord de libre-échange Canada-États-Unis (ALÉ); (2) d'étendre à tous les pays signataires de l'ALÉNA (c'est-à-dire le Mexique)

8 S.C. 1988, c. 65.
9 S.C. 1985, c. 20.

la portée de l'engagement qu'il a pris dans le cadre de l'ALÉ de ne pas soumettre les acquisitions indirectes à l'examen; et (3) d'élever le facteur d'indexation de manière à tenir compte, à compter de 1995, de la croissance économique réelle aussi bien que de l'inflation.

L'article 2006 de l'ALÉNA et l'annexe 2106 (Industries culturelles) précisent que, sous réserve de l'article 302 (Élimination des droits de douane), les industries culturelles seront, pour ce qui concerne le Canada et les États-Unis et pour les fins de l'ALÉNA, assujetties aux dispositions de l'ALÉ et que ces dispositions s'appliqueront entre le Canada et toutes les autres Parties de l'ALÉNA. Les passages du chapitre 11 qui visent l'investissement ne s'appliquent donc pas aux industries culturelles canadiennes. En conformité de l'article 179 de la Loi de mise en oeuvre de l'ALÉNA, l'article 24 de la *Loi sur Investissement Canada* (LIC)[10] est modifié de manière à permettre l'entrée en vigueur de l'article 2106 et de l'annexe 2106 de l'ALÉNA concernant les industries culturelles. L'ALÉ obligeait le Canada a acquérir à sa juste valeur marchande toute entreprise culturelle acquise indirectement par un investisseur américain et dont celui-ci devait se départir à la suite d'un examen en vertu de la LIC. Un nouvel article de la LIC fait écho à cette obligation et en étend la portée à tout investissement d'une Partie de l'ALÉNA.

L'article 178 de la Loi de mise en oeuvre de l'ALÉNA énumère les modifications apportées à la LIC. Cet article corrige la formule d'indexation du seuil d'examen des acquisitions directes, étend à tous les investisseurs des Parties signataires les avantages inhérents à la hausse de ce seuil et à l'affranchissement des acquisitions indirectes de la procédure d'examen et définit les termes connexes. Les modifications permettent aussi au gouvernement de se porter acquéreur d'une entreprise culturelle dont un investisseur d'une Partie à l'ALÉNA pourrait être forcé de se départir; cette clause figurait déjà dans l'ALÉ et l'ALÉNA en étend la portée à toutes les Parties signataires. Les modifications entraînant la hausse des seuils visent particulièrement les articles 14.1 et 14.2. Elles créent également l'article 14.3, qui suspend l'application des articles 14.1 et 14.2 (qui établissent la relation entre la LIC et l'ALÉ) tant que l'ALÉNA restera en vigueur.

___

10 *Supra* note 9.

La *Loi sur l'arbitrage commercial* (LAC)[11] permet l'application des Règles d'arbitrage de la CNUDCI et réglemente les arbitrages commerciaux, notamment en ce qui concerne la révision judiciaire et la mise en oeuvre des sentences, quand la Couronne, du chef du Canada, en est une des parties intéressées. L'article 50 de la Loi de mise en oeuvre de l'ALÉNA modifie l'article 5 de la LAC de manière à en assurer l'application dans les litiges soumis à l'arbitrage en vertu de l'ALÉNA.

[11] L.R.C. 1985, c. 17 (2e Suppl.).

Canadian Practice in International Law / La pratique canadienne en matière de droit international public

At the Department of Foreign Affairs in 1994-95 / Au ministère des Affaires étrangères en 1994-95

compiled by / préparé par
PHILIPPE KIRSCH*

ARMED CONFLICT

Detentions and Hostages

In a memorandum dated June 2, 1995, the Legal Bureau wrote:

Two aspects of the recent events in Bosnia-Herzegovina raise legal questions. These are the legality of: (i) the hostage-takings and other acts and threats by the Bosnian Serb forces; and (ii) the detention of members of the Bosnian Serb forces as "prisoners of war" (POWs) by United Nations peacekeepers.

The taking of United Nations peacekeepers as hostages and the use of the peacekeepers as human shields are prohibited under conventional and customary international law, irrespective of whether the conflict is international or internal in character.

* Philippe Kirsch, Legal Adviser, Department of Foreign Affairs and International Trade, Ottawa. The extracts from official correspondence contained in this survey have been made available by courtesy of the Department of Foreign Affairs and International Trade. Some of the correspondence from which extracts are given was provided for the general guidance of the enquirer in relation to specific facts that are often not described in full in the extracts within this compilation. The statements of law and practice should not necessarily be regarded as a definitive statement by the Department of Foreign Affairs and International Trade of that law or practice.

These crimes are punishable under customary international law and the Geneva Conventions by states on whose territories the offenders are found and by the International Criminal Tribunal for the Former Yugoslavia (the Yugoslav Tribunal) which has jurisdiction to prosecute war crimes and crimes against humanity, including the offences committed by the Bosnian Serb forces.

As the United Nations peacekeepers in Bosnia-Herzegovina are not combatants, they should avoid characterizing Bosnian Serb detainees as POWs. By characterizing them as POWs, the peacekeepers weaken the position of the United Nations that the peacekeepers are neutral nonparties to the conflict.

(1) *Obligations of the Parties to the Conflict*

In 1991 and subsequently, the six Republics of the former Federal Republic of Yugoslavia signed a series of accords under the auspices of the International Committee of the Red Cross in which they agreed to apply the concepts of international humanitarian law to the conflict in Croatia, and later in Bosnia-Herzegovina. Subsequently, the parties to the conflict in Bosnia-Herzegovina also agreed to be bound by international humanitarian law, including provisions of the Geneva Conventions and Additional Protocol I.

In addition, the Security Council has stated in its resolutions that the Geneva Conventions apply to the situation in the former Yugoslavia and the International Criminal Tribunal for the former Yugoslavia has, as its subject matter jurisdiction, "grave breaches" of the Geneva Conventions, as well as other laws and customs of war. The latter, in our view, includes provisions of Additional Protocols I and II of the Geneva Conventions. Finally, the fundamental guarantees set out in the Geneva Conventions and Additional Protocol 1, including prohibitions against murder, torture and hostage-taking, have been recognized as forming part of customary international law and are, therefore, binding on all the parties to the conflict.

The Bosnian Serb forces are "dissident" or "unorganized" armed forces and do not represent a recognized government or state. As such, they cannot formally become a Party to the Geneva Conventions. In addition, Bosnian Serb representatives have recently "renounced" all agreements and United Nations resolutions related to the conflict. Consequently, the obligations that apply most clearly to the Bosnian Serb forces are those recognized as customary international law.

(2) *Rights and Obligations of the United Nations Peacekeepers*

United Nations peacekeepers in general, and the peacekeepers currently in Bosnia-Herzegovina in particular, are neither combatants nor civilians. They have a *sui generis* status and are not *specifically* covered under the Geneva Conventions. That said, there is a strong argument that certain general provisions of the Geneva Conventions offer peacekeepers international protection. As there is some uncertainty about whether the conflict in Bosnia-Herzegovina is international or internal in character, we discuss below the possible protection afforded peacekeepers under both regimes.

(a) International armed conflict

If the conflict in Bosnia-Herzegovina is international in character, the United Nations peacekeepers are likely protected under Additional Protocol I of the Geneva Conventions (*Protection of Victims of International Armed Conflict*), in particular, under the provision on fundamental guarantees set out in Article 75. This provision, which, in our view, represents customary international law, provides as follows:

(1) [P]ersons who are in the power of a Party to the conflict and who do not benefit from more favourable treatment under the Conventions or under this Protocol shall be treated humanely in all circumstances and shall enjoy, as a minimum, the protection provided by this Article[.]

(2) The following acts are and shall remain prohibited at any time and in any place whatsoever, whether committed by civilian or military agents:

(a) violence to the life, health or physical or mental well-being of persons, in particular:

(i) murder

(ii) torture of all kinds, whether physical or mental . . .

(b) outrages upon personal dignity, in particular humiliating and degrading treatment . . .

(c) the taking of hostages . . .

(e) threats to commit any of the foregoing acts.

As these guarantees are available to all persons who are in the power of a party to a conflict and who do not benefit from more favourable treatment under the Conventions or under Protocol I, they would apply to the United Nations peacekeepers currently being detained. The activities in question, i.e., the hostage-taking and detention of the peacekeepers, as well as the threats against them and the fact that they are/ were being used as human shields, are in violation of a number of these guarantees. In particular, they violate sub-paragraphs 2 (b) (outrages upon personal dignity) and (c) (the taking of hostages) and are likely in violation of sub-paragraphs 2 (a) (ii) (torture) and 2 (e) (threat to commit murder and corporal punishment).

Therefore, notwithstanding that (a) the Bosnian Serbs, as a dissident armed force, are not, strictly speaking, bound by the obligations in Additional Protocol I; (b) that they have denounced any agreements they had previously entered into with the United Nations; and (c) that they take the position that the United Nations is not neutral and that the peacekeepers are POWs, it is clear that their actions involve fundamental breaches of international law.

(b) Non-international armed conflict

If the conflict was internal in character, Protocol II (Protection of Victims of Non-International Armed Conflict) and Common Article 3 of the Geneva Conventions would apply.

Both Protocol II (Article 4) and Common Article 3 state that persons taking no active part in the hostilities are protected against, *inter alia*, the taking of hostages, outrages upon personal dignity and violence to life and person, in particular, murder, mutilation, cruel treatment and torture.

Quite clearly, the hostage-taking and threats by the Bosnian Serb forces against the United Nations peacekeepers in Bosnia-Herzegovina contravene these provisions. . . .

Breaches of the obligations referred to above are war crimes at customary international law and, as such, are punishable in the state where an offender is found. If that state cannot or will not punish the accused, it may extradite the accused to a state that is in a position to do so. In addition, the Yugoslav Tribunal, established by United Nations Security Counsel resolution in 1993, has jurisdiction to prosecute war crimes and crimes against humanity, including the types of offences committed by the Bosnian Serb forces referred to above. The Office of the Prosecutor of the Tribunal has indicated that it is investigating Bosnian Serb leaders Karadzic and Mladic in connection with the Bosnian Serb actions in question.

The *United Nations Convention on the Safety of United Nations and Associated Personnel*, which was adopted by the General Assembly by consensus in December 1994, obliges states parties to prosecute, or to extradite to another state that is prepared to prosecute, persons responsible for ordering or carrying out attacks against United Nations peacekeepers. The taking of United Nations peacekeepers as hostages and using them as human shields would fall clearly within the definition of crimes under the Convention. Unfortunately, the Convention is not yet in force and is unlikely to be for at least a year. . . .

The taking of hostages and torture, mental or physical, of detainees is clearly contrary to international humanitarian law. This is true whether the armed conflict in question is international or non-international in character. The prohibition applies whether the victims are civilians, combatants or United Nations peacekeepers. As a result, by taking peacekeepers as hostages and using them as human shields, the Bosnian Serb forces have violated international law. Such actions are punishable by states on whose territory the accused are found under customary international provisions on war crimes and by the Yugoslav Tribunal.

Terrorism

In a memorandum dated March 16, 1995, the Legal Bureau wrote:

(2) There is no definition of "terrorism" in international law, customary or treaty-made; there are only examples of acts amounting to terrorism. Those agreements which have actually set out to identify acts which are terrorist in nature have only addressed specific manifestations of the phenomenon, rather than trying to set out criteria by which any acts might be adjudged as terrorist or not terrorist. Examples of recent agreements that address specific manifestations of terrorism are: the Convention on Offences Committed Aboard Aircraft; the Convention on the Suppression of the Unlawful Seizure of Aircraft; the Convention Against the Taking of Hostages; and the Convention for the Suppression of Unlawful Acts Against the Safety of Maritime Navigation.

(3) The most recent attempt, in an international forum, to address the issue of international terrorism came during the 49th Session of the United Nations General Assembly, which adopted, without a vote, a "Declaration on Measures to Eliminate International Terrorism" (resolution 49/60). Terrorism was not defined; however, "criminal acts intended or calculated to provoke a state of terror in the general public, a group of persons, or particular persons for political purposes" were declared unjustifiable. This language is similar, though not identical, to that used by a number of learned authors to define terrorism.

(4) The United Nations Declaration made reference to the 1937 Convention on the Prevention and Punishment of Terrorism, the most determined attempt by the international community to date to define terrorism comprehensively. The Convention never came into force, however, as only one State ratified it.

(5) In part, the failure of the international community to address the issue in a decisive manner stems from competing and often contradictory interests: e.g., the peaceful resolution of disputes, on the one hand, and the right to self-determination or national liberation, on the other. The problem has often been stated in the following way: "One man's terrorist is another man's freedom fighter."

(6) Learned authors do not agree on the essential elements of terrorism. The creation or attempt to create fear or terror seems to be present in most attempts to define terrorist acts. Whether those directly affected or a wider group must be the targets of the terror, whether the violence must be systematic or can be random, and the nature of the acts of violence themselves continue to be disputed.

(7) In the absence of an internationally accepted definition of terrorism, the categorisation of an act, not otherwise enumerated in an international agreement as an act of terrorism, becomes more of a political statement than a legally maintainable charge. . . .

(8) The aforementioned conventions deal only with acts committed by individuals or by groups, not with acts of states or with the acts of individuals or groups acting in an official capacity on behalf of states. Indeed, given the requirement under many of those agreements that parties prosecute or extradite terrorists, it is inconceivable that a state's actions could be covered by them. The position that states cannot commit acts of international terrorism, as opposed to sponsoring such acts, is widely supported in the legal literature. It is worth noting, however, that the United Nations Declaration on Terrorism, in a preambular paragraph, refers to "acts of international terrorism . . . in which states are directly or indirectly involved". While the Declaration neither defines "terrorism" nor "directly involved," it may be an indication of support for the idea that states can commit acts of international terrorism directly.

(9) The emphasis on the individual is a reflection of the fact that the international law on terrorism has flowed from that of piracy. Attempts to expand the application of measures against terrorism to include acts by governments, such as the Saudi Arabian proposal to have the Convention for the Suppression of Unlawful Acts Against the Safety of Maritime Navigation include State acts, have been rejected. . . .

(10) Under customary international law "state terrorism" — that is, acts committed by government officials in the course of their duties — referred only to acts directed against the population of the state. There was no international dimension to the problem. Efforts to expand this definition to include objectionable acts taken by states on the international level — e.g., coercive diplomacy — have not found acceptance. (11) Increasingly, the phrase "state-sponsored terrorism" has come into use. By definition, however, the state must act through a third party. The state sponsors or aids the terrorist but does not involve itself in the terrorist acts in an official capacity. The extent of state involvement may be substantial but, in the end, it can amount to no more than "surrogate warfare." Sanctions under international law would be directed primarily at the third party.

INTERNATIONAL COURT OF JUSTICE

Advisory Proceedings before the International Court of Justice

In a memorandum dated February 6, 1995, the Legal Bureau wrote:

(1) . . . [T]he only bodies that may resort to the ICJ for an advisory opinion are the General Assembly, the Security Council, and those U.N. organs specifically authorised to do so: e.g., ECOSOC, the Trusteeship Council, all the specialised agencies, the IAEA, etc. That only the Secretary-General is allowed to forward such requests to the Court is further evidence of the U.N.'s monopoly of access to advisory proceedings.
(2) The Court itself referred to this fact in the *Northern Cameroons* case (1963), stating that it could not give an advisory opinion at the request of a State. Presumably, it wanted to avoid States "testing the water" in contemplation of initiating contentious proceedings.
(3) A State may, nevertheless, sponsor a request for an advisory opinion before the General Assembly. Theoretically, it might also do so before the Security Council or, less directly, through one of the authorised organs of the U.N. The General Assembly is the usual route . . .
(4) The Assembly must pass a resolution requesting an advisory opinion, following its normal procedure. It is unclear whether such a resolution would require a simple majority or, as an "important matter" under Article 18 of the U.N. Charter, two-thirds of the vote in order to pass. In connection with the *South-West Africa* case (1949), however, the President of the General Assembly ruled that such a vote was a purely procedural matter and, as such, only required a simple majority. The only time an enlarged majority was required, with respect to the *Treatment of Indians in the Union of South Africa* case (1946), was when the reference to the Court was proposed as an amendment to an existing resolution for which a two-thirds majority was required.
(5) Although a single state can propose such a resolution, the normal practice has been for more than one state to sponsor it. . . .
(6) The ICJ Statute places no restriction upon the matters with respect to which an advisory opinion may be sought, other than that it be a "legal

question." This has been interpreted, however, as meaning any legal question *within the competence of the body seeking the advisory opinion.* Consequently, challenges have been made as to the General Assembly's competence or authority to refer an international agreement to the Court for an advisory opinion in the absence of consent from all of the State parties to that agreement.

(7) The ICJ has set a wide scope for the Assembly's competence. In *Peace Treaties* (1950) the U.N. had no role in the treaty in question. Nonetheless, the Court determined that the issue at stake was human rights, a matter in which the U.N. had a definite interest. Moreover, it said that "no State . . . *can prevent the* giving of an Advisory Opinion which the United Nations considers to be desirable in order to obtain enlightenment as to the course of action it should take."

(8) In the *Reservations* case (1951), in which interpretation of the Genocide Convention was sought, the ICJ held that the General Assembly had played an integral role in the Convention's creation and implementation and that this was a "permanent interest of direct concern to the United Nations which has not disappeared with the entry into force of the Convention." Besides which, reference to the Court would have in no way impaired States' independent right to seek the Court's interpretation of the Convention.

(9) In light of the foregoing, it is hardly surprising that opinions on abstract issues are permitted under Article 65 of the ICJ Statute. Indeed, questions on construction or on general international law have been far more common under this provision than those on real-life disputes have been. That is not to say, however, that the abstract questions were not based upon real and pressing issues. Likely, the General Assembly finds it more politically acceptable to seek advice in general terms. At the same time, the Court would find it next to impossible to pass judgment, albeit non-binding, on parties which did not consent to the adjudication of their dispute.

(10) Nevertheless, a ruling is precedent-setting. Although there may be no way to enforce the judgment, the propaganda value is manifest. Even if of no consequence vis-a-vis the dispute which was behind the reference, such decisions have tended to clarify the norms of international law and, presumably, affect the subsequent conduct of relations between States.

Intervention and Discontinuance before the International Court of Justice (ICJ)

In a memorandum dated July 6, 1995, the Legal Bureau wrote:

(1) International Court of Justice (ICJ) caselaw indicates that a successful intervention in a dispute before the Court must fall within very narrow parameters. Where specific provisions of a convention to which the intervening State is a party are being interpreted, as opposed to simply being applied to facts, that State has a *prima facie* right to intervene. Alternatively, if a direct and close link is established between the interests of the State seeking to intervene and the subject matter of the dispute, intervention may also succeed. The Court has consistently refused to

allow interventions that seek clarification of broad principles of international law or the general application of conventions, unless these are specifically at issue in a case before it. Although the interest in the Court's decision of the successful intervener must be nearly as great as that of a party to the dispute, and it may intervene even in the face of opposition from the parties, the ICJ has made it clear that an intervener is always an incidental player in the matter before it. It is doubtful, therefore, that an intervener could force the parties to see the case through to its conclusion should they decide between themselves to discontinue it. . . . Could Canada successfully intervene in the *Bosnia* v. *Serbia* case under Article 62 of the ICJ Statute?

(4) Likely not. While there are few decisions in this regard, the fact that so few applications have been made under this provision would seem to suggest that an even higher threshold must be met than under Article 63 before standing will be extended.

(5) Nicaragua's intervention in the *Case Concerning the Land, Island and Maritime Frontier Dispute* between El Salvador and Honduras has been the only successful intervention under Article 62. Although basing its claim to intervene on four issues, Nicaragua was only successful with respect to the status of the waters of the Gulf of Fonseca. Those waters had been the subject of a previous case before the Central American Court of Justice (CACJ) between all three countries and, in the ICJ case, Nicaragua felt it necessary to intervene in order to reiterate its claims and to safeguard its legal interests.

(6) The 1981 *Continental Shelf* decision was the first to extensively consider an Article 62 intervention. There, Malta failed to prove that it had the requisite interest. Tunisia and Libya had turned to the Court to spell out principles of international law which could then be used by them in negotiations to delimit their respective shares of the continental shelf. Malta sought to intervene because it felt that the judgment would be precedent-setting for the resolution of maritime boundary disputes in the region.

(7) The Court held that this was not sufficient to allow Malta to intervene and made the following points:

    (1) Malta's interest in the relevant legal principles was no different from that of any other State within the region. It was not seeking a determination of its own claims, so its interests would not really be affected.

    (2) The history of Article 62 suggested that it was intended to allow the intervener to participate *as a party* and not just to submit legal arguments that might have a prejudicial effect upon the parties.

    (3) If the intervener wishes to participate in the case, it must put its own claims under scrutiny and, also, establish the existence of a jurisdictional link between its interests and the dispute before the Court.

    (4) The Court only considers specific issues, from which general conclusions concerning other States' rights should not be drawn.

(8) While the Court was unanimous in advancing the foregoing reasons for its ruling, there was some disagreement with respect to the weight that

each was to be accorded and, indeed, to their precise implications — for example, whether the relationship between the intervener's situation and the dispute be such that the outcome of the case need only *affect* it, rather than be *determinative* of it.

(9) The 1981 *Continental Shelf* case stands for the proposition that there must be a close proximity between the dispute and the interests of the intervener. Article 81, paragraph 2 of the 1978 ICJ Rules spells this out: "The application . . . shall set out . . . the interest of a legal nature which the State applying to intervene considers may be affected by the decision in that case." It also indicates, by requiring the intervener to set out the object of its intervention, that some impact upon the intervener's rights — which it seeks either to prevent, alleviate, or ensure — must be demonstrated. The Nicaraguan case reinforced this point.

(10) The 1981 *Continental Shelf* decision also considered the question of whether, because of the consensual nature of litigation before the ICJ, the Court had the jurisdiction to allow intervention in the absence of the consent of the parties. The Court decisively dealt with this issue by ruling that parties, by submitting to the Court's jurisdiction, had consented to all of the provisions of its Statute, including the possibility of interventions under Articles 62 and 63.

(11) It is clear that the Court does not interpret Article 62 as giving it unfettered discretion to permit interventions for policy reasons, but as enabling it to examine the relevant circumstances to see if these fit the criteria of "an interest of a legal nature which may be affected by the decision."

(12) A successful intervention under this Article would, therefore, require a strong link to the particular fact situation. This link need not be sufficient to allow the intervener to participate as a full party, but its interest would have to be distinct and more immediate than that of all other States that did not seek to intervene. The 1981 *Continental Shelf* decision, as well as the existence of Article 63, would seem to preclude intervention solely for the purpose of shaping or clarifying international law. The Nicaraguan decision provides the definitive statement in this regard: "[*The Court] does not consider that an interest of a third State in the general legal rules and principles likely to be applied by the decision can justify an intervention*" [emphasis added].

(13) Should Canada decide to intervene in the case currently before the ICJ between Bosnia and Yugoslavia (Serbia and Montenegro) to seek a declaration from the Court to the effect that rape amounts to genocide within the meaning of the Convention on the Prevention and Punishment of the Crime of Genocide (the Genocide Convention), it would, therefore, have to do so pursuant to Article 63. Could Canada successfully intervene in the *Bosnia* v. *Serbia* case under Article 63 of the ICJ Statute?

(14) Canada could not intervene under this Article until a question as to the construction of the Convention arises. The procedure to be followed by a State wishing to avail itself of the right conferred by Article 63 is set out . . . by Article 82 of the 1978 ICJ Rules . . .

(15) The cases . . . in particular *Haya de la Torre* and *The S.S. Wimbledon*, have stated that a party to an international agreement may intervene "as

of right" in a case before the ICJ by virtue of Article 63 of the ICJ Statute. Article 82, paragraph 3, of the ICJ Rules of 1978 strengthens this right by allowing parties to a convention to assert their right to intervene even if they were not notified by the Registrar under Article 63 of the Statute. (16) In the *Wimbledon* case, the PCIJ awarded standing to Poland under Article 63 solely on the basis that it was a signatory to the Treaty of Versailles, even though Poland had originally framed its claim in terms of the Court's discretionary power under Article 62. Afghanistan's claim to intervene in the *Trial of Pakistani Prisoners of War* case was summarily dismissed on the same basis: i.e., that it was not a party to the agreements at issue.

(17) In *Haya de la Torre*, this principle was upheld but was qualified slightly by the additional requirements that the issue over which intervener status is sought be "before the Court" and relevant to the case; that is, that it be "at issue."

(18) These requirements narrow the scope for intervention under Article 63. Merely being a party to the convention at issue is not sufficient to enable a would-be intervener to obtain such status. Rather, the case must involve actual interpretation of the convention's provisions and not just its application to a particular fact pattern.

(19) In the context of any attempted intervention in the Bosnia-Serbia dispute, the issue for Canada will be whether the construction of the Genocide Convention is *in question*. The answer to this question will depend on the pleadings of the parties to the dispute. Article 63, paragraph 1, requires the ICJ Registrar to notify all State parties when a question of construction arises but, in the present case, the Registrar has remained silent. This is not to be accorded significant weight, however, in light of Article 82 of the Rules which allows intervention even if no notice is given. It does suggest, however, that in the Registrar's mind at least, the construction of the Convention has not yet been put into question.

(20) In light of the foregoing, even though a party to the Genocide Convention, Canada may have difficulty in obtaining standing as an intervener in the *Bosnia* v. *Serbia* case, unless the interpretation of the Convention is specifically brought into question. It should be borne in mind, moreover, that Canada would be bound by any construction the court put upon the Convention. . . . Could Canada, if granted intervener status, compel the ICJ, Bosnia, and Serbia to continue with the case?

(21) Likely not. Discontinuance is governed by Rules 88 and 89 of the 1978 ICJ Rules. Rule 89 is not of particular concern here as it deals with an attempt to discontinue the case by the applicant's *unilateral* withdrawal. Rule 88, however, relates to an agreement by the *parties* to discontinue the action. . . .

(22) If Canada, as an intervener, were a party to the action, it might conceivably succeed in blocking the discontinuance of the case under Article 88 of the Rules. However, the caselaw would seem to indicate that an intervener is not a party.

(23) In *Haya de la Torre*, the Court stated that "every intervention is incidental to the proceedings in a case." This case and Article 63(1) of the ICJ Statute suggest that the intervener's interest lies in the construction of the convention to which the intervener is a party, not in the

resolution of the particular dispute. Therefore, if the principals were not prepared to proceed, the interest of the intervener in obtaining a judicial construction of the convention is unlikely to be enough to compel the principals to continue with the case.

(24) Even Nicaragua's successful intervention was tempered by the statement that it did not "by reason only of being an intervener, become also a party to the case." The Court went on to say that it would breach a fundamental principle of consensual jurisdiction if the intervener was permitted to become a party, in effect creating a new case, without the consent of the original parties.

(25) The Article 63 right arises only because the intervener's interests, in the form of the construction of a convention to which it is party, are at stake. Once that threat is removed, it would seem logical that that right is also extinguished.

INTERNATIONAL ECONOMIC LAW

General Agreement on Tariffs and Trade — Non-discriminatory Administration of Quantitative Restrictions

In a memorandum dated October 21, 1994, the Legal Bureau wrote:

Article XIII establishes a series of rules for the non-discriminatory administration of quantitative restrictions. The most relevant provisions of Article XIII . . . may be summarized as follows:
· any restriction on the importation of a product is to be applied on a most favoured nation (MFN) basis
· in applying import restrictions to a product, the importing party "shall aim" at a distribution of trade in the product approaching as closely as possible the shares which the various other contracting parties might be expected to obtain in the absence of such restrictions
· wherever practicable, quotas representing the total amount of permitted imports (whether allocated among supplying countries or not) shall be fixed
· in cases in which a quota is allocated among supplying countries, the country applying the restrictions may seek agreement on the allocation of the quota with other contracting parties having a substantial interest in supplying the product
· in cases where such an agreement is "not reasonably practicable," the importing party "shall allot to contracting parties having a substantial interest in supplying the product shares based upon the proportions, supplied by such contracting parties during a previous representative period, of the total quantity or value of imports of the product
[It could be argued] that Article XIII is largely hortatory, imposing only a vague, "best efforts" kind of unenforceable obligation to "aim" at a distribution of trade approaching the shares which the contracting parties might be expected to obtain in the absence of restrictions. In our view, we would be on strong grounds to counter such an argument with the following points:

- paragraph 1 of Article XIII, which states the basic obligation of the Article, is in no way hortatory: "No . . . restriction shall be applied" on imports unless the like product of all third countries is similarly restricted. This paragraph creates a binding obligation, and the subsequent paragraphs of the Article merely elaborate upon and give greater precision to the basic obligation of Article XIII:1
- the use of the word "aim" in other provisions of GATT 1947 indicate the intent of the drafters to impose binding obligations through the use of this word. The word is used in two other places in the GATT. Article XXVIII:4(d) states that if an agreement cannot be reached on a tariff modification dispute, the matter may be referred to the Contracting Parties and, "[u]pon such reference, the *contracting parties* shall promptly examine the matter and submit their views to the contracting parties primarily concerned with the aim of achieving a settlement [emphasis added]. Similarly, Interpretative Note Ad Article XXVIII refers to affected parties participating in Article XXVIII negotiations with an applicant contracting party "with the aim of reaching agreement." In neither case have the drafters of the GATT used the word "aim" in a purely hortatory sense. We would argue that the use of the "shall aim" in Article XIII:2 similarly imposes a binding obligation on the United States to attempt to reach the distribution of trade called for in this Article, which it has not done. Indeed, the use of the word "aim" in Article XIII creates a stronger obligation than that imposed in Article XXVIII, since it is preceded by the mandatory "shall"
- in any event, the term "shall aim" is followed by language which unambiguously imposes obligations: "In applying import restrictions to any product, contracting parties shall aim at a distribution of trade in such product approaching as closely as possible the shares which the various contracting parties might be expected to obtain in the absence of such restrictions"
- in cases in which a quota is allocated among supplying countries, the contracting party applying the restrictions may seek agreement with respect to the allocation of shares in the quota with all other contracting parties having a substantial interest in supplying the product concerned. In cases in which this method is not reasonably practicable, the contracting party concerned shall allot to contracting parties having a substantial interest in supplying the product shares based upon the proportions, supplied by such contracting parties during a previous representative period, of the total quantity or value of imports of the product.

General Agreement on Tariffs and Trade — Self-Initiation of Anti-Dumping and Countervailing Duty Investigations and the World Trade Organization

In a memorandum dated November 21, 1994, the Legal Bureau wrote:

The only GATT Panel that has specifically addressed the requirements for the self-initiation of an anti-dumping or countervailing duty investigation is the one that considered the countervailing duty investigation undertaken by the United States in 1991 on softwood lumber imports from Canada (SCM/162, 19 February 1993). That Panel considered that the requirement for "special circumstances" in support of self-initiation "had to be interpreted in the light of the main purpose of the initiation provisions in Article 2:1 (of the Subsidies Code), which was to ensure that investigations were normally initiated through a petition procedure. A self-initiation in circumstances occurring so rarely that this main purpose was not undermined could therefore . . . be considered to be covered by Article 2:1."

Concerning the standard of evidence required for self-initiation, the Panel considered that there was no justification for requiring a higher standard in cases of self-initiation than in cases initiated by petition. The Panel interpreted the term "sufficient evidence" in the context of the initiation of a countervailing duty investigation to mean "evidence that provides a reason to believe that a subsidy exists and that the domestic industry is injured as a result of subsidized imports."

There is sufficient similarity between Article 2:1 of the Subsidies Code and the self-initiation provisions in Article 5 of the World Trade Organization (WTO) Agreement on Implementation of Article VI of the General Agreement on Tariffs and Trade 1994 (Anti-Dumping Agreement) to support an assumption that the principles outlined above would also govern the self-initiation of an anti-dumping investigation.

General Agreement on Tariffs and Trade — Customs Valuation Methods

In a memorandum dated July 6, 1995, the Legal Bureau wrote:

Article VII of GATT 1994 must be interpreted in the light of the Customs Valuation Agreement. The Customs Valuation Agreement elaborates rules for the application of the provisions of Article VII "in order to provide greater uniformity and certainty in their implementation." It appears in Annex 1A to the WTO Agreement and therefore prevails to the extent of any conflict with a provision of the GATT 1994. By implication, the Customs Valuation Agreement is the most authoritative interpretation of how to apply the provisions of Article VII.

The Customs Valuation Agreement sets out five valuation methods which are ranked in a hierarchical order. Article 1 states the primary valuation method: "the customs value of imported goods shall be the transaction value, that is the price actually paid or payable for the goods when sold for export to the country of importation adjusted in accordance with the provisions of Article 8." The primary method must be used provided that there are no restrictions on the disposition or use of the goods by the buyer, that the sale or price is not subject to some condition or consideration for which a value cannot be determined, that no parts of the proceeds of any subsequent resale accrue to the seller, and that the buyer and the seller are not related. Even in circumstances of sales between related persons, the transaction value should be used unless the relationship influenced the price. In such a sale, the transaction value must be accepted when the importer demonstrates that the price closely approximates the transaction value in sales to unrelated buyers of identical or similar goods for export to the same country of importation.

North American Free Trade Agreement — Accession

In a memorandum dated March 31, 1995, the Legal Bureau wrote:

NAFTA Article 2204(1) provides for accession by any country or group of countries "subject to such terms and conditions as may be agreed between such country or countries and the Commission."

NAFTA Article 2001 establishes the NAFTA Free Trade Commission (consisting of cabinet-level representatives of the Parties or their designees), and provides in paragraph 4 that all decisions of the Commission shall be taken by consensus, except as the Commission may otherwise agree.

Any applicant for membership in NAFTA . . . would have to reach agreement with the NAFTA Free Trade Commission on terms and conditions of accession. This process would involve (1) setting the terms and conditions within the NAFTA Free Trade Commission, i.e., establishing what would be expected from [the applicant state]; and (2) following negotiations, a determination whether [the applicant state] has met such terms and conditions. Both decisions would be subject to the consensus rule (unless the Commission by consensus agreed to derogate from this rule, which is highly unlikely). It should be emphasized that in the process of setting the terms and conditions for accession, Mexico and the United States could be expected to put forward their own demands, in addition to Canada's. All these would be reflected in the terms and conditions that would be set by the NAFTA Free Trade Commission before accession negotiations are opened.

Even if it was decided by the NAFTA Free Trade Commission that an applicant for accession had met the terms and conditions set by it, a NAFTA country could still, by virtue of NAFTA Article 2204(2), prevent application of the Agreement as between itself and the acceding state (though not between the other NAFTA countries and the acceding State). NAFTA Article 2204(2) provides that the Agreement "shall not apply between any Party and any acceding country or group of countries if, at the time of accession, either does not consent to such application."

North American Free Trade Agreement — Expropriation Provisions

In a memorandum dated June 12, 1995, the Legal Bureau wrote:

Article 1605 sets out the Parties' obligations with respect to expropriation of investments. It reads as follows:

Neither Party shall directly or indirectly nationalize or expropriate an investment in its territory by an investor of the other Party or take any measure or series of measures tantamount to an expropriation of such an investment, except:

(a) for a public purpose;
(b) in accordance with due process of law;
(c) on a non-discriminatory basis; and
(d) upon payment of prompt, adequate and effective compensation at fair market value.

In contrast to direct expropriation and nationalization, there is scant international jurisprudence on measures "tantamount to an expropriation." The words "tantamount to" suggest that the measure has the equivalent effect of an expropriation. It has been suggested that a state may indirectly expropriate property by unreasonably interfering in the use of property or with the enjoyment of its benefits, even though legal title to the property is not affected.

It is generally acknowledged that taxation is a taking of property, but one that is a justifiable exercise of the state's taxing power and for which no compensation is due. Indeed, under the NAFTA, an investor cannot make a claim for investor-state arbitration on the basis that a tax measure constitutes an expropriation where the Parties have determined that the measure is not an expropriation. However, it is also acknowledged that a tax measure must be *bona fide*, non-discriminatory, and not designed to cause an alien to abandon an investment to the state or to sell it at a distress price. . . .

There is no clear threshold for a determination of unreasonableness, but international arbitral tribunals have held that interference is unreasonable when property rights have been rendered so useless that they must be deemed to have been expropriated.

JURISDICTION

Extraterritoriality — Helms/Burton Bills and International Law

In a May 1995 memorandum, the Legal Advisor wrote:

[It has been] argued that the Hickenlooper amendment established the principle that the United States would use its courts to place into question the illegal taking of the property of United States nationals abroad. The purpose of this paper is to examine the international legal considerations that are relevant to this argument. We will consider the following doctrines: A. The Act of State Doctrine and the Hickenlooper amendment [and] D. Reprisal and Retorsion. . . .

(A) Act of State and the Hickenlooper Amendment

The Hickenlooper amendment does not constitute a precedent for the actions now proposed by the Helms/Burton bills. While a case can be made that the legislative branch can limit the application of the act of state doctrine, the Hickenlooper amendment is not a precedent for creating a right in the United States founded on an unlawful taking of property in another state's territory.

In a 1964 case, *Banco Nacional de Cuba* v. *Sabbatino*, the United States Supreme Court declared that the judicial branch of the United States government would not examine the validity of a taking of property by a foreign sovereign government irrespective of the legality in international law of that action. A similar conclusion was reached in 1986 by the House of Lords in the United Kingdom in *Williams & Humbert Ltd* v. *W & H Trade Marks (Jersey) Ltd.* In both *Sabbatino* and *W & H Trade Marks* the courts accepted and enforced the consequences of the compulsory acquisition without considering its merits. In the *Sabbatino* case, Cuba had confiscated a shipload of sugar in Cuba which was subsequently delivered to the United States. Sabbatino, the receiver appointed by the former owner, asserted a right to the proceeds of the sale, while Banco de Cuba sought enforcement of the bill of lading pursuant to which the sugar had been sold.

The United States Supreme Court's ruling in the *Sabbatino* case was widely criticized in the United States by academics and practitioners and was overruled by Congress in an amendment to the Foreign Assistance Act known as the Hickenlooper Amendment. This amendment, slightly modified, appears now in 22 USC s. 2370 (e)(2). The text provides, "no court in the United States shall decline on the grounds of the federal act of state doctrine to make a determination on the merits giving effect to the principles of international law in a case in which a claim of title or other right to property is asserted by any party . . . based upon . . . an act of that state in violation of the principles of international law."

The Hickenlooper amendment is far more modest than Helms/Burton and has been given a narrow interpretation by United States courts. The comments on the Third Restatement of the Foreign Relations Law of the United States indicate that the courts have generally held that the amendment applies to claims to title to specific property before the court, but does not apply to claims to compensation for taking of property not before the court. Moreover, if a court determines that the act of state doctrine is inapplicable, the burden of proof that a violation of international law has occurred is on the party making the assertion. Claims by persons who were nationals of the taking state would not come under the amendment because they would not raise an issue under international law. The Hickenlooper amendment did not seek to impose sanctions for the unlawful taking of the property of United States nationals by a foreign government; it merely refused to lend the support of United States courts to the enforcement of such unlawful takings.

International law does not require a state to assist in the enforcement of rights to property taken contrary to international law, so the Hickenlooper amendment does not contravene international law in this respect. Indeed, as it has been interpreted, the Hickenlooper amendment is a conflict of laws rule, rather than a rule of public international law, since it deals with commercial rights by seeking to find the appropriate legal rule to apply. . . .

(D) Reprisal and Retorsion

International law permits a state to take reprisals against another state, within certain limits, for wrongs done to its nationals or their investments in the territory of that other state. However, the Helms/Burton proposals cannot be justified as reprisals because they go well beyond the limits contemplated by international law. In particular, the measures are aimed at persons in Canada and other OECD countries in a manner that retroactively affects property rights, and are inconsistent with the basic international law standard of fair and equitable treatment.

International law has as a fundamental principle that a state is responsible for internationally unlawful acts, and that a breach of an international act gives rise to a requirement for reparations. This rule was clearly stated by the Permanent Court of International Justice in the *Chorzow Factory* case in 1928. However, the enunciation of this principle does not clarify what the consequences are if a state fails to make reparations.

It is a common complaint that international law lacks effective means of enforcement. It seeks to cope with violations through diverse means of dispute settlement. The United Nations Charter accords priority to the peaceful resolution of disputes rather than the enforcement of law. Inevitably, the victims of violation have resorted to self help and countermeasures. Schachter observes that judicial decisions on self-help have been few and scholarly analysis relatively sparse. Indeed, Chapter IX of Schachter's recent text on International Law in Theory and Practice makes a notable contribution in this regard. . . .

To be legitimate a reprisal must, according to Schachter, meet the following conditions:

(a) it must be directed to obtaining redress for the wrong committed. It loses its legality if it is directed to producing an outcome extraneous to the violation and the situation created by the illegal act. On the other hand, reprisals are permitted even if the parties have agreed to other means of peaceful settlement. Once arbitration or judicial settlement are underway, reprisals are normally ruled out unless there is a continuing injury to the complaining state which the tribunal is unable to alleviate during litigation.

(b) it should be implemented in a good faith manner: following advance notification, based on a good faith belief that a violation has occurred. There are some who argue that a reprisal is unlawful if a tribunal subsequently finds that there was no violation.

(c) reprisals must not be disproportionate to the violations to which they respond. In this respect one should note that the tribunal in the United States/France Air Services arbitration ruled that a reprisal which had more serious consequences that the original violation was not disproportionate.

(d) if the reprisal involves non-performance of a treaty obligation, certain special considerations apply

   (i) The Vienna Convention provides that material breach of a treaty permits the other party to suspend the treaty but it specifically provides that this rule does not apply in respect of any agreement that prohibits reprisals against persons protected by such agreements.

   (ii) If the treaty has specific provisions providing for non-compliance to be dealt with by specified organs, there may be an inference that it was the intent of the parties to leave questions of violations exclusively to such organs.

   (iii) If the reprisal is a cross-reprisal under another agreement, and other parties would be affected, such reprisal would probably not be appropriate; indeed some commentators argue that for treaty regimes involving collaboration in economic, social and technical matters, the autonomy of the specialized legal regime should prevail over the principle of reprisals.

(e) a reprisal may be taken by a state not directly affected by a breach if the violation has an *erga omnes* character.

(f) in some circumstances measures may properly be taken against nationals of the offending state provided they do not relate to international obligations for the protection of human rights.

The Helms/Burton proposals cannot be justified in terms of this analysis. . . .

The Helms/Burton proposal to provide a claim against persons dealing in confiscated United States property does not appear to be limited to obtaining redress for the wrong committed. One of the sponsors has made it clear that the legislation is aimed at Canada and Canadian trade with Cuba. This outcome is entirely extraneous to the wrong committed. While the illegal taking of the property of United States nationals is the basis for the prohibition on dealing with such property, the measure affects Cuba's trading partners, and companies that have entered into commercial transactions in good faith with Cuban companies many decades after the takings occurred.

The extension of the legislation to the property of Cubans who subsequently became United States citizens is entirely outside the permissible limits for a reprisal.

The reprisals are also disproportionate: they could exceed the value of the property several times over; and they include restrictions upon the entry into the United States of persons who traffic in the confiscated property. The long delay between the reprisals and the offence to which they relate is also relevant, since it is hard to justify a severe reprisal 36 years after the illegal act, even if a timely reprisal of the same magnitude might have been proportionate. The fact that the reprisals aim to injure the economic interests of persons engaged in peaceful commercial activity in Cuba is also disproportionate because it attacks economic activity which is only distantly related to the issue upon which the United States seeks redress. The creation of legal liability for such peaceful activity by third parties is disproportionate to the offence complained of.

Reprisals against Cuba can not justify breach of United States obligations against Canada under the NAFTA. . . .

The reprisals are directed at persons from third countries. While limited reprisals against an offending state's own nationals are permitted, reprisals against third country nationals fall outside the criteria enumerated by Schachter. The United States has never claimed that trade with Cuba by third countries is unlawful under international law.

TREATIES

Interpretation — Amendment through a Protocol or an Exchange of Notes

In a memorandum dated October 3, 1994, the Legal Bureau wrote:

An amendment in the form of a Protocol or an exchange of notes is acceptable as both qualify as a treaty within the meaning of the Vienna Convention on the Law of Treaties. In the present case we would prefer an exchange of notes as the proposed amendments are minor in nature and lend themselves to this form of amendment as opposed to drafting an entire Protocol. . . .

An international agreement can take the form of a single formal agreement, such as a treaty, convention or protocol, or be embodied in two related instruments, such as in an exchange of notes. Both forms qualify as international agreements within the meaning of Article 2(1) of the Vienna Convention on the Law of Treaties: "'treaty' means an international agreement concluded between States in written form and governed by international law, whether embodied in a single instrument or in two or more related instruments and whatever its particular designation."

The essential element of an international agreement between states is their intention to create binding obligations under international law. A variety of names can be used when referring to a treaty (convention, protocol or agreement). In international diplomacy, each one has certain connotations as to the nature of the treaty, but the various names are of no legal significance. All agreements between states that are intended to be binding under international law are treaties, no matter what they are called. The term protocol is often used to designate a form of international agreement that is used to complete a treaty. However, it is an autonomous instrument and the procedure for its entry into force is distinct from that of the treaty on which it is based.

An exchange of notes is an agreement between states embodied in two related instruments. Typically, it takes the form of an exchange of diplomatic notes between the Minister of Foreign Affairs of one state and the Ambassador of another.

Interpretation — Evidentiary Requirements for the Use of Preparatory Works in Trade Disputes

In a memorandum dated May 15, 1995, the Legal Bureau wrote:

One of the most cogent and concise discussions of interpretive methodology as it relates to agreements between sovereign states can be found in McNair's treatise on the law of treaties. He notes that many arbitrators and judges have attempted to apply principles derived from the private law of contracts to the interpretation of international agreements. According to McNair, this has obscured the main task of an interpreter of international agreements: to give effect to "the expressed intention of the parties, that is, their intention as expressed in the words used by them in the light of the surrounding circumstances." Therefore, the first task of an interpreter of a treaty is to elucidate "the meaning of the text of the treaty which must be taken as the authentic expression of the parties' intention." Indeed, the International Court of Justice has held that "the first duty of a tribunal which is called upon to interpret and apply the provisions of a treaty, is to endeavour to give effect to them in their natural and ordinary meaning in the context in which they occur."

While exercising caution, the Permanent Court of International Justice and the International Court of Justice have not excluded resort to documents "such as memoranda, minutes of conferences, and drafts of the treaty under negotiation" for the purpose of interpreting the treaty, or finding support for their own interpretation of the treaty. The traditional practice of international tribunals was endorsed in the Vienna Convention on the Law of Treaties (the "Vienna Convention"). Article 32 of the Vienna Convention states that:

> Recourse may be had to supplementary means of interpretation, including the preparatory work of the treaty and the circumstances of its conclusion, in order to confirm the meaning resulting from the application of article 31, or to determine the meaning when the interpretation according to article 31:
> (a) leaves the meaning ambiguous or obscure; or
> (b) leads to a result which is manifestly absurd or unreasonable.

The Vienna Convention, and in particular Articles 31 and 32, are applicable to the interpretation of the NAFTA.

Supplementary means such as the preparatory work or official statements may be used to interpret a term that is "ambiguous or obscure," or to "confirm the meaning resulting from the application of Article 31." In the *Durum Wheat* case, the United States argued that, since the terms in question were clear and unambiguous, resort to Article 32 of the Vienna Convention was not necessary. The Panel disagreed. Noting that after a series of meetings the Parties had not resolved their differences and that the oral hearing "reflected very sharp differences between the Parties," the Panel relied on Article 32, "either to confirm the ordinary meaning of the words or to resolve any ambiguity."

Interpretation — Legal Status of Arrangements and Memoranda of Understanding

In correspondence dated April 10, 1995, the Legal Bureau wrote:

Arrangements and memoranda of understanding are less formal instruments than international agreements (treaties), although they represent significant political and moral commitments to be honoured by the signatories.

The primary advantage of such instruments is that they provide greater administrative flexibility than international agreements. Moreover, these instruments enable government departments and agencies to function more effectively by fostering close working-level contacts with their counterparts in other countries.

The following is an overview of Canada's position regarding the legal status of arrangements and memoranda of understanding:
· Unlike international agreements (treaties), arrangements and memoranda of understanding do not create formal legal obligations between sovereign states under international law.

· The execution of an arrangement or memorandum of understanding is a politically binding act.
· Canadian government departments may negotiate and conclude arrangements and memoranda of understanding without obtaining Cabinet approval or an Order-in-Council.

It is important to note that in addition to the title of an instrument, the intent of the drafters and the language of the document may be taken into account in determining its legal status. Therefore, language that could lead to confusion as to the status of an instrument under international law should be avoided. For example, terms such as "agreement," "agree," "shall," "must," and "obligations" should be avoided. Also, the phrase "come into effect" should be used rather than "enter into force."

Interpretation — Agreement on the Application of Sanitary and Phytosanitary Measures

In a memorandum dated February 8, 1995, the Legal Bureau wrote:

It should be explained at the outset that in the new structure of the World Trade Organization (WTO), the Agreement on the Application of Sanitary and Phytosanitary Measures (SPS) and the General Agreement on Tariffs and Trade 1994 (GATT 1994) are included in a series of agreements that are annexed to the Marrakesh Agreement Establishing the World Trade Organization. All WTO Members are bound by the obligations of the SPS as well as the GATT 1994, by virtue of their membership. . . .

[T]he SPS builds on the GATT and, according to its concluding preambular paragraph, elaborates "rules for the application of the provisions of GATT 1994 which relate to the use of sanitary or phytosanitary measures, in particular the provisions of Article XX(b)."

It should be appreciated that in WTO dispute settlement proceedings WTO Members may plead provisions from different WTO Agreements before a panel. This is different from the situation as it previously existed in the GATT. The so-called Tokyo Round Codes (e.g., the previous Agreement on Technical Barriers to Trade) had their own individual dispute settlement mechanisms which were separate from that of the GATT itself. With the arrival of the WTO, there is now one integrated dispute settlement mechanism for all WTO Agreements. Thus, if [a] case were to go to WTO dispute settlement, the GATT 1994 and the SPS Agreement could both be invoked simultaneously.

Interpretation — Compatibility of the Canada-United States Agreement on the Transboundary Movement of Hazardous Waste and the Basel Convention on the Control of Hazardous Wastes and other Wastes and their Disposal

In a report dated December 1994, the Legal Bureau wrote:

The Basel Convention acknowledges that in certain cases the environmentally sound management of hazardous wastes may necessitate their disposal in another country besides that in which they were generated. One of the principles behind the development of the Canada-United States Agreement is that the transboundary movement of hazardous waste between Canada and the United States contributes to regionally efficient and environmentally sound management of these wastes, regardless of on which side of the border the wastes were generated. The salient feature of the geographic relationship between the two countries is that they share a common border several thousand miles in length and that most Canadian communities lie along that common border. Consequently, most sites where hazardous wastes are generated in Canada will be closer to the United States than to other parts of Canada.

There are two types of risks associated with the transboundary movement and disposal of hazardous wastes: the danger of an accident during transportation and the danger of an accident during disposal. In many cases, in order to reduce transportation distances and the likelihood of an accident during transportation, it is preferable to manage hazardous waste at the nearest suitable facility for treatment, storage or disposal, which may be located in the other country. Furthermore, in the case of hazardous wastes that may require specialised facilities for treatment and disposal, the appropriate facilities may only exist and be economically viable in an area where there is a certain critical mass of that particular type of waste, which may be on the other side of the boundary.

Therefore, due to the particular geographic relationship between Canada and the United States and to practical exigencies, it is frequently more efficient and environmentally sound to transport hazardous waste across the border to the other country for storage, treatment, disposal or recycling. The Canada-United States Agreement exists to facilitate such movements and the regulations implementing it ensure that transboundary movements of hazardous wastes are carried out in an environmentally sound manner. . . .

The Agreement is predicated on the mutual recognition that the domestic systems of regulation in both countries ensure that the management of hazardous wastes shall be conducted in an environmentally sound manner. . . .

The Canada-United States Agreement applies to all wastes that are subject to control under the legislation in both countries. In Canada the Transportation of Dangerous Goods Regulations and the Export and Import of Hazardous Wastes Regulations contain extensive lists of products and wastes subject to controls, as well as detailed hazardous criteria supported by prescribed tests. The criteria were adopted from the United Nations Recommendations on Transport of Dangerous Goods and from the definitions in the Basel Convention. In order to include "other wastes," as defined in the Basel Convention, as well as hazardous wastes, the Agreement was amended in 1992, just before it came into force for Canada. As provided for in the Hazardous Wastes Regulations, the Agreement covers both recovery and final disposal.

Like the Basel Convention, the Canada-United States Agreement requires advance notification and consent for transboundary movements of hazardous wastes. . . .

In the case of Canada, the Export and Import of Hazardous Waste Regulations require that Canadian importers, exporters and carriers carry environmental impairment liability insurance in prescribed amounts to cover the shipment of hazardous wastes from the moment they are sent from the generator/exporter to the time an authorised facility (including a facility in Canada if the wastes are returned) accepts delivery of the hazardous waste. The insurance is in respect of any damages to third parties for which the exporter, importer or carrier is responsible and any costs imposed by law on the exporter, importer or carrier to clean up the environment in respect of any hazardous waste that is released to the environment. Thus, the Agreement fulfils the Basel Convention requirement that all waste shipments be insured. . . .

Consistent with the provisions of the Basel Convention, both Canada and the United States require that all shipments of hazardous wastes be accompanied by manifests or tracking documents containing relevant information about the shipment in question. These manifests serve to track the shipment from its point of origin to its final destination in either country. The Agreement also ensures the co-operation of both countries in the monitoring and spot-checking of transboundary shipments of hazardous waste to ensure, as far as possible, that such shipments conform to the requirements of the applicable legislation and the Agreement. In Canada, in addition to being controlled by the Department of the Environment, shipments are subject to being checked by provincial police or provincial environment ministries at any time.

In the case of shipments that may be returned by the country of import or transit, the Agreement requires that the country of export re-admit the hazardous waste in question. In implementation of the related provisions of the Basel Convention, the Hazardous Waste Regulations require that the Canadian exporter make other arrangements or return the waste if it cannot be disposed of as foreseen, and include an undertaking to that effect in the notice of the transboundary movement. There has been very good co-operation between both countries in the implementation of all these provisions. . . .

In summary, the Canada-United States Agreement establishes a comprehensive set of controls with simplified administrative procedures between two industrialized countries with similar political, legal and economic infrastructures. It takes into account the fact that both countries have an extensive body of environmental legislation and well-trained personnel to respond to any issues associated with the movement of waste between the two countries, including technically competent staff to initiate inspection/investigation. Together with the related sets of regulations, the Agreement provides for the environmentally sound transboundary movement and disposal of hazardous wastes, as between Canada and the United States.

The Agreement and the implementing regulations incorporate all the main elements of the Basel Convention: prior notification and consent; prohibition of shipments without consent; prohibition of exports where the country of import has prohibited imports of hazardous waste; shipments only by authorised persons to authorised facilities; the use of tracking documents; adherence to safety rules and procedures during transportation; the requirement of environmentally sound management; and the possibility of returning the waste if it cannot be disposed of as foreseen.

In the eight years since its introduction, despite the large number of transboundary movements between the two countries, the Agreement has been smoothly implemented without any untoward incidents. In view of all the features outlined above, it is clear that the *Canada-United States Agreement on the Transboundary Movement of Hazardous Waste*, which allows the two Parties to control transboundary movements across their common border, is compatible with the environmentally sound management of hazardous wastes and other wastes as set forth in the provisions of the Basel Convention.

Interpretation — Protocol to the Migratory Birds Convention

In a memorandum dated May 16, 1995, the Legal Bureau wrote:

The Protocol between the Government of Canada and the Government of the United States of America Amending the 1916 Convention between the United Kingdom and the United States of America for the Protection of Migratory Birds in Canada and the United States . . . was initialled in Parksville, British Columbia, April 27, 1995. . . .

(2) The primary purpose of the Protocol is to bring the 1916 Convention into conformity with Canadian constitutional law regarding aboriginal harvesting. This goal was achieved in Article II 4(a)(i) which permits harvesting of migratory birds by Aboriginal peoples of Canada subject to existing aboriginal and treaty rights under section 35 of the Constitution Act, 1982. The United States would only agree to such a clause on the condition that such harvesting was also subject to the general principles of conservation elaborated in the chapeau to Article II.

Parliamentary Declarations in 1994-95 / Déclarations parlementaires en 1994-95

compiled by / préparé par
SAPARD V. M. T. N. KALALA*

1 Les droits de la personne / Human Rights

(a) India / Les Indes

Mr. Gurbax Singh Malhi (Bramalea-Gore-Malton): ... my question is for the Minister of Foreign Affairs. Recently, several Canadian citizens have been arrested or harassed while travelling in India. There is evidence that the Indian authorities are detaining individuals without charge. Coincidentally this harassment and unfounded police interrogation are directed particularly at Canadians of Sikh origin. Will the minister on behalf of the Government of Canada send a strong message to the Indian government to put an end to this practice and human rights violations with minorities in India?

Hon. Christine Stewart (Secretary of State (Latin America and Africa)): . . . the Canadian government is very concerned about the detention of some Sikh Canadians who have been travelling to India. To be more specific, recently there was a case in which a Canadian was held for about a week and others recently for shorter periods of time. . . .

Our High Commissioner in New Delhi has followed up on every case of detention that he has been aware of and through him and other officials here in Ottawa we have relayed to the government in India our concern about this issue and hope that it will be dealt with.

(House of Commons Debates, March 3, 1995, p. 10329)
(Débats de la Chambre des communes, le 3 mars 1995, p. 10329)

2 Les différents internationaux et le maintien de la paix / International Disputes and Peacekeeping

(a) La Bosnie / Bosnia

M. Michel Gauthier (Roberval): Le premier ministre peut-il confirmer que les cinquante-cinq Casques bleus canadiens devenus en otage sont

---

x

* Common Law Section, Faculty of Law, University of Ottawa / Section de common law, Faculté de droit, Université d'Ottawa.

395

traités convenablement et que les négociations devant permettre leur libération sont toujours dans l'impasse avec les autorités serbes?

Le très hon. Jean Chrétien (premier ministre): . . . les cinquante-cinq soldats canadiens ne sont pas, à strictement parler, en otage. Ils sont gardes dans les postes qu'ils occupaient et ils continuent à faire le travail qu'ils faisaient auparavant dans les territoires en question.

(Débats de la Chambre des communes, le 28 novembre 1994, p. 8342)

(House of Commons Debates, Novembre 28, 1994, p. 8342)

M. Michel Gauthier (Roberval): . . . les cinquante-cinq Casques bleus canadiens se retrouvent avec une mobilité extrêmement réduite. Le premier ministre pourrait-il nous indiquer si les autorités serbes ont réagi officiellement à la demande de cessez-le-feu à Bihac faite par les États-Unis, la Russie, la France et la Grande Bretagne?

Le très hon. Jean Chrétien (premier ministre): . . . les informations indiquent que les Serbes accepteraient un cessez-le-feu indéfini, alors que les Musulmans de Bosnie veulent avoir un cessez-le-feu pour une période de trois mois. En ce moment, les discussions continuent pour essayer d'en venir à une entente. Ce qui est encourageant, c'est que les deux parties veulent un cessez-le-feu. Il s'agit maintenant de déterminer si c'est pour une période indéterminée ou pour une période fixe.

(Débats de la Chambre des Communes, le 28 novembre 1994, p. 8342)

(House of Commons Debates, November 28, 1994, p. 8342)

Mr. Elwin Hermanson (Kindersley-Lloydminster): . . . Canadians are appalled that some of our peace-keepers are being held hostage and were targeted in a rocket attack yesterday.

In September the Minister of National Defence informed the House that he had renewed Canada's engagement in Yugoslavia conditionally for six months. . . . Since the situation on the ground has changed and the safety of our troops is threatened and the ability of the UN to carry out its mandate has been undermined, will the minister reconsider Canada's participation?

Right Hon. Jean Chrétien (Prime Minister): . . . I had the occasion to say earlier that the Canadian role there is very useful. There will be a discussion this weekend in Budapest where the heads of state will be meeting. It will certainly be one of the items discussed.

The Canadian position has always been that we want to maintain our troops there as long as there is no lifting of the arms embargo. We are to review our commitment every six months. The commitment we made in September will be maintained until February and we will review our position in due course.

In the meantime, I will discuss this next week, especially with the French and the British who are in the same position as we are. We have decided to have a discussion before making the final decision. I will be in a position to report more next week.

(House of Commons Debates, Novembre 28, 1994, p. 8343)
(Débats de la Chambre des Communes, le 28 novembre 1994, p. 8343)

M. Michel Gauthier (Roberval): . . . on apprend que les forces serbes bosniaques ont intensifié leur offensive sur l'enclave musulmane de Bihac où 70 000 personnes sont littéralement assignées en compagnie de 1200 Casques bleus impuissants. Pendant ce temps, l'étau se resserre considéralement sur les Casques bleus a Visoko et l'armée serbe bosniaque menace de les bombarder dans les quarante-huit heures.

Le premier ministre confirme-t-il l'information à l'effet que l'armée serbe bosniaque s'apprête à bombarder la base des Casques bleus canadiens à Visoko?

Le très hon. Jean Chrétien (premier ministre): . . . nous n'avons pas d'indication à l'effet que les Serbes s'apprêtent a reprendre leur attaque sur la base de Visoko. Nous espérons que tout le monde va garder son sang-froid, que les combats vont cesser et qu'on va accepter un cessez-le-feu dans les plus brefs délais.

Les soldats canadiens sont là, non pas pour faire la guerre, mais pour des raisons humanitaires, pour distribuer de la nourriture et des médicaments à la population. Ils ont fait un excellent travail jusqu'aujourd'hui et ni les Serbes ni les Musulmans n'ont de raison d'attaquer nos vaillants soldats.

(Débats de la Chambre des Communes, le 29 novembre 1994, p. 8426)
(House of Commons Debates, November 29, 1994, p. 8426)

Mr. Jim Hart (Okanagan-Similkameen-Merritt): . . . in reaction to the French government's call for a withdrawal of peacekeepers from Bosnia/La Bosnie, the Prime Minister said: "Probably they want to reassure their own people." Those are the Prime Minister's words. I ask the Prime Minister: does this government wish to reassure Canadians now that the hostages are free by moving to withdraw our troops?

Right Hon. Jean Chrétien (Prime Minister): . . . I said that it is very important for everyone to plan to make sure that if there is a situation, for example the lifting of the embargo, we said we were to go. If there were to be some other disastrous situation, we have to have a plan . . . for our troops [to] be evacuated. We have been in contact too with NATO and the UN to make sure the plans are ready if evacuation is needed. I hope it will not be needed, but it is very good to do the planning now in case we have the need later.

(House of Commons Debates, December 8, 1994, p. 8828)
(Débats de la Chambre des Communes, le 8 décembre 1994, p. 8828)

Mr. Bob Mills (Red Deer): . . . as we have already heard today, reports out of Bosnia indicate that the fighting has risen to the highest level in three years. . . . My question is for the Minister of National Defence. For the safety of our peacekeepers, will the government pull our forces out now?

Hon. David M. Collenette (Minister of National Defence and Minister of Veterans Affairs): The situation in the former Yugoslavia is of great concern. . . . However, there is still good work to be done by UNPROFOR, and the Canadian government is still committed. We are consulting with our allies to see whether or not the mission should continue and if changes are required that could be implemented.

(House of Commons Debates, May 17, 1995, p. 12719)

(Débats de la Chambre des Communes, le 17 mai 1995, p. 12719)

L'hon. Lucien Bouchard (chef de l'opposition): . . . à la suite de la réunion du Groupe de contact sur la Bosnie, les pays alliés du Canada ont décidé de riposter aux affronts des Serbes bosniaques en renforçant l'action des forces de paix par une redéfinition de leur mandat et en privilégiant la voie diplomatique pour obtenir la libération de près de 400 Casques bleus, dont dix Canadiens. Le ministre des Affaires étrangères du Canada emboîtait le pas à l'OTAN ce matin, mais sans toutefois énoncer concrètement la position canadienne quant au renforcement du mandat des Casques bleus.

Ma question s'adresse au premier ministre. À la lumière du débat d'urgence autorisé hier, peut-il nous indiquer quelles instructions concrètes il a envoyées à son ministre des Affaires étrangères qui nous représentera demain à l'autre réunion prévue par l'OTAN?

Le très hon. Jean Chrétien (premier ministre): . . . J'ai eu l'occasion hier en cette Chambre d'expliquer qu'il était nécessaire qu'à ce moment-ci les Nations Unies donnent de nouvelles directives aux troupes pour éviter la répétition des actes d'enlèvement qu'on a connus et peut-être redéfinir leur mandat de telle sorte que les troupes puissent agir plus facilement en cas d'urgence que par la passé. Je sais qu'aujourd'hui même, aux Nations Unies, le Secrétaire général doit déposer devant le Conseil de sécurité des nouvelles à ce sujet. Nous avons eu l'occasion au cours de la fin de semaine de faire valoir le point de vue du Canada en la matière. Nous verrons ce que le Conseil de sécurité déterminera. Là-bas, nos troupes sont sous le commandement des Nations Unies et ce sont les Nations Unies qui donnent les instructions qui s'imposent.

Le secrétaire général m'a confirmé qu'il était nécessaire de redéfinir le rôle de nos soldats, de les regrouper de façon à ce qu'ils soient en positions de se défendre plus facilement. Nous verrons ce que les Nations Unies décideront plus tard cette semaine. Quant au ministre des Affaires étrangères, il suit les instructions des énoncés que nous avons émis en cette Chambre au cours du débat, hier, par le ministre de la Défense et mes réponses à la période des questions, hier.

(Débats de la Chambre des Communes, le 30 mai 1995, p. 13001)

(House of Commons Debates, May 30, 1995, p. 13001)

L'hon. Lucien Bouchard (chef de l'opposition): . . . si le ministre des Affaires étrangères est uniquement inspiré et éclairé par ce que vient de dire le premier ministre, il va ramener demain à Bruxelles parce qu'il n'y a pas grand-chose de clair là-dedans, c'est extrêmement ambigu. Il y a d'autres pays qui, eux aussi, font partie des forces de l'ONU et qui ont pris des décisions concrètes. Par exemple la France, la Grande-Bretagne, les États-Unis ont envoyé des troupes supplémentaires ainsi que des équipements plus adéquats là-bas. Je demande au premier ministre de nous dire si son gouvernement a dépêché ou dépêchera d'urgence des équipements additionnels, notamment des blindés plus lourds et des armes, afin que nos Casques bleus puissent se défendre et mener à bien leur mission de paix.

Le très hon. Jean Chrétien (premier ministre): . . . actuellement nous n'avons pris aucune décision en ce sens. Nous croyons que nos troupes, là où elles sont placées actuellement, ont ce qu'il faut pour pouvoir réagir, surtout si leur mandat est redéfini. Nous n'avons pas décidé d'envoyer des troupes additionnelles à ce moment-ci.

(Débats de la Chambre des Communes, le 30 mai 1995, p. 13001)
(House of Commons Debates, May 30, 1995, p. 13001)

Mr. Bob Mills (Red Deer): . . . Lord Owen, the chief European negotiator in Bosnia, who is himself withdrawing from this war torn country, argues that, if there is no peace settlement by autumn, then UN forces will be forced to leave Bosnia. Given the circumstances and that Canada's commitment to Bosnia ends in September, will the government assure Canadians today that after three and a half long years in Bosnia all our troops will be home with their families by fall or sooner?

Hon. David M. Collenette (Minister of National Defence and Minister of Veterans Affairs): . . . with respect to Lord Owen, we do regret very much that he now feels unable to continue with his duties. He has done outstanding work, but it is frustrating and very demanding. However, we still believe that a negotiated settlement to this problem is the answer, not a military solution. We will not be moved by any deadlines set by anyone, whether it is the Bosnian Serbs or any other party.

(House of Commons Debates, June 1, 1995, pp. 13126-27)
(Débats de la Chambre des Communes, le 1er juin 1995, pp. 13126-27)

L'hon. Lucien Bouchard (chef de l'opposition): . . . réunis à Paris samedi, les ministres de la Défense de l'Union européenne et de l'OTAN ont convenu de créer une nouvelle force de réaction rapide chargée de protéger et de porter assistance aux Casques bleus en Bosnie. Or, on apprend que la Russie, membre du Groupe de contact sur la Bosnie, s'oppose à la création d'une telle force de réaction rapide. Le premier ministre peut-il nous indiquer si son gouvernement appuie officiellement la création d'une force et si le Canada y participera concrètement?

Le très hon. Jean Chrétien (premier ministre): . . . le ministre de la Défense et le ministre des Affaires étrangères ont indiqué clairement que le Canada appuyait l'initiative prise par les Anglais et les Français, mais le gouvernement canadien n'a pas décidé, à ce jour, de contribuer des troupes ou de l'équipement. Nous continuons nos consultations et une décision sera prise éventuellement, qu'elle soit affirmative ou négative.

(Débats de la Chambre des Communes, le 6 juin 1995, p. 1321)

(House of Commons Debates, June 6, 1995, p. 1321)

(b)   Le Burundi / Burundi

Mme Maud Debien (Laval-Est): . . . ma question s'adresse au ministre des Affaires étrangères. Le Burundi est en proie à de vives tensions depuis le meurtre, en octobre 1993, de son premier président démocratiquement élu. Ces derniers mois, les conflits entre les deux principales ethnies ont fait quelque 50 000 morts et tout indique qu'une autre crise se prépare. L'assassinat récent du ministre de l'Énergie et des Mines envenime la situation et le pays se trouve actuellement dans un grave climat d'insécurité.

Le ministre peut-il faire le point sur la situation qui prévaut actuellement au Burundi et peut-il nous indiquer quels sont les moyens envisagés par l'ONU et le Canada pour prévenir une éventuelle crise?

L'hon. André Ouellet (ministre des Affaires étrangères): . . . les craintes exprimés par l'honorable député au sujet de la situation au Burundi, malheureusement, sont bien fondées. Il est regrettable de constater que ces conflits ethniques qui ont sévi et créé tant de massacres au Rwanda menacent d'être transportés dans un pays voisin, et ce drame que nous avons vu risque d'être répété. C'est pourquoi le gouvernement du Canada a multiplié ses interventions auprès des Nations Unies que cet organisme régional s'implique immédiatement pour tenter de trouver des solutions à cette crise de plus en plus menaçante.

(Débats de la Chambre des Communes, le 15 mars 1995, p. 10513)

(House of Commons Debates, March 15, 1995, p. 10513)

Mme Maud Debien (Laval-Est): . . . le ministre nous a fait part des différentes démarches qu'il a effectuées auprès, entre autres, du Secrétaire des Nations Unies hier, lors d'un comité, demandant d'envoyer des troupes supplémentaires au Rwanda afin de rétablir l'équilibre dans la région. On sait que le Conseil de sécurité a rejeté la demande du Canada. Ce que je voudrais demander au ministre c'est ceci: Peut-il s'engager à intervenir à nouveau auprès du Conseil de sécurité de l'ONU afin de rassembler, à court terme, les forces multinationales nécessaires à la prévention de ce conflit?

L'hon. André Ouellet (ministre des Affaires étrangères): La réponse est oui, monsieur le Président. Dans le cas où les Nations Unies ne pourraient d'elles-mêmes intervenir, nous avons entrepris des démarches auprès de l'Organisation de l'unité africaine, afin de voir si une démarche régionale ne serait pas plus propice pour amener un certain nombre de pays intéressés à ce qui se passe au Rwanda et au Burundi à intervenir, avec évidemment l'appui et le support des Nations Unies, mais le faisant sur une base régionale plutôt que sur une base globale des Nations Unies.

(Débats de la Chambre des Communes, le 15 mars 1995, p. 10513)
(House of Commons Debates, March 15, 1995, p. 10513)

(c) Haiti / Haïti

Mr. Bob Mills (Red Deer): . . . the minister committed personnel and money, lots of money toward the building of Haiti. I believe the Canadian people need to know what the costs are going to be, what our commitment is going to be, and how long we are going to be there.

Hon. André Ouellet (Minister of Foreign Affairs): Mr. Speaker . . . Canada supports the UN resolutions with regard to Haïti/Haiti. Indeed, we support the Governors Island agreement which calls for the sending of Canadian police forces to Haiti to train the Haitian police forces . . . Second, we have approved the UN resolutions, which will allow — in the second phase of the implementation of resolution 940 of the United Nations — the involvement of military personnel under the auspices of the United Nations. This has not yet been realized. When this second phase takes place, we will respond.

(House of Commons Debates, September 19, 1994, p. 5818)
(Débats de la Chambre des Communes, le 19 septembre 1994, p. 5818)

3 *La politique du maintien de la paix / Peacekeeping Policy*

Mme Maud Debien (Laval-Est): . . . le ministre pourrait-il nous indiquer quelles actions ont été entreprises par le gouvernement pour aider à stopper l'escalade du conflit interethnique au Burundi et, entre autres, pour favoriser la création d'une commission d'enquête internationale sur les événements d'octobre 1993, tel que souhaité, le mois dernier, par les participants à la Conférence régionale sur le Burundi?

L'hon. André Ouellet (ministre des Affaires étrangères): . . . encore une fois, je pense qu'il est important de rappeler que le gouvernement n'a pas attendu que l'opposition nous pose une question en cette Chambre pour agir. Ma collègue, la secrétaire d'État, s'est rendue au Burundi pour participer à une conférence avec des représentants d'autres pays préoccupés par cette question ainsi que par celle du Rwanda. Nous avons nommé, il y a déjà plusieurs semaines, un ambassadeur itinérant spécial pour ces questions, l'ambassadeur Dusseault, qui visite [la] semaine après le Burundi, le Zaïre, le Rwanda et d'autres pays intéressés par [ce qui] se passe là-bas. Bien sur, le Canada veut éviter un bain de sang. Il est certain que ces conflits ethniques sont répréhensibles, mais je rappellerai à l'honorable député que les efforts que nous avons faits, tant aux Nations Unies qu'auprès de l'Organisation de l'Unité africaine, pour tenter d'emmener d'autres pays à agir avec le Canada, ne peuvent pas être imputés au non-intérêt du Canada. Au contraire, nous sommes très intéressés, nous sommes très préoccupés, mais le Canada seul ne peut pas régler ce problème ethnique qui perdure en Afrique.

(Débats de la Chambre des Communes, le 23 mars 1995, p. 10900)
(House of Commons Debates, March 23, 1995, p. 10900)

Mr. Bob Mills (Red Deer): . . . Can the Minister assure us that we will now take the lead and work with the OAS and the UN in a leadership role regarding the solution to the Haiti problem?
Hon. André Ouellet (Minister of Foreign Affairs): Certainly, under the auspices of the UN, we could give leadership in playing a very constructive role[.]

(House of Commons Debates, September 19, 1994, p. 5818)
(Débats de la Chambre des Communes, le 19 juin 1994, p. 5818)

M. Stéphane Bergeron (Verchères): le premier ministre . . . peut-il nous indiquer si le Canada est disposé à envisager la proposition faite par le secrétaire général des Nations Unies . . . à l'effet de réduire le nombre de Casques bleus et de procéder à un redéploiement?
Le très hon. Jean Chrétien (premier ministre): . . . la situation est évidemment très compliquée à ce moment-ci dans cette partie du monde. Le Canada, comme le disait le secrétaire parlementaire, fait partie d'un groupe de pays qui sont présents sur le terrain, et nous avons convenu qu'il n'y aurait aucun retrait sans consultation avec nos partenaires. Les Français ont indiqué qu'ils songeaient à se retirer, mais je suis sûr que s'ils veulent le faire, ce ne sera pas unilatéralement, comme ils nous ont déjà demandé de ne pas le faire unilatéralement. Toute suggestion émanant du secrétaire général des Nations Unies mérite que nous la prenions en considération parce que ce sont des troupes qui sont sous le commandement des Nations Unies.

(Débats de la Chambre des Communes, le 17 mai 1995, p. 12718)
(House of Commons Debates, May 17, 1995, p. 12718)

4   Les relations diplomatiques / Diplomatic Relations

(a)   La politique des affaires étrangères / Foreign Affairs Policy

Hon. Lucien Bouchard (Leader of the Opposition): . . . my next question is directed to the Minister of Foreign Affairs. Could the Minister tell us whether or not Canada has taken diplomatic steps to reach a peaceful resolution in the conflict with the European Union that will respect the pressing goal of protecting and conserving current stocks of turbot threatened by overfishing on the part of European ships?
L'hon. André Ouellet (ministre des Affaires étrangeres): . . . il est absolument clair que le gouvernement du Canada veut poursuivre par la voie diplomatique, et toutes les avenues diplomatiques dont nous disposons, les discussions avec les représentants de l'Union européenne et plus particulierement avec l'Espagne. Il est clair que notre ambassadeur

en Espagne, notre ambassadeur aupres de l'Union européenne, et des representants de mon ministère ici à Ottawa, sont entrés en contact avec les ambassadeurs des pays de l'Union européenne pour expliquer notre position, dire de façon très claire que l'objectif que nous poursuivons est la conservation et tenter de trouver une solution à l'amiable dans les plus brefs délais.

(House of Commons Debates, March 13, 1995, p. 10383)

(Débats de la Chambre des Communes, le 13 mars 1995, p. 10383)

Mr. Svend J. Robinson (Burnaby-Kingsway): Mr. Speaker . . . I want to ask the Prime Minister if he will assure the House that at the summit he will raise two specific issues. First, will he raise the issue of the exclusion of Cuba from the summit and the continued illegal and immoral blockade by the United States of that country. Second, given the very critical situation in Chiapas, Mexico, will the Prime Minister urge at the summit an open dialogue and peaceful negotiated, non-military settlement in Chiapas?

Right Hon. Jean Chrétien (Prime Minister): . . . on the question of Mexico we have already mentioned many times to the authorities there that we want them to negotiate a settlement with the people of that province. I am informed that the dialogue is going better than it was some months ago. But I will press the issue with the newly elected president if I have the occasion. As far as Mr. Castro and Cuba not being present are concerned, we would have had no problem seeing him there. It was decided that he was not to be invited and I was not the one inviting people to that summit.

(House of Commons Debates, December 8, 1994, p. 8832)

(Débats de la Chambre des Communes, le 8 décembre 1994, p. 8832)

M. Stéphane Bergeron (Verchères): . . . ma question s'adresse au ministre des Affaires étrangères. L'impasse perdure toujours dans le conflit sur la pêche au turbot qui oppose le Canada à l'Union européenne. Le ministre des Affaires étrangères a invoqué hier une série d'initiatives diplomatiques afin de reprendre le dialogue avec les représentants de l'Union européenne. Le ministre des Affaires étrangères peut-il nous faire part du résultat des initiatives diplomatiques qu'il invoquait hier et nous indiquer si ces initiatives pourront permettre un déblocage des négociations en vue d'un règlement du différend?

L'hon. André Ouellet (ministre des Affaires étrangères): . . . il est certain que nous voulons poursuivre dans la mesure du possible les démarches diplomatiques que nous avons entreprises. La détermination du gouvernement canadien est on ne peut plus claire à l'effet de vouloir protéger les ressources du poisson qui sont menacées par une surpêche. Je peux assurer l'honorable député que le gouvernement du Canada ne reculera pas à cet égard.

(Débats de la Chambre des Communes, le 14 mars 1995, p. 10468)

(House of Commons Debates, March 14, 1995, p. 10468)

L'hon. Lucien Bouchard (chef de l'opposition): . . . je ne sais pas s'il y a présentement des négociations informelles entre les diplomates canadiens et leurs vis-à-vis européens, je souhaiterais qu'il y en ait. Mais, je demanderais au ministre si le Canada a entrepris des pourparlers et des tentatives pour que des négociations formelles s'amorcent rapidement entre ses représentants et ceux de l'Espagne et de l'Union européenne?

L'hon. André Ouellet (ministre des Affaires étrangères): . . . il me fait plaisir d'informer cette Chambre qu'en effet, une équipe dirigée par le sous-ministre des Affaire étrangères du Canada est à Bruxelles, pour justement entreprendre des négociations avec les représentants de l'Union européenne. Nous sommes prêts, nous sommes disposés et nous voulons régler cette question d'une façon diplomatique. Il est clair que nous recherchons deux objectifs. Le premier objectif est bien sûr de nous assurer que les mesures de conservation qui nous tiennent à coeur seront respectées et par conséquent, nous espérons nous entendre avec nos amis de l'Union européenne pour mettre en place un mécanisme de surveillance, de vérification qui sera efficace. Également, je peux profiter de l'occasion pour dire que dans un esprit de coopération, nous sommes prêts à revoir, avec les représentants de l'Union européenne, le partage du quota que nous avons obtenu à l'occasion des dernières négociations.

(Débats de la Chambre des Communes, le 15 mars 1995, p. 10511)
(House of Commons Debates, March 15, 1995, p. 10511)

Ms. Judy Bethel (Edmonton East): . . . my question is for the Secretary of State for Latin America and Africa. It was reported today that an American congressman suggested Canada defer to U.S. foreign policy on Cuba. He was supporting a bill before Congress that would push countries that ignore the U.S. embargo. How will this bill affect Canadian companies doing business in Cuba?

Hon. Christine Stewart (Secretary of State for Latin America and Africa): The United States has draft legislation in place right now which will have a negative effect, especially on the principals and families of some Canadian companies investing in Cuba.

(House of Commons Debates, March 17, 1995, p. 10667)
(Débats de la Chambre des Communes, le 17 mars 1995, p. 10667)

5 Le droit de la mer / Law of the Sea

(a) Les pêcheries / Fisheries

Mr. Ron MacDonald (Dartmouth): . . . my question is for the Minister of Fisheries and Oceans. In the last eight months this government has taken extraordinary conservation measures to halt the destruction of fish stocks on both coasts. These measures include shutting down entire commercial fisheries, standing up to the Americans on the west coast Pacific salmon treaty, and even convincing the Northwest Atlantic Fisheries Organization to have a moratorium on straddling stocks on the nose and tail of the Grand Bank. Since NAFO is meeting again this week in my riding of

Dartmouth to decide on next year's fishing plans, will the minister stay true to his course? What position will he be taking to the table to ensure that those stocks which are still perilously close to extinction are going to be protected?

Hon. Brian Tobin (Minister of Fisheries and Oceans): . . . given that this important international multilateral meeting is being held in the member's constituency, there is no question the resolve of the Government of Canada will be under his scrutiny as chairman of the fisheries committee. Therefore we will take a position of integrity and new ethics in conservation to the table. We will stand fast for strong rules to protect Canada's fish stocks to seek a reduction in Greenland halibut harvesting off our waters.

(House of Commons Debates, September 19, 1994, p. 5821)
(Débats de la Chambre des Communes, le 19 septembre 1994, p. 5821)

L'hon. Lucien Bouchard (chef de l'opposition): . . . Ma question s'adresse au ministre des Pêches et des Océans. À la faveur de l'inspection au ministre qui à suivi l'arraisonnement du navire espagnol Estai, le ministre des pêches peut-il nous indiquer si les agents de Pêches et Oceans ont relevé des irrégularités qui pourront être mises en preuve au soutien de la position canadienne?

L'hon. Brian Tobin (ministre des Pêches et des Océans): En ce qui concerne les prises trouvées dans l'Estai, il est maintenant évident que jusqu'à 70 p.100 des poissons sont petits et immatures. Cette question est important pour les pêcheurs de partout en Nouvelle-Écosse, à Terre-Neuve, au Nouveau-Brunswick, à l'île-du-Prince-Édouard et dans la province de Quebec. Les pêcheurs d l'Atlantique sont unanimes à vouloir que des mesures efficaces soient prises.

(Débats de la Chambre des Communes, le 13 mars 1995, p. 10383)
(House of Commons Debates, March 13, 1995, p. 10383)

L'hon. Lucien Bouchard (chef de l'opposition): . . . pour démontrer le serieux et la fermeté de la position canadienne, le ministre confirme-t-il que son gouvernement refusera la libération du navire arraisonné posée par l'Union européenne comme condition préealable à la reprise des pourparlers avec le Canada?

Hon. Brian Tobin (Minister of Fisheries and Oceans): . . . the government is proceeding today to do all things required in a very normal and appropriate way in Canadian law. That is the action we are taking today and that is the action we shall continue without fail over the hours and days ahead.

(House of Commons Debates, March 13, 1995, p. 10383)
(Débats de la Chambre des Communes, le 13 mars 1995, p. 10383)

L'hon. Lucien Bouchard (chef de l'opposition): . . . Le ministre des Pêches peut-il nous indiquer si, en échange de la libération du navire espagnol, le

Canada à obtenu que les chalutiers européens respectent le moratoire de soixante jours demandé par le Canada sur la pêche au turbot?

Hon. Brian Tobin (Minister of Fisheries and Oceans): This morning, the master, or the owner, of the Estai posted bond in the order of $500,000 against his vessel. This is in addition to the $8,000 bail posted against the captain of the vessel a day or two ago. . . . . This is in keeping with the procedures of the Canadian judicial system, procedures that have been followed in similar circumstances with other vessels of similar size, shape and value. As a result of the bond being posted, the vessel and the crew are free to leave at any time. In addition to the bond being posted, some 130 tonnes of product have been removed from the vessel and are being held by the crown as evidence. They will be held in a storage facility and will be disposed of by the court at the end of the judicial proceedings. There has been no negotiation, nor should there be in terms of the judicial proceedings themselves. I know the honourable Leader of the Opposition would agree with this. The proceedings have been conducted as they ought to be by the court in the normal manner. Now that both a bond has been posted and there is no fishing on the nose and tail of the Grand Banks, this may well be an opportunity for talks. The Minister of Foreign Affairs and the Prime Minister have given instructions to a negotiating team in Brussels[.]

(House of Commons Debates, March 15, 1995, pp. 10510-11)

(Débats de la Chambre des Communes, le 15 mars 1995, pp. 10510-11)

L'hon. Lucien Bouchard (chef de l'opposition): . . . je demanderais au ministre si, dans le contexte de la libération du chalutier Estai, le Canada à tenté d'obtenir, ou le cas échéant obtenu de l'Union européenne, ou de l'Espagne, la garantie que leurs chalutiers ne pêcheront pas le turbot pendant toute la durée des négociations à venir avec le Canada?

Hon. Brian Tobin (Minister of Fisheries and Oceans): Canada has made it clear since the beginning of this difficulty between Canada and the EU that we will not negotiate while fish are being caught. I was pleased to note yesterday we had four or five days in a row of no fishing on the nose and tail of the Grand Banks. For a few hours last night one vessel did cross over into the area . . . but this morning it had pulled back. Bond has been posted on this vessel and it will sail out of harbour without a net, thus without the ability to fish, since the net was cut.

(House of Commons Debates, March 15, 1995, p. 10511)

(Débats de la Chambre des Communes, le 15 mars 1995, p. 10511)

Mrs. Bonnie Hickey (St. John's East): . . . my question is for the Minister of Fisheries and Oceans. On Monday, March 27 the United Nations conference on the straddling and highly migratory fish stocks reconvenes. The recent fishing of the Spanish fleet on the nose and tail of the Grand Bank clearly shows the urgency for a bidding convention to end the threat of foreign over-fishing. Can the minister tell the House what Canada hopes to achieve in these crucial meetings next week?

Hon. Brian Tobin (Minister of Fisheries and Oceans): Mr. Speaker. . . . This conference has now been ongoing for two years. It has made very substantial progress to the point at which we now have more than 80 per cent of all the countries participating in New York at the UN conference supporting the proposal endorsed and in some respect authored by Canada for a binding convention that would give us effective rules, transparent rules to govern the ways distant water fishing fleets behave on the high seas. We hope for a success and a completed conference this year, but even if a convention comes in 1995 it will take several years for it to gain ratification. In the interim we must have effective means to protect those fragile and fast disappearing straddling stocks.

(House of Commons Debates, March 24, 1995, p. 10954)
(Débats de la Chambre des Communes, le 24 mars 1995, p. 10954)

M. Francis G. LeBlanc (Cape Breton Highlands-Canso): . . . ma question s'adresse au ministre des Pêches et des Océans. La récente entente entre le Canada et l'Union européenne pour conserver et protéger les stocks de poissons dans l'Atlantique fut l'objet d'une réunion de l'Organisation des Pêches de l'Atlantique Nord-Ouest la semaine dernière à Toronto. Le ministre qui à été largement responsable pour l'élaboration de la position canadienne peut-il informer la Chambre des suites de ces rencontres et du soutien de l'OPANO en ce qui concerne les objectifs cruciaux du Canada.

L'hon. Brian Tobin (ministre des Pêches et des Océans): . . . la réunion de l'OPANO élargit la nature de l'entente de conservation du flétan noir à une entente qui protège toutes les espèces de poissons de fond de l'Atlantique nord-ouest. Elle élargit l'entente conclue entre le Canada et l'Union européenne à une entente avec les quinze membres de l'OPANO. Je crois qu'il est nécessaire que je parle avec les pêcheurs québécois à certaines occasions[.]

(House of Commons Debates, June 12, 1995, p. 13598)
(Débats de la Chambre des Communes, le 12 juin 1995, p. 13598)

6 Trade / Le commerce

(a) Free Trade Agreement / L'accord de libre-échange

M. Ghislain Lebel (Chambly): . . . ma question s'adresse au ministre des Affaires étrangères. En proposant dans son budget l'imposition d'une taxe de 3 $ par véhicule de 1,50 $ par personne entrant aux États-Unis, le gouvernement américain à soulevé une opposition unanime au Canada, où l'on juge cette taxe tout à fait incompatible avec l'Accord de libre-échange nord-américain. Le ministre des Affaires étrangères peut-il nous indiquer quelle a été la réaction du gouvernement américain, à la suite de la protestation faite par le Canada, via son ambassade à Washington?

Hon. Roy MacLaren (Minister for International Trade): . . . as indicated to the House yesterday, we have raised this issue with the United States trade representative. We did so last week and we have done so more formally with the State Department. Our protests have been duly noted, but the response has been generally that the proposed measure has no chance of passing through the U.S. Congress.

(House of Commons Debates, February 8, 1995, p. 9328)
(Débats de la Chambre des Communes, le 8 février 1995, p. 9328)

M. Stéphane Bergeron (Verchères): Le 1ᵉʳ janvier dernier, les États-Unis ont profité de la création de l'Organisation mondiale du commerce pour imposer au Canada des nouvelles restrictions sur les importations du sucre, menaçant ainsi plus de 2 400 emplois. Par ailleurs, un projet de loi piloté par le sénateur Jesse Helms se trouve actuellement devant le Congrès américain et vise à interdire l'accès au marché américain à toute entreprise qui entretient des relations commerciales avec Cuba. Pendant que le sucre américain inonde notre marché à un point tel que le ministère du Revenu à senti le besoin d'initier une enquête en dumping, est-ce que le ministre du commerce international peut nous dire ce qu'il entend faire concrètement pour empêcher l'adoption du projet de loi Helms?

Hon. Roy MacLaren (Minister for International Trade): We have been vigorous in our protests about the Helms bill. They have taken a variety of forms. We followed the traditional one of protesting to the United States State Department. The Prime Minister had occasion to raise the matter during heads of government meetings. For my part, I have on a number of occasions pressed the matter with the United States Trade Representative. The result of our protests and those of European countries, Japan and other major trading partners of the United States has been to encourage the administration to seek a revision of the bill in such a way as to meet our trading concerns.

(House of Commons Debates, June 21, 1995, p. 14317)
(Débats de la Chambre des Communes, le 21 juin 1995, p. 14317)

L'hon. Lucien Bouchard (chef de l'opposition): . . . je demande au premier ministre s'il souscrit à la suggestion faite par les députés qui siégeaient au comité et qui, au lendemain de la ratification de l'ALÉNA, s'empressent de proposer l'abolition des postes de délégués commerciaux aux États-Unis et au Mexique?

Le très hon. Jean Chrétien (premier ministre): . . . [au] contraire, nous avons signé l'ALÉNA. Suite aux discussions que j'ai eues, par exemple, avec le président du Chili et le président du Mexique, nous favorisons l'entrée du Chili dans l'ALÉNA parce que nous croyons qu'il est important qu'il y ait plus de pays que seulement trois dans cette association. Nous en discuterons davantage lors du sommet qui aura lieu le mois prochain à Miami.

(Débats de la Chambre des Communes, le 21 novembre 1994, p. 8036)
(House of Commons Debates, November 21, 1994, p. 8036)

Mr. Barry Campbell (St. Paul's): . . . my question is for the Minister for International Trade. Both the Prime Minister and the Minister for International Trade have spoken recently about the need to strengthen economic ties between North America and Europe. Would the Minister for International Trade please bring the House up to date on the status of this initiative?

Hon. Roy MacLaren (Minister for International Trade): . . . the Prime Minister some months ago raised the question of closer economic ties between Europe and North America, including the possibility of an eventual free trade agreement. He did so because on this side of the House we recognize that . . . the era of the cold war having passed, the security emphasis is no longer so central to our relationship and should be further underpinned by closer economic ties. In addition, we are a government that recognizes the possibilities of going beyond the commitments we made in the World Trade Organization to reduce trade barriers. We believe that initiative could be embodied in a freer trade agreement with Europe [similar to the agreement to which we] have already committed . . . over a longer period with Asia Pacific and the western hemisphere.

(House of Commons Debates, June 9, 1995, p. 13532)

(Débats de la Chambre des Communes, le 9 juin 1995, p. 13532)

(b) GATT and WTO / Le GATT et L'OMC

Mr. Charlie Penson (Peace River): . . . The government has taken the position that GATT takes precedence over NAFTA. That is because we have imposed new tariffs as high as 350 per cent on butter and other supply managed goods. Does this not put us in a very difficult position when arguing against new U.S. tariffs on sugar?

Hon. John Manley (Minister of Industry): . . . on behalf of the Minister for International Trade, let me say that we are conducting these discussions with a very high regard for Canadian interests which will be defended in all aspects of the continuing discussions.

(House of Commons Debates, March 15, 1995, p. 10517)

(Débats de la Chambre des Communes, le 15 mars 1995, p. 10517)

Mr. Paul Zed (Fundy-Royal): . . . Can the minister explain to the House the basis for the investigation into the dumping and subsidization of sugar imports and the benefits which the sugar producers can expect to receive from this important action?

Ms. Susan Whelan (Parliamentary Secretary to Minister of National Revenue): . . . today the department initiated a dumping subsidy investigation into imports of sugar from Korea, the European Union and the United States. This investigation was initiated in response to allegations filed by the Canadian Sugar Institute that sugar imports are being dumped into Canada, and that foreign refiners have been receiving government subsidies which allow them to sell at prices which are sometimes below the cost of production. The alleged practices have reduced profit levels, [and] forced Canadian refiners to reduce prices to unreasonable levels and to lay off workers. Therefore, the department will now investigate the allegations and should they be proven accurate, apply an extra duty which will take away the unfair advantage enjoyed by imports and once again provide a level playing field for Canadian refiners.

(House of Commons Debates, March 17, 1995, p. 10663)

(Débats de la Chambre des Communes, le 17 mars 1995, p. 10663)

Treaty Action Taken by Canada in 1994 / Mesures prises par le Canada en matière de traités en 1994

compiled by / préparé par
ANDRÉ BERGERON*

I BILATERAL

Antigua and Barbuda
Agreement between the Government of Canada and the Government of Antigua and Barbuda on Social Security (with Administrative Arrangement). Ottawa, September 2, 1992. *In force* January 1, 1994. CTS 1994/6

Argentina
Agreement between the Government of Canada and the Government of the Argentine Republic for Co-operation in the Peaceful Uses of Nuclear Energy. Ottawa, June 21, 1994.

Convention between the Government of Canada and the Government of the Argentine Republic for the Avoidance of Double Taxation and the Prevention of Fiscal Evasion with Respect to Taxes on Income and on Capital (with Protocol). Buenos Aires, April 29, 1993. *Entered into force* December 30, 1994. CTS 1994/24

Exchange of Notes between Canada and Argentina constituting an Agreement for the Avoidance of Double Taxation on Profits Derived from Sea and Air Transportation. Buenos Aires, August 6, 1949. *Entered into force* August

6, 1949. (CTS 1949/5). *Terminated* December 31, 1994.

ASEAN
Agreement between the Governments of the member Countries of the Association of Southeast Asian Nations and the Government of Canada on Economic Co-operation. Singapore, July 28, 1993. *Entered into force* April 1, 1994. CTS 1994/16

Chile
Film and Television Co-Production Agreement between the Government of Canada and the Government of the Republic of Chile. Santiago, September 2, 1994. *Applied provisionally* from September 2, 1994.

China
Treaty between the Government of Canada and the Government of the People's Republic of China on Mutual Legal Assistance in Criminal Matters. Beijing, July 29, 1994.

Agreement between the Government of Canada and the Government of the People's Republic of China for Co-operation in the Peaceful Uses of Nuclear Energy (with Annexes), Peking, Novem-

* Treaty Registrar, Legal Advisory Division, Department of Foreign Affairs / Greffier des Traités, Directions des consultations juridiques, Ministère des Affaires étrangères.

ber 7, 1994. *Entered into force* November 7, 1994. CTS 1994/27.

Commission for Environmental Co-operation

Headquarters Agreement between the Government of Canada and the Commission for Environmental Co-operation. Montreal, September 2, 1994. *Entered into force* September 2, 1994. CTS 1994/21.

Estonia

Agreement between the Government of Canada and the Government of the Republic of Estonia on Trade and Commerce. Ottawa, June 27, 1994.

Finland

Protocol between the Government of Canada and the Government of the Republic of Finland amending their Agreement on Social Security done at Ottawa, October 28, 1986 (with Administrative Arrangement). Ottawa, November 2, 1994

France

Procès-verbal Applying the March 27, 1972 Agreement between Canada and France on their Mutual Fishing Relations (with Annexes). Paris, December 2, 1994.

Exchange of Notes between the Government of Canada and the Government of the Republic of France constituting an Agreement on Cooperation in the Management of the Fisheries Resources within the Framework of the Northwest Atlantic Fisheries. Paris, December 2, 1994.

Agreement between the Government of Canada and the Government of the Republic of France Relating to the Development of Regional Co-operation between Canadian Atlantic Provinces and the French Territorial Collectivity of St. Pierre and Miquelon. Paris, December 2, 1994. *Entered into force* December 2, 1994. CTS 1994/33.

Hungary

Convention between the Government of Canada and the Government of the Republic of Hungary for the Avoidance of Double Taxation and the Prevention of Fiscal Evasion with Respect to Taxes on Income and on Capital. Budapest, April 15, 1992. *Entered into force* October 1, 1994. CTS 1994/15.

Protocol to the Tax Convention between the Government of Canada and the Government of the Republic of Hungary signed on April 15, 1992. Budapest, May 3, 1994

India

Treaty between the Government of Canada and the Government of the Republic of India on Mutual Assistance in Criminal Matters. Ottawa, October 24, 1994.

Italy

Protocol amending the Convention between the Government of Canada and the Government of Italy for the Avoidance of Double Taxation with Respect to Taxes on Income and for the Prevention of Fiscal Evasion. Ottawa, March 20, 1989. *Entered into force* February 22, 1994. CTS 1994/11.

Japan

Exchange of Notes between the Government of Canada and the Government of Japan constituting an Agreement amending the Canada-Japan Air Services Agreement, signed at Ottawa on January 12, 1955, as amended (with Annex). Ottawa, June 2, 1994. *Entered into force* June 2, 1994. CTS 1994/12.

Korea

Treaty on Extradition between the Government of Canada and the Government of the Republic of Korea. Ottawa, April 15, 1994.

Treaty between the Government of Canada and the Government of the Republic of Korea on Mutual Legal Assistance in Criminal Matters. Ottawa, April 15, 1994. *Entered into force* February 1, 1995.

Latvia

Agreement between the Government of Canada and the Government of the Republic of Latvia on Trade and Commerce. Ottawa, August 10, 1994.

Lithuania

Agreement between the Government of Canada and the Government of the Republic of Lithuania on Trade and Commerce. Vilnius, August 8, 1994.

Agreement between the Government of Canada and the Government of the Republic of Lithuania for Co-operation in the peaceful Uses of Nuclear Energy (with Annexes). Vilnius, November 17, 1994.

Luxembourg

Protocol to the 1986 Convention on Social Security between Canada and Luxembourg. Ottawa, February 6, 1992. *Entered into force* January 1, 1994. CTS 1994/8.

Mexico

Agreement between the Government of Canada and the Government of the United Mexican States for Co-operation in the Peaceful Uses of Nuclear Energy (with Annexes). Mexico, November 16, 1994.

Mongolia

Agreement between the Government of Canada and the Government of Mongolia on Trade and Commerce. Ottawa, June 8, 1994. *Entered into force* October 6, 1994. CTS 1994/25.

Netherlands

Protocol Amending the Convention between Canada and the Kingdom of the Netherlands for the Avoidance of Double Taxation and the Prevention of Fiscal Evasion with Respect to Taxes on Income (with Protocol). The Hague, March 4, 1993. *Entered into force* July 30, 1994. CTS 1994/32.

Philippines

Agreement on Social Security between the Government of Canada and the Government of the Republic of the Philippines. Winnipeg, September 9, 1994.

Poland

Agreement between the Government of Canada and the Government of the Republic of Poland concerning Military Relations. Ottawa, March 28, 1994.

Treaty between Canada and the Republic of Poland on Mutual Legal Assistance in Criminal Matters. Ottawa, September 12, 1994.

Romania

Agreement between the Government of Canada and the Government of Romania concerning Military Relations. Ottawa, June 7, 1993. *Entered into force* January 24, 1994. CTS 1994/10.

Exchange of Notes between the Government of Canada and the Government of the Socialist Republic of Romania constituting an Agreement amending their Agreement for Co-operation in the Development and Application of Atomic Energy for Peaceful Purposes, done at Ottawa, October 24, 1977. Bucharest, October 12, 1994. *Entered into force* October 12, 1994. CTS 1994/23.

Russia

Agreement between the Government of Canada and the Government of the Russian Federation on Economic Co-operation. Moscow, May 8, 1993. *In force* December 7, 1994.

Spain

Treaty between Canada and Spain on Mutual Assistance in Criminal Matters. Madrid, July 4, 1994.

St. Kitts and Nevis

Agreement on Social Security between Canada and the Federation of St. Kitts and Nevis (with Administrative Arrangement). Ottawa, August 17, 1992. *Entered into force* January 1, 1994. CTS 1994/9.

Sweden

Agreement on Film and Video Relations between the Government of Canada and the Government of Sweden. Stockholm, October 17, 1994.

Convention on Social Security between Canada and the Swiss Confederation (with Final Protocol). Ottawa, February 24, 1994.

Switzerland

Convention on Social Security between Canada and and the Swiss Confederation (with Final Protocol). Ottawa, February 24, 1994.

Thailand

Treaty between the Government of Canada and the Government of the Kingdom of Thailand on Mutual Legal Assistance in Criminal Matters. Ottawa, October 3, 1994. *Entered into force* October 3, 1994. CTS 1994/20.

Ukraine

Agreement between the Government of Canada and the Government of Ukraine on Trade and Commerce. Kiev, March 31, 1994.

Agreement on Friendship and Co-operation between Canada and Ukraine. Kiev, March 31, 1994.

Agreement between the Government of Canada and the Government of Ukraine concerning Military Relations. Ottawa, October 24, 1994. *Entered into force* October 24, 1994. CTS 1994/29.

Agreement between the Government of Canada and the Government of Ukraine on Economic Co-operation. Ottawa, October 24, 1994.

Agreement between the Government of Canada and the Government of Ukraine for the Promotion and Protection of Investments. Ottawa, October 24, 1994.

United Kingdom

Exchange of Letters constituting an Agreement between the Government of Canada and the Government of the United Kingdom of Great Britain and Northern Ireland Establishing the Terms and Conditions of Reciprocity in Social Security between Canada, Jersey and Guernsey (with Schedule). Ottawa, February 5 and 12, 1993. *Entered into force* January 1, 1994. CTS 1994/5.

Exchange of Letters constituting an Agreement on Consolidated Arrangements concerning Social Security between the Government of Canada and the Government of the United Kingdom of Great Britain and Northern Ireland (with Schedule). Ottawa,

October 18, 1994. *Notes signed* October 11 and October 18, 1994.

United States of America

Exchange of Notes constituting an Agreement between the Government of Canada and the Government of the United States of America to Facilitate Co-operation between Military Services of the two countries. Washington and Ottawa, August 19, 1994. *Entered into force* August 19, 1994.

Exchange of Notes between the Government of Canada and the Government of the United States of America constituting an Agreement concerning the Establishment of a Jointly Staffed Undersea Surveillance Facility in Halifax, Nova Scotia (with Memorandum of Understanding). Ottawa, May 30, 1994. *Entered into force* May 30, 1994. *Notes signed* March 23 and May 30, 1994. CTS 1994/17.

Exchange of Notes between the Government of Canada and the Government of the United States of America constituting an Agreement regarding the Allocation of Television Channels. Ottawa, June 23, 1952. *In force* June 23, 1952. *Notes signed* April 23 and June 23, 1952. CTS 1952/13. *Terminated* January 5, 1994.

Exchange of Notes between the Government of Canada and the Government of the United States of America constituting an Agreement amending the Agreement concerning the Allocation of Television Channels dated June 23, 1952. Washington, April 7, 1982. *Entered into force* April 7, 1982. *Notes signed* February 26 and April 7, 1982. CTS 1982/23. *Terminated* January 5, 1994.

Agreement between the Government of Canada and the Government of the United States of America on Co-operation in the Boreal Ecosystem-Atmosphere Study (BOREAS). Washington, April 18, 1994. *Entered into force* April 18, 1994. CTS 1994/26.

Exchange of Notes between the Government of Canada and the Government of the United States of America concerning the 800 MHz band and amending the 1952 Agreement regarding the Allocation of Television Channels, as amended, and the 1962 Agreement concerning the Coordination and use of Radio Frequencies above Thirty Megacycles Per Second, as amended (with Annex). Washington, November 2, 1993 and January 4, 1994. *Entered into force* January 4, 1994.

Exchange of Notes between the Government of Canada and the Government of the United States of America constituting an Agreement relating to the Television Broadcasting Service. Washington, November 3, 1993 and January 5, 1994. *In force* January 5, 1994.

Venezuela

Treaty between the Government of Canada and the Government of the Republic of Venezuela on the Serving of Penal Sentences. Caracas, January 24, 1994.

Vietnam

General Agreement on Development Co-operation between the Government of Canada and the Government of the Socialist Republic of Vietnam (with Annexes). Ottawa, June 21, 1994. *Entered into force* June 21, 1994. CTS 1994/18.

Agreement on Economic Co-operation between the Government of Canada and the Government of the Socialist Republic of Vietnam. Ottawa, June 21, 1994.

Zimbabwe

Agreement between the Government of Canada and the Government of the Republic of Zimbabwe for the Avoidance of Double Taxation and the Prevention of Fiscal Evasion with Respect to Taxes on Income, Capital and Capital Gains. Harare, April 16, 1992. *Entered into force* December 15, 1994. CTS 1994/31.

II MULTILATERAL

Adoption

Convention on Protection of Children and Co-operation in Respect of Inter-

country Adoption. The Hague, May 29, 1993. *Signed* by Canada April 12, 1994.

Aviation

Protocol on the Authentic Quadrilingual Text of the Convention on International Civil Aviation (Chicago, 1944). Montreal, September 30, 1977. *Acceded to* by Canada March 23, 1994.

Commerce

North American Free Trade Agreement between the Government of Canada, the Government of the United Mexican States and the Government of the United States of America. Ottawa, December 17, 1992. *Signed* by Canada December 17, 1992. *Entered into force* for Canada January 1, 1994. *Signed* at Ottawa December 11 and 17, at Mexico, D. F. December 14 and 17 and at Washington, D. C. December 8 and 17, 1992. CTS 1994/2.

Agreement Establishing the World Trade Organization (WTO). Marrakesh, April 15, 1994. *Signed* by Canada April 15, 1994. *Ratified* by Canada December 30, 1994.

Agreement on Government Procurement (with Appendices). Marrakesh, April 15, 1994. *Signed* by Canada April 15, 1994.

International Bovine Meat Agreement (with Annex). Marrakesh, April 15, 1994. *Signed* by Canada April 15, 1994. *Ratified* by Canada December 30, 1994.

Defence

Agreement to amend the Protocol of Signature (re: Article 56, paragraph 9,) to the Agreement of 3 August 1959, as amended by the Agreements of 21 October 1971 and 18 May 1981, and without prejudice to the Agreement of 18 March 1993 to Supplement the Agreement between the Parties to the North Atlantic Treaty Regarding the Status of their Forces with Respect to Foreign Forces stationed in the Federal Republic of Germany. Bonn, May 16, 1994. *Signed* by Canada May 16, 1994.

Exchange of Notes constituting an Agreement amending the Agreement of June 19, 1951 between the parties to the North Atlantic Treaty (NATO) regarding the Status of their Forces, the Supplementary Agreement of August 3, 1959 and the Agreements related thereto. Bonn, September 25, 1990. *Signed* by Canada September 25, 1990. *Entered into force* for Canada January 4, 1994. CTS 1994/30.

Exchange of Notes constituting an Arrangement (constituting an Agreement for Canada) between the Governments of Canada, Belgium, and the Netherlands and the Government of the Federal Republic of Germany concerning the Status and Access of Canadian, Belgian, and Dutch Forces in Berlin. Bonn, September 23, 1991. *Signed* by Canada September 23, 1991. This treaty never entered into force and will not be published. *Terminated* September 12, 1994.

Exchange of Notes constituting an Agreement concerning the Agreement of June 19, 1951 between the parties to the North Atlantic Treaty Organization (NATO) regarding the Status of their Forces, the Supplementary Agreement of August 3, 1959 and the Agreements related thereto. Bonn, September 12, 1994. *Signed* by Canada September 12, 1994.

Environment
Agreement Establishing the Inter-American Institute for Global Change Research. Montevideo, May 13, 1992. *Signed* by Canada March 25, 1993. *Entered into force* for Canada March 12, 1994. CTS 1994/28.

Amendment to the Montreal Protocol on Substances that Deplete the Ozone Layer. Copenhagen, November 25, 1992. *Ratified* by Canada March 16, 1994. *Entered into force* for Canada June 14, 1994. CTS 1994/13.

North American Agreement on Environmental Co-operation (with Annexes). Ottawa, September 14, 1993. *Signed* by Canada September 14, 1993. *Entered into force* for Canada Janu-

ary 1, 1994. *Signed* at Ottawa September 12 and 14, 1993, at Mexico, D. F., September 8 and 14, 1993 and at Washington, D. C., September 9 and 14, 1993. CTS 1994/3.

United Nations Convention to Combat Desertification in Those Countries Experiencing Serious Drought and/or Desertification, Particularly in Africa. Paris, October 14, 1994. *Signed* by Canada October 14, 1994.

United Nations Framework Convention on Climate Change. New York, May 9, 1992. *Signed* by Canada June 12, 1992. *Ratified* by Canada December 4, 1992. *Entered into force* for Canada March 21, 1994. CTS 1994/7.

Fisheries
Agreement to Promote Compliance with International Conservation and Management Measures by Fishing Vessels on the High Seas. Rome, November 24, 1993. *Acceptance* by Canada May 20, 1994.

Health
Agreement to Ban Smoking on International Passenger Flights. Chicago, November 1, 1994. *Signed* by Canada November 1, 1994.

Labour
Convention concerning Minimum Standards in Merchant Ships (Convention 147). Geneva, October 29, 1976. *Ratified* by Canada May 25, 1993. *Entered into force* for Canada May 25, 1994.

North American Agreement on Labour Co-operation (with Annexes). Ottawa, September 14, 1993. *Signed* by Canada September 14, 1993. *Entered into force* for Canada January 1, 1994. *Signed* at Ottawa September 12 and 14, 1993, at Mexico, D. F., September 8 and 14, 1993 and at Washington, D. C., September 9 and 14, 1993. CTS 1994/4.

Navigation
International Convention on Salvage. London, April 28, 1989. *Signed* by Canada June 11, 1990. *Ratified* by Canada November 14, 1994.

Nuclear
Convention on Nuclear Safety (IAEA). Vienna, September 20, 1994. *Signed by* Canada September 20, 1994.

Pollution
Protocol to the 1979 Convention on Long-Range Transboundary Air Pollution on Further Reduction of Sulphur Emissions. Oslo, June 13, 1994. *Signed* by Canada June 14, 1994.

Postal Matters
Acts of the 21st Universal Postal Congress. Seoul, August 31, 1994. *Signed by* Canada August 31, 1994.

Fifth Additional Protocol to the Constitution of the Postal Union. Montevideo, June 23, 1993. *Signed by* Canada June 23, 1993. *In force* January 1, 1994.

Safety of Personnel
Convention on the Safety of United Nations and Associated Personnel. United Nations, December 9, 1994. *Signed* by Canada December 15, 1994.

Science
Agreement to Establish a Science and Technology Centre in Ukraine. Kiev, October 25, 1993. *Ratified* by Canada June 17, 1994. *In force* July 16, 1994.

Settlement of Disputes
Convention for the Pacific Settlement of International Disputes. The Hague, October 18, 1907. *Ratified* by Canada May 10, 1994. *Entered into force* for Canada July 9, 1994. CTS 1994/14.

Telecommunications
Optional Protocol on the Compulsory Settlement of Disputes Relating to the Constitution of the ITU, to the Convention of the ITU and to the Administrative Regulations, Nice, 1992. Geneva, December 22, 1992. *Signed* by Canada December 22, 1992. *Ratified* by Canada June 21, 1993. *Entered into force* for Canada July 1, 1994.

Constitution and Convention of the International Telecommunication Union (ITU). Geneva, December 22, 1992. *Signed* by Canada December 22, 1992. *Ratified* by Canada June 21,

1993. *Entered into force* for Canada July 1, 1994.

Textiles
Protocol Maintaining in Force the Arrangement Regarding International Trade in Textiles. Geneva, December 9, 1993. *Signed* by Canada December 21, 1993. *Ratified* by Canada March 2, 1994. *Entered into force* for Canada March 2, 1994. *Applied provisionally* by Canada as from 1 January 1994. CTS 1994/22.

Use of Force
Convention on Prohibitions or Restrictions on the Use of Certain Conventional Weapons which may be Deemed to be Excessively Injurious or to have Indiscriminate Effects (with Protocols). Geneva, October 10, 1980. *Signed* by Canada April 10, 1981. *Ratified* by Canada June 24, 1994. *Entered into force* for Canada December 24, 1994. CTS 1994/19.

1 BILATÉRAUX

Antigua et Barbuda
Accord de sécurité sociale entre le gouvernement du Canada et le gouvernement de Antigua et Barbuda (avec Arrangement Administratif). Ottawa, le 2 septembre 1994. *En vigueur* le 1er janvier 1994. RTC 1994/6.

Argentine
Convention entre le gouvernement du Canada et le gouvernement de la République d'Argentine en vue d'éviter les doubles impositions et de prévenir l'évasion fiscale en matière d'impôts sur le revenu et sur la fortune (avec Protocole). Buenos Aires, le 29 avril 1993. *En vigueur* le 30 décembre 1994. RTC 1994/24

Échange de Notes entre le Canada et l'Argentine comportant un Accord visant à éviter la double imposition des bénéfices provenant du transport maritime et aérien. Buenos Aires, le 6 août 1949. *En vigueur* le 6 août 1949. RTC 1949/5. *Terminé* le 31 décembre 1994.

Accord de coopération entre le gouvernement du Canada et le gouvernement de la République d'Argentine concernant les utilisations pacifiques de l'énergie. Ottawa, le 21 juin 1994.

ANASE
Accord de coopération économique entre le gouvernement du Canada et les gouvernements des États Membres de l'Association des Nations de l'Asie du Sud-Est. Singapour, le 28 juillet 1993. *En vigueur* le 1ᵉʳ avril 1994. RTC 1994/16.

Chili
Accord de coproduction entre le gouvernement du Canada et le gouvernement de la République du Chili. Santiago, le 2 septembre 1994. *Appliqué à titre provisoire* avec effet à compter du 2 septembre 1994.

Chine
Traité d'entraide judiciaire en matière pénale entre le gouvernement du Canada et le gouvernement de la République populaire de Chine. Beijing, le 29 juillet 1994.

Accord de coopération entre le gouvernement du Canada et le gouvernement de la République populaire de Chine en matière d'utilisations pacifiques de l'énergie nucléaire (avec Annexes). Beijing, le 7 novembre 1994. *En vigueur* le 7 novembre 1994. RTC 1994/27.

Commission de coopération environnementale
Accord de Siège entre le gouvernement du Canada et la Commission de coopération environnementale. Montréal, le 2 septembre 1994. *En vigueur* le 2 septembre 1994. RTC 1994/21.

Corée
Traité d'entraide entre le gouvernement du Canada et le gouvernement de la République de Corée. Ottawa, le 15 avril 1994. *En vigueur* le 1ᵉʳ février 1995.

Traité d'extradition entre le gouvernement du Canada et le gouvernement de la République de Corée. Ottawa, le 15 avril 1994.

Espagne
Traité d'entraide judiciaire en matière pénale entre le Canada et le Royaume d'Espagne. Madrid, le 4 juillet 1994.

Estonie
Accord de commerce entre le gouvernement du Canada et le gouvernement de la République de l'Estonie. Ottawa, le 27 juin 1994.

États-Unis d'Amérique
Échange de Notes constituant un Accord entre le gouvernement du Canada et le gouvernement des États-Unis d'Amérique concernant l'établissement à Halifax (Nouvelle Écosse) d'une installation conjointe de surveillance sous-marine (avec Mémoire d'entente). Ottawa, le 30 mai 1994. *En vigueur* le 30 mai 1994. *Notes signées* les 23 mars et 30 mai 1994. RTC 1994/17.

Échange de Notes constituant un Accord entre le gouvernement du Canada et le gouvernement des États-Unis d'Amérique visant à faciliter la coopération entre les Forces armées des deux pays. Washington et Ottawa, le 19 août 1994. *En vigueur* le 19 août 1994.

Échange de Notes entre le gouvernement du Canada et le gouvernement des États-Unis d'Amérique concernant un Accord relatif a l'allocation de réseaux. Ottawa, le 23 juin 1952. *En vigueur* le 23 juin 1952. *Notes signées* les 23 avril et 23 juin 1952. RTC 1952/13. *Terminé* le 5 janvier 1994.

Échange de Notes entre le gouvernement du Canada et le gouvernement des États-Unis d'Amérique constituant un Accord modifiant l'Accord signé le 23 juin 1952. Washington, le 7 avril 1982. *En vigueur* le 7 avril 1982. *Notes signées* les 26 février et 7 avril 1982. RTC 1982/23. *Terminé* le 5 janvier 1994.

Échange de Notes entre le gouvernement du Canada et le gouvernement des États-Unis d'Amérique constituant un Accord relatif aux services de télédiffusion. Washington, le 3 novembre 1992 et le 5 janvier 1994. *En vigueur* le 5 janvier 1994.

Échange de Notes entre le gouvernement du Canada et le gouvernement des États-Unis d'Amérique constituant un accord sur la réallocation de la bande des 800 MHz et modifiant l'Accord de 1952 au sujet de l'attribution de canaux de télévision, tel que modifié, et l'Accord de 1962 concernant la coordination et l'utilisation des fréquences radiophoniques de plus de trente mégacycles par seconde, tel que modifié (avec Annexe). Washington, le 2 novembre 1993 et le 4 janvier 1994. *En vigueur* le 4 janvier 1994.

Accord entre le gouvernement du Canada et le gouvernement des États-Unis d'Amérique concernant la coopération dans le cadre de l'étude de l'atmosphère et des écosystèmes boréaux (BOREAS). Washington, le 18 avril 1994. *En vigueur* le 18 avril 1994. RTC 1994/26.

Finlande
Protocole entre le gouvernement du Canada et le gouvernement de la République de Finlande modifiant leur Accord sur la sécurité sociale fait à Ottawa le 28 octobre 1986 (avec Arrangement administratif). Ottawa, le 2 novembre 1994.

France
Procès-verbal d'application de l'Accord relatif aux relations réciproques entre le Canada et la France en matière de pêche du 27 mars 1972 (avec Annexes). Paris, le 2 décembre 1994.

Échange de Notes entre le gouvernement du Canada et le gouvernement de la France constituant un Accord relatif à la coopération en matière de gestion des ressources halieutiques dans le cadre de l'Organisation des pêches de l'Atlantique Nord-Ouest. Paris, le 2 décembre 1994.

Accord entre le gouvernement du Canada et le gouvernement de la République française relatif au développement de la coopération régionale entre les provinces atlantiques canadiennes et la collectivité territoriale française de Saint-Pierre et Miquelon. Paris, le 2

décembre 1994. *En vigueur* le 2 décembre 1994. RTC 1994/33.

Hongrie
Convention entre le gouvernement du Canada et le gouvernement de la République de Hongrie en vue d'éviter les doubles impositions et de prévenir l'évasion fiscale en matière d'impôts sur le revenu et sur la fortune. Budapest, le 15 avril 1992. *En vigueur* le 1er octobre 1994. RTC 1994/15.

Protocole à la Convention fiscale entre le gouvernement du Canada et le gouvernement de la République de Hongrie signée le 15 avril 1992. Budapest, le 3 mai 1994.

Inde
Traité d'entraide judiciaire en matière pénale entre le gouvernement du Canada et le gouvernement de la République de l'Inde. Ottawa, le 24 octobre 1994.

Italie
Avenant à la Convention fiscale entre le gouvernement du Canada et le gouvernement de l'Italie en vue d'éviter les doubles impositions en matière d'impôts sur le revenu et de prévenir les évasions fiscales. Ottawa, le 20 mars 1989. *En vigueur* le 22 février 1994. RTC 1994/11.

Japon
Échange de Notes constituant un Accord entre le gouvernement du Canada et le gouvernement du Japon modifiant l'Accord relatif aux services aériens entre le Canada et le Japon, signé à Ottawa le 12 janvier 1955, tel que modifié (avec Annexe). Ottawa, le 2 juin 1994. *En vigueur* le 2 juin 1994. RTC 1994/12.

Lettonie
Accord de commerce entre le gouvernement du Canada et le gouvernement de la République de Lettonie. Riga, le 10 août 1994.

Lituanie
Accord de commerce entre le gouvernement du Canada et le gouvernement

de République de la Lituanie. Vilnius, le 8 août 1994.

Accord entre le gouvernement du Canada et le gouvernement de la République de Lituanie pour la coopération dans l'usage pacifique de l'énergie nucléaire. Vilnius, le 17 novembre 1994.

Luxembourg
Avenant à la Convention de 1986 sur la sécurité sociale entre le Canada et le Luxembourg. Ottawa, le 6 février 1992. *En vigueur* le 1er janvier 1994. RTC 1994/8.

Mexique
Accord de coopération entre le gouvernement du Canada et le gouvernement des États-Unis mexicains en matière d'utilisations pacifiques de l'énergie nucléaire (avec Annexes). Mexique, le 16 novembre 1994.

Mongolie
Accord de Commerce entre le gouvernement du Canada et le gouvernement de la Mongolie. Ottawa, le 8 juin 1994. *En vigueur* le 6 octobre 1994. RTC 1994/25.

Pays-Bas
Protocole modifiant la Convention, y compris son Protocole, entre le Canada et le Royaume des Pays-Bas en vue d'éviter les doubles impositions et de prévenir l'évasion fiscale en matière d'impôts sur le revenu. La Haye, le 4 mars 1993. *En vigueur* le 30 juillet 1994. RTC 1994/32.

Philippines
Accord sur la sécurité sociale entre le gouvernement du Canada et le gouvernement de la République des Philippines. Winnipeg, le 9 septembre 1994.

Pologne
Accord entre le gouvernement du Canada et le gouvernement de la République de Pologne au sujet des relations militaires. Ottawa, le 28 mars 1994.

Traité d'entraide judiciaire en matière pénale entre le Canada et la République de Pologne. Ottawa, le 12 septembre 1994.

Roumanie
Accord entre le gouvernement du Canada et le gouvernement de la Roumanie au sujet des relations militaires. Ottawa, le 7 juin 1993. *En vigueur* le 24 janvier 1994. RTC 1994/10.

Échange de Notes entre le gouvernement du Canada et le gouvernement de la Roumanie constituant un Accord modifiant leur Accord concernant la coopération dans le développement et l'utilisation de l'énergie atomique à des fins pacifiques, fait à Ottawa le 24 octobre 1977. Bucarest, le 12 octobre 1994. *En vigueur* le 12 octobre 1994. RTC 1994/23.

Royaume-Uni
Échange de Lettres constituant un Accord entre le gouvernement du Canada et le gouvernement du Royaume-Uni de Grande-Bretagne et d'Irlande du Nord établissant les termes et conditions de réciprocité en matière de sécurité sociale entre le Canada, Jersey et Guernesey (avec Annexes). Ottawa, les 5 et 12 février 1993. *En vigueur* le 1er janvier 1994. RTC 1994/5.

Échange de Lettres constituant un Accord sur les arrangements codifiés en matière de sécurité sociale entre le gouvernement du Canada et le gouvernement du Royaume-Uni de Grande-Bretagne et d'Irlande du Nord (avec Annexes). Ottawa, le 18 octobre 1994. *Notes signées* les 11 octobre et 18 octobre 1994.

Russie
Accord de coopération économique entre le gouvernement du Canada et le gouvernement de la Fédération de Russie. Moscou, le 8 mai 1993. *En vigueur* le 7 décembre 1994.

Saint-Kitts-et-Nevis
Accord de sécurité sociale entre le Canada et la Fédération de Saint-Kitts-et-Nevis (avec Arrangement administratif). Ottawa, le 17 août 1992. *En vigueur* le 1er janvier 1994. RTC 1994/9.

Suède
Accord sur les relations cinématographiques et audiovisuelles entre le gouvernement du Canada et le gouvernement de la Suède. Stockholm, le 17 octobre 1994.

Suisse
Convention de Sécurité sociale entre le Canada et la Confédération suisse (avec Protocole final). Ottawa, le 24 février 1994.

Thaïlande
Traité d'entraide judiciaire entre le gouvernement du Canada et le gouvernement du Royaume de Thaïlande. Ottawa, le 3 octobre 1994. *En vigueur* le 3 octobre 1994. RTC 1994/20.

Ukraine
Accord de Commerce entre le gouvernement du Canada et le gouvernement de l'Ukraine. Kiev, le 31 mars 1994.

Accord d'amitié et de coopération entre le gouvernement du Canada et le gouvernement de la République d'Ukraine. Kiev, le 31 mars 1994.

Accord de coopération économique entre le gouvernement du Canada et le gouvernement de l'Ukraine. Ottawa, le 24 octobre 1994.

Accord entre le gouvernement du Canada et le gouvernement de l'Ukraine au sujet des relations militaires. Ottawa, le 24 octobre 1994. *En vigueur* le 24 octobre 1994. RTC 1994/29.

Accord entre le gouvernement du Canada et le gouvernement de l'Ukraine pour l'encouragement et la protection des investissements. Ottawa, le 24 octobre 1994.

Vénézuéla
Traité entre le gouvernement du Canada et le gouvernement du Vénézuéla sur l'exécution des sentences pénales. Caracas, le 24 janvier 1994.

Vietnam
Accord de coopération économique entre le gouvernement du Canada et le gouvernement de la République socia-

liste du Vietnam. Ottawa, le 21 juin 1994.

Accord général sur la coopération au développement entre le gouvernement du Canada et le gouvernement de la République socialiste du Vietnam (avec Annexes). Ottawa, le 21 juin 1994. *En vigueur* le 21 juin 1994. RTC 1994/18

Zimbabwé
Accord entre le gouvernement du Canada et le gouvernement de la République du Zimbabwé en vue d'éviter les doubles impositions et de prévenir l'évasion fiscale en matière d'impôts sur le revenu, sur la fortune et sur les gains en capital. Harare, le 16 avril 1992. *En vigueur* le 15 décembre 1994. RTC 1994/31.

II MULTILATÉRAUX

Adoption
Convention sur la protection des enfants et la coopération en matière d'adoption internationale. La Haye, le 29 mai 1994. *Signé* par le Canada le 12 avril 1994.

Aviation
Protocole concernant le texte authentique quadrilingue de la Convention relative à l'aviation civile internationale (Chicago, 1944). Montréal, le 30 septembre 1977. *Adhésion* par le Canada le 23 mars 1994.

Commerce
Accord de libre-échange nord-américain entre le gouvernment du Canada, le gouvernement des États-Unis Mexicains et le gouvernement des États-Unis d'Amérique. Ottawa, le 17 décembre 1992. *Signé* par le Canada le 17 décembre 1992. *En vigueur* pour le Canada le 1er janvier 1994. *Signé* à Ottawa les 11 et 17 décembre, à Mexico les 14 et 17 décembre et à Washington les 8 et 17 décembre 1992. RTC 1994/2.

Accord instituant l'Organisation mondiale du commerce (OMC). Marrakesh, le 15 avril 1994. *Signé* par le

Canada le 15 avril 1994. *Ratifié* par le Canada le 30 décembre 1994.

Accord relatif aux marchés publics (avec Annexes). Marrakesh, le 15 avril 1994. *Signé* par le Canada le 15 avril 1994.

Accord international sur la viande bovine (avec Annexe). Marrakesh, le 15 avril 1994. *Signé* par le Canada le 15 avril 1994. *Ratifié* par le Canada le 30 décembre 1994.

Défense

Accord modifiant le Protocole de signature (article 56, paragraphe 9) de l'Accord du 3 août 1959 modifié par les Accords du 21 octobre 1971 et du 18 mai 1981, sans préjujés à l'Accord du 18 mars 1993, complétant la Convention entre les États Parties au Traité de l'Antlantique Nord sur le statut de leurs Forces, en ce qui concerne les Forces étrangères stationnées en République fédérale d'Allemagne. Bonn, le 16 mai 1994. *Signé* par le Canada le 16 mai 1994.

Échange de Notes constituant un Accord relatif à la Convention du 19 juin 1951 entre les États Parties au Traité de l'Atlantique Nord (OTAN) sur le statut de leurs Forces, à l'Accord du 3 août 1959 complétant cette Convention, y compris les accords qui s'y rapportent. Bonn, le 25 septembre 1990. *Signé* par le Canada le 25 septembre 1990. *En vigueur* pour le Canada le 4 janvier 1994. RTC 1994/30

Échange de Notes constituant un Arrangement entre les gouvernements du Canada, de la Belgique et des Pays-Bas et le gouvernement de la République fédérale d'Allemagne concernant le statut et l'Accès des Forces canadiennes, belges et néerlandaises à Berlin. Bonn, le 23 septembre 1991. *Signé* par le Canada le 23 septembre 1991. Ne sera pas publié — n'est jamais entré en vigueur. *Terminé* le 12 septembre 1994.

Échange de Notes constituant un Accord modifiant l'Accord constitué

par l'Échange de Notes du 25 septembre 1991 relatif à la Convention du 19 juin 1951 entre les États parties au Traité de l'Atlantique Nord (OTAN) sur le statut de leurs Forces et à l'Accord supplémentaire du 3 août 1959 complétant ladite Convention, y compris les Accords qui s'y rapportent. Bonn, le 12 septembre 1994. *Signé* par le Canada le 12 septembre 1994.

Droit de la guerre

Convention sur l'interdiction ou la limitation de l'emploi de certaines armes classiques qui peuvent être considérées comme produisant des effets traumatiques excessifs ou comme frappant sans dicrimination (avec Protocoles). Genève, le 10 octobre 1980. *Signée* par le Canada le 10 avril 1981. *Ratifiée* par le Canada le 24 juin 1994. *En vigueur* pour le Canada le 24 décembre 1994. RTC 1994/19.

Environnement

Accord nord-américain de coopération dans le domaine de l'environnement (avec Annexes). Ottawa, le 14 septembre 1993. *Signé* par le Canada le 14 septembre 1993. *En vigueur* pour le Canada le 1er janvier 1994. *Signé* à Ottawa, les 12 et 14 septembre 1993, à Mexico, D.F., les 8 et 14 septembre 1993 et à Washington, D.C., les 9 et 14 septembre 1993. RTC 1994/3.

Accord relatif à la création d'un institut interaméricain de recherches sur les changements à l'échelle du globe. Montevideo, le 13 mai 1992. *Signé* par le Canada le 25 mars 1993. *En vigueur* pour le Canada le 12 mars 1994. RTC 1994/28.

Amendement au Protocole de Montréal relatif à des substances qui appauvrissent la couche d'ozone. Copenhague, le 25 novembre 1992. *Ratifié* par le Canada le 16 mars 1994. *En vigueur* pour le Canada le 14 juin 1994. RTC 1994/13.

Convention-cadre des Nations Unies sur les changements climatiques. New York, le 9 mai 1992. *Signée* par le Canada le 12 juin 1992. *Ratifiée* par le

Canada le 4 décembre 1992. *En vigueur* pour le Canada le 21 mars 1994. RTC 1994/7.

Convention des Nations-Unies sur la lutte contre la désertification dans les pays gravement touchés par la sécheresse et/ou la désertification, en particulier en Afrique. Paris, le 14 octobre 1994. *Signée* par le Canada le 14 octobre 1994.

Navigation
Convention internationale de 1989 sur l'assistance. Londres, le 28 avril 1989. *Signée* par le Canada le 11 juillet 1990. *Ratifiée* par le Canada le 14 novembre 1994.

Nucléaire
Convention sur la sûreté nucléaire. Vienne, le 20 septembre 1994. *Signée* par le Canada le 20 septembre 1994.

Pêche
Accord visant à favoriser le respect par les navires de pêche en haute mer des mesures internationales de conservation et de gestion. Rome, le 24 novembre 1993. *Accepté* par le Canada le 20 mai 1994.

Pollution
Protocole à la Convention de 1979 sur la pollution atmosphérique transfrontière à longue distance, relatif à une nouvelle réduction des émissions de soufre. Oslo, le 13 juin 1994. *Signé* par le Canada le 14 juin 1994.

Postes
Actes du 21ième Congrès de l'Union postale. Séoul, le 31 août 1994. *Signés* par le Canada le 31 août 1994.

Cinquième protocole additionnel à la Constitution de l'Union postale des Amériques, de l'Espagne et du Portugal. Montevideo, le 23 juin 1993. *Signé* par le Canada le 23 juin 1993. *En vigueur* le 1er janvier 1994.

Règlement des différends internationaux
Convention pour le règlement pacifique des conflits internationaux. La Haye, le 18 octobre 1907. *Ratifiée* par le Canada le 10 mai 1994. *En vigueur*

pour le Canada le 9 juillet 1994. RTC 1994/14

Santé
Accord sur l'interdiction de fumer à bord des vols internationaux de transport de passagers. Chicago, le 1er novembre 1994. *Signé* par le Canada le 1er novembre 1994.

Science
Accord instituant un centre pour la science et la technologie en Ukraine. Kiev, le 25 octobre 1993. *Signé* par le Canada le 25 octobre 1993. *Ratifié* par le Canada le 17 juin 1994. *En vigueur* le 16 juillet 1994.

Sécurité du personnel
Convention sur la sécurité du personnel des Nations Unies et du personnel associé. Nations Unies, le 9 décembre 1994. *Signée* par le Canada le 15 décembre 1994.

Télécommunications
Constitution et Convention de l'Union internationale des télécommunications (UIT). Genève, le 22 décembre 1992. *Signées* par le Canada le 22 décembre 1992. *Ratifiées* par le Canada le 21 juin 1993. *En vigueur* pour le Canada le 1er juillet 1994.

Protocole facultatif concernant le règlement obligatoire des différends relatifs à la Constitution de l'Union internationale des télécommunications, à la Convention de l'Union internationale des télécommunications et aux Règlements administratifs, Nice 1992. Genève, le 22 décembre 1992. *Signé* par le Canada le 22 décembre 1992. *Ratifié* par le Canada le 21 juin 1993. *En vigueur* pour le Canada le 1er juillet 1994.

Textiles
Protocole portant maintien en vigueur de l'arrangement concernant le commerce international des textiles. Genève, le 9 décembre 1993. *Signé* par le Canada le 21 décembre 1993. *Ratifié* par le Canada le 2 mars 1994. *En vigueur* pour le Canada le 2 mars 1994.

Appliqué à titre provisoire à compter du 1ᵉʳ janvier 1994. RTC 1994/22.

Travail

Accord nord-américain de coopération dans le domaine du travail (avec Annexes). Ottawa, le 14 septembre 1993. *Signé* par le Canada le 14 septembre 1993. *En vigueur* pour le Canada le 1ᵉʳ janvier 1994. *Signé* à Ottawa, les 12 et 14 septembre 1993, à Mexico, D.F., les 8 et 14 septembre 1993 et à Washington, D.C., les 9 et 14 septembre 1993. RTC 1994/4.

Convention concernant les normes minima à observer sur les navires marchands (Convention 147). Genève, le 29 octobre 1976. *Ratifiée* par le Canada le 25 mai 1993. *En vigueur* pour Canada le 25 mai 1994.

Cases / La jurisprudence

Canadian Cases in
Public International Law in 1994-95 /
La jurisprudence canadienne en matière de
droit international public en 1994-95

compiled by / préparé par
KARIN MICKELSON*

Interpretation of United Nations Convention Relating to the Status of Refugees

Thamotharampillai v. Minister of Employment and Immigration [1993] 3 F.C. 99. Federal Court Trial Division.

The applicant came to Canada from Sri Lanka in 1984 and was deemed to be a Convention refugee in the following year. He obtained permanent resident status in 1986. In 1990, he was convicted of conspiracy to traffic in a narcotic and sentenced to three years' imprisonment. A conditional deportation order was obtained against him. Mr. Thamotharampillai again claimed Convention refugee status. The Convention and Refugee Determination Division (CRDD) of the Immigration and Refugee Board reached a decision that the applicant, despite having a "well-founded fear of persecution," was not a Convention refugee within the meaning of the Immigration Act, R.S.C. 1985, c. I-2 because of the operation of Article 1(F)(c) of the United Nations Convention Relating to the Status of Refugees. Article 1(F)(c) provides that the Convention definition of refugee "shall not apply to any person with respect to whom there are serious reasons for considering that . . . he has been

* Faculty of Law, University of British Columbia

guilty of acts contrary to the purposes and principles of the United Nations." This was an application for judicial review of that decision.

The critical issue was whether the CRDD had erred in law in preferring a broad interpretation of Article 1(F)(c) to the more restrictive interpretation adopted by the United Nations High Commissioner for Refugees in its *Handbook on Procedures and Criteria for Determining Refugee Status under the 1951 Convention and the 1967 Protocol relating to the Status of Refugees.* The *Handbook* notes that the purposes and principles of the United Nations set out fundamental standards that are intended to govern the conduct of the member states of the Organization in relation to each other and in relation to the international community, adding (at 106), "From this it could be inferred that an individual, in order to have committed an act contrary to these principles, must have been in a position of power in a member State and instrumental to his State's infringing these principles." The *Handbook* goes on to point out that this clause has rarely been interpreted and should be applied with caution due to its very general character.

The CRDD acknowledged that the *Handbook* carries considerable authority, but asserted that it is not binding. It noted that the wording of Article 1(F)(c) does not indicate that the offender had to have held a position of power within his or her country. Having previously emphasized recent United Nations initiatives aimed at combating the drug problem, and having reached the conclusion that the fight against the illegal traffic of narcotics is one of the purposes of the Organization, albeit not one that is specifically identified in its Charter, the CRDD asserted (at 107) that it was entirely reasonable "to reach the determination that someone that has committed a serious criminal act that is clearly against major initiatives of the United Nations is not worthy of the protection of the country of refuge in which he committed such an act."

While expressing some doubts about the CRDD's determination that the fight against drug trafficking was one of the purposes of the United Nations, Gibson, J. asserted that it is an activity within the ambit of those purposes. Gibson, J. (at 111) reiterated a number of the points made by the CRDD in reaching its determination, emphasizing the fact that the crime "involved significant international implications" and was a crime that "within Canada, potentially had fearful social, cultural and humanitarian repercussions, to say nothing of its economic repercussions." Thus, the Convention and Refugee Determination Division had properly exercised its discretion in denying the applicant Convention refugee status.

It should be noted that Mr. Thamotharampillai's involvement in the trafficking operation was characterized as relatively minor by the trial judge. This fact appears to have had little or no impact on the decisions either of the CRDD or of Gibson J.

Diplomatic Immunities

Laverty v. *Laverty* (1994), 32 C.P.C. (3d) 91. Ontario Court of Justice (General Division).

Mr. Laverty was a customs agent serving with the United States Embassy in Ottawa. Mrs. Laverty had sought and obtained, on an unopposed basis, two interim orders affecting Mr. Laverty and the matrimonial home. Mr. Laverty then argued that, because of his status as a diplomatic agent he, the members of his household, and the matrimonial home enjoyed immunity from the jurisdiction of the court. This position was supported by the government of Canada.

The court rejected the argument raised on behalf of Mrs. Laverty on the basis of Article 31(1)(a) of the Vienna Convention on Diplomatic Relations (Schedule I of the Foreign Missions and International Organizations Act, S. C. 1991, c. 41), which creates an exception to immunity for private property owned by the diplomatic agent of the receiving state so long as it is not held for the purposes of the mission. Cunningham, J. noted that Article 31(1)(a) must be read in the context of the other provisions of the Convention. Among the provisions cited were Article 31, which sets out the basic rule that a diplomatic agent enjoys immunity from the civil and administrative jurisdiction of the receiving state subject to certain stated exceptions, and Article 30, which stipulates that the private residence of the diplomatic agent is to enjoy the same protection as the premises of the diplomatic mission, which under Article 22(1) are inviolable and under Article 22(3) are immune from search, requisition, attachment, or execution. Unless the property in question could be attached without infringing upon the inviolability provisions of the Convention, no exception to immunity would exist. Moreover, the court noted that the interim orders obtained by Mrs. Laverty were not orders against the land itself but rather against Mr. Laverty, who held an interest therein. Thus, this was not "a real action relating to private immovable property" within the meaning of the exception contained in Article 31(1)(a).

The court also rejected a constitutional argument that the Foreign Missions and International Organizations Act encroached upon jurisdiction specifically reserved to the provinces.

The court expressed disapproval of the decision of the United States government to decline to waive diplomatic immunity in this case, and referred to the obligation of the United States government "to ensure that Mrs. Laverty and her children are not left out in the cold." Cunningham, J. (at 100) expressed the hope that Mrs. Laverty would be ensured "easy and cost effective access to the appropriate U.S. court," noting, "She should not have to chase Mr. Laverty around the United States seeking to enforce rights which, were it not for diplomatic immunity, she might do easily."

Treaties — Operation and Effect — Domestic Application

R. v. Rebman (R.) et al. (1994), 122 Nfld. & P.E.I.R. and 379 A.P.R. 111. Newfoundland Supreme Court Trial Division.

A number of French fishermen from St. Pierre and Miquelon, who were charged with illegally fishing in Canadian waters, attempted to invoke as a defence the provisions of a 1972 treaty between Canada and France. The treaty authorized fishermen from St. Pierre and Miquelon to fish in Canadian waters, subject to Canadian fishing regulations. The court held that it did not have jurisdiction to interpret the treaty because the treaty had not been incorporated into Canadian law.

Canadian Cases in
Private International Law in 1994-95 /
La jurisprudence canadienne en matière de
droit international privé en 1994-95

compiled by / préparé par
JOOST BLOM*

A Jurisdiction / Compétence des tribunaux

1 Common Law and Federal

(a) Jurisdiction *in personam*

Service ex juris — *constitutional validity of rules authorizing service*

MacDonald v. *Lasnier* (1994), 21 O.R. (3d) 177. Ontario Court, General Division.

The plaintiff, a resident of Ontario, was injured as a passenger in an automobile that was in an accident in Valleyfield, Quebec. He was taken to hospital in Valleyfield and treated there. He subsequently returned to Ontario. He brought this action in Ontario against the Valleyfield physician and hospital, for allegedly misdiagnosing his injuries and thus causing him pain and suffering in Ontario. Service of the writ was effected on the defendants in Quebec under Ontario Civil Procedure Rule 17.02(h), which authorizes service *ex juris* without leave if the claim is "in respect of damage sustained in Ontario arising from a tort or breach of contract, wherever committed." The defendants argued that such service contravened the requirement that a court can only take jurisdiction over a case that has a real and substantial connection with the province (*Morguard Investments Ltd.* v. *De Savoye*, [1990] 3 S.C.R. 1077; *Hunt* v. *T & N plc*, [1993] 4 S.C.R. 289).

Cunningham, J. accepted this argument and held that the Ontario court had no jurisdiction. The Supreme Court of Canada

---

* Faculty of Law, University of British Columbia.

had made it clear that the territorial reach of judicial jurisdiction was subject to a limitation based on real and substantial connection. Here the hospital's sole place of business was in Quebec, the doctor was licensed to practise in, and was regulated by, the province of Quebec, the standard of care applicable was that of Quebec, the doctor was a resident of Quebec, and probably all of the defendants' witnesses and documentary evidence would be from Quebec. The accident occurred in Quebec, as did the alleged misdiagnosis. The only connection with Ontario was the fact that the plaintiff allegedly endured pain and suffering there. The onus of displacing the plaintiff's choice of forum was on the defendant. The defendants in this case had met that onus. The court did not have jurisdiction and the action was stayed. Counsel had advised that there was no prescription difficulty in Quebec and a new action could be commenced there.

Alternatively, Cunningham, J. held that the action should be stayed on the ground of *forum non conveniens.* As far as liability was concerned, most if not all the witnesses lived in Quebec. As for the quantum of damages, there appeared to be no significant difference in the assessments of general and special damages between Ontario and Quebec. Since no motor vehicle claim was involved, the evidence of the driver, who like the plaintiff was from Ontario, was of diminished relevance. What medical witnesses there might be from Ontario could more easily give their evidence in Quebec than the Quebec witnesses could give theirs in Ontario. The possibility of language difficulty alone would seem to be of sufficient weight in that regard. Finally, the plaintiff lost no substantial juridical advantage by having to proceed in Quebec. The speed of obtaining a trial date would, if anything, be greater there.

Note. The judgment is not altogether clear on whether the first ground of the decision, based on the absence of a real and substantial connection with Ontario, was seen as constitutionally negating the court's jurisdiction or merely as indicating the proper interpretation of Rule 17.02(h). If the court had no jurisdiction at all, as the *Morguard* and *Hunt* cases imply, the proper result would seem to be a dismissal of the action rather than a stay. The case also illustrates the broad overlap between the criteria for constitutionally permitted jurisdiction, based on real and substantial connection, and the criteria for determining the *forum conveniens* for the action. The two matters are distinct, however. The former deals with the *minimum* requirements for exercising jurisdiction, whereas the latter deals with whether the action is *most appropriately* brought in one or the other of two courts, each of which may have a real and substantial connection with the litigation.

Service ex juris — *claims for which service is authorized* — *general*

Tortel Communication Inc. v. *Suntel Inc.* (1994), 120 D.L.R. (4th) 100, [1995] 1 W.W.R. 457. Manitoba Court of Appeal.

The plaintiffs, Ontario corporations, brought this action on a debt allegedly due to them by Suntel, a Georgia, U.S.A., corporation, and by a Grand Cayman corporation for which Suntel acted as agent. The debt was said to have arisen out of the short delivery by Suntel of telephones to the plaintiffs in Toronto, and for service work that the plaintiffs did in Ontario on Suntel's behalf in repairing telephones supplied directly by Suntel to the Manitoba Telephone System (MTS) and another company. None of the contracts in question was made or performed in Manitoba, and none of the parties had a presence in Manitoba. Nevertheless, the plaintiffs sued in Manitoba because they discovered that MTS owed money to Suntel, and the plaintiffs were able to garnish this debt as a consequence of having brought their action in the Manitoba court. The Court of Appeal, affirming the chambers judge, held that the Manitoba court had no jurisdiction. Philp, J.A., with whom Lyon, J.A. concurred, said that the mere presence of unrelated funds in Manitoba might be a juridical advantage to a foreign party, but it was not a legitimate one if it was the sole foundation of jurisdiction. The plaintiffs' action had no real and substantial connection with Manitoba. Moreover, their claim fell under none of the categories for which service *ex juris* was permitted without leave under Manitoba Queen's Bench Rule 17.02, and it was not an appropriate case to give leave for service *ex juris.* Twaddle, J.A. agreed, but added that the presence of an asset belonging to the defendant within the jurisdiction might support service *ex juris* if it was also shown that, without the security provided by the Manitoba asset, any judgment the plaintiff might obtain elsewhere would probably remain unsatisfied.

Note. See also *Janke* v. *Budd Canada Inc.* (1994), 28 C.P.C. (3d) 42 (Man. Q.B.), aff'd (1994), 31 C.P.C. (3d) 1 (Man. C.A.), another case that fitted none of the categories for service *ex juris* without leave, and was held to involve no real and substantial connection between the defendant or the action and the province. In respect of pleading the grounds for service *ex juris*, see *Stewart Estate* v. *Stewart Estate*, [1994] 8 W.W.R. 196, [1994] N.W.T.R. 276 (S.C.) (failure to plead the correct grounds for service *ex juris* without leave was held to make service irregular, not a nullity).

Service ex juris — *claims for which service is authorized — breach of contract in the province*

Note. See *Aerial Sign Co.* v. *Steel Art Signs Ltd.* (1994), 31 C.P.C. (3d) 392 (Alta. Q.B. (M.C.))

Service ex juris — *claims for which service is authorized — necessary or proper party*

Jan Poulsen & Co. v. *Seaboard Shipping Co.* (1994), [1995] 2 W.W.R. 633, 100 B.C.L.R. (2d) 175. British Columbia Supreme Court.

The plaintiff, a Norwegian company, brought this action in breach of contract against Seaboard Vancouver, a British Columbia company, and its English subsdiary company, Seaboard London. The claim was for brokerage and consulting services allegedly provided by the plaintiff to the defendants in respect of the financing and construction of a lumber-carrying ship. Seaboard London applied to have service *ex juris* on it set aside, or for a declaration that British Columbia had no jurisdiction over the claim against it, or should decline jurisdiction.

Campbell, A.C.J.S.C., held the action should continue. He applied *Bushell* v. *T & N plc* (1992), 67 B.C.L.R. (2d) 330 (noted in (1992), 30 C.Y.I.L. 408), in holding that where the defendant disputed service *ex juris*, the plaintiff had the onus of showing that British Columbia was the *forum conveniens*. The plaintiff here said that Seaboard London was "a necessary or proper party to a proceeding properly brought against some other person duly served in British Columbia" (British Columbia Rules of Court, R. 13(1)(j)). The action against Seaboard Vancouver was "properly brought" because the plaintiff had pleaded a good cause of action against Seaboard Vancouver. A chambers judge had so held on an application to strike out the statement of claim as disclosing no reasonable cause of action. It was unnecessary that the plaintiff show a "probable cause of action" against both the party in and the party outside the province. As to whether the "necessary or proper party" test was met, the criterion was the same as that applied to the joinder of parties — namely, whether the same cause of action was pleaded against both the foreign and the domestic defendant. That was the case here. The plaintiff having showed a good arguable case falling within the rule for service *ex juris*, jurisdiction *simpliciter* was established.

On the further question of *forum non conveniens*, the plaintiff had met the onus of showing that British Columbia was the *forum conveniens*. The judge referred to a variety of factors supporting the conclusion. The plaintiff, if forced to sue Seaboard London in England, would lose the significant juridical advantage of oral pre-trial examination. Given the complexity of the underlying transactions in this case, this was of particular importance. While the plaintiff, being foreign, had no special claim to the juridical advantages of British Columbia, it was not unfair that it should gain those advantages in light of the fact that the plaintiff was suing in Seaboard Vancouver's home jurisdiction. Seaboard London, as a closely controlled subsidiary of Seaboard Vancouver, could reasonably expect by virtue of that corporate connection to be called upon to defend actions against it in the home jurisdiction of its parent company. A number of Seaboard London's directors lived in the province, as did a former director who was potentially a material witness. So far in the proceedings, the plaintiff had made significant gains in the British Columbia courts, and should not be deprived of the juridical advantages conferred thereby. The final test for the appropriateness of taking jurisdiction was whether the plaintiff had shown that doing so would preserve a measure of fairness and justice sufficient to meet the reasonable expectation of the national and international communities. The plaintiff had met that onus.

Service ex juris — *claims for which service is authorized* — *damage sustained in the province*

de Vlas v. Bruce (1994), 18 O.R. (3d) 493, 25 C.P.C. (3d) 140. Ontario Court, General Division.

The plaintiffs were the parents, brothers, and sisters of a man who died as a passenger in an automobile that was involved in a single-car accident in Alberta, where the deceased lived. The defendant, the driver, was also an Alberta resident. The plaintiffs' claims were for funeral and burial expenses, loss of income for the family in attending to the funeral arrangements, travelling and car rental expenses, and long distance telephone expenses. They also included claims for pecuniary benefits that they would have received from their son and brother, and for loss of his guidance, care, and companionship. The claims were based on section 61 of the Family Law Act, R.S.O. 1990, c. F.3. The defendant applied to set aside the service *ex juris* of the statement of claim on him, and to have the action stayed on the ground of *forum non conveniens*. The plaintiffs relied on Ontario Civil Procedure Rule 17.02(h), which authorizes service *ex juris* without leave if the claim is "in respect of damage sustained in Ontario arising from a tort or breach of contract, wherever committed."

MacPherson, J. held the Ontario court had jurisdiction and refused the stay. The location of key witnesses in the action was roughly a neutral factor, since the witnesses on the plaintiffs' losses would be from Ontario and the defendant's on liability would be from Alberta. The geographical factors did not point to either province as being the only natural forum. There would be no multiplicity of proceedings, since the plaintiffs had made no claims in Alberta and had received no benefits from anyone in Alberta. The law applicable to the plaintiffs' claims, the judge held, was the law of Ontario. Thus in terms of convenience and expense, Ontario was the proper forum for the action. In addition, the plaintiffs had two advantages in Ontario that they would not have in Alberta proceedings. One was the lower cost of litigation; the plaintiffs were of modest means and it would be difficult if not impossible for them to initiate and sustain an action in Alberta. The other was that section 61 of the Family Law Act was broader than the equivalent provisions in the Fatal Accidents Act of Alberta. Some of the claims by the brothers and sisters might not be allowed in Alberta, and, for some items, the damages awarded in Ontario might be higher than in Alberta, where they were subject to statutory caps.

Note. MacPherson, J.'s conclusion that the plaintiffs' claims were governed by Ontario law was based on the law as it stood before *Tolofson* v. *Jensen*, noted below, under D.1(c) Tort. That case has now eliminated the application of the *lex fori* and has laid down that liability in tort, at least for torts that take place entirely within one jurisdiction, is governed by the *lex loci delicti* alone. The implications of this decision for a case like *de Vlas* v. *Bruce* are not altogether clear. MacPherson, J. specifically decided that the family members' claims under the Family Law Act were independent claims in the sense that they could be brought even though the deceased's estate was making no claim. If they are independent claims, it is arguable that they represent a distinct statutory tort of damage to a deceased's immediate family members. The locus of that tort could be argued to be in the province where the family members are injured, presumably the province where they live. It could also be argued to be in the province where the deceased was killed.

In relation to Ontario R. 17.02(h), see also *MacDonald* v. *Lasnier*, noted above under the heading *Service* ex juris — *constitutional validity of rules authorizing service.*

Service ex juris — *claims for which service is authorized* — *action on contract and defendant has assets in the province*

Note. See *Mercer Int'l Inc.* v. *Larsen* (1994), 25 C.P.C. (2d) 110 (B.C.S.C.), involving British Columbia Rule 13(1)(m), which authorizes service *ex juris* for a claim founded on a contract where the defendant has assets in the province. The defendant's shares in the plaintiff corporation were held not to be assets in the province merely because the transfer agent for the shares had an office in the province.

Declining jurisdiction — arbitration agreement

Note. A number of cases concerned stays of judicial proceedings pursuant to the International Commercial Arbitration Acts of the provinces, implementing the UNCITRAL Model Law on International Commercial Arbitration. Article 8 of the Model Law requires a stay unless the arbitration agreement is null and void, inoperative, or incapable of being performed. In *Kvaerner Enviropower Inc.* v. *Tanar Industries Ltd.*, [1995] 2 W.W.R. 433, 24 Alta. L.R. (3d) 365 (C.A.), the court rejected an argument that the arbitration agreement in that case, providing for arbitration in Baltimore, was void because the dispute concerned a builder's lien on property in Alberta. The Alberta legislation was not construed to make such disputes non-arbitrable. A similar result, again in relation to a builder's lien dispute, was reached in *BWV Investments Ltd.* v. *Saskferco Products Inc.* (1994), 119 D.L.R. (4th) 577 (Sask. C.A.). There, actions by other parties who were not bound by the arbitration agreement were also stayed, because their claims turned on the issues to be decided in the arbitration. Both decisions emphasized the policy, which is expressed in the UNCITRAL Model Law, of giving effect to the parties' right to arbitrate their disputes if they choose. In *Globe Union Industrial Corp.* v. *G.A.P. Marketing Corp.* (1994), [1995] 2 W.W.R. 696 (B.C.S.C.), the argument was that the arbitration agreement was void because the contract in which it was contained was void. This was rejected on the ground that Article 16 of the Model Law makes it clear that the validity of the arbitration agreement is to be treated as independent of the validity of the main agreement.

Declining jurisdiction — forum non conveniens — *defendant served in the jurisdiction*

Note. In *Discreet Logic Inc.* v. *Canada (Registrar of Copyrights)* (1994), 55 C.P.R. (3d) 167 (FCA), a stay was refused in a copyright dispute that, although rooted in an agreement made in Australia, concerned two companies' businesses in Canada. Moreover, courts in both Australia and the United States had ordered adjournments or stays of proceedings on the same subject matter on the assumption that it would be litigated in Canada.

See also *Dairy Producers Co-operative Ltd.* v. *Agrifoods Int'l Co-operative Ltd.*, [1994] 7 W.W.R. 596, 122 Sask. R. 191 (Q.B.), in which a defendant served at a place of business in Saskatchewan, in an action by a Saskatchewan corporation, was unsuccessful in showing that the court was *forum non conveniens.*

Declining jurisdiction — forum non conveniens — *defendant served* ex juris

Frymer v. *Brettschneider* (1994), 115 D.L.R. (4th) 744, 19 O.R. (3d) 60. Ontario Court of Appeal.

This litigation related to a trust established in 1979 by Henry Tuchman, who then lived in Florida. After a life interest to himself, all the estate interests would go to a separate trust of which his two daughters from his first marriage, Carol and Nancy, were the sole beneficiaries. His second wife, Sheila Schechtman, was not provided for under the trust. Originally there were two trustees but after Tuchman's death one resigned, leaving Tuchman's first wife's brother, Mervyn, as sole trustee. The trust was prepared by Florida lawyers and was expressly governed by Florida law. Tuchman died in 1986. His will made no provision for his wife Sheila either. Shortly after his death, she entered into two agreements with Carol, Nancy, and Mervyn. Both agreements were prepared by Florida lawyers and were expressly governed by Florida law. Essentially, they provided for Sheila to receive $50,000 cash from the trust assets and the income on another $200,000 for her lifetime. Upon Sheila's death the capital would be divided between Carol and Nancy. In return for what she would receive under the agreements, Sheila agreed to forego her rights against Tuchman's estate as surviving spouse, rights under Florida law that could have exceeded the provision the agreements made for her. The money set aside for Sheila was invested by the trust with a mutual fund whose head office was in Toronto. Nancy and Carol each borrowed money from the trust, secured by mortgages on their respective homes, which were both in Ontario. The trust assets consisted of intangibles that could be moved at the will of the trustee. The present action was brought by Carol in Ontario to have the agreements with Sheila set aside on the basis of undue influence and lack of independent legal advice, and to have Mervyn, a resident of Alberta, removed as trustee. Sheila was served in Quebec, where she now lived, and Mervyn was served in Alberta, where he lived. Sheila and Mervyn applied to have the service *ex juris* on them set aside under Ontario Civil Procedure Rule 17.06(2)(c), which allows the court to decline jurisdiction "where it is satisfied that . . . Ontario is not a convenient forum for the hearing of the proceeding."

The Court of Appeal unanimously upheld the motions judge's decision that Ontario was *forum non conveniens,* because most of the witnesses, namely the lawyers who drafted the agreements, were residents of Florida, and the real dispute concerned a trust and agreements that were drafted in Florida and were governed by Florida law. Although Florida had no reciprocal enforcement legislation in respect of Ontario judgments, the trustee had undertaken to abide by the decision of the Florida courts in respect of Carol's claims. The three judges differed, however, as to the proper test to apply in these cases. Arbour, J.A., with whom McKinlay, J.A. concurred, held that *Amchem Products Inc.* v. *British Columbia (Workers' Compensation Board),* [1993] 1 S.C.R. 897 (noted in (1993), 31 C.Y.I.L. 405), had overruled earlier authority to the effect that *forum non conveniens* was an issue to be approached in two stages, the first involving the defendant's showing that a foreign court was a more convenient forum, and the second involving the plaintiff's showing that a stay of the action in Ontario would deprive the plaintiff of a legitimate personal or juridical advantage. The test as propounded in *Amchem* was the same whether service was effected *ex juris* or in the jurisdiction, and was a single test designed to find whether there clearly was a more appropriate forum than the domestic forum chosen by the plaintiff. All factors relevant to finding the closest connection with the action and the parties, including the parties' respective advantages in either jurisdiction, were to be considered.

The question of which party bore the burden of proof on the issue of *forum non conveniens* depended on the interpretation of the rules. It was a question that would seldom matter, because the strength of the relevant factors would determine the issue. Where it did matter, however, the proper approach was that if the plaintiff chose a forum in which the defendant was resident and jurisdiction was therefore "as of right," the defendant had the burden of showing that another forum was a more convenient one. If the plaintiff chose to bring a foreigner into the jurisdiction, typically in a case of service *ex juris*, the burden would be on the plaintiff to establish that Ontario was the appropriate forum if the choice of forum was challenged by the defendant. This accorded with the principles of comity upon which the doctrine of *forum non conveniens* rests. The wording of Rule 17.06(2)(c), referring to the court being "satisfied that . . . Ontario is not a convenient forum," did not alter this conclusion. The rule did not purport to deal with all instances where *forum non conveniens* might be in issue, and should not be regarded as altering the law on a discretion that was essentially based on principles of international comity and had a history as part of the court's inherent powers, quite apart from any rule of court. Weiler, J.A. disagreed with the conclusion on burden of proof, and would have held that the burden was on the defendant in any case where service *ex juris* was effected without leave under Rule 17.02.

Note. Arbour, J.A. makes the burden of proof on the issue of *forum non conveniens* depend on the residence of the defendant rather than on the place where the defendant was served. Both Canadian authority (*Bushell* v. *T & N plc* (1992), 67 B.C.L.R. (2d) 330 (C.A.) (noted in (1992), 30 C.Y.I.L. 408)) and English authority (*Spiliada Maritime Corp.* v. *Cansulex Ltd.* (1986), [1987] A.C. 460 (H.L.)) have made the burden of proof in relation to *forum non conveniens* turn on whether service was in the jurisdiction (in which case the defendant must show that there is another more appropriate forum to obtain a stay) or *ex juris* (where the plaintiff must show that the local forum is clearly more appropriate than any alternative forum). Arbour, J.A.'s language suggests that the defendant should have the onus of proof if that person resides in the province, whether service was in the province or *ex juris.* More significantly, the plaintiff should have the onus of proof if the defendant is resident outside the province, whether that party is served while temporarily present in the jurisdiction or *ex juris.*

Note. In *Confederation Trust Co.* v. *Discovery Tower II Ltd.* (1994), 95 B.C.L.R. (2d) 309 (C.A.), the court held that an action in British Columbia for foreclosure of a mortgage on British Columbia immovable property could not be stayed on *forum non conveniens* grounds because British Columbia was the only possible forum for such an action. The personal action for the debt was, however, stayed pending the conclusion of related proceedings in Ontario. *Dino* v. *Albertson's Inc.* (1994), 28 C.P.C. (3d) 15 (Ont. Gen. Div. (M.C.)) refused a stay in an action by an Ontario resident in respect of personal injuries suffered when the plaintiff fell in a supermarket in Florida while on holiday. Florida was not shown to be a more appropriate forum. The defendant was a chain that was used to being sued all over the United States anyway; the plaintiff did not have the money to bring the action in Florida; and the plaintiff's daughter was also making a claim in respect of her expenses in looking after the plaintiff in Ontario.

Other *forum conveniens* decisions involving service *ex juris* were *Touchbourne* v. *Philbrook* (1994), 151 N.B.R. (2d) 377 (Q.B.); *G. N. Johnston Equipment Co.* v. *Remstar Int'l Inc.* (1994), 151 N.B.R. (2d) 184 (Q.B.); *Johnson* v. *Hall* (1994), 136 N.S.R. (2d) 60, 29 C.P.C. (3d) 232 (S.C.T.D.).

Declining jurisdiction — lis alibi pendens

Note. See *Cytoven Int'l N.V.* v. *Cytomed-Peptos* (1994), 87 F.T.R. 88.

(b)   Actions relating to property

Title to immovables outside the province

Note. In *Lauser* v. *Lauser* (1993), 2 E.T.R. (2d) 243 (B.C.S.C.), the court stayed litigation concerning a trust agreement, although it was made in British Columbia and the parties were residents of the province, because the agreement was in respect of inherited interests in immovable property in Germany. The trust obligations could not be determined without first determining the issues of inheritance rights and title in respect of the German property, which only a German court could do.

(c)   Matrimonial actions

Divorce — jurisdiction

Note. See *Al-Hashemy* v. *Gheddah* (1994), 121 Sask. R. 62 (Q.B.).

Divorce — corollary orders — jurisdiction to vary

Note. See *Ralph* v. *Ralph* (1994), 122 Nfld. & P.E.I. R. 153 (Nfld. S.C.T.D.).

(d)   Infants and children

Custody and access — jurisdiction

Note. See *Bradley* v. *Bradley* (1994), 121 Nfld. & P.E.I. R. 74 (P.E.I. S.C.), and *Duffy* v. *Duffy* (1994), 125 Nfld. & P.E.I. R. 117 (P.E.I. S.C.), applying the Uniform Custody Jurisdiction and Enforcement Act. Jurisdiction to make a custody order was declined in the former case, and held not to exist in the latter. In *Gratto* v. *Wittner* (1994), 114 D.L.R. (4th) 99, 3 R.F.L. (4th) 189 (Alta. C.A.), the court, applying the Uniform Extra-Provincial Custody Orders Act, held that the Alberta courts had jurisdiction to vary a custody order previously made in British Columbia. As a consequence of the custodial parent's having moved with the child to Alberta, the child's real and substantial connection with British Columbia had been severed.

Child abduction — Hague Convention

Thompson v. *Thompson,* [1994] 3 S.C.R. 551, 119 D.L.R. (4th) 253. Supreme Court of Canada.

A father, resident in Scotland, applied to the Manitoba Queen's Bench under the Child Custody Enforcement Act, S.M. 1982, c. 27 (the CCEA), for the return of his son, who had allegedly been wrongfully removed to or detained in Manitoba by the mother, contrary to the Hague Convention on the Civil Aspects of International Child Abduction (1980) (the Convention), which was implemented in Manitoba by the CCEA. The mother and father, both Scots, then respectively 17 and 22, had been married in Scotland in February 1991. Their son was born in March 1992. They separated in September 1992. Each parent applied to the Sheriff Court in Scotland for custody. On November 27, 1992, the mother was awarded interim custody, with interim access to the father. In the light of evidence that the mother was thinking of emigrating to Manitoba, where her parents had recently settled, the court ordered that the child remain in Scotland pending a further court order. The mother had not attended the hearing; her lawyer told her only that she had custody and the father had visitation rights. On December 2, 1992, before she received a report from her solicitor as to the details of the court's decision, the mother took the child to visit her parents in Manitoba. Within two months, the mother had decided to stay in Manitoba and had enrolled in high school there. On February 3, 1993, she applied to the Manitoba court for custody of her son. On the same day, the Scottish court resumed its custody proceedings. The mother deposed in the present action that she had not known of these proceedings. Her lawyer received no instructions and accordingly withdrew. The Scottish court awarded custody to the father. On February 25, 1993, he applied to the Scottish central authority under the Hague Convention for the return of the child. He also, in March 1993, entered pleadings in the Manitoba proceedings, replying to the mother's application for custody with an application for a return of the child under the CCEA and the Hague Convention.

The Manitoba Queen's Bench and the Court of Appeal held that the child should be returned to Scotland. This decision was upheld 8-0 by the Supreme Court of Canada. La Forest, J. gave the majority judgment. L'Heureux-Dubé, J., McLachlin, J. concurring, agreed with the majority judgment except for certain *obiter dicta* about the relationship between the court's powers as defined by the Hague Convention itself and by the CCEA as implementing statute.

La Forest, J. noted that the Hague Convention, like other treaties, should be interpreted in the light of the *travaux préparatoires* and other evidence as to what the state parties to it must have intended. So construed, the statement in the Preamble of the Convention that the "interests of children are of paramount importance in matters relating to their custody" was not to be taken as giving a court jurisdiction to consider the best interests of the child as they would be considered at a custody hearing. The provisions of the Convention showed that prompt return was intended to be predominant. It was also clear from the Preamble and Article 3, and from the *travaux préparatoires*, that the primary object of the Convention was the enforcement of custody rights as distinct from access rights. The enforcement of access rights was left to the administrative channels of central authorities designated by the state parties and was meant to be achieved by co-operation of the authorities rather than by the return of the child.

Since the Hague Convention was concerned with custody rights, the question was whether the mother's removal or detention of her son in this case was wrongful in the sense of violating custody rights. Courts in Canada and England had taken three approaches to cases where a child had been removed by a custodial parent contrary to a non-removal clause in the order giving him or her custody. One was to say that the removal was in violation of custody rights because it was contrary to conditions imposed on the removing parent's own right of custody. This was not entirely compatible with the drafting of the Convention, which in Article 3 implied that the rights breached must have belonged to someone other than the breaching party. The second approach was to say that by a non-removal clause the access parent gained a right of custody within the meaning of the Convention. The third approach, which La Forest, J. preferred, was to say that the effect of including a non-removal clause in an interim custody order was to give the court itself a right of custody within the meaning of the Convention. The court is vested with jurisdiction to determine who should have custody of a child and, on a temporary basis, orders the non-removal of the child in order to preserve that jurisdiction. The preservation of access rights is just a corollary effect of the clause.

In this case, it seemed clear that the non-removal clause had been inserted into the custody order of November 27, 1992, to preserve jurisdiction in the Scottish courts to decide the issue of custody on its merits in a full hearing. Thus the Scottish court became "an institution or any other body, either jointly or alone, under the law of the State in which the child was habitually resident immediately before the removal or retention" having custody rights within the meaning of Article 3. The mother's removal of the child from Scotland was therefore wrongful and the court was obliged under Article 12 to order the child's return "forthwith."

La Forest, J. stressed that the approach might well be different if a court inserted a non-removal clause in a permanent order for custody. That would usually be intended to ensure permanent access. The right of access, although important, was not given the same level of protection by the Convention as rights of custody. Moreover, the return of a child in the care of a person having permanent custody would ordinarily be far more disruptive to the child. Enforcing such non-removal clauses would also have serious implications for the mobility rights of the custodial person.

Although the finding of wrongful removal decided the case, La Forest, J. also said, obiter, that the Scottish court's order of February 3, 1993, would not of itself have been sufficient to make the mother's detention of the child in Canada wrongful. A wrongful retention began from the moment of the expiration of the period of access, where the original removal was with the consent of the rightful custodian of the child. An *ex parte* court order in the country of habitual residence might clarify the requesting state's opinion that indeed the continuing retention of the child was wrongful, but it could not convert a retention that, as far as the Convention was concerned, was not wrongful into one that was wrongful. There was nothing in the Convention requiring the recognition of an *ex post facto* custody order of a foreign jurisdiction, and the *travaux préparatoires* were consistent with this interpretation.

The mother argued that if the removal of the child was wrongful, the court should nevertheless refuse to order the child's return to Scotland because there was a "grave risk" that this would "expose the child to physical or psychological harm or otherwise place the child in an intolerable situation" (Article 13(1)(b) of the Convention), or because the court should be "satisfied that [the] child would suffer serious harm" (CCEA section 5). La Forest, J. thought that the differences in terminology of the Convention and of the implementing statute were not so great as to mandate the application of a significantly different test of harm. There was no doubt here that the child would suffer some psychological harm in being torn from his mother's custody and thrust into that of his father, especially since the Scottish court might ultimately award final custody back to the mother. Even if it appeared that there would not be harm amounting to an "intolerable situation," in the long term a court could, as Australian and English courts had done, impose conditions on the return of the child to ameliorate any short-term harm to the child. In this case, the court accepted the father's undertakings that he would not take physical custody of his son upon the son's return to Scotland and not until a court permitted such custody; and that he would take such proceedings as would enable the Scottish court to determine the issue of care and control of the child, on an interim or final basis, within five weeks of the child's return.

Finally, as to the relationship between the terms of the Convention and the implementing statute, La Forest, J. held that the two sets of terms operated independently of one another, in the sense that an application made under the Convention was governed by the Convention's terms and not those of the statute, and vice-versa. However, where the provisions of the statute were selected, it would not be improper to look at the Convention as determining the attitude that should be taken by the courts, since the legislature's adoption of the Convention indicated its judgment that international child custody disputes were best resolved by returning the child to its habitual place of residence.

L'Heureux-Dubé, J., with whom McLachlin, J. concurred, gave a separate opinion in which she differed from La Forest, J. on the question whether, if a court was obliged to order the return of a child "forthwith" under the Convention, it might nevertheless award interim custody to the wrongfully removing or retaining parent in the best interests of the child. The dissenting judge in the Court of Appeal would have made such an order in favour of the mother, on condition that she commence custody proceedings in Scotland within two months. La Forest, J. thought that there was no jurisdiction to make an interim custody order because the authority to do so, provided for in section 6 of the CCEA, existed only in proceedings under the statute as distinct from those under the Convention. He did not, however, rule out the possibility that a court might achieve a similar result under the Convention by giving a period of time for compliance with the order for the return of the child. L'Heureux-Dubé, J. thought that the "interplay" between the Convention and the CCEA was best interpreted as allowing a transitory interim custody order to be made where that was in the best interests of the child, provided that it did not hamper the objectives of the Convention or delay the return of the child to the point of frustrating the purpose of the Convention.

Note. Alberta, Saskatchewan, New Brunswick and Nova Scotia have implemented the Convention by means of a Uniform Act promulgated by the Uniform Law Conference of Canada: International Child Abduction Act, S.A. 1986, c. I-6.5; International Child Abduction Act, S.S. 1986, c. I-10.1; International Child Abduction Act, S.N.B. 1982, c. I-12.1; Child Abduction Act, S.N.S. 1982, c. 4. Quebec has not implemented the Convention as such but enacted equivalent provisions: Loi sur les aspects civils de l'enlèvement international et interprovincial d'enfants, S.Q. 1984, c. 12. British

Columbia, Manitoba, Ontario, Prince Edward Island, and New-foundland have adopted the Convention as part of a more general statute dealing with the civil aspects of child abduction: Family Relations Act, R.S.B.C. 1979, c. 121, Part 2.2 [added by S.B.C. 1982, c. 8, as am. by S.B.C. 1985, c. 72, s. 20]; Child Custody Enforcement Act, S.M. 1982, c. 27 (now R.S.M. 1987, c. C360); Children's Law Reform Act, R.S.O. 1990, c. C.12, s. 46; Custody Jurisdiction and Enforcement Act, S.P.E.I. 1984, c. 17; Children's Law Act, S.N. 1988, c. 61. Of the last five statutes, those in British Columbia and Manitoba have no express provision that the provisions of the Convention prevail over those of the Act if there is a conflict between them. The other three statutes do have such a provision.

Other cases applying the Hague Convention were *Hoge* v. *Hoge* (1994), 162 A.R. 397 (C.A.) (no wrongful removal or detention of child from Montana because mother agreed to Alberta-resident father's taking custody for a time, and father had a right to invoke Alberta court's jurisdiction to obtain custody himself), and *Z.(D.)* v. *Z.(J.)* (1994), 99 B.C.L.R. (2d) 287 (S.C.) (child ordered returned to Germany; allegations of grave risk of harm not made out).

(e)   Antisuit injunctions

Note. See *Nyquvest* v. *Rutkowski* (1994), 163 A.R. 307 (Alta. Q.B.), where an injunction was granted against the continuation of a parallel action in Florida between the same parties.

2   Québec

(a)   Lieu de l'introduction de l'action

Défendeur étranger — préjudice subi au Québec — art. 3148 C.C.Q. (1991)

P. J. Clayman Canada Inc. c. *Gibson Textile Dryers Ltd.,* [1994] A.J.Q. 830, N° 2304. Cour supérieure du Québec.

La demanderesse avait remis certains tissus à teindre à la défenderesse, dont la place d'affaires était en Ontario. Lorsque la défenderesse a retourné les tissus, la demanderesse a constaté que la teinture était inadéquate et que les tissus étaient inutilisables. La demanderesse a alors intenté une action en dommages au Québec contre la défenderesse. La Cour a rejeté l'exception déclinatoire de la défenderesse. Malgré le fait que la défenderesse soit domiciliée en Ontario, que le contrat soit intervenu en Ontario et que le travail

a été effectué en Ontario, le préjudice a été subi par la demanderesse au Québec. Cela était suffisant pour donner compétence
aux tribunaux québécois en vertu de l'article 3148 C.C.Q.

Arrêts concernant les anciennes règles de compétence (art. 68 C.P.)

Note. Veuillez voir *Van Den Brink N.V.* c. *Heringer*, [1994] A.J.Q.
830, N° 2306 (biens en transit au Québec); *Les Équipements Eustache
Lamontagne Ltée* c. *Les Équipements Belarus du Canada Ltée*, [1994]
R.D.J. 599, [1994] A.J.Q. 994, N° 2819 (C.S.) (application des
anciennes règles à une action intentée par l'émission du bref avant
le 1ᵉʳ janvier 1994, bien que l'action n'était pas signifiée à la
défenderesse jusqu'au 2 février 1994); *Thompson* c. *Masson*, [1995]
R.J.Q. 329 (C.A.) (rejetant l'appel de *Masson* c. *Thompson*, noté
dans (1994), 32 A.C.D.I. 375) (naissance de toute la cause d'action
au Québec).

(b)   Demande en matière familiale

Enfants — garde

*Droit de la famille — 2094 (1994), [1995] R.J.Q. 107. Cour
supérieure du Québec.*

Le Tribunal était saisi de trois requêtes concernant la garde d'un
enfant ainsi que les droits d'accès. Comme l'enfant habitait depuis
deux ans et demi en Ontario avec l'intimé, son père, en vertu d'une
ordonnance intérimaire, le Tribunal a soulevé la question de la
compétence de la Cour supérieure compte tenu de l'article 3142
C.C.Q. La Cour supérieure a cependant déjà rejeté une requête
pour exception déclinatoire dans laquelle le père alléguait divers
faits au soutien du renvoi du dossier devant le tribunal de l'Ontario.
La Cour supérieure avait alors conclu qu'elle était toujours saisie
d'une requête du père en changement de garde d'enfant et qu'elle
ne pouvait avoir perdu compétence du fait que la garde de l'enfant
avait été confiée au père par une ordonnance intérimaire.

Dans le présent jugement, la Cour a décidé à se dessaisir du
dossier. C'était à tort que la mère a soutenu que l'article 3142
C.C.Q., qui prévoit que les tribunaux québécois sont compétents
pour statuer sur la garde d'un enfant domicilié au Québec, devait
s'appliquer en fonction de l'intérêt de l'enfant. Seul doit être
considéré le domicile de l'enfant. Aux fins de l'article 3142 C.C.Q.,
le domicile est déterminé par les articles 76 à 80 et 192 C.C.Q. En
l'espèce, comme les deux parties étaient légalement tuteurs de

l'enfant, celui-ci avait, aux termes de l'article 80 C.C.Q., son domicile chez l'une ou chez l'autre. Il fallait alors s'en remetrre aux articles 77 et 78 C.C.Q. et conclure qu'il avait son domicile là où il résidait habituellement. Le fait que le père ait la garde de l'enfant en vertu d'une ordonnance intérimaire n'affectait pas le fait du domicile de ce dernier. C'était donc le tribunal du lieu de ce domicile qui était compétent pour statuer sur les questions relatives à la garde. Même si la Cour supérieure avait déjà été saisie de la demande, elle ne le demeurait pas car, en vertu de la Loi sur l'application de la réforme du Code civil, la loi nouvelle avait un effet immédiat dès son entrée en vigueur. Enfin, l'article 3135 C.C.Q., qui prévoit qu'un tribunal peut décliner compétence, ne s'appliquait pas en l'espèce car, pour ce faire, il aurait d'abord fallu que la Cour supérieure soit compétente. Il en était de même de l'article 3136 C.C.Q., qui prévoit qu'un tribunal, même s'il n'est pas compétent, peut entendre un litige si celui-ci présente un lien suffisant avec le Québec dans le cas où on ne peut exiger qu'elle y soit introduite. En effet, comme deux tribunaux ontariens avaient déjà été saisis d'instances entre les parties relativement à la garde de l'enfant, on ne saurait prétendre que les requêtes dont était saisie la Cour supérieure ne pouvaient être entendues par le tribunal de l'Ontario. Quant à l'impossibilité d'intenter le litige dans cette dernière province, il faudrait qu'il y ait une intervention du tribunal québécois pour établir que justice ne pouvait être rendue à l'étranger ou pour faire la preuve d'une cause de nécessité. Il manquerait alors un lien suffisant avec le Québec, l'enfant ayant son domicile en Ontario.

Note. Veuillez voir aussi *Droit de la famille — 1995*, [1994] R.D.F. 469, [1994] A.J.Q. 336, N° 979 (C.S.).

(c)   Litispendance

Gordon Capital Corp. c. *Garantie (La), compagnie d'assurance de l'Amérique du Nord*, [1994] A.J.Q. 842, N° 2337. Cour supérieure du Québec.

Le 15 juillet 1993, Gordon a intenté une action dans le district de Montréal contre les compagnies d'assurances défenderesses, leur réclamant une indemnité d'assurance de 39 381 235 $. Le 16 juillet 1993, elle a déposé au greffe de la Cour de l'Ontario, division générale, une action recherchant les mêmes condamnations contre les défenderesses, fondées sur les mêmes contrats d'assurance et sur la même cause. Le 29 juillet 1993, la défenderesse La Garantie a déposé au greffe de la Cour de l'Ontario, division générale, une action de nature déclaratoire qui aurait, suivant les règles de procédure du Québec, le caractère d'une défense aux deux actions de Gordon. Les deux autres défenderesses sont intervenues à l'action de La Garantie. Cette action a été signifiée à Gordon le 29 juillet 1993 à son siège social de Toronto. L'action de Gordon intentée au Québec a été signifiée le 30 juillet 1993 aux bureaux des trois défenderesses situés à Montréal et l'action de Gordon intentée en Ontario n'avait pas encore été signifiée. Les défenderesses ont demandé le rejet de l'action de Gordon aux motifs de litispendance et de prescription ou, subsidiairement, la suspension de cette action jusqu'au jugement final dans les procédures en cours en Ontario.

La Cour a rejeté la requête des défenderesses en rejet de l'action, et aussi leur requête en suspension de l'action. L'action de Gordon intentée devant la Cour de l'Ontario n'était pas une instance pendante parce que cette action n'avait pas été signifiée. Quant à l'action de Gordon intentée au Québec et à l'action de La Garantie intentée en Ontario, le forum était déjà fixé et établi le 15 juillet 1993. Au surplus, la requête en litispendance des défenderesses n'était pas pertinente. Le 29 juillet 1993, La Garantie savait déjà que Gordon avait intenté une action contre elle. L'action de Garantie intentée en Ontario, qui était de la nature d'une défense déclaratoire, ne pouvait se superposer à celle de Gordon. Il y avait un rapport entre ces actions et une connexité vraisemblable mais il ne s'agissait pas d'un cas de litispendance.

Quant à la demande des défenderesses en vue d'obtenir la suspension des procédures intentées au Québec par Gordon, l'article 27 C.C. prévoyait que tout étranger, bien que ne résidant pas au Québec, peut y être poursuivi pour l'exécution des obligations qu'il aurait contractées même en pays étranger. Or, si un étranger peut être poursuivi au Québec pour des obligations contractées à l'étranger, *a fortiori* les défenderesses qui avaient leur domicile et leur résidence au Québec pouvaient y être poursuivies pour le même genre d'obligations contractées non pas dans un pays étranger mais dans une province du Canada. De plus, en vertu de l'article 68 du Code de procédure civile, le forum naturel est d'abord celui du domicile du défendeur et non celui où a été conclu le contrat. En l'espèce, les domiciles réels de deux des défenderesses étaient situés au Québec et non en Ontario. Gordon avait eu le libre choix suivant l'article 68 C.P. d'intenter son action au Québec.

L'article 2190 C.C. ne pouvait s'appliquer à la défenderesse Chubb. Lorsque la prescription de deux ans alléguée a été acquise en sa faveur, Chubb avait déjà son domicile à Montréal. La prescription de trois ans prévue à l'article 2495 C.C. était, selon l'article 2500 C.C., d'ordre public absolu, et une interprétation large du mot "domicile" devait être privilégiée plus qu'une interprétation restrictive, suivant laquelle une société "étrangère" pourrait être considérée comme domiciliée au Québec en raison de son établissement commercial.

Note. Veuillez comparer *Guarantee Co. of N. America* v. *Gordon Capital Corp.* (1994), 18 O.R. (3d) 9 (Gen. Div.), noté dans (1994), 32 A.C.D.I. 366.

(d) *Forum non conveniens* — article 3135 C.C.Q. (1991)

Application de l'article 3135 — action intentée avant le 1er janvier 1994

Banque Toronto-Dominion c. *Arsenault*, [1994] R.J.Q. 2253. Cour supérieure du Québec.

L'action de la banque, fondée sur un billet à demande souscrit à Montréal par les défendeurs, a été intentée avant le 1er janvier 1994. La banque soutenait que l'article 3135 C.C.Q. ne s'applique pas à une action intentée avant l'entrée en vigueur du Code Civil du Québec. La Cour a décidé que l'article 3135 s'appliquait, et a suspendu les procédures au Québec.

L'exception de *forum non conveniens* n'était pas une règle de droit substantif liée à la compétence des tribunaux. Il s'agissait d'une règle de courtoisie, d'une mesure de collaboration judiciaire internationale qui n'affecte pas la compétence initiale d'un tribunal. Elle fait partie des règles d'organisation judiciaire et relève strictement de la procédure. L'article 3135 était donc applicable en l'espèce. Les circonstances de l'affaire militaient en faveur d'un dessaisissement au profit du tribunal ontarien. Le fait que les défendeurs résidaient au Québec et qu'ils y possédaient des biens n'était pas un facteur déterminant compte tenu des désavantages et des inconvénients qu'ils subiraient s'ils avaient à s'y défendre. Une action en dommages a en effet été intentée en Ontario en 1993 contre un promoteur immobilier et certaines institutions financières par trente investisseurs, dont les quatre défendeurs, résidants du Québec. Sans l'arrêt des procédures au Québec, les défendeurs seraient pénalisés du fait qu'ils ne pourraient plus tirer le même avantage de l'action commune intentée en Ontario. On ne saurait prétendre que l'action sur billet promissoire de la banque était simple et qu'il suffisait aux défendeurs de produire une défense. Pour se défendre adéquatement, ils auraient à répliquer par une demande reconventionnelle, réclamant les dommages qu'ils réclamaient déjà en Ontario. Ils devraient de plus assigner des témoins qui résidaient en Ontario. Enfin, un danger de jugements contradictoires militait en faveur d'une suspension des procédures au Québec.

Défendeur domicilié au Québec

Malden Mills Industries Inc. c. *Huntingdon Mills (Canada) Ltd.,* [1994] R.J.Q. 2227. Cour supérieure du Québec.

Malden a intenté un recours au Massachusetts contre Hoschek, qui, après avoir été congédié, est allé travailler pour Huntingdon, qui était une compagnie concurrente. Malden a également intenté un recours au Québec en injonction interlocutoire contre Huntingdon, alléguant que celle-ci employait le mis en cause, Hoschek, en contravention avec une clause de non-concurrence. Huntingdon a demandé au Tribunal de décliner compétence, bien qu'elle ait son siège social au Québec, au motif que les contrats qui liaient Malden et le mis en cause stipulaient que c'était la loi du Massachusetts qui s'appliquait. Elle a ajouté que la majorité des témoins résidaient au Massachusetts et que le recours était vexatoire. Enfin, elle a allégué que les autorités du Massachusetts étaient plus à même de trancher le litige.

La Cour a rejeté la requête en exception déclinatoire. Le nouvel article 3135 C.C.Q. codifie la doctrine de *forum non conveniens.* Toutefois, la discrétion accordée au tribunal par cet article doit être exercée dans des cas exceptionnels et à la demande d'une partie puisque la règle générale veut que le forum naturel soit le domicile du défendeur. En l'espèce, les motifs invoqués par Huntingdon n'etaient pas suffisants pour que le Tribunal décline compétence. D'abord, à ce stade-ci, le Tribunal ne pouvait conclure que les procédures étaient abusives ou vexatoires. Ensuite, le fait que plusieurs témoins résidaient à l'étranger pénalisait davantage Malden que Huntingdon. Il n'y avait pas non plus possibilité de jugement contradictoire entre le recours devant le tribunal étranger et le recours devant celui du Québec puisque les trois identités ne se retrouvaient pas ici. Finalement, le Tribunal ne croyait pas que les tribunaux du Massachusetts soient mieux en mesure de trancher le litige. Il n'y avait aucun facteur de rattachement entre Huntingdon et les tribunaux du Massachusetts et, qui plus était, le mis en cause invoquait devant le District Court au Massachusetts le fait que, en vertu de la clause de non-concurrence, les tribunaux du Massachusetts n'avaient pas compétence pour entendre la demande de Malden contre lui.

Note. Veuillez voir aussi *H. L. Boulton & Co. S.A.C.A.* c. *Banque Royale du Canada* (1994), [1995] R.J.Q. 213 (C.S.), dans laquelle la Cour a décliné compétence dans une action intentée par une compagnie vénézuélienne, avec une place d'affaires à Vancouver, contre la banque concernant une lettre de crédit confirmée par celle-ci à Vancouver. Le paiement devait aussi avoir lieu à Vancouver. Le bénéfice de la lettre de crédit a été transféré à la demanderesse pour effectuer paiement pour le transport par la demanderesse du bois du Vénézuéla à la Corée. Bien que la banque avait son siège social au Québec, il se dégageait de la preuve une impression nette tendant vers un seul forum étranger, soit la Cour suprême de la Colombie-Britannique. De plus, en droit international privé, en matière de lettre de crédit, c'est l'endroit où la lettre de crédit est payable qui constitue le *situs*.

Défendeur étranger — établissement au Québec

Rosdev Investments Inc. c. *Allstate Insurance Co. of Canada*, [1994] R.J.Q. 2966. Cour d'appel du Québec.

Rosdev, qui avait son siège social au Québec, a poursuivi Allstate en remboursement d'un emprunt ayant servi au refinancement d'un immeuble situé au Québec. Allstate a invoqué l'incompétence des tribunaux du Québec au motif que l'une des clauses du contrat prévoyait qu'il était soumis aux lois et aux tribunaux de l'Ontario. Elle a ajouté qu'elle était domiciliée en Ontario, que ses témoins y résidaient, ainsi que les membres du personnel qui avaient traité avec Rosdev, et que les derniers détails de l'entente ont été mis au point en Ontario. Elle soutenait que son établissement situé au Québec se spécialisait non pas dans le domaine du financement d'entreprises mais uniquement dans celui de l'assurance. Elle prétendait que, même si le Tribunal arrivait à la conclusion qu'il avait compétence, il devrait, en vertu de l'article 3135 C.C.Q., déférer l'affaire aux tribunaux de l'Ontario.

La Cour d'appel a décidé que la Cour supérieure du Québec avait compétence. La clause du contrat n'indiquait aucunement que les tribunaux de l'Ontario auraient compétence exclusive sur les parties. Le texte prévoyait que le contrat serait interprété selon les lois de l'Ontario et que Rosdev consentait à être poursuivie en Ontario, mais cet article ne s'appliquait que dans les cas de poursuite par Allstate. L'action instituée par Rosdev était une action personnelle à caractère patrimonial et c'était l'article 3148 C.C.Q. qui s'appliquait, particulièrement ses paragraphes 2 (un défendeur qui est une personne morale qui n'est pas domiciliée au Québec mais qui y a un établissement, et la contestation est relative à son activité au Québec) et 3 (une faute a été commise au Québec, un préjudice y a été subi, un fait dommageable s'y est produit ou l'une des obligations découlant d'un contrat devait y être exécutée). Il était exact que la contestation entre les parties ne relevait pas du domaine de l'assurance mais elle relevait d'activités de Allstate au Québec. En édictant un double critère à l'article 3148 paragraphe 2 C.C.Q., le législateur n'avait pas voulu lier l'activité à l'établissement mais plutôt à la cause de la contestation entre les parties.

Le moyen de *forum non conveniens* fondé sur l'article 3135 C.C.Q. est aussi rejeté. Cet article est discrétionnaire et d'application exceptionnelle. La Cour n'etait pas convaincue que l'administration de la justice serait mieux servie si le Tribunal déclinait juridiction. Allstate avait un établissement au Québec, elle y détenait des créances et elle y exerçait plusieurs activités. Elle possédait donc plusieurs facteurs de rattachement, et les critères des articles 3148 paragraphe 2 et 3148 paragraphe 3 étaient respectés.

Droit de la famille — 2032, [1994] R.J.Q. 2218. Cour supérieure du Québec.

La femme et le mari, de nationalité belge, se sont mariés en France en 1988 et leur régime matrimonial était assujetti aux lois de la Belgique. Leurs enfants, nés en Amérique du Sud, ont été adoptés selon les lois de la Belgique et étaient des citoyens belges. En août 1993, ils sont arrivés au Canada à titre d'immigrants reçus. La femme est retournée en Belgique à plusieurs reprises afin de s'occuper des affaires et de la gestion d'un institut dont elle était administratrice. Dernièrement, elle était retrounée définitivement en Belgique avec les enfants et y a intenté des procédures en divorce. Le mari a contesté la compétence des tribunaux belges et a intenté des procédures en séparation au Québec. La femme a demandé à la Cour de décliner compétence en appliquant la doctrine de *forum non conveniens*. À titre de mesure de rechange, elle a demandé au Tribunal une ordonnance de sursis tant et aussi longtemps que les tribunaux belges ne se seront pas prononcés sur les mesures accessoires.

La Cour a rejeté l'exception déclinatoire mais a accueilli la requête pour sursis de procédures. Les tribunaux du Québec n'avaient pas compétence pour entendre une demande en divorce parce que les parties n'étaient pas demeurées 12 mois au Québec. Il y avait néanmoins une juridiction pour entendre les procédures en séparation. Il suffit que l'un des époux ait son domicile ou sa résidence au Québec à la date de l'introduction de l'action (articles 3145 et 3146 C.C.Q.). Mais, en appliquant l'article 3135 C.C.Q., les tribunaux belges étaient beaucoup mieux placés pour statuer sur l'ensemble du litige. Il n'y avait pas eu de changement de domicile de l'une ou l'autre des parties. N'était pas suffisant le fait de vendre une maison à l'étranger pour en acheter une autre ici, d'avoir obtenu le statut d'immigrant reçu, d'avoir emmené les enfants au Québec et de les avoir inscrits à l'école. La totalité des intérêts financiers et personnels de la femme étaient en Belgique. De plus, advenant le cas où il y aurait une dissolution du régime matrimonial, ce serait les lois belges qui s'appliqueraient. Toutefois, afin d'éviter la possibilité que les tribunaux de chaque pays déclinent compétence, une ordonnance de sursis (article 3137 C.C.Q.) des procédures en séparation serait prononcée le temps que les tribunaux belges prennent position. Advenant le cas où les tribunaux belges se saisissent des procédures de divorce déjà intentées, il y aurait lieu de donner à l'article 3135 C.C.Q. sa pleine application et de décliner juridiction sur la base de *forum non conveniens*.

Note. Veuillez voir aussi *Droit de la famille — 2054*, [1994] A.J.Q. 885, Nº 2378 (C.S.); [1994] A.J.Q. 873, Nº 2433 (C.A.).

B   Procedure / *Procédure*

1   Common Law and Federal

(a)   Proof of foreign law

Proof of foreign statutes

Note. In *Royal Trust Co.* v. *H. A. Roberts Group Ltd.*, [1995] 4 W.W.R. 305 (Sask. Q.B.), the provision in the Saskatchewan Evidence Act, R.S.S. 1978, c. S-16, s. 3(1) (similar to provisions in other provinces), providing for proof of the "contents" of a foreign statute by means of an officially printed copy of the statute, was held not to authorize taking those contents as proof of the foreign law itself. Another provision, s. 3(2) (again with at least a partial equivalent in some other provinces), authorizing the court to take judicial notice of the law of another province, was held not to require the court to do so.

(b)   Evidence obtained locally for foreign proceeding

Letters rogatory

Note. See *Henry Bacon Building Materials Inc.* v. *Royal Canadian Mounted Police* (1994), 98 B.C.L.R. (2d) 59 (S.C.).

2   Québec

(a)   Action au Québec — preuve de la loi étrangère

Note. Veuillez voir *Desert Palace Inc.* c. *Bavary*, [1994] A.J.Q. 863, N° 2404 (C.S.) (droit de contre-interroger un expert juridique).

(b)   Poursuite dans un pays étranger — commission rogatoire

Note. Veuillez voir *Somerset Pharmaceuticals Inc.* c. *Clayman*, [1994] A.J.Q. 862, N° 2402 (C.S.).

C   Foreign Judgments / Jugements étrangers

1   Common Law and Federal

(a)   Conditions for enforcement by action or registration

Jurisdiction of original court — real and substantial connection with the foreign jurisdiction

Note. Default judgments, in cases where the defendant was served *ex juris* and did not submit to the original court's jurisdiction, have been declared by the Supreme Court of Canada to be enforceable, at least as far as Canadian judgments are concerned, if there was a real and substantial connection between the litigation and the province where the judgment was rendered (*Morguard Investments Ltd.* v. *De Savoye*, [1990] 3 S.C.R. 1077). Lower courts have since applied the principle to non-Canadian judgments as well. (Until now, all these judgments have been from either the United States or the United Kingdom.) Cases this year that have applied the *Morguard* principle were: *Webb* v. *Hooper*, [1994] 7 W.W.R. 124, 19 Alta. L.R. (3d) 269 (Q.B. M.C.) (Kentucky judgment held not enforceable because the only connection with Kentucky was the plaintiff's residence; the defendant's business dealings with the plaintiff, out of which the action arose, were centred in California and Colorado); *Clancy* v. *Beach,* [1994] 7 W.W.R. 332, 92 B.C.L.R. (2d) 82 (S.C.) (British Columbia residents held liable on Colorado judgment arising out of their business activities in Colorado and elsewhere); and *Pfaff* v. *Performax Systems Ltd.* (1994), 93 Man. R. (2d) 230 (Q.B.) (agreement by Manitoba-resident defendant to distribute goods for Ontario-resident plaintiff in parts of Ontario; action on contract brought in Ontario; judgment held enforceable; an express choice of Manitoba law to govern the contract was not an implied exclusion of Ontario jurisdiction).

(b) Enforcement by registration under uniform reciprocal enforcement of judgments legislation

Conditions for registration — jurisdiction of original court-defendant neither resident nor carrying on business in the jurisdiction

Note. In *917294 Ontario Inc.* v. *167644 Canada Inc.* (1994), 28 C.P.C. (2d) 114 (Sask. Q.B.), an Ontario judgment was held not registrable because the defendant was not resident, did not carry on business in the original jurisdiction, and had not submitted to the jurisdiction; the *Morguard* "real and substantial connection" test was inapplicable in Saskatchewan because the common law recognition rules were supplanted by the Foreign Judgments Act, R.S.S. 1978, c. F-18. A similar decision was *T. D. I. Hospitality Management Consultants Inc.* v. *Browne* (1994), 117 D.L.R. (4th) 289, [1994] 9 W.W.R. 153 (Man. C.A.). A Manitoba agent who accepted a telephone booking from an Alberta inn for a performance at the inn by a musical group was held not to have been carrying on business in Alberta. The inn's Alberta default judgment against the agent could not be registered. The *Morguard* test might have led to a different result, but it applied only to a common law action, not to registration under the Reciprocal Enforcement of Judgments Act, R.S.M. 1987, c. J20, which had more restrictive jurisdiction rules.

Conditions for registration — jurisdiction of original court — submission by agreement

Note. See *Bank of Credit & Commerce Int'l (Overseas) Ltd.* v. *Gokal* (1994), [1995] 2 W.W.R. 240, 99 B.C.L.R. (2d) 176 (C.A.), in which the registration of an English judgment was governed by the Canada-United Kingdom Convention, as implemented by Part 2.2 of the Court Order Enforcement Act, R.S.B.C. 1979, c. 75, not by the uniform Reciprocal Enforcement of Judgments Act, also implemented by Part 2 of the same statute. An agreement that the contract was to be "subject to the exclusive jurisdiction of the English courts" was held to have been a submission to the English court's jurisdiction for the purposes of either statute.

(c) Enforcement by registration under reciprocal enforcement of maintenance orders legislation

Scope of legislation — nature of order

Note. An order for costs in an Alberta maintenance proceeding was held not registrable as a maintenance order, but only as an ordinary money judgment under the reciprocal enforcement of judgments legislation: *British Columbia (Attorney General)* v. *Houle* (1994), 1 B.C.L.R. (3d) 215 (S.C.).

Registration of final order — effect

Note. See *Parent* v. *Litalien* (1994), 158 A.R. 235 (Q.B.) (no power to vary registered final order from Quebec).

Confirmation proceeding — local court's power to vary

Note. See *White* v. *White,* [1994] 7 W.W.R. 249 (Sask. Q.B.), in which a provisional order for child maintenance from Alberta was confirmed, but the amount was reduced by the Saskatchewan court, taking into account the factors relevant to the obligation under Saskatchewan law, such as the fact that both parents shared the obligation to maintain the child.

(d) Defences to enforcement or registration

Public policy

Note. In *Riese* v. *Mueller* (1995), 3 B.C.L.R. (3d) 228 (C.A.), the defendants sold certain land in Manitoba to a purchaser in Germany through a German real estate agent. The German agent sued in Manitoba for the agreed commission and obtained a default judgment. When the agent sued on the Manitoba judgment in British Columbia, the defendants argued that enforcement would be against public policy because the plaintiff had not been licensed as a real estate agent in Manitoba. The British Columbia court rejected the argument on the ground that the agent's work was all done in Germany and there was no evidence that, under these circumstances, the Manitoba licensing statute applied. The court left for another day the question whether the public policy defence might be qualified in Canada by the full faith and credit obligation that, according to recent authority, the courts owed in respect of judgments from other parts of Canada.

Collateral agreement not to enforce

Note. In *Black Gold Potato Sales Inc.* v. *Garibaldi* (1994), 29 C.P.C. (3d) 78 (Ont. Gen. Div.), the enforcement of a United States federal court consent judgment from Ohio was defended on the ground that the judgment creditor had promised, as part of the consent agreement, that the judgment would be only "of local effect." These words were held to be without legal significance either in Ohio or in Ontario. Moreover, the debtor did not take any steps to ensure non-enforceability of the judgment in Ontario, such as asking the United States court to make the alleged collateral agreement part of the judgment.

2 Québec

Reconnaissance des décisions étrangères rendue avant le 1ᵉʳ janvier 1994

Note. Veuillez voir *V.P.C. Promotion S.A.* c. *Bagyn,* [1994] A.J.Q. 495, N° 1457 (C.S.) (nouvelle procédure par requête applicable, tandis que les conditions pour la reconnaissance sont ceux de la loi ancienne).

D   *Choice of Law (Including Status of Persons) / Conflits de lois (y compris statut personnel)*

1 Common Law and Federal

(a) Characterization

Procedural and substantive rules

Note. See the note about *Canadian Deposit Insurance Corp.* v. *Canadian Commercial Bank,* below, under (d) Property (movables — transfer — security interests).

(b)   Legal personality

Note. See *International Assn. of Science & Technology for Development* v. *Hamza*, [1995] 6 W.W.R. 75, 28 Alta. L.R. (3d) 125 (C.A.) (capacity of unincorporated Swiss companies to sue in Alberta).

(c)   Tort

Tort outside the province

Tolofson v. *Jensen, Lucas* v. *Gagnon* [1994] 3 S.C.R. 1022, 120 D.L.R. (4th) 289. Supreme Court of Canada.

This was a consolidation of two actions, brought in different provinces, in respect of automobile accidents that had occurred outside the forum province. In *Tolofson* v. *Jensen*, the plaintiff, then twelve years old, was seriously injured in 1979 in Saskatchewan in the course of an automobile trip with his father. They lived, then and now, in British Columbia. Their British Columbia-registered automobile, driven by the father, collided with another automobile, registered in Saskatchewan and driven by a Saskatchewan resident. In 1987, more than eight years after the accident, the plaintiff sued his father and the Saskatchewan driver in British Columbia. The defendants raised two defences based upon Saskatchewan law. One was that the limitation period for the action had expired one year after the accident. The other was that a gratuitous passenger could not recover damages from a driver in the absence of proof of "wilful and wanton misconduct." (Both these statutory rules had been repealed by the time of the action.) Both the trial judge and the British Columbia Court of Appeal held, on a determination of the issue as a preliminary point of law, that these rules did not apply, because the actions against both defendants were governed by the law of British Columbia. This was based on the rule in *Phillips* v. *Eyre* (1870), L.R. 6 Q.B. 1 (Ex. Ch.), as applied by the Supreme Court of Canada in *McLean* v. *Pettigrew*, [1945] S.C.R. 62. Under this rule an action lies on a tort outside the province if (1) the wrong would have been actionable by the *lex fori* if committed in the forum, and (2) the defendant's act or omission was "not justifiable," meaning subject to some legal penalty, civil or criminal, under the *lex loci delicti*. Here the defendants' acts or omissions had been, according to the pleadings, actionable negligence in Saskatchewan or at least punishable as provincial highway offences.

In *Lucas* v. *Gagnon*, the plaintiff and her two children were passengers in an automobile driven by her husband that was involved in an accident in Quebec. The family were residents of Ontario and the automobile was registered there. The plaintiff, on behalf of herself and the children, sued the husband for damages in Ontario. She originally also sued the Quebec-resident driver of the other vehicle involved in the collision, but discontinued her action. The husband's cross-claim against the Quebec resident was, however, still on foot. The husband raised the defence that under the law of Quebec any delictual action in respect of an automobile accident is barred, under a no-fault insurance scheme. The plaintiff had, in fact, claimed and received benefits under that scheme. The lower courts, again applying *McLean* v. *Pettigrew*, [*supra*] had held that the plaintiff's claim against her husband was governed by Ontario law, subject only to a showing that he had committed some punishable wrong according to the law of Quebec. The Quebec bar to a civil action therefore did not defeat the plaintiff's claim.

The Supreme Court of Canada, overruling *McLean* v. *Pettigrew*, held unanimously that the claims were governed, not by the *lex fori*, but by the law of the province where the accident occurred. The court also held, again reversing long-standing authority, that statutes of limitation should be characterized as substantive even if they were worded so as to bar the action as distinct from extinguishing the obligation.

On the choice of law issue, after reviewing the extensive precedents in the field, La Forest, J., speaking for the court, considered the question of principle. He thought that ideas such as the legitimate expectations of the parties, or "fairness," were usually invoked to support one or other approach to choice of law, but what exactly these ideas meant never seemed to be examined. He suggested that a rational and workable system of private international law should be based on firmer ground. On the international plane, the underlying reality was the territorial limits of law under the international legal order. Much the same could be said of the federal system, subject to constitutional imperatives and other structural elements. Courts had evolved rules of jurisdiction that governed and limited the exercise of jurisdiction over extraterritorial and transnational transactions. From the general principle that a state has exclusive jurisdiction within its own territories and that other states must under principles of comity respect the exercise of its jurisdiction within its own territory, it seemed axiomatic that, at least as a general rule, the law to be applied to torts was the law of the place where the activity occurred, that is, the *lex loci delicti*.

There could be cases where the locus of the tort itself posed thorny problems, such as where the act was separated in space from its consequences; in such a case, it might well be that the consequences would be held to constitute the wrong. Difficulties might also arise where the wrong directly arose out of some transnational or interprovincial activity. There territorial considerations might become muted; they might conflict and other considerations might play a determining role. But, in the two cases here, the defining activity that constituted the wrong took place within a single province.

Application of the *lex loci delicti* was supported by practical considerations. The rule had the advantage of certainty, ease of application, and predictability. It would seem to meet normal expectations. And it avoided the confusion that would stem from states routinely applying their own law to activities taking place elsewhere. In a modern world of easy travel and with the emergence of a global economic order, chaotic situations would often result if the principle of territorial jurisdiction were not, at least generally, respected. *McLean* v. *Pettigrew* reflected a rule by which the forum country applied its own law to activities beyond its borders, and which invited forum shopping. It should be overruled.

The current English rule, which required that the wrong be civilly actionable both by the *lex loci delicti* and by the *lex fori*, was also seen as inapposite. The requirement that the wrong be actionable by the *lex fori* might have some merit, especially if it was flexibly applied, as the English courts seemed to do. But, at least within Canada, there was little need for a rule to bar actions unknown to the law of the forum. Consitutional restrictions on the jurisdiction of the courts of a province meant that an action would have a real and substantial connection with the forum jurisdiction, and the doctrine of *forum non conveniens* should be sufficient to control the bringing of actions before an inappropriate court. Application of the *lex loci delicti* alone should therefore be the general choice of law rule.

La Forest, J. considered whether the *lex loci delicti* rule should be subject to an exception. One means of obtaining flexibility was to adopt the approach of some American states, based upon a qualitative weighing of the relevant contacts with the competing jurisdictions. The extreme uncertainty of this approach made it undesirable. There might be room for a more narrowly defined exception where the parties were nationals or residents of the forum, and it was in these cases that courts in other countries often departed from the *lex loci delicti*. In many instances, however, this seemed to be motivated by a view that some aspect of the *lex loci delicti* was contrary to the public policy of the forum. This said little more than that the court did not approve of the law that the legislature in the other jurisdiction had chosen, on grounds that seemed reasonable to it, to adopt for its territory. It might be unfortunate for the victim of a tort that it took place in one jurisdiction rather than another, but such differences were a concomitant of the territoriality principle. While the underlying principles of private international law were order and fairness, order comes first. It is a precondition to justice. There was no reason why the circumstance that the parties came from the forum province should displace the application of the *lex loci delicti*. It was worth noting, as well, that the "public policy" differences in tort law tended to disappear over time. The biggest differences between provinces now, as far as liability for automobile accidents was concerned, was in insurance schemes, and this only created problems of quantum, not liability. Arguments of judicial convenience were also unconvincing grounds for making an exception in favour of the law of the forum. There might be some reason for admitting an exception in the international sphere, especially if it was reciprocally negotiated in an international instrument such as the Hague Convention on Traffic Accidents (to which Canada was not a signatory). In relation to domestic litigation, however, there was little to gain and much to lose in the judges creating an exception to the *lex loci delicti* rule. (La Forest, J. noted, however, that Article 3126 of the 1991 Civil Code of Quebec includes an exception that, where the wrongdoer and the victim "have their domiciles or residences in the same country, the law of that country applies.")

Turning to the federal context, La Forest, J. said that Canada's constitutional arrangements would seem to support a rule that was certain and that ensured that an act committed in one part of the country would be given the same legal effect throughout the country. The mobility of Canadians and the many common features of the law of the various provinces as well as the essentially unitary nature of Canada's court system were further reasons why there was no need for an invariable rule that the matter also be actionable according to the law of the forum. Concerns about constitutional validity also militated in favour of a strict *lex loci delicti* rule. It was doubtful whether a province had the constitutional capacity to impose liability in negligence for activities that took place wholly within another province and conducted by residents of that province or of a third province. Even if those involved were the forum province's own residents, it was arguably constitutionally impermissible for both the province where the activities took place and the province of residence of the parties to deal with civil liability arising out of the same activities. Assuming that both provinces had legislative power in these circumstances, it would open the possibility of conflicting rules in respect of the same incident. La Forest, J. expressed no conclusions on these issues, but thought that they argued against the court's devising a choice of law rule that might possibly raise intractable constitutional problems.

Major, J., with whom Sopinka, J. agreed, gave a short concurring judgment in which he disagreed only with La Forest, J.'s foreclosing an exception to the *lex loci delicti* rule in domestic, as distinct from international, cases. Major, J. thought that the possibility of an exception should be kept open, even with respect to domestic cases.

On the characterization of the Saskatchewan limitation statute, La Forest, J. said the common law's treatment of limitation statutes as procedural, if they were drafted in terms of barring the action rather than extinguishing the right, was obsolete. It apparently rested on two reasons. One was that foreign litigants should not be given advantages that were not available to forum litigants. (This related to the English preference for the *lex fori* in conflict situations.) The other reason was the rather mystical view that a common law cause of action gave the plaintiff a right that endured forever, and that the limitation statute only barred the remedy in the courts of the jurisdiction that had enacted the statute. Neither of these reasons fitted the modern context. The notion that foreign litigants should be denied advantages not available to forum litigants was at odds with the proposition that the law defining the character and consequences of the tort is the *lex loci delicti*. The view of limitations statutes as directed to the remedy was being eroded by Canadian courts in other contexts. For the purposes of determining the retroactive effect of lengthening the limitation period, the courts had treated the expiry of the former limitation period as creating a right in the defendant, and so denied the plaintiff the benefit of the new limitation rule. The purpose of the substantive/procedural classification was to determine which rules would make the machinery of the forum court run smoothly, as distinguished from rules that determine the rights of *both* parties. Rules as to whether the limitation bar must be pleaded were legitimately viewed as procedural, but the bar itself should henceforth be treated as substantive for choice of law purposes. The suggestion that a foreign limitation law might contravene the public policy of the forum should be rejected. To permit the court of the forum to impose its views over those of the legislature, which is endowed with power to determine the consequences of wrongs that take place within its jurisdiction, would invite the forum shopping that is to be avoided if courts are to attain the consistency of result that an effective system of conflict of laws should seek to foster. In *Tolofson* v. *Jensen*, the plaintiff's action was therefore statute barred.

As for *Lucas* v. *Gagnon*, it was clear that the Quebec automobile insurance legislation creating the no-fault scheme was intended to apply to all persons who had an accident in Quebec regardless of their province of residence. The Quebec and Ontario governments had negotiated reciprocal arrangements as to insurance coverage that were consistent with this assumption. The automobile insurance legislation was so clear that it also overrode the general choice of law rule in Article 3126 C.C.Q., cited above. Therefore the law of Quebec, as the *lex loci delicti*, barred the plaintiffs' claims in *Lucas* v. *Gagnon*.

Note. The Supreme Court of Canada has decided few choice of law cases. *Tolofson* v. *Jensen* is without doubt the most important choice of law decision it has ever made, in terms both of its scope of analysis and of its implications.

It is suggested that La Forest, J.'s founding of the choice of law rule on the principle of territoriality of law is not compelling. The principle of territoriality of law is problematic, to say the least, even in public international law. In private international law, it is most closely associated with the notion of "vested rights," which long since lost its appeal to courts and writers. Whatever appeal the idea of territorial limits of law may have in the context of torts, it is virtually unworkable as far as other fields of civil obligations are concerned.

A more solid-looking foundation for the *lex loci delicti* rule is La Forest, J.'s concept of a rigidly co-ordinated choice of law system within Canada, in which an act committed in one part of Canada ought to have the same legal effect throughout the country. But this principle, if taken to its logical conclusion, is a denial that choice of law rules form part of the civil law of each province. If in a given case the courts of each province must reach the same result, leaving procedural differences aside, the choice of law rules must be nationally uniform. The court stops short of saying this uniformity is constitutionally mandated. It does not suggest that Article 3126 of the Quebec Civil Code is constitutionally invalid because it puts the Quebec choice of law rule on a different footing from the common law choice of law rule laid down by the court. If, however, provinces are free to alter their choice of law rules by statute so as to deviate from the national rule, the principle of national uniformity would seem, at bottom, to be hardly more than a desideratum, not the fundamental factor the court seems to make it.

That said, *Tolofson* v. *Jensen* is in many respects a decision to be applauded. It finally eliminates the *Phillips* v. *Eyre* rule from Canadian law. The re-characterization of limitation statutes as substantive is eminently sensible. Whatever the strengths of its theoretical underpinnings, a strict *lex loci delicti* rule in relation to liability for automobile accidents within Canada has much to be said for it. The interprovincial insurance arrangements are based on it. It would strike most people as fair enough, provided they can insure themselves against the risk of lower standards of compensation if they have an accident in a province other than their own. How far *Tolofson* v. *Jensen* lays down a choice of law rule for other types of tort is open to question. La Forest, J. himself admitted that the *lex loci delicti* principle might not work well where the locus of the tort was unclear, or where the territorial considerations were more muted, as in truly interprovincial or international activities. (As an example of a case where the locus of the tort might be debatable, even in respect of an automobile accident, see *de Vlas* v. *Bruce*, above, under A.1(a), Jurisdiction *in personam*.) These *obiter dicta*, together with his comments on possible constitutional constraints on what courts can do by way of choice of law, will no doubt be much discussed and litigated in the coming years.

Subrogation to tort claims

Note. The choice of law rules that apply to rights of subrogation are unclear. A court struggled with the issue in *Fortus* v. *Allegretti*, [1994] 10 W.W.R. 194, 22 Alta. L.R. (3d) 221 (Q.B.). The Ontario Hospital Insurance Plan (OHIP) asserted its statutory right of subrogation in respect of benefits paid to an Ontario resident who had been injured in an Alberta automobile accident. The court refused to recognize OHIP's claim because the accident occurred in Alberta, the defendant was an Alberta resident, and the action was brought in Alberta. Ontario law did not have the most significant relationship to the issue, and Alberta law did not regard OHIP as having a common law right of subrogation under the circumstances. In a separate action, however, the court held that, in respect of the victim there, OHIP did have a common law right of subrogation. (The latter victim paid premiums for coverage, whereas the former victim did not.)

(d)   Property

Movables — transfer — security interests

Note. In *Canada Deposit Insurance Corp.* v. *Canadian Commercial Bank* (1994), 121 D.L.R. (4th) 360, [1995] 1 W.W.R. 395 (Alta. Q.B.), a Canadian bank had granted the Bank of Canada a security interest over foreign currency loans made by its California branch and over collateral property situated in California. The interest was not perfected. The validity of the security interest was challenged, and the question, posed as a preliminary question of law, was by which law the validity should be determined. The court held that California law, as the *lex situs* of the property in which the interest was to be created, governed the question of whether the security interest was a valid property right. Alberta law, as the *lex fori*, governed questions of priority among creditors. Thus the effect of the non-perfection depended on the proper characterization of the relevant California rule. If under California law the consequence of non-perfection was to invalidate the interest, the California rule would apply. If, on the other hand, non-perfection was regarded by California law as relating only to the question of priorities among creditors, the California rule would not apply, since that issue was for Alberta law to decide.

Matrimonial property

Note. See *Adam* v. *Adam* (1994), 7 R.F.L. (4th) 63 (Ont. Gen. Div.), determining the parties' last common habitual residence (held to be Zimbabwe) for the purpose of applying its law to the division of their family assets under the rule in s. 15 of the Family Law Act, R.S.O. 1990, c. F.3.

Succession — movables and immovables — different intestacy rules

Note. Vak Estate v. *Dukelow* (1994), 117 D.L.R. (4th) 122, 4 E.T.R. (2d) 1 (*sub nom. Putlic Trustee* v. *Dukelow*) (Ont. Gen. Div.), was an application for directions by the administrator of an estate of a woman who died intestate in Manitoba, where she lived. The estate included $131,000 worth of movable property in Manitoba, and an immovable property in Ontario worth $42,000. Her husband survived her. The issue was the preferential share to which he ought to be entitled. Under Manitoba law he was entitled to $50,000 as a first charge on the estate, with the residue to be divided equally between himself and his wife's son from an earlier marriage. Under Ontario law his first charge on the estate was $75,000, with the residue also going equally to himself and the son. Kinsman, J. held, following *Re Thom* (1987), 40 D.L.R. (4th) 184 (Man. Q.B.) (noted in (1988), 26 C.Y.I.L. 431), that the husband's right to a $75,000 preferential share under Ontario law should be applied, but with a deduction for the preferential share already given to him under the law of Manitoba. The first $50,000 from the Manitoba assets should therefore go the husband, plus the first $25,000 from the sale of the Ontario immovable. The judge showed some impatience with the traditional choice of law rules. The relevant connecting factor for succession to movable property was said to be habitual residence rather than domicile (which may have made no difference on the facts). It might also make sense, the judge said, for courts to apply a single law to the distribution of the estate rather than apply one law to the movables and potentially a different law, the *lex situs*, to any immovable. According to the judge that issue did not have to be addressed here, but the only explanation of the actual decision is that the *lex situs* was in fact applied to decide the distribution of the Ontario immovable; otherwise, there would have been no ground for awarding the husband the extra $25,000 of preferential share.

2   Québec

(a)   Biens

Hypothèque mobilière conventionelle — cession d'une universalité de créances

Note. Veuillez voir *Antares Electronics Inc. (Syndic de)*, [1994] A.J.Q. 1092, N° 3040 (C.S.). La Cour a décidé qu'en l'espèce la validité et l'effet des garanties créées étaient assujetis aux lois de l'Ontario, soit que s'appliquait l'ancienne règle de l'article 6(2) C.C. (meubles sont régis par la loi du domicile du propriétaire), soit que s'appliquait l'article 3105 C.C.Q. (la validité d'une sûreté grevant un meuble corporel utilisé dans plus d'un État ou celle grevant un meuble incorporel est régie par la loi de l'État où était domicilié le constituant au moment de sa constitution). Mais la créance en question, un remboursement d'impôt, était exclue de la cession par la loi fédérale sur la gestion des finances publiques.

Book Reviews / Recensions de livres

Anti-dumping and Anti-trust Issues in Free-trade Areas. By G. Z. Marceau.
Oxford and New York: Clarendon Press, 1994. Pp. xli, 343

International Trade and Investment Law in Canada. By Robert K.
Paterson and Martine M. N. Band, with Jock A. Finlayson and
Jeffrey S. Thomas. 2d ed. Scarborough, ON: Carswell, 1994
(Looseleaf)

The Regulation of International Trade. By Michael J. Trebilcock and
Robert Howse. London and New York: Routledge, 1995. Pp. 510

That Canada is a mature trading nation whose main international
economic interest lies in having clear and enforceable rules governing international trade and investment seems only gradually to be
taking hold of the political imagination of Canadians. In 1992,
more than 25 per cent of Canada's GNP was accounted for by
exports of goods and services. In the same year, Canada ranked as
the seventh largest exporter and eighth largest importer in the
world, although, with the emergence of the newly industrialized
countries of the Asia-Pacific region, its relative share of world trade
has been declining for a number of years. As is well known, the bulk
of this trade — 78 per cent of exports and 71 per cent of imports, in
1992 — is with the United States and, more significantly still, much
of this, perhaps the largest part, is non-arm's-length.[1] The American
relationship has been growing steadily in relative importance and
absolute size since the 1950s and has picked up significantly in the
wake of the Free Trade Agreement (FTA) in 1989 and the North
American Free Trade Agreement (NAFTA) in 1994. As a consequence of Canada's dependency on trade, Canadian governments
historically have been strong supporters of multilateral trading
institutions and have long been in favour of a predictable international trading order. Paradoxically, this economic interest is not

1 Much of this information is taken from the first chapter of R. Paterson, M. Band,
et al, *International Trade and Investment Law.* It is written by J. Finlayson and is an
excellent, concise survey of Canada in the international trading system.

reflected in the image Canadians have of their country in the way that it is, for example, in the case of the Dutch.

The reluctance of Canadians to embrace their identity as a trading nation is founded on a concern that international economic relationships might entail too great a loss of political, economic, cultural, and social sovereignty. The spectre of American hegemony in these spheres has been a particular worry. This fear lay at the basis of the Trudeau government's attempts in the 1970s to pursue the third option,[2] which was the foundation of his government's Foreign Investment Review Act.[3] It has informed Canadian public policy since Macdonald's National Policy and, in its current form, is expressed in apprehension over the coming changes to social, health, and cultural policy. In Macdonald's day, it was the need to make, rather than import, manufactured goods. In Trudeau's, it was a reaction against the branch-plant economy thereby created.

Even if the political accommodation of the idea of Canada as a trading nation has not yet been fully achieved, it seems very unlikely that an anti-globalization or anti-free trade political agenda could capture much political support in the foreseeable future. It is difficult to imagine the country returning to the negative view it held of free trade with the Americans in the 1988 federal election.[4] Witness, for example, the lack of credibility in the Liberal Red Book's promise to "renegotiate" NAFTA and the scepticism attendant on the Chrétien government's half-hearted effort to keep that promise. The economic nationalism of the 1960s and 1970s seems to have lost its political resonance.

Time will tell whether these developments have been all to the good. Adjustment has caused a lot of Canadians much hardship. Social policy is clearly lagging in innovation. It is still not clear where we are headed, although recent signs indicate continued devolution of significant areas of social policy to the provinces. But,

2 In February to June 1976, Canada negotiated and concluded a framework agreement with the European Community (*The Framework Agreement on Commercial and Economic Co-operation*, July 6, 1976. Can. T. S. 1976 (No. 35)), hoping thereby to increase its trade with the EEC and lessen its reliance on trade with the United States.

3 S.C. 1973-74, c. 46.

4 Opposition to the FTA failed to carry the day only because it was split and could not win in a first-past-the-post electoral system. David Peterson, premier of the province most likely to gain the most from free trade over the long run, also opposed the FTA, as did, perhaps more understandably, organized labour in Canada.

looking back, it is remarkable that Canada in 1988 was one of only three OECD countries (the other two being Japan and the United States) that was not a member of a free trade area and the only major industrialized country without liberalized access to a market of 100 million people. How things have changed since then!

Perhaps the way forward is to see the new trading environment as a guarantor of sovereignty, not a threat to it, based on the view that there is more liberty in order than in independence or solitude. In advancing the understanding of Canada's interest in an intelligently ordered world trading environment, the books under review subtly and implicitly suggest as much. They also demonstrate a maturing of Canadian legal scholarship on international trade and investment law that parallels the developments in national self-image just described. Each makes a substantial contribution to the legal and economic literature on international trade and investment.

The Trebilcock and Howse book is a broad and in-depth treatment of international trade and investment regulation. It is written for "serious students of law, economics, politics, and public policy," and introduces them to "the institutions and rules that govern trade between sovereign states" (preface). Trebilcock and Howse write from a "new liberal institutionalist perspective," one based on the view that "rules, norms and institutions matter a great deal" (*ibid*). Their evaluation of the world trading order is not, they say, premised "upon a naive or unquestioning adherence to the economic theory of the gains from trade . . . but on a [sensitivity] to the qualifications to and limits on the case for free trade, as well as the complexities involved in determining the domestic interest in these matters — including concerns about unemployment, worker adjustment, the quality of life and values of human rights and environmental protection" (*ibid*). I quote these statements from the preface because they convey accurately the sense of this book. In terms of style, structure, coherence, and substance, the book is a great success. Page after page, the analysis is measured, detailed, balanced, insightful, and engaging.

The book starts, thoughtfully, with a brief intellectual history of international trade theory and policy. The method of the first chapter is illustrative of the balanced approach of the book as a whole. The subject matter is positioned as "intellectual history" — that is, not merely economics or political science, but a history of the political and economic explanations of trade. The chapter

informs us of the origins of trade theory in the Scottish Enlightenment thought of Hume, Smith, and Ricardo and their critical
analysis of mercantilist theory, and guides us through the factor
proportions theory of comparative advantage into the 1960s product cycle theory. The presentation of this familiar material is followed by arguments that qualify the theory of comparative advantage — the infant industry argument, the idea of the optimal tariff,
strategic trade theory, etc. — then, by an evaluation of the traditional arguments against open economies — job losses and wage
depression, cultural homogenization, loss of sovereignty, etc. All are
dealt with in a knowledgeable and erudite way. The chapter then
concludes with an institutional history of trade policy. The intellectual and ethical perspective of the writing in this chapter is appeal-
ing. Positioned as intellectual history, the ideas are offered as partial
views and helpful fragments, not dogmatically as "the" theory of
trade. This well-informed but intellectually modest approach, here
as elsewhere, is one of the book's major strengths.

The second chapter illustrates another of the book's strengths. It
provides a brief overview of the major elements of international
trade law and policy, including the basic principles of the GATT, the
FTA, NAFTA, and the European Union (EU). This introductory
survey, by providing the basic structure of ideas upon which the rest
of the book hangs, contributes to its underlying thesis that the
regulation of international trade is a single, integral subject. Many
treatments of the subjects examined in this book do not succeed in
achieving that goal.

After an examination of the economics of exchange rates and the
balance of payments, and a brief history of the institutional arrangements that deal with them, followed by a similar treatment of tariffs
and the effects of tariff reduction on an MFN and regional basis,
the remainder of the material in the book is organized thematically:
anti-dumping (Chapter 5), subsidies, countervail, and government
procurement (Chapter 6), safeguards and domestic adjustment
(Chapter 7), agriculture (Chapter 8), services (Chapter 9), TRIPs
(Chapter 10), trade and investment (Chapter 11), trade and
developing countries (Chapter 12), trade and the environment
(Chapter 13), the movement of people (Chapter 14), and dispute
resolution (Chapter 15), followed by a concluding set of arguments
in Chapter 16.

The book is replete with arguments on trade policy and the
economic and political implications of trade policy. The authors

skilfully articulate their ideas in clear, precise prose and demonstrate a mastery of their multidisciplinary approach to international trade regulation. Their detailed descriptions of institutional arrangements are not easily or readily available from other sources. For example, the GATT bargaining structures before the Kennedy round (1964-67) (product-by-product) and after the Kennedy round (linear, and, to some extent, sector-by-sector) are described in detail, and the economic and game theoretic implications of these methods of negotiation are explored in a way that helps explain the current shape of world trade law. Overall, their multidisciplinary and balanced approach integrates the entire broad subject of international trade.

The GATT system is evaluated throughout from their "new liberal institutionalist" perspective. That perspective emphasizes that "multilateralism should . . . be seen as a decentralized framework for the negotiation and maintenance of mutually advantageous bargains among states" (preface). It is opposed to the "liberal internationalist" perspective, which tends to regard every arrangement that falls short of maximizing global welfare (by failing to constrain short term national self-interest) as a failure or near failure. Rather, the GATT is regarded as an arrangement of institutions and practices — a process — that, by "reducing information, transaction, surveillance and verification costs," facilitates value-maximizing arrangements between states. Judged from this perspective, and taking realistic account of the political and cultural environment in which the GATT system operates, the authors judge the system a success.

This book includes a fascinating evaluation of regional trading blocs. The authors ask whether these arrangements are likely to lead to freer trade worldwide in the long term. That, after all, is the rationale for these blocs in GATT Article XXIV. The authors evaluate the extensive literature and come to a cautiously sceptical view of this development. The mechanics of regionalism leading to multilateralism, presumably, would be the development of large blocks in a first stage, followed, in a second stage, by a process in which these blocks would negotiate a larger liberal trading order. Trebilcock and Howse doubt the reality of this scenario. Their reasons are compelling.

First, they argue, the prospects for intraregional trade expansion in many potential trading blocks — notably, the Caribbean, South Pacific, Africa, and Latin America — are minimal, due to the similarity in natural endowments. Regional blocks, therefore, might simply end up closing these regions out of large segments of the world economy. Second, regionalists argue that multilateralism is plagued by the "convoy problem," with the least able holding up the whole group. In contrast, they praise regionalism as a "migrating bird formation," with each regional trading group dominated by a single major market leading the whole to deeper integration. This structure, argue Trebilcock and Howse, may not be as conducive to profound economic integration as regionalists think. This is because (a) the cultural sovereignty concerns of the weaker partners in the group are likely to prevent deeper integration, and (b) the extreme unlikelihood that the larger partner in the group would be willing to modify significantly any element of its economic law. The authors suggest that the level of integration achieved in the EU is a *sui generis* case explained largely by the fact that there are several leaders in that group and, of course, by the fact that it is a specific product of European history. The case of the Canadian/ American relationship, they argue, seems more realistic. Third, the trade diversion resulting from regional arrangements may, in fact, exacerbate the costs of adjustment to new inter-regional arrangements. Finally, the incremental approach of regionalism, building up from small to larger economic blocks, is hindered by the reluctance that the first movers in the group may feel toward making open-ended commitments to future unknown parties to the agreement. To reduce the risks inherent in this position, first movers will hedge their commitments by bargaining for veto rights on the admission of new members. This in turn entails a full multi-party negotiation at a subsequent stage with, at some point, the same level of organizational difficulty said to attend the multilateral convoy. On the basis of these arguments, the authors suggest that continued support for the GATT system is required.

The same level of analysis is brought to bear in other chapters of the book. There is, for example, an in-depth economic critique of anti-dumping laws and realistic and not-so-realistic suggestions for their reform.[5] On this score the authors see the Australian-New Zealand Closer Economic Relations Trade Agreement (ANZCERTA)

---

[5] Much of this critique draws on previous work by the authors. See S. Hutton and M. J. Trebilcock, *An Empirical Study of the Application of Canadian Antidumping Laws: A Search for Normative Rationales* (Toronto, ON: Ontario Centre for International Business, Trade Law Programme, 1990); M. J. Trebilcock and Robert C. York, *Fair Exchange: Reforming Trade Remedy Laws* (Toronto: C.D. Howe Institute, 1990).

as the way forward. New Zealand and Australia agreed in 1990 to cease anti-dumping actions and to deal henceforth with these question under harmonized provisions dealing with the abuse of dominant positions. They therefore agree with Warner's proposal[6] in favour of a harmonized anti-dumping regime between Canada and the United States.

The subsidy and countervail issue is dealt with by a thorough evaluation of all the reasons that have been offered in favour of countervailing duty laws, especially the fair trade rationales.[7] They criticize the various methods of conceptualizing countervailing duty law — the cash flow approach, the entitlement approach and the Uruguay round effort to provide a taxonomy of subsidies — all of which they justly condemn for "normative incoherence." They suggest a regime at the GATT level similar to the EU system of administrative review of state aids. Such a regime would respond responsibly to the problem of subsidies on a case-by-case basis, evaluating the cases in light of political and social realities.

The chapter on safeguards contains a lengthy analysis of labour market adjustment reforms and brings that analysis to bear on the reform of safeguards law at the GATT level. The NAFTA example here, as in the chapter on environmental law, is marshalled.

The study concludes with a discussion of what the authors regard as the three major challenges facing international trading order today, namely: (1) disciplining protectionism disguised as fair trade law; (2) integrating the former east bloc countries into the liberal economic order; and (3) managing the interrelationship between regional accords and the multilateral system. These arguments pick up on themes developed extensively throughout the book.

Like the Trebilcock and Howse book, the Marceau book has a strong policy orientation. The author is a Canadian lawyer currently working with GATT. The book appears (it is not so stated) to have been produced originally as a thesis for the author's doctorate in law at the University of London. It is clear, however, that the book has benefited from the author's more recent practical experience in the area — she completed a stage at the Competition Directorate of the EEC Commission, for example. The book's objective is to

---

6 See P. Warner, "The Canada-US Free Trade Agreement: The Case for Replacing Anti-dumping with Antitrust" (1992) 23 Law and Policy in International Business 791.

7 This chapter also draws on previous work. See M. J. Trebilcock, *Proposed Policy Directions for the Reform of the Regulation of Unfair Trade Practices in Canada* (Ottawa: Information Canada, 1976).

provide an in-depth analysis of the legal implications of Article XXIV.8(b) of the GATT (requiring that "duties and other restrictive regulations of commerce . . . are eliminated on substantially all the trade between the constituent territories" of a free trade area) for anti-dumping action and competition laws. This is a fascinating topic, since the interaction between competition policy and trade policy will become increasingly important in the post-Uruguay round. The author does a marvellous job reviewing and analyzing the material.

The book begins with a review of the legal and economic implications of dumping. Here the author explores the well-known conceptual and practical difficulties in defining "dumping." Ostensibly, the definition ought to be tied to some economic rationale for sanctioning dumping, but, as both this book and the Trebilcock and Howse book affirm, it is difficult to identify any sound basis in competition policy for anti-dumping laws. Viewing dumping as a form of international price discrimination would not justify making it illegal, since the importing country is the lower price country. As such, it does not suffer by virtue of the discrimination and probably has little reason to advance global welfare by requiring its consumers to pay more. Viewing it as predation, the only other plausible economic justification, also seems implausible; in the vast majority of cases of current applications of anti-dumping laws, predation was simply not present.[8] These difficulties are reflected in the jurisprudence and doctrine on the definition, which the author reviews in some depth.

The second chapter reviews the international control of restrictive business practices other than dumping. Her objective here is to assess whether, given the weak case for anti-dumping laws, there is any basis at the international level to include what is of value in them in international or domestic competition laws. Here Marceau reviews the international efforts to regulate competition, as well as the national laws and the extraterritorial application of national laws in Canada, the United States, and the EU. There is also a comprehensive review of agreements in place between states to cooperate in the application of their competition laws. She takes the view that the European proposals for "positive comity" are to be preferred. According to this view, instead of a state applying its law in an extraterritorial fashion, it should request the state where the anti-competitive practice occurs to intervene by applying its own

<hr>

[8] See S. Hutton and M. Trebilcock, *supra*, note 5.

competition laws against the offending parties for the benefit of both states.

Chapters 3 and 4 of the book look at the differences in the treatment of restrictive business practices between domestic and external policies. Marceau first (in Chapter 3) thoroughly examines the differences between the treatment of price discrimination and predation in domestic versus external regulation of various states and the EU. What emerges, of course, is such a divergence of treatment that most anti-dumping laws violate the national treatment obligation of the GATT. This claim is made in respect of both procedural law and substantive law. Anti-dumping laws diverge in their treatment of substantive questions (the existence of predation, the causation of injury, and the definition of markets), and procedural questions (whether trial is in a regular court or by an administrative tribunal, time constraints, and interim and final relief). Marceau observes, however, that even if there were full compliance with the GATT national treatment obligation, anti-dumping laws would still remain a significant impediment to international trade. This conclusion is based on her review of the different legal cultures generating these norms and therefore the different objectives each sets for competition policy. She therefore argues in favour of an international effort to harmonize competition law.

Chapter 4 examines the context for a possible harmonization of anti-dumping laws by describing the main elements of anti-dumping law in the United States, Canada, the European Union, and Mexico. And Chapter 5 examines the legal, political, and economic basis of free trade areas under customary international law and the GATT. These two chapters lay the ground for the examination of the treatment (in Chapter 6) of internal trade measures in free trade areas — that is, in EFTA, in the EEA (and in its predecessor the EEC-EFTA FTAs), in the ANZCERTA, in the EEC, and under the FTA and NAFTA, with their regime of binational panel review. The study ends with chapters advancing the author's preferred solution, which is an abolition of anti-dumping laws and an international harmonization of national competition laws, which would contain only those elements from anti-dumping legislation justified as abusive price discrimination. This should occur, in her view, at least in the free trade areas, but preferably on an international basis.

One very useful feature of the Marceau book is the detailed bibliographies at the end of each chapter, which make this text an excellent resource for further work in this area.

The Paterson and Band book is a second edition of R. Paterson's book that was published in 1986.[9] Its policy orientation is much less pronounced than that of the other two, and, although its scope is similar to that of the Trebilcock and Howse book — it covers most of international trade and investment law — it does so almost exclusively from the point of view of Canadian law or Canadian concerns. Consequently, it will be of interest to readers requiring an in-depth treatment of Canadian law. The book is, nonetheless, quite ambitious. In terms of topics, it deals with the GATT, the FTA, NAFTA, the Canadian public law of international trade, Canadian customs law, Canadian law of import and export controls, government procurement in Canada, Canadian anti-dumping and countervail law, export financing in Canada, foreign direct investment law in Canada, and investment insurance. The appendices include some useful documents, such as the Bilateral Investment Treaty between Canada and the former USSR.

Throughout, the description and analysis are informative, useful, and readable. The book is a collaborative effort, but, for the most part, the level, tone, and quality of presentation are even. This is an excellent resource book on Canadian law.

The book is produced in looseleaf format, and the authors express the intention of adding further chapters. They might consider including, for example, chapters on transfer pricing, antitrust and competition policy, international employment law, international bankruptcy, and dispute settlement. None of the private law aspects of international trade is treated in any of the books. Perhaps it is another subject.[10] Similarly, a larger orientation toward American subject matter in some of these domains would be useful to Canadian lawyers. These are merely suggestions for additions, not criticisms for omissions.

On the whole, it is encouraging to see the Canadian scholarship in this area growing and maturing so well.

DAVID P. STEVENS
Faculty of Law, McGill University

---

[9] R. K. Paterson, et al., *Canadian Regulation of International Trade and Investment* (Toronto: Carswell, 1986).

[10] *Cf.* J. G. Castel, A. L. C. de Mestral, and W. C. Graham, *The Canadian Law and Practice of International Trade, with Particular Emphasis on Export and Import of Goods and Services* (Toronto: Emond Montgomery Publications, 1991), which attempts to do just this.

International Responses to Traumatic Stress: Humanitarian, Human Rights, Justice, Peace, and Development Contributions, Collaborative Actions, and Future Initiatives. Edited by Yael Danieli, Nigel S. Rodley, and Lars Weisaeth. Amityville, New York: Baywood Publishing Company, 1996

Despite admonitions to the contrary, we do tend to judge books by their covers. This important volume, which is essentially about the victims of human rights abuses and their emotional suffering, has the look and feel of a psychology textbook. Once past the deceptive cover, it reveals an original contribution to human rights law in the form of a series of essays published to mark the fiftieth anniversary of the United Nations — what Roger Clark and Daniel Nsereko call, in their concluding chapter, "an essay in imagination."

The book, which is crowned with a foreword by Boutros Boutros-Ghali, brings together some of the most distinguished commentators in the field of human rights and its periphery. The word "periphery" is not chosen pejoratively. This book is hard to classify because it addresses a number of specialized fields, including the rights of victims, protection of children, violence against women, and stress experienced by aid workers and peacekeeping forces. Further, it provides a general overview of the international legal basis for the protection of human rights.

The chapters are organized by tandems along specific themes, the first dealing with the role of the United Nations and the second with the role of non-governmental organizations (NGOs). Thus, in eight pairs of chapters the following subjects are addressed: criminal law in a general sense, human rights violations, forced displacement, armed conflict, natural disasters, children, women, and health activities.

Traumatic stress is described as the consequence of "exposure to extreme events and attempts to cope with their sequelae." As Clark and Nsereko note, the term is not to be found in the United Nations instruments and had not even been coined when the organization was set up at the close of the Second World War. Although some limited attention is given to natural disasters, the focus is on human rights abuses in their most extreme form: genocide, war, ethnic cleansing, torture.

Sometimes, contributors focus essentially on the rights of "victims," as if the issue is indistinct from that of traumatic stress. But obviously the theme is larger, as the very interesting articles on the psychological problems of those involved in humanitarian relief make clear. But perhaps more reflection should have been given to the issue of defining what is meant by the term "victim." For example, large numbers of the "refugees" who fled Rwanda following the 1994 genocide were, in fact, perpetrators of the most heinous crimes known to humanity. They brought with them hundreds of thousands who were surely uninvolved in any serious wrongdoing, although the latter, having in a sense subsequently allied themselves with these criminals, have possibly become accomplices after the fact. Are they victims? Some of the contributors to this volume seem to think so. If they are, do they deserve the same treatment as genuinely innocent victims? The answers provided by this volume are, to say the least, unclear.

One approach to the problem is the classic Red Cross vision, which is largely neutral with respect to the previous conduct of so-called victims. The contribution of the International Committee of the Red Cross is set out in an article by Pascal Daudin and Hernan Reyes that is subtitled "How Visits by the ICRC Help Prisoners Cope with the Effects of Traumatic Stress." This useful contribution focuses on methodology, but begs the more fundamental philosophical question. In a large humanitarian law sense, of course, "prisoners" may be deemed victims. In a somewhat different human rights law context, prisoners may be detained for good and sufficient cause, and an exaggerated attention to their well-being may be misunderstood by their victims and itself considered an abuse of human rights.

Irwin Waller, in his chapter on the contribution of NGOs with respect to the victims of crime, and Elsa Stamatopoulou, in her chapter on the United Nations and human rights, get closer to the heart of this conundrum. The difficult issue is the struggle against impunity for human rights abuses, and its relationship to the rights of victims. Waller makes the helpful observation that victims are not principally interested in vengeance, but rather with personal security. Stamatopoulou discusses the importance of compensation for victims, and in an appendix to her text, she recommends a number of principles, including a "right of reparation."

This approach to the issue is essentially judicial, and we are entitled to ask whether legal remedies really do help victims to heal their emotional wounds. The conventional wisdom recognizes that the battle against impunity makes at least a contribution in this respect. Indeed, vigorous public condemnation of human rights violators is important to the mental health of victims. But this is surely only a small part of the picture. Punishment of the offender cannot really help ease the physical suffering of an innocent child whose leg is blown off by an anti-personnel mine; why then should it allay the attendant psychological suffering? This issue will surely be more fully developed in subsequent work in the field, for which this volume is very much a pathfinding study.

Collections of this nature frequently suffer from inconsistency in the standards of contributions, but the obviously careful editing of *International Responses to Traumatic Stress* has kept this problem to a minimum. An exceptional and truly helpful addition is the index, which is usually absent in volumes of this type. A spot check, however, showed the index to be incomplete. For example, a very useful discussion on the problems of refugee workers in Rwandan refugee camps, in the chapter by Barbara Smith, Inger Agger, Yael Danieli, and Lars Weisaeth, cannot be traced under "Rwanda" or "Zaire," although it appears under "Goma." Nor is there any reference in the index to the International Tribunal for Rwanda, although it is discussed on page 67 in the exhaustive study on victims in the United Nations crime prevention and criminal justice program by Eduardo Vetere and Irene Melup.

The multidisciplinary approach of this volume is a great strength and will make it valuable to a broad readership. International lawyers will particularly appreciate the thorough discussions of the relevant norms concerning the protection of victims of human rights abuses, as well as the many insights into the activities and roles of different United Nations bodies and non-governmental organizations.

WILLIAM A. SCHABAS
Département des sciences juridiques, Université du Québec à Montréal

Le Comité international de la Croix-Rouge et la protection des victimes de la guerre. Par F. Bugnion. Genève: Comité international de la Croix-Rouge, 1994. Pp. 1438

Du Comité international de la Croix-Rouge (CIRC), il est peu dire qu'il a largement dépassé le dessein pour lequel il avait été conçu. Commission de cinq membres à l'origine, l'institution fut créée en février 1863 par la Société genevoise d'Utilité publique, dans le seul but de rédiger un mémoire qui développerait les propositions faites par H. Dunant dans *Un Souvenir de Solférino*. Il était prévu que ledit mémoire serait présenté lors du Congrès international de bienfaisance qui allait se tenir à Berlin la même année. Son mandat accompli, le Comité était appelé à disparaître. Mais, l'Histoire devait en décider autrement.

Grâce à près de cent cinquante ans d'action au service des victimes des conflits armés, des situations de troubles intérieurs et de tensions internes, le Comité international s'est mérité une place sur la scène internationale. Il est ainsi doté d'un statut d'observateur auprès de l'ONU depuis 1990. En 1993, il s'est lié à la Suisse par un accord de siège qui garantit son indépendance par rapport aux autorités helvétiques et lui confère les privilèges et immunités octroyés aux organisations internationales installées sur le territoire de la Confédération.

Aujourd'hui, le CICR oriente ses activités à partir de trois grands axes:

· Le Mouvement international de la Croix-Rouge et du Croissant-Rouge, du fait de ses activités en son sein
· Le droit humanitaire tant en ce qui concerne son développement progressif et sa codification, qu'en ce qui a trait à sa diffusion
· La protection des victimes des conflits armés, des situations de troubles intérieurs et de tensions internes.

C'est cette dernière voie, du moins en ce qu'elle concerne les conflits armés, que F. Bugnion a choisi de suivre pour nous entretenir du Comité international et de son oeuvre.

Divisé en trois livres, l'ouvrage de F. Bugnion relate d'abord l'histoire du Comité de Solférino à Hiroshima (livre premier). À travers les événements de l'époque, l'auteur explique comment le Comité est passé du rôle de promoteur d'une idée à celui d'un rouage essentiel au fonctionnement, ainsi qu'au développement, des mécanismes humanitaires qu'il a contribué à créer. On y apprend notamment que la neutralisation des infirmiers volontaires dépêchés à la suite des armées par les Comités de secours aux blessés s'avéra être le seul point de friction lors de la Conférence diplomatique qui est à l'origine de la première Convention de Genève (1864). Certains délégués en effet doutaient qu'ils fussent autorisés à signer une Convention dans laquelle des secouristes volontaires seraient mentionnés. En définitive, ceux-ci furent assimilés au personnel sanitaire des armées. Il est intéressant ici de faire un parallèle entre cette controverse et celle concernant l'application de la *Convention pour la sécurité du personnel des Nations Unies et du personnel associé* (1994) au personnel des ONG à but humanitaire. Lors des négociations ayant conduit à l'adoption de la Convention, en effet, plusieurs États voyaient d'un très mauvais oeil son application à ce personnel.[1] On constate ainsi que la méfiance des États à l'égard des sociétés de secours bénévoles existait en 1864 et que cela n'a guère changé depuis.

Le livre second est consacré à la place qu'occupe le CICR dans le droit international humanitaire. Il s'agit alors pour l'auteur de préciser les tâches et les prérogatives du Comité international à la lumière du droit international humanitaire contemporain. Cet examen comprend huit parties dont certains développements sur les sources, y compris les sources coutumières, relatives aux compétences et aux obligations du CICR; les offres de service du Comité international; la protection des blessés, malades ou naufragés, des prisonniers de guerre et des détenus civils, ainsi que des populations civiles; la mise en oeuvre du droit humanitaire et le CICR, etc. De cet examen des tâches et des prérogatives du Comité, il ressort notamment qu'il n'a pas hésité, quand cela servait l'intérêt des victimes, à invoquer des règles conventionnelles encore à l'état de projet et que ses interventions ont contribué au développement de ces principes. Cette attitude à l'égard du droit international en formation pourra paraître peu orthodoxe à certains. Elle s'explique par une préoccupation essentielle: la protection des victimes des conflits armés, qui dans certains cas ne peut attendre la lente progression du droit laissée à la seule initiative des États.

Le livre troisième traite du statut juridique du Comité international, de sa composition ainsi que de ses rapports avec la Confédération helvétique. Après avoir démontré que le Comité international jouit d'une personnalité juridique internationale de type fonctionnel et avoir décrit les droits et les obligations qui en découlent, l'auteur explique comment, à travers son histoire, le Comité est demeuré une institution suisse quant à sa composition, en dépit de certaines tentatives en sens contraire. C'est dans ce contexte que sont abordés les rapports entre le Comité et la Fédération des Sociétés de la Croix-Rouge et du Croissant-Rouge. Enfin, l'auteur consacre quelques pages aux rapports généralement harmonieux qui existent entre le Comité international et la Suisse. À cet égard, il

---

[1] *Cf.* C. Emanuelli, "La Convention sur la sécurité du personnel des Nations Unies et du personnel associé: des rayons et des ombres," (1995) 4 R.G.D.I.P. 849.

est cependant souligné que s'il existe une relation particulière entre le CICR et la Suisse, celle-ci n'est pas de nature à créer un lien de subordination entre eux.

Rédigé dans un style dynamique, ponctué d'interrogations et de réflexions personnelles, le texte de F. Bugnion s'avère d'une lecture agréable, et même facile, en dépit de sa longueur, de ses nombreux détails et de ses multiples références. Ce texte passionnant s'accompagne d'une table des traités, d'une table des décisions arbitrales ou judiciaires, d'une longue bibliographie des sources publiées et non publiées, des témoignages et des travaux. Il inclut aussi un index des noms de personnes, un index des noms des lieux, ainsi qu'un index analytique.

Le tout constitue une mine de renseignements extrêmement utiles pour quiconque veut mieux connaître le CICR et son oeuvre. Au début de son ouvrage, l'auteur nous dit du Comité international qu'il s'agit d'une institution mal connue, souvent confondue avec d'autres. Il ne fait aucun doute qu'une telle confusion ne saurait subsister après avoir lu l'ouvrage ici recensé.

CLAUDE EMANUELLI
Faculté de droit, Université d'Ottawa

Precautionary Legal Duties and Principles in Modern International Environmental Law. By Harald Hohmann. London: Graham & Trotman, 1994. Pp. xvii, 377. ISBN 1-85333-911-3

In a review of this book's original German version,[1] I referred to it as "one of the more comprehensive and interesting reviews of international environmental law currently available" and expressed the hope that an English translation would make it accessible to a broader readership. The present volume, published in Graham & Trotman's International Environmental Law & Policy Series, now offers this English translation. It has been updated from the German version, notably with respect to the outcome of the 1992 Earth Summit. However, most additions and changes are brief, at times confined to additional comments in footnotes, so that Hohmann's new book is perhaps not quite the "second edition" he promises in

---

[1] "Preventive Legal Obligations and Principles in Modern International Environmental Law (Praeventive Rechtspflichten und-prinzipien des modernen Umweltvoelkerrechts)" (1993) 18 Queen's L. J. 491-501.

the foreword. It also carries over the touchstones for disagreement present in its old incarnation so that I will, again, beg to differ with some of Hohmann's key themes and arguments. Nonetheless, what was true for the original version is equally true for the translation: this is a volume worth the reader's while.

The book pursues two closely related goals. First, it seeks to trace a general paradigm shift in international environmental law from a preoccupation with the allocation of resources to an emphasis on environmental protection. Second, it sets out to demonstrate that, along with other modern environmental protection principles, the precautionary principle has established itself in customary and treaty law. Hohmann's account, based on detailed analysis of a wealth of material, forcefully makes the first point. With respect to the second goal, Hohmann's approach and conclusions invite a number of more critical observations, to be explored briefly in this review.

The book is divided into four chapters. The first chapter is brief and serves mainly to set the stage for the book's approach and the themes to be explored. Hohmann postulates that "traditional" international environmental law has gradually been replaced by "modern" international environmental law. In his view, the former was based on a "narrow anthropocentric" approach, protecting primarily human life and health, general human welfare, and economic interests. By contrast, he sees modern international environmental law as being characterized by a "reformed or broader anthropocentric" approach, recognizing the intrinsic value of nature and protecting it for its own sake. Hohmann provides a brief overview of the evolution of German environmental law, in which the precautionary principle has some of its roots. As Hohmann explains, the concepts of prevention and precaution are used interchangeably in Germany. The larger concept of prevention appears to be a matter of degree, its normative content varying according to the threshold at which action is required. Thus, while "prevention" ("Prävention") relates to concrete danger, "precaution" ("Vorsorge") goes further, requiring action in case of a mere "concern or risk potential" and, therefore, even in the face of scientific uncertainty. In the international arena, only the latter concept has become known as the precautionary principle.

Chapter 2 is the most substantial and also the most engaging part of the book. Marking the 1972 Stockholm Conference on the Human Environment as the watershed between the two, Hohmann persuasively documents the evolution from "traditional" to "modern" international environmental law. He reviews early case law and a series of international declarations and guidelines, but places most emphasis on the work of three bodies that have played significant roles in identifying rules of customary international environmental law: the International Law Association (ILA), the Institut de Droit International (IdI), and the International Law Commission (ILC). Based upon this review, Hohmann then identifies a number of "principles of precaution and resource conservation" and argues that many of these concepts, commonly labelled as "soft law," are actually binding as customary international law.

It is here that the book, while being at its most controversial, is also the most interesting and most likely to stimulate a lively debate among international environmental lawyers. In Hohmann's view, much of the literature on international environmental law is "static" and inclined to accept only a core of firmly established customary principles, rather than taking account of the dynamic development of international environmental law. One can wholeheartedly welcome Hohmann's careful effort to document and analyze the developments of the last two decades. However, one may disagree with his harsh view of the literature, in particular given that Hohmann draws his conclusions regarding the customary nature of a broad range of new principles on the basis of a theory of the formation of customary law that is perhaps a little too "dynamic." Building upon Ago's theory of "spontaneous law" and Suy's theory of "instant custom," he suggests that conventional theory places too much emphasis on (external) state practice, failing to accord appropriate weight to "diplomatic practice" and documents such as conference declarations, guidelines, and the work of the afore-mentioned recording and codifying bodies. According to Hohmann, such documents contain *opinio juris* and suffice to generate binding legal obligations if the following four conditions are met: (1) "solidification" through continual use, which increasingly clarifies the rule; (2) absence of any regional limitation; (3) adoption by the community of states through acceptance or at least acquiescence; and (4) citation in subsequent agreements or declarations.

Most international environmental lawyers, all too familiar with the slow and painstaking process of customary lawmaking in the face of pressing environmental concerns, will agree that Hohmann's view holds considerable moral appeal. One can also credit him with taking a clear position in the perennial and controversial debate about the legal quality of "soft law." However — and Hohmann is quite aware of this (p. 170, note 20a)[2] — his approach is debatable in a number of respects. First, it seeks to create binding rules where, arguably, the states involved specifically sought to avoid binding themselves by choosing a non-binding ("soft") format. Therefore, second, Hohmann's approach may actually have the opposite effect from the one desired by him. Rather than lead to more rapid formation of customary law, it may slow down the process because, outside of more narrowly defined treaty contexts, states will be reluctant to participate in the development of broad and generally binding principles. Given the experience of the past decade, it must also be asked — and this is a question that Hohmann does not really explore — what would be gained by making "soft" principles binding. Even without clearly identified legal quality they have served useful functions in organizing state behaviour, shaping environmental policy, merging positions, and thus, ultimately, in preparing the ground for binding customary or treaty law. Third, even if one agrees with Hohmann's theory, one may be reluctant to agree with some of his conclusions. For example, can the work of private organizations, such as the ILA or the IdI, really "establish" customary law, as Hohmann seeks to argue for a limited range of situations? Similar doubts are in order with respect to the work of the ILC. One need only point to the manifold objections that states typically have, even once the ILC finally adopts a set of rules, and to the fact that ILC rules are intended to become binding only as treaties subsequently signed by states.

Chapter 3 of the book is devoted to a review of international environmental protection agreements. Regional and global agreements are surveyed with a view to ascertaining the extent to which they endorse and develop the principles identified in Chapter 2. Hohmann's coverage is comprehensive, if perhaps at times somewhat cursory. However, that is hardly surprising, given his effort to include agreements to protect rivers, lakes, endangered species, the environment more generally, soil, air, and the atmosphere. The review confirms the trends highlighted in the previous chapters, finding that more recent agreements place increasing emphasis on

[2] In this update to the German edition, Hohmann writes: "I must admit that we are on safer legal grounds when we demand State practice (external practice) as an additional requirement of customary law, and I would integrate State practice if asked to write an expert legal opinion."

prevention and even precaution. Hohmann correctly observes that this is particularly true for the Earth Summit documents. Yet, a more cautious analysis of these documents may have been desirable. Hohmann draws sweeping conclusions as to the customary nature of certain principles. For example, at one point he concludes that the *(Rio) Declaration on Environment and Development* of 1992 "ended numerous academic debates over whether international law recognizes inter-generational equity and the right to development, and whether the precautionary principle as well as the principle of sustainable development are already established in international law." He goes on to observe (p. 321) that "[s]till needed . . . are academic efforts to define the exact impacts of these principles."[3] In my view, the legal nature of each of these principles remains controversial. And, while Hohmann's conclusions are consistent with his theory of customary law formation, he does not quite live up to his own demand that the "exact impact" of the principles be defined by the academic literature. He devotes relatively little attention to sustainable development, a notion that may well be too broad to be capable of becoming custom at any stage, and may thus more appropriately be seen as a policy principle. More surprising is Hohmann's failure to fully explore a number of ambiguities remaining within the precautionary principle. For example, on p. 341, he concludes that the precautionary duties of states are "unconditional in that they are triggered by mere *prima facie* cases of risks and, thus, independently of costs/economic criteria and of proofs of thresholds, causality and full scientific certainty." At least with respect to the cost effectiveness of precautionary measures, this conclusion is at odds with the text of the *Rio Declaration,* cited by Hohmann earlier in the book (p. 321).[4] At a more general level, Hohmann maintains that the elusiveness of the "exact political and legal implications" of the precautionary principle does not prevent the conclusion that it is binding as custom (p. 344). However, it would seem that these ambiguities, in the contrary, lend support to the more "traditional" view that we are still dealing with "soft" concepts, programs, and crystallizing agents, rather than with bind-concepts, programs, and crystallizing agents, rather than with binding principles. In fact, the *Rio Declaration* itself speaks of the "precautionary approach," rather than the "precautionary principle."

[3] Note references omitted in quote.

[4] At this point, Principle 15 is quoted as stating: "lack of full scientific certainty *shall* [*sic*] not be used as a reason for postponing cost-effective measures."

The book's final chapter is short. It briefly reviews recent literature on the precautionary principle and then draws together the main conclusions as to the evolution of international environmental law and the emergence of new principles. Overall, despite the concerns raised in this review, Hohmann's book is a valuable contribution to the international environmental law literature. It provides a systematic and thorough review of recent developments, and, precisely because it dares to offer a provocative approach to its topic, it is interesting reading. Beyond consistent development of its thesis, the book offers a wealth of "incidental" information. Extensive footnotes and a comprehensive bibliography provide useful leads for further research. The reader will also find the volume to be a useful source of information on the work of the ILA, the IdI, and the ILC, as well as on international documents that relate to the protection of the environment. Nevertheless, due to the focus and theoretical underpinnings of the text, some caution is warranted. This book will be more useful to readers with some knowledge of international environmental law than to those seeking an introduction to the field.

JUTTA BRUNNÉE
Faculty of Law, University of British Columbia

Introduccion al derecho international: Relaciones Exteriores de los Ordenamientos Juridicos. Par Antonio Boggiano. Buenos Aires: La Ley, 1995. Pp. 743

Antonio Boggiano, l'auteur de cet ouvrage intitulé "Introduction au droit international," est un éminent juriste, très connu dans son pays d'origine: l'Argentine. Il y a occupé le poste de président de la Cour Suprême. Il est également bien connu sur la scène internationale où il a oeuvré, en particulier, au sein des Conférences de droit international privé de la Haye et des Conférences Interaméricaines de Droit International Privé (CIDIP).

Cet ouvrage est le reflet de l'expérience d'un auteur qui a vécu, en Amérique latine, à deux grandes époques. La première a été dominée par une philosophie isolationniste, de protection des économies nationales derrière des barrières politiques, économiques et juridiques établies à cet effet. Les théories sous-jacentes étaient alors celles de Raul Prebish (politique de substitution aux

importations); de Carlos Calvo (soumission des contrats d'investissements étrangers à la loi et à la juridiction des États récipien-
daires) et du Président Monroe (Hégémonie des États-Unis sur les
affaires de l'Amérique — qui a d'ailleurs pratiquement duré
jusqu'à la fin de la guerre froide et l'entrée du Canada à l'OEA en
1990). C'est également la période où le conflit entre les États
partisans de l'application de la loi du domicile et ceux favorables à
celle de la loi de la nationalité au statut personnel de l'individu, a
fait échouer la première tentative Pan-Américaine de codification
du Droit international privé, mieux connue sous le nom de "Code
Bustamante."

La deuxième époque, qu'a également vécue Antonio Boggiano,
est au contraire celle de l'ouverture des frontières à l'économie de
marché, de la suppression des barrières économiques (GATT et
OMC), de l'intégration économique régionale (Mersocur) et du
libre échange (ALADI, ALÉNA).

C'est vers cette deuxième période qu'est résolument orienté le
livre d'Antonio Boggiano. Il y mesure, en effet, les conséquences de
l'interdépendance des États sur l'évolution du droit international.
Il ne s'agit plus de démontrer, comme autrefois, l'intérêt du droit
international privé face à un univers cloisonné, mais bien de souli-
gner son enracinement dans le droit interne des États et par conséquent dans la pratique quotidienne du droit. Ce phénomène
résulte des relations étroites que le nouvel ordre économique a fait
naître entre le droit international, les droits internes et les divers
ordonnancements juridiques. L'auteur en arrive à la conclusion
qu'aujourd'hui le droit international se prolonge dans les droits
internes et inversement.

C'est par cette profonde réflexion sur l'état du droit international et sur son évolution que commence l'ouvrage. Il ne s'agit pas
d'un long exposé, mais d'une synthèse magistrale, extrêmement
dense, d'une centaine de pages seulement, que seul permet un
long mûrissement basé sur une très riche expérience. Cette
démonstration, délibérément pragmatique, s'appuie sur des exemples très variés d'application tirés de la jurisprudence de la Cour
suprême d'Argentine. L'auteur établit ainsi la relation étroite qui
existe désormais entre le droit international et le droit interne.

Cette démonstration débute par le principe de l'intégration des
divers traités internationaux dans le droit interne (I et II); de ceux
qui uniformisent les droits internes ou les divers critères de rattachement à ces derniers (IV); de ceux qui établissent une coopéra-

tion juridictionnelle internationale en matières civiles, pénales, fiscales ou administratives (V); de ceux qui prévoient une intégration économique (VI). Elle se poursuit par de nombreux autres exemples (VII à XVI) et se termine par une conclusion où est résumée la thèse de l'auteur. Celle-ci reprend, en l'illustrant d'exemples jurisprudentiels argentins, la pensée de Shearer, citée en exergue de son ouvrage par Antonio Boggiano: *"Nothing is more essential to a proper grasp of the subject of International law than a clear understanding of its relations to state law. A thorough acquaintance with this topic is of the utmost importance."*

La deuxième partie de l'ouvrage d'Antonio Boggiano est un appendice de plus de cinq cent pages qui contient une soixantaine d'arrêts de la Cour suprême d'Argentine, choisis en vue d'illustrer l'étroitesse des rapports entre le droit international et le droit interne. Par leur diffusion, l'auteur a cherché, ainsi qu'il l'explique dans son avant-propos, à suivre l'exemple d'autres publications telles que: *Decisions of the Bundesver fassungsgericht — Federal Constitutional Court — Federal republic of Germany Vol. I, Part I/II: International Law and Law of the European Communities*, 1952-1989, Karlsruhe, 1992, ou PICONE et CONFORTI, *La Guirisprudenza Italiana di diretto internazionale publico*, Repertorio 1960-1987, Napoli, 1988.

Il est à souhaiter que ce genre de livre de réflexion et de référence à la jurisprudence internationale des différents États se multiplie, en particulier en matière de droit uniforme. En effet, l'élaboration d'une véritable jurisprudence internationale cohérente est à ce prix. À cet égard, et comme l'exprime clairement Antonio Boggiano: "La jurisprudence étrangère n'est pas de droit étranger, mais de droit uniforme" (à la page 37).

En conclusion, nous pensons que le livre d'Antonio Boggiano sera des plus utiles pour les juristes chevronnés en raison de la profondeur de la réflexion et des nombreuses décisions qu'il rend accessible par leur publication. C'est un ouvrage qui se situe au deuxième degré de la connaissance et de la pensée juridique. De ce fait, il aurait davantage mérité le titre de "Réflexion sur le droit international," que celui d'"Introduction au droit international." Par son niveau, il nous apparaît, en effet, peu accessible à de jeunes étudiants n'ayant encore jamais été exposés au droit international. Il fera, par contre, le délice des autres.

LOUIS PERRET
Faculté de droit, Université d'Ottawa

International Law as Law of the United States. By Jordan J. Paust.
Durham, NC: Carolina Academic Press, 1996. Pp. xi, 491. ISBN
0-89089-862-6

In recent years, both American and foreign international lawyers
have been concerned about some of the United States' activities,
and have questioned the allegiance of the United States to international law. They have been worried at the intervention in Vietnam,
the invasions of Grenada, Panama, and Haiti, the abduction of
alleged drug traffickers and other offenders from third states, the
bombing of Libya, and the successful or attempted assassinations of
foreign heads of state, including Allende and Castro. It is with a
sense of true satisfaction, therefore, that they have turned to Professor Paust's *International Law as Law of the United States,* especially
as he points out in his Preface:

With respect to international law and presidential power, the views of the
Founders and overwhelming trends in judicial and other opinion are
quite clear and affirm that (1) the President is bound by international
law, (2) no President has openly admitted violating international law
absent some allegedly compelling need to do so under a preemptive
constitutional or statutory mandate, and (3) presidential illegalities (by
themselves) cannot change constitutional duty. Nonetheless, quite
recently some have raised a question whether our President or others in
Executive officialdom should be able to violate international law. In a
related vein, the Executive (here, primarily the Department of Justice)
recently began to exert a claim of Executive freedom, not to violate
treaties as such, but to ignore customary international law under a
question-begging concept of "controlling" executive action — and some
lower federal court judges have been confused or misled concerning the
origins of such a concept. Clearly these latter claims, if followed more
generally, would play havoc with the well-received notion of international
law as law of the United States (p. viii).

The book is directed at United States lawyers, and others may
find it difficult to appreciate at times, particularly when Paust
discusses specific constitutional or statutory issues without always
spelling out the section in question. The extensive citation of what
appears to be every possible relevant judicial decision, which results
in 292 pages of footnotes against 184 of text, does not make the
problem any simpler. However, enough jurisprudential and philosophical issues are discussed to make it worthwhile for non-Ameri-
cans to look at this seminal work. For example, in discussing the
nature and significance of international customary law, Professor
Paust reminds us that

the subjective element of customary law (i.e., *opinio juris*) is to be gathered from patterns of generally shared legal expectation among humankind, not merely among official State elites. . . . The expectations of all human beings ("mankind," "the world," "the people") are not only relevant but; they also provide the ultimate criterial referent . . . (even if apathetic "inaction" is the form of participation for some, a form that simply allows others a more significant role) (p. 2).

Professor Paust does not, however, give any indication of how or by what criteria these "others" are selected. This is especially important, in view of his statement that "universality of expectation or unanimity are not required, although the norm will be universal in obligation" (p. 2). It is submitted that recent developments with regard to the extent of the territorial sea culminating in UNCLOS 1982 do not appear to support this assertion.

It is also a little difficult to accept without reservation Professor Paust's view that "since each nation-state, *indeed each human being,* is a participant in the attitudinal and behavioural aspects of dynamic customary international law, *each* may initiate a change in such law or, with others, reaffirm its validity" (p. 3, emphasis added). It might have been helpful if he had indicated how "each human being" can play this creative role insofar as customary international law is concerned. His case is not advanced by the suggestion that "[w]hen the General Assembly passes a unanimous or nearly unanimous resolution, the chances are obviously greatly increased that one has an evidence of the opinion of mankind" (p. 4). Surely the real situation is that the politicians in power at the time claim to speak for everyone, even though their successors may repudiate whatever they might have said. Moreover, these same politicians, particularly in the field of human rights, often make statements or cast votes to elicit the public's support, even when they have no intention of giving effect to what they have said or done.

Most lawyers are aware of the way in which the United States distinguishes between the effect of self-executing and non-self-executing treaties, especially when compared with those countries that invariably require legislation to give effect to treaty obligations. Paust's analysis of the history of this distinction and the manner in which judicial comment created it is fascinating. He argues that the distinction has no validity, since by the United States Constitution all treaties are *law* of the land equal in status with any other law, unless the treaty itself requires legislative action to give it effect. He maintains:

It seems clear that the text of the Constitution, the predominant views of the Founders, and early and modern trends in judicial decisions all demand that certain notions of several textwriters with respect to the inherently non-self-executing nature of certain types of treaties . . . be abandoned. The constitutionally preferable view is that no treaty is inherently non-self-executing except those which seek to declare war on behalf of the United States. . . . [I]t also seems clear that all treaties are self-executing except those (or the portions of them) which, by their terms considered in context, require domestic implementing legislation or seek to declare war on behalf of the United States. All treaties are supreme federal law, but some treaties, by their terms, are not directly operative (pp. 63-4).

It is well known that in United States practice, since treaties and statutes are of equal validity, the "last in time" rule operates, even though the courts will seek to avoid a contradiction between a later statute and an earlier treaty. Nevertheless, it is well to be reminded that, "when there is an unavoidable clash between a treaty and the U.S. Constitution, our courts will apply the Constitution domestically even though such action places the United States in violation of international law at the international level, and the same pertains to international customary law" (p. 81), and that the "views of the Founders and overwhelming trends in legal decision inform the meaning of Article II, Section 3 of the Constitution and affirm emphatically that the President cannot lawfully violate international law. In view of the actual trends and the legal policies at stake, there is simply no viable counter-argument. The President must obey and faithfully execute such law" (p. 153). Despite this emphatic statement, it cannot be questioned that a number of recent events, including for example the closing of the PLO office to the United Nations, lead one to question whether the Executive — or even all levels of the judiciary — acting in the name of the president is aware of this interpretation of the legal position.

It is perhaps surprising, in view of the history of segregation and the struggle for civil and equal rights or the attitude to "un-American" activities in the United States, to find Professor Paust stating that

the actual use of human right precepts in U.S. history has been substantial and concern for human rights has been associated with most major politico-legal developments in the United States over the last two-and-one-half centuries. Not surprisingly, then, one can also discover a rich, often splendid history of use of human right and equivalent phrases by U.S. courts over the last two hundred years (p. 212).

It cannot be ignored that the use of grandiloquent phrases does not always coincide with practical reality, although it may be surprising "that there has been an increasing use of human rights precepts in the last thirty years" (*ibid.*). However, when examining the United States' judicial record on human rights, it must be remembered that, regardless of the language used, including reference to the "natural" rights of all persons, most of the decisions mentioned by Paust concern the rights of United States citizens under the constitution and against American authorities. For the most part, the same rulings could be cited without any suggestion that there is a relationship with international law. In this connection, we may question Paust's belief that the Universal Declaration of Human Rights of 1948, particularly Article 8 concerning the right to an effective remedy, "is applicable by its terms in the context of U.S. domestic legislation" (p. 198). This belief evades the issue of the obligatory character of the Declaration, almost implying that without it there might be no legal right to an effective remedy in the United States, and disregards the history of the common law, which would contradict many of the dicta cited by Paust himself (see, e.g., p. 200, reference to *Christian County Court* v. *Rankin & Tharp*, 69 Ky 606 (1869)). Is it true that in the twentieth century human rights law "internationally . . . and, as part of such law, [grants] individuals the express right to an effective remedy in national tribunals" (p. 204)?

Finally, in respect of his arguments on human rights, it is questionable where Professor Paust finds support for his assertion that in today's international law:

When a state violated human rights law it must know and expect that its intentional acts in violation of international law — including obligations under the U.N. Charter and other human rights instruments — are outside the sphere of protectable sovereign acts, and that it can be held responsible, and that it can be judged by law and in fora other than its own. . . . It is the state's intentional and illegal conduct coupled with such knowledge and expectation that results in an implicit waiver of protection (p. 211).

At a time when the *ad hoc* tribunal at The Hague possesses, and is exercising, competence to try those accused of genocide, it is interesting to note Paust's criticisms of the United States' ratification of the Genocide Convention. In his view, the wording of the instrument of ratification, based as it is on a Senate "understanding," is "fundamentally incompatible with the object and purpose of the Genocide Convention and leave[s] the United States effort at meaningful adherence to the treaty and customary international law a laughable disgrace" (pp. 295-98). In fact, the whole of

Chapter 6 on "Congress and Genocide" is an indictment, as are Paust's comments regarding the United States' adherence to the Covenant on Civil and Political Rights (p. 361). If, as he claims, such a reservation to the treaty will be void *ab initio*, an attempted "declaration of the same nature must also be void and of no effect" (p. 366), and surely one must conclude that the United States has not, in fact, become a party to the Covenant. This claim is hardly consistent with Paust's attempts to uphold respect for human rights as part both of customary international law and of the law of the United States, regardless of treaty. With respect, it is submitted that the view that "certain rights reflected in the Covenant which have now become not merely customary international law (which are also protected through the U.N. Charter), [are] also peremptory norms as *jus cogens*" (p. 368), would probably not receive universal acceptance — at least not without further specification. It would also be useful if Paust were to explain how "the International Court of Justice . . . might press the matter or assure more formally that it is to be declared void ab initio" (p. 373).

Chapter 10 constitutes a brief but effective summary of the law concerning bases of jurisdiction. It is strange, however, that the discussion of objective territorial jurisdiction — the "effect" or "continuing" theory — makes no reference to the invasion of Panama and subsequent seizure and trial of Noriega.

NATO's IFOR in Bosnia has been criticized for failing to arrest alleged war criminals. On this failure, it is as well to recall the opening paragraph of Paust's Chapter 11, "Universality and the Enforcement of International Criminal Law":

Today it is generally recognized that customary international law of a peremptory nature places an obligation on each nation-state to search for and bring into custody and to initiate prosecution of or to extradite all persons within its territory *or control* who are reasonably accused of having committed, for example, war crimes, genocide, breaches of neutrality and other crimes against peace (p. 405).

While the comment concerning "breaches of neutrality" may be controversial, there is no question as to the validity of the rest of the statement. However, does difficulty in arresting such persons amount to mitigation in failing to effect their capture? It would be interesting to know how well the following statement expresses the views of most American international lawyers:

In view of . . . recognitions concerning universal jurisdiction and enforcement responsibility as well as the incorporation of customary international law as supreme law of the land, one can recognize that a prior Administration's policy of *denaturalizing* and *deporting* alleged Nazi war criminals or, in a few cases, extraditing them was on balance misguided and a national disgrace. Not only is such an abnegative policy generally violative of international law, but it is also generally subversive of global efforts, however halting and incomplete, to seek out and bring to trial all persons reasonably accused of having committed war crimes. The effort to declare a then present head of state [unidentified here] *persona non grata* was equally misguided and shockingly inadequate. Mere deportation and exclusion of aliens is hardly responsive to this nation's and the President's peremptory duty to seek out and to initiate prosecution of all persons reasonably accused of war crimes or, alternatively — as the only viable alternative — to extradite them for the purpose of prosecution elsewhere (p. 408).

It does not take much effort to suggest that the surest way of ensuring a successful trial was in pursuit of the policy here so bitterly condemned. In the same way, one might ask whether it is in fact "well-recognized" that no nation state can lawfully grant any sort of immunity for violations of international law. More specifically, it has also been recognized that a domestic pardon or grant of amnesty for war crimes is legally inoperative, just as any domestic effort to "exonerate" war criminals" (pp. 413-14). Presumably, therefore, the decision of the occupying powers to cease war crimes trials after the Second World War and to "rehabilitate" accused personnel was invalid and had no effect!

There is an increasing trend among many countries to enter agreements for the transfer of nationals who are imprisoned, and the United States has played a major role in this sphere. If Paust is correct, then such treaties entered into by the United States, including that with Canada, are hardly worth the paper they are written on. He contends that, since the prisoners concerned have been tried in a foreign jurisdiction for offences defined by that jurisdiction and often by processes not according with United States concepts of due process, there is no right for any federal or state authority to hold such transferred Americans in incarceration. In fact, he asserts, all such treaties are unconstitutional and void (Chapter 13).

It should be clear from the above that there is probably not a great deal in this work of major significance for the non-American reader. Particularly is this so since so much of it is directed to constitutional analysis, while frequently one is left with the feeling that, rather than being an exposition of *International Law as Law of the United States*, it is the international law of the United States as

Paust would like to see it. This is evidenced in his approach to human rights and is manifest in his analysis of the Ninth Amendment in Chapter 8. Regardless of these criticisms, there is enough of interest to warrant the attention of all international lawyers and perhaps provoke some of them into producing a similar work on international law as law in their own countries.

L. C. GREEN
United States Naval War College

The Charter of the United Nations. Sous la direction de Bruno Simma. Oxford: Oxford University Press, 1995. Pp. xlix, 1258. £140 / CDN$405. ISBN 0-19-825703-1

Ce livre est la version traduite et mise à jour du commentaire de la Charte des Nations Unies publié en langue allemande en 1991 par C.H. Beck.[1] Il s'agit d'une collaboration entre soixante juristes germanophones allemands, suisses, et autrichiens, sous la direction générale de Bruno Simma. On compte parmi les auteurs plusieurs sommités du droit international, dont Michael Bothe, Felix Ermacora, Hermann Mosler, Karl-J. Partsch, Ignaz Seidl-Hohenveldern et Christian Tomuschat, pour ne mentionner que ceux-là. La publication d'une version anglaise de l'ouvrage a permis à la plupart des auteurs de réviser, à des degrés variables, leur texte afin d'y incorporer les développements importants survenus entre 1990 et 1994, y compris la fin de la Guerre froide, l'invasion du Kuwait par l'Iraq, la crise somalienne, et le conflit yougoslave. Bien au-delà de ces événements récents, cet ouvrage met enfin à la disposition des lecteurs anglophones un commentaire de la Charte qui puisse succéder à l'ouvrage monumental de Goodrich, Hambro et Simons publié il y aura bientôt trente ans.[2] Il propose de plus une alternative au commentaire publié en français sous la direction de Jean-Pierre Cot et Alain Pellet, *La Charte des Nations Unies*, dont la seconde édition remonte à 1991.[3]

[1] *Charta der Vereinten Nationen: Kommentar* (Munich: C.H. Beck, 1991).

[2] Leland Goodrich, Edvard Hambro & Anne Simons, *Charter of the United Nations: Commentary and Documents*, 3d ed. (New York: Columbia University Press, 1969).

[3] Jean-Pierre Cot & Alain Pellet (dir.), *La Charte des Nations Unies: commentaire article par article*, 2ᵉ éd. (Paris: Economica, 1991).

Le livre dirigé par Simma adopte, sauf exception, une structure tout à fait classique. Les textes de la Charte de l'ONU et du Statut de la Cour internationale de Justice sont reproduits dans les premières pages du volume, afin de permettre une consultation rapide des textes de base, suivis du commentaire lui-même, article par article. Pour chaque article, on reprend d'abord le texte de la disposition, ensuite les références aux documents officiels des Nations Unies pertinents, particulièrement les travaux préparatoires, une table des matières du commentaire, et finalement une courte bibliographie très ciblée, avec des références surtout en allemand, en anglais, et en français. Les commentaires eux-mêmes adoptent souvent un plan-type, avec des sections distinctes sur l'historique, l'interprétation et la pratique se rapportant à la disposition concernée. On identifie clairement au bas de chaque page l'auteur du commentaire.

L'attrait principal de ce genre d'ouvrage, un survol de la portée donnée à ce texte fondamental qu'est la Charte de l'ONU, constitue du même coup sa limite insurmontable, c'est-à-dire le caractère nécessairement incomplet de l'analyse que l'on y propose. Le but à atteindre consiste donc à présenter les principales questions soulevées par l'interprétation et l'application de la Charte, d'une manière brève et claire qui n'obscurcit pas leur complexité. Ceci est réussi de manière remarquable par le commentaire dirigé par Bruno Simma. Cela vaut autant pour les dispositions extrêmement complexes ou qui ont fait l'objet de débats doctrinaux, par exemple l'article 2 paragraphe 4, que pour les dispositions qui sont restées lettre morte depuis l'adoption de la Charte, par exemple l'article 47. Quant à l'article 2 paragraphe 4, prohibant l'usage de la force, le commentaire relate brièvement (pp. 108-11) l'évolution historique de la prohibition, discute de sa portée par rapport aux moyens économiques et politiques, des notions de "relations internationales" et de "menace," des diverses exceptions à cette règle, et de problèmes particuliers comme les guerres de libération nationale, l'intervention d'humanité, la protection des nationaux à l'étranger, et la responsabilité pénale individuelle (pp. 111-28). Quant à l'article 47 sur le Comité d'état-major, le commentaire s'étend assez longuement (pp. 645-51) sur les travaux préparatoires mouvementés de la disposition et du désaccord régnant entre les superpuissances, qui explique le coma prolongé de ce comité (malgré quelques soubresauts lors de la crise Iraq-Kuwait).

En plus du commentaire article par article, les directeurs de l'ouvrage ont jugé utile d'inclure trois sections spéciales sur des thèmes difficilement assignables à un seul article de la Charte. On retrouve ainsi en exergue du commentaire une section sur l'interprétation de la Charte (pp. 25-44), qui soulève entre autres les difficultés d'interprétation d'un texte adopté en cinq versions authentiques, avec de nombreuses références à la pratique de la Cour internationale de Justice. On inclut ensuite une section sur le droit des peuples à disposer d'eux-mêmes (pp.56-72), qui décrit l'évolution de ce droit et analyse son contenu, en n'évitant aucune des questions épineuses soulevées par ce droit (par exemple son statut de *jus cogens* ou ses implications pour les États tiers). Finalement, pour une raison moins manifestement évidente, on ajoute une section spéciale sur les opérations de maintien de la paix (pp. 565-603). Celle-ci consiste pour moitié en une longue énumération de toutes les opérations entreprises par l'ONU à ce jour, suivie d'une discussion de divers problèmes soulevés par de telles opérations, dont leur constitution, fonction, base juridique et financement. Le niveau de ces sections spéciales s'apparente à celui des diverses encyclopédies de droit international, c'est-à-dire de très haut calibre.

Un des principaux dangers qui menacent ce genre d'entreprise est le manque de cohésion de l'ensemble, en raison de la diversité des auteurs (ici au nombre de soixante!) qui rédigent souvent leur texte de manière concurrente. En l'espèce, comme il s'agit après tout d'une "deuxième" édition, on était en droit de s'attendre à ce que les auteurs parcourent l'ouvrage au-delà de leur propre contribution pour effectuer les recoupements qui s'imposent. En l'occurrence, même si l'on retrouve effectivement de tels recoupements ici et là dans les commentaires, chaque article reste largement indépendant du tout. Le recoupement, s'il y en a un, se fait plutôt avec le commentaire dirigé par Cot et Pellet auquel on réfère constamment! Il s'agit d'une faiblesse presque inévitable pour ce genre de projets, mais qui est d'autant plus à déplorer que la structure même de l'ouvrage pousse à une consultation à la pièce et non à une lecture suivie, et que le lecteur risque de manquer des développements connexes incorporés dans le commentaire d'un autre article.[4]

---

[4] Par exemple, on discute de l'applicabilité du droit à la légitime défense (art. 51) à la guerre de libération nationale dans la section sur le droit des peuples à disposer d'eux-mêmes, sans aucun recoupement entre cette section et le commentaire de l'art. 51.

Malgré quelques faiblesses, largement inhérentes à l'entreprise elle-même, le commentaire dirigé par Bruno Simma est un solide ouvrage apportant une contribution importante à la doctrine de droit international. Non seulement constitue-t-il le premier commentaire systématique de la Charte des Nations Unies en langue anglaise depuis trois décennies, mais encore rend-il à la littérature juridique publiée en allemand la place qui lui revient. Il s'agit d'une source fiable sur laquelle les juristes expérimentés pourront se reposer à titre d'ouvrage général de référence ou pour débuter une recherche touchant à l'application de la Charte des Nations Unies.

RENÉ PROVOST
Faculté de droit, Université McGill

Conflict of Laws in Western Europe: A Guide through the Jungle. By Mathias Reimann. Irvington, NY: Transnational, 1995. Pp. xxvi, 198, including tables. US$65.00 ISBN 1-57105-005-1

Professor Reimann describes his aim in this work as "generally to introduce the practitioner, teacher, or student to the basic features of Western European rules on international cases in private as opposed to public law." The result is a jewel of a book. Although it is written for a United States audience, with frequent comparisons to American conflicts law, it will be equally useful to Canadian and other non-European readers. In fact, to them it offers not only a compendium of European conflict of laws but also some new insights into American law. Although it is avowedly not an in-depth analysis, the detailed references are plentiful enough that they offer a good starting point for anyone trying to understand how a particular conflicts problem would be approached in a Western European country.

To anyone familiar with the picture in the United States, it seems slightly surprising that the Western European conflict of laws would be described by comparison as a "jungle." The complexity Professor Reimann highlights is not in the rules themselves; they are often much clearer than their American equivalents. The jungle refers partly to the fact, relatively unfamiliar to American lawyers, that private cross-border disputes are almost all international rather than interstate (Canadians are more used to this). It also refers partly to the huge array of sources that make up European private international law. There are bilateral and multilateral treaties on uniform private law or on private international law that, for many years, the continental European countries have embraced more enthusiastically than have their common law counterparts. There are also quite divergent national traditions of private international law. Then, added to this already untidy picture is the law of the European Union (more correctly, as Professor Reimann points out (at xxiv), the law of the European Community and the European Union), composed of the constitutive treaties (principally the Rome and Maastricht Treaties), the treaties dealing specifically with jurisdiction and the enforcement of judgments in civil matters (Brussels Convention), the law applicable to contractual obligations (Rome Convention), and the regulations and directives emanating from the Union's lawmaking agencies.

Professor Reimann gives an admirably concise overview of the pattern of law in each of the three major fields of private international law: jurisdiction, choice of law, and foreign judgments. Also, a short chapter highlights some of the distinctive characteristics of court procedure, including the continental tradition that foreign law is a matter for the judge to investigate rather than for the parties to prove. Even as elaborate a feature as the Rome Convention on the Law Applicable to Contractual Obligations gets enough coverage that the uninitiated reader is given a good sense of how it functions. For reasons of space, factual examples are few, but there is a particularly nice one (at pp. 98-100) involving residents of an EU country who, while at home, sign a lease on a Florida condominium for their holiday and are later injured on the premises. The question addresses the validity of an exculpatory clause in the lease. The Rome Convention applies, but does not invalidate the clause; nor does the plaintiffs' own national law; but the EU directive on unfair terms in consumer contracts (1993) might have availed the plaintiffs, if their country had legislated in response to the directive.

As valuable as the chapters that actually outline the law is the general part that deals in four chapters with "Conflict of Laws and the Civil Law Culture," "The International Context," "The Levels of Conflicts Law," and "The Types of Rules." Aside from the material that they provide for understanding the European law, they clearly sketch the differences in legal culture between the United States and Europe (particularly the European civil law jurisdictions). Even for a Canadian common lawyer, who may have a nodding acquaintance with the civil law through Quebec, there are many useful insights to be gained.

Private international law is the area where different legal traditions interact with one another. The opportunities for comparative study are many, but, for a common law readership, the literature on comparative private international law is sparse. Professor Reimann's modestly self-described "primer" (at xv) fills a real need for the practising legal community as well as for those with an academic interest in this fascinating and increasingly important field.

JOOST BLOM
Faculty of Law, University of British Columbia

Analytical Index / Index Analytique

THE CANADIAN YEARBOOK OF
INTERNATIONAL LAW

1995

ANNUAIRE CANADIEN
DE DROIT INTERNATIONAL

(A) Article; (NC) Notes and Comments; (Ch) Chronique;
(PR) Practice; (C) Cases; (R) Review
(A) Article; (NC) Notes et commentaires; (Ch) Chronique;
(PR) Pratique; (J) Jurisprudence; (R) Recension de livre

Accord de libre-échange Canada-É.-U.
   Voir FTA
Accord de libre-échange nord-
   américain. *Voir* ALÉNA /
   NAFTA
agriculture, l'ALÉNA et, 347-48
ALÉNA. *Voir aussi* Canada; NAFTA
   agriculture et, 347-48
   banques et, 356
   commerce des services et, 348-51
   investissement et, 362-67
   et modifications à la législation
      canadienne, 367-69, 384-85,
      407-10
   et Déclarations parlementaires,
      407-10
"Another Kick at the Can: Tuna/
   Dolphin II" by Torsten H.
   Strom (A), 149-83
anti-dumping, 75, 82-84, 407-10,
   469-78
*Anti-dumping and Anti-trust Issues in
   Free-trade Areas* by G. Z.
   Marceau (R), reviewed by
   David P. Stevens, 469-78
"At the Department of Foreign
   Affairs in 1994-95 / Au
   ministère des Affaires
   étrangères en 1994-95"
   compiled by / préparé

par Philippe Kirsch (PR),
   371-94
Ayllón, Sergio, "NAFTA Disputes
   Settlement and Mexico:
   Interpreting Treaties and
   Reconciling Common and
   Civil Law Systems in a Free
   Trade Area" (A), 75-122

Band, Martine M. N., *International
   Trade and Investment Law in
   Canada* (R), reviewed by David
   P. Stevens, 469-78
Beijing World Conference on Women:
   Declaration and Platform for
   Action, 123-48
Bergeron, André, "Treaty Action
   Taken by Canada in 1994 /
   Mesures prises par le Canada
   en matière de traités en 1994"
   (PR), 411-24
Blom, Joost, "Canadian Cases in
   Private International Law in
   1994-95 / La jurisprudence
   canadienne en matière de
   droit international privé en
   1994-95" (C), 429-67
Boggiano, Antonio, *Introduccion al
   derecho international: Relaciones
   Exteriores de los Ordenamientos*

Juridicos (R), recension de
Louis Perret, 489-91
Bosnia
hostages in, 372-74, 380, 395
peacekeeping in, 260-61, 275-76
Bugnion, F., *Comité international de la
Croix-Rouge et la protection des
victimes de la guerre, Le,* (R),
recension de Claude
Emmanuelli, 481-84
Burundi, conflits ethniques, 400-01

Canada
Bill C-26 for marine management,
305-30
cases in, 425-28
cases in private international law,
429-67
cases in public international law,
425-28
choice of law in, 457-67
common law jurisdiction in, 429-45
international trade in, 469-73
Law of the Sea in, 404-07
et l'ORD, 243, 244
politique étrangère, 353-55
procedure in, 453-54
property in, 439, 465-66
trade and investment in, 478
treaties in, 388-94, 411-24, 428
Canada-U.S. Free Trade Agreement.
See FTA
"Le Canada et le système monétaire
international en 1994"
préparé par / compiled by
Bernard Colas (Ch), 353-59
"Canadian Cases in Private
International Law in 1994-95 /
La jurisprudence canadienne
en matière de droit
international privé en
1994-95" compiled by /
préparé par Joost Blom (C),
429-67
"Canadian Cases in Public
International Law in 1994-95 /
La jurisprudence canadienne
en matière de droit
international public en
1994-95" compiled by /
préparé par Karin Mickelson
(C), 425-28

"Canadian Practice in International
Law / La pratique canadienne
en matière de droit
international public: At the
Department of Foreign Affairs
in 1994-95 / Au ministère des
Affaires étrangères en
1994-95" compiled by /
préparé par Philippe Kirsch
(PR), 371-94
"Canadian Practice in International
Law / La pratique canadienne
en matière de droit
international public:
Parliamentary Declarations in
1994-95 / Déclarations
parlementaires en 1994-95"
compiled by / préparé par
Sapard V. M. T. N. Kalala
(PR), 395-410
"Canadian Practice in International
Law / La pratique canadienne
en matière de droit
international public: Treaty
Action Taken by Canada in
1994 / Mesures prises par le
Canada en matière de traités
en 1994" compiled by /
préparé par André Bergeron
(PR), 411-24
The Charter of the United Nations sous la
direction de Bruno Simma
(R), recension de René
Provost, 498-501
children
abuse of, 440-45
custody and access of, 440
and rights of the girl child, 124
Chircop, Aldo, "Legislating for
Integrated Marine
Management: Canada's
Proposed Oceans Act of 1996"
(NC), 305-31
"Chronique de Droit international
économique en 1994 / Digest
of International Economic Law
in 1994: Commerce" préparé
par / compiled by Martin St-
Amand (Ch), 343-51
"Chronique de Droit international
économique en 1994 / Digest
of International Economic Law
in 1994: Le Canada et le

système monétaire international en 1994" préparé par / compiled by Bernard Colas (Ch), 353-59

"Chronique de Droit international économique en 1994 / Digest of International Economic Law in 1994: Investissement" préparé / compiled by par Pierre Ratelle (Ch), 361-69

Colas, Bernard, "Chronique de Droit international économique en 1994 / Digest of International Economic Law in 1994: Le Canada et le système monétaire international en 1994" (Ch), 353-59

Comité de Bâle sur le contrôle bancaire, 353, 356, 357-59

Comité international de la Croix-Rouge (CICR). *Voir aussi* Red Cross; Victimes de conflits armés, 482-83

Le Comité international de la Croix-Rouge et la protection des victimes de la guerre par F. Bugnion (R), recension de Claude Emmanuelli, 481-84

comity, international, 14, 18-19
  and the United States, 26
  and conflict with nationhood, 33-38

"Commerce" préparé par / compiled by Martin St-Amand (Ch), 343-51

commerce. *See also* trade
  ALÉNA / NAFTA and, 343, 345-51, 407-10
  in Canada, 469-73
  et droit international, 343-51
  FTA and, 344

Conflict of Laws in Western Europe: A Guide through the Jungle by Mathias Reimann (R), reviewed by Joost Blom, 501-03

countervailing duty and dumping, 82-84

Cour internationale de justice. *Voir aussi* International Court of Justice (ICJ)
  statut, 499

"Cyclops Meets the Privy Council: The Conflict in the Conflict of Laws" by Ed Morgan (A), 3-39

declining jurisdiction, 435-39

deference, principle of, in Canadian and American systems, 109-10

Dispute Settlement Body (DSB). *See also* Organe de règlement des différends (ORD); Organisation Mondiale du Commerce; World Trade Organization
  creation of, 149 n. 3

diversité biologique, 281-304

droits de la personne. *Voir* human rights

droit international. *Voir aussi* international law
  interne, 490-91
  privé, 490

environment, 150-52, 160-63, 165, 168-72, 180-82
  et concept de patrimoine commun à l'humanité (PCH), 285-89
  et Convention sur la diversité biologique, 281-83
  gestion équitable et, 296-300, 320-21, 416, 422
  law, international, 484-89
  and trade, 472

equality, 124
  barriers to, 132-33

equal rights, 127

ex juris, 429-35

Extraordinary Challenge Committee (ECC), 88-90, 97-100

free trade. *See* FTA, NAFTA

"From the Margins to the Mainstream: The Beijing Declaration and Platform for Action" by Marcia Waldron (A), 123-48

FTA, 77, 80
  Chapter 19 of the, 81-96
  dispute settlement procedure of the, 84-88
  and dumping and countervailing duty disputes, 82 n. 14, 83-84
  and the Extraordinary Challenge Committee, 88-90

and the *Softwood Lumber* dispute, 92
and trade law and policy, 472

GATS, 355-56
GATT
  and the anti-dumping code, 84
  Article III of the, 165-72, 243,
    381-84
  Article XX arguments of the,
    162-65, 175-82
  Article XX exceptions of the,
    157-60
  and the environment, 150
  purpose of the, 182
  and Tuna/Dolphin I and II, 149-82
  and WTO, 151-52, 409-10
  and world trade, 473-74, 476
gender rights, 126, 132-40, 144-46
green traders, 168

Haiti, costs to Canada, 401
Helms-Burton Bills, 385-88, 408
Hohmann, Harald, *Precautionary Legal
    Duties and Principles in Modern
    International Environmental Law*
    (R), reviewed by Jutta
    Brunnée, 484-89
Howse, Robert, *The Regulation of
    International Trade* (R),
    reviewed by David P. Stevens,
    469-78
human rights
  abuses, victims of, 479-81
  and barriers to equality, 132
  and Beijing Conference, 123-48
  and civil and political rights, 128,
    146
  and culture, 136-38
  of the girl child, 124
  John Peters Humphrey, tribute to,
    333-41
  interrelation of all, 128
  and the marginalization of women,
    135, 140-47
  and parliamentary declarations,
    395
  and peacekeepers, 271
  protection of, 479
  and systemic inequalities, 130
  and violence against women, 130
  of women, 123-48
  women's rights and men, 129
Humphrey, John Peters, 333

and human rights manuscript,
    334-41

immunity, diplomatic, 427-28
International Court of Justice (ICJ)
  concept of progressive
    development, 207-10
  emerging constitutional role of,
    217-19, 376-81, 496
  as international lawmaker, 198-210
international law
  American and foreign international
    lawyers, 492
  in Canada, 371-94
  customary, 492-93
  and human rights, 494-96
  and international criminal law, 496
  private, 501-03
  and territorial modifications, 42-43
  violation of, 494
*International Law as Law of the United
    States* by Jordan J. Paust (R),
    reviewed by L. C. Green,
    492-98
*International Responses to Traumatic
    Stress: Humanitarian, Human
    Rights, Justice, Peace, and
    Development Contributions,
    Collaborative Actions, and Future
    Initiatives* edited by Yael
    Danieli, Nigel S. Rodley, and
    Lars Weisaeth (R), reviewed by
    William A. Schabas, 479-81
*International Trade and Investment Law
    in Canada* by Robert K.
    Paterson and Martine M. N.
    Band, with Jock A. Finlayson
    and Jeffrey S. Thomas (R),
    reviewed by David P. Stevens,
    469-78
*Introduccion al derecho international:
    Relaciones Exteriores de los
    Ordenamientos Juridicos* par
    Antonio Boggiano (R),
    recension de Louis Perret,
    489-91
"Investissement" préparé / compiled
    by par Pierre Ratelle (Ch),
    361-69
investissement, 361-69
  modifications à la législation
    canadienne, 367-69
Iraq/Kuwait conflict, 260, 276

"John Peters Humphrey — A
Tribute" (NC), 333-41
judgments, competing foreign, 6-27

Kalala, Sapard V. M. T. N., "Canadian
Practice in International Law /
La pratique canadienne en
matière de droit international
public: Parliamentary
Declarations in 1994-95 /
Déclarations parlementaires en
1994-95" (PR), 395-410
Kindred, Hugh, "The Protection of
Peacekeepers" (NC), 257-80
Kindred, Hugh, "Legislating for
Integrated Marine
Management: Canada's
Proposed Oceans Act of 1996"
(NC), 305-31
Kirsch, Philippe, "Canadian Practice
in International Law / La
pratique canadienne en
matière de droit international
public: At the Department of
Foreign Affairs in 1994-95 /
Au ministère des Affaires
étrangères en 1994-95" (PR),
371-94

Law of the Sea, 305-30, 404-07
"Legislating for Integrated Marine
Management: Canada's
Proposed Oceans Act of 1996"
by Aldo Chircop, Hugh
Kindred, Phillip Saunders, and
David VanderZwaag (NC),
305-31
libre-échange. *Voir* ALÉNA; FTA;
NAFTA

McWhinney, E., 185, 190, 197-98,
199-210
Marceau, G. Z., *Anti-dumping and Anti-
trust Issues in Free-trade Areas*
(R), reviewed by David P.
Stevens, 469-78
Marceau, Gabrielle, "La Première
année de l'Organe de
règlement des différends de
l'Organisation mondiale du
commerce" (NC), 223-55

marine management legislation, 305
and Bill C-26 (1996), 305-07
jurisdiction of, 308-13
and marine science, 324-26
and zones, 309-11
marine science, and Bill C-26 (1996),
324-28
Mercure, Pierre-François, "Le rejet
du concept de patrimoine
commun de l'humanité afin
d'assurer la gestion de la
diversité biologique" (NC),
281-304
"Metamorphoses: Judge Shigeru Oda
and the International Court of
Justice" by Michael Reisman
(A), 185-221
Mexico
and the *amparo*, 112
and Chapter 19 in Mexican law,
100-13
and *Cut-to-Length Steel* decision,
114-21
and NAFTA dispute settlement,
75-121
Mickelson, Karin, "Canadian Cases in
Public International Law in
1994-95 / La jurisprudence
canadienne en matière de
droit international public en
1994-95" (C), 425-28
Morgan, Ed, "Cyclops Meets the Privy
Council: The Conflict in the
Conflict of Laws" (A), 3-39
municipal law, territorial
modifications, 41

NAFTA. *See also* Canada; ALÉNA
and agriculture, 347-48
and anti-dumping, 75
binational panel review process of,
79-81
Chapter 19 of, 96-118
deference, principle of, in, 109-10
and parliamentary declarations,
407-10, 470-72
Pork and *Swine* cases and, 119
remand procedure of, 111-13
and *Softwood Lumber* case, 119
"NAFTA Disputes Settlement and
Mexico: Interpreting Treaties
and Reconciling Common and
Civil Law Systems in a Free

Trade Area" by J. C. Thomas and Sergio Lopez Ayllön (A), 75-122
North-American Free Trade Agreement. *See* NAFTA; ALÉNA

Oda, Judge Shigeru, 185-220
  decisions of, 210-17
  dissenting opinions of, 210-17
  legal formation of, 191
  personality of, 186-98
  style of, 194-96
Organization Mondiale du Commerce (OMC), 79, 223-55, 353, 409-10. *See also* World Trade Organization (WTO)
  changements causés par l'ORD, 229-34
  pouvoirs des conseils, 228
  structure institutionnelle, 227-29
  structure juridique, 224-27
Organe de règlement des différends (ORD), 223
  première année, 234-45
  pluralité des plaignants, 244

Pardo, Arvid, 286-88
"Parliamentary Declarations in 1994-95 / Déclarations parlementaires en 1994-95" compiled by / préparé par Sapard V. M. T. N. Kalala (PR), 395-410
Paterson, Robert K., *International Trade and Investment Law in Canada* (R), reviewed by David P. Stevens, 469-78
Patrimoine commun de l'humanité (PCH), 282-84
  concept of, 285
  contenu juridique, 287-89
  développement durable, 289-93, 292 n. 44
  facteurs extérieurs au débat, 293
  genèse, 285-87
  principes, 288-89
  ressources génétiques, 293-300
Paust, Jordan J., *International Law as Law of the United States* (R), reviewed by L. C. Green, 492-98

pays en voie de développement (PED), 241-42, 281-304
peacekeepers, protection of, 257-80
  and civilian personnel, 262
  death of, 257
  and human rights, 271
  injured personnel, 278
  and international criminal laws, 271
  and military personnel, 259
  obligations and rights, 372-74, 395-402
  and police personnel, 261
Precautionary Legal Duties and Principles in Modern International Environmental Law by Harald Hohmann (R), reviewed by Jutta Brunnée, 484-89
"La Première année de l'Organe de règlement des différends de l'Organisation mondiale du commerce" par Gabrielle Marceau et Alain Richer (NC), 223-55
progressive development, concept of, and the ICJ, 207-10
"The Protection of Peacekeepers" by Hugh M. Kindred (NC), 257-80

Québec, jurisprudence
  biens, 466-67
  famille et enfants, 446-47
  forum non conveniens, 449-53
  jugements étrangers, 457
  jurisdiction of, 445-46
  litispendance, 447-49

Ratelle, Pierre, "Chronique de Droit international économique en 1994 / Digest of International Economic Law in 1994: Investissement" (Ch), 361-69
Red Cross, 269, 481-84
refugees, status of, 425-27
The Regulation of International Trade by Michael J. Trebilock and Robert Howse (R), reviewed by David P. Stevens, 469-78
"Le Rejet du concept de patrimoine commun de l'humanité afin d'assurer la gestion de la diversité biologique" par

Pierre-François Mercure (NC), 281-304

Reimann, Mathias, *Conflict of Laws in Western Europe: A Guide through the Jungle* (R), reviewed by Joost Blom, 501-03

Reisman, Michael, "Metamorphoses: Judge Shigeru Oda and the International Court of Justice" (A), 185-221

Richer, Alain, "La Première année de l'Organe de règlement des différends de l'Organisation mondiale du commerce," (NC), 223-55

St-Amand, "Chronique de Droit international économique en 1994 / Digest of International Economic Law in 1994: Commerce" (Ch), 343-51

Saunders, Phillip, "Legislating for Integrated Marine Management: Canada's Proposed Oceans Act of 1996" (NC), 305-31

Strom, Torsten H., "Another Kick at the Can: Tuna/Dolphin II" (A), 149-83

système monétaire international, 353-59

territorial modifications, external in Canada, 59-64
in non-communist federal states: admissions, 53-54
secessions or breakups, 54-64, 65-73
in post-communist federal states, 64-73
in Switzerland, 60
territorial modifications, internal in Canada, 49
in non-communist federal states, 44-53
in Switzerland, 49-53
"Territorial Modifications and Breakups in Federal States" by Luzius Wildhaber (A), 41-74

Thomas, J. C. and Sergio Lopez Ayllön, "NAFTA Disputes Settlement and Mexico: Interpreting Treaties and Reconciling Common and Civil Law Systems in a Free Trade Area" (A), 75-122

Tiers-Monde, pays du, 296 n. 55

Tolba, Mostapha, 283-85

trade. *See also* commerce
in Canada, 469-73
challenges of international, 475
international, 94

"Treaty Action Taken by Canada in 1994 / Mesures prises par le Canada en matière de traités en 1994" compiled by / préparé par André Bergeron (PR), 411-24

Trebilock, Michael J., *The Regulation of International Trade,* (R), reviewed by David P. Stevens, 469-78

United Nations
and the Beijing Conference, 123-48
charter of, 200-02, 204, 206, 498-501
civilian personnel, 262
and the Convention on the Law of the Sea, 306-07
et le Convention sur la diversité biologique, 281-302
and equality rights, 127
and the Geneva Convention, 270
military personnel of the, 259
peacekeepers of the, 257-80, 401-02
police personnel of the, 261
and safety of personnel, 272-75
and the Vienna Convention, 239

United States
import embargo, 161, 170
territorial modifications after Civil War, 57

VanderZwaag, David, "Legislating for Integrated Marine Management: Canada's Proposed Oceans Act of 1996" (NC), 305-31

violence against women, 130
state responsibility toward, 130

Waldron, Marcia, "From the Margins to the Mainstream: The Beijing Declaration and

Platform for Action'' (A),
123-48
Wildhaber, Luzius, "Territorial
Modifications and Breakups in
Federal States'' (A), 41-74
women's rights
and gender inequality, 131
and men, 129
and the role of the United Nations,
141

state responsibility toward, 130
universality of, 139
and violence, 130, 137
World Trade Organization (WTO)
79, 223-55, 353, 409-10. *See
also* Organization Mondiale du
Commerce (OMC)
and agreements on anti-dumping,
104

Index of Cases /
Index de la jurisprudence

Adam v. Adam, 465

Aerial Sign Co. v. Steel Art Signs Ltd., 432

Affaire Différend frontalier. Voir Burkina Faso c. Mali

Al-Hashemy v. Gheddah, 440

Allen v. Lynch, 20

Amchen Products Inc. v. British Columbia (Workers Compensation Board), 20, 437

Antares Electronics Inc. (Syndic de), 466-67

Arrowmaster Inc. v. Unique Farming Ltd., 20

Asylum case (Colombia v. Peru), 35

Babulal Parate v. State of Bombay, 47

Banco Nacional de Cuba v. Sabbatino, 385

Bank of Bermuda Ltd. v. Stutz, 17

Bank of Credit & Commerce Int'l (Overseas) Ltd. v. Gokal, 455-56

Banque Toronto-Dominion c. Arsenault, 449-50

Barber v. Barber, 26

Batavia Times Publishing Co. v. Davis, 17

Becquet v. MacCarthy, 17

Black Gold Potato Sales Inc. v. Garibaldi, 457

BMW Investments Inc. v. Saskferco Products Inc., 435

Bosnia v. Serbia, 378, 379, 380

Boundary Dispute Concerning the Taba Area case, 205

Bradford v. Rice, 22

Bradley v. Bradley, 440

British Columbia (Attorney General) v. Houle, 456

Burkina Faso c. Mali, 69

Bushell v. T & N plc, 432, 438

Cameroon v. U.K., 205, 376

Canada v. U.S. (Delimitation of the Maritime Boundary in the Gulf of Maine Area). See Gulf of Maine case

Canada, Pérou et Chili c. CE (Différend au sujet des coquilles St-Jacques), 243

Canadian Deposit Insurance Corp. v. Canadian Commercial Bank, 457, 465

CE, Canada et États-Unis c. Japon (Taxes imposées sur certaines boissons alcooliques), 244

Certain Phosphate Lands in Nauru. See Nauru v. Australia

Certain Softwood Lumber Products from Canada. See Softwood Lumber case

Chisholm v. Georgia, 57

Chorzow Factory case, 387

Christian County Court v. Rankin & Tharp, 495

Clancy v. Beach, 20, 455

Colombia v. Peru, 35

Confederation Trust Co. v. Discovery Tower II Ltd., 439

Continental Shelf case. See Tunisia v. Libyan Arab Jamahiriya

Cook v. Cook, 26

Cooper v. Aaron, 58

Cottington's case, 8

C.P.R. v. Western Union Telegraph Co., 8

Croft v. Dunphy, 7

Cut-to-Length Steel, Originating In or Exported from the United States of America, 75, 104, 114-21

Dairy Producers Co-operative Ltd. v. Agrifoods Int'l Co-operative Ltd., 436

de Vlas v. Bruce, 433-35, 464

Desert Palace Inc. c. Bavary, 454

Dimock v. Revere Copper Co., 21, 23, 24, 25

Dino v. Albertson's Inc., 439

Discreet Logic Inc. v. Canada (Registrar of Copyrights), 436

Don v. Lippmoun, 11

Droit de la famille — 1995, 447
Droit de la famille — 2032, 452-53
Droit de la famille — 2094, 446-47
Duffy v. *Duffy*, 440
Durum Wheat case, 390

Earth Island Institute v. *Mosbacher*, 153
East Timor case. *See Portugal* v.
  Australia
Eggleton v. *Broadway Agencies Ltd.*, 17
El Salvador v. *Honduras* (Nicaragua
  Intervening), 212, 214, 219, 378
Emmanuel v. *Symon*, 9-10, 11, 14, 19
Équipements (Les) Eustache Lamontagne
  Ltée c. *Équipements (Les) Belarus du*
  Canada Ltée, 446
Ex parte Siebold, 58
Eyster v. *Gaff*, 22

Fabrielle Wallcoverings and Textiles Ltd.
  v. *North American Decorative Products*
  Inc., 20
Federal Republic of Germany v. *Denmark*,
  207
Federal Republic of Germany v.
  Netherlands, 207
Finland v. *Denmark* (Passage through
  the Great Belt), 215
Fortus v. *Allegretti*, 464-65
Fresh, Chilled, or Frozen Pork from
  Canada, (Pork case), 119, 120
Frymer v. *Brettschneider*, 436-39

Globe Union Industrial Corp. v. *G.A.P.*
  Marketing Corp., 435
Goddard v. *Gray*, 9
Gordon Capital Corp. c. *Garantie (La)*,
  compagnie d'assurance de l'Amérique
  du Nord, 447-49
Gratto v. *Wittner*, 440
Guarantee Co. of N. America v. *Gordon*
  Capital Corp., 449
Guinea-Bissau v. *Senegal* (Arbitral
  Award), 213
Gulf of Fonseca case, 212, 214
Gulf of Maine case, 214

H. L. Boulton & Co. S.A.C.A. c. *Banque*
  Royale du Canada, 451
Haya de la Torre case, 379, 380
Henry Bacon Building Materials Inc. v.
  Royal Canadian Mounted Police, 454
Herring/Salmon case, 164

Hilton v. *Guyot*, 18
Hoge v. *Hoge*, 445
Hollister v. *Abbott*, 22
Hunt v. *T & N plc*, 429-30

In re Berubari Union and Exchange of
  Enclaves, 47, 55
In re Trepca Mines Ltd., 17
Indian Endurance case, 4
Indyka v. *Indyka*, 12
International Assn. of Science and
  Technology for Development v. *Hamza*,
  458

Jan Poulsen & Co. v. *Seaboard Shipping*
  Co., 432-33
Janke v. *Budd Canada Inc.*, 431-32
Johnson v. *Hall*, 439
Johnston Equipment Co. v. *Remstar Int'l*
  Inc., 439
Judgment of 20 December 1974 in the
  Nuclear Tests Case. See New Zealand v.
  France

Kvaerner Enviropower Inc. v. *Tanar*
  Industries Ltd., 435

Land, Island and Maritime Frontier
  Dispute. See El Salvador v. *Honduras*
  (Nicaragua Intervening)
Lauser v. *Lauser*, 439
Laverty v. *Laverty*, 427
Le Mesurier v. *Le Mesurier*, 14
Lockerbie case. *See Libyan Arab*
  Jamahiriya v. *U.K.*, 212
Lucas v. *Gagnon*, 458-64
Libyan Arab Jamahiriya v. *Malta*, 213
Libyan Arab Jamahiriya v. *U.K.*, 212,
  213, 219

MacDonald v. *Lasnier*, 429-31, 435
Mackenzie v. *Hare*, 58
McLean v. *Pettigrew*, 458-61
McMickle v. *Van Straaten*, 20
Madzimbamuto v. *Lardner-Burke*, 56
Maganthai v. *Union of India*, 47
Malden Mills Industries Inc. c.
  Huntingdon Mills (Canada) Ltd.,
  450-51
Marcotte v. *Megson*, 17
Marshall v. *Houghton*, 17
Masson c. *Thompson*, 446
Matter v. *Public Trustee*, 17

Mercer Int'l Inc. v. *Larsen*, 435
Milhaukee County v. *M.E. Whiteco.*, 8
Military and Paramilitary Activities case. See *Nicaragua* v. *U.S.*
Milleken v. *Mayer*, 26
Moran v. *Pyle National (Canada) Ltd.*, 19
Morguard Investments Ltd. v. *De Savoye*, 16, 17, 19, 24, 27, 429-30, 454
Mortished case, 213
Moses v. *Shore Boar Builders Ltd.*, 20

Nauru v. *Australia*, 215, 218
New York v. *Fitzgerald*, 17
New York v. *United States*, 58
New Zealand v. *France* (*Nuclear Tests* case), 195, 215, 219
Nicaragua v. *Honduras* (Border and Transborder Armed Actions), 214
Nicaragua v. *U.S.*, 214
North Sea Continental Shelf case. See *Federal Republic of Germany* v. *Denmark; Federal Republic of Germany* v. *Netherlands*
Northern Cameroons case. See *Cameroon* v. *U.K.*
Nyquvest v. *Rutkowski*, 445

Ontario Inc. v. *167644 Canada Inc.*, 455
Owens Bank Ltd. v. *Bracco*, 4

Parent v. *Litalien*, 456
Patrician Reference (*Re Resolution to Amend the Constitution*), 63
Peace Treaties case, 377
Pfaff v. *Performax Systems Ltd.*, 455
Philips v. *Eyre*, 458, 464
P. J. Clayman Canada Inc. v. *Gibson Textile Dryers Ltd.*, 445-46
Pork case. See *Fresh, Chilled, or Frozen Pork from Canada*
Portugal v. *Australia*, 199, 216
Public Trustee v. *Dukelow*. See *Vak Estate* v. *Dukelow*

Qatar v. *Bahrain Boundary* (Maritime Delimitation) (1994), 215-16
Qatar v. *Bahrain Boundary* (Maritime Delimitation) (1995), 215-16
Quebec Veto Reference, A.G. Que. and A.G. Can. (*Re Objection by Quebec to a Resolution to Amend the Constitution*), 63

R. v. *Rebman (R.) et al.*, 428
Ralph v. *Ralph*, 440
Ram Kishore v. *Union of India*, 55
Re Thom, 466
Re Whalen and Neal, 17
Red Raspberries from Canada case, 120
Reparations case, 278
Request for an Examination of the Situation in Accordance with Paragraph 63 of the Court's Judgment of 20 December 1974 in the Nuclear Tests Case (*New Zealand* v. *France*), 195
Reservations case, 377
Riese v. *Mueller*, 456-57
Rosdev Investments Inc. c. *Allstate Insurance Co. of Canada*, 451-52
Royal Trust Co. v. *H. A. Roberts Group Ltd.*, 453-54

S.S. Wimbledon case, 379, 380
Schibsby v. *Westenholz*, 8, 9, 11
Schooner Exchange (The) v. *McFadden*, 7
Section 337 case, 173, 174, 179
Showlag v. *Mansour*, 3, 6, 7, 8, 9, 27, 28, 34, 36
Sirdar Gurdyal Singh v. *Rajah of Faridkote*, 11-12
Softwood Lumber case, 119
South-West Africa case, 276
Spencer v. *The Queen*, 18
Spiliada Maritime Corp. v. *Cansulex Ltd.*, 438
Sri Kishan v. *State*, 47
State of West Bengal v. *Union of India*, 47
Steward v. *Green*, 22
Stewart Estate v. *Stewart Estate*, 432
Stoddard v. *Accurpress Manufacturing Ltd.*, 20
Sutton v. *Leib*, 25, 26, 27

T.D.I. Hospitality Management Consultants Inc. v. *Browne*, 455
Texas v. *White*, 58
Thai Cigarette case, 173
Thamotharampillai v. *Minister of Employment and Immigration*, 425
Thompson c. *Masson*, 446
Thompson v. *Thompson*, 440-45
Tolofson v. *Jensen*, 434, 458-64
Tortel Communication Inc. v. *Suntel Inc.*, 431-32

Touchbourne v. *Philbrook*, 439
Traders Group Ltd. v. *Hopkins*, 17
Travers v. *Holley*, 14
Treatment of Indians in the Union of South Africa case, 376
Treinies v. *Sunshine Mining Co.*, 23, 26, 27
Trial of Pakistani Prisoners of Wars case, 380
Tuna/Dolphin I case, 149-60, 165-82
Tuna/Dolphin II case, 160-82
Tunisia v. *Libyan Arab Jamahiriya*, 199, 204, 207, 213, 214, 378, 379

United Kingdom v. *Norway (Fisheries)*, 207, 214
United States — Prohibition of Imports of Tuna and Tuna Products from Canada. See U.S.-Canada Tuna case
United States — Section 337 of the Tariff Act of 1930. See Section 337 case
United States of America v. *Ivey*, 20
United States Restrictions on Imports of Tuna (1991). *See Tuna/Dolphin I*
United States Restrictions on Imports of Tuna (1994). *See Tuna/Dolphin II*

United States v. *Curtiss-Wright Export Corp.*, 58
U.S.-Canada Tuna case, 181

V.P.C. Promotion S.A. c. *Bagyn*, 457
Vak Estate v. *Dukelow (sub nom. Public Trustee* v. *Dukelow)*, 466
Van Den Brink N.V. c. *Heringer*, 446
Vénézuéla/Brésil c. *États-Unis* (Différend sur l'essence), 243

Walsh v. *Herman*, 17
Webb v. *Hooper*, 454
Wedley v. *Quist*, 17
Weiner v. *Singh*, 17
Weir's case, 8, 9
White v. *White*, 456
WHO Headquarters case, 212
Williams & Humbert Ltd. v. *W & H Trade Marks (Jersey) Ltd.*, 386

Yakimetz case, 213

Z.(D.) v. *Z.(J.)*, 445